r
14. 7. 08

DIETRICH BONHOEFFER WORKS, VOLUME 13

London: 1933–1935

This series is a translation of
DIETRICH BONHOEFFER WERKE
Edited by
Eberhard Bethge†, Ernst Feil,
Christian Gremmels, Wolfgang Huber,
Hans Pfeifer, Albrecht Schönherr,
Heinz Eduard Tödt†, Ilse Tödt

This volume has been made possible through the generous support in the United Kingdom of the following individuals, churches, foundations, and organizations: His Grace the Most Reverend Dr. Rowan Williams, Archbishop of Canterbury; Lord Carey of Clifton; the Dean and Chapter of Westminster Abbey; the Dean and Chapter of Chichester Cathedral; the Baptist Union of Great Britain; the Evangelical Lutheran Church of Geneva (English-Speaking Congregation); the Moravian Church of Great Britain; the Mallinckrodt Foundation; the Kaiser Wilhelm II Fund; the German Christ Church, London; the German YMCA, London; the Allchurches Trust; St. Paul's German Evangelical Reformed Church Trust; the Synod of the German Lutheran Church in Great Britain; Spurgeon's College; the Bonhoeffer Society (British Section); Bloomsbury Central Baptist Church, London; Tyndale Baptist Church, Bristol; Michael Docker; Alan Dowsett; Brian Frost; Susan Howatch; Alan and Helen Lamb; David and Margaret Thompson; Peter Walker; and George Wedell. Support in the United States has come from the Lilly Endowment, Inc.; the Thrivent Financial for Lutherans Foundation; the Bowen H. and Janet Arthur McCoy Foundation; the Lutheran Theological Seminary at Philadelphia; and numerous members and friends of the International Bonhoeffer Society.

DIETRICH BONHOEFFER WORKS

General Editors
Victoria J. Barnett
Barbara Wojhoski

DIETRICH BONHOEFFER

London

1933–1935

Translated from the German Edition
Edited by
HANS GOEDEKING, MARTIN HEIMBUCHER,
AND HANS-WALTER SCHLEICHER

English Edition
Edited by
KEITH CLEMENTS

Translated by
ISABEL BEST

Supplementary Material Translated by
DOUGLAS W. STOTT

FORTRESS PRESS   MINNEAPOLIS

DIETRICH BONHOEFFER WORKS, Volume 13

Originally published in German as *Dietrich Bonhoeffer Werke*, edited by Eberhard Bethge et al., by Chr. Kaiser Verlag in 1994; Band 13, *London: 1933—1935*, edited by Hans Goedeking et al. First English-language editing of *Dietrich Bonhoeffer Works*, Volume 13, published by Fortress Press in 2007.

The publication of this work was subsidized in part by a grant from the Goethe-Institut Inter Nationes, Munich

Jacket design: Cheryl Watson
Cover photo: Dietrich Bonhoeffer. © Chr. Kaiser/Gütersloher Verlagshaus, Gütersloh, Germany.
Internal design: The HK Scriptorium, Inc.
Typesetting: Ann Delgehausen, Trio Bookworks

Library of Congress Cataloging-in-Publication Data

Bonhoeffer, Dietrich, 1906–1945.
    [London, 1933–1935. English.]
    London, 1933–1935 / Dietrich Bonhoeffer ; translated from the German Edition ; edited by Hans Goedeking, Martin Heimbucher, and Hans-Walter Schleicher ; English edition edited by Keith Clements ; translated by Isabel Best ; supplementary material translated by Douglas W. Stott.
    p. cm.—(Dietrich Bonhoeffer works; v. 13)
    ISBN-13: 978–0–8006–8313–9 (alk. paper)
    ISBN-10: 0–8006–8313–7 (alk. paper)
    1. Bonhoeffer, Dietrich, 1906-1945--Correspondence. 2. Theologians—Germany—Correspondence. 3. Theology. 4. Lutheran Church—Sermons. 5. Sermons, German—Translations into English. I. Title.
    BX4827.B57A2513 2007
    230'.044092--dc22
    [B]   2007015501

The paper used in this publication meets the minimum requirements of American National Standard for Information Sciences—Permanence of Paper for Printed Library Materials, ANSI Z329.48-1984.

Manufactured in the U.S.A.
11   10   09   08   07   1   2   3   4   5   6   7   8   9   10

CONTENTS

London: 1933–1935

Part 1
Letters and Documents

Part 2
Reports and Lectures

Part 3
Sermons and Meditations

GENERAL EDITOR'S FOREWORD TO DIETRICH BONHOEFFER WORKS

THE GERMAN THEOLOGIAN AND PASTOR Dietrich Bonhoeffer has become one of the most influential Christian thinkers of all time. Barely twenty-seven years of age when the Nazi regime came to power in Germany, Bonhoeffer emerged immediately as a radical Protestant voice against the ideological cooptation of his church. He was one of the earliest critics of the Nazi regime and an outspoken opponent of the pro-Nazi "German Christians." From 1933 to 1935, he served as pastor of two German-speaking congregations in England, leading them to join the Confessing Church, the faction within the German Protestant Church that opposed the nazification of the Christian faith. He returned to Germany to become director of a small Confessing Church seminary and, after the Gestapo closed it, continued to work illegally to educate Confessing clergy. Throughout the 1930s, he attended ecumenical meetings, effectively becoming the voice of the Confessing Church throughout the European and American ecumenical world. In 1939, his ecumenical friends urged him to accept a position in New York. Rejecting the security of a life in exile, Bonhoeffer chose instead to join the ranks of the German conspiracy to overthrow the regime, like his brother Klaus and his brothers-in-law Hans von Dohnanyi and Rüdiger Schleicher. He was arrested and imprisoned in April 1943 and executed in the Flossenbürg concentration camp in April 1945.

In a eulogy published shortly after Bonhoeffer's death, his former professor and friend Reinhold Niebuhr wrote that Bonhoeffer's story "is worth recording. It belongs to the modern acts of the apostles. . . . Not only his martyr's death, but also his actions and precepts contain within them the hope of a revitalized Protestant faith in Germany. It will be a faith religiously more profound than that of many of its critics; but it will have learned to overcome the one fateful error of German Protestantism, the complete dichotomy between faith and political life."[1]

Throughout his brief life, Bonhoeffer wrote hundreds of letters, sermons, and biblical reflections in addition to his published theological works. After 1945, Bonhoeffer's former student and close friend Eberhard Bethge began to publish selected documents, including Bonhoeffer's prison writings, and to reissue books published in his lifetime. In translation, these works—*Discipleship, Ethics*, and *Letters and Papers from Prison*—became classics, finding a wide readership among Christians throughout the world. In the ensuing decades, Niebuhr's prescient assessment that Bonhoeffer's life and work offered lasting insights for modern Christian experience and witness has been more than fulfilled.

Yet there was a growing sense that these works should not stand alone, a realization of the significance of the biographical and historical context of his thought. Bonhoeffer's papers included lecture notes made by his students, documents from the German Church Struggle and ecumenical meetings, circular letters that were sent to his seminarians, sermons, and an extensive correspondence with theologians and religious leaders in Europe and the United States. Bethge published several early compilations of some of these documents (*Gesammelte Schriften* and *Mündige Welt*) and incorporated additional material into his magisterial biography of Bonhoeffer, which appeared in English in 1970 and in a revised and unabridged edition in 2000.

Bethge and leading Bonhoeffer scholars in Germany decided to publish new annotated editions of Bonhoeffer's complete theological works, together with most of the documents from the literary estate, including historical documents and correspondence to Bonhoeffer. The *Dietrich Bonhoeffer Werke* series was published by Chr. Kaiser Verlag, now part of Gütersloher Verlagshaus. The first German volume, a new edition of Bonhoeffer's dissertation, *Sanctorum Communio*, appeared in 1986; the final volume, Bonhoeffer's complete prison writings, appeared in April 1998. The seventeenth volume, an index for the entire series, appeared in 1999; it also includes documents discovered after the earlier volumes had been published. Whenever possible these documents have been integrated into the appropriate volumes of the English edition; documents that continue to be discovered are published in the *Dietrich Bonhoeffer Yearbook*.

Discussion about an English translation of the entire series began as soon as the first German volumes appeared, and in 1990 the International

---

[1.] Reinhold Niebuhr, "The Death of a Martyr," *Christianity and Crisis* 5, no. 11 (1945): 6–7.

Bonhoeffer Society, English Language Section, in agreement with the German Bonhoeffer Society and Fortress Press, undertook the English translation of the German *Dietrich Bonhoeffer Werke*. The project began with an initial grant from the National Endowment for the Humanities, with Robin Lovin serving as project director, assisted by Mark Brocker. An editorial board was formed for the *Dietrich Bonhoeffer Works*, English edition, staffed by Wayne Whitson Floyd Jr. as general editor and Clifford J. Green of Hartford Seminary as executive director. Floyd, at that time director of the Dietrich Bonhoeffer Center at the Lutheran Theological Seminary in Philadelphia, served as general editor from 1993 to 2004, overseeing publication of the first seven volumes as well as volume 9. Victoria J. Barnett, director of church relations at the U.S. Holocaust Memorial Museum, joined the project as associate general editor in 2002 and became general editor in 2004, joined by Barbara Wojhoski, a professional editor who prepared the manuscripts of the final volumes for publication.

The *Dietrich Bonhoeffer Works*, English edition (*DBWE*) is the definitive English translation of Bonhoeffer's theological and other writings. It includes much material that appears for the first time in English, as well as documents discovered after the publication of the original German volumes. *DBWE* is a significant contribution to twentieth-century theological literature, church history, and the history of the Nazi era. Particularly in their portrayal of the daily implications of the Protestant Church Struggle in Nazi Germany and the response of Christians outside Germany, these volumes offer a detailed and unique glimpse of Bonhoeffer's historical context and its great challenges for the churches and for all people of conscience.

The translators of the *DBWE* volumes have attempted throughout to render an accurate and readable translation of Bonhoeffer's writings for contemporary audiences while remaining true to Bonhoeffer's thought and style. Particular attention has been paid to the translation of important theological, historical, and philosophical terms. Bonhoeffer's language and style are often reflective of his age, particularly with regard to gendered language, and this can be discerned in the historical and church documents. Nonetheless, in translating his theological writings, we have decided to use gender-inclusive language, insofar as it is possible without distorting Bonhoeffer's meaning or unjustifiably dissociating him from his own time.

Each volume includes an introduction written by the *DBWE* volume editor(s), footnotes provided by Bonhoeffer, editorial notes added by the German and the *DBWE* editors, and the original afterword written by the editor(s) of the German edition. Additions to or revisions of the German editors' notes are enclosed in square brackets and initialed by the editor of the respective volume. When any previously translated material is quoted in an

editorial note in altered form—indicated by the notation [trans. altered]—
such changes should be assumed to be the responsibility of the translator(s).
When available, existing English translations of books and articles in German and other languages are cited in the notes.

Bonhoeffer's own footnotes, which are indicated in the body of the text by
plain, superscripted numbers, are reproduced in precisely the same numeri-
cal sequence as they appear in the German critical edition, complete with his
idiosyncrasies of documentation. In these, as in the accompanying editorial
notes, the edition of a work used by Bonhoeffer himself can be determined
by consulting the bibliography at the end of each volume.

A list of frequently used abbreviations appears at the front of each volume.
Each volume also includes a chronology of important dates relevant to that
volume as well as an index of scriptural references, an index of persons with
biographical information, and an index of subjects. A bibliography at the
end of each volume includes archival sources, sources used by Bonhoeffer,
literature consulted by the editors, and other works relevant to that volume,
providing complete information for each written source that Bonhoeffer or
the various editors have mentioned in the current volume.

Bonhoeffer's literary estate—the archives, collections, and personal
library of materials that belonged to him and survived the war—was cataloged by Dietrich Meyer and Eberhard Bethge and published as the *Nachlaß
Dietrich Bonhoeffer*. Most of the documents cited in the *Nachlaß* are collected in
the Berlin Staatsbibliothek; some are in other archives. All documents listed
in the *Nachlaß*, however, have been copied on microfiches at the Bundesarchiv in Koblenz and in the Bonhoeffer collection at Burke Library, Union
Theological Seminary, New York. References to any of these documents are
indicated within the *DBWE* by the abbreviation *NL*, followed by the corresponding catalog number. Books in the bibliography from Bonhoeffer's own
library are indicated by the abbreviation *NL-Bibl.*

Volumes 1–7 of the English edition, which contain only Bonhoeffer's own
writings, retain his original organization of the material, either as chapters
or as sections or unnumbered manuscripts. Volumes 8–16 contain collected
writings from a particular period of Bonhoeffer's life, including correspondence from others and historical documents. With the exception of volume
8, these final volumes are divided into three sections, with the documents
in each section arranged chronologically: (1) Letters, Journals, Documents;
(2) Essays, Seminar Papers, Papers, Lectures, Compositions; (3) Sermons,
Meditations, Catechetical Writings, Exegetical Writings. Documents are
numbered consecutively within the respective sections. In editorial notes
these items are labeled by the *DBWE* volume number, followed by the section

number, the document number, and finally the page and/or note number, for example, *DBWE* 9, 1/109, p. 179, ed. note 1, refers to the English edition, volume 9, section 1, document 109, page 179, editorial note 1.

The *DBWE* also reproduces Bonhoeffer's original paragraphing; exceptions are noted by the ¶ symbol indicating a paragraph break added by the editors of the English edition or by conventions explained in the introductions written by the editor(s) of specific volumes. The pagination of the *DBW* German critical edition is indicated in the outer margins of the pages of the translated text. Where it is important to give readers a word or phrase in its original language, a translated passage is followed by the original, enclosed in square brackets. All biblical citations come from the New Revised Standard Version (NRSV) unless otherwise noted. Where versification of the Bible used by Bonhoeffer differs from the NRSV, the verse number in the latter is noted in the text in square brackets.

The publication of the *Dietrich Bonhoeffer Works,* English edition, would not have been possible without the generous support of numerous individuals and institutions. The verso of the half-title page of each volume provides a list of supporters of that particular volume. The series as a whole is indebted to many individual members and friends of the International Bonhoeffer Society and to family foundations, congregations, synods, seminaries, and universities. Special thanks are due the following foundations and donors for major grants: the National Endowment for the Humanities; the Lilly Endowment, Inc.; the Thrivent Financial for Lutherans Foundation; the Aid Association for Lutherans; the Stiftung Bonhoeffer Lehrstuhl; the Bowen H. and Janice Arthur McCoy Charitable Foundation; and Dr. John Young and Ms. Cleo Young. The Lutheran Theological Seminary at Philadelphia and its former Auxiliary provided space and ongoing support. Particular thanks goes to our publisher, Fortress Press, and its ever-helpful and skilled staff, particularly its editorial director, Michael West, and his predecessor, Marshall Johnson.

The existence of this series in English and other languages is testimony to the international community of those who have found Dietrich Bonhoeffer to be a profoundly important companion in their own journey. That community would not exist without the wisdom, generosity, and dedication of Eberhard Bethge (1909–2000) and his wife, Renate. Bethge was himself a pastor in the Confessing Church. After 1945, he became convinced that the future of a living church in Germany depended on its addressing its failures under Nazism and in a new understanding of Bonhoeffer's lasting question, Who is Christ for us today?

The editors of this English edition are particularly grateful to the original editorial board of the German edition, composed of Eberhard Bethge†, Ernst Feil, Christian Gremmels, Wolfgang Huber, Hans Pfeifer, Albrecht Schönherr, Heinz Eduard Tödt†, and Ilse Tödt. As liaison between the German and the English editorial board, Hans Pfeifer has given steadfast and congenial support to his colleagues on both sides of the Atlantic. The editors of the individual German volumes have been generous with their time and expertise. As work on *DBWE* has proceeded, a new generation of Bonhoeffer scholars in Germany has assisted us as well: Christine Kasch, Andreas Pangritz, Holger Roggelin, Christiane Tietz, Ralf Wuestenberg.

We remain grateful to those whose original translations of Bonhoeffer's words introduced most of us to his work. It is only fitting, however, that this English edition be dedicated, finally, to the remarkable group of scholars who over the years have devoted their time, their insights, and their generous spirit to the translation, editing, and publication of these volumes. That dedication should begin with a special acknowledgment of the capable editorial leadership of Wayne Whitson Floyd Jr., who brought eight volumes to publication, and to Clifford J. Green, whose steady hand has guided the project throughout its existence and ensured the financial foundation for its completion.

The translators who have brought Bonhoeffer's words to new life in these volumes are Victoria Barnett, Douglas Bax, Claudia and Scott Bergmann-Moore, Isabel Best, Daniel W. Bloesch, James H. Burtness†, Lisa Dahill, Peter Frick, Barbara Green, David Higgins, Reinhard Krauss, Peter Krey, Nancy Lukens, Mary Nebelsick, Marion Pauck, Martin Rumscheidt, Anne Schmidt-Lange, Douglas W. Stott, and Charles West.

Since its inception, the following people have served on the *DBWE* Editorial Board: H. Gaylon Barker, Victoria Barnett, Mark Brocker, Keith Clements, Wayne Whitson Floyd Jr., Peter Frick, Clifford J. Green, John W. de Gruchy, Barry Harvey, Geffrey B. Kelly, Reinhard Krauss, Michael Lukens, Larry Rasmussen, H. Martin Rumscheidt, and Barbara Wojhoski. The following have served on the Advisory Committee: James H. Burtness†, John D. Godsey, Barbara Green, James Patrick Kelley, Robin W. Lovin, Nancy Lukens, Paul Matheny, and Mary Nebelsick.

In September 1943, Dietrich Bonhoeffer wrote his parents from prison: "In ordinary life we hardly realize that we receive a great deal more than we give, and that it is only with gratitude that life becomes rich. It is very easy to overestimate the importance of our own achievements in comparison with what we owe to others."[2] Everyone who has worked on this project will, I believe, find meaning in those words. It is a privilege to have been part of this long, deep, and rich conversation with Bonhoeffer's thought and now to extend that conversation to the readers of these volumes, shaped above all by gratitude for Bonhoeffer's life and witness.

Victoria J. Barnett

[2.] *LPP*, 109.

ABBREVIATIONS

ADBC	Archives of the Dietrich Bonhoeffer Church, London
BA	Bundesarchiv
DB-ER	*Dietrich Bonhoeffer: A Biography* (Fortress Press, rev. ed., 2000)
DBW	*Dietrich Bonhoeffer Werke*, German edition
DBWE	*Dietrich Bonhoeffer Works*, English edition
EZA	Evangelisches Zentralarchiv, Berlin
GS	*Gesammelte Schriften*
KJV	King James Version
LKA EKvW	Landeskirchliches Archiv der Evangelischen Kirche in Westfalen, Bielefeld
LPL	Lambeth Palace Library, London
LPP	*Letter and Papers from Prison* (Simon & Schuster, 1997)
LW	*Luther's Works*, American edition
NL	*Nachlaß Dietrich Bonhoeffer*
NL-Bibl.	Restbibliothek Bonhoeffers in *Nachlaß Dietrich Bonhoeffer* (supplement to the literary estate of Dietrich Bonhoeffer)
NRS	*No Rusty Swords* (Collins; Harper & Row, 1965)
NRSV	New Revised Standard Version
NSDAP	Nationalsozialistische Deutsche Arbeiterpartei; the Nazi Party
PAM	*Predigten—Auslegungen—Meditationen* (Chr. Kaiser, 1984–85)
SA	Sturmabteilung (Nazi storm troopers)
SBL	Schroders Bank, London, Archives
WA	Weimarer Ausgabe (Weimar edition), Martin Luther
ZEKHN	Zentralarchiv der Evangelischen Kirche in Hessen und Nassau, Darmstadt

KEITH CLEMENTS

EDITOR'S INTRODUCTION TO THE ENGLISH EDITION[1]

"Now I have been here for eight days, have to preach every Sunday, and get news almost every day from Berlin as to how things stand. It's enough to tear one apart."[2] From the first days of his pastoral duties in London, Dietrich Bonhoeffer sensed that the German Church Struggle would continue to make demands on him. Developments in the Third Reich also overshadowed the other work that he hoped to pursue and influence from London: his involvement in the ecumenical movement. "Perhaps," he hoped, "this can also be a way of giving some real support to the German church."[3] The stay in London, which Bonhoeffer initially viewed as a withdrawal from the clashes over the direction of the church in Germany, became a new phase in his intensive participation in that struggle. Bonhoeffer's collaboration with his clergy colleagues in the Association of German Evangelical Congregations in Great Britain and Ireland, his influence on ecumenical developments and decisions prior to the Fanø ecumenical conference in August 1934, and finally his close contact with family and friends in Germany all bore the marks of the conflict that hit the churches under National Socialism. And in all these spheres—in line with what at the time was still his isolated opting for decisive resistance against the *Gleichschaltung* (bringing into line) of the churches—Bonhoeffer sought to bring energetic and effective influence to bear. From this perspective, Bonhoeffer's decision after a year and a half in London to return to Germany and become director of an

---

[1.] This is a translation of the introduction to the German edition, with some revisions and additional information for readers added by Keith Clements.

[2.] Letter of Dietrich Bonhoeffer to Karl Barth, October 24, 1933 (1/2).

[3.] Letter to Karl Barth, 1/2.

1

illegal Confessing Church seminary for preachers was simply a continuation of his involvement in the Church Struggle.

The present volume impressively documents Bonhoeffer's engagement in the Church Struggle from London and the means with which he pursued it. The documents cover the entire period of Bonhoeffer's stay in London, from October 16, 1933, to April 15, 1935, and witness to both the intensity and the diversity of Bonhoeffer's engagements during his London period. The bulk of the material consists of his correspondence: letters to and from his contacts in Berlin, both friends and foes in the Church Struggle; exchanges with the ecumenical staff in Geneva and with important English allies such as George Bell, bishop of Chichester; and not least the frequent messages of support and encouragement between himself and his family members in Germany. This volume also includes records and minutes of meetings of the congregational councils of Bonhoeffer's two London parishes, as well as of the meetings with other German pastors and congregations in Britain; excerpts from the diaries of Bonhoeffer's friend and London colleague Julius Rieger; reports from the important international ecumenical conferences in which Bonhoeffer was engaged in 1934; and over twenty sermons he preached to his London congregations. All this material provides readers an opportunity to step into, and in a measure to experience, a dramatic slice of history as it was actually lived day by day, even hour by hour. It also reveals something of the different facets of Bonhoeffer's personality as, at one and the same time, he lived out the roles of theologian, radical campaigner for the integrity of the church in the face of Nazism, ecumenical peace activist, devoted pastor, tireless helper of refugees, and affectionate son, grandson, brother, and friend.

In 1933 there were in fact six German congregations in London (not including a Methodist one). Bonhoeffer came to London to be pastor of two of them. The German Church, Sydenham, in the southeast suburbs, belonged to the United tradition (that is, embracing both the Lutheran and the Reformed confessions). The building dated from 1875 and stood in Dacres Road, a few minutes' walk from the manse on Manor Mount in Forest Hill, where Bonhoeffer lived for his eighteen months in London. Relatively affluent, reflecting the social ambience of Sydenham, the congregation included diplomats, prosperous merchants, and business people. Sunday attendance averaged thirty to forty.

During some years of financial constraint, however, the Sydenham Church had shared its pastor with the St. Paul's German Reformed Church in London's East End. This community had a history dating back to the early eighteenth century. Its present building was in Goulston Street, Aldgate. The congregation was a somewhat different social mix from that of Sydenham:

tradespeople, small shopkeepers, and the like. There had been much inter-
marriage with the native population over the generations, and for many of
the community English was now their first or only language. Bonhoeffer
therefore often preached here in English. The attendance averaged about
fifty. There was a strong musical tradition with a fine choir. With a more
informal atmosphere than the Sydenham Church, a close-knit circle of inter-
related families, a social life built around the choir and a fondness for outings and picnic excursions, St. Paul's had much of the ambience of a typical
English free church of that era. Both the Sydenham Church's and the St.
Paul's building were destroyed in the bombing of London during the Second World War. The Sydenham Church was rebuilt as the Dietrich Bonhoeffer Church, opened in 1959.

The German Church Struggle

The German Church Struggle (*Kirchenkampf*), which forms both the context
and the content of so much of Bonhoeffer's activity while in London, was the
conflict between those who attempted the nazification of the ethos, beliefs,
and principles of governance of the German Protestant churches and those,
such as Bonhoeffer, who resisted these attempts. The struggle effectively
began well before Adolf Hitler's accession to power in January 1933. Along
with the rising tide of political right-wing nationalism during the late 1920s,
there was a movement that sought to inject the Nazi ideology into Protestantism. This was led by the Faith Movement of German Christians, generally known in short as the German Christians (*Deutsche Christen*), not to
be confused with the German Faith Movement that offered an alternative
pseudoreligion of nationalism rather than aiming to take over the churches
directly.[4]

During 1931–32, Bonhoeffer had already joined theological battle with
the German Christians, particularly over their attempts to make the concepts
of nation, race, and people (*Volk*) fundamental items of Christian belief—so-
called orders of creation intended by God as fundamental to human existence and therefore to be preserved in their "purity" at all costs. Bonhoeffer
saw this as a false doctrine of creation that supplanted the biblical and Reformation insistence on *Christ* as the key to understanding the divine purpose
for human existence in all its dimensions. In this as in other respects, he was
a close ally of Karl Barth, the Swiss Reformed theologian who taught in Bonn
from 1930 until his suspension in 1934. With his call for a reversal from

---

[4.] [Wherever it is used in *DBWE*, the term "German Christian" refers to this ideological movement.—KC]

nineteenth-century liberalism and a new emphasis on God as unknowable save through revelation in Christ, Barth had a dramatic impact on Protestant theology in the wake of the First World War.

After Hitler became chancellor on January 30, 1933, the German Christian campaign to capture control of the German Evangelical Church began in earnest. Their aim was to create a truly "Germanic" church conforming to the new Nazi order, "completing the work of Martin Luther." Not only was there enthusiasm for making the categories of nation, race, and *Volk* central in the ethos and preaching of the church, but they demanded very concrete changes in church law. In particular, the so-called Aryan paragraph had to be introduced, corresponding to the new Nazi civil service laws, whereby people of "non-Aryan" (i.e., Jewish) descent would be banned from the ministry and other church positions. The German Christians also sought the introduction of the *Führerprinzip* (the Nazi authoritarian "leadership principle") into church government.

The German Church Struggle was very much shaped by the historical complexities of the German church scene. Since the Reformation, Protestantism in Germany had comprised many wholly autonomous regional churches (*Landeskirchen*). Such churches had been formed on the principle of *cuius regio, eius religio*, that is, the religion of a population within a given region was determined by the ruler or government of that territory. Of the twenty-eight regional churches that existed in 1933, twenty were Lutheran in confession, two Reformed, and the remaining six were United—among them the Old Prussian Union Church established in 1817, which was by far the largest and included eight provincial churches. While some forms of cooperation among them had been devised, one could speak only very loosely of the "German Evangelical Church" as an umbrella term for these churches collectively. But it was the long-held dream of many Protestants that there should indeed be a unified church structure embracing all the regional churches (with proper safeguards for their distinctive features and some degree of autonomy). The desire for a German Evangelical Church in reality as well as in name had wholly worthy motives, especially the desire for a more effective Protestant witness in Germany as a whole (though perhaps some were primarily anxious to counter the evident solidity of the Roman Catholic presence). But this desire was highly susceptible to co-optation by nationalist political ambitions and the German Christian agenda in particular. On July 11, 1933, a constitution of the German Evangelical Church, as consisting of the regional churches and theologically based on the scriptures and the confessions of the Reformation, was accepted by the government.

But it was precisely on the issue of what that theological foundation meant and how this church should be governed that battle was already joined between the German Christians and their opponents. A crucial factor bequeathed by history to this battlefield lay in the German Protestant understanding of the church as a *Volkskirche*—a "people's" or "national" church (as distinct from a "gathered" church of believers). The principle of *cuius regio, eius religio* meant that one confessional tradition had a privileged position in each region or (in Prussia) province and was recognized collectively as the church of that region, the church into which people would be baptized at birth and of which they would claim membership, however nominal their active allegiance might be. With the formation of one German Evangelical Church structure, there was now the possibility of speaking, as never before, of a *Volkskirche* for the whole German *Volk*. But whereas previously a *Volkskirche* had its distinct theological identity defined by the confession (Lutheran, Reformed, or United), and on this basis could claim to shape the life of the *Volk*, the demand was now being made by the nationalist ideologues for the character of the *Volk* to shape the church. The church was to be coordinated with the new German Reich in every respect.

The summer of 1933 was a tumultuous time for the German churches. Hitler appointed Ludwig Müller, a devoted Nazi whose previous church experience was as a naval chaplain, as his plenipotentiary in church affairs, with the charge of bringing about the unification of Protestantism within the one new Reich Church. Müller's sympathies with the German Christians were all too clear. The bullying tactics of the German Christians (who had their own militaristic uniforms: black jackets, riding breeches, and high boots), combined with Müller's oscillation between heavy-handedness and evasiveness, provoked widespread opposition. This opposition was at first expressed through a group of young pastors and students, the Young Reformation movement sympathetic to Karl Barth. During the summer of 1933, there were hectic weeks of ecclesiastical political struggle for the leadership of the church. The first bishop of the Reich Church, elected by representatives of all the regional churches, was Friedrich von Bodelschwingh, a widely respected figure who was director of the famous Bethel Institute for the physically and mentally handicapped near Bielefeld. But the German Christians mounted a campaign of lying and intimidation that led him to resign. Ludwig Müller was imposed as his replacement by dubious means, and in the church elections in July 1933, which many opponents charged were rigged, the German Christians won a decisive majority of seats on synods throughout the country. Thus the September 1933 synod of the Old Prussian Union— the so-called brown synod because so many delegates appeared in brown SA uniforms—was dominated by the German Christians. By this time, Martin Niemöller, a much-decorated First World War submarine commander, now pastor of the Dahlem church in Berlin, had emerged as the main leader of the opposition. Niemöller formed the Pastors' Emergency League, which soon had six thousand members.

The central issue in the Church Struggle concerned the nature of the German Evangelical Church as newly constituted in July 1933. For the church opposition, the imposition of the Aryan paragraph and the nazified forms of governance demanded by the German Christians and sanctioned by Müller were a clear departure from that constitution, grounded as it was in the scriptures and Reformation confessions. At the famous free synod of Barmen that convened in late May 1934, the opposition met around this principle and, largely under Karl Barth's inspiration, drew up the Barmen Theological Declaration. The Barmen declaration reaffirmed the confessional foundation of the German Evangelical Church, and its six theses declared that the true church was faithful to God's word in Jesus Christ, in sharp contrast to a church that became subservient to contemporary ideologies, political developments, and events as alternative sources of God's revelation. The Barmen declaration became the theological foundation document of the Confessing Church. The Barmen synod was followed in October 1934 by a second Confessing Synod in Dahlem, Berlin, which even more explicitly affirmed the Confessing Church's claim to be the true Evangelical Church of Germany, and those gathered in Dahlem began to set up separate structures of church governance, including the training of clergy, thus paving the way for the establishment of five Confessing preachers' seminaries. After the Dahlem synod, the Confessing Council of Brethren, the governing council of the Confessing Church, invited Bonhoeffer to return to Germany as director of one of those seminaries.

The Significance of Bonhoeffer's Role

The German editors' afterword is included in this volume and provides additional information on this historical background for Bonhoeffer's period in London. But two points should be emphasized here. First, the claim of the Confessing Church—certainly as understood by Bonhoeffer—was not that it was a separate church from the German Evangelical Church, but that it alone constituted that church, by virtue of remaining faithful to its confessional basis. In the view of Bonhoeffer and other Confessing Christians, those Protestants who did not adhere to Barmen and either acquiesced to or supported Müller's leadership and the German Christian takeover represented not the German Evangelical Church but a heretical body deserving no title other than "Reich Church"—even if they continued to hold office in the German Evangelical Church. The Confessing opposition, therefore, did not see itself as founding another church alongside the Reich Church, but rather regarded itself as the only true expression of the German Evangelical Church. In its eyes, the Reich Church had no claim to either theological or legal validity.

Second, at this stage in the Church Struggle many if not most of those in the opposition were careful to distinguish between their resistance to the nazification of the church and any form of political resistance to the state and the new Nazi order. Indeed, even people such as Martin Niemöller at this stage saw no contradiction between asserting loyalty to the new Reich and opposition to Müller and the German Christians.[5] This may seem surprising to observers from a later generation and from outside the German scene. Indeed, at the time many people in the English-speaking world, where intense interest was taken in the press reports of what was happening in Germany, were hailing the church opposition as a kind of political resistance to "Hitlerism" per se. The situation was more complex, however. The Confessing Church was not directly opposing Hitler and the Nazi regime. Nonetheless, insofar as the church opposition was resisting the complete incorporation of the church into the Nazi system, it can be seen as standing against the completely totalitarian claims of the Nazi state. In that way, even if not intentionally so, the Confessing Church remained a highly visible thorn in the side of Nazi Germany.

It should also be said that we do not find Bonhoeffer himself making professions of loyalty to the regime. He was on the radical wing of those in the church opposition to the German Christians, insisting that there could be no compromise or retreat from the stand taken at Barmen and absolutely no recognition of the Reich Church, either in Germany or by the ecumenical movement abroad. This radical stand led him not only into confrontation with the Reich Church authorities in Berlin (as is evidenced in numerous documents in this volume) but also into increasing tension with those Protestant leaders who wished to keep their regional churches "intact" rather than face the risk of division over the confession.

When he returned to Germany in April 1935, Bonhoeffer was entering a far more polarized scene within the opposition than had been the case when he left for London in October 1933. This polarization was to widen during his time as seminary director at Finkenwalde from 1935 to 1937 and thereafter, when the Confessing seminaries had become illegal and theological training continued as an underground movement.[6] By 1939 Bonhoeffer was seriously contemplating the possibility of involvement in political

---

[5.] [See, for example, ed. note 10. See also Barnett, *For the Soul of the People*, 57–63. —KC]

[6.] [These periods are covered by *DBW* 14 and 15.—KC]

resistance as an option for himself, and shortly thereafter his work for the resistance began.

During Bonhoeffer's time in London, events in the German Evangelical Church were coming to a head. Thousands of pastors joined in support of the Pastors' Emergency League declaration against the church "Aryan paragraphs." The November 13, 1933, Sports Palace rally of the German Christians—at which prominent German Christians called for the removal of Hebrew scriptures from the Bible and the radical nazification of the church—revealed their true colors. The ongoing attempts by Reich Bishop Müller's church regime to force the creation of a German Christian–governed Reich Church empowered the church opposition that, despite its internal divisions, was to constitute itself as the Confessing Church in the course of 1934. Bonhoeffer impatiently followed the course of his friends in Germany and tried to implement their decisions in the German congregations in Great Britain and at the ecumenical level. Bonhoeffer viewed the April 22, 1934, Ulm declaration as the opposition's long-overdue claim to be the legitimate Protestant Church in Germany against the German Christian usurpers.[7] He sensed that the Barmen Theological Declaration was the necessary expression "of a restoration of Reformation theology," a foundation that he believed would require further strides into uncharted theological territory.[8] In his preparations for the Fanø conference, Bonhoeffer was already in practice anticipating the schism that was eventually achieved at the Dahlem synod in October 1934.[9]

The political developments also kept the well-informed and critical London observer on his toes. Bonhoeffer regarded Germany's withdrawal from the League of Nations in the autumn of 1933—celebrated even by the church opposition[10]—as a dangerous step toward war. He sensed that the attempted National Socialist putsch in Austria was a warning signal of the threat Hitler's evil posed to all of Europe. And he saw the murders

---

[7.] See his letter of July 12, 1934, to Henry Louis Henriod, 1/125. [The Ulm declaration, issued by the churches of Württemberg and Bavaria and the Old Prussian Union churches, was a preliminary to the Barmen declaration one month later and accused the Reich Church of harassing its opponents in the churches and misrepresenting the situation. The full text of the Ulm declaration can be found in Cochrane, *Church's Confession under Hitler*, 235–36.—KC]

[8.] See his letter of July 13, 1934, to Reinhold Niebuhr, 1/127.

[9.] See his letter of July 4, 1934, to Théodore de Félice, 1/122.

[10.] [In October 1933, the Pastors' Emergency League issued a statement, signed by Martin Niemöller, congratulating Hitler. The statement stressed that the church opposition was concerned only with church-related matters and reiterated its loyalty to Hitler and his regime. See *DB-ER*, 323.—KC]

of June 30, 1934, as the dismal writing on the wall about what could be expected from the regime at home as well.[11]

The letters and documents in the extensive first part of this volume enable us to follow in detail the workings of Bonhoeffer's mind as he reacted to events in his homeland, actively and effectively intervening in these conflicts at the highest level. The Reich Church leaders seem to have suspected as much when at the last moment they hesitated to let Bonhoeffer go to London.[12] Here was a man who knew how to combine his activities as a local pastor with far-reaching involvement in national church politics and international ecumenical activities. In these minutes of meetings and letters, we can glean how Bonhoeffer led not only his London clergy colleagues but the entire Association of German Congregations in England on a collision course with the German Christian church leaders in Berlin. This began in November 1933 with the threats of withdrawal by both the Bradford pastors' conference and the Association of Congregations,[13] culminating one year later in the decision by a large majority of the German Protestant congregations in England that their association should join the Confessing Church.[14]

The twenty-eight-year old Bonhoeffer won the trust of his colleagues and of the highly regarded president of the Association of Congregations, Baron Bruno von Schröder, surprisingly quickly. At the same time, Bonhoeffer's counterpart in church political matters in Berlin, Theodor Heckel, became almost completely discredited with the London congregations. As a senior consistory official in the Reich Church administration, Heckel was already responsible for the oversight of congregations abroad when Bonhoeffer took up his work in London. Because of Bonhoeffer's firsthand information, Heckel's attempts to appease the congregations abroad and prevent them from taking sides in the Church Struggle became increasingly less credible.[15] Shortly after his visit to London in February 1934, Heckel was appointed a bishop and the director of the newly established Church Foreign Office. If his appearance in England had already given rise to uneasiness and distrust, his promotion by the Reich bishop discredited him even further.[16]

[11.] [This is a reference to the murders of several Catholic figures in connection with the Röhm putsch.—KC] See 1/146, ed. note 3, as well as the letter to Erwin Sutz of September 11, 1934, 1/147. See also *DB-ER*, 323.

[12.] See *DB-ER*, 321.

[13.] See 1/20.

[14.] See 1/159.

[15.] Cf. Heckel's letter of January 31, 1934, 1/65.

[16.] Regarding Heckel's visit, see 1/74, as well as Baron Schröder letter of February 19, 1934 (1/77) and Bonhoeffer's of March 18, 1934 (1/82).

Bonhoeffer was received with a remarkable degree of trust and understanding by George Bell, bishop of Chichester, who at the time was also president of the Ecumenical Council for Life and Work. Bonhoeffer had made Bell's acquaintance briefly in 1932. Two weeks after Bonhoeffer's arrival in London, Bell invited him for a meal at the Athenaeum club,[17] and shortly thereafter Bonhoeffer was the bishop's guest at Chichester. A friendship developed in which Bonhoeffer could safely express his views about the essentials of the German Church Struggle. Bell followed developments in Germany with keen interest and was grateful that he could consult this expert informant quickly and at any time, not least because Bonhoeffer was fluent in English and Bell himself hardly knew German. Bonhoeffer was therefore involved behind the scenes, motivating and advising, in a series of effective interventions by the bishop on behalf of the Confessing Church opposition.

Organization of the Material and Commentary in *London: 1933–1935*

The reader coming fresh to the period covered by this volume may not always find it easy to grasp the identities of the personalities involved nor to picture the contours of the entire context and the issues that were at stake. In addition to the historical review provided in the afterword, historical clarifications have been added to many of the footnotes, citing authoritative works available in English that offer a fuller understanding of Bonhoeffer's role and the wider history of the German Church Struggle. Preeminent here are Eberhard Bethge's *Dietrich Bonhoeffer: A Biography* and Klaus Scholder's two-volume *The Churches and The Third Reich.* Indeed, these may be regarded as essential background reading. The editor ventures also to suggest his own *Bonhoeffer and Britain,* which includes an extensive chapter on Bonhoeffer's London period and in fact is intended to be a companion to this volume at the more popular level. The index of persons includes pertinent biographical and historical information for everyone mentioned in the text and the notes.

In view of the wide range of Bonhoeffer's activities, the German editors have included in part 1 correspondence and some documents written by third parties. These documents illustrate Bonhoeffer's influence and show the effects of some of his initiatives. They include the letters and protests addressed to the Reich Church government in the name of the Association

---

[17.] See *DB-ER,* 356.

of Congregations in Britain or from the London pastors,[18] communications about the congregations' decision to break away from the Reich Church as well as the reactions from Berlin,[19] and Bell's "Ascension Day message" to the member churches of Life and Work on May 10, 1934, which was initiated (and coedited) by Bonhoeffer.[20]

Part 2, which includes Bonhoeffer's lectures and essays from this period, is inevitably thinner than in other volumes of the *Bonhoeffer Works*. Bonhoeffer's teaching activity was in abeyance during his time in London. Because of his contributions to the August 1934 ecumenical conference on the Danish island of Fanø, however, this volume does include texts that have had a lasting impact down to the present day. Several texts in the first part of the volume illustrate Bonhoeffer's involvement in the preparations for the conference. As one of the three international secretaries of the ecumenical youth commission, Bonhoeffer was responsible for running the youth conference that took place in conjunction with the main conference in Fanø. From the correspondence (which until now has been published only in fragments) with Théodore de Félice, the Geneva-based secretary of the youth commission, we learn something of Bonhoeffer's own concerns, as well as about his role in the discussions preceding the major joint conference of the Ecumenical Council for Life and Work with the working group of the World Alliance. Bonhoeffer's appeal to the ecumenical movement to make decisions of "conciliar" quality—on the one hand, carrying forward the confessional declarations of the Church Struggle and, on the other, as a powerful peace testimony—made history.[21] It may be said that this really only began to bear fruit half a century later, in the ecumenical conciliar process on Justice, Peace, and the Integrity of Creation. But what Bonhoeffer viewed as the integral relationship between the battle for the confession in Germany and the wider ecumenical movement was also a powerful and energizing memory when in the 1970s the World Council of Churches set up its special fund to combat racism. Not for nothing was the witness against apartheid sometimes called "the Church Struggle in South Africa."[22]

[18.] See, for example, 1/20.2, 1/20.3, and 1/49.

[19.] See 1/160, 1/162, 1/167, and 1/176–1/184.

[20.] See 1/103, as well as the intense correspondence between Bonhoeffer and Bell from April 15 to May 16, 1934: 1/89, 1/90, 1/92, 1/95, 1/97–1/99, 1/106, and 1/107.

[21.] See Weizsäcker, *Die Zeit drängt*; Heino Falcke, "Vom Gebot Christi and Konzilsgedanke," in Gremmels and Tödt, *Die Präsenz des verdrängten Gottes*, 101–19; Huber, "Ein ökumenisches Konzil"; Reuter, *Konzil des Friedens*; and Mayer, "Was wollte Dietrich Bonhoeffer in Fanø?"

[22.] [See de Gruchy and de Gruchy, *Church Struggle in South Africa*, esp. 119, 140, and 260, as well as de Gruchy, *Bonhoeffer for a New Day*, 353–65.—KC]

Bonhoeffer's address at the Fanø ecumenical meeting, "The Church and the Peoples of the World,"[23] until now classified with the sermons, must after thorough inquiry be viewed as a lecture. As contemporary conference reports make clear, Bonhoeffer gave this speech as the third of four introductory papers to the discussion of "The Church and the Peoples of the World" on August 28, 1934. The recollection of some participants of a morning meditation[24] probably refers to the devotions at the beginning of the youth conference on August 23, in which Bonhoeffer possibly used the same text from Psalm 85:9.[25] As in his other sermons, in this meditation Bonhoeffer probably kept closer to an exposition of the biblical text, whereas the text heads his conference lecture more like a motto.

Since Bonhoeffer looked after two of the six German congregations in London, he had to preach twice each Sunday, at St. Paul's Reformed Church in the East End and at the German Church, Sydenham, in southeast London. We owe the preservation of the twenty-three sermons and addresses in part 3 largely to the fact that Bonhoeffer sent the manuscripts to his theological colleague and friend Elisabeth Zinn in Germany. These sermons show us a preacher who, for all the intensity and concern for the political and church developments at home, applies himself first and foremost to drawing the listener into his concentrated dialogue with the promises and claims of the gospel. Indeed, no greater impact from this volume can be expected than from these samples of Bonhoeffer's powerful preaching.

The German editors conducted research for this volume in archives in Germany and abroad. Consequently, some documents that were published in the earlier *Gesammelte Schriften* (Bonhoeffer's collected writings) on the basis of copies or in abbreviated form have now been corrected and completed on the basis of the original texts. A few previously unpublished pieces supplement and clarify our existing knowledge of Bonhoeffer's activity during this period. In some instances, the originals could not be found in the relevant collections and archives; in these cases, the version presumed closest to the document has been used. A photocopy was generally sufficient to establish the text, but where there were problems deciphering it, recourse to the original was sometimes necessary. In three cases we have used existing English translations made at the time: 1/141 ("From the Report on the Fifth International Youth Conference"), 2/2 ("Theses Paper for the Fanø

[23.] See 2/3.

[24.] See *DB-ER*, 387–89.

[25.] See the minutes of the ecumenical youth meeting, 1/141. For a more extensive analysis of Bonhoeffer's role at the Fanø conference, see Heimbucher, "Christusfriede— Weltfrieden," chap. 2.

Conference"), and 2/3a ("Report on the Theological Conference in Bruay-en-Artois").

This volume also includes newly discovered material not included in the original German edition: correspondence between Bonhoeffer and Heinrich Lebrecht, a "non-Aryan" pastor who sought Bonhoeffer's help in immigrating to England, as well as Bishop Theodor Heckel's revealing comment on this; Bonhoeffer's correspondence with his brother-in-law Walter Dreß; letters from Hardy Arnold to his father, Eberhard Arnold, founder of the pacifist Bruderhof community, about conversations with Bonhoeffer in England; letters from Wilhelm Lütgert to Adolf Schlatter that give a particular perspective on the Church Struggle and the role of "radicals" such as Bonhoeffer; and Bonhoeffer's own report on the small Bruay conference that followed the Fanø conference in 1934. It cannot be assumed that there are no further relevant materials still awaiting discovery.

Bonhoeffer's spelling and punctuation were retained by the German editors throughout (any obvious slips being corrected without comment) even in his sermon scripts, unless it affected understanding. Allowing for the obvious needs of translation, this English edition has attempted to be faithful to this aim. The most obvious result of this policy for English-speaking readers is in those letters and sermons that Bonhoeffer himself wrote in English. Bonhoeffer was very fluent in English, but inevitably there are points where his command of the language is not perfect, either in spelling, grammar, or style, and no attempt has been made to correct these. All material originally in English is indicated in the notes.

Following the German edition, the editor of this English edition has closely followed Bonhoeffer's paragraph divisions, however unusual this may sometimes seem. An exception to this rule has been made in some of the sermons, where it was judged that the reproduction of whole pages of continuous text without paragraph breaks could not always convey the impression of a spoken homily nor encourage the reader to engage with the movement of thought in the discourse. The beginning of a new paragraph not in the original text is indicated by the symbol ¶.

Each corresponding page of the German critical edition is given in the outer margin of the page of the translated text. Emphases in the original texts are indicated with italics. The related biblical texts have been placed in small type at the head of the sermons in part 3 unless they were written in full by hand in the manuscript. Translations of biblical texts follow the New Revised Standard Version (NRSV), except where an English-original document cites an earlier version such as the King James Bible. Texts of writers other than Bonhoeffer appear in smaller type. Text omitted in the German edition is indicated by three ellipsis points enclosed in square brackets. In cases where the original German word may be of significance to scholars, it is included in the text in square brackets.

Translation Issues

Several points of translation should be noted. First, "Evangelical" (*Evangelisch*) in the German context generally means "Protestant" as distinct from "Catholic" rather than a certain type of Protestantism, as in some parts of the English-speaking world. In this context, the German Evangelical Church refers to the Protestant Church of Germany, which includes the regional Lutheran, Reformed, and United churches. Throughout *DBWE*, "German Evangelical Church" refers to that national institution; *evangelisch* is otherwise translated here as "Protestant." Second, readers will note the interchangeable use of "Confessing Church" and "Confessional Church" as terms for the sector of German Protestantism that constituted itself as a church in opposition to the German Christians and their goal of the nazification of Christianity. It is now generally accepted that the truer rendering of *Bekennende Kirche* is "Confessing Church," and this term is used throughout in our translation from the German. At the time of the Church Struggle, however, "Confessional Church" was frequently used by English speakers such as George Bell and by Bonhoeffer himself when writing in English, and in such cases that rendering has been retained.

In many instances, the names of ecumenical organizations and offices reflect the changing terminology of that era. During the period covered by this volume, the ecumenical movement was still constituting itself, and Bonhoeffer and his correspondents refer at various points to the "universal council," "Life and Work," and the "ecumenical council." These terms are all references to the Universal Christian Council for Life and Work, the governing body of the ecumenical movement whose offices were located in Geneva. In 1938 this body then became incorporated into the "World Council of Church in process of formation."

The translation and clarifications of terms from the Nazi era pose a challenge for everyone who deals academically with this era. Much of the early Church Struggle, for example, focused on debates about the status of "Aryans" and "non-Aryans"—distinctions that have no legitimacy but were at the heart of Nazi ideology and therefore played a powerful role. Bonhoeffer, of course, consistently opposed this ideological and false distinction; this opposition was the foundation of his battle against the "Aryan paragraph" in the German church before he left for London. Thus where these terms appear, they have been enclosed in quotation marks, although quotation marks are not used in the original text. The editors of this English edition have also attempted to indicate to readers other terms with loaded ideological meaning, such as *Volk.*

A most important feature, as in all volumes in the series, is the critical apparatus supplied through footnotes that indicate sources, variant readings, provisional versions discarded by Bonhoeffer, cross references, explanatory historical notes, and so on. In most instances the first note for a text comprises information on where the document can be found and also, when appropriate, its reference number in the catalog of the Bonhoeffer literary estate (*Nachlaß*, abbreviation *NL*) compiled by Eberhard Bethge and Dietrich Meyer. Information on the format of the document is also given, along with references to copies already available and any pertinent information on the historical background. Information about letterheads and memoranda— when they are contemporary or biographically well testified—is given in the citations and not in the text. More precise postal information is omitted from the address and date in the text. Signatures that can be inferred from the document but are missing from the basic version as, for example, in a carbon copy, appear in square brackets.

This English edition reproduces as exactly as possible the critical apparatus of the German original, with certain additions. When possible, English editions of German works cited either by Bonhoeffer himself or by the German editors have been identified. At certain points the English editor has augmented the original German notes, either with additional relevant information or explanations of points likely to be less familiar in the English-speaking world or—very occasionally—where a correction seemed necessary. All such additions by the English editor are placed in square brackets followed by "KC."

Acknowledgments

The editor of this volume has throughout had the immense benefit of continual guidance and advice from Victoria Barnett, general editor of the English edition of the *Dietrich Bonhoeffer Works*, and Barbara Wojhoski, who has had the final responsibility in preparing the manuscript for publication. Almost the entire main text and the afterword (the *Nachwort* of the German edition) were translated by Isabel Best of Nyon/Geneva, and high praise is due her for the skill and diligence with which she has undertaken this task—one that she has repeatedly declared to the editor to have been as inspiring as it was challenging. Martin Conway of Oxford acted as a consultant in the earlier stages of drafting the translation, and his comments were greatly appreciated by the translator and the editor alike. One item in the volume, however, required an unusual degree of specialist skill, namely, the poem that Franz

Hildebrandt wrote in sixteenth-century *Lutherdeutsch* for Bonhoeffer's birthday in February 1934. The translation of this into a rendering redolent of sixteenth-century English was undertaken by Professor Mark McCulloh of Davidson College and Julie Woestehoff, executive director of Parents United for Responsible Education, after preliminary work by Douglas Stott and Victoria Barnett. Letters to Bonhoeffer originally in French were translated by Professor Vicki Mistacco of Wellesley College. Finally, the editor wishes to thank Kenneth Walker of London for supplying a translation of the German editors' foreword that has been adapted for this introduction.

Because this volume is a rendering into English of the German edition, no words of appreciation can adequately convey the debt owed to the German editors: Hans Goedeking, Martin Heimbucher, and Hans-Walter Schleicher. It will be very evident to the reader just how much assiduous labor went into their edition in terms of locating original sources, checking variant editions in the sources, and researching historical background and detail. They have also been most helpful to the translator and the editor in offering many perceptive and valuable comments on the translation in its penultimate stages, as has Hans Pfeifer of Freiburg, the liaison between the German and the English editorial board. We can only hope that our work may in some degree at least do justice to the impressively high standards of scholarship set by our German colleagues. In turn, we join them in appreciation of the help they received in their own work from a great many individuals and institutions. In particular, the late Eberhard Bethge, the close friend and biographer of Dietrich Bonhoeffer, was always ready to help them with information from his rich store of memory and checked doubtful readings against the original materials. Herbert Anzinger assisted editorially with the volume and patiently and carefully helped overcome complicated editorial problems. Holger Roggelin cooperated unselfishly in the essential archival inquiries. Those responsible for the Lambeth Palace Library in London, for the archives of the World Council of Churches in Geneva, as well as for the archives of the Dietrich Bonhoeffer Church in London generously allowed inspection of their resources. The late Jørgen Glenthøj laid the foundation for the biographical information in the index of names.

The editor of the present volume thanks the staff of the Lambeth Palace Library and the Library and Archives of the World Council of Churches in Geneva for yet further assistance. John Godsey assisted in tracking down English translations for the footnotes. Pushpa Iyer typed the documents that were originally in English so that they could be edited for this volume. G. Clarke Chapman devotedly attended to the listing of biblical citations and to refining the biograms in the index of names. Last but not least, Andrea Havaz and Ruthann Gill on the staff of the Conference of European Churches in

Geneva came to the editor's rescue on several critical occasions when his computer literacy manifested its limitations

Conscious of the privilege of being invited to undertake this work and in the hope that it will further the knowledge of the rich legacy of Dietrich Bonhoeffer's life and witness, the editor and his colleagues gratefully offer this volume to the English-speaking world.

Keith Clements
Geneva, November 2005

PART 1
Letters and Documents

1. To Baron Bruno Schröder[1]

11

[London,] October 24, 1933

Dear Baron Schröder,

Thank you very much for your letter.[2] Certainly I shall be happy to take over as secretary of the Association of Congregations, if that is your wish. Of course, I am completely new to the organization and have just been discussing with my fellow pastor Wehrhan whether it would not be more advisable to ask one of the more experienced gentlemen. Pastor Wehrhan tells me that you are not receiving visitors at present, so with your permission I shall ask you about it again after a little time.

In the meantime, my dear Baron, allow me to present to you my very best wishes.

Your humble servant,
D. Bonhoeffer

2. To Karl Barth[1]

London, October 24, 1933

Dear Professor Barth,

I am now writing you the letter that I meant to write six weeks ago and which would then, perhaps, have had entirely different consequences for the course of my personal life. Why I did not write then is almost incomprehensible to me *now*. I know only that two things were factors at that time. I knew that you were busy with a thousand other matters, and it seemed to me, during those heated weeks,[2] that the fate of one individual was so utterly trivial that I simply could not imagine it being important enough to write

---

12

[1.] ADBC, GV 5, 2; handwritten; return address: "Pastor Dr. D. Bonhoeffer, 23, Manor Mount S.E. 23." Baron Schröder was chairman of the Association of German Evangelical Congregations in Great Britain and Ireland.

[2.] Letter of October 12, 1933, in which Schröder asked Bonhoeffer to serve as acting secretary of the Association of Congregations. *NL*, A 41,1 (1).

[1.] Karl Barth-Archiv, Basel; handwritten; see also *NL*, A 41,9 (28); typewritten copy; previously published in *Evangelische Theologie* 15 (1955), 234–36; *Mündige Welt*, 1:112–14; *GS* 2:130–34. For Barth's reply, see 1/16.

[2.] The reference is to the founding of the Pastors' Emergency League and the World Alliance conference in Sofia; both occurred in the weeks following the "brown synod" of the Old Prussian Church in September 1933. Cf. *DB-ER*, 304–23. [This synod was termed the "brown synod" because so many of the church delegates appeared in brown SA uniforms.—KC]

about to you. Second, however, I think there was also a bit of fear involved. I knew that I would simply have had to do what you would have told me, and I wanted to be free, so I suppose I simply withdrew. Today I know that that was wrong and that I must beg your pardon. I made my decision "freely," but without really being free in relation to you. I had meant to ask you whether I should go to London to take up a pastorate. I would have believed that you would tell me the right thing, and you alone, except for one person who is so deeply involved in my personal destiny and would have been caught up in my uncertainty.[3]

I have always wanted to be a pastor, as I have mentioned to you several times.[4] This matter of London was raised with me in July.[5] I accepted with reservations, came here for two days, found the congregations in rather a neglected state, and remained uncertain. When the matter had to be decided in September, I said yes.[6] The formal agreement is loose; six months' notice required for resignation. I have taken only a leave of absence from the university.[7] I cannot foresee at this point the extent to which I shall have to make a firmer commitment to the congregation. At the same time I also received an offer of a pastorate in east Berlin[8] and was certain of the vote there. Then came the Aryan paragraph in the Prussian church,[9] and I knew that I could not accept that pastorate for which I had been longing, particularly in that part of the city, if I was unwilling to give up my unconditional opposition to *this* church. It would have meant the loss of credibility before the congregation from the outset. It would have meant abandoning my solidarity with the Jewish Christian pastors—my closest friend is one of them and is currently without a future, so he is now coming to join me in England.[10]

13

[3.] According to Eberhard Bethge (*GS* 2:131), this was Franz Hildebrandt. It may, however, refer to Elisabeth Zinn.

[4.] Regarding Bonhoeffer's encounters with Barth, see *DB-ER*, 175–86.

[5.] On July 30 Bonhoeffer was interviewed in London and preached at Sydenham and St. Paul's churches (see *DB-ER*, 298).

[6.] See Bonhoeffer's August 17, 1933, letter to the Church Federation office. *DBW* 12 (1/85), 115.

[7.] While he was pastor of the two overseas congregations in London, Bonhoeffer also remained a lecturer at Friedrich Wilhelm University in Berlin. On August 20, 1933, the dean of the theological faculty there granted him a leave for the winter semester 1933–34; see *DBW* 12, (1/87), 118. See also the confirmation of this by the congregational council, 1/38.

[8.] The Lazarus Church in east Berlin (see *DB-ER*, 252.)

[9.] On September 5 the new Prussian general synod voted to introduce the "Aryan paragraph" in the church. "Non-Aryan" pastors and church officials were to be excluded from church positions.

[10.] Franz Hildebrandt. Cf. his letter of the same date (October 24) to Martin

So the alternatives were lecturer *or* pastor, and in any case, not as pastor in the Prussian church. I cannot give you a full account of my motives for and against, even though I am still dealing with them and perhaps shall never put them fully behind me. I hope I have not gone away out of pique at the situation of our church and in particular at the position taken by our group. In any case, it probably would not have taken long until I was forced to a formal parting of the ways with my friends—but really, I think all that spoke much more against London than in its favor. If it is at all desirable, after such a decision, to find well-defined reasons for it, I think one of the strongest was that I no longer felt inwardly equal to the questions and demands that I was facing. I felt that, in some way I don't understand, I found myself in radical opposition to all my friends;[11] I was becoming increasingly isolated with my views of the matter, even though I was and remain personally close to these people. All this frightened me and shook my confidence, so that I began to fear that dogmatism might be leading me astray—since there seemed no particular reason why my own view in these matters should be any better, any more right, than the views of many really good and able pastors whom I sincerely respect. And so I thought it was about time to go into the wilderness for a spell, and simply work as a pastor, as unobtrusively as possible. At the time it seemed to me more dangerous to make a gesture than to retreat into silence.[12] That is how it came about. There was one other symptom for me as well, and that is that the Bethel Confession, into which I truly had poured heart and soul, met with almost no understanding.[13] I am sure that I did not take this personally, however; there was not the least reason to do so. It just made me insecure about what I was doing.

14

Then about ten days before I was to leave, the church chancellery office telephoned to say that sending me abroad was creating difficulties, because of my attitude of opposition toward the German Christians.[14] Fortunately

---

Niemöller: "I (want to) follow Bonhoeffer in the foreseeable future as his guest at his new home, and then see what to do" (*GS* 2:227); see also the certificate for Hildebrandt, 1/5.

[11.] In Berlin, Bonhoeffer and Hildebrandt had called in June for an interdict (boycott on funeral services) in protest against the state-appointed church commissioner [August Jäger—KC], and in September they advocated schism (separation from the heretical church) in view of the church Aryan paragraphs. On neither occasion did they meet with understanding from within the church opposition (see *DB-ER*, 299 and 307).

[12.] The sentence "At the time . . . into silence" was added in the margin.

[13.] Cf. *DB-ER*, 303; *GS* 2:91–119; *DBW* 12:362–408.

[14.] [The so-called Faith Movement of German Christians (*Deutsche Christen*), which was seeking to nazify the Protestant churches and bring them into conformity with the new Nazi order.—KC]

I was able to have a conversation with Müller in person,[15] in which I said that of course I could not change my position and would much rather stay there than sail under false colors, and also that I could not represent the German Christians abroad. At my request this was all noted for the files. I can't tell you what a poor impression M[üller] made on me. He said to reassure me, "By the way, I have already arranged for the existing difficulties to be dismissed." However, he remained uncertain as to what to do about me, and I hoped that the decision would simply be made elsewhere and was quite relieved. The next day I received word that I should go. Fear of the Oikumene—how disagreeable.

Now I have been here for eight days, have to preach every Sunday, and get news almost every day from Berlin as to how things stand. It's enough to tear one apart. And now you will soon be in Berlin,[16] and I cannot be there. I even feel as though, by going away, I have been personally disloyal to you. Perhaps you won't be able to understand this at all, but for me it is an enormous reality. Yet at the same time I am infinitely happy to be working in a congregation, even one so far away. I am also hoping that here I will be able to get some real clarity about ecumenical issues, for I plan to continue that type of work while I am here. Perhaps this can also be a way of giving some real support to the German church.

I have no idea yet how long I shall have to stay on here. If I knew I was really needed there in Berlin—it's so terribly hard to know what we should do. "We do not know what to do, but . . ." 2 Chronicles.[17]

So, now this letter has been written. These are only personal matters, but I did want you to know about them. If I were ever to hear a word from you again, it would be wonderful. I think a great deal about you and your work and where we should be without it. Would you be so kind as to write me your very honest opinion of all this? I think I would be open even to sharp words and grateful for them. I'd like to write to you again about the matter, when my typewriter comes. This way it's heavy going for you to read.

In gratitude as always, I remain
Yours very sincerely,
Dietrich Bonhoeffer

[15.] Conversation with Reich Bishop Ludwig Müller on October 4, 1933. Cf. the letter to Heckel of the same date, *DBW* 12 (1/107); see also *DB-ER*, 321.

[16.] On October 30, 1933, Barth lectured at the Berlin Choral Academy (*Singakademie*) on "Reformation as Decision-Making" (cf. Busch, *Karl Barth: His Life from Letters and Autobiographical Texts*, 230–31; see also *Theologische Existenz heute*, no. 3, Munich 1933).

[17.] 2 Chron. 20:12: "We do not know what to do, but our eyes are on you." Cf. Bonhoeffer's sermon on this verse for the Sunday after Ascension Day, 1932; *GS* 1:133–39, *PAM* 1:273–80, and *DBW* 11 (3/8).

3. From Friedrich Siegmund-Schultze[1]

Flims-Waldhaus (Graubünden)
October 28, 1933

Dear Colleague,

I hear from Miss Lepsius[2] that you have arrived in London. Several people had told me that you were planning to take up a pastorate in London. But I also heard all kinds of rumors, which arise so easily these days both inside and outside Germany. Some very important persons in the ecumenical movement had received false reports alleging, for instance, that you were to be sent to a concentration camp and that it was not yet certain that you would be able to avoid this.[3] I would be most grateful if at some point you could give me an idea of the actual facts (i.e., that you went of your own free will to take up a pastorate in London and that this also reflects the wishes of the present church leadership), so that in two or three cases where I need to provide correct information I can give it according to what I hear from you.

Professor Richter has written me at length about Sofia.[4] I have also heard a good deal from other people. I can understand how these things took place. But you will agree with me that the resolution passed in Sofia will have rather far-reaching consequences for the position of the World Alliance in Germany.[5] Since it would not be honorable for us to keep this resolution a secret in Germany, the "German Christians" aren't going to be kindly disposed toward any thinking within the German branch of the World Alliance that identifies with this trend in the world organization. Because I anticipate all sorts of struggles over this, I would be most grateful if you would give me your thoughts on it, even after the fact. Perhaps there are also other things that happened in Sofia that it would be important for

16

[1.] EZA 51/D III u/2; carbon copy. Cf. *NL*, A 28,4 (8); previously published in *Mündige Welt*, 5: 66–67, and *GS* 6: 341–43.. [Friedrich Siegmund-Schultze had been arrested by the Gestapo on June 21, 1933, and deported "on the charge of helping Jews in ninety-three cases" (Klaus Scholder, *Churches and the Third Reich*, 1:257–58).—KC] He sought to regain his health in the Swiss mountain climate. See Bonhoeffer's reply, 1/8.

[2.] Siegmund-Schultze's secretary in Berlin.

[3.] Cf. *DB-ER*, 296, and Bonhoeffer's letter of October 10, 1933, reassuring Bishop Ammundsen that this was not the case, *DBW* 12 (1/110).

[4.] Julius Richter and Bonhoeffer were the German participants at the World Alliance conference in Sofia, Bulgaria, September 1933; see *DB-ER*, 313.

[5.] Among other things, the Sofia conference decided that the theme for the major conference in 1934 [i.e., the Fanø conference—KC] should be the peace question, and that Bonhoeffer should be one of the main speakers. On the Jewish issue a resolution was passed that sharply criticized the Aryan paragraph [as well as the Nazi anti-Jewish laws in general—KC] and accused the German church of "a denial of the explicit teaching and spirit of the gospel of Jesus Christ." See Boyens, *Kirchenkampf und Ökumene* 1:66–67 and 312, and *DB-ER*, 313.

me to know. In any case, I would be grateful to have your own personal view of what took place there.

Today I also have a particular request to make, one that you can probably easily fulfill from London. I have heard somewhat contradictory news of remarks made by Bishop Hossenfelder[6] during his conversations in London. Among other things I have received a confidential report of his talk with the archbishop of Canterbury, to which I will need to give a reply. It would be very important to me if you could let me know whatever you can find out about Bishop Hossenfelder's mission in London. Perhaps you could also write to me explicitly what was reported about it in the papers and magazines, that is, what could eventually be quoted elsewhere, and what is confidential or at least should be kept confidential. It is most important to me to be able to answer correctly the questions that I have also received about this matter.

My old friends in the World Alliance, of course, are making even more use of me than before for all sorts of communications. I have therefore brought my secretary[7] here and am doing quite a bit of writing about these matters. I am also trying to keep *Ekklesia* going.[8] I have just sent your new address to Klotz. Evidently he has been delayed in printing Bell's book[9] by Christmas publications that have to be finished first.

I wish you a good start in your new work with all my heart. It is hard to be abroad, watching events in our homeland that are so drastic and difficult to imagine. From outside the country, one has a better possibility of seeing them objectively, but one does miss the ability to be involved on a daily basis. I hope that experiencing this together with a German congregation will give you the possibility of working spiritually with a group of Germans in the creation of a new order that, I am convinced, will not be so much fulfilled in the outward forming of our age, but rather in the working out of a whole new shape for the future.

Cordially, I remain
Yours,
S[iegmund]-S[chultze]

[6.] Hossenfelder had been delegated by Reich Bishop Ludwig Müller to try to establish good relations with the Church of England. See *DB-ER*, 355.

[7.] Possibly Miss Lepsius, see ed. note 2.

[8.] Siegmund-Schultze was editor of *Ekklesia*, a "collection of self-descriptions of Christian churches," Gotha/Leipzig, from 1934.

[9.] George Bell, *Brief Sketch of the Church of England*, 1929; German translation in *Ekklesia*, vol. 2: "Die anglikanische Kirche," 1934. It was translated by Elisabeth Reinke, Dietrich Bonhoeffer, and Bertha Schulze.

4. From Baron Bruno Schröder[1]   18

November 1, 1933

Dear Pastor Bonhoeffer,

My thanks for your letter of the twenty-fourth of last month.[2] I shall be most happy to have a visit from you sometime soon here in the City and will ask my secretary to send you a date and time at which I would like to see you, if convenient for you.

Your obedient servant,
[Bruno Schröder]

5. Certificate for Franz Hildebrandt[1]

London, 3.XI. 33

The Pastor of the German Church
of Sydenham and St. Paul's in London
Dr. Dietrich Bonhoeffer.
23, Manor Mount, S.E. 23, London

This is to certify that I have invited my friend Pastor Dr. Franz Hildebrandt, to come to London and to stay with me as long as he wants. He will during the time he is here take up studies of the English language and of English Churchlife. I guarantee for him in any respect.

Dr. Dietrich Bonhoeffer, Pastor
[Two seals:]   19
St. Paul's German Reformed Church
    Goulston St. Aldgate, E.
German Evangelical Church of Sydenham
    Christ for all, and all in him[2]

[1.] ADBC, GV 5, 3; carbon copy; from London. See also *NL*, A 41,1 (2); typewritten.
[2.] See 1/1.

[1.] National Library of Scotland, estate of Franz Hildebrandt; ACC 9251, no. 22[a–c]; typewritten; in original English, including errors. Bonhoeffer had been the German pastor of the two congregations, St. Paul's German Reformed Church in Aldgate, London, and the German Evangelical Church of Sydenham, London, for ten days. He used the seals of both churches to request an extended residence permit for his friend Pastor Franz Hildebrandt from the British authorities in London.
[2.] [Although written in English, the heading of this letter uses the German seals of the two congregations. The German original of the motto "Christ for all, and all in him" is *Alles allen und in Christus.*—KC]

I beg to repeat this invitation for the month of August and September. Being myself on holiday in Danmark where my friend is coming from I am unable to confirm this invitation with my church seal.

August 22nd. 34.   Dietrich Bonhoeffer, Pf.[3]

6. Minutes of a Meeting of the Congregational Council of the Sydenham Church[1]

Meeting of the Congregational Council[2]
Friday, November 3, 1933, at 8:30 P.M. in the Parish Hall
Present: Mrs. Schlund, Mr. Voigt, Mr. Lorenz, Mr. Brown, the pastor

The meeting was opened with a prayer. The pastor was unanimously requested to chair the meeting. The minutes of the last meeting[3] were approved. The pastor thanked those in attendance for coming and asked permission to put several questions to them for discussion.

1.) How can the children and youth of the church be encouraged to attend? An attempt should be made to hold a Sunday school after the worship service. Special events should be planned for the young people, and they should be personally invited by the pastor. A new address list for this purpose is urgently needed. Musical evenings, and later also evening lectures, should be organized. Christmas should be an occasion for the young people themselves to participate in the work of the church. The question of whether to have a nativity play[4] was considered.

2.) Christmas and New Year's Eve services. An attempt should be made this year to have a Christmas Eve service in the afternoon. However, there were doubts as to whether this could be carried out. There should also be an afternoon service on New Year's Eve.

[3.] The sentence beginning "I beg to" was added by Bonhoeffer when he met Hildebrandt on Fanø in Denmark in August 1934, shortly before the conference that was held there. Cf. Hildebrandt's contribution in Zimmermann, *I Knew Dietrich Bonhoeffer*, 39.

[1.] ADBC, Minute Book of the German Evangelical Church of Sydenham in London; written in Bonhoeffer's own hand. See *NL*, A 41,3 (2).

[2.] ["Meeting of the Congregational Council" is the English term used here and elsewhere in this volume for *Vorstandssitzung der Gemeinde*.—KC]

[3.] Chaired by Pastor Singer, Bonhoeffer's predecessor.

[4.] Here Bonhoeffer was drawing on his experience as a student pastor in Barcelona; see *DBW* 10:119–20, 134, and 137. On Christmas Eve 1933, the Sydenham Church did in fact have its first nativity play; see *DB-ER*, 330.

3.) The pastor asked if he might post the numbers of the hymns to be sung during worship on the notice boards. This request was granted. A possible change in the liturgy was considered.

4.) The pastor was granted permission to convert his storage room into a guest room.[5]

5.) Mr. Voigt presented some bills to be paid. The meeting was adjourned at 9:45 P.M.

Bonhoeffer

7. Minutes of a Meeting of the Congregational Council of St. Paul's Church[1]

Quarterly Meeting
on Monday November 6, 1933, at 7 P.M.
in the Church Sacristy

Present: Messrs. G. Henne, E. Henne, Blumenstock, Eisemann, Nette, Klugmann, Compton, Neubert, Goetz, Dickens, Klotz, Neubert, Weber, and the pastor

At the suggestion of the treasurer, the pastor was asked to serve as chair. He opened the meeting with a prayer. The account books were examined and found to be correct. The pastor then asked if he might put some questions with regard to encouraging the youth to come to church. The question of holding a Sunday school was thoroughly considered, but it was decided that concentrating on the religious instruction in the Saturday classes, plus the confirmation classes, was more appropriate. A nativity play with the children should be kept in mind for Christmas.[2] The vestry members will help in bringing the youth closer to the church. The meeting was adjourned at 7:45 P.M.

Dietrich Bonhoeffer, Pastor

21

[5.] In his flat in the German parsonage; see 1/5.

[1.] ADBC, Minute Book of St. Paul's German Evangelical Reformed Church, London, November 6, 1933; in Bonhoeffer's handwriting. See *NL*, A 41,3 (1); typewritten copy.

[2.] Cf. 1/6.

8. To Friedrich Siegmund-Schultze[1]

London, November 6, 1933

Dear Professor Siegmund-Schultze,

Many thanks for your letter.[2] I would like to reply right away to your various questions. The matter of the pastorate in London for me came up during the summer and was unrelated to church politics. In the end my acceptance of it was also without any particular relation to the church political situation. However, I cannot claim that I was fulfilling the wishes of the present church government, as you suggest, since a few days before I was due to leave,[3] they made an attempt to use my position in the Wittenberg appeal[4] against me, as well as the Sofia resolution[5] and, third, my memorandum on the Aryan paragraph at the time of the General Synod.[6] They told me that, having taken such positions, I could not be sent abroad. I said only that I would, of course, retract nothing of what I had said, and I insisted on speaking with the Reich bishop. I said to him that under no circumstances could I represent the German Christians, that I would continue to express my position in ecumenical conversations, and that if he expected anything different from me, I would prefer that he forbid me to go. He was very amicable and said he would make the decision himself. The next day it appeared as though they were really going to stop me. But on the following day the fear that the congregations here would break away gained the upper hand, and I was asked to go to London. I then permitted my conversation with the Reich bishop and the opinions I had put forward to be placed on record, so that I could have an absolutely free hand and did not need in any way to see myself as the emissary of a German Christian church[7]—quite the contrary, in fact. Of course, I would not bring the Church Struggle into my congregations here, and it is equally clear that at ecumenical meetings I must continue as

22

[1.] EZA 51/D III u/2; typewritten. See also *NL*, A 28,4 (8); typewritten copy; previously published in *Mündige Welt*, 6:67–68; *GS* 6:343–46.

[2.] Of October 28, 1933; see 1/3.

[3.] The reference is to discussions with Theodor Heckel and Ludwig Müller on October 4, 1933. Cf. *DB-ER*, 321–22.

[4.] Bonhoeffer's was the first signature on the September 27, 1933, manifesto of the Pastors' Emergency League, "To the National Synod of the German Evangelical Church in Wittenberg" [which opposed the Aryan paragraph—KC]. Cf. *NL*, A 38,6. Previously published in *GS* 2:74–76. See also *DB-ER*, 309–10, 319–20.

[5.] See 1/3, ed. note 5.

[6.] Leaflet addressed to the "brown synod" of the Old Prussian Church on September 5, 1933: "The Aryan Paragraph and the Church," *NL*, 38,5. Previously published in *GS* 2:62–69. See also *DB-ER*, 304–6.

[7.] [I.e., a church controlled by the so-called German Christian movement.—KC]

always to speak personally, as one who can only represent a small minority. Afterward the Clerical Ministry[8] once more started a terrible row about my being sent abroad; Secretary Theodor[9] almost lost his job over it, I heard afterward. But after all the Reich bishop had taken the decision upon himself, and so here I am.

No, I have not actually been in a concentration camp, although on the occasion of the church election the highest police authority raised the prospect that a colleague and I might be sent there.[10] Perhaps this is what the rumor is about.

Now a word about Sofia. In fact I regard the resolution as it stands as both good and defensible, and objectively I would not be able to retreat on the wording. At Henriod's request I had a private conversation in my room, lasting several hours, with Toureille, Bouvier, W. A. Brown, Ammundsen, [and] Atkinson. On this occasion I spoke very frankly about the Jewish question, the Aryan paragraph in the church, and the general synod, and also about the question of the future of the minority, and met with a great deal of understanding. I believe that in essence it is thanks to this meeting—which, by the way, Prof. Richter[11] most likely does not, and should not, know about (mainly because of what he said in Zurich[12]—this, of course, I tell you in confidence)—that the resolution did take the moderate form in which we now have it. The others were naturally aware that during those very days the situation in Germany was so tense that we could only expect the weighty interventions that did subsequently take place. Incidentally, during this little meeting we decided on a plan to send a delegation to the German church government, and this is still being pursued here in London. A few days ago

23

[8.] [*Geistliches Ministerium*; this was a governmental council with United, Lutheran, and Reformed representatives, appointed by Reich Bishop Müller.—KC]

[9.] Theodor Heckel.

[10.] In response to the protests by Bonhoeffer and Gerhard Jacobi to the head of the Prussian Gestapo against the confiscation of the Young Reformers' election leaflets in July 1933 (*DB-ER*, 295). The group "Gospel and Church" had first listed themselves on the church election lists as "Evangelical Church." The German Christians had obtained an injunction against the use of the name that applied to all election material and flyers. On July 18, 1933, five days before the church elections, Bonhoeffer and Jacobi got Gestapo head Rudolf Diels to return the materials, on the condition that the title of the group be changed. Diels had to return the materials because there was no formal legal basis for impounding them if the name were changed.

[11.] Professor Julius Richter, member of the International Committee of the World Alliance for Promoting International Friendship through the Churches

[12.] [This may be a reference to Richter's remark to Siegmund-Schultze that Reich Bishop Müller had shown an "astonishing sign of understanding" in allowing Bonhoeffer to go to London. See *DB-ER*, 321.—KC]

I was at a meeting with all the ecumenical people here.[13] It seems to me questionable whether the G. C.[14] will seriously attack the Sofia resolution, since there has been some embarrassment within their own ranks about the Aryan paragraph. I don't know by what means the resolution was officially conveyed to the church government, but I do know that they received a copy. I really don't think we need be afraid of spreading it about as much as we can. *Junge Kirche*,[15] too, ought to publish the text.

Hossenfelder[16] had no discussion at all with Canterbury.[17] Chichester[18] told me about this in detail the day before yesterday. Canterbury refused because he wished to avoid any misunderstanding about, or misuse of, such a reception—which he apparently regarded as not improbable. Hossenfelder saw Gloucester,[19] who was evidently rather taken with him. Chichester told me in confidence that a misunderstanding developed during the conversation with regard to the possibility of English bishops attending the consecration of the Reich bishop, which was cleared up later through correspondence. Hossenfelder came to London at the invitation of the Oxford movement,[20] about which he was very enthusiastic. Obviously the reception was nothing much. He wanted to make a speech in a German parish hall where the trustees included some eminent Jews, but this was prevented.[21] Instead, after a dinner given by Hoesch,[22] to which parsons and church elders had been invited, he gave a speech that was quite inept and made little impression. The newspapers took almost no notice of Hossenfelder's presence, besides the fact that he was visiting the Oxford movement, and to my knowledge even that only amounted to four or five lines in two newspapers. His obvious intention of ingratiating himself with the English church has, just as obviously, failed.

I'm so very glad to hear that you are feeling better. About how long do you expect to remain abroad? I have no idea of my own plans concerning

---

[13.] At the meeting of the World Alliance's Executive Committee and the Universal Council for Life and Work, November 2–4, 1933, in London. See *DB-ER*, 356.

[14.] [German Christians.—KC]

[15.] [*Junge Kirche* (Young Church) was a monthly journal published by the Young Reformation movement, strongly opposed to the German Christians.—KC]

[16.] See 1/3, ed. note 6.

[17.] The archbishop of Canterbury, Cosmo Gordon Lang.

[18.] The bishop of Chichester, George Bell, at Bonhoeffer's first meeting with him in London.

[19.] The bishop of Gloucester, Arthur Cayley Headlam.

[20.] A popular evangelistic missionary movement led by the American Frank Buchman.

[21.] Cf. *DB-ER*, 355.

[22.] Leopold von Hoesch was the German ambassador in London.

this at this point. These days it is hard even to predict what will be happening in eight days, and as for the week after, who knows?

With my heartiest good wishes, I remain
Yours sincerely,
Dietrich Bonhoeffer

9. To Henry Louis Henriod[1]

25

London, November 9, 1933

My dear Henriot,[2]

Having kept to the deadline of four days,[3] as you see I am looking to improve my reputation with you. The following addresses in Berlin will most likely lead you to a great deal of the information you are looking for: 1. Pastor Jacobi, Berlin W. 50, Achenbachstraße 18; 2. Pastor Niemöller, Dahlem, Cäcilienallee no. ?; 3. Pastor Häfele, Immanuel Church, Berlin NE. Jacobi can give you more addresses.

Yours sincerely,
Dietrich Bonhoeffer

10. From Friedrich Siegmund-Schultze[1]

Flims-Waldhaus, November 10, 1933

My dear colleague,

I very much appreciated your letter of November 6.[2] In response, may I raise a few more questions:

Could you please send me a copy of your memorandum on the Aryan paragraph,[3] which you wrote at the time of the general synod?

[1.] WCC Archives, World Alliance, Letters from Dietrich Bonhoeffer, 12; typewritten. Previously published in *GS* 6:341.

[2.] The misspelling occurs in the original document.

[3.] Apparently in reply to a letter (not extant) from Henriod, who was planning a visit to Berlin in the hope of contact with the church opposition. On the plans (again abandoned) for an ecumenical delegation to Germany, see 1/4 and Bell's November 4, 1933, letter to Koechlin (Bell and Koechlin, *Briefwechsel*, 80), as well as the reference to Henriod's visit to Berlin in spring 1934, in Winterhager's May 22, 1934, letter to Félice, 1/109.

[1.] EZA 51/D III u/2; typewritten; see also *NL*, appendix D 1,4 (1). Previously published in *GS* 6:346–47.

[2.] See 1/8.

[3.] The August 1933 leaflet "The Aryan Paragraph in the Church," *GS* 2:62–69; previously published in *DBW* 12 (2/16).

Would you be so kind as to keep me informed about the progress of plans to send a delegation to the German church government?

26   Will you actually be able to keep your post as German youth secretary of the World Alliance?[4] I personally would be very glad if you could do so. I am only afraid that in Germany people will say that this post should be held by someone working in a youth organization or who is, in any case, in direct contact with German youth work. I would be grateful to you if you could let me know at some point if you have given thought to this, or whether someone else has approached you with any thoughts about it. In any case, I would take a position on this entirely in accordance with your wishes and opinions.

I have hardly been able to express to you how pleased I have been about your work in the World Alliance throughout these last few years and how grateful I am for it. I do hope that at some time before too long we shall have more of a chance to share our thoughts on these matters than has been possible at the most recent conferences. For the next few months I shall have to stay quiet here high up in the mountains, but in the spring I hope to be able to travel and perhaps come to London.

I recently had a letter from the Reverend Fox, the general secretary of the British Association for the World Alliance. He wrote that he had heard you were coming to London. I would hope very much that you might be able to call on him as soon as possible. But perhaps you have already met him in the meantime. In fact I have just heard as much from him.[5]

With all good wishes again for your work,
Yours,
F. Siegmund-Schultze

11. Vote to Call Dietrich Bonhoeffer as Pastor

11.1 From the Minute Book of the Sydenham Church[1]

Congregational Assembly on November 12, 1933, at the Church in Dacres Road, following the Worship Service

The congregation, having been duly invited to an assembly following this
27   morning's worship service in order to vote on the calling of a pastor, met in

[4.] Since 1931 Bonhoeffer had been one of the three international youth secretaries of the World Alliance. Cf. *DB-ER*, 200, and *DBW* 11:314–67.

[5.] This last sentence was added by hand.

[1.] ADBC, Minute Book of Sydenham Church, 30; in Bonhoeffer's own hand. See *NL*, 41,3 (2); typewritten copy.

assembly, and the presence of a quorum was established. Mr. Lorenz, chairing the meeting in place of the pastor, who was not present in the room, called the meeting to order. After a few introductory words, a voice vote was taken, and the chairman determined that Pastor Lic. Dietrich Bonhoeffer, on the basis of his sermons preached here,[2] has been unanimously elected as pastor of the Sydenham Church. He then informed the pastor of this decision, and the latter expressed his thanks to the congregation. The meeting was then adjourned.

Bonhoeffer

11.2 Letter from the Congregation to the Church Chancellery[3]

London E.1, November 13, 1933

At the general assembly of our congregations in Sydenham and St. Paul's churches, held after yesterday's worship service, Pastor Dietrich Bonhoeffer was unanimously called as pastor, succeeding Pastor Singer, who has resigned for health reasons. We hereby request confirmation.

P. Voigt
Treasurer and Vice-Chairman
Congregational Council of Sydenham Church

Treasurer and Vice-Chairman
Congregational Council of St. Paul's Church, Aldgate
G. Henne

28

12. To George Bell[1]

London, 16. XI. 33

Mylord,

I thank you very much for your kind invitation to come to Chichester on November 21st. It is indeed a great pleasure for me to come. May I ask you what time would be convenient for you for my arrival?

[2.] Cf. 3/1 and 3/2.

[3.] EZA 5/1315; typewritten. The return address reads: "St. Paul's German Evangelical Church, London E.1, 3, Goulston Street, Aldgate"; however, the vice-chairmen of both the St. Paul's and the Sydenham congregation signed the letter to the German Evangelical Church Federation office in Berlin-Charlottenburg.

[1.] LPL, Bell Papers 42, 1 and 2; typewritten; in original English, including errors. See also *NL*, A 42,1(1); typewritten copy; previously published in *GS* 2:138–39.

You certainly know of the recent events[2] within the German church and I think that there is a great likelihood for a separation[3] of the minority from the Reichskirche, and in this case an action of ecumenic support would certainly be of immense value in this tense situation. There is no doubt that any sort of separation would become at once a strong political issue, and for this reason would probably be dealt with by the government in an exclusively political way. It seems to me that the responsibility of the ecumenic work has perhaps never been so far-reaching as in the present moment.

If the ecumenic churches would keep silent during those days, I am afraid that all trust put into it by the minority would be destroyed. Undoubtedly—Müller is now in a very precarious situation, and a strong demand from the side of the ecumenic churches could be the last hope for the Christian Churches in Germany. We must not leave alone those men who fight—humanly spoken—an almost hopeless struggle. I get news with every mail and also by telephone. If I may, I will forward to you the recent informations.

In the enclosed paper you will find some very typical formulations of the Teutonic Christians.[4]

I think one ought to try to drive a wedge between Müller and the radicals. On the other hand one cannot rely by any means on Müller's personal theological insight and so it is dangerous to put too much trust into such a break.

With many thanks, I remain, Mylord, Yours very sincerely
Dietrich Bonhoeffer

29

[2.] The Sports Palace rally held by the German Christian Faith Movement on November 13, 1933, in Berlin, was followed by the resignation of many German Christians from the movement. See Scholder, *Churches and the Third Reich*, 1:551–54. [Some of the German Christian speakers at the rally called for extreme changes, including the removal of the Old Testament from the Bible and extensive revision of hymns and liturgies to remove all "Jewish influences" from the Christian tradition. These radical demands created an uproar in the churches, and prominent theologians (including Friedrich Gogarten, Gerhard Kittel, and Heinrich Bornkamm) who had previously supported the movement now repudiated it. Hundreds left the German Christian movement, and membership in the Pastors' Emergency League jumped correspondingly, reaching six thousand by the end of 1933. See Helmreich, *German Churches under Hitler*, 147–48.—KC]

[3.] Six months later the Confessing Church assembled for its first national synod at Barmen; see *DB-ER*, 371–72, and Scholder, *Churches and the Third Reich*, 2:142–56.

[4.] Not extant.

13. From George Bell[1]

17th November, 1933

Dear Dr. Bonhoeffer,

I am delighted that you can come to Chichester on Tuesday, November 21st. The best plan would be that you should come to Brighton. There are trains from Victoria to Brighton every quarter of an hour. I am at a Committee at Brighton that afternoon. If you could catch the train from Victoria at 3., reaching Brighton at 4., I would send my car to meet you at the station. My Chaplain Mr. Mason, a young clergyman, will be standing by the car and will look out for you if you would look out for him. Then you will come on to Church House in Brighton and have tea, and we could drive to Chichester together and have a talk on the way.

I appreciate what you say about the oecumenical movement and its task just now. Have you seen my letter to Bishop Müller? I enclose the English original text and a German translation. It was printed in full in "The Manchester Guardian" on Monday, and the main portions appeared in "The Times" and other papers.[2] Bishop Müller knew it was to be published and I received no objection. Dr. Schönfeld tells me that he has seen Bishop Müller and Bishop Schöffel, and that my letter had made an impression. I understood from Schönfeld that Bishop Müller was going to send me a preliminary reply and that he might possibly ask for a delegation from the oecumenical movement to visit Berlin and see Church leaders.[3] But I have heard nothing more.

Yours sincerely,
[George Cicestr]

[1.] LPL, Bell Papers 42, 3; carbon copy; in original English, including errors. See also *NL*, A 42,2 (1); copy; excerpt in *GS* 2:139.

[2.] Letters from Bell to the editors of the *Times* and the *Manchester Guardian*, October 23, 1933.

[3.] In 1934 nothing came of Müller's intentions of receiving a delegation from the ecumenical council in Berlin.

30   **14. To Théodore de Félice**[1]

London, November 17, 1933

Dear Mr. de Félice,

Please send the announcement of the competition[2] first to Mr. Fritz Söhl-mann, Berlin N. 22, and Dr. Winterhager, Hohenzollerndamm 199, Schmar-gendorf, who are standing in for me during my absence from Berlin.[3]

Yours sincerely,
Dietrich Bonhoeffer

15. To George Bell[1]

London, 19. XI. 33

Mylord,

may I thank you once more for your great kindness. I will take—as you told me[2]—the train for Brighton which leaves London at three o'clock and I shall certainly find out your chaplain at the station. In case I should need an evening dress for your meeting I should be very much obliged to you if you would then kindly let me know about it.

Very respectfully yours,
Dietrich Bonhoeffer

[1.] WCC Archives, World Alliance, Letters from Dietrich Bonhoeffer, 13; typewritten. See also *NL*, A 40, 1 (1); typewritten copy.

[2.] Cf. Minutes of the Youth Commission, Paris, January 31–February 1, 1934, and the Report of the Youth Commission for Fanø, World Alliance VI. A prize competition of the Youth Commission, World Alliance for Promoting International Friendship through the Churches, was limited to the European countries. Over three hundred entries were submitted.

[3.] Bonhoeffer thus remained European Youth Secretary for the World Alliance.

[1.] LPL, Bell Papers 42, 4; typewritten; in original English, including errors. See also *NL*, A 42,1 (2); typewritten copy.

[2.] See 1/13.

16. From Karl Barth[1]

31

November 20, 1933

My dear colleague,

From this salutation you will gather that I have no intention of regarding your going off to England as anything other than a perhaps personally necessary interlude. Since your mind was set on this, you were quite right not to seek any wisdom from me before doing it. I would have advised against it, unconditionally and certainly bringing up the heaviest artillery I could muster. And now that you have come to me with this after the fact,[2] I truly cannot do otherwise than call to you, "Get back to your post in Berlin straightaway!" What is this about "going into the wilderness," "keeping quiet in the parish ministry," and so forth at a moment when you are needed in Germany? You, who know as well as I do that the opposition in Berlin, indeed the church opposition in Germany as a whole, is on such shaky footing spiritually! That every honest man should have his hands full with making it sharp and clear and solid! That it all may be about to come apart, not because the German Christians are really so strong and clever, but because their opponents themselves are so stubborn and thickheaded and hopelessly lacking in principle![3] Under no circumstances should you now be playing Elijah under the juniper tree[4] or Jonah under the gourd;[5] you need to be here with all guns blazing!

¶What's the point of singing my praises—from the other side of the Channel? What's the point of the message I received from your student,[6] just as I was in the midst of tussling with our splendid "Council of Brethren" of the Emergency League[7]—instead of your being here and standing up to these brethren along with me? You see, that was the second time I have been in Berlin in the past few weeks,[8] and I think I now know fairly accurately what is going on there. I tried

---

32

[1.] Karl Barth-Archiv, Basel; carbon copy; from Bonn. Previously published in *Mündige Welt*, 1:114–16, and *GS* 2:134–37.

[2.] See 1/2.

[3.] Cf. Barth's previous sharp criticism of the Young Reformation movement in *Theologische Existenz heute*, June 1933 (Scholder, *Churches and the Third Reich*, 1:437).

[4.] 1 Kings 19:4: "But he himself went a day's journey into the wilderness, and came and sat down under a solitary juniper tree. He asked that he might die . . ." [NRSV trans. altered].

[5.] Jon. 4:5–11.

[6.] Neither the student nor the message has been identified.

[7.] Reference is to an argument between Barth and Martin Niemöller, on November 14, 1933, in Berlin, about what course the church opposition should take following the Sports Palace scandal (cf. Scholder, *Churches and the Third Reich*, 1:554–56).

[8.] The first time was October 30–31 to lecture on "Reformation as Decision" and for several formal discussions with Berlin opposition pastors (Scholder, *Churches and the Third Reich*, 1:537–41).

earnestly to pull the steering in a different direction, and in some ways partly succeeded, but for things to have turned out for the good I would have needed a very, very different kind of success. So for the second time I was quite depressed as I left that scene. Why weren't you there pulling together on the rope that I, virtually alone, could hardly budge? Why aren't you here all the time, when there is so much at stake that calls for a few brave souls to keep watch, whether the occasion is great or small, and try to save whatever can be saved? Why, why? You see, as I said, I'm quite ready to assume that your going away was personally necessary for you. But I would then like to ask, what does a "personal necessity" actually mean at this moment? Reading your letter, I believe I can see that you, like the rest of us—yes, _all_ of us!—are suffering under the enormous difficulty of "making straight paths for our feet"[9] through the present chaotic situation. But shouldn't it be clear to you that this is no reason to withdraw from the chaos; that perhaps we are called to man our positions _in and with_ our uncertainty, even if we stumble and go astray ten or a hundred times over, or however well or badly we then serve our cause? I am simply not happy with your putting your own private problem at center stage at this point, in view of what is at stake for the German church today. Won't there be time enough _afterward_, when, God willing, we are beginning to come out on the other side of this mess, to work off the various complexes and scruples from which you are suffering, as others are suffering as well? No, to all the reasons and apologies that you may still have to offer, I can only and shall always have the same answer: And what of the German church? And what of the German church?—until you are back in Berlin, manning your abandoned machine gun like a loyal soldier. Haven't you seen yet that we have now entered a time of altogether _un_dialectical theology, which is totally unsuited to holding back, saying, "Maybe—or maybe not!"[10] in which instead, any biblical saying you like positively cries out to us, lost and damned sinners that we are, that we have only to believe, believe, believe?! Shouldn't you—with your fine theological skills, and then being the very image of a German—be a little embarrassed in the presence of a man like Heinz Vogel, who, though wizened and excitable, is always there, waving his arms around like a windmill and shouting, "Confession, confession!"—whether in strength or weakness matters little, but witnessing indeed in his own fashion?[11]

33

[9.] Heb. 12:12–13a: "Therefore lift your drooping hands and strengthen your weak knees, and make straight paths for your feet."

[10.] Barth is alluding to theological reservations that he himself had held in the past.

[11.] At the Pastors' Emergency League discussion with Barth on October 31, 1933, Heinrich Vogel had called for spontaneous approval of his draft confession, "Eight Articles of Evangelical Doctrine." See Scholder, _Churches and the Third Reich_, 1:688.

I really cannot offer you the prospect of sharing in a triumph, when I ask you to come back to Germany. Everything here could not be more arduous and disagreeable. As soon as one gets even slightly involved in tactical or historical philosophical thinking, one sees clearly at every moment that—the sea is raging and demanding its own[12]—all our efforts are in vain; the German church is lost anyway. In the next numbers of the new essay series, which will have more or less current things of mine in nos. 3 and 4, [13] you will see how much trouble I myself have staving off weariness. But you know, this is just not the time to grow weary. So it is even less the time to go to England! What in the world are you supposed to be doing or hoping to do there? Just be glad I don't have you here in front of me, because then I'd find an entirely different way of putting it to you forcefully that you need to drop all these quirks and special considerations, however fascinating, and think only of one thing: that you are a German, that your church's house is on fire, that you know enough, and know well enough how to say what you know, to be able to help, and in fact you ought to return to your post by the next ship! Well, let's say, with the one after that. But I cannot tell you explicitly and urgently enough that you belong in Berlin and not in London.

Since you have written me only that you are now over there, I will write you, for now, nothing more than just this: that you should be in Berlin.

Unfortunately I shall have to ask Gertrud Staewen[14] to send me your address, so this letter will take some time to reach you. Please be so good as to understand it in just the way I mean it. If you did not matter so much to me, I would not have taken you by the collar in this fashion.

Yours sincerely,
Karl Barth

My greetings to Mr. Hildebrandt. It only became clear to me afterward that he is the man who wrote the book "Est,"[15] in which he is supposed to have said some nasty things about me. I have not read it and therefore am quite ready to forgive him everything.

[12.] Line from Schiller's *William Tell*, act 1, scene 1.

[13.] Reference to *Theologische Existenz heute*, the series of monographs edited by Karl Barth and Eduard Thurneysen. No. 3: Karl Barth, "Reformation as Decision Making." No. 4: Karl Barth, "Celebrating Luther in 1933."

[14.] Cf. Busch, *Karl Barth: His Life from Letters and Autobiographical Texts*, 250.

[15.] Hildebrandt, *EST: Das lutherische Prinzip*, 1931.

17. To Gerhard and Sabine Leibholz[1]

[London,] Thursday[, November] 23, [1933]

Dear Gert, dear Sabine,

I wanted to write to you especially in view of next Sunday. I am just working on my Remembrance Sunday[2] sermon,[3] and it makes me think once more of you and those days in March.[4] The text is beautiful, from the Wisdom of Solomon, chapter 3:1ff. Read it sometime. I am preaching only on the brief sentence in it, ". . . but they are at peace." It would have been a good choice for your father, too. I am tormented even now by the thought that I didn't do as you asked me as a matter of course.[5] To be frank, I can't think what made me behave as I did. How could I have been so horribly afraid at the time? It must have seemed equally incomprehensible to you both, and yet you said nothing. But it preys on my mind, because it's the kind of thing one can never make up for. So all I can do is ask you to forgive my weakness then. I know now for certain that I ought to have behaved differently. Remembrance Sunday is particularly moving this time because, after all that has happened during the past months, one feels such a tremendous longing for real peace at last, in which all the misery and injustice, the lying and cowardice will come to an end, in which the struggle is over and all is quiet, resting in a strong hand. But it is certainly dangerous to let oneself get carried away, and we have to live by hope as never before. We really must not lose courage. I believe that your father, Gert, would probably have lived through even these times with an unwavering and much stronger confidence in the future than most of us have. But it must be wonderful to be at peace, as Hans said at the time. You have a bit of such peace at home with your children, and I have a bit of it in my parish. And for this we should be truly grateful. I hope things will be well for you. I think about you often, even though I seldom write. My thanks to you for your letters. Dear Gert, I forgot your birthday in the rush

[1.] *NL*, A 39,4 (2); handwritten; the text suggests it was sent from London, probably in November 1933; previously published in *GS* 6:290–91.

[2.] [The German *Totensonntag* (literally: "Sunday of the Dead") is here translated as "Remembrance Sunday" but is not to be confused with the day of this title in Britain and other countries when war dead are commemorated.—KC]

[3.] See 3/3.

[4.] The reference is to the funeral of Gerhard Leibholz's father, who died on April 11, 1933.

[5.] Bonhoeffer had consulted his church district general superintendent, who advised him strongly against conducting the funeral service for Leibholz's Jewish father, and Bonhoeffer had followed this advice. See *DB-ER*, 275–76.

of moving, even with it marked on my calendar. I'm sorry! My love to the children, and love to both of you as well.

Dietrich

18. To George Bell[1]

London, 25. XI. 33

My Lord Bishop,

The two days which I spent in your home meant so much to me that I beg to thank you once more for this opportunity which you so kindly gave to me. I have received your letter,[2] and I shall certainly keep all you told me to myself. Things in Germany are getting on—as it seems—more slowly than one could expect, and I am almost afraid that the influence of the radical German Christians becomes once more very strong, and that Müller will 36 yield under this heavy pressure.[3] I shall give you new information as soon as something important will occur.

I remain, Mylord, yours very sincerely
Dietrich Bonhoeffer

19. To George Bell[1]

London, Nov. 27th 1933

My Lord Bishop,

may I draw your attention to the enclosed leaflets.[2] Three pastors[3] have been dismissed only because of their sincere confession to Christ as the only

---

[1.] LPL, Bell Papers 42, 5; typewritten; in original English, including errors. See also *NL*, 42,1 (3); copy; previously published in *GS* 2: 139–40.

[2.] Not extant.

[3.] On November 22 and 23, 1933, the German Christians held a conference in Weimar. The radical wing, under its "Reich leader" Hossenfelder, decided to hire a special railway carriage to take fifty people to Berlin to lobby and pressure Reich Bishop Müller to follow the radical German Christian line. Cf. Scholder, *Churches and the Third Reich*, 1:559–61.

[1.] LPL, Bell Papers 42, 6; handwritten; in original English, including errors. See also *NL*, 42,1 (4); copy.

[2.] Not extant.

[3.] Three pastors were suspended from their parish ministries for publicly reading the November 19, 1933, pulpit announcement of the Pastors' Emergency League, which condemned the events at the Sports Palace. See also Wilhelm Niemöller, *Kampf und Zeugnis der Bekennende Kirche*, 79–80.

Lord of the Church. One of them, Pastor Wilde is father of seven children. The case is not decided yet definitely, but perhaps the moment has come when the ecumenical movement ought to provide for subsidies and financial support for those who will lose their positions for the only reason of their being confessors of their faith. Things are becoming very acute. Schöffel has resigned, Prof. Fezer has left the German Christian Movement.[4]

Yours, My Lord, very sincerely,
Dietrich Bonhoeffer

37   **20. Pastors' Conference in Bradford**[1]

20.1 Notes Taken by Julius Rieger[2]

Bonhoeffer:

In July 1933 the Christian Student Association[3] was to have been taken over by the German Christians. A few of the SA[4] men protested. A delegation, consisting of Bonhoeffer, two SA men, and a pastor, then went to the ministry.[5] Rust was not there; they met with a minister director Gerullis. The next day there was a student assembly with about nine hundred to one thousand students present.

[4.] Cf. Scholder, *Churches in the Third Reich*, 1:562–64.

[1.] The German pastors working in Great Britain met from November 27 to 30 in Bradford, Yorkshire, for their annual conference. See *DB-ER*, 338–40. [For more on the Bradford conference, see Moore, *Celebrating Critical Awareness.*—KC]

[2.] *NL*, A 41,4: typewritten transcription of shorthand notes; previously published in *GS* 6:304–7.

[3.] According to *DB-ER*, 286, this was not the German Student Christian Association (Deutscher Christlicher Studentenverband, DCSV), but rather the June 1933 attempt by a "German Christian Students' Fighting League" to get "the German Student Association" in Berlin to join the German Christian movement "spontaneously." During the summer of 1933, however, there were fleeting efforts from some within the DCSV toward joining the German Christians.

[4.] [SA is the abbreviation for *Sturmabteilung* (storm troopers), the uniformed and armed branch of the Nazi Party responsible for much of the violence and intimidation being carried out at the time. A number of church members and even clergy were SA members at the beginning of the Nazi period, however, and not always in agreement with Nazi church policies. By 1934 party leaders were discouraging church membership in the SA; a May 1939 order required all clergy and theological students to resign. See Helmreich, *German Churches under Hitler*, 126, 144, and 219. For an example of a Confessing Church pastor who joined the SA, see Barnett, *For the Soul of the People*, 40. See also ed. note 11.—KC]

[5.] The Prussian Ministry for Cultural Affairs directed by Bernhard Rust; on this delegation, see *DB-ER*, 286.

We held an(other) event in the New Aula[6] at which Hirsch and Schumann were invited to speak.[7]

The election was held soon afterward.[8] Flyers were confiscated. Bonhoeffer and a colleague were summoned to the office of the secret police;[9] there they were told that if any of the pastors said anything more against the German Christians, the two of them would be held responsible.

The election results are completely false, because the election took place under disgraceful conditions of terror. There were clear orders from the Party, in many places at least, that every Party member had to vote.

At eleven-thirty at night, Hitler clearly took a stand on behalf of the German Christians.[10] This was the first time it was clear to us that the political government was behind them as well. Seventy-five percent voted for the German Christians.

The German Christians marched into the general synod in uniform.[11] The draft church regulations[12] had been brought in shortly beforehand, so that nobody had a chance to prepare for them. Werner was elected.[13] At every "Who wishes to speak?" Eckert, who appeared to be slightly drunk, would make a motion, immediately followed by a motion that there should be no discussion. Beforehand, four vice presidents had been elected who were all German Christians.[14]

Then the Aryan paragraph was brought up. Deissmann took the floor and said some trivial rubbish. Niemöller asked to speak but was turned down. (Niemöller's brother, a lieutenant captain[15] whose [NSDAP] membership card was around no.

38

[6.] [Assembly Hall.—KC]

[7.] On this assembly, organized by a "Working Committee of Protestant Students," see *DB-ER*, 287.

[8.] The German Evangelical Church elections on July 23, 1933.

[9.] Cf. 1/8, ed. note 10.

[10.] This was in a broadcast on all German radio stations the night before the election, from the Bayreuth festival; cf. Scholder, *Churches and the Third Reich*, 1:446–47.

[11.] The general synod of the Old Prussian Church, September 5–6, in Berlin (the "brown synod" [so called because of the number of those present in brown SA uniforms.— KC]). Regarding the synod proceedings, see Scholder, *Churches and the Third Reich*, 1:470–73.

[12.] Among others, the "Church Law on the Legal Position of Clergy and Church Officials," which included the "Aryan paragraph."

[13.] The synod elected as its president Friedrich Werner, who shortly afterward was also named president of the Old Prussian Evangelical Church Council.

[14.] Two, in fact, were chosen as Werner's deputies: Joachim Hossenfelder and August Jäger.

[15.] [Wilhelm Niemöller had joined the Nazi Party during the 1920s and was also an early member of the German Christians; he broke with the movement by the end of 1933. See Bergen, *Twisted Cross*, 13.—KC]

3000, was thrown out because he was German Christian and had spoken against Hossenfelder. They then asked him back in, but he refused.)

Koch presented the group's declaration[16] and was shouted down. He left the podium. The group left the hall.

In the group's absence, all the resolutions were unanimously adopted. Hossenfelder was elected bishop of Brandenburg. The national synod members were elected, sixty people, none of whom was a member of the opposition. At the end, Müller[17] said he would show people where they belonged.

The next day, the group met and quite seriously considered the question of schism.[18] Knak and others prevailed over the more radical members.

Then came the national synod.[19] Church President Koch was there.[20]

The day before, a few pastors from Berlin met and drafted a protest statement regarding the Aryan paragraph and the suppression of the opposition.[21] This statement was sent to Müller. Müller read a report (on the church situation?) that was downright ridiculous. The second, ceremonial part followed.

39   During the lunch break a telegram was sent to Müller, requesting him to address the issues.

(Insert: the Young Reformation Movement–Fellowship of Young Theologians, later the Emergency League.)[22] There was a break from 1 to 4 P.M. Bonhoeffer eavesdropped on the ongoing negotiations from the back of the balcony. There was a scene between the Lutheran bishops and Hossenfelder. The Lutheran bishops didn't want Müller, but Hossenfelder had been won over to his cause. The Lutheran bishops said Müller was unacceptable for reasons of conscience. Hossenfelder retorted, "Conscience is neither here nor there; Müller is Reich bishop." It

---

[16.] The "Gospel and Church" party, from which the Pastors' Emergency League emerged after the general synod.

[17.] Ludwig Müller, who was named a regional bishop under the "Bishops' Law" that had just been passed by the synod.

[18.] [Reference to the opposition faction.—KC] Bonhoeffer and Franz Hildebrandt in particular had pleaded in vain for an "immediate move to resignations from office" (see *DB-ER*, 292).

[19.] The national synod of the German Evangelical Church on September 27, 1933, in Wittenberg; regarding the proceedings, see Scholder, *Churches and the Third Reich*, 1:488–92.

[20.] [Karl Koch was president of the regional church of Westphalia; this was the equivalent of a bishop in the Lutheran churches.—KC]

[21.] "To the National Synod of the German Evangelical Church." Previously published in *GS* 2:74–76. Regarding its origin, see J. Schmidt, *Martin Niemöller im Kirchenkampf*, 127–28.

[22.] At this point Bonhoeffer is apparently giving information about coalitions among the opposition groups at the beginning of the Church Struggle. The "Fellowship of Young Theologians" was started primarily on the initiative of Bonhoeffer's students in Berlin.

was announced afterward that Müller had been elected unanimously. Hossenfelder declaimed: "I greet thee, my Reich bishop!"

Meiser wrote to Schreiner[23] that Neurath should be persuaded to report that the Aryan paragraph would be impossible to implement abroad.

Wurm gave a sermon on the "cogite intrare."[24]

The reason the national synod did not deal with the Aryan paragraph is that the Foreign Ministry intervened beforehand![25]

Some 100–120 pastors were meeting every Monday at Jacobi's house. A minority kept pressing for a decision.

At the beginning of September, Merz, Sasse, and Bonhoeffer drafted a confession.[26] Its intent was spoiled by attempts to thwart it and by the strange course of action taken by Bodelschwingh.[27] It is now being published, after having the (original) intent spoiled by a few pastors.

Only four weeks ago there was actually a proposal to put the Emergency League under the authority of the Reich bishop![28]

The Bethel Confession covered the ground from the doctrine of the Trinity to 40 eschatology. Where were the doctrinal errors [Irrlehre] found? Examples:

1. Justification: In the speech Müller gave, he said that on Judgment Day, God would only ask a person if he had been a decent fellow and had served his people

[23.] Bonhoeffer's colleague in Liverpool, Karl Heinz Schreiner, had been informed about this by Bishop Meiser; see ed. note 25.

[24.] Wurm preached at the synod's festive opening worship service in the Schloßkirche, on Matt. 22:2–14; cf. Schäfer, *Die evangelische Landeskirche in Württemberg*, 2:386ff.

[25.] On September 22, 1933, the state Ministry of Foreign Affairs urged the "acting leadership of the German Evangelical Church" not to adopt a resolution enacting the Aryan paragraph (see Nicolaisen and Kretschmar, *Dokumente zur Kirchenpolitik des Dritten Reichs*, 1:132). [Evidently the government was displaying some sensitivity to opinion in the ecumenical world and its diplomatic implications, not least in the U.S., Scandinavia, and Britain. The World Alliance conference in Sofia, Bulgaria, held in September 1933 (which Bonhoeffer attended), had passed a resolution protesting against anti-Jewish measures taken by the German state and the application of the Aryan paragraph in the church. The backlash in Germany to the Sofia resolution had in turn prompted increased concern abroad.—KC]

[26.] Reference is to the Bethel Confession ("August version"). Cf. Müller, *Bekenntnis und Bekennen*, 36–44 and 82–117. Reprint of a 1933 copy in *GS* 2:91–119; cf. *DBW* 12, 2/15.

[27.] [Bonhoeffer believed that Bodelschwingh acted to water down the Bethel Confession. See *DB-ER*, 303.—KC]

[28.] In an article in *Junge Kirche* at the end of October 1933, Walter Künneth called for the "readiness for legal co-operation specifically in this Reich church, specifically in this Volk and their national revival, specifically in Hitler's state." Scholder, *Churches and the Third Reich*, 1:535–36; see also 674, ed. note 56.

[Volk].[29] From Müller one keeps hearing about trusting in God and assuming one's responsibility.[30] It is completely Enlightenment, faded, estranged from Christ.

2. The cross: Wienecke said the cross was the highest symbol for the sentence "Public interest comes before self-interest." The Bethel Confession, on the other hand, says that the cross is absolutely not a symbol for anything, but is rather the act of God.[31]

3. The Spirit: It is the spirit of National Socialism that renews the church. Here spirit always means ethos. Stapel has the notion of the law of the people [Volks-Nomos].[32] The crypt is below, the cathedral on top of it. The people's law is below and on top of it the Christian law and the altar. First nature's grace, then Christ's grace. First creation, then redemption. This goes back to liberal theology. What is decisive is that the filioque is missing.[33] The filioque means that the Spirit proceeds from the Father and the Son. The German Christians want to introduce a nature spirit, a folk [Volk] spirit, into the church, which is not judged by Christ but rather justifies itself. The doctrine of the filioque was brought to Germany by Charlemagne in his fight against pagan religion.[34] Now it appears that German paganism is flaring up again. It is a struggle between Germanic folk religiosity and the church. By its very nature, the German Christian tendency is always in the folk direction.

Is there a revelation of God that is independent of Christ in the Scriptures and the preaching of the church? Is there an independence with regard to nature, blood, race, ethnic [völkisch] characteristics? Or should all those things be ques-

---

[29.] Cf. article 6/2 of the Bethel Confession, "On Justification and Faith," *DBW* 12:388–91 (2/15). See also Müller, *Bekenntnis und Bekennen*, 101–2.

[30.] Cf. Ludwig Müller's proclamation to the national synod, in Norden, *Der deutsche Protestantismus*, 110–14.

[31.] See article 5 of the Bethel Confession, "On Christ," *DBW* 12:384–87 (2/15). See also Müller, *Bekenntnis und Bekennen*, 100.

[32.] See esp. Stapel, *Der christliche Staatsmann*, 159 and 174–85, as well as Bonhoeffer's discussion of it in 1932, *GS* 5:331–34.

[33.] [In the traditional Western form of the Niceno-Constantinopolitan Creed (381) the Holy Spirit is stated to proceed from the Father "and the Son" (*filioque*). This was a point of major significance to Bonhoeffer, Barth, and other "Confessing" theologians who saw in contemporary German quasi-religious, nationalistic ideologies the detaching of "Spirit" (German *Geist*) from a specifically *Christocentric* anchorage in the Trinitarian faith.—KC] See article 6 of the Bethel Confession, "On the Holy Spirit," *DBW* 12:387–88 (2/15). See also Müller, *Bekenntnis und Bekennen*, 100.

[34.] Bonhoeffer is pointing to the relevance of the Aachen synod's decision in 809 for the Church Struggle.

tioned? They do not justify; they have some relative validity, but no ultimate validity.

Althaus, Hirsch, Schlatter, Fezer: the revelation through Christ in the church 41
(and?) in preaching (must?) be rejected; instead we have the revelation in the fullness of the creation.[35]

Bishop Peter talked to others and applauded during Krause's speech (and?)
Lörzer's.[36] Bishop Peter had friendly conversation with the others. In the assembly there was no protest from Peter.

In Stolzenhagen and in Golzow[37] Pastor Wilde, on November 19, as an act of confession and witness, held congregational assembly in place of worship service. Sincere friend of the German people's chancellor. "Before God and this Christian congregation I accuse the Reich bishop, Hossenfelder, Peter, and the other German Christians of having violated the honor of the church by their principles and of having enacted church laws that are contrary to the spirit of the teaching of Christ." He was then denounced to Bishop Thom in Cammin.[38]

20.2 Declaration to the Reich Church Government[39]

Bradford, November 29, 1933

The German Protestant pastors assembled today at the pastoral conference in Bradford are pleased and note with satisfaction that the Reich bishop, in his statement of November 14, spoke strongly in favor of the purity of doctrine.[40]

Despite this statement, we consider the recent decisions made by the church 42

[35.] Like Barth, Bonhoeffer saw "natural theology" as claiming a revelation *besides* that of "Christ in the church," the central theological problem in the disputes of 1933; see Scholder, *Churches and the Third Reich*, 1:414–40. [Cf. also 2/4.—KC]

[36.] At the infamous Sports Palace rally of the Berlin German Christians on November 13, 1933; see Scholder, *Churches and the Third Reich*, 1:550–53. See also 1/12, ed. note 2.

[37.] In Pomerania.

[38.] Pastor Wilde was suspended from service; see 1/19. See also *Junge Kirche* (1933): 394–95.

[39.] EZA 5/1265; typewritten; cf. also ADBC, GV 13, 15; and *NL*, 41, 4 (4); copy. Previously published in *GS* 2:147–48.

[40.] In this statement Ludwig Müller attempted to distance himself from the Sports Palace rally. He also stripped the regional German Christian leader (*Gauobmann*) Krause of his church offices. The text of that announcement is in Gauger, *Chronik der Kirchenwirren*, 1:109–10.

[41.] After the Sports Palace scandal, Müller initially continued his attempts to strengthen his position with the German Christian movement and to get government offices to take action against the pastors in the Emergency League. See J. Schmidt, *Martin Niemöller im Kirchenkampf*, 155–56.

government, recent events within the "German Christian Faith Movement,"[41] as well as public and private statements on the occasion of the visit of senior church leaders to England,[42] as cause for a statement on our part. We are deeply troubled about the future of the church and of our congregations.[43]

1. We hope and expect from all those who hold church office and positions of leadership that, in accordance with the Reich bishop's promise, they will acknowledge the doctrine of belief in justification by grace alone through Jesus Christ—which is the sole basis of Reformation thought—as the teaching of the church in word and deed, and that this basic position on the part of all church officeholders will from now on be evident beyond all doubt, even to anyone outside and unconnected with the church.

2. We hope and expect that the formal principle of the German Reformation—that the sole standard for the faith is set by the Holy Scriptures of the New and Old Testaments—will remain fully unscathed in every sense. There is a very grave danger that confidence in the church leadership will be disrupted if members of the church government cast serious doubt on the validity of this Reformation principle, either through their public behavior, which is beyond our comprehension, or if they give their support to any such efforts to destroy our inalienable heritage from the German Reformation.

We would like to point out that any doubt cast on the inviolable principles of the Reformation, in regard to both form and content, will cause serious disturbances in the life of the German Protestant congregations in Great Britain and without doubt will dissolve the close relationship between the German Protestant diaspora in England and the home church.

In indignation and shame over these attacks on the substance of the Protestant faith, we express our hope and expectation, for the sake of the unity and purity of the church, in this Luther anniversary year 1933 and on the occasion of the enthronement [Inthronisierung] of the Reich bishop, that the German Evangelical Church will remain for all time the church of the Reformation.

G. Schönberger, London   K. H. Schreiner, Liverpool
Julius Rieger, London   M. Böckheler, Hull
W. Hansen, Bradford   Dietrich Bonhoeffer, London

43

[42.] See 1/3, ed. note 6.

[43.] Bonhoeffer's draft for the preceding paragraph says, ". . . however, we still don't understand that the Reich bishop is still the sponsor of the German Christian movement, whose Reich leaders silently watched while the church's confession was attacked unbearably in the form of mockery of the Bible and the cross of Christ; and they found it right that Dr. Krause's successor in the movement should be the very person [Pastor Tausch of Berlin] whose behavior at [the Sports Palace] expressed only approval" (*DB-ER*, 339).

20.3 Cover Letter by Friedrich Wehrhan[44]

London, S.W.13, December 3, 1933

The enclosed declaration by the German pastors in Great Britain, unanimously adopted at the pastoral conference in Bradford, was intended to have been presented in Berlin by myself, representing the Association of German Evangelical Congregations in Great Britain and Ireland, on the occasion of the Reich bishop's consecration.[45]

Since my journey to Berlin did not take place, I have been asked to send the declaration by post.

To my regret, I was not able to take part in the pastoral conference, as I was ill in the hospital in Germany. However, I associate myself in every respect with my colleagues' declaration.

That the influential lay circles within our congregations are in complete agreement with their pastors is a fact known to us. I take the liberty of passing on to you a letter from the president of our Association of Congregations, Baron Bruno von Schröder, which I received the other day with his express request that it be copied and conveyed to the Reich Church government, as follows:

"As President of the Association of German Evangelical Congregations in Great Britain, and in my capacity as a member of the vestries of *Christ Church* and the *Hamburg Lutheran Church* in Dalston, I would like to inform you that I fully support the position taken by the pastors, and that the content of their letter expresses precisely my own feelings about the matter.

"With all sympathy for the new Germany and the great confidence that I have in our Führer, my conscience compels me to take a position on this issue, and I would like to do so by writing this letter to you, in which I express complete agreement with the content of the letter signed by the pastors.

"I should like to point out, furthermore, that the two Protestant churches with which I am associated here only joined the home church a few years ago. They did so precisely to show the desire that our Protestant churches have for a close contact with the home church.[46] But I must also point out that our statutes and founding documents etc., etc., give us the full liberty to resign from the Church Federation should we so desire. I do not wish to characterize that as a threat; it is only a statement of what our rights are.

44

[44.] ADBC, GV 13, 16; typewritten copy; see also *NL*, A 41,4 (5); typewritten copy.

[45.] The installation of the Reich bishop was to have taken place on December 3, 1933, but was postponed several times and was finally held on September 23, 1934.

[46.] The London congregations had been members of the German Evangelical Church Federation since 1928. See 1/74, ed. note 8.

"I hope with all my heart that this dispute will be resolved as soon as possible, for it damages the church whose interests we all have at heart."

This letter from the president of our Association of Congregations expresses the views of all our congregational councils and congregations and is occasion enough for the concern expressed in our declaration about the ties of the German congregations in this country with the home church, which are a necessity of life for them, and for which we pastors have fought throughout all the hard years since the war with all the strength and love we could muster.

(Signed) Fr. Wehrhan
Pastor of the German Evangelical Christ Church
and the German Ev.–Lutheran St. Mary's Church

21. Dietrich Bonhoeffer and Franz Hildebrandt to Martin Niemöller[1]

London, November 30, 1933

Dear Brother Niemöller,

We would have much preferred to ring you up again straightaway so as to embrace you in fellowship from our side, with all the force of our youth, imploring you not to hand over the control of the ship, at this critical moment, to those who will certainly steer it once again into uncharted seas and only give back the helm when it is too late.[2] Only the admirals can do the job now.[3] The course you set last summer seemed to us to be the only hope for the Council of Brethren to take a radical offensive instead of getting bogged down in tactics. Today may be the last moment for saving the church, and we shall all stand guilty in two years' time if we let it pass (who can tell what will happen even in the next fourteen days?). False shame and timidity brought about our downfall once before, last June.[4] If neither you

45

[1.] *NL*, A 41,9 (13); typewritten copy; bearing the notice "Original in the files of Martin Niemöller, Bielefeld" (not found). Previously published in *GS* 2:149–50.

[2.] After the resignations of the remaining members of the Clerical Ministry (Hossenfelder, Otto Weber, and Friedrich Werner) on November 30, 1933, there appeared to be an opportunity to replace the German Christian church government. [Their resignations were in the wake of the uproar about the Sports Palace rally. See 1/12, ed. note 2.—KC] Martin Niemöller now tried to get the regional church leaders who were not (or no longer) in the German Christian movement to work with him, with the immediate aim of restoring constitutional order under their leadership. For this reason Niemöller turned down the request that he himself join a new church cabinet (see J. Schmidt, *Martin Niemöller im Kirchenkampf*, 157–58).

[3.] Reference to Niemöller's past as a submarine commander.

[4.] During the debates at that time about the future form of the German Evangelical Church and concerning Friedrich von Bodelschwingh, Martin Niemöller also considered

nor Jacobi grasp the opportunity now, it won't be long until the same old mess is irrevocably swept back in.

What is indispensable now is for the synod to be dissolved immediately, and for the entire church to be cleansed of this entire plague—solely according to the perspective of strict doctrinal disciplinary proceedings[5] (with a panel of Sasse as Lutheran, Barth as Reformed)—and the strictest bar on membership, to clear out all the old and new half-baked Christians from our ranks.[6] Precisely because this is about doctrine and not about jobs, it really doesn't matter if a few ignorant folk gossip about a chase for jobs. Who will believe that! Only Luther's language, not Melanchthon's,[7] can help today—precisely where the authorities are concerned. Everyone now expects serious people to know they must bear responsibility and assume the leadership; the Bavarians and the gray old men[8] have given us ample evidence of what they are capable of at the critical moment.

Please also listen to the voices from the Wild West, not just the tame one,[9] and be assured of our warmest best wishes and great concern for you.

Dietrich Bonhoeffer and Franz Hildebrandt

22. Dietrich Bonhoeffer and Franz Hildebrandt to Erich Seeberg[1]

sincerely request support for jacobi as churches minister since he alone as trusted spokesman for the pastors guarantees a calming and clarification of the church situation

respectfully bonhoeffer hildebrandt

---

the possibility of a schism, in the form of a coalition outside the church of those pastors and congregations that were faithful to the confession (J. Schmidt, *Martin Niemöller im Kirchenkampf*, 83–84). [The debate about Bodelschwingh was in the context of the election of the Reich bishop. Church moderates, including those in the Pastors' Emergency League, elected Bodelschwingh as Reich bishop; this election was undermined by a vicious German Christian campaign against Bodelschwingh, who then resigned; Ludwig Müller was then elected. See Helmreich, *German Churches under Hitler*, 135–39.—KC] Since then, Bonhoeffer and Hildebrandt had been focusing on the practical consequences of this course (cf. *DB-ER*, 307–9.)

[5.] [Cf. Bonhoeffer's letter to Henriod of January 2, 1934, 1/40.—KC]

[6.] The Pastors' Emergency League.

[7.] In the Reformation disputes, Melanchthon's position had been more conciliatory than Luther's.

[8.] This indicates their reservations about some regional church representatives such as bishops Hans Meiser, Karl Koch, and Theophil Wurm (cf. 1/133).

[9.] The "tame" West refers to the regional church of Westphalia.

[1.] BA Koblenz, NL 248 (Erich Seeberg) 94, fol. 33; telegram, sent from London on November 30, 1933, at 11:35 P.M.; received in Berlin-Grünewald on December 1, 1933.

23. From the *Gemeindebote*[1]

Sydenham Evangelical Church in Dacres Road,
December 3, 1933

On Sunday, December 3, 1933 (first Sunday in Advent), a Sunday school will again be held for the first time in some years, following the morning worship service, from 12:15 to 1 P.M. in the church. I cordially request you to invite all the children whom you can reach to come along to this first effort and would also ask the parents to be there this time so that we can discuss the question of a convenient time. I would also like to try to prepare a nativity play[2] for Christmas with the children. For this, of course, we would require a few twelve- to fourteen-year-old girls and boys to play the main roles. But every child is hereby warmly invited to take part.

47

A small group has been found that would like to start a four-part choir, mainly to practice older choral music and occasionally be available to sing in our worship services. Who would like to join us? Who can read music well enough to sing fairly easy pieces? Please get in touch with me anytime.

Another request: who is prepared to make flowers available from time to time to decorate the altar?

Finally, I would again ask that decisions be made soon on participation in confirmation classes, by those to whom this would apply.

Dietrich Bonhoeffer, Pastor

24. The London Pastors to Martin Niemöller[1]

London, December 4, 1933

dismayed to hear of breach[2] in council of brethren stop jacobi's exclusion from negotiations would compel us to resign immediately and thwart imminent membership of german pastors in england jacobi as most level-headed

[1.] ADBC, *Gemeindebote für die deutschen evangelischen Kirchen in Großbritannien*, no. 49 (December 3, 1933): 8. See also *NL*, 41,8 (3); copy.

[2.] Cf. 1/6.

[1.] *NL*, A 41,9 (14); copy of telegram (original not found). Previously published in *GS* 2:150.

[2.] Between Niemöller and Jacobi. See Niemöller's reply to this on December 9, 1933, 1/25.

must be given prominence stop shameful fence sitting why flight from the responsibility[3] brotherly greetings

the Londoners

25. Martin Niemöller to the German Pastors in Great Britain[1]   48

Berlin-Dahlem, December 9, 1933

My dear brothers,

Thank you for your kind letter of the fifth of this month[2] and the copy of the declaration to the Reich Church government, which we have been glad to read.

With regard to your fear that the Emergency League and its members might fail to assume their responsibility,[3] you may set your minds at rest. The brothers in the Emergency League are agreed, however, that what we need in the church government is not strong individuals—not even those coming from our side—but rather persons who have a *church* behind them. From this point of view, it would be impossible for one individual from among us to take a seat in the cabinet, which furthermore has been organized in a wholly new way. We have been firmly resisting all compromises of that sort.[4]

You may be assured that we are acting without regard for personal issues, and that the Emergency League, the Lutheran bishops as representatives of intact churches, and the Church of Westphalia are *united* in our actions.

We would, of course, be very glad to welcome you as members of the Emergency League.

On behalf of the Emergency League, I extend warm brotherly greetings to you all.

(signed) Niemöller, Pastor

[3.] Cf. J. Schmidt, *Martin Niemöller im Kirchenkampf,* 157 and 475.

[1.] *NL,* A 41,2 (1); typewritten copy. Previously published in *GS* 2:150–51. See also 1/20.2, 1/20.3, and 1/21. Addressed to "The German Pastors in Great Britain, c/o Pastor Wehrhan, London."

[2.] Not extant; probably a cover letter accompanying the declaration from the Bradford clergy meeting (1/20.2).

[3.] See 1/21 and 1/24.

[4.] The Reich bishop had decided to appoint Hans Lauerer, Hermann Beyer, Otto Weber, and Friedrich Werner to the new Clerical Ministry (see Scholder, *Churches and the Third Reich,* 1:568). [Scholder refers to this council as the "Clergy Ministry."—KC]

26. Franz Hildebrandt and Dietrich Bonhoeffer
to Martin Niemöller[1]

London, December 15, 1933

Dear Brother Niemöller,

With every letter and every newspaper we read, our thoughts fly to you in Berlin
and especially to Dahlem. Perhaps you are thinking that at our age, and because we
are over here, we don't have an adequate view of the situation. You may be right.
In any case, there is one thing we cannot understand, that at this critical moment
there is some kind of personal tension or substantive disagreement between you
and Jacobi,[2] with the likes of Müller, Meiser, Beyer enjoying the scrap[3] while we,
as spectators, are left disconsolate. Surely all human hopes for the church depend
on the two of you, at least, acting together, as the proven leaders from last summer. If there were anything we could do from here to help dispel these clouds,
we would certainly be very glad—knowing that we are united with both of you in
caring about what really matters, our concern for the new church.

Yours in heartfelt fellowship,
Hildebrandt

Dear Brother Niemöller,

I just wanted to let you know briefly that I think of you a great deal and in
quiet moments contemplate the immense responsibility that weighs on you.
The clarity of the course you set during the summer continues to make the
two of us hopeful that our side won't be found at the last moment "not knowing how to be winners," and that we won't allow ourselves to be dragged away
from the purity of our theological stance.[4] Now is the time when we must be
radical on all points, including the *Aryan paragraph*, without fear of the possible disagreeable consequences for ourselves. If we are untrue to ourselves
in any way at this point, we shall *discredit* the entire struggle of last summer.
Please, please, *you* be the one who makes sure that everything is kept clear,
courageous, and untainted.

In heartfelt solidarity and with many greetings for the Advent season,
Sincerely yours in friendship,
D. Bonhoeffer

[1.] LKA EKvW, BA 431/II; handwritten by Hildebrandt and Bonhoeffer on the same
sheet of paper. See also *NL*, A 41,9 (15); typewritten copy. Previously published in *GS*
2:151–52. See Niemöller's reply, 1/37.

[2.] Cf. J. Schmidt, *Martin Niemöller im Kirchenkampf*, 157.

[3.] [Hildebrandt uses the phrase "den tertius gaudens."—KC]

[4.] Here Bonhoeffer is arguing in the spirit of Karl Barth's *Theologische Existenz heute.*

49

27. The German Pastors in London to August Marahrens and Hans Meiser[1]

Expect Lutheran bishops to preserve gospel for Christian youth and honor of German Evangelical Church.[2] Congregations here extremely perturbed. German   50 pastor of London Wehrhan.

Telegram sent on December 19, 1933.

28. Theodor Heckel to Friedrich Wehrhan[1]

Berlin-Charlottenburg, December 20, 1933

In your letter of December 3, 1933,[2] Reverend Pastor, you enclosed a declaration from the German pastors in Great Britain and also informed the church government about a letter from the president of the Association of Congregations, Baron Bruno von Schröder. The events that have since occurred testify to the existence of the earnest desire not only to uphold the full authority of Bible and confession as the inviolable foundations of the church but also to bring peace to the church.[3] I respectfully ask to be permitted to inform you, the president of the Association of Congregations, and you, Reverend Gentleman, that the responsible church leadership is fully aware of the special nature and situation of the German Protestant congregations in Great Britain and is concerned to do everything it can to preserve fellowship with them in full measure. It therefore derives considerable pleasure and satisfaction from the evidence in this declaration of the German Protestant pastors' complete unanimity in confessing to the fundamentals of the Protestant Church.

For the Church Foreign Office
(signed) Dr. Heckel

[1.] ADBC, GV 13, 17; typewritten copy. Previously published in *Mündige Welt*, 5:149.

[2.] This refers to the forced incorporation of the Evangelical Youth organization into the Hitler Youth, which Reich Bishop Müller and Baldur von Schirach agreed on in a personal meeting on December 19, 1933, without prior notice to the various governing bodies of the Evangelical Church. Cf. Scholder, *Churches and the Third Reich*, 1:578.

[1.] ADBC, GV 13, 22; copy; cf. *NL*, A 41,2 (2). Letterhead: The Reich Church Government, K. M. II 3348; addressed to "Pastor Wehrhan, Reverend Pastor, London S.W. 13"; no salutation.

[2.] See 1/20.3.

[3.] In the meantime, Hossenfelder had resigned from his office as vice president of the Clerical Ministry, and the [German Christian] "faith movement" had been removed from some church leadership positions, but the other demands of the "confessional front" had not been met. Cf. Scholder, *Churches and the Third Reich*, 1:570–71.

51   **29. From the Reich Church Government**[1]

Berlin-Charlottenburg, December 20, 1933

To Pastor Dr. Bonhoeffer

This office has received a communication from the congregational councils of Sydenham and St. Paul's churches to the effect that, at an assembly of both congregations following worship on November 12, 1933, you were unanimously elected as their pastor. I therefore look forward to the further receipt of a notarized copy of the minutes of this assembly and the election. In sending it, would you please also inform us of your plans concerning resignation from the post you presently hold in Germany, or the arrangements you have made in this regard.[2]

30. To Théodore de Félice[1]

London S.E. 23, December 21, 1933

Dear Mr. de Félice,

I have been ill and have not been able to plan for January in order to reply to you. It would indeed be quite convenient for me if the commission meeting were held in Paris.[2] I could then combine my attendance with other important matters. Of course, London would also be convenient, but I would prefer Paris.[3]

With best wishes for Christmas,
Yours sincerely,
Dietrich Bonhoeffer

[1.] EZA 5/1316; typewritten draft; file reference: KM II 3153; initialed by "He(ckel) 19.12. B(esig) 18.12." According to office records, it was sent on December 21, 1933. See the reply, 1/45.

[2.] In the draft, a further clause is crossed out: "as well as how you envision your return, later, to a position in Germany."

[1.] WCC Archives, World Alliance, Letters from Dietrich Bonhoeffer 13; handwritten. Cf. *NL*, A 40,1 (1). Previously published in *Mündige Welt*, 5:224.

[2.] Meeting of the Ecumenical Youth Commission, January 31–February 1, 1934 (minutes of this meeting are in the WCC Archives, World Alliance, Youth Commission IV).

[3.] Among other things, Bonhoeffer planned a visit to Jean Lasserre in Bruay, which, however, did not take place until September 1934; see letter of September 11, 1934, to Erwin Sutz, 1/147.

31. To Julie Bonhoeffer[1] 52

London, December 21, 1933

Dear Grandmama,

Thank you very much for your letter.[2] It's especially nice of you to take the trouble to write such a long one. I'm always so happy when I get a letter from you, because then I can be sure you are well.

This Christmas will be a very quiet and restful one for you all. And that's good after a year like this. This year we have such an awful lot to put behind us, so as not to be bitter and let it spoil our mood. But I've been thinking recently that by the time one is your age and has seen so many things come and go, one "may gain a wise heart," as the Bible says,[3] and take a longer perspective. During these past weeks as the authoritarian church regime has been falling apart, I could not help feeling rather ashamed. Not that I believe that the line we have been following was wrong—on the contrary, it is in fact being proved right. Rather, it was because we had been so incredibly shortsighted and regarded as hard certainties things that collapsed into nothingness when the moment came. We can certainly learn a lot from this. I am hoping very much that by the end of this year the church will have been "cleansed." But then the work really begins, and there will be no lack of fresh difficulties and conflicts. Even so, to some extent we can take heart as we move on into the coming year. I do not yet know when I will next come home. Something could happen quite suddenly, at any moment, in the church situation, which would require me to come. I don't really hope that it will. Yet I hope all the more to see you all again soon.

Have a good rest during these days.

With all my good wishes, gratitude, and love,
Dietrich

[1.] *NL*, A 39,4 (1); handwritten, on paper with letterhead—crossed out by Bonhoeffer—of the "German Evangelical Church of St. Paul."

[2.] Not extant.

[3.] Ps. 90:12. [This psalm had always been read in the Bonhoeffer household on New Year's Eve; see *DB-ER*, 36.—KC]

53 **32. From Théodore de Félice**[1]

Geneva, December 22, 1933

Dear Sir,

Since the anticipated dates for the Youth Commission are not convenient for some of its members, in agreement with M. Henriod we propose to you February 15 (all day) and February 16 (morning only). The meeting in this case would take place in Paris.

I would be grateful if you could give me your opinion of this date.

Very cordially yours,
Th. de Félice

33. From Paula Bonhoeffer[1]

December 22, 1933

My dear Dietrich,

I wanted my letter to reach you right on Christmas Eve, but I'm afraid I'll not succeed in that! Well, be that as it may, you know we are thinking of you, thinking of your work and all the things you are concerned about, and wishing you a very happy Christmastime, doing things you have to do and that are fulfilling for you.

If the contents of our Christmas packages bring you some joy, we will be pleased. I shan't tell you anything about them, just in case this letter reaches you *before* you open them. Just one I'll give away—on Monday Mr. Hildebrandt is bringing you something I've been making especially, a jar of paté de foie gras, the same as we shall be having here. On Christmas Eve we'll be celebrating at 7:30 P.M. Hans-Walter and Renate[2] will be allowed to join us. We will ring you at 10 o'clock; I'm already looking forward to that. On Christmas Day everyone will be here again except the Dreßes,[3] because his mother is coming for dinner. The evening will be quiet, but in the afternoon we'll all play Lotto, Snap, etc. with the children.

54 The day after Christmas we are invited to the Dohnanyis'[4] in the afternoon to see a play in the truly delightful puppet theater the two of them have built. In the

---

[1.] WCC Archives, World Alliance, Letters to Dietrich Bonhoeffer; carbon copy; written in French.

[1.] *NL*, C 1/4–5; handwritten; from Berlin.
[2.] Hans-Walter Schleicher and Renate Schleicher, later married to Eberhard Bethge.
[3.] Walter and Susanne ("Susi") Dreß.
[4.] Hans and Christine von Dohnanyi.

evening the Goltzes[5] are coming to see us. Then we shall have one more quiet day at home before leaving on Thursday for a week in Göttingen.[6] We had also planned a visit to Karl-Friedrich's,[7] but now Mother Dohnanyi[8] is going there, and since we have never had a time with the children when she was not there, we decided not to go this time. Karl-Friedrich's chances of moving here have come to naught, since the position for which he was being considered will not be in his field at all, but in another altogether. Klaus will have to celebrate by himself, since he is still in Kischinev,[9] where he was hoping to win a case, at least he was the day before yesterday. I will be glad when he gets back.

Hainchen[10] has just been here, as we were able to be some help in sorting out her right to a pension, but she hasn't had a final decision yet. I feel so sorry for her.

You will certainly have a lot of work these next few days.

God keep you, and much love to you at Christmas from
Your Mother

34. From Karl Bonhoeffer[1]

December 22, 1933

Dear Dietrich,

I trust you will have this letter by the day after tomorrow, when you will be celebrating Christmas Eve with the others in your house. Our thoughts will be very much with you. Tomorrow evening, too, when we decorate the tree we will miss you—including your help in doing the work. Hans Dohnanyi is still convalescing, Rüdiger[2] is not supposed to climb ladders, and Claus[3] will only turn up as Father Christmas on the twenty-fourth. I assume he will be leaving Kischinev tomorrow. He has been away a long time—almost too long for his practice, but I hope he will come home satisfied. We expect to be together with the grandchildren as usual

55

[5.] Rüdiger Graf von der Goltz and his wife, Hannah, Paula Bonhoeffer's sister.

[6.] To visit Gerhard ("Gert") and Sabine Leibholz.

[7.] Karl-Friedrich and Grete Bonhoeffer.

[8.] Elisabeth von Dohnanyi.

[9.] In Bessarabia; present-day Chiṣinău, Moldova.

[10.] Elke Heidenhain was a family friend of the Bonhoeffers from their time in Breslau and still lived in Silesia.

[1.] *NL*, C 1/4–5; handwritten; from Berlin.

[2.] Rüdiger Schleicher; this was the result of a war injury.

[3.] Klaus Bonhoeffer.

after the celebration; the two eldest, Hans-Walter and Renate, will be allowed to join in celebrating Christmas Eve here with their grandparents. Some of the traditional foie gras should be making its way to you.

I assume, from my memories of English Christmas cards, that you will be having plum pudding. It is a vivid part of my childhood recollections, with its blue flame, from my Grandmother Tafel's[4] house and the English ladies she had staying with her. All in all, as far as the family is concerned, we have reason to be thankful that in spite of everything we can celebrate Christmas in good health and knowing that all our children are launched in their careers. I expect you will be getting news of your brothers and sisters directly from them, so I do not need to report on them. Just now the Dohnanyi children are making a din in the corridor, exiled here to leave their mother free to get ready for the Christ Child.[5]

I hope our things have arrived safely by courier. I am also sending you a copy of a photo of my grandfather Bonhoeffer[6] as a boy; Eugen B.[7] sent it to us. These days more than ever, one ought to have one's ancestral gallery on the wall.[8]

You must be having lots of visitors from over here, who can keep you up to date on what is happening in the church better than I can. I still have Barth's letter[9] to you. Do you want to have it back, or shall I keep it for you here? It is striking testimony to a fiery spirit. As to the matter itself, I don't venture to comment. I only think that it can also be extremely valuable to be able to look at things from the outside, whence, perhaps, some influence can be brought to bear, and particularly to save oneself for the right moment. That you find satisfaction in your endeavors there in the parish ministry is also a comforting thought for us. Someone called Otto Hasse[10] has just telephoned here to wish you a happy Christmas. He was sorry he could not speak to you, and I promised to pass along his greeting to you. Apparently he is one of your confirmands. This letter must catch the post. Have a lovely Christmas Eve, and much love from

Your Father

[4.] Karoline Friederike Tafel, née Oswald.

[5.] [In Germany it is the Christ Child, rather than Father Christmas or Santa Claus, who brings the gifts that children receive at Christmas.—KC]

[6.] Sophonias Franz Bonhoeffer.

[7.] Eugen Bonhoeffer.

[8.] An ironic allusion to the research people had to do after 1933 to prove their "Aryan" descent.

[9.] See 1/16.

[10.] Illegible; could also be Hesse, not identified.

35. Report on the Christmas Celebration
at the London Seamen's Mission[1]

56

Christmas Celebration at the Seamen's Mission in London

Just in time last Monday evening,[2] the fog lifted to allow the parish hall of St. Paul's Church to fill with sailors, parishioners, and friends of the congregation, who had come at Pastor Rieger's invitation to the big Seamen's Mission Christmas celebration. The four London pastors were there; Pastor Schönberger had brought his church choir and men's choir, Pastor Wehrhan his flugelhorn, all glad to help make the evening a happy one for all who were gathered. Dr. Rüter, an official representing the German embassy, welcomed the sailors warmly, spoke of many things both cheery and serious, and received grateful applause. Pastor Wehrhan spoke on behalf of the General Committee of the Seaman's Mission, pointing out what is really the mission's most important task by introducing the anthem, impressively sung by the Dalston Men's Choir: "Christ, Lord, come to us on the sea." Later the young seamen themselves sang a few lively songs. The spiritual centerpiece of the evening was the Christmas play about the three kings, taken from the Munich amateur theatre[3] and enacted with great devotion by a group of young people and children from St. George's Church. It was not theater for its own sake, but rather complete immersion in the theme—that was what made this performance so impressive. The three kings, according to old folk tradition, are three poor creatures who go from house to house on Christmas Eve, singing and begging. On their way home, their pockets finally full, they come across the home of a poor family—a young mother with a newborn baby, the father, and two children who have returned almost empty-handed 57 from their begging and are asking about the Christ Child.[4] Almost like the desolate question that the little son of a proletarian family, in their cold, bare, rented cellar room on Christmas Eve, is supposed to have asked his mother, who is sick in bed: "Mother, why does the Christ Child only bring gifts to rich families who can buy things themselves anyhow?" Into such a situation our odd three kings have entered, and here Christmas comes for them too. They pour out their treasures—knowing that Christ was born in poor surroundings—and through becoming poor once more, they become truly rich.

[1.] *NL*, Anh. D 1,6 (2), in private possession of Rudolf Weckerling; handwritten by Bonhoeffer; December 1933.

[2.] On December 25, 1933.

[3.] The play was Adolf Wurmbach's *Wir sind die drei Könige mit ihrem Stern* (We are the three kings with their star).

[4.] [See 1/34, ed. note 5.—KC]

We thank those who, through this play, brought the Christmas message home to us once again. The evening ended with some announcements and good words from Pastor Rieger.

B.[onhoeffer]

36. To George Bell[1]

Dez. 27th, 33

My Lordbishop,

thank you very much for your most kind Christmas greetings. It means very much to me indeed to know that you are sharing all the time the sorrows and the troubles which the last year has brought to our church in Germany. So we do not stand alone, and whatever may occur to one member of the Church universal, we know that all the members suffer with it. This is a great comfort for all of us; and if God will turn back to our church sometime now or later, then we may be certain, that, if one member be honoured, all the members shall rejoice with it.[2]

Things in Germany are going on more slowly than we expected. Müller's position is, of course, very much endangered. But he seems to try to find closer contact with the state to be sure of its protection in case of danger. Only from this point of view I can understand his last agreement with the Hitleryouth.[3] But it seems as if the State is nevertheless very much reserved and does not want to interfere once more. I do not think personally that Müller can keep his position and it will certainly be a great success if he falls. But we must not think that the fight is settled then. On the contrary, it will without any doubt start anew and probably sharper than before with the only advantage that the fronts have been cleared. The trend towards nordic heathenism is growing tremendously, particularly among very influential circles; and, I am afraid, the opposition is not united in their aims. In Berlin they are going to form an Emergency Synod under the leadership of Jacobi next Friday.[4] This is meant to be a legal representation of the oppositional

58

[1.] LPL, Bell Papers 42, 7 and 8; handwritten, on paper with Bonhoeffer's address in Berlin crossed out; from London; in original English, including errors. See also *NL*, A 42,1 (5); typewritten copy. Previously published in *GS* 1:182–83.

[2.] 1 Cor. 12:26.

[3.] Müller had sent a telegram to Hitler on December 20, 1933: "I have just completed the incorporation of the Evangelisches Jugendwerk into Hitler Youth, in agreement with the Youth Leader authorized by you" (Scholder, *Churches and the Third Reich*, 1:578).

[4.] In early January the preparatory committee in Berlin-Brandenburg met for the first time under Jacobi's leadership. See Meier, *Der evangelische Kirchenkampf,* 1:167.

congregations against the illegal synods of last August and September.[5] Jacobi is probably the wisest of the oppositional leaders in the moment and I put much trust into what he is doing. There is a great danger that people who have had a very indefinite attitude towards the German Christians last summer, jeopardize now the success of the opposition by mingling in and seeking their own personal advantage.

The letter of Müller[6] is as expected very weak and anxious, it really does not mean anything at all. It does not come out of a sound theological but much more of political argumentation—though one always has to realise that his position now is so difficult as never before.

If you allow me I shall be only too glad to come once more to Chichester 59 to see you.[7] I am still having continuous information by telephone and airmail from Berlin.

Please, give my most respectful regards to Mrs. Bell.

I remain, in sincere gratitude, My Lord, Yours truly

Dietrich Bonhoeffer

37. Martin Niemöller to Franz Hildebrandt[1]

Berlin-Dahlem, December 27, 1933

Dear Brother Hildebrandt,

I would like to send my greetings to you and Bonhoeffer before the end of the year, even though on several occasions your various communications[2] did add stress when my life was already more than stressful enough!—But I know you meant well, even if you were obviously proceeding on the basis of false information.

In actual fact there were no personal differences of any kind between me and Jacobi. There was only a parting of the ways, to the extent that Jacobi believed he saw an opportunity where I saw a trap: the bishops, together with the other church leaders except those who were German Christians, had proposed that the

---

[5.] The Prussian general synod held its first meeting after the elections on September 5 and 6, 1933; the national synod convened on September 27 in Wittenberg.

[6.] Reference is to his letter of December 8, 1933. Müller was reacting to a letter of October 23 from Bell. Bell then replied on January 18, 1934, with even more intense complaints on behalf of the Universal Council on Life and Work. The letters from October and December 1933 were reprinted in a brochure from Life and Work, "Minutes of the Meeting of the Executive Committee in Novi Sad, Yugoslavia, 1933," 39–42. Bell's January 1934 reply has been reprinted in Boyens, *Kirchenkampf und Ökumene*, 1:315–17.

[7.] "Me" in the original letter.

[1.] Original not found. Previously published in *GS* 2:152–54.

[2.] See, for example, 1/21, 1/24, and 1/26.

Reibi[3] have a full-fledged cabinet. This must have been pretty awkward for the Reibi, since it turned out that behind this cabinet proposal stood a united front of church leaders, the provincial church of Westphalia, and the Pastors' Emergency League.

There was great consternation, and the camarilla around Müller tried to break up this front by negotiating separately with its different factions. In the course of which, Oberheid said to me: How would you yourself like to take over this united cabinet?

I did not take the question seriously and could not do otherwise than say no immediately, since we were committed to the others involved and to the proposals made by the bishops.[4] It was here that Jacobi began to protest: he thought I should have said yes.— There you have the source of the fable of my shying away from responsibility!

Jacobi and I had another, slight disagreement on participation in the "arbitration panel"; Jacobi was supposed to be on it, and at first he wanted to be. This discussion went on for about a week and ended with Jacobi's seeing that we could not possibly take on even part of the responsibility for the Reibi and his new cabinet. So that took care of that. In the meantime the new cabinet has fallen apart, since they could not find a Lutheran as a minister; Weber[5] resigned a few days ago, so now only Beyer[6] and Werner[7] are left in the cabinet. The Reibi made another attempt to save himself by sacrificing the Protestant Agency for Youth. But he won't have any luck with that either; it will only lead to another attack on him. This Reich bishop crisis can hardly be covered up anymore.

As for the new organization of things, I am not in favor of appointing people prominent in the Emergency League, lest we cause the wavering German Christian front to take a new hard line. We must first see about restoring calm and order within the church, so that in the near future we shall once more be in a position to elect a true church synod. That, in my opinion, will be the proper time for setting up the new. We are planning not on going back to the old system but rather on having an unmistakably transitional solution, with limited powers and responsibilities. Otherwise we shall have schism on the basis of still not properly

60

[3.] The common nickname for Reich Bishop Ludwig Müller, "Reibi" was an abbreviation for "Reich Bishop." [This nickname for Müller, of course, also sounds like "Rabbi." It is difficult today to discern the extent to which this might have also reflected anti-Judaic prejudices, but the term was certainly used in a derogatory manner.—KC]

[4.] On this affair, see Bonhoeffer's letter of March 18, 1934, to Heckel, 1/82, as well as the reply of April 17, 1934, from the Church Foreign Office, 1/91.

[5.] Otto Weber.

[6.] Hermann Wolfgang Beyer.

[7.] Friedrich Werner.

defined fronts from the other side. Of course, all the Prussian bishops must go, and the law[8] with them! But I'd rather not specify beyond that.

I am also hopeful that we can steer this course with full unanimity in the ranks of the Emergency League! It appears to be plain to everyone by now that the Reibi is impossible, but how we are to get rid of him is still very much a question. The Christmas holidays have unfortunately brought the whole thing to a standstill, and at the moment I cannot see how we are to get it moving again.

In any case, we have no intention of entering into compromises or being satisfied with half measures, since that certainly will not help the church. I trust the two of you are still of the same opinion!

I am under great pressure with the Emergency League work, since Captain   61
Schulze[9] is leaving as of January 1 and no one has yet been found to take over from him.[10]

Enough for now; it's midnight yet again. Best regards to you from back home.

Yours as ever,
Niemöller

38. Minutes of Congregational Council Meetings

38.1 Sydenham Church, December 29, 1933[1]

Meeting of the Congregational Council
on December 29, 1933, in the Parsonage

Present: Mrs. Schlund, Mr. Voigt, Mr. Brown, Mr. Heydorn

The pastor opened the meeting with a prayer.

He then informed the vestry about a letter from Dr. Heckel of the Church Foreign Office,[2] asking what the pastor planned to do about resigning from

---

[8.] This refers to the "Bishops' Law" passed by the Old Prussian general synod on September 5, 1933, which replaced the office of general superintendent in Old Prussia with ten bishoprics under the jurisdiction of Ludwig Müller, who was named regional bishop (*Landesbischof*) (cf. *DB-ER*, 306–7). [Müller was only named regional bishop of the Old Prussian Union regional church at this synod, under one of the provisions in the Bishops' Law; he had not held that office previously. See Helmreich, *German Churches under Hitler*, 144.—KC]

[9.] Martin Schulze.

[10.] "This was the first indication to Hildebrandt that he would have to return to Berlin to assist Niemöller in administration of the Emergency League" (Bethge, *GS* 2:154, ed. note 1).

[1.] ADBC, Minute Book of Sydenham Church, 30–31; handwritten by Bonhoeffer.
[2.] See 1/29.

his post as lecturer [Privatdozent] at the University of Berlin. The pastor said that he had expressed the wish to retain this position for the time being and repeated this wish. The vestry authorized the pastor to write to Dr. Heckel informing him that the congregation gave its consent for the pastor to retain the position of lecturer until further notice.[3]

The meeting was then adjourned.

Bonhoeffer

38.2 St. Paul's Church, January 1, 1934[4]

Extraordinary Meeting on January 1 at 7 P.M.

Due to fog, only a few gentlemen were present: G. Henne, Blumenstock, Klugmann, Streitberger, Weber, Neubert, Klotz

62   The pastor opened the meeting with prayer. He then informed the council that one of its long-time members, Mr. Brenner, had died. The council members rose for a moment in honor of the deceased. The pastor then presented a letter from Dr. Heckel of the Church Foreign Office, asking for information about the pastor's resignation from his previous employment as lecturer at the University of Berlin. The pastor also presented a reply he had written,[5] which had already been approved by Sydenham Church, in which he said that the congregation had no objection to the pastor's retaining the post of lecturer in Berlin. This letter was approved by the council. The meeting was adjourned at 8 P.M.

Dietrich Bonhoeffer, Pastor[6]

39. To Erich Seeberg[1]

January 2, 1934

Dear Professor Seeberg,

I have been meaning for a long time to write and thank you for the letter you wrote me in September, with its really surprising news that pleased me

---

[3.] See 1/45.

[4.] ADBC, Minute Book of St. Paul's Church, 21; handwritten by Bonhoeffer.

[5.] Draft letter written by Bonhoeffer on the back of a draft of the minutes of the meeting at St. Paul's, which corresponds to the January 3, 1934, version (1/45), except for insignificant details.

[6.] This was followed by the signatures of twelve elders and council members.

[1.] *NL*, A 39,1 (10); typewritten, from London, with handwritten date and salutation. For the reply, see 1/51.

greatly.[2] To be frank, I had always felt that I was regarded as something of an outsider within the faculty, not as though I really belonged there. It warms my heart to know that apparently my impression was incorrect, and I thank you for letting me know about it.

I must also beg your pardon for our suddenly firing off a telegram[3] to you. We stood under the strong impression here that, at a crucial moment, the whole opposition struggle was coming apart for personal reasons, and did not know to whom we might turn for help, if not to you.   63

It now looks as though things are rapidly being cleared up. Our view from here is that Müller's resignation is absolutely necessary. And we had better not retreat one step from this demand, or else the whole court theology around this new periodical[4] will regain the upper hand, and that is a thousand times more dangerous than all of the Krause church.[5] Shouldn't a doctrinal disciplinary committee composed of academic theologians, in conjunction with the opposition, be convened as soon as possible, which can make a charge of heretical teaching[6] stick, not just against the German Christian bishops but also particularly against these court theologians? Otherwise we shall never be rid of this poison, and I really cannot see why only the poor devils who parrot it should suffer while the originators of the entire falsehood are allowed to go on talking with impunity. Isn't it high time we began thinking quite explicitly about this?

Finally, with your permission, a personal question on my own behalf. Do you feel that any material interest would be served if I were to lecture next

---

[2.] Letter of August 20, 1933, to Bonhoeffer from Erich Seeberg (*GS* 2:124; *DBWE* 12, 1/87). The "surprising news" from Seeberg, who was dean of the theological faculty in Berlin, was that in the negotiations concerning Arthur Titius's successor for the chair for systematic theology, Bonhoeffer's name had been proposed "with great appreciation." In the end, Arnold Stolzenburg was appointed.

[3.] See 1/22.

[4.] *Deutsche Theologie*, Stuttgart, 1934. The editorial board consisted of Hermann Wolfgang Beyer, Heinrich Bornkamm, Karl Fezer, Friedrich Gogarten, Ernst Haenchen, Emanuel Hirsch, Gerhard Kittel, Helmuth Kittel, Hanns Rückert, Friedrich Karl Schumann, Otto Weber, and Arthur Weiser. A special issue on Luther had already appeared in November 1933.

[5.] Reinhold Krause, the regional German Christian leader (*Gauobmann*) for greater Berlin, was the main speaker at the Sports Palace rally on November 13, 1933. On November 14 he was stripped of all his offices in the Brandenburg church and in the German Christian movement; see Scholder, *Churches and the Third Reich*, 1:557–58. Cf. 1/20.2, ed. note 40.

[6.] Cf. 1/40.

semester? I find myself in a serious inner conflict about this and would be most grateful for your personal advice.

Once again I thank you, highly esteemed Professor, and remain

Very respectfully yours,
Dietrich Bonhoeffer

64　**40. To Henry Louis Henriod**[1]

[London] S.E. 23, 2. Jan. 34

Dear Henriod!

A happy New Year to you and to our common work! Since we met last[2] things have changed very rapidly. The process of cleansing has gone on faster than any of us would have thought. And it is very satisfactory to me to see that the aims of the opposition become more and more radical and to the point. Müller must be done away with and with him all his bishops, and what seems most important almost of all—the new court-theologians[3] (you find their names in the new periodical: Deutsche Theologie) must all undergo a "Irrlehreverfahren," "Lehrzuchtverfahren";[4] for they are the real source from which the poison goes out. As long as they are allowed to speak out their heretical christianity as approved teachers of the church, we shall never get rid of the german christian ideology. I personally do not believe that with the settlement of the struggle with the German Christians the dangerous time for the church is over. On the contrary, it is only the beginning of much more serious and dangerous fights in the near future. But—anyway—the fronts become clear and that is all we want.

The youth commission meeting Febr. 15th will probably have to deal already with more or less clear conditions in Germany, and I hope that we can make from this meeting a very important step forward in connecting our youth work with the new Church Government. But we will talk about that personally.

[1.] WCC Archives, World Alliance, Letters from Dietrich Bonhoeffer, 15; handwritten; in original English (except for the salutation "Lieber Henriod!" and the references appearing in German in the letter), including errors. See also *NL*, A, 40,1 (2); typewritten copy. Previously published in *Mündige Welt*, 5:225, and *GS* 6:347–49.

[2.] In Sofia, Bulgaria, September 15–20, 1933; see *DB-ER*, 311–17.

[3.] Cf. 1/39, ed. note 4.

[4.] [These German terms refer to investigations and disciplinary procedures for alleged teaching of heresy in the church.—KC]

I can only start today with my outlines for Budapest.[5] It was too much work hitherto.

We all must keep praying for our christian church and I thank you for all fellowship which I know I have with you in this regard. May the New Year bring us a clearer vision of what our aim may be in the future under changed conditions. 65

Yours very sincerely
Dietrich Bonhoeffer

41. To Théodore de Félice[1]

London S.E. 23

Dear Mr. de Félice,

February 15 in Paris will suit me very well! This meeting will surely be a very important one for our work in Germany, since by then hopefully we shall have clearly defined conditions, and I trust that this will allow us to integrate all this work firmly into the international work. We had best speak of these plans when we are together—that will be very important.

Yours sincerely,
Dietrich Bonhoeffer

42. George Bell to the Editor of *The Round Table*[1]

2nd January, 1934

Dear Sir,

I received your letter of December 28th yesterday, though I was away from home.

I am delighted that you propose to secure an article on the crisis in the Ger- 66
man Protestant Church, for the March "Round Table." I wish I could write it, but I simply have not got the time before March. I should however like to suggest a man who would do the article with great ability and first-hand knowledge. He is

---

[5.] The meeting was actually held in Paris from January 31 to February 1, 1934.

[1.] WCC Archives, World Alliance, Letters from Dietrich Bonhoeffer, 16; handwritten. Cf. *NL*, A 40,1 (3); typewritten copy. Undated, probably early January 1934, since in his letter to Henriod of January 2, 1934 (1/40), Bonhoeffer was also expecting "the fronts [to] become clear."

[1.] LPL, Bell Papers 5, 86; carbon copy, in original English, including errors. Cf. also *NL*, A 42,3 (1); typewritten copy. *The Round Table* [under the overall editorship of Lord

Dr. Dietrich Bonhoeffer, 23 Manor Mount, Forest Hill, S.E. 23. For the last three months about, he has been German Pastor in London. I know him well and he was introduced to me by Professor Adolf Deissmann of Berlin as "one of our best young theologians." He speaks English perfectly. He is under 30. He spent a year in U.S.A. for theological purposes. He knows the personnel of the German Church at Berlin extremely well and is a follower of Karl Barth. He is also in almost daily touch with the situation in Berlin. Further he is one of the earliest members of the Pastors Emergency League, now swollen to 6,000 members, and his name is actually the first of the twenty or so signatures to the famous manifesto which the pioneers of the Pastors Emergency League presented to the Prussian Synod in September.[2] I do not think you could get anyone to write an article of the kind you want with more authority, and you can be very certain of his ability. I would gladly help him in any way that was useful. If you liked I would write to him myself and make the proposal. But that is just as you please. He would quite understand the points which you set out in your letter to me, and I could send on your letter as it stands to him if you liked. He and I would probably discuss the article together, as he is coming to stay with me again shortly.

Yours faithfully,

[George Cicestr]

43. Emil Karow to the Consistory of the Mark Brandenburg[1]

[Berlin-]Charlottenburg, January 2, 1934

The student chaplain at the technical college, Lecturer Dr. Dietrich Bonhoeffer, carried on his efforts to provide services to the students during the summer semester 1933, as previously. He came to see me and told me of his regret that he

67

Lothian (Philip Kerr); the general editor was John Dove; cf. 1/53.—KC] was a quarterly journal in which important issues in political life were discussed, around a different theme in each issue. A few days later Bonhoeffer persuaded Bell that he was unable at that time to write an article about the Church Struggle in Germany for any British newspaper or magazine. In a letter of January 6, 1934, to Hermann Beyer (1/47), Bonhoeffer stated that there was no connection between himself and reports appearing in the *Times*.

[2.] This refers to the leaflet (see *GS* 2:141 and *DBW* 12, 1/105) that was posted on trees in Wittenberg on September 27, 1933, when the national synod was meeting. An early version was published in English in Macfarland, *New Church and the New Germany*. Cf. also *DB-ER*, 319.

[1.] EZA 14/1623; typewritten on letterhead of "The Bishop of Berlin," addressed to "The Evangelical Consistory of the Mark Brandenburg." See also *NL*, A 30 (14). Previously published in *GS* 6:220.

had not only been unable to expand the work, but that, on the contrary, there had been less demand for his services than in previous semesters. He offered hours when he was available for private consultation, plus working groups and lectures. The response was only quite modest.

Bonhoeffer left Berlin in October 1933. A suitable person to take over the work at the technical college on behalf of the church has not been found. The experience we have had, particularly during the last semester, causes me to doubt whether what we have been doing is at all the right thing for a technical college. After a long conversation with Prof. Dr. Stolzenburg, I would like to propose that we set our sights on offering a teaching position at the college, for a Protestant with theological training, on questions of worldview and personal values. Perhaps the students would be more open to such an approach, and the person could also be available for pastoral counseling and for working groups. But this is a question that needs to be decided in consultation with the Consistory of the Evangelical Church and the Ministry for Education and Cultural Affairs.

Karow

44. To George Bell[1]

3. Jan. 34

My Lord Bishop,

thank you very much for your kind invitation for Friday night.[2] I should like very much indeed to come. But there is just in the present moment so very much work in the congregation that I hardly can leave this place in this week. If any time in the near future would be suitable for you, I shall certainly be able to arrange it and come with the greatest pleasure. It would interest me immensely what you think of the situation of Bishop Muller and of what would be wise to do. May I ask you to let me know whether any other day would suit you.

With the best wishes for the New Year I remain in sincere gratitude My Lord, Yours

Dietrich Bonhoeffer

[1.] LPL, Bell Papers 42, 9; handwritten; from London, on stationery with letterhead (crossed out) formerly used by Bonhoeffer as student pastor in Berlin; in original English, including errors. See also *NL*, A 42,1 (6); copy.

[2.] On January 5, 1934.

68   **45. To Theodor Heckel**[1]

London, January 3, 1934

Dear Senior Consistory Councilor[2] Heckel:

In response to your letter of December 20,[3] permit me to reply as follows. I had already stated, in response to an inquiry from the church government immediately before my departure for London, that I am on leave from the University of Berlin until further notice. However, I immediately convened a meeting of the congregational councils of both Sydenham and St. Paul's Church to discuss the contents of your letter.[4] The council was and is informed of the fact that I am on leave from my position as lecturer. The only question was whether the purpose of your letter is to make a change in this state of affairs, which the vestry does not consider necessary.

The wording of the present letter was established during the meeting at the request of the vestry. The minutes of the two elections[5] were sent by yesterday's post. By the way, the work here is going well and gives me great pleasure.

Very respectfully,
your obedient servant,
Bonhoeffer

46. From George Bell[1]

4th January, 1934

My dear Bonhoeffer,

Very many thanks for your letter.[2] I am very anxious to see you at an early date, for I have an important proposal with regard to a long article in a very important periodical to put before you.[3] As it turns out, I shall be away myself tonight
69   and probably tomorrow night, for personal reasons. Could you send me your

---

[1.] EZA 5/1316; typewritten; erroneously dated 1933 in the original. Previously published in *Mündige Welt*, 5:129, and *GS* 6:288.

[2.] [Heckel, a senior official in the Berlin Consistory, had responsibility for liasing with overseas ministries such as the one in London. He was appointed bishop on February 21, 1933.—KC]

[3.] See 1/29.

[4.] See 1/38.

[5.] See 1/11.

[1.] LPL, Bell Papers 42, 10; carbon copy, from Chichester; in original English, including errors. See also *NL*, A 42,2 (2); typewritten copy. Previously published in *GS* 2:142.

[2.] See 1/44.

[3.] Cf. 1/42 and 1/53.

telephone address on a postcard, so that I may talk to you? When are you most likely to be in?

I want you to reserve yourself for a luncheon engagement which has been suggested, if you will, on Tuesday, January 23rd, at 1.15. Let me know about this.

Yours sincerely,

[George Cicestr]

47. To Hermann Wolfgang Beyer[1]

London, January 6, 1934

Dear Professor Beyer:

From a very reliable source I have learned that outrageous rumors are circulating within the church leadership, even going so far as to imply that I am connected with the reports in the *Times* about the church situation in Germany. I must say I am amazed that it is possible for any obscure persons,   70 as unscrupulous as they are ignorant, to have their slanderous statements accepted in high places without a trace of proof.

¶I hereby declare to you that I had and have nothing whatever to do with the reporting in any English newspaper. I do not even know who the clearly outstanding reporter for the *Times* is. Furthermore, I really don't need to turn to foreign papers to express my opposition to the "German Christians"—the Wittenberg declaration[2] should have made that clear enough. However, if there is not an immediate end to these false accusations, I shall consider

---

[1.] ZEKHN 62/1002; carbon copy. See also *NL*, A 41,9 (3); copy. Previously published in *GS* 2:154–55. Addressed to "Church Minister Prof. Dr. Beyer, Berlin-Charlottenburg, Marchstr. 2." In fact, Beyer had withdrawn from this office [in the Clerical Ministry—KC] shortly before. See *DB-ER*, 362. See Beyer's reply of July 30, 1934 (1/130). On the same carbon copy there is a handwritten note from Franz Hildebrandt to Martin Niemöller (undated, but probably January 6 as well; see the following telegram, 1/48), which reads: "Dear Brother Niemöller, this copy is for your information and edification—indicating the way in which certain people back home are working against Bonhoeffer! By the way, thanks very much for your letter, we were very pleased to receive it and agree entirely. If things continue as in the Emergency League's December 29 declaration [on December 30 in Würzburg, the Emergency League's officers had demanded that Reich Bishop Müller resign from office—KC], we need have no doubt of success. Hopefully the bishops will not again go back on their ultimatum and retract it? [on December 22, Meiser, Wurm, and Bodelschwingh had already advised Müller to take an unlimited leave—KC]. (It looks that way according to today's *Times*.) Perhaps we shall hear from you again soon. Best regards, from Bonhoeffer as well, yours ever, Hildebrandt." [See also Bonhoeffer's letter of January 6 to his brother-in-law Walter Dreß (1/47a) for his vigorous reaction to this rumor.—KC.]

[2.] Declaration of September 27, 1933; see *GS* 2:74–76. The first version of the pamphlet from August 1933 was in *GS* 2:62–69.

myself compelled to come to my own defense in some appropriately effective way within Germany.

I am addressing this letter to you because I am sure that you will be concerned to use your influence for clarity, openness, and decency within the Church Struggle and to oppose the spread of any slander.

Yours most respectfully,

B.[onhoeffer]

17:121 **47a. To Walter Dreß**[1]

London, January 6, 1934[2]

Dear Walter,

Just a short note to thank you very much [for] your letters, including the one for Christmas. I was delighted to hear that you are planning to visit me in April. That's great! But don't be like most people—where things just stay at the planning stage! Then we could have the leisure to talk about all sorts of other things. So, you are very welcome indeed at any time, you will give me the honour and pleasure of your visit. Can't you bring your "old lady"[3] with you—I have got a guest room for two people and I suppose she would enjoy London as well and it will be to me[4] an all the greater pleasure.[5] Tell her she should get our parents to give her this journey as a late Christmas or a praenumerando[6] birthday present. It would be really nice if both of you came! So pluck up your courage and resolve to do it! I have just written to Seeberg.[7] I am sure you know of it. But in the meantime a shameless and despicable slander has come my way. I have sent copies of the response I

[1.] Literary estate of Walter and Susanne Dreß; handwritten letter, with typewritten date and heading: "The Rev. Dr. Dietrich Bonhoeffer"; envelope addressed "Dr. W. Dreß, Instructor, Berlin-Lichterfelde, Prettauerpfad 15, Germany"; first publication in *DBW* 17:121. German edited by Hans Goedeking. The page number in the margin refers to *DBW* 17.

[2.] The date is not clear; the envelope is postmarked January 12, 1934, while the date in the letter has been typed over and could be read as either "6.I." or "6.II. [February 6,] 1934." The reference to Christmas makes the January date more likely.

[3.] Susanne Dreß. [This and the preceding sentence are in Bonhoeffer's English.—KC]

[4.] The original has an extra "be" here.

[5.] "You are very welcome . . . pleasure" written in English.

[6.] "Anticipated."

[7.] See 1/39.

wrote Beyer to Niemöller, Seeberg, Heckel, Stolzenburg, Opitz, and my parents.[8] A fine pack of scoundrels,[9] attacking behind my back—I can only spit, how disgusting!

All good wishes to you both!

Yours,

Dietrich

48. The German Evangelical Pastors in London to the Reich Church Government[1]

Following today's *Times* report[2] extremely worried about relations of churches here with home church request elucidation facts. German pastors in London January sixth.

Telegram sent on January 6, 1934.

49. Friedrich Wehrhan to the Reich Church Government[1]

For the sake of the gospel and our conscience we associate ourselves with the Emergency League proclamation[2] and withdraw our confidence from Reich Bishop Müller. German pastors in London.

Fr. Wehrhan

Telegram sent on January 7, 1934

[8.] See 1/47, ed. note 1.

[9.] ["Pack of scoundrels" refers to the officials in the church government who were spreading rumors about Bonhoeffer. See 1/47.—KC]

[1.] ADBC, GV 1, 3; typewritten copy. See also *NL*, A 41,1 (17); typewritten copy. Cf. *DB-ER*, 341.

[2.] The report described a gathering of the church opposition (Emergency League and bishops from southern Germany) in Halle at which the plans to separate from the Reich Church were apparently abandoned for the time being, because of the rumors that Ludwig Müller was counting on a Ministry for Church Affairs (*Kirchenministerium*) dominated by extremist German Christians, that Hitler was very annoyed about the expected schism and, due to the Reich bishop's threats, would ban any public criticism of his church policies in the future (the "muzzling decree"). Cf. J. Schmidt, *Martin Niemöller im Kirchenkampf*, 162–63.

[1.] ADBC, GV 13, 25; typewritten; see also *NL*, 41,2 (3). Previously published in *GS* 2:158. Cf. *DB-ER*, 341.

[2.] Proclamation of the Emergency League of January 4, 1934, calling for disobedience to the Reich bishop's decrees. It was intended to be read from church pulpits on January 7 or 14, in opposition to the "muzzle decree," the January 4, 1934, "Law to restore order in the German Evangelical Church." Cf. Scholder, *Churches and the Third Reich*, 1:570–82.

50. From Hans Besig[1]

Berlin-Charlottenburg, January 8, 1934

Dear Pastor Bonhoeffer,

The two excerpts from the minutes regarding your election to the ministry of Sydenham and St. Paul's churches[2] have been passed on to me from Senior Consistory Officer[3] Dr. Heckel. According to the regulations governing the diaspora churches, before a clergyman's service abroad is ratified, the German Evangelical Church must contact the offices of the regional church responsible for him and request its affirmation that it is prepared, after at least six years' satisfactory service abroad—in case of necessity, earlier—to assist him in obtaining placement as a pastor within Germany. In view of your special circumstances due to your having entered the academic teaching profession, I am doubtful as to whether this assurance of backing from the regional church, which in any event would require us to delay your ratification by several weeks in order to procure it, is of value to you.[4] In case it is not, I would like to ask you to inform us officially—*without making any reference to this letter*—that you relinquish the assurance of subsequent benefits within Germany according to §10, paragraph 3 of the Church Federation law regarding the union of German Evangelical church communities, congregations and clergy outside Germany with the Church Federation of June 17, 1924 (pp. 16ff. in the Legal Principles). The ratification of your election to ministry can then take place right away. I am sending separately as printed matter a section of the "Legal Principles" for your information.

We have just received your letter of January 3, 1934,[5] to Dr. Heckel. This office has no intention of bringing about any change in your relationship with the University of Berlin. The inquiry was intended only to clarify whether, following

72

[1.] *NL*, A 39,2 (3); typewritten. Previously published in *Mündige Welt*, 5:131–32. Cf. also EZA 5/1316; typewritten draft with note: "with oral agreement of OKR [Oberkirchenrat] Heckel."

[2.] See 1/11.

[3.] [See 1/45, ed. note 2.—KC]

[4.] See 1/43. In the draft version (EZA 5/1316) this sentence first appeared as follows: "Since you were a university teacher before you moved to London, you have probably never served in any regional church; I cannot assess whether this assurance of backing from a regional church is of value to you."

[5.] See 1/45.

your election as a pastor in London, you retained any relationship with your previous field of endeavor or intended to give it up.[6]

With best wishes, also from Senior Consistory Councilor Dr. Heckel, I remain,

Yours sincerely,

B.[esig]

51. From Erich Seeberg[1]

Berlin C2, January 9, 1934

Dear Mr. Bonhoeffer,

I am quite ready to postpone the decision as to whether you should lecture next semester. Since you ask for my personal advice, I would say that it seems to me better for you to stay in London next semester. Presumably we are now entering into a last major period of ecclesiastical conflict, and I think it would be in your interest not to wear yourself out too soon in this church conflict. I think it is important overall to keep back some men who will then be fresh and able to come forward when the time arrives for genuine rebuilding. On the other hand, I can naturally understand that in a tense situation such as the present one, you think of helping and taking a hand in the work yourself; and certainly I am persuaded that you would be personally enormously effective in these struggles, both among the pastors here and with our students. But when I weigh the one against the other, I do think that the duty to preserve one's strength is greater than that which calls one into the midst of the battle. Moreover, I entirely agree with your estimation of the real background of the situation. How I wish that the pastors would finally understand that here, too, the theologians are still the ones who can move things forward. And it is completely clear to me that the German church can neither tolerate Mr. Müller's zigzag course internally nor be properly represented by it to the outside world.

With all best wishes, to Mr. Hildebrandt as well,

Sincerely yours,

Erich Seeberg

[6.] In the draft version, this sentence follows, later crossed out: "Difficulties for the G.E.C. [German Evangelical Church]—particularly as a consequence of the supervisory relationship—will surely not emerge through the arrangement with the university?"

[1.] *NL,* Anh. D 1,5 (7); typewritten on letterhead of the "Theological Faculty of the Friedrich Wilhelm University of Berlin. The Dean." See Bonhoeffer's letter of January 2, 1934 (1/39).

52. Baron Bruno Schröder to Ludwig Müller[1]

January 9, 1934

As a loyal son of my old homeland and its Führer events in the German Evangelical Church fill me with gravest concern stop Rooted in the biblical Gospel our congregations much as they love their home church cannot tolerate that the church's foundation be shaken or that pastors be persecuted by the church government for obeying their consciences in fighting for this foundation stop I fear fateful consequences in the shape of secession of German churches abroad from their home church which for the sake of the hitherto community of faith I would utterly deplore[2]

Baron Bruno von Schröder
President
Association of German
Evangelical Congregations
in Great Britain and Ireland

74　　## 53. Lancelot Mason to the Editor of *The Round Table*[1]

12th January, 1934

Dear Sir,

Pastor Bonhoeffer, the German Pastor in London, who was originally asked to write the article on the German Church for "The Round Table," writes to the Bishop this morning[2] to say that though he is unable to write the article himself, he would be very glad to give any help that he can in the matter. He says that if you and Lord Lothian would like him to meet you at lunch he would be free on January 16th but not January 23rd. I have told him that I would write to you to let you know this, and that I would ask you to get into touch with him about the place and time of lunch on January 16th[3] if you want him to meet you. Pastor Bonhoeffer's address is: 23 Manor Mount, Forest Hill, London, S.E. 23. Telephone number:—

[1.] ADBC, GV 3, 1; carbon copy; from London. Cf. *DB-ER*, 342.

[2.] Alternative closing sentences, rejected in the final version, may be found in the files of ADBC, GV 3, 1.

[1.] LPL, Bell Papers 5, 103; carbon copy; from Chichester; in original English, including errors. Cf. also *NL*, 42,4 (2); carbon copy of notes. Lancelot Mason was George Bell's chaplain [see 1/12—KC]. This letter was addressed to John Dove; see 1/42, ed. note 1.

[2.] Not extant.

[3.] Cf. *DB-ER*, 363. The meeting took place on January 16; the draft for the article was written by Koechlin. After Bonhoeffer's letter of January 6, 1934, to Beyer (1/47), it was

I will of course let you know as soon as ever an answer comes from Pastor Koechlin.

Yours faithfully,

[L. Mason]

Chaplain

54. To Karl-Friedrich Bonhoeffer[1]

Dear Karl Friedrich,

Once again this letter is going to be late, and I wanted to answer your letter some time ago. So let me begin by wishing you a happy New Year, which I hope is going to bring you back here sometime. In any case, you can count on finding some peace and time to relax here. Actually England is not a   75 good place to be these days, because one is close enough to want to take part in everything and too far away for active participation. And during the past weeks this has made things exceptionally difficult for me. I have just read about Barth's dismissal in the *Times*.[2] I can hardly believe it's true. But if it is, perhaps I ought to come home, so that there's at least someone at the universities who's prepared to say these things. Somehow this stay in England—although I am really enjoying the work here, within its very narrow limits—feels like a sort of intermezzo to me. But I had actually been thinking that the next step might take me, at last, to India and the Far East. From here it seems so much nearer. And since I am becoming more convinced every day that in the West Christianity is approaching its end—at least in its present form, and its present interpretation—I should like to get to the Far East before coming back to Germany.[3]

Besides my parish work, I have conversations and various plans with English church people, including a few interesting politicians,[4] and countless German visitors, most of them Jews, who know me from somewhere and want something from me. I must have written already that a Dr. Steiner was here, whom you directed to me.

---

indeed impossible for him to fulfill Bell's request that he write a background article for *The Round Table*.

[1.] *NL*, A 39,4 (4); handwritten; from London. January 13, 1934, was Karl-Friedrich Bonhoeffer's birthday. Excerpt in *GS* 2:157–58.

[2.] The *Times* of January 13, 1934.

[3.] On Bonhoeffer's plans to go to India, see *DB-ER*, 406–9.

[4.] For example, with Lord Lothian on January 16, 1934.

Otherwise, Hildebrandt is staying here, which is very nice for me, as well as for the past two weeks a student from Berlin.[5] So I hardly have a chance to be lonely; this is also prevented by the numerous telephone conversations back and forth between here and Berlin.

So, now you know a bit more about me once again. And I must close, because it's Saturday and I still have more to do on my sermon.

I wish you all a happy New Year. I was very pleased with the picture!

Many greetings to you and Grete.[6]

Dietrich

76   **55. Friedrich Wehrhan to Baron Bruno Schröder**[1]

London, January 14, 1934

My dear Baron,

In view of the news in the papers here, and especially of reports that Pastor Bonhoeffer[2] has received by telephone directly from Berlin, we have decided to convene a meeting of the congregational council members and trustees of all the German congregations in London, to be held next Wednesday[3] at 8 P.M. in St. Mary's Church, at which we will discuss the situation with them and perhaps make decisions. We can hardly hope to welcome you among us, although we can scarcely do without your advice. We have notified the pastors from outside London and hope that they also will take part in this gathering. I have also invited Mr. Martens, as a member of the council of St. Mary's Church.

If it's agreeable to you, I and certainly Pastor Schönberger as well would be prepared to come and see you again before this meeting. The discussion will in any case be in accordance with your thinking, and I will report to you about it immediately afterward and ask for a statement of your own opinion.

May the Lord God and our Lord Jesus Christ stand by our precious Protestant church in this time of deep crisis and lead it toward what God intends for it!

I remain sincerely and respectfully yours,

Fr. Wehrhan, Pastor

[5.] The student was Wolf-Dieter Zimmermann. See Zimmermann, *I Knew Dietrich Bonhoeffer*, 77–78.

[6.] Grete Bonhoeffer, née von Dohnanyi.

[1.] ADBC, 13, 27; typewritten on letterhead of Christ Church (crossed out). See also *NL*, A 41,2 (4). Previously published in *GS* 6:307–8.

[2.] "Bonhöffer" in the original.

[3.] January 17, 1934.

56. The German Evangelical Pastors in London to the President of the German Reich[1]

London, January 15, 1934

Your Excellency, Mr. President:

As pastors of the German Protestant congregations in England, conscious of our responsibility toward the German Evangelical Church and the German Reich, we 77 feel obligated to present to your Excellency our view of the church dispute in Germany.

In this Luther anniversary year 1933, the "German Christians" have brought a spirit into the church and its governance that has shaken the foundations of the church. Despite all retractions, the Holy Scriptures and the Confession have been dishonored and have not been defended by the church government. Yet it was on the basis of the biblical gospel that our congregations were founded by our forefathers and, with tenacity and loyalty to the heritage of the Reformation, have been preserved to this day.[2] The most recent events have brought our congregations into the deepest concern, for they cannot bear that these foundations should be shaken.

Baron Bruno von Schröder, as chairman of the Association of German Evangelical Congregations in Great Britain and Ireland, has already expressed his concern over events in the mother church in a telegram[3] to the Reich bishop. He pointed out that the question has arisen in all seriousness whether the congregations here can remain within the German Evangelical Church in the face of the most recent church policy measures. As pastors we have had to decide, for the sake of the gospel and our conscience, to send a telegram[4] to the Reich bishop withdrawing our confidence from him.

For centuries our Protestant congregations have been the staunchest carriers of German heritage [Deutschtum] here in England. If the Evangelical Church here were to dissolve its ties with the mother church, we are firmly convinced that this would have a shattering effect on the ties of the German colony with its homeland,

---

[1.] ADBC, GV 13, 18; typewritten copy, addressed to "His Excellency the President of the German Reich [Paul von Hindenburg—KC], Berlin"; the return address is that of Fritz Wehrhan, who also signed the text composed by Bonhoeffer and Franz Hildebrandt (see *DB-ER*, 344); printed in the *Gemeindebote für die deutschen evangelischen Kirchen in Großbritannien* of January 21, 1934. See also *NL*, A 41,2 (4); copy. Previously published in *GS* 2:159–60.

[2.] This sentence is missing in the Association of Congregations copy but appears in the *Gemeindebote für die deutschen evangelischen Kirchen in Großbritannien*.

[3.] See 1/52.

[4.] See 1/49.

quite apart from the fact that our English neighbors regard this church quarrel as the event that, more than any so far, has damaged their esteem for Germany.

We implore you, Mr. President, now, at the eleventh hour, to avert the terrible danger for the sake of church unity and of the Third Reich, which we and our congregations gladly welcomed and which we support with all our might. As long as Reich Bishop Müller continues in office, the danger of secession remains imminent.

Copies of this letter, which we also are taking the liberty of publishing in the next issue of the German Evangelical Congregations' parish newsletter, are being sent to the Reich chancellor and to Reich ministers Baron von Neurath, Dr. Frick, and Count Schwerin von Krosigk, as well as to the Reich bishop.

Yours most respectfully and obediently,
The German Evangelical Pastors in London

57. Baron Konstantin von Neurath to Friedrich Wehrhan[1]

Berlin, January 17, 1934

Dear Pastor Wehrhan,

Thank you very much for your letter of January 15,[2] which I received today with its enclosures. I too have followed with considerable concern what has been happening in Germany's Evangelical Church. In particular I am aware of the ominous repercussions of these developments, both for the German Protestant congregations abroad and for the opinion of the entire Protestant world with regard to the new Germany. Insofar as there is any possibility of influencing the course of the disputes within the Evangelical Church, I have endeavored to do so.[3] I hope that at this point we are not too far from seeing peace restored. However, I would strongly advise the German Evangelical churches in Great Britain to delay for the time being the drafting of their proposed resolutions.

This comes with the assurance of my highest esteem and best wishes.

Sincerely yours,
(signed) Baron von Neurath

[1.] ADBC, GV 13, 31; typewritten copy. Cf. also *NL*, A 41,2 (5); copy. Previously published in *GS* 6:308.

[2.] Baron von Neurath had received a copy of the letter to the Reich president (1/56).

[3.] Cf. *DB-ER*, 344, and Scholder, *Churches and the Third Reich*, 2:29.

58. From Paula Bonhoeffer[1]

January 17, 1934

Dear Dietrich,

You must have received our telegram[2] by now. Jacobi had phoned Barth, and
Barth had said to him that he knew nothing about it, but that the rumor succeeded   79
in getting lots of nice flowers sent to him.[3] It was surely the wish that fathered
such a rumor.

As far as I have heard at this point, the letter[4] you wrote has met with great
approval from Jacobi and Seeberg and our Dahlem friend.[5] Lietzmann, when
Papa told him about it, was also very much in agreement and said this was a case
where one could not spell it out clearly enough.[6] What Stolzenburg said, I expect
I shall find out from Walter.[7] Walter is now getting involved very courageously.
In Greifswald a decision was made by sixty-two theology professors from many
different universities to come out with a protest.[8] It said that the latest church
regulations "for various reasons could not meet with their approval as teachers
and educators of student pastors." Then came the announcement from the Ministry of Cultural Affairs that professors, as civil servants, are not entitled to criticize
the church regulations in any way.[9] This was sent to the heads of all the university
departments of theology. I think it is going to cause yet more reactions.

Müller's audience with the Reich chancellor has been postponed from today
until tomorrow.[10] At the moment all we can think about is how to make him
realize sufficiently before the meeting that the bishops' truce is not in fact a *true
peace*. I may have found a way of doing this, with Uncle Rudi's[11] help: we hope
that our Dahlem friend[12] may get an audience with the old gentleman.[13] So now

[1.] *NL*, C 1,4–5; handwritten; from Berlin.

[2.] Not extant.

[3.] There were rumors that Barth had been dismissed; cf. Busch, *Karl Barth*, 241–42.
See also 1/54, including ed. note 2.

[4.] Letter from the London pastors to the Reich president (1/56).

[5.] Martin Niemöller.

[6.] This sentence was added at the bottom of the page, with a mark indicating its inser-
tion here in the text.

[7.] Walter Dreß.

[8.] [It is unclear what protest is meant here.—KC]

[9.] Above all, against the so-called muzzle decree. See Scholder, *Churches and the Third
Reich*, 1:579–80 and 2:23–24.

[10.] Cf. Scholder, *Churches and the Third Reich*, 2:33. The Reich chancellor [Hitler]
abruptly cancelled his audience with the Reich bishop on January 17, 1934.

[11.] Count Rüdiger von der Goltz, Paula Bonhoeffer's brother-in-law.

[12.] Martin Niemöller.

[13.] Reich president Paul von Hindenburg.

once again we can only wait and see, but our Dahlem friend is stouthearted and full of confidence in the future, all things considered.

You will be pleased to hear that there was a most excellent review of your *Creation and Fall*[14] in the Kreuz newspaper last week. Susi[15] told me about it, and I am going to try and get a copy. Walter has borrowed your book from Rost, whose comments about you, by the way, were not really made in ill will, but in my opinion just stupidly, or innocently, as they say.[16]

Opitz is at the camp in Zossen[17] with Max Delbrück; they are sharing a room there. He talked to him unsuspectingly about you and apparently had high praise for your talents and abilities, but thought it a bad thing that people like you don't stay here.

Do write to Winterhager when you get a chance; he's so conscientious.—I'll write again soon. The Dohnanyis have just come, Papa is at a meeting, and I must get this into the post.

So goodbye for now, my dear. I'll write again soon. Please give my regards to Mr. Hildebrandt and thank him for his letter.[18] I'll write to him soon as well but would like to find time to visit his parents first.

Any news about your passport?

Love,
Mother

59. From Hans Schönfeld[1]

January 17, 1934

Dear Dr. Bonhoeffer,

At the last meeting of the Research Commission of the Ecumenical Council[2] on January 10 and 11, it was proposed that you be invited to take part in the next

---

[14.] This was the review of Bonhoeffer's *Creation and Fall* (*DBWE* 3) by a Dr. Uhl from the University of Budapest (*Kreuzzeitung* 86, no. 11 [January 13, 1934]: 14.)

[15.] Susanne Dreß.

[16.] [The background for this comment is unclear.—KC]

[17.] This was an SA [cf. 1/20.1, ed. note 4—KC] "defense fitness" course for lecturers. [Depending on the political sympathies of the rectors, these courses were compulsory at some universities; a February 7, 1934, decree made SA service compulsory for all university students.—KC]

[18.] Not extant.

[1.] WCC Archives, World Alliance, Letters to Dietrich Bonhoeffer; carbon copy; from Geneva; ref. number: FA 27 34.

[2.] The Research Department of the Ecumenical Council for Practical Christianity (Life and Work) had existed since 1930 and was based in Geneva; Hans Schönfeld, a

ecumenical study conference on "Church, State, and the Peoples of the World," which will be held from April 8 to 14 somewhere near Paris, or near Mulhouse in Alsace.[3] As agreed with Mr. Henriod, you would participate as an adviser representing the World Alliance, as will Canon Hodgson, representing the Lausanne movement, and Dr. Oldham, representing the International Missionary Council. I am having sent to you for your information two brief memoranda with perspectives and points for preparation for the study conferences. I hope to be able to see you in London some time between January 23 and 26, so that we can discuss this in more detail. From the provisional schedule you will get some idea of how 81 we are planning to proceed. Besides knowledgeable representatives from the various movements, some theological advisers such as Professors Brunner, Althaus, and Berdyaev will also take part. Later on I will be able to give you more exact information.

With best regards,
Yours sincerely,
(signed) Dr. H. Schönfeld
Director, Research Department

60. To George Bell[1]

Jan. 17th, 34

My Lord Bishop,

it is my strong desire to thank you most heartily for your letter which I have just read in the Times.[2] I am sure, it will be of very great importance for the decisive meeting of today.[3] We German pastors in London have sent a telegram[4] to Hindenburg, Hitler, Neurath, Frick, Müller, saying that only

---

German ecumenist with degrees in theology and political economics, was full-time director. It was particularly concerned with the exchange of basic information on social ethics and with organizing conferences.

[3.] On the study conference in Paris, see 1/114.

[1.] LPL, Bell Papers 42, 11; handwritten with corrections, on Berlin letterhead; from London; in original English, including errors. Cf. also *NL*, A 42,1 (7); copy. Previously published in *GS* 2:142–43.

[2.] Letter to the editor of the *Times*, January 17, 1934. Cf. *DB-ER*, 363. The precipitating events included the Reich bishop's "muzzle decree," the reintroduction of the Aryan paragraph, the pulpit proclamation by Emergency League pastors, bannings of assemblies, and Cultural Affairs Minister Rust's decree that no university professor was permitted to criticize the church government.

[3.] The reception of church leaders by Hitler was first scheduled for January 17, 1934, "today," but it actually took place on January 25.

[4.] Letter from the London pastors to the Reich president (1/56).

the removal of Müller could pacify the highly excited German congregations here in England.

You have certainly seen the new order of Rust[5] forbidding all professors of theology to take part in the opposition against Müller and to be members of the Pastor's Emergency League. If this order is the beginning of a state action against the opposition, then, I think, your letter should be enforced by a most drastic disapproval of Müller's policy and approval and support for the opposition, directed to President von Hindenburg as a "membrum praecipuum" of the protestant church.[6] Any delay of time would then probably be of great danger. A definite disqualification of Müller by the ecumenical movement would perhaps be the last hope—humanly spoken—for a recovery of the german church. It may be, of course, that Rust's order is one of the many attempts from the side of the Prussian government to anticipate the decision of the Reich and to overrule the Reich government.

The first prints of your book in German have just arrived.[7]

I thank you once more for your help. Yours very respectfully,

Dietrich Bonhoeffer

61. From George Bell[1]

18th January, 1934

My dear Bonhoeffer,

Ever so many thanks for your kind letter.[2] I have to-day written a letter to the Reichsbischof,[3] a copy of which I enclose. It has gone by air mail—two copies, one to Jebenstrasse 3, the other to Marchstrasse 2, under direction to Wahl.

I am considering the question whether it would be a wise and legitimate action on my part to send a copy of this letter to President Hindenburg.[4] If so, I wonder whether it would be embarrassing you if I asked you to translate the letter into

---

[5.] See 1/58, ed. note 9.

[6.] Here Bonhoeffer is alluding to the Reformation model of the *cura religionis* as applied to the German princes: Hindenburg was to be addressed concerning his responsibility in the Church Struggle, not on the basis of the worldly office he held, but rather as a "preeminent" member of his church.

[7.] Cf. 1/3, ed. note 9.

[1.] LPL, Bell Papers 42, 12; carbon copy; from Chichester; in original English, including errors. Cf. *NL*, A 42,2 (3). Previously published in *GS* 2:143–44.

[2.] Of the day before, see 1/60.

[3.] Reprinted in Boyens, *Kirchenkampf und Ökumene*, 1:315–16. Bell also wrote a letter dated January 17, 1934, to the *Times*.

[4.] Cf. 1/60, ed. note 6; also 1/62.

German—both the covering letter to the President and the letter to Bishop Müller. I particularly do not want you to do anything injudicious. I shall probably in any case send copies of my letter to Bishop Müller in English to Deissmann and Dibelius, but one is anxious not to embarrass one's friends, and even that may be unwise. Will you, if you think there is anything in it, translate both the covering letter and the letter to Bishop Müller into German, and let me have the copies by return of post? But use your own judgement, and if you would rather have nothing to do with it, I shall understand.[5]

Yours ever,
[George Cicestr]

62. To George Bell[1]

London

My Lord Bishop!

Thank you very much for your wonderful letter to Reichsbischof Müller.[2] One feels that it comes out of such a warm and strong desire to stand for the Christian cause and to "open the mouth for the dumb in the cause of all such as are appointed to destruction" (Proverbs 31,8),[3] that it must undoubtedly be convincing for everybody.

I am sending you the translations of the letters and I am absolutely convinced that it would be of immense value, if Hindenburg would learn to know this point of view. It has always been the great difficulty to have a free discussion with him about that matter, because there were many people who wanted to prevent it. So it is all the more important, that he gets your letter.

Once more many thanks.

I am always Yours very respectfully
Dietrich Bonhoeffer[4]

[5.] After Bonhoeffer's reservations about writing for *The Round Table* (cf. 1/53), Bell hesitated to involve him in this action.

[1.] LPL, Bell Papers 42, 13; handwritten; undated, presumably of January 19, 1934; in original English, including errors. Cf. also *NL*, A 42,1 (8); copy. Previously published in *GS* 2:144.

[2.] Cf. 1/61, ed. note 3.

[3.] Prov. 31:8 became a leitmotif of Bonhoeffer's attitude toward the Nazis. [The King James Version of this text, which Bonhoeffer is effectively quoting here, perhaps from memory, has "thy mouth," not "the mouth."—KC] Cf. *DBWE* 4:237; also 1/147.

[4.] Handwritten on a separate slip of paper: "To His Excellency Reich President von Hindenburg, Berlin, Wilhelmstraße."

63. The Office of the Reich President to Friedrich Wehrhan[1]

Berlin W 8, January 19, 1934

Dear Pastor Wehrhan:

84   The Reich president has asked me to acknowledge with thanks his receipt of your letter[2] regarding the situation in the German Evangelical Church, with the comment that the Reich president follows the events in the Evangelical Church with the closest attention.

With German greetings[3]

(signed) Meissner

64. To Théodore de Félice[1]

Dear Mr. de Félice,

This date is agreeable to me. In fact I plan to be in Paris[2] a little before that and will pay for my own lodgings.

My best regards, and all good wishes for your work at this disastrous moment![3]

Yours,

Dietrich Bonhoeffer

[1.] ADBC, GV 13, 30; typewritten copy; letterhead: "Office of the Reich President—The Secretary of State." Addressed to Pastor Wehrhan. Cf. also *NL,* A 41,2 (6); copy. Previously published in *GS* 6:308–9.

[2.] Cf. 1/56.

[3.] [Like "Heil Hitler," this became a common closing to letters in Nazi Germany.—KC]

[1.] WCC Archive, World Alliance, Letters from Dietrich Bonhoeffer, 17; handwritten; undated, after January 25,1934; from London. Cf. *NL,* A 40,1 (2). Previously published in *GS* 6:349.

[2.] Cf. 1/30 and 1/32.

[3.] This letter was presumably written after the chancellor's reception [of the church representatives] on January 25, 1934. The "disastrous moment" would be a reference to this reception (and its consequences). On January 25, Hitler had finally received the leaders of the regional churches as well as Martin Niemöller, spokesman of the Pastors' Emergency League. Immediately beforehand, Göring had tapped a telephone conversation between Niemöller and Künneth, which was then read to the assembled church leaders. [Niemöller had made a number of unguarded remarks about possible strategies for the church opposition to Ludwig Müller, and the church leaders in the meeting (Bishops Meiser, Wurm, and Marahrens) were immediately placed on the defensive. Among other things, this incident revealed to the church opposition the extent to which they were under state police observation.—KC] The chancellor's reception thus ended very differently than the church opposition had anticipated—by reinforcing the position of Ludwig Müller rather than weakening

65. Theodor Heckel to the German Congregations and Pastors Abroad[1]

Berlin-Charlottenburg, January 31, 1934

"On Thursday, January 25, 1934, Reich Chancellor Adolf Hitler received Reich Bishop Ludwig Müller and the bishops of the regional Evangelical churches in order to speak with them.

"The Reich bishop invited all the leaders of the German Evangelical Church for a conversation on Saturday, January 27. As the result of the long discussion that took place in full unanimity,[2] the leaders of all the German Evangelical regional churches made the following declaration:

"Under the influence of that great hour when *the heads of the German Evangelical Church met the Reich chancellor,* they reaffirmed unanimously their *unconditional loyalty to the Third Reich and its Führer.* They condemn most strongly any intrigue involving criticism of state, Volk, or movement,[3] because such criticism is calculated to imperil the Third Reich. In particular they condemn the use of the foreign press to present the false view that the controversy within the church is a struggle against the state. *The assembled heads of the church take up a united stand behind the Reich bishop* and declare themselves willing to enforce his policies and decrees in the sense desired by him, *to hinder church-political opposition to them,* and to consolidate the authority of the Reich bishop by all available constitutional means."

Although I assume that these proclamations have already been made known to you, I would nevertheless like to point out to you once again the significance of these facts. In particular I must urgently impress upon the clergy abroad the necessity for the greatest possible discretion in regard to church politics.[4] Just as the soldier at the front is not in a position to assess the overall plan but must carry out the duties that immediately concern him, so I expect the clergy abroad to dis-

85

---

it or even causing his dismissal. [Indeed, the outcome was a meeting two days later (see 1/65) between Müller and the three bishops (without Niemöller), at which the bishops signed a statement of loyalty to the Reich bishop and pledged "unconditional fidelity to the Third Reich and its Führer" (Scholder, *Churches and the Third Reich,* 2:44). It was a decisive event in sharpening the divisions within the church opposition.—KC] Cf. Scholder, *Churches and the Third Reich,* 2:39–48.

[1.] ADBC, GV 4, 2; carbon copy; letterhead "German Evangelical Church K.K. III 334/34." See also *NL,* A 41,2 (7). Previously published in *GS* 6:309–10. This letter was sent to all congregations and clergy abroad.

[2.] Müller and Oberheid had in fact taken bishops Meiser and Wurm by surprise; the bishops tried cautiously, from Berlin, to distance themselves from this declaration of loyalty.

[3.] [This refers to the Nazi movement. Regarding *Volk,* see the editor's introduction, pp. 4–5.—KC]

[4.] Heckel is referring here primarily to the protests, telegrams, and petitions from London.

tinguish between their own particular task and the task of the church authorities in shaping the German Evangelical Church at home. I assure you that the independence of German Protestant work abroad is very carefully observed here. Yet, of course, when it comes to the structure of the entire German Evangelical Church in its homeland, the rules to be followed certainly cannot be determined only from abroad. Establishing and reinforcing the authority of the German Evangelical Church must be a major concern at the present time for all persons who are involved. The more rapidly and decisively this takes place, the more it will benefit the German Protestant communities abroad.

for the Foreign Affairs Office
(signed) Dr. Heckel

86   **66. From Franz Hildebrandt**[1] **(in "Luther-Deutsch")**[2]

My deare Dove:[3]

If thou shouldst moan / Like a true dove / So must we truly dare to growle / More than the beares in the wilde / And stande at the ready, the ready, the ready / I saye / for salvation cometh / For it is still far beyonde us[4] / But such is thy gain /

[1.] *NL*, Anh. D 1,8 (3); handwritten birthday letter for February 4, 1934; written from Berlin after January 28, 1934. There is in Hildebrandt's commonplace book for 1934 a draft of this letter with numerous small differences. The transcription in *NL* A 41,9 (8) is based on this draft, which forms the basis for the version published in *GS* 6:291–93.

[2.] ["Luther-Deutsch" is the German of the sixteenth century particularly associated with the literary style of the reformer Martin Luther, whose translation of the Bible into the vernacular greatly influenced the development of the German language. Hildebrandt, Bonhoeffer's friend from Berlin who stayed with him for some time in London (see 1/21, 1/22, 1/26; also Zimmermann, *I Knew Dietrich Bonhoeffer*, 38–40, and *DB-ER*, 328), here humorously parodies the Luther style as a birthday gift to Bonhoeffer. With the humor, however, a serious point is also being made. The rightful ownership of Luther's legacy was a contentious issue in the Church Struggle, with the German Christians claiming that their program of creating a purely "Germanic" church was simply "completing the work of Martin Luther." Here Hildebrandt is in effect saying, "*This* is what Luther would say to you today," and therewith also satirizing much that was happening in the Church Struggle. (Hildebrandt had employed for similar purpose a passage in Luther-Deutsch in an earlier letter to Bonhoeffer; see *DBW* 10, 1/138). The text also speaks eloquently of how someone close to Bonhoeffer recognized his friend's sense of isolation and his need of encouragement as the struggle intensified. To retain in English the flavor of parody, the translation here has been done in a style redolent of the early sixteenth century, both in vocabulary and spelling. The translation was done by Douglas Stott and Victoria Barnett, with the assistance of Mark McCulloh and Julie Woestehoff.—KC]

[3.] [Evidently a reference to Bonhoeffer's pacifism.—KC]

[4.] This is a play on Isa. 59:11, a text "that we had a lot of fun with" (Hildebrandt): "We all growl like bears; like doves we moan mournfully. We wait for justice, but there is none; for salvation, but it is far from us."

when thou hatest the works of the Nicolaitans / Which I too hate[5] / Especiallay since they do meaneth / They would do it / Since at the last our deedes are such follye[6] / And now raise the magna passio domini / To his personne / Col. I. v. XXIV[7] / And little Hans and little Heintz / and every Thom, Dick, and Harry / Max and Moritz[8] / Threaten poor Nicolao[9] / who yet is nary / Afraid[10] / and also knoweth full well / That speakinge and silence / have their season[11] / Which in sooth thy epistle[12] quite mightily proveth / Although it seemeth to me / As somewhat dry / And more of a preacher than Solomon[13] / And yet I would not press on any man / That he heareth Luther's sermoning / Verily, nor that he receive it as the truthe / That would a great abomination be.

And there would be much to tell / Of Gog and Magog[14] / And theire ways (markest thou well / That Gog's ways [arts][15] are not everyman's ways) / But let them sport themselves as they may / The madde hunters [jäger][16] / In wood and over the heath/heathen[17] / Yet it must be fulfilled / That which stands writ Matt. XXIII / Ye shall not let yourselves be named rabbi.[18]

[5.] This is a play on Rev. 2:6: "you hate the works of the Nicolaitans, which I also hate."

[6.] This is a reference to Luther's hymn "Out of the depths I cry to you" (*Aus tiefer Not*): "The holiest deeds can naught avail / Of all before thee living" (*Lutheran Book of Worship*, 295). [Perhaps also an allusion to Ecclesiastes; see ed. note 11.—KC]

[7.] Col. 1:24: "I am now rejoicing in my sufferings for your sake, and in my flesh I am completing what is lacking in Christ's afflictions for the sake of his body, that is, the church."

[8.] *Max und Moritz* is a popular German children's book about two mischievous boys who torment their elders. [In this context is seems likely that "Max and Moritz" and "Hans and Heintz" refer to figures in the Church Struggle.—KC]

[9.] The reference to "Nicolao" (Niemöller) picks up on the earlier reference to the Nicolaitans. Niemöller had been placed on a leave of absence on January 27, 1934.

[10.] The draft reads: "is merry and of good cheer."

[11.] Eccles. 3:1 and 7: "For everything there is a season . . . a time to keep silence, and a time to speak."

[12.] Letter not extant.

[13.] [A reference to the preacher Solomon (Ecclesiastes), not King Solomon.—KC]

[14.] According to Rev. 20:8, the peoples of the earth led by Satan into battle at the end of time.

[15.] The German here (*gog arten*) is a play on the name of Friedrich Gogarten, one of the founders of dialectical theology and a supporter of the German Christians in 1933.

[16.] This pun on the German word *Jäger* (hunter) refers to August Jäger [whom the Nazi regime appointed to oversee the Prussian churches; cf. 1/89—KC].

[17.] The German here (*ober der heyden*) refers to Heinrich Oberheid, a prominent German Christian bishop. [It also seems to be a play on the German *Heide/Heiden* from which the English words *heath/heathen* are derived. The pun here, of course, would be about the Church Struggle, in which the Confessing Christians and German Christians viewed each other as heathen.—KC]

[18.] "Reibi" (here Hildebrandt uses *reybi*) was the common nickname for Reich Bishop Ludwig Müller; cf. Matt. 23:8: "But you are not to be called rabbi."

87   Milk have I given thee / And no solid foode[19] / That I will surely say to thee / For thou canst not digest it / And thou needeth full sore / Someone to teach thee / That Max [is] not Moritz / And each day does not an evening bring / May they sleepe and doze / In Laodicea[20] / The lazy glutinous swine / With their mys and their wormes[21] / We will certainly not place [our] light / Under the bushel[22] / That is not hard for a body to prove.

Shall, then, I prove it to you / My deare Dove / That would well soothe thee / Thou surely wished once to fare to India[23] / So that thou couldest burn thy wives / (whose number is legion / That almost no one can speake it) / And thou wouldst outstretch thy belly in the sun / Puff on a pipe / Let the mice be shooed [scheuchen] away[24] / By the shieks [scheichen] / O childe / What knowest thou / Of all that.

So that thou cannot change / That thou wert born here / And as a naked childe / And true Adam / Of two years / Once sat in the tub and gazed / At thy deare mother / Who lately showed me this deare picture[25] / As if to say / Childe / I do not know it either.[26]

So often I say it to thee / Like the same one / Who made this / And was here with us / And fought[27] / So that the feathers flew[28] / Here / Here / Here / Is thy proper place[29] / And thou shouldst bring all your puppets along / George[30] and

---

[19.] Cf. 1 Cor. 3:2.

[20.] The church in Laodicea, recipient of the message of Rev. 3:14ff.

[21.] The German text here (*meysen und wurmern*) is a wordplay on the names of Bavarian bishop Meiser and Württemberg bishop Wurm.

[22.] The German for "bushel" (*Scheffel*) is a wordplay on the name of Johann Simon Schöffel, a Lutheran member of the Provisional Church Administration. Cf. Matt. 5:15.

[23.] A reference to Bonhoeffer's plans to visit India; see 1/54 and 1/93. [Note again the allusion in "My deare Dove" to Bonhoeffer's pacifism, which led to his interest in Gandhi.—KC]

[24.] [In the Sydenham vicarage Bonhoeffer "fought a losing battle against an invasion of mice" (*DB-ER*, 328).—KC]

[25.] A photograph of two-year-old Dietrich in the bathtub.

[26.] This was an expression frequently used by Bonhoeffer.

[27.] The reference is to Karl Barth at the church opposition meeting in Berlin on January 23, 1934 (cf. Scholder, *Churches and the Third Reich*, 2:36–39). [By all accounts Barth was very combative at the meeting.—KC]

[28.] The German here (*das die fetzern vlogen [dass die Fetzen flogen]*) is a wordplay on the name of Karl Fezer, the German Christian with whom Barth argued at the Berlin meeting.

[29.] [This may well be a reference to Barth's strong argument against Bonhoeffer's taking a position in England.—KC] See Barth's letter to Bonhoeffer, 1/16.

[30.] George Bell.

his pupil . . .[31] / And the Rigorosum[32] / And the man from the propeller-driven steamer[33] / Should soon be on his waye / So that one may speake [about this] with him / Berta,[34] however, / I pray thee / Beg thee as well / Leave her behind.

While I now cannot myself / With my own mouth (or however you name it / Snout / Mug / Trap) / Wish thee joy and good fortune on Sunday / That costs me too deare / So one should put the lovely music / On the player[35] / Sing and make merry / This thou shouldst know / I will think on thee / Yea, in perpetuity / And it pains me as it doth thee / That I have had to forego / The wryting[36] / Even though I would / How much more / Would I stay with [by] you.

In the middle of the years / I have not the time therefore / I hope to thinke   88
on it againe / One thing is needed sore / That we pray heartily and plentily / Our common song / Oh, my Lord Jesus / Thy nearness / Especially the first and fifth verse[37] / Which filled me with solace and comfort / When we sang it here / At Septuagesima[38] / And brother Eberhard[39] / also did a wondrous / Sermon to it / Col. III v. 16–17.[40]

Greetest thou our friends / And staye the olde thou for my sake / In the cominge yeare as well.

Thy little calff

[31.] Uncertain reading.

[32.] The rigorosum is the doctoral examination; Julius Rieger was facing it at the time.

[33.] This reference is unclear.

[34.] A reference to Berta Schulze. [Schulze had studied together with Bonhoeffer and became his secretary and housekeeper in London until (in Hildebrandt's words) "her 'intentions' toward Dietrich led to her dismissal." Roggelin, *Franz Hildebrandt*, 64.—KC].

[35.] Hildebrandt sent Bonhoeffer a recording of Schubert's *Trout Quintet* for his birthday.

[36.] This refers to the work that was being planned on Hildebrandt's book "Christianity and Humanity," which he had to interrupt after his return from London.

[37.] From the hymn by Christian Gregor, verse 5: "Thou reachest down to us Thy wounded hand / And at Thy cross, dear Lord, ashamed we stand / Remembering all Thy truth through weal and woe / Until our eyes with tears must overflow / Of thanks and praise" (Christian Classics Ethereal Library at Calvin College;

http://www.ccel.org/w/winkworth/life/htm/h091.htm).

[38.] Sunday, January 28, 1934.

[39.] Eberhard Röhricht.

[40.] Col. 3:16–17: "Let the word of Christ dwell in you richly . . ."

67. From Sabine Leibholz[1]

Göttingen, February 1, 1934

Dear Dietrich,

I don't know where you will be on your birthday this year. So I am writing to London, even though you may actually be in Paris.[2] Mama was going to send me your address there ahead of time, but I still have not heard from her and must post this letter if you are to have it for your birthday. Anyway, this year we all know what we wish you, and ourselves as well! For the two of us here, this matter[3] is closer to our hearts than anyone imagines.

¶It is a pity that we "don't have time" to write more often. There is so much one would like to know. Mama writes that it wouldn't make sense to telephone you either, because it is "so expensive."[4] How are you getting on personally? Are you well looked after in your house? What is it like, living there? Have you found nice people in your congregation with whom you can get together often? Does preaching in two churches keep you very busy? Or do you have time for your own work; or is it hard to find enough quiet for academic work? Do write me sometime about what you do every day. Here we are on very good terms with the theologian Bauer (professor of New Testament), who, although quite isolated, still keeps his upright stance and is a very unprejudiced, strong character. You would like him. Now for a bit about us. We are fine; after all sorts of flu and children's colds, today we have snow again. The children in the park with sleds. And now we have our brand new car! But when it's snowing like this we are still very cautious with it. Gert is very happy with it. We live very quietly; besides Gert's lectures, we are working hard on our English and Italian.[5] Gert makes up for his lack of talent for languages by speaking boldly and thus learns quickly. Sometimes in the evening a young Italian who doesn't know a word of German comes to see us, and we almost learn more from him than in the lessons. We have lots of visitors in the evenings, especially students. Usually we talk politics, but sometimes we make music. Tomorrow again eight young people are coming to supper. Sometimes they innocently bring along a good friend whom we don't know about, and we just have

89

[1.] *NL*, Anh. D 1,3 (there with incorrect date); handwritten. [Sabine Leibholz was Bonhoeffer's twin sister and had married Gerhard (Gert) Leibholz, a "non-Aryan," in 1926. Cf. 1/17. For the background of her correspondence with Bonhoeffer in this volume and her perspective on the overall Bonhoeffer family experiences, see her memoirs, *The Bonhoeffers: Portrait of a Family.*—KC]

[2.] Bonhoeffer actually was in Paris from January 31 to February 1, 1934, at a meeting of the Ecumenical Youth Commission (WCC Archives, World Alliance IV).

[3.] The church opposition.

[4.] The quotation marks are presumably used to indicate another reason for not writing, namely, postal censorship [and likewise also the tapping of telephones—KC].

[5.] This suggests that they were already considering emigration.

to quickly fit him in! I will write more another time about the children. I would like to have Marianne skip a year. School is so boring for her in a class of fifty children. But they'll certainly make this difficult for me. Always having top marks bores her so that she's getting lazy. They make her seventh in the class, but that's all we can expect these days.[6] I don't have to be a conceited mother to know that she deserves better, and those ahead of her are no match for her in the work they are doing. She is not in the least ambitious and always says "all the children are just as good in everything."

Marianne wants to write you a birthday letter on her own.

We are sending you Max von Scheler,[7] which you will certainly find interesting if you have not already read it. Hoping that things will go well for you, and wishing you a better year this year.

With all my heart,
Your Sabine

68. From Karl Bonhoeffer[1]

February 2, 1934

Dear Dietrich,

Well, we won't be able to celebrate your birthday together day after tomorrow, after all. We had really been counting on it quite confidently. So perhaps our   90
birthday wishes will arrive too late. But on Sunday you will scarcely have time to read them or to celebrate anyway. May this new year be a good one for you and for that which is closest to your heart! At the time when you decided to study theology, I sometimes thought to myself that a quiet, uneventful pastor's life, as I knew it from that of my Swabian uncle and as Mörike[2] describes it, would really almost be a pity for you. So far as uneventfulness is concerned, I was greatly mistaken. That such a crisis should still be possible in the ecclesiastical field seemed to me, with my scientific background, to be out of the question. But in this as in many other things, it appears that we older folks have had quite wrong ideas about the solidity of so-called established concepts, views, and things; however, I don't believe that everything that seemed good to us now belongs on the scrap heap. In any case, you gain one thing from your calling—and in this it resembles mine—liv-

---

[6.] This indicates discrimination because of her "non-Aryan" father.
[7.] Max Scheler, *On the Eternal in Man.*

[1.] *NL,* C 1(4–5); handwritten; from Berlin
[2.] The reference is to Pastor Meyding, an uncle (by marriage), with whom Karl Bonhoeffer had spent time as a child. Meyding's parish was in Cleversulzbach, where Eduard Mörike [nineteenth-century pastor and poet—KC] had also been pastor.

ing relationships to human beings and the possibility of meaning something to them, in more important matters than medical ones. And of this nothing can be taken away from you, even when the external institutions in which you are placed are not always as you would wish.

Here I seem to be coming to a quiet phase, in the midst of all the agitation and activity, and I hope it will bring clarity. It would be nice if you and your colleagues there could come and see us for a few days. I am glad that this semester is almost over. It was quite turbulent emotionally, and because of the new laws[3] in many respects one is compelled into all sorts of new thoughts. I must post this letter, so I will close with all good wishes, hoping you have a nice evening on your birthday.

Your Father

91

69. From Théodore de Félice[1]

Geneva, February 3, 1934

Dear Friend,

Wednesday evening, when I returned to my hosts, I found a letter addressed to me, which I opened and began reading the beginning but without understanding anything at first. Then I saw that there was written on it "pass on to Dr. B.," and I concluded that it was certainly meant for you.[2]

I intended to give it to you at the beginning of Thursday's session,[3] but I apologize for not thinking about it at all in the midst of our more intense discussions after you arrived. Not having your address in Paris, and not knowing by heart the London one, I had to wait for my return to Geneva to return it to you, with my kindest regards,

Very cordially yours,
Th. de Félice

[3.] The "Law for the Prevention of Genetically Ill Progeny" came into force on January 1, 1934, prescribing forced sterilization (eventually performed on some 350,000 to 400,000 persons), and placed a leading German psychiatrist such as Karl Bonhoeffer in an especially difficult conflict.

[1.] WCC Archives, World Alliance, Letters to Dietrich Bonhoeffer II; carbon copy; written in French.

[2.] Letter not extant.

[3.] Cf. the minutes of the meeting in Paris, January 31–February 1, 1934, in the report of the Ecumenical Youth Commission for the Working Group of the World Alliance for Promoting International Friendship through the Churches and the Universal Council on Life and Work, WCC Archives, World Alliance II.

70. From Eric Gray Hancock[1]

London S.W. 17. Febr. 4th 1934

Dear Dr. Bonhoeffer

Dr. Winterhager has asked me to send you a copy of Beverly Nichol's "Cry Havoc"[2] with his very best wishes for your birthday and desires to draw your attention specially to pp. 168 and 169 (the end of paragraph III) of this book.[3]

The book will be following in the course of a day or two as printed matter.

I should like to add my own good wishes to those of Dr. Winterhager and trust that I may have an opportunity of meeting you in the near future.

Yours sincerely
Eric Gray Hancock

92

71. From Paula Bonhoeffer[1]

February 5, 1934

Dear Dietrich,

I decided to put a few words in with my little birthday package after all! I had thought surely you would be in Paris on the fourth; you had written us that at some point. So then we all begged for your address in Paris,[2] but in vain since you were in London after all. We could just as well have sent the package last week, but I was worried about the cake. You'll be thinking that I sound like Berta![3] But that's the way it is when one is trying to do something right and sees how dim one has actually been.

At least we could wish you happy birthday by telephone and hear that, after a hard day's work,[4] you had spent the evening in good company—that was lovely.

[1.] *NL*, C 24, 1–1; handwritten; in original English, including errors. Previously published in *GS* 6:293–94.

[2.] Nichols, *Cry "Havoc."* The title stems from Shakespeare, *Julius Caesar*, 3.1.270–73: "And Caesar's spirit . . . shall . . . Cry 'Havoc!' and let slip the dogs of war."

[3.] This passage tells the story of Robert Mennel, a conscientious objector to military service, who at the beginning of his prison experience received encouragement only from the soldiers imprisoned with him, who told him to stick to his convictions.

[1.] *NL*, C 1 (4–5); handwritten; from Berlin.

[2.] Bonhoeffer was in Paris only from January 31 to February 1; cf. 1/69.

[3.] Berta Schulze, who was very attentive to Bonhoeffer during this time, cf. 1/66, ed. note 34.

[4.] On his birthday, Sunday, February 4, 1934, Bonhoeffer had to preach in the morning in Sydenham and in the evening at St. Paul's.

They all were here for the evening just for that purpose—except Susi and Walter this time, unfortunately; he is usually much more uncomplicated and sensible about these things.[5] The development of the church question has been all-consuming for him, and he does his duty conscientiously. He was planning to visit you in March; do let us know whether you would rather he did or not.—He is probably not very sure whether he can afford it financially. He could stay with you, for meals as well, couldn't he? We still have in mind to visit in April—perhaps two weeks on "Whigt," and then, after your return from Paris, on to you in London.[6] But who can tell how it will all turn out. The Dohnanyis haven't made up their minds yet either.

Are you planning on lecturing here in the summer semester? But for the time being I am still thinking we shall see each other here even before that. I am going to see Gerhard[7] again later today and discuss with him whether he thinks it would be good for you to come calling here, together with George.[8] Franz[9] was very much in favor of that. I was thinking it might be better if he came later, or perhaps before; I'll write you what Gerhard says. It is really a pity that the lads in Swabia have dissolved their league.[10] A circular letter to all the relatives is about to be sent by Uncle Ludwig,[11] as the eldest in the family, and everyone will be required to join in. I believe he will think twice about taking this step; otherwise he might find himself confronted with the "Loving Relatives" comedy.[12]

I must get this package in the post. I had the pillow stuffed very firmly, to use for your back on the couch. The weaving is from Warmbrunn,[13] sent for my

---

[5.] Susanne, née Bonhoeffer, and Walter Dreß. Bonhoeffer's mother is conveying the news that Dreß had distanced himself from the German Christians.

[6.] The Isle of Wight in the English Channel, a popular holiday resort because of its climate. Bonhoeffer planned to attend the Ecumenical Study Conference in Paris until April 14; cf. 1/64.

[7.] Gerhard Jacobi.

[8.] George Bell; apparently there were still plans for an ecumenical delegation on the church dispute; cf. *DB-ER*, 363.

[9.] Franz Hildebrandt.

[10.] On February 2, 1934, the Council of Brethren in Württemberg had decided that the Pastors' Emergency League in Württemberg should dissolve itself. See Scholder, *Churches and the Third Reich*, 2:45.

[11.] Presumably Ludwig Müller.

[12.] A comedy by Julius Benedix. Schummrich, the protagonist, finds himself the odd man out while the other characters pair off and marry. At the end of the play, "Schummrich (looking at each couple in turn) [says]: 'Well, what's left for me?' The curtain falls."

[13.] The wife of Paula Bonhoeffer's youngest brother (von Hase) had a weaving shop in Bad Warmbrunn.

birthday. The picture is one I am glad for you to have.—The brass bowl is to remind you of your evenings as a student! The cake speaks for itself.—I hope that in the meantime a big envelope sent by air and express mail, with letters and photos of the rooms downstairs, has reached you.

God bless you,
Your Mother

Yesterday Hildebrandt preached in Christ Church in place of Niemöller, who has been suspended—he did very well.

72. Minutes of a Meeting of the Congregational Council of St. Paul's Church[1]

94

Quarterly Meeting
on Monday, February 5, 1934, 7:30 P.M.
in the sacristy, St. Paul's Church

Present: Messrs. Neubert, Klotz, L. Goetz, C. Blumenstock, G. Henne, E. Henne, Streitberger, Dickens, Klugmann, Eisemann, Weber

The pastor opened the meeting with prayer. The minutes of the previous meeting[2] were read, approved as correct, and signed. The treasurer presented the accounts, which were examined and approved as correct. Mr. Henne shared some news from correspondence he had received and read a letter of thanks from the family of Mr. Brenner, recently deceased. The question of increasing the number of Congregational Council members was discussed, and Mr. Henne was requested to undertake some preliminary discussions. The meeting was closed with prayer.

Dr. Dietrich Bonhoeffer, Pastor[3]

[1.] ADBC, Minute Book of St. Paul's Church, 122; handwritten.

[2.] Of November 6, 1933; see 1/7.

[3.] This is followed by the signatures of thirteen vestry members (differing from the above list of those present).

73. Preparations for the Conference with Theodor Heckel

73.1 Friedrich Wehrhan to Baron Bruno Schröder[1]

London S.W.13, February 5, 1934

My dear Baron,

With your permission, I am enclosing the memorandum drawn up today by the London pastors[2] in full unanimity on our position regarding the Church Struggle.

I also send enclosed, for your attention, a letter from Dr. Heckel[3] that was addressed to all pastors. Dr. Heckel's visit to you[4] and, as we have heard, to the embassy as well, has given us the alarming impression that those in Berlin are trying to impose themselves between us and our congregations. However, we have the encouraging impression that in this matter we and our congregations are in full agreement.

It is certainly important to us to consolidate and strengthen the authority of the German Evangelical Church; thus we wish for a church government that can be respected by all groups within the church, especially the most loyal and faithful churchgoers.

Most sincerely and respectfully yours,
Fr. Wehrhan, Pastor

73.2 Memorandum from the Pastors in London[5]

1. It has not been made at all clear whether the new constitution of the Evangelical Church enacted on June 11, 1933,[6] entitles the German Evangelical Church Federation to transfer its authority—freely recognized in an agreement with the German Evangelical congregations in Great Britain—to another, newly created body, without seeking the assent of the other free party to the agreement. There is reason to doubt whether this new constitution has not created a situation requiring a new agreement. Until this question has been clarified, the German Evangelical congregations in Great Britain do not consider that decrees enacted by the Reich bishop and/or the Reich Church government are binding upon the churches abroad.

[1.] ADBC, GV 13, 37; typewritten. Cf. also *NL*, A 41,1 (26); carbon copy.

[2.] See 1/73.2.

[3.] Of January 31, 1934; cf. 1/65.

[4.] Heckel's visit immediately before the conference.

[5.] ADBC, GV 13, 38; carbon copy; handwritten heading "Memo 5/2/34." See also *NL*, A 41,5 (2–4). Previously published in *GS* 6:310–12.

[6.] Constitution of the German Evangelical Church, reprinted in Beckmann, *Kirchliches Jahrbuch 1933–1944*, 27ff.

2. The Reich bishop and the governments of the majority of the German Evangelical churches have only been able to take up and exercise their powers through the use of force. This constitutes such a severe threat to the substance of the Evangelical Church that fruitful work on its part can only be possible, it seems to us, when all measures and appointments undertaken by the use of force are unconditionally rescinded. Since last month the Reich bishop even called for assistance from the police,[7] it is clear that he is not willing to renounce the seeking of such help to strengthen his position.

3. The German Evangelical congregations in Great Britain are seized by a deep mistrust in light of the fact that the German Evangelical Church is now headed by a man who until recently, as the patron of the "Faith Movement of German Christians," obviously felt himself at one with the theology, the will, and the actions of this movement.

96

By decree of the Reich bishop, in an unchristian application of certainly legitimate governmental principles, the Aryan paragraph was introduced into some regional Protestant churches, was suspended, and then reimposed.[8] This paragraph contradicts the clear meaning of the scriptures and is only one symptom of the danger to the pure gospel and the confession that is posed by the "German Christians."

4. In regard to the Reich bishop's incorporation of the Evangelical Youth into the Hitler Youth,[9] there is considerable doubt as to his right to do so. Furthermore, we see a serious danger that young people will become estranged from the church, causing the church to lose its next generation of members, and that the youth will be deprived of the chance to belong to a Christian community of their peers.

5. The Reich bishop's language, as reported even in the daily press, which is otherwise allowed to say so little, includes such expressions as "Pfaffen" and "shriveled-up fellow citizens."[10] For pastors who are already subjected to enough hostility in their daily work, such insults out of the mouth of their highest minister really do not allow any confidence to grow.

[7.] On January 7, 1934, Müller and Jäger had demanded that Gestapo chief Diels take police action against pastors belonging to the Emergency League. See Scholder, *Churches and the Third Reich*, 2:29; and J. Schmidt, *Martin Niemöller im Kirchenkampf*, 164–65.

[8.] In his January 4, 1934, "muzzle decree," Müller had rescinded his previous suspension of the Aryan paragraph for church officials and pastors (cf. Scholder, *Churches and the Third Reich*, 2:20).

[9.] In December 1933. See Scholder, *Churches and the Third Reich*, 1:575–78.

[10.] See Joachim Gauger, *Chronik der Kirchenwirren*, 1:134. There are similar observations repeated in Scholder, *Churches and the Third Reich*, 2:29. [The German here, *Pfaffen*, combines the German words here for "pastor" (*Pfarrer*) and "monkey" (*Affe*); the derogatory term *Pfaffen* was used during the Third Reich by Hitler and other Nazi leaders to refer to the clergy.—KC]

6. All the pastors here support Baron von Schröder's proposal that the Reich bishop should give a written personal guarantee not only that the conditions we have laid down as a basis for our remaining within the German Reich Church will retain their validity in the future but also that all measures he has taken by force will be rescinded retroactively.

London, February 5, 1934.

The four pastors of the London congregations[11]

97   **74. Conference with Representatives of the Reich Church Government**

74.1 Minutes Recorded by Benjamin Locher[1]

Minutes of conference of the German Evangelical Pastors in Great Britain with the representatives of the German Evangelical Church: Senior Consistory Councilor Heckel, Pastor Krummacher, and Dr. Wahl.

1. Session on February 8, 1934

Present: Dr. Heckel, Pastor Krummacher, Dr. Wahl, Pastors Wehrhan, Schönberger, Rieger, Bonhoeffer, Schreiner, Steiniger, Böckheler

Pastor Wehrhan opens the session with words of welcome and explains that those present are meeting not as theologians but as representatives and leaders of their congregations.

Pastor Schönberger wants to know, as a point of order, why Dr. Heckel as the church's representative has visited the chairman of the Association of Congregations, Baron v. Schröder, without first making contact with the pastors.[2]

Dr. Heckel replies that he has been charged by the Reich bishop to inform the baron about the situation in the church, since the Reich bishop has received a telegram from the baron.[3]

Pastor Wehrhan asks Dr. Heckel to explain, with reference to his last intervention, what is meant by "general plan."[4]

Dr. Heckel begins by asking two questions. (1) Should the representative of the German Evangelical Pastors' Conference in England who would be attending the

---

[11.] Friedrich Wehrhan, Julius Rieger, Gustav Schönberger, and Bonhoeffer.

[1.] *NL*, A 41,5 (1); carbon copy. Previously published in *GS* 6:312–19. Benjamin Locher, who took these minutes, was attending the conference as Schönberger's vicar. Regarding Heckel's visit, see *DB-ER*, 346–54.

[2.] See 1/73.1.

[3.] See 1/52.

[4.] Of January 31, 1934; see 1/65.

consecration of the Reich bishop make a formal statement? What was his authority to do so? (the limits thereof)[5]

Pastor Wehrhan replies that there was no intention, on such an official occasion, to speak about the reservations of the congregations.

Dr. Heckel then asks question (2), why copies of the letter of January 15, 1934,[6] to the Reich president had been sent to this particular selection of recipients.

Pastor Wehrhan replies that there had been no answers to various urgent inquiries by telegram, and that he had wanted to make sure of finally reaching those   98 who made the decisions.

Pastor Rieger: The appeal to the Reich president was meant to avoid the involvement of political authorities.

Dr. Heckel then sets forth the "overall plan" of the German Church; cf. Decree KK III 334/34 of January 31, 1934.[7]

(1) German Protestantism to be brought together in one organization by a process parallel to that of the centralization being pursued by the German state.

(2) The administrative centralization of youth work, home missions, Protestant social organizations, etc.

(3) Theological study of contemporary problems, especially the relationship of law and gospel.

This overall plan agreed to by all church leaders. "I leave open the question of whether agreement in such cases is wholly spontaneous or whether it takes place under the impression of quite specific things."

Independence of the congregations abroad. It is not possible to have partisan church-policy groups abroad. The Diaspora Law regarding churches abroad[8] remains in force.

Authority of the German Evangelical Church. The chancellor is of the opinion that Protestant unity has come too late; he predicts the collapse of this Protestantism in five months if the top-level crisis develops into a chronic dispute. This calls for support for unity and establishment of outwardly orderly conditions.

[5.] The parenthetical note reads *Limitierung,* but the word may be *Legitimierung,* or "justification." Regarding the plans for Wehrhan to participate, see 1/20.

[6.] See 1/56.

[7.] See 1/65.

[8.] After the establishment of the German Evangelical Church Federation, the June 17, 1924, "Church Federation law regarding the ties of German Evangelical church organizations, congregations and clergy outside Germany to the Church Federation" (Merzyn, *Das Recht der EKD,* 122–30) had governed relationships between the German Evangelical Church and the congregations abroad. Although Heckel considered this law to be the basis for his office's jurisdiction over the churches, the congregations abroad, especially the Association of Congregations in England, were concerned to preserve their fundamental autonomy (see also 1/52, 1/65, and 1/77).

Overall background. "I have been empowered to inform you that there is no cause for further concern in the matter of the Aryan paragraph."

Detailed *report* on the *consequences of the Sports Palace demonstration.*[9] Hossenfelder's dismissal.[10] Failure of the attempt at a complete turnaround (Clerical Ministry) to consist of Niemöller,[11] Lauerer, Koch). Offer made to Künneth without success. Provisional Cabinet, Civil Service Law[12] rejected by both sides as being reactionary and/or not without legal flaws. Ultimatums from the opposition rejected by Müller, but he is prepared to negotiate. Fixed list of nominations for church leadership presented by the opposition.[13]

The agreement on the *youth work* sanctioned by the church leaders. Hitler had described the amalgamation of the Evangelical Youth with the Hitler Youth as his best Christmas present.[14]

Hitler's position. Müller the man most highly esteemed by the National Socialist Party. Chancellery reception.[15] (Niemöller's telephone conversation: "Hitler is just now visiting the old gentleman. Extreme unction. Buttered up. When he comes into the outer office, he'll be handed a memorandum, and the old gentleman will say, 'Here are your marching orders.' We have it all splendidly worked out.") Then Göring's intervention in the meeting. Hitler: "This is completely unheard of. Rebellion. I will not allow my leader's circle to be broken. I will attack this rebellion with every means at my disposal." Niemöller: "But we are all enthusiastic about the Third Reich." Hitler: "I'm the one who built the Third Reich. You just attend to your sermons!"—Hitler asks about objections to the Reich bishop. The church leaders are silent. Hitler: "It pains me deeply that the Protestant church isn't moving ahead faster. I am much closer to it than to the Catholic Church." This was followed by the swearing of a loyalty oath to the Führer. Niemöller managed to speak with Göring. Result: the opposition lost this round.

[9.] [Cf. 1/12, ed. note 2.—KC]

[10.] On December 20, 1933, Hossenfelder had to give up all his church offices as well as the Reich leadership of the German Christian movement (cf. Scholder, *Churches and the Third Reich,* 1:570–71). [This was part of the backlash against the German Christians following the Sports Palace rally.—KC]

[11.] On this so-called attempt to bring Niemöller into a new clerical ministry, cf. 1/37 and 1/82. [See also 1/8, ed. note 8.—KC]

[12.] The restoration of the November 16, 1933, civil service law for church officials, including the "Aryan paragraph."

[13.] On these efforts to appoint a new church leadership, see J. Schmidt, *Martin Niemöller im Kirchenkampf,* 154–55.

[14.] On the handover of the Evangelical Youth work to the "Hitler Youth," which was entirely the work of Müller, see Scholder, *Churches and the Third Reich,* 1:575–78.

[15.] On Hitler's reception for the Protestant church leaders on January 25, 1934, see Scholder, *Churches and the Third Reich,* 2:40–42. See also 1/60; 1/64, ed. note 3; and 1/65.

Incriminating evidence against pastors in the opposition.[16] Foreign influence
(an English and a Swedish bishop).[17] "Niemöller was satisfied with the way things
had gone"[18] (trip to Barmen).

The situation at present is that to oppose Müller is tantamount to opposing　　100
the state. Müller's audience with Hitler and Hindenburg.[19] In July the Young
Reformation movement had been sacrificed; now it is the Emergency League. This
is the consequence of wrong thinking on the part of southern German Lutheranism. Schöffel too a victim of the southern German bishops.[20] This concludes the
second stage.

Today this must be recognized realistically, and the best theological minds must
get together and apply themselves to confessional work within the German Evangelical Church. If Niemöller will not go along, it will all end dreadfully.

Emergency decrees[21] only being applied in extreme cases; to date there have
only been leaves of absence, no dismissals, from office.

Pastor Bonhoeffer's response: Dr. Heckel had only addressed church policies
and tactical matters, not the questions of principle arising from the confessions.
Is Müller really representative of the church (after applying the Aryan paragraph,
suspending it, and then applying it again, after his use of force and the position he
has taken on the problem of youth work)?? Is not the most urgent church policy
task for today to secede from such a church?

Dr. Heckel replied, with regard to the problem of the Old Testament, that it
presented an unresolved theological task.

The decree of Cultural Affairs Minister Rust on freedom of speech for university professors[22] still allows publications such as *Junge Kirche* or Künneth's *Nation
vor Gott* to appear.

With regard to the discussion on the *Aryan paragraph*:

[16.] In the days preceding the chancellery reception, the Gestapo was observing the
church opposition.

[17.] This refers to the interventions of Bell (see *DB-ER*, 363) and Eidem (see Meiser,
Verantwortung für die Kirche, 109).

[18.] Following the chancellery reception, Niemöller took the position in a circular letter that there was no reason "to be dissatisfied with the results so far" (Scholder, *Churches
and the Third Reich*, 2:42).

[19.] On February 2, 1934; cf. Scholder, *Churches and the Third Reich*, 2:51.

[20.] Schöffel resigned from the Reich church government Clerical Ministry on November 24, 1933 (cf. Scholder, *Churches and the Third Reich*, 1:563).

[21.] On January 26, 1934, Ludwig Müller assumed all governing powers of the Old
Prussian Union Church. This was followed on February 3 by his orders for transfers and
suspensions of clergy, affecting sixty-eight pastors by mid-month (cf. Niesel, *Kirche unter
dem Wort*, 22–23).

[22.] Cf. 1/60, ed. note 2.

The proposal not to enforce the Aryan paragraph came not from the Lutheran but rather from the German Christian bishops. Relations with the Reich in any case preclude discussion of the Aryan paragraph.

Rieger interjected that for various organizations (the swim club, philharmonic orchestra), it seemed possible to disobey the state's Aryan paragraph. Why cannot the church do the same?

Dr. Heckel's reply: "For that to happen, Hitler's stance would have to be different." The legality of the emergency degree has been strongly questioned. In any case, by agreement with all the German bishops, the Aryan paragraph was not being implemented.[23] In summary: I. The Aryan paragraph applies not to the Reich Church but only to the regional churches. 2. It applies only to the professional clergy. 3. It would not be systematically applied abroad. 4. Therefore there is no cause for worry about the future.

With regard to the charge of *dictatorship* (force) in the church: the Reich bishop's recent emergency decree was necessary, if the church authorities were to continue their functions; in the church senate, for instance, there had been five different parties.[24] There had been only leaves of absence, not dismissals, from office. Bishops are certainly not being dismissed because of the opposition, but only because of their own incompetence. Our struggle today is against the romanizing of the church, comparable to that in the years 1530–80 (FC stage).[25] The Reich bishop himself did not want the Aryan paragraph.

With regard to the charge of failure in the *youth work* problem: The incorporation of the Evangelical Youth into the Hitler Youth had been accomplished in some places without any friction (Bavaria, East Prussia, the Rhineland).

With regard to the personality of the Reich bishop: the language used by the Reich bishop was only the "soldier's slang" of our age. Bishop Glondys praised the Reich bishop's strategic foresight. The work abroad is really close to the Reich

---

[23.] Speaking to church leaders on January 27, 1934, Müller described the nonimplementation of the Aryan paragraph in the regional churches as a "sacrifice" made by the German Christians for the sake of church politics (see Meiser, *Verantwortung für die Kirche*, 247–48).

[24.] In the January 26, 1934, "Ordinance to Ensure Unified Leadership of the Old Prussian Union Church," Müller personally assumed authority over the church senate of the Old Prussian Union as well as authority over the Evangelical High Council in Berlin (Beckmann, *Kirchliches Jahrbuch 1933–1944*, 46–47). On February 5 he dissolved the High Council and dismissed Friedrich Werner.

[25.] Formula Concordiae, the Formula of Concord of 1577. [This is a highly significant doctrinal text in the history of Lutheranism. It aimed at ending deep controversies and divisions among Lutherans in the wake of Luther's death in 1546 and the military defeat of Lutheran princes and estates in 1547, and in the face of strong political pressures from both Roman Catholic and Calvinist sides. See Kolb and Wengert, *Book of Concord*, esp. 481–85.—KC]

bishop's heart; otherwise it would not have been possible to have a man like Pastor Krummacher in the Church Foreign Office.

Dr. Wahl said, with regard to the *legal question*, that the German Evangelical Church is the lawful successor to the Church Federation.

Dr. Heckel is asking for, if not a vote of confidence, at least a declaration of allegiance in which each of the German pastors would affirm his regard for the whole. The vote of no confidence seems to him to be a sign of radicalism.

2. Session on February 9, 1934

Present: Dr. Heckel; Pastor Krummacher; Dr. Wahl; Pastors Wehrhan, Schönberger, Dr. Rieger, Dr. Bonhoeffer, Schreiner, Steiniger, Böckheler; Vicar Locher

Pastor Wehrhan opened the meeting with an exposition of the situation resulting from the negotiations up to this point. He stated expressly that Dr. Heckel's account of matters to date corresponded very largely with the reports carried in   102 the *Times*; only the events of the last week had no longer been clearly reported therein. Hence there could be no question of the London clergy having been driven into opposition by misrepresentations in the foreign press. He called for a clear policy.

Pastor Schönberger then read the declaration of the London pastors on the present situation (see appendix 1).[26]

Dr. Heckel curtly refused to engage in further discussion on the basis of this declaration.

Pastor Wehrhan suggested that Baron v. Schröder's[27] draft statement, which formed the basis of the pastors' declaration, be read.

Pastor Schönberger did so, with the remark that the two declarations were in accord with each other.

Dr. Heckel said that he found the second declaration substantially milder.

Pastor Schönberger explained the individual points of the pastors' declaration. Dr. Heckel addressed himself to the legal question, declaring that it was in effect resolved on the basis of the Diaspora Law, which was still valid. The German Evangelical Church had no intention of meddling in the affairs of the German churches in England; hence the latter should refrain from meddling in the affairs of the German Evangelical Church.

Pastor Bonhoeffer explained that meddling was not the issue under discussion, but rather a preeminently theological concern for us to have an inner bond and unity, on the basis of faith, with the German church.

Dr. Heckel wanted to know whether all the pastors present stood by this declaration.

[26.] Declaration by the German Evangelical Pastors in Great Britain; see 1/74.2.

[27.] On Schröder's draft statement, see ed. notes 32 and 35.

Pastor Schreiner declared that he personally no longer did so. For him, all its concerns had been clearly answered by Dr. Heckel's replies. He had the impression that the opposition of the London pastors was based on the principle of opposition itself.

Pastor Wehrhan strongly repudiated this accusation.

Pastor Böckheler suggested that the points in the declaration could be formulated as inquiries.

Pastor Rieger said he also felt that setting conditions was not a fitting way to address these concerns to the German church, but that even without being stated in this form, the doubts would remain.

Pastor Schönberger pointed out that the pastors' text formulates loyalty and a firm relationship of trust as clearly distinct from each other. The form of the text could, however, be changed to that of inquiries.

103   *Pastor Wehrhan* felt that even the legal question had not been clarified at all. For example, when the constitution of the Church Federation was changed, it was not done at all according to the constitutional forms that are required for such changes. This, he said, strengthened his fear that other laws still standing today—i.e., for us, the Diaspora Law—are not safe from arbitrary changes. There then followed a general discussion about the way pastors had been treated by the church authorities. *Pastor Schönberger* asked Dr. Heckel to respond to something he had heard from a trustworthy source: whether it were true that one of the pastors least in sympathy with the German Christians only received his assignment to a parish after he had joined the German Christians, under pressure from his regional church office. *Dr. Wahl* interjected, "Those are the kind of stories you are using to stir up public opinion around here!" *Pastor Schönberger* immediately protested, whereupon *Wahl* said he had not meant the "you" personally.

In reply to the question, *Dr. Heckel* denied categorically the possibility of such influence being exerted.

Dr. Heckel then read a declaration that he himself had composed, in which the pastors here would state that they accepted his explanations and were reassured (see appendix 2).[28] This declaration did not meet with approval from the pastors.

Pastor Schönberger said he found all this "reassurance" very far from reassuring.

Pastor Bonhoeffer pointed out that this declaration included only what Dr. Heckel himself considered to be important, while ignoring practically all the critical points raised by the pastors here. There was no need, he said, for assurances about the autonomy of the churches abroad, since that had never been in question, nor had that ever been the motive for the doubts raised by the pastors in England about the present church government.

[28.] See 1/74.3.

Dr. Heckel replied to the rejection of his declaration with deep regret that no agreement had been reached: "I cannot go home empty-handed."

He gave an explanation for each of the points in his declaration and suggested that it be duplicated and each pastor present be given a copy to study more carefully.

Dr. Heckel then said that those in opposition must realize that they were aligning themselves with the Prague emigrants[29] and proceeded to give examples of the treasonable actions of the latter.

104

Pastor Wehrhan proposed that the pastors relinquish their own statement as the basis for negotiations and that they acknowledge Dr. Heckel's declaration. However, he said he could not give his own agreement without first consulting Baron von Schröder.

Pastor Schönberger declared that he also could not act without the baron's approval, but that one could not count on his agreement since the baron had clearly expressed his unconditional approval of the pastors' own statement. He asked Dr. Heckel whether he would agree to publication of this statement in order to reassure the congregations. He said he could not sign anything unless it could also be made public. An honest transaction would not be harmed by publication (in the church newsletter) when necessary.

Dr. Heckel replied, "You will have to leave the NSDAP[30] first." He would not agree to publication of the statement and proposed an abridged version, but Pastor Schönberger would not accept it. The discussion appearing without hope of any further issue, at this point three of the participants—Pastors *Rieger, Bonhoeffer,* and *Steiniger*—took their leave.

Pastor Schönberger assumed responsibility for copying and distributing Dr. Heckel's declaration.

Dr. Heckel asked him to add this sentence below the declaration: "During the session of February 9, 1934, this declaration was unanimously agreed to by all the German Evangelical pastors in England."

Pastor Schönberger strongly protested against adding this final sentence, in view of the course that the discussion had taken. Only the comparison of the church opposition to the activities of the emigrants had hindered the individual pastors from speaking out more clearly.

No agreement was reached on this point, and the session was adjourned.

(See also, as appendix 3, the six points subsequently drafted by London pastors Wehrhan, Dr. Rieger, Bonhoeffer, and Schönberger.)[31]

[29.] This was a derogatory term applied collectively to the political opponents of Nazism who fled in 1933.

[30.] [The Nazi Party.—KC]

[31.] The declaration by the pastors in London; see 1/74.5.

105 **74.2 Declaration by the Pastors in Great Britain**[32]

The following points form the basis on which the congregations here would be ready to join the new Evangelical Church:

1. The Evangelical Church stands on the ground of the Reformation.

2. It is founded on the Holy Scriptures of the Old and New Testaments.

3. The Aryan paragraph is *not* recognized by the German Evangelical pastors in Great Britain,[33] and they expect it not to be implemented anywhere[34] by the Reich Church.

4. The German Reich Church does not dismiss any pastor in Germany who accepts the above points, except in the case of other, serious offenses against discipline.

5.[35] The pastors declare that, following the dissolution of the Church Federation, they have no further obligation to the Reich Church; they are nevertheless prepared, on the basis of the above and in Christian love and fellowship, to remain in the Reich Church.

6. The German Evangelical churches in Great Britain, declaring themselves prepared to be members of the new Reich Church, nevertheless declare specifically that, as is already the case, they have the right to resign their membership in this association of churches at any time.

London, February 9, 1934

74.3 Declaration by Theodor Heckel[36]

Because of the steps taken by the *Association of German Evangelical Congregations in England* and the German Evangelical pastors in London during January of this
106 year,[37] I gave a full report on the overall situation in the church to a meeting of the German Evangelical clergy in England on February 8.

[32.] ADBC, GV 4, 6; carbon copy; see *NL*, A 41,5 (4). Previously published in *GS* 6:320. Original title: "Minutes of the Discussions between the German Evangelical Pastors of Great Britain with Consistory Councilor Dr. Heckel." The declaration is based on a February 9, 1934, draft by Baron Schröder [*NL*, A 41,5 (2)]. The differences between it and the subsequent version are documented in the editorial notes that follow.

[33.] Schröder's draft does not have "Great Britain."

[34.] Schröder's draft does not have "anywhere."

[35.] Points 5 and 6 replace the moderate point 5 in Schröder's draft: "The pastors declare that they are not bound to the Reich Church by their acceptance of the Church Federation but are nevertheless prepared, on the basis of the above and in Christian love and fellowship, to participate in the Reich Church."

[36.] ADBC, GV 4, 4; carbon copy; see *NL*, A 41,5 (5). Previously published in *GS* 6:319–20.

[37.] Cf. 1/48, 1/49, 1/52, and 1/56.

On this occasion I declared to them as instructed, with the understanding that my remarks would not be used publicly, that with respect to the *Aryan paragraph*, aside from the fact that there had been no normative Reich Church regulation as yet, there was no longer any cause for anxiety.

Insofar as the German Evangelical churches in England showed concern about alterations to the Bible, I denied that the German Evangelical Church had any such intention.

With regard to the existing membership status of the German Evangelical congregations in England, I represented the position that the legal basis of their membership, as provided for in the Diaspora Law for churches abroad, had not undergone any change as a result of the German Evangelical Church's constitution taking effect.

On receiving the assurance that the German Evangelical clergy in England are willing to recognize the authority of the German Evangelical Church, I declared my willingness to propose to the Reich bishop a written statement to the effect that the existing confessional status of the German Evangelical churches in England, as well as the autonomy guaranteed them within the framework of the relationship that has existed up to now, will be preserved by the German Evangelical Church.

During the session of February 9, 1934, this declaration was unanimously agreed by all the German Evangelical pastors in England.[38]

74.4 Baron Bruno Schröder to Theodor Heckel[39]

February 9, 1934

Dear Dr. Heckel,

Before you leave England again, I would like you to know that I was very pleased to see you here and to have the opportunity of discussing with you the questions   107 concerning our Evangelical Church.

As chairman of the *Association of German Evangelical Congregations in Great Britain and Ireland*, I would like to express my opinion that, above all, I would not like to see these problems of the church get thrown together with political issues. In my view, the church stands apart from politics and is governed only according to the will of our Lord and Savior. Insofar as I may as a foreigner, I stand politically wholly on the side of the Social Nationalists, who have already done so much good for our old Fatherland.

[38.] Heckel added this last sentence to his declaration, despite Schönberger's protest, after Bonhoeffer and two other colleagues had left the meeting (see 1/74.1, p. 111).

[39.] ADBC, GV 4, 7; carbon copy; see *NL*, A 41,1 (27). In the bottom margin is the following address: "To the honorable Consistory Councilor Dr. Heckel, presently at Garland's Hotel, 15, Suffolk Street, S.W.1."

For the rest, I hope with all my heart that the differences of opinion in Germany will be resolved soon, for nothing could be a heavier blow to our Evangelical Church than not to be united within itself.

With very best wishes, I remain
Yours sincerely and respectfully,
[B. Schröder]

74.5 Declaration by the Pastors in London[40]

In order to avoid any possible misunderstandings, the undersigned German Evangelical pastors in London make the following statement concerning the declaration by the representative of the German Evangelical Church, Bishop Dr. Heckel, of February 8, 1934:

1. Contrary to what is stated in the final sentence, this declaration was *not* unanimously agreed by all the German pastors in England, since Pastor Hansen of Bradford did not attend the conference.

2. After Dr. Heckel read his declaration aloud, Pastors Bonhoeffer and Schönberger immediately raised objections.

3. No vote was taken, nor did any signing of the declaration take place.

4. The declaration was not presented in writing to any of the pastors in attendance.

5. Discussion of this declaration was severely hindered by the pastors' being under the apprehension that they might risk incurring political defamation.

6. Not all the pastors who were present were informed about the addition of the final sentence.

In connection with Dr. Heckel's declaration, the undersigned respectfully request answers to the following questions:

1. During the conference, Dr. Heckel made the following statement: "I have been empowered to inform you that there is no further cause for concern in the matter of the Aryan paragraph." Permit us to inquire, what is then the meaning of the reinstatement of the General Synod's statute of September 6, 1933, which contains the Aryan paragraph?[41] We have been made aware that this statute is in force by the dismissal of Pastor Niemöller, which was based on this statute.[42]

[40.] ADBC GV 4, 8; typewritten copy; cf. *NL,* A 41,5 (6). Previously published in *GS* 6:320–22. This text must have been composed *after* February 21, 1934, the date of Heckel's consecration as bishop.

[41.] Cf. 1/73.2, ed. note 8.

[42.] Niemöller was temporarily suspended by the Reich bishop on January 27, 1934, and was removed from office on February 10 [effective March 1] (cf. J. Schmidt, *Martin Niemöller im Kirchenkampf,* 186–87). [Niemöller's suspension was not due to the Aryan

Furthermore, how can the aforementioned statement by Dr. Heckel be reconciled with the introduction or reintroduction of the Aryan paragraph in various regional churches?

2. On inquiring about the suspension or dismissal of pastors, we have received the answer that only leaves of absence have been ordered. In this regard we ask today how we are to understand the news of suspensions and/or dismissals of a considerable number of pastors, which we regularly find confirmed[43] not only in the foreign newspapers but also in the newsletters of the German churches?

3. There is a rumor among German lay circles in Holland that Dr. Heckel has raised accusations regarding the actions of the pastors in London, and that the possibility of withdrawal of passports has been mentioned. We can scarcely believe this rumor and therefore request clarification.

75. From George Bell[1]

10th February, 1934

My dear Bonhoeffer,

I enclose a copy of a letter to Schonfeld[2] for your information. I should very much like to see you, for I want your help with regard to the Round Table article which is now in manuscript.[3] Would it be at all possible for you to spend Wednesday, February 14th, here, arriving at 11 A.M.? The article has to be in the printer's hands by Thursday, and if you could stay Wednesday night as well, we could get on I think.

I rang you up last night but you were out.

Yours ever,

[George Cicestr]

109

---

paragraph, however, but was the direct result of his clash with Müller in the wake of the meeting with Hitler. Niemöller took legal action to contest his suspension and won reinstatement (Scholder, *Churches and the Third Reich*, 2:48–49).—KC]

[43.] Cf. ed. note 21.

[1.] LPL, Bell Papers 42, 15; carbon copy; from Chichester; in original English, including errors. See also *NL*, A 42,2 (4). Previously published in *GS* 2:145.

[2.] Not extant. Possibly connected with Schönfeld's plan to send an ecumenical observer to Germany. Cf. Bell and Koechlin, *Briefwechsel*, 112–13, but also Boyens, *Kirchenkampf und Ökumene*, 1:108.

[3.] Bell had arranged with the editor of *The Round Table* to expand Koechlin's article [see 1/53, ed. note 3—KC], which it was to publish, with some background information about events in the Church Struggle. See Bell and Koechlin, *Briefwechsel*, 107–8.

76. To George Bell[1]

My Lord Bishop,

thank you very much for your very interesting letter. I should like to come to Chichester on Wednesday very much, but last night, I received a telephone call from Germany and I was asked most urgently to come to Germany for a meeting which shall take place tomorrow afternoon at Hannover.[2] The Emergency League will take its decision about its future, separation, etc. So I will leave to night and shall unfortunately not be able to come to see you on Wednesday. I shall be back probably on Saturday. If you wish some information from a German I should propose to telephone to Pastor Rieger, my colleague, Greenwich 2613. I will try to read the paper still before I leave and to make some notes.[3] I am very sorry not to be able to help you as much as I should like to.

Yours very respectfully,
Dietrich Bonhoeffer

77. Baron Bruno Schröder to Theodor Heckel[1]

110

London, February 19, 1934

Dear Consistory Councilor Heckel:

My thanks for your kind letter,[2] which I received this morning. I can only assure you that your visit here was a great pleasure for my wife and myself.

The thorough discussion that you had here with regard to the situation in the church has in any case contributed to understanding on both sides, and I hope we will now make progress in this matter. As you know, I am a man of patience and have no wish to hurry anything. I must now consult with the various congregations and ultimately bring them to an agreement. Thus I rely on your kindness in continuing to have patience as well, because new points keep coming up that I must try to clear away.

[1.] LPL, Bell Papers 42, 16 and 17; handwritten; from London; undated but written on February 12, 1934; in original English, including errors. Cf. also *NL*, A 42,1 (9). Previously published in *GS* 2:145.

[2.] Meeting of the Council of Brethren of the Pastors' Emergency League in Hanover on February 13, 1934. See *DB-ER*, 364.

[3.] Koechlin's article appeared in *The Round Table: A Quarterly Review of Politics of the British Commonwealth* 24, no. 94 (March 1934): 319–33.

[1.] ADBC, GV 4, 9; carbon copy.
[2.] Not extant.

For example, today there is again an article in the *Times*[3] by its Berlin correspondent, which I am enclosing. I ask you please to tell me frankly whether this is true. If it is, it would completely contradict what you said in your declaration,[4] of which you so kindly left me a copy.

In regard to the declaration itself, I do not want any misunderstandings to arise in the future. Thus I ask you please to let me know whether we are to understand the phrase "used in the press" to mean that nothing must be allowed to be printed, but that we have the right to discuss the matter with our congregations, as long as nothing is said from the pulpit or altar.

Then you are demanding that the German Evangelical clergy here agree to preserve the authority of the German Evangelical Church. That you may take for granted, but I would like to add the words "as long as the church remains as it is now." Just as an example, it would be difficult to persuade the pastors and congregations here to follow the German Evangelical Church if it should suddenly decree that the crucifix be removed from its altars.

Please be so kind as to write to me regarding these points. In the meantime my wife and I send you our best regards, and I remain, 111

Sincerely and respectfully yours,
[Bruno Schröder]

78. From George Bell[1]

24th February, 1934

My dear Bonhoeffer,

I am very anxious to see you. I wonder whether you have returned from your wanderings? I hope very much you are better, for I was very sorry to learn from Pastor Rieger that you had fallen a victim to a chill or influenza.[2] I am in London on Wednesday evening and Thursday[3] morning. What would suit me best of all

---

[3.] On February 19, 1934, the *Times* carried a detailed report on dismissals and suspensions of pastors and superintendents in Pomerania and Silesia.

[4.] See 1/74.3.

[1.] LPL, Bell Papers 42, 18; carbon copy; in English, including errors. See also *NL*, A 42,2 (5); copy. Previously published in *GS* 2:146.

[2.] Bonhoeffer had gone to Hanover on February 13, 1934, to take part in a meeting of the Pastors' Emergency League that had been called at short notice. He then continued on to Berlin, where he fell ill with influenza (cf. *DB-ER*, 264).

[3.] March 1, 1934.

would be if you could come and have breakfast with me at the Athenaeum[4] at 9 o'clock on Thursday morning. Is that too outrageous?

Yours ever,
[George Cicestr]

79. To George Bell[1]

March 14th, 1934

My Lord Bishop,

112   may I just let you know, that I was called last week again to Berlin—this time by the Church Government.[2] The subject was the ecumenic situation. I also saw Niemöller, Jacobi, and some friends from the Rhineland. The free Synod in Berlin[3] was a real progress and success. We hope to get ready for a Free National Synod until 18th of April in Barmen. One of the most important things is that the Christian Churches of the other countries do not lose their interest in this conflict by the length of time. I know that my friends are looking to you and your further actions with great hope. There is really a moment now as perhaps never before in Germany in which our faith into the ecumenic task of the churches can be shaken and destroyed completely or strengthened and renewed in a surprisingly new way. And it is you, My Lord Bishop, on whom it depends whether this moment shall be used. The question at stake in the German Church is no longer an internal issue but is the question of existence of Christianity in Europe; therefore a definite attitude of the ecumenic movement has nothing to do with "intervention"—but it is just a demonstration to the whole world that Church and Christianity as such are at stake. Even if the information of the newspapers is becoming of less interest, the real situation is as tense, as acute, as responsible as ever before. I shall only wish you would see one of the meetings of the Emergency League

---

[4.] The prestigious club in Pall Mall, London, where Bell often used to invite people for conversations [and which was also used by J. H. Oldham, another of Bonhoeffer's important London contacts, and a number of other Anglican bishops—KC].

[1.] LPL, Bell Papers 42, 20; handwritten; from London; in original English, including errors. See also *NL*, A 42,1 (10). Previously published in *GS* 1:184–85.

[2.] Bonhoeffer had been summoned to Berlin by Theodor Heckel and asked to sign a declaration to refrain from any future ecumenical activities, which he refused to do. Cf. 1/82 and 1/93, also *DB-ER*, 365.

[3.] On March 7, 1934, the first confessional synod of Berlin-Brandenburg was held in Dahlem and chaired by Gerhard Jacobi (cf. Meier, *Der evangelische Kirchenkampf*, 281, and Scholder, *Churches and the Third Reich*, 2:62).

now—it is always inspite of all gravity of the present moment a real upheaval to one's own faith and courage.

Please do not be silent now! I beg to ask you once more to consider the possibility of an ecumenic delegation and ultimatum. It is not on behalf of any national or denominational interest that this ultimatum should be brought forward but it is in the name of Christianity in Europe. Time passes by very quickly and it might soon be too late.[4] The 1st of May the "Peace in the Church" shall be declared by Müller![5] Six weeks only.

I remain, My Lord Bishop, Yours very gratefully and respectfully
Dietrich Bonhoeffer

113

80. To Hans Besig[1]

London, March 15, 1934

Honored Consistory Councilor:

On the basis of your letter of January 8, 1934,[2] it was my understanding that you were only expecting an official communication from me in the case of my agreement with the suggestion that you so kindly made to me. However, in order to make the matter perfectly clear, I would now like to come back to this and to say explicitly that I do not believe I should relinquish my assurance from the regional church of being reemployed as a pastor there, insofar as it is customary and possible. The fact that I have worked as a university lecturer docs not, to me, indicate that I necessarily have any commitment to a further career as such.

My respect and thanks once again for your kind offer. I hope that this letter has now clarified the matter.

I remain most sincerely and respectfully yours,
Bonhoeffer

[4.] On March 14, Bonhoeffer also sent a letter (not extant) to Henriod, which Henriod quoted in a letter of March 16, 1934, to George Bell as follows: "I know of very many leading men whose names I may not mention in this letter, who expect almost everything from a definite step from the side of the Oecumenical movement. It might soon be too late." Cited in *GS* 6:349, ed. note 5.

[5.] Ludwig Müller actually published his "Message on Peace in the Church" on April 13, 1934. Cf. Beckmann, *Kirchliches Jahrbuch 1933–1945*, 62–63. See also 1/50.

[1.] EZA 5/1316; typewritten; handwritten note by the recipient: "Recommend await clarification of the situation." Previously published in *GS* 6:288–89.

[2.] See 1/50.

114   **81. From Henry Louis Henriod**[1]

Geneva, March 16, 1934[2]

My dear Bonhoeffer,

Thank you for your letter of March 14th.[3] As you say, the situation is becoming more critical and some action should be taken up without any delay by the Oecumenic movement. I have discussed your letter fully with Dr. Schönfeld and we have consulted also one or two other leaders and Christian workers here.

I have written a few days ago already to the Bishop of Chichester, urging him to follow up his correspondence with Bishop Heckel[4] by a strong letter. I am writing him to-day asking for a small conference of leading theologians, most of whom would be in Paris at the beginning of April for our Study conference on Church and State—a conference which would be separate from that Study Week, and to which the Reichsbischof would be asked to send delegates,[5] so that straight forward questions can be put to them and strong statements made, which will make it possible for an outspoken disapproval of the attitude adopted by the Church and probable action by the Churches belonging to the Oecumenic movement. This would follow up naturally steps taken before and might lead to a delegation to Berlin. If the Bishop of Chichester prefers to have a delegation go to Berlin—which I doubt very much, as most of the members of our Administrative Committee were not in sympathy with this method—I would fall in with him of course.

At the same time we are preparing as fast as we can documentation on the attitude of other Churches toward the present German situation, which can be used in the press and thus become known in Germany.

It is not in my competence to prepare for a delegation or to send an ultimatum without the consent of my committee and as you know, the Bishop of Chichester was asked to take up responsibility in the direction of relationships with Germany and I am keeping in close touch with him.

Those who stand for the Gospel in Germany should not get desperate. There
115 are declarations and messages which are coming out from various countries by pastors and others, which will indicate how much deep feeling there is outside Germany with regard to the situation of the government of the German Church.

[1.] WCC Archives, World Alliance, Letters to Dietrich Bonhoeffer; carbon copy; in original English, including errors. Cf. *NL*, Anh. D 1,4 (8); photocopy. Previously published in *GS* 1:185–86.

[2.] [In the original the city and date are in French.—KC]

[3.] Not extant, but see 1/79, ed. note 4.

[4.] See Boyens, *Kirchenkampf und Ökumene,* 1:317–19 and 321; and Scholder, *Churches in the Third Reich,* 2:76–77.

[5.] On the planning in Geneva for an ecumenical delegation, see Boyens, *Kirchenkampf und Ökumene,* 1:108; and Scholder, *Churches in the Third Reich,* 2:78.

I can only repeat that stronger action might have been taken earlier if our best trusted friends in Germany had not urged us again and again even these last few days, not to break relationships with the German Church, as it is our only means of influencing the situation by getting at the present government again and again with strong criticisms.

If you have to return to Germany, please let me know before you leave London your address, and whether one can write to you and comparatively freely.

Through our press service and through every means we have at our disposal, we are doing our utmost to pass on the truth as we receive it with regard to the German situation.

I shall be away from Geneva in Austria, Hungary and Czechoslovakia up till Easter time. I trust that you keep in close touch with the Bishop of Chichester. As you say the issue is plainly Christian and it touches the future of Christianism in Europe. You can count on my full sympathy and we know how terrific the situation must be for those who suffer bodily, mentally as well as in their soul. May God give us His clear lead so that we act at every point according to His will and for His cause.

Yours ever,
Henry Louis Henriod

82. To Theodor Heckel[1]

London, March 18, 1934

Dear Bishop Heckel:

In response to your inquiry,[2] I take the liberty of replying as follows: The communication that you received from Pastor Niemöller[3] relates to two things. First, in the meeting with the German pastors in England on February 8, 1934,[4] during your detailed report on developments in the German church in the past month, you mentioned that at one time Pastor Niemöller

116

[1.] *NL*, A 41,5 (8); typewritten copy. Previously published in *GS* 2:160–62. See the reply, 1/91.

[2.] Not extant.

[3.] Heckel's inquiry refers to a letter of March 11, 1934, to him from Martin Niemöller: "Dear Colleague: I have learned from Pastor Bonhoeffer that you have informed the bishop of Chichester that at one point I turned down a formal offer from the Reich bishop of a position in the 'Clerical Ministry.'—I have no wish to hide from you, even when I otherwise have no intention of pursuing our former connection, that this piece of news is untrue, and that it would have been easy enough for you, before spreading these kinds of false reports abroad, to have asked me to confirm to you the actual state of affairs. Respectfully, (signed) Niemöller" (*NL*, D 2).

[4.] See 1/74.

had received an offer to join the Clerical Ministry [Geistliche Ministerium]. When I interjected that according to my personal information such an offer had been made only casually in a private conversation with Dr. Oberheid, you replied that Dr. Oberheid had been officially authorized to make this offer. I then replied that I had been otherwise informed.[5] Furthermore, I know that, following the aforementioned meeting with the German pastors, the lord bishop of Chichester was informed of this same offer made to Pastor Niemöller and of the reasons for his refusal. After consulting the lord bishop, I can provide you with the exact wording, if you wish. In view of the significance that the fact of such an offer would have in assessing the entire policy of the church in the last few months and in its development, I needed—also in the interest of my colleagues here—to insist on clarifying the truth of this matter. I therefore showed your account of it to Pastor Niemöller and asked for his response. His answer confirmed my previous information. It is understandable that the utmost clarity about this matter is important to Niemöller, and that he needs to counter any rumor about it wherever he can. We here are also very concerned that this matter be reported in such a way that no lack of clarity remains.

To return, as promised, to our discussion in Berlin,[6] I just want to say to you that I still feel that, with my ordination vow and the statement I made to the Reich bishop and yourself before I came over here,[7] I have said everything I can. I therefore cannot sign such a revocation as you are requesting from me. I cannot see any compelling reason that would relieve me of this purely ecclesiological, theological, ecumenical work to which I have had a commitment for years. However, as a matter of fact, you may perhaps be pleased to know that, because of parish work, I am no longer sure I will be able to participate in the Paris conference[8] and that I have not heard anything more about a reception with the archbishop of Canterbury[9] and have concluded that nothing will come of it, at least for the present.

Most respectfully yours,
Dietrich Bonhoeffer

[5.] Bonhoeffer's information was correct. On Oberheid's "offer," see also J. Schmidt, *Martin Niemöller im Kirchenkampf*, 157–58.

[6.] See 1/79, ed. note 2.

[7.] Letter from Bonhoeffer to Heckel of early October 1933, *GS* 2:125 and DBW 12, 1/107. See also *DB-ER*, 321.

[8.] Cf. 1/86.

[9.] On March 28, 1934, Bonhoeffer nevertheless did speak with Archbishop Lang. He received the invitation after his letter to Heckel had already been sent. See *DB-ER*, 365–66.

83. From the Diary of Julius Rieger[1]

March 23, 1934

Spoke with Bonhoeffer. He has been invited to visit the archbishop of Canterbury (Dr. Lang) on Monday, March 26. The archbishop is said to have heard that Bonhoeffer knows about Germany and the situation in the German church, and he wanted to be informed about it.

Bonhoeffer spoke with Chichester yesterday. Eidem, Ammundsen, and Chichester want to approach the Reich bishop with questions in the form of an ultimatum. Henriod in Geneva especially is pursuing this matter very actively.[2]

Mistake in Chichester's letter to the *Times*[3] ("German Christians" instead of "National Socialists"). Chichester said he had this information in this form from another source. "National Socialist," he said, would actually be a stronger term, because "German Christian" was still a Christian category, whereas "National Socialist" was purely political.

84. From the *Gemeindebote* [1]   118

London, St. Paul's German Evangelical Church

On Palm Sunday, March 25, at 6:30 P.M., our church choir will sing Maunder's passion oratorio *Olivet to Calvary*.[2]

On Good Friday, March 30, at 6:30 P.M. we will have a passion prayer service. An old German passion play will be enacted by members of our congregation.

The same passion play will be presented on Good Friday at 4 P.M. in the German Evangelical Church of Sydenham.

All members and friends of both congregations are cordially invited to these celebrations.

D. Bonhoeffer

[1.] *NL*, A 41,9 (18); typewritten copy by Julius Rieger. Previously published in *GS* 6:322–23.

[2.] See 1/81.

[3.] See Boyens, *Kirchenkampf und Ökumene*, 1:321–22.

[1.] ADBC, *Gemeindebote für die deutschen evangelischen Kirchen in Großbritannien*, no.12 (March 25, 1934): 4. See also *NL*, A 41,8 (3); typewritten copy.

[2.] [A relatively simple choral work of 1904 by J. H. Maunder. Together with J. Stainer's *Crucifixion*, it enjoyed wide popularity in Anglican and (especially) free churches in England as a Passiontide devotion during much of the twentieth century.—KC]

85. From the Diary of Julius Rieger[1]

March 28, 1934

On March 26, Bonhoeffer spoke with the archbishop.[2] Lang knew that the prospect of this interview had made trouble for Bonhoeffer in Berlin (Heckel).[3] Lang asked for an account of this and "wanted to know about a great many other things." Recognition of the existing church is out of the question as far as Lang is concerned. That would mean, for example, that Lang would refuse to receive Heckel. The conversation lasted about three-quarters of an hour and ended by the archbishop's saying he hoped he would soon see Bonhoeffer again.

A conference had been planned to discuss peace issues,[4] but it broke down, first of all, because no one knows who should be invited from Germany. What is not wanted is an official church delegation. So the conference is being postponed. (Information from Dietrich B.)

85a. To Heinrich Lebrecht[1]

April 1, 1934

Dear Colleague,

It is not easy to find the right answer to your inquiry.[2] The regular pastorates in England are all occupied at the moment, although it is possible that some changes may occur in the near future. Our congregations here have the great advantage of complete financial autonomy; thus they are largely

---

[1.] *NL*, A 41,9 (18); typewritten copy made by Julius Rieger. Previously published in *GS* 6:323.

[2.] See *DB-ER*, 365–66.

[3.] See 1/83.

[4.] See Bell and Koechlin, *Briefwechsel*, 117.

[1.] In possession of Marianne Lebrecht, London. Typewritten and signed by hand. Return address: "Dr. Pastor Bonhoeffer., 23, Manor Mount, SE 23 ("SE 23" replaces "1934," corrected by hand). First published in Lebrecht, *Verschweigen oder kämpfen*, 76. The volume relates the life of Heinrich Lebrecht, a pastor in the Confessing Church who was personally affected by the Nazi racial laws. Edited here by Hans Pfeifer.

[2.] Lebrecht's inquiry as to whether there was a vacant post as pastor of a German Evangelical congregation in England was presumably occasioned by the new church constitution of September 1933 in Hesse and the establishment of the "German Christian" Evangelical Church of Nassau-Hesse the following November. Lebrecht had worked with three other Confessing pastors on the drafting of a "Statement on the Situation in the Church" in early January 1934 and had to reckon with reprisals (cf. Lebrecht, *Verschweigen oder kämpfen*, 24–26 and 74–75, as well as his letter of July 5, 1935, to Bonhoeffer, *DBWE* 14, 1/8a).

independent of Berlin. However, every call to a pastor is supposed to be confirmed by Berlin, even though this only concerns the pension scheme; my own call, for example, has not been confirmed, and I no longer expect that it will be.[3] I am afraid that an official application to the German Evangelical Church will not do you any good either. The people in charge there are *very* cautious.[4]

However, at the point where you as a non-Aryan are forced to leave your post as pastor, I believe that in the English church here many doors will be opened to you.[5] I urge you to let me know *immediately* when that happens. I am sure I will be able to help.

I should tell you, by the way, that two other colleagues who are in the same situation, one of whom has been a close friend of mine for years,[6] have already asked me the same thing, and for the time being I have not had any other information to give them either.

With greetings and best wishes,

Sincerely yours,
Dietrich Bonhoeffer

[3.] The German congregations in England had a contract with the German Reich Church (prior to 1933, the German Evangelical Church Council) concerning the calling of pastors. From a list provided by the Reich Church, congregations could choose a German pastor, who would be given a leave of absence for the time he worked abroad (and credited during this period toward his pension). Bonhoeffer himself had obtained his post in London on the recommendation of the Reich bishop and the head of the Church Foreign Office, Theodor Heckel, and then through his call by the two London congregations. Bonhoeffer had refused to sign the declaration of loyalty to the Reich Church government demanded by Reich Bishop Müller (see *DB-ER*, 321). For this reason the Church Foreign Office, contrary to the law, withheld its official confirmation of his call.

[4.] [For Heckel's response to an inquiry on Lebrecht's behalf to the Reich Church Foreign Office, see 1/144a.—KC]

[5.] In 1938, Lebrecht did in fact receive an invitation from Bishop Bell to come to England with his family; see Lebrecht, *Verschweigen oder kämpfen*, 72.

[6.] Franz Hildebrandt; see *DB-ER*, 138; also 1/66. On Bonhoeffer's efforts on behalf of "non-Aryan" pastors, see his letter of recommendation to Bishop Bell on behalf of Ernst Gordon, September 8, 1935 (*DBW* 14, 1/25); also Ernst Gordon, *And I Will Walk at Liberty: An Eye-Witness Account of the Church Struggle in Germany, 1933–1937*.

119   **86. To Hans Schönfeld**[1]

attendance conference[2] very difficult wire whether my presence absolutely requisite

=bonhoeffer=

87. To Henry Louis Henriod[1]

April 7, 1934

My dear Henriod,

The day before yesterday I wired Schönfeld to ask if it is absolutely necessary that I come to Paris.[2] There are two very serious cases in the congregation[3] that would make it quite difficult for me to be away at this time. On the other hand, I would have found a way if it had made a difference with regard to the church situation in Germany, but this does not seem to be the case. Moreover, I had not received Brunner's paper etc., which was to be sent so that I could prepare my comments for the discussion. Besides that, I had
120   not even known until today where this affair is being held, so I felt rather uncertain about the whole thing.

I would very much have liked to discuss the situation with you again; the slowness of ecumenical procedure is beginning to look to me like irresponsibility. A decision has got to be made some time, and it's no good waiting indefinitely for a sign from heaven, for the solution to the difficulty to fall into one's lap. Even the ecumenical movement has to make up its mind and

---

[1.] *NL*, A 40,1 (11); photocopy of a telegram; according to *GS*, the original [in English] is in the WCC Archives but has not been found. Sent from London on April 3,1934. Recipient's note: "[Received from] London, 17.50 [hrs]." Previously published in *GS* 6:349–50. There is a handwritten note on the telegram by Henry Louis Henriod: "Dr. Schönfeld, please wire. He would be very useful, but we should not press if it makes the situation too difficult for him. Henriod." On the back is the draft of a reply by Schönfeld: "Your presence [crossed out: 'attendance'] Paris conference not necessary. Schönfeld."

[2.] See 1/59.

[1.] WCC Archives, World Alliance, Letters from Dietrich Bonhoeffer, no. 18; photocopy of a typescript. Previously published in *Mündige Welt*, 5:226–27, and *GS* 6:350–51. See also *NL*, A 40,1 (13); typewritten copy.

[2.] See 1/59 [and 1/86—KC].

[3.] On the day this was written, nineteen-year-old Gertrud Lütgens died of appendicitis. She was from Hamburg and had been in London since October 1933. Bonhoeffer buried her on April 11, 1934, in the "New Cemetery" [the correct name is Bromley Hill Cemetery—KC] in Bromley, S.E., according to the register of burials of Sydenham Church, 146.

is therefore subject to error, like everything human. But to put off acting and taking a position simply because you are afraid of erring, while others—I mean our brethren in Germany—have to reach infinitely difficult decisions daily, seems to me almost to go against love. To delay or fail to make decisions may be more sinful than to make wrong decisions out of faith and love. "Lord, first let me go . . ." it says in the gospel;[4] how often we use that as a pretext!—and in this case it really is now or never. "Too late" means "never." Should the ecumenical movement fail to realize this, and if there are no "men of violence" to "take the kingdom of heaven by force" (Matthew 11:12), then the ecumenical movement is no longer church, but a useless association for making fine speeches. "If you do not believe, surely you shall not be established,"[5] but to believe means to decide. And can there still be any doubt as to which way that decision should go? For Germany today it is the confession, as it is the confession for the ecumenical movement today. Let us shake off our fear of this word—the cause of Christ is at stake; are we to be found sleeping?[6]

I am writing this to you because your last letter to me[7] seemed to be hinting at much the same thing. And if all the "wise," the elders, and the influential are unwilling to join us here and are held back by all kinds of considerations—then it is you who must attack, you who must go forward. Don't let yourself be stopped or misled; after all, if we're really honest with ourselves, we do know in this case what is right and what is wrong. Someone has got to show the way, fearlessly and unflinchingly—why not you? There is much more at stake here than just personal and administrative difficulties. Christ is looking down at us and asking whether there is anyone left who confesses faith in him. I think I am right in believing that you and I both see things this way.   121

With all best wishes,
Yours very sincerely,
Dietrich Bonhoeffer

[4.] Luke 9:59.

[5.] Isa. 7:9 [NRSV: "If you do not stand firm in faith, you shall not stand at all." —KC].

[6.] Cf. Mark 13:36.

[7.] Letter of March 16, 1934, from Henriod (1/81).

88. From the *Gemeindebote*[1]

London, St. Paul's Reformed Church

Our church soiree will be held Monday, April 16, at 7 P.M., in the parish hall at 3 Goulston Street, E.1. The Saturday school children will give a play, and our choir will sing. All members and friends of our church are cordially invited.

DR. *Dietrich Bonhoeffer*, Pastor

89. To George Bell[1]

15th April 1934

My Lord Bishop,

It is on the urgent request of one of my german friends, whose name I would rather mention to you personally, that I am writing to you again. I have received yesterday this letter[2] which has upset me very much indeed and I do think it is necessary that you know how our friends in Germany are feeling about the present situation and about the task of the ecumenic movement[3] now. This letter is really an outcry about the last events in the german church and a last appeal for a unmisunderstandable word[4] of the ecumenic movement. This man who speaks for a few thousand others states quite francly: "in the present moment there depends everything, absolutely everything on the attitude of the Bishop of Chichester." If such a feeling arises in Germany, it means that the moment has definitely come for the ecumenic movement either to take a definite attitude—perhaps in the way of an ultimatum or in expressing publicly the sympathy with the oppositional pastors—or to loose all confidence among the best element of the german pastors—an outlook which terrifies me more than anything else. It is for this very reason that I am repeating to you this statement of my friend. Of course, pastors in Germany do not realise all the implications which are connected with such a step taken by the ecumenic movement, but they certainly have a very fine feeling for the right spiritual moment for the churches abroad to speak their word.

[1.] *Gemeindebote für die deutschen evangelischen Kirchen in Großbritannien*, April 15, 1934. See also *NL*, A 41,8 (3); typewritten copy.

[1.] LPL, Bell Papers 42, 22; typewritten, with corrections by hand; in original English, including errors. See also *NL*, A 42,1 (11); typewritten copy. Previously published in *GS* 1:187–89.

[2.] Not extant.

[3.] "Ecumenic movement" replaces "churches."

[4.] "Word" replaces "attitude."

Please, do not think our friends in Germany [are] loosing all hope, it is only humanly spoken when they look to the ecumenic movement as their "last hope" and it is on the other hand for the ecumenic movement the moment to give a test of its reality and vitality.

As to the facts there is firstly the appointment of Dr. Jäger,[5] which is considered to be an ostentatious affront to the opposition and which means in fact that all power of the church government has been handed over to political and party authorities. It was much surprising to me that the Times gave a rather positive report about this appointment.[6] Jäger is in fact the man with the famous statement about Jesus being only the exponent of Nordic race etc.[7] . . . He was the man who caused the retirement of Bodelschwingh and who was considered to be the most ruthless man in the whole church government.[8] Furthermore he is—and remains—the head of the church-department in the Prussian Ministry of Education and a leading member of the Party. So this appointment must be taken as a significant step towards the complete assimilation of the church to the state and party. Even if Jäger should try to make himself sympathetic to the churches abroad by using mild words now, one must not be deceived by this tactic.

The situation in Westphalia seems even to be much more tense than we know.[9] I could tell you some details personally.

On the other hand it is still the great danger that the attempt of the Churchgovernment to win the sympathy of the leading men of the churches abroad will succeed—as we know of one such case[10]—because many of

123

[5.] On April 12, 1934, August Jäger had been appointed "legal administrator" (*Rechtswalter*) in Ludwig Müller's Clerical Ministry, charged with "bringing to completion the legal unity of the German Evangelical Church" (see Beckmann, *Kirchliches Jahrbuch 1933–1944*, 62).

[6.] The *Times* of April 13, 1934, called Jäger's appointment "A New Move" and a consolidating intervention by the Party and state in the "German Church Chaos."

[7.] In calling for participation in the July 1933 church elections, Jäger announced: "The appearance of Jesus in world history ultimately represents a burst of Nordic light in the midst of a world tormented by symptoms of degeneracy" (Gauger, *Chronik der Kirchenwirren*, 1:91).

[8.] On Jäger's role, as state commissioner for the Prussian church, in the forced resignation of Bodelschwingh as Reich bishop in June 1933, see Scholder, *Churches and the Third Reich*, 1:350–56.

[9.] On March 16 the Westphalian provincial synod had been dissolved by the state police, since the Confessing Church majority led by Westphalian church president Koch had opposed integration into the Reich Church. On the same day the Westphalian confessional synod had constituted itself, and a few days later 140 congregations had placed themselves under its governance. See Meier, *Der evangelische Kirchenkampf*, 1:312.

[10.] Arthur C. Headlam, bishop of Gloucester and leading member of Faith and Order, had contacts with the German Christians and was seeking support from the British public for Hitler's Germany.

them do not have enough knowledge to see what is going on behind the scenes. It is therefore that the mentioned letter proposes very strongly, if you could not send a letter to all other churches connected with the ecumenic movement warning them to take any personal step towards a recognition of the German Churchgovernment and giving them the real christian outlook of the situation which they want. The Reichsbishop himself is reported to have said, if we get the churches abroad on our side, we have won.

Excuse this long letter, but everything looks so frightfully dark. It is always a great comfort to me that I may tell you francly and personally our feelings. I hope to have the chance to hear from you soon.

With deep gratitude, I remain yours very respectfully
Dietrich Bonhoeffer

124   **90. To George Bell**[1]

16th April 1934

My Lord Bishop,

may I just add a few words to my letter of yesterday—with regard to the recent decree of Müller.[2] The only reason by which it can be explained is this: the church government has become aware of the fact, that the secession of the Westphalian church could no longer be detained,[3] and it was a clever move to delay once more this decision by issuing this new decree. That this offer of peace can not be taken seriously at all, can be proved by a comparison with the Good Friday message.[4] There Müller refuses an "amnesty," today he has changed once more his mind. The new amnesty is not even complete, Niemöller and other important pastors do not come under the decree.[5] It

---

[1.] LPL, Bell Papers 42, 23; typewritten; from London; in original English, including errors. See also *NL*, A 42,1 (12); typewritten copy. Previously published in *GS* 2:169. On the letter is a handwritten note by the recipient: "*Answered 20/4/34.* Lunch Time? Or Friday 6 [o'clock] in London?" Office note "ack[nowlege]d. 18/4/34."

[2.] On April 13, Reich Bishop Müller had published a "Message on Peace in the Church." There he announced that the actions pending "for reasons of church policy" against church officials were to be called off (Beckmann, *Kirchliches Jahrbuch 1933–1944*, 62–63).

[3.] See 1/89, ed. note 9.

[4.] On March 24, Müller had published a "Statement to Pastors," in which he expressed the view that if they would just concentrate on their parish work, the "church political troubles" among their colleagues could be "healed" (*Junge Kirche* 2, no. 7 [April 9, 1934]: 281).

[5.] According to the "Church Decree on Pacification of the Situation in the Church," also published on April 13, 1934, "actions with national political implications" were to be exempt from the amnesty (Beckmann, *Kirchliches Jahrbuch 1933–1944*, 63).

is undoubtedly the only intention of this decree to split up the opposition and then to go on freely. The Arianclause is still in force, since the law of Nov. 16th is expressly[6] once more cancelled.[7] So we can watch this move only with the greatest mistrust.

I remain, My Lord Bishop, yours very respectfully
Dietrich Bonhoeffer

91. From Hans Wahl (on behalf of Theodor Heckel)[1]   125

Berlin-Charlottenburg, April 17, 1934

Dear Pastor Bonhoeffer:

I am replying to your letter of March 18 to Bishop Dr. Heckel[2] on his behalf, as follows:

It is an established fact that, at the time of Dr. Oberheid's conversation with Pastor Niemöller, Dr. Oberheid did inform him that the Reich bishop was considering conferring on him, Pastor Niemöller, a position in the clerical ministry. Dr. Oberheid asked Pastor Niemöller whether he was prepared to accept such an appointment. The response to that question was no. This was an informal inquiry, such as is generally customary in such matters, but it does provide the basis in fact that at that time Pastor Niemöller was offered an appointment to the Clerical Ministry. There was nothing said in London about a "formal" offer. Stated in this way, the matter takes on an entirely different aspect.

I leave it to you to communicate the above to Pastor Niemöller. No correspondence with him is planned by this office.

Yours sincerely,
Wahl

[6.] The text actually says "expressively."

[7.] In the decree mentioned above, Müller reconfirmed his January 4, 1934, annulment of the "Decree on the Legal Conditions affecting Clergy and Church Officials of November 16, 1933," in which the Reich Church government—yielding to protests from the Pastors' Emergency League and from the ecumenical community—had temporarily suspended the application of the Aryan paragraph (Meier, *Der evangelische Kirchenkampf*, 1:122 and 125).

[1.] *NL*, A 41,5 (9); typewritten on letterhead "German Evangelical Church–Foreign Office." Previously published in *GS* 2:162–63.

[2.] See 1/82.

92. To George Bell[1]

My Lord Bishop,

126

thank you very much for your kind letter and invitation to Chichester.[2] Unfortunately I could not change another arrangement made for Tuesday[3] and so I could not come. In the meantime things are going on rapidly in Germany and the information I get are more optimistic than ever before, at least with regard of the stand of the opposition.[4] The last number of our Churchpaper "Junge Kirche" brings your letter to the Times and in addition to that a few voices from Sweden and Switzerland.[5] Today I have received the answer of the Emergency League in Berlin to the Peace-offer of the Reichsbishop and I have dared to translate it for you as well as I could, because I thought it very important.[6] I think the moment has come, that

---

[1.] LPL, Bell Papers 42, 24; typewritten, probably on April 25, 1934, on letterhead of the "Association of German Evangelical Congregations in Great Britain and Ireland"; in original English, including errors. See also *NL*, A 42,1 (13); typewritten copy. Previously published in *GS* 2:170.

[2.] Not extant, but see Bell's notes written on Bonhoeffer's letter of April 16, 1934, 1/90, ed. note 1.

[3.] Probably Tuesday, April 24, when Bonhoeffer gave a lecture at the German YMCA in London on "Youth and the Church" (see *GS* 3:292).

[4.] On "Ulm Day" [This refers to a meeting in the southern German city of Ulm of representatives from Württemberg, Bavaria, Prussia, and many individual confessing congregations, which then passed the Ulm declaration. The text of this declaration can be found in Cochrane, *Church's Confession*, 235–36.—KC], April 22, 1934, the "confessional front"—in protest against the Reich Church's interference in the regional church of Württemberg—declared itself "as the lawful Evangelical Church of Germany before the whole of Christendom" (Beckmann, *Kirchliches Jahrbuch 1933–1944*, 65–66). [See also Bell's mention of the Ulm declaration, 1/97.—KC]

[5.] *Junge Kirche* (1934): 342–47. In a letter written [on March 19—KC] and published on March 20 in the *Times*, Bell had protested against the misinterpretation of his February 8 conversation with Heckel's delegation; one could not speak, he said, of an undisturbed relationship between the German Evangelical Church and the ecumenical council. [Bell's actual words were: "It appears that this note, which advocated a common study of 'various problems now before the churches,' has been widely used in Germany as evidence that all is well in the relations between the German Evangelical Church and other Churches represented on the Universal Council for Life and Work. It should therefore be stated very plainly that no such inference must be drawn."—KC] He insisted that there had been no mitigation of the grievances he had listed to Heckel; on the contrary, the Reich Church government was moving further in the direction of "absolute autocracy." Cf. Boyens, *Kirchenkampf und Ökumene*, 1:321–22. [See also the *Times*, March 20, 1934.—KC]

[6.] Meeting on April 16, 1934, the Council of Brethren of the Free Evangelical Synod of Berlin-Brandenburg (chaired by Gerhard Jacobi) had emphatically rejected the Reich bishop's April 13 message "On Peace in the Church" (see 1/90, ed. note 2), saying that the solution sought by the Reich bishop obscured "the real fault, need and danger of the

you should and could speak a final word to this conflict. There are thousands
who are anxious to hear that word soon. May I come to the Athenaeum[7] on   127
Friday[8] at 6 o'clock. If I do not hear anything else, I shall be there.

I remain, My Lord Bishop, yours very sincerely
Dietrich Bonhoeffer

92a. From Heinrich Eberhard ("Hardy") Arnold[1]

35 Dunless Road, Edgbaston, Birmingham
April 27, 1934

Dear Mr. Bonhoeffer,

I too have heard about you on various occasions, in London as well through Henry
Ecroyd[2] and his wife. She is a daughter of the late professor _____[3] in Heidelberg. I don't know whether you know her very well.

---

church" [Bonhoeffer's translation—KC]. Müller's separation of the church's confessional
stance from its external order was unacceptable. The Reich bishop's dictatorship, modeled
on the secular Führer principle, could not be tolerated in the Protestant church. Moreover, the council's statement continued, the present church government owed its policy
to the erroneous and violence-promoting teachings of the German Christians and thus
could claim no ecclesiastical legitimacy. Therefore, the Council of Brethren was demanding "a radical revision of the church revolution of 1933" [Bonhoeffer's translation—KC].
All forceful infringements on the freedom of the clergy must be reversed, said the council, not to secure the ministry and the living of pastors, but to save the church "since it is
not the need of the pastors but the need of the church which makes our confession and
resistance necessary. We cannot yield a single step from the necessary way" [Bonhoeffer's
translation—KC]. The original statement in German is reprinted in K. D. Schmidt, *Die
Bekenntnisse und grundsätzlichen Äusserungen zur Kirchenfrage*, 2:60ff. Bonhoeffer enclosed
a complete English translation of the statement in his letter to Bell (LPL, Bell Papers
42, 32–34; 5 pages, handwritten; cf. *NL,* A 42, 1 [13/enclosure]; typewritten copy). [The
excerpts quoted in this note are taken from his English version.—KC]

[7.] Cf. 1/78, ed. note 4.

[8.] April 27, 1934.

[1.] *NL,* Anh. D1, 7 (6); handwritten, unpublished. Hardy Arnold, son of Eberhard
Arnold, was then in Birmingham for the summer semester 1934, where he was taking education courses with the help of a scholarship from the Society of Friends (Quakers). He
was also seeking donations for the school in the Alps recently founded by the Bruderhof
community (see ed. note 4, as well as Hardy Arnold's letter of June 14, 1934, to Eberhard
Arnold, 1/114a). Special thanks to Dr. Martin Heimbucher for information and advice on
this Bruderhof correspondence.

[2.] Uncertain reading.

[3.] A space was left here, presumably for the purpose of filling in the professor's name
later.

Unfortunately I returned to Birmingham only yesterday, after helping to set up our new children's home in Liechtenstein.[4] So I did not get your kind letter of April 7[5] until yesterday and am hastening to reply. If you have already made your trip to Birmingham, I would like to come to see you in London, either with one of those cheap trains, or maybe not until June when I [shall be leaving] England[6]

93. To Erwin Sutz[1]

London, April 28, 1934

My dear Sutz,

I have just destroyed the remains of a letter to you that I started more than four weeks ago and never finished. I hope this one will not meet the same fate! Many thanks for your kind letters[2] and the pictures, which I have placed in my series of striking portraits of promising young men—you'll be complaining, there's that cheeky Berliner again, but seriously it was *very* nice of you to think of me. In the last few months, I have often longed for the quiet of your mountain parish,[3] even though for several months I have appeared to be some distance away from the action myself. But that is only the way it looks. All the church things going on in Germany have their effect here and their ecumenical implications, and that keeps us pretty well in check. Besides, I have to keep going back to Germany from time to time; once it was for the Emergency League, and the next time because the church regime[4] ordered me to fly to Berlin and put before me some sort of declaration that I would refrain from all ecumenical activity from now on, which I didn't sign.[5] This sort of thing is disgusting. They'd give anything to get me

---

[4.] On December 29, 1933, the National Socialists withdrew the Bruderhof's permit to run its private school in Sannerz. The Bruderhof then took all its children to Liechtenstein, where on March 19, 1934, they moved into the sanatorium at the resort on the Alm Silum. See Baum, *Against the Wind*, 234–35.

[5.] Not extant.

[6.] The rest of the letter is missing.

[1.] Literary estate of Erwin Sutz, Herrliberg, Switzerland; handwritten. See also *NL*, A 29,4 (13); typewritten copy. Excerpted in *GS* 1:39–41. Letterhead: "Association of German Evangelical Congregations in Great Britain and Ireland."

[2.] Not extant.

[3.] In Wiesendangen, Switzerland, in the canton of Zurich, near Winterthur.

[4.] [Bonhoeffer's word here is *Kirchenregiment*; usually he and others speak of a church government (*Kirchenregierung*).—KC]

[5.] On February 13, 1934, Bonhoeffer had participated in a meeting of the Pastors' Emergency League in Hanover (see 1/76). Two weeks later Heckel summoned him to Berlin (see 1/82 and *DB-ER*, 364–65).

away from here, and for that reason alone I am digging in my heels. But all   128
that doesn't matter; it's not very interesting for you.

What is going on in the church in Germany you probably know as well as
I do. Nat. Socialism has brought about the end of the church in Germany
and has pursued it single-mindedly. We can be grateful to them, in the way
the Jews had to be grateful to Sennacherib.[6] For me there can be no doubt
that this is clearly the reality that we face. Naive, starry-eyed idealists like
Niemöller still think they are the real Nat. Socialists[7]—and perhaps it's
a benevolent Providence that keeps them under the spell of this delusion.
Maybe it is even in the interest of the Church Struggle, for anyone who is still
at all interested in this struggle. For some time it hasn't even been about what
it appears to be about; the lines have been drawn somewhere else entirely.
And while I'm working with the church opposition with all my might, it's
perfectly clear to me that *this* opposition is only a very temporary transitional
phase on the way to an opposition of a very different kind, and that very few
of those involved in this preliminary skirmish are going to be there for that
second struggle. I believe that all of Christendom should be praying with us
for the coming of resistance "to the point of shedding blood"[8] and for the
finding of people who can suffer it through. Simply suffering is what it will
be about, not parries, blows, or thrusts such as may still be allowed and possible in the preliminary battles; the real struggle that perhaps lies ahead must
be one of simply suffering through in faith. Then, perhaps then God will
acknowledge his church again with his word, but until then a great deal must
be believed, and prayed, and suffered. You know, it is my belief—perhaps it
will amaze you—that it is the *Sermon on the Mount* that has the deciding word
on this whole affair. I think that Barth's theology—and surely Brunner's   129
ethics[9] too—have delayed recognition of this a little while, but have certainly also made it possible. I wish I could talk all these things over with you
again now, three years on.[10] So very much has completely changed, and
perhaps I wasn't really hearing you then, perhaps I just argued things away,
so it's partly my fault that you haven't been going ahead of me all this time

---

[6.] Cf. 2 Kings 18:13–19:37 and Isaiah 36–38, also 1/147.

[7.] At a March 1934 meeting of the inner circle of the Pastors' Emergency League,
Martin Niemöller had proposed a discussion about whether Emergency League members
should join the Nazi Party as a united group, in order to counter the political defamation
they were experiencing (cf. J. Schmidt, *Martin Niemöller im Kirchenkampf,* 181).

[8.] Heb. 12:4: "In your struggle against sin you have not yet resisted to the point of
shedding your blood."

[9.] Emil Brunner, *Divine Imperative.* [The original German edition, *Das Gebot und die
Ordnungen,* had appeared in 1933.—KC]

[10.] Sutz and Bonhoeffer had been students together at Union Theological Seminary
in New York in 1930–31. See *DB-ER,* 152–53.

and showing me the way in this regard. I can't yet see clearly, only shadowy outlines of what is happening and what should happen, but your constant, ongoing questioning has not been the least of that which has brought me to where I am. I have found a few people who are continuing, along with me, to ask these questions. Please write and tell me sometime how you preach about the Sermon on the Mount. I'm currently trying to do so, to keep it infinitely plain and simple, but it always comes back to *keeping* the commandments and not trying to evade them. *Following*[11] Christ—what that really is, I'd like to know—it is not exhausted by our concept of faith. I'm doing some writing that I think of as a "spiritual exercise"—only as a first step.[12] Please help me with this. How long I shall remain a pastor, and how long in this church,[13] I don't know. Possibly not very long. This winter I'd like to go to India.[14]

Couldn't you come over here sometime? Well, that's enough—perhaps all this seems quite mad to you. Please just write again, and then I'll write some more.

With many thanks, sincerely your old friend
Dietrich Bonhoeffer

130   **94. From Charles Freer Andrews**[1]

Selly Oak
Birmingham
April 29, 1934

Dear Pastor Bonhoeffer,

I am so sorry not to have written before. I have been away in Denmark, Sweden and the Netherlands and also in Switzerland and have not had a moment to write to you. I should very much like to have a talk with you before I go out to South

---

[11.] [In German, *Nachfolge*. See ed. note 12.—KC].

[12.] These are some of the early preliminary reflections on Bonhoeffer's *Discipleship* (*Nachfolge*, 1937), *DBWE* 4.

[13.] [Bonhoeffer uses here *Kirche*, not *Gemeinde* (local church or congregation), and thus could be taken to be implying that he was dubious about remaining a pastor in the German Evangelical Church as a whole. But the final sentence of the paragraph would seem to indicate that it was his continuance in the London pastorate that was primarily or more immediately in question.—KC]

[14.] Bonhoeffer hoped to visit Mahatma Gandhi; cf. 1/54, 1/94, 1/127, 1/154, and 1/158.

[1.] *NL*, Anh. D 1, 4 (9); photocopy of the handwritten text; in original English, including errors. Bonhoeffer had met Andrews [an Anglican priest with strong Quaker leanings,

Africa but the days now are so few and my own engagements are so uncertain that I am hardly able to fix any time to see you. But I feel strongly that you ought to go to Woodbrooke if possible and meet Mr. Horace Alexander 144 Oak Tree Lane Selly Oak, Birmingham, who can tell you all about the "peace" movement in India.[2] I am likely to be at Woodbrooke up to May 6 but even that is not quite certain. I sail for South Africa on May 11. It is just possible that I may go away next Sunday[3] to my sisters to say goodbye.

Could you possibly visit Woodbrooke and see our friends there who both love and know India and also are trying to follow the Sermon on the mount? There are two especially Jack Hoyland and Horace Alexander. *Do* write to the latter and arrange a visit even if you cannot see me.

Yours very sincerely
C. F. Andrews

95. To George Bell[1]   131

May 1st 1934

My Lord Bishop,

referring to our conversation last Friday,[2] I thought it might be of interest to you and perhaps even for the circular letter that you see the new seal of our German Church.[3] It needs no comments.

---

confidant of Gandhi, and friend of Rabindranath Tagore—KC] in August 1932 at the World Alliance meetings in Geneva and Gland, Switzerland (see *DB-ER*, 252–53). This letter is obviously related to Bonhoeffer's plan to go to India in the winter of 1934–35 (see 1/93, ed. note 14).

[2.] After the failure of the [second] Round Table Conference in London in late 1931, Gandhi and his satyagraha movement struggled—using fasting as a method of nonviolent resistance—against the partition of India that was being sought by the British colonial regime.

[3.] Sunday, May 6, 1934.

[1.] LPL, Bell Papers 42, 25; handwritten; in original English, including errors. See also *NL*, A 42,1 (14); typewritten copy. Previously published in *GS* 2:171. On the stationery is a handwritten note by Bell's office: "German Church—answered 3/5/34."

[2.] Conversation at the Athenaeum on April 27, 1934 (cf. 1/92). Apparently Bonhoeffer's proposal for an ecumenical pastoral letter was first concretely discussed at this time (cf. 1/89 and 1/103).

[3.] The seal of the "German Evangelical Church—The Reich Bishop" contained, in addition to the Christian symbol of the cross, the Luther rose and a swastika (see the illustration in *GS* 2:32).

Secondly, I have just received the message from my Berlin student friends that they have to prove their Aryan ancestry and descent in order to be admitted to the theological examinations.

Thirdly, two letters of leading oppositionals foretelling a very dark near future. The government seems to be willing to maintain Müller at any cost, even with force. In Saxonia [the] situation seems to be most critical.[4]

There is an idea going about in Berlin concerning the organisation of a Council of all parties and to bring about the split on such an occasion.

I hope very much that your letter will contain a word of sympathy for the suppressed opposition overthere. It would help them much. Sometimes they seem to be rather exhausted.

I remain, My Lord Bishop,
Yours very respectfully
Dietrich Bonhoeffer

132 **96. From the Diary of Julius Rieger**[1]

May 2, 1934

On Friday, April 13, there was a crisis in the cabinet. Schacht[2] is said to have threatened to resign, and apparently Hitler wanted to let him go. But Schmitt[3] is said to have declared that, in solidarity with Schacht, he too would resign if Schacht did so. In the end, it appears they managed to arrive at some sort of agreement (source Bonhoeffer).

[4.] The provincial synod of Saxony, at its March 16, 1934, meeting—which the Confessing Church group "Gospel and Church" did not attend—had implemented the integration measures introduced by "Legal Administrator" (*Rechtswalter*) Jäger. Then, on May 4, 1934, despite vigorous protests, the provincial church of Saxony was completely taken over by the Reich Church (cf. Meier, *Der evangelische Kirchenkampf*, 1:205 and 306).

[1.] *NL*, A 41,9 (18); typewritten copy. Previously published in *GS* 6:324.
[2.] Reich Bank president Hjalmar Schacht.
[3.] Reich Minister for Economic Affairs Kurt Paul Schmitt.

97. From George Bell[1]

2nd May 1934

My dear Bonhoeffer,

I send you a draft letter to members of the Oecumenical Council.[2] I should be most grateful if you would tell me how it strikes you. I think myself it is too long. I hope it is properly balanced. Any points which you think might be better expressed, or omitted or added, will be most thankfully received. I should naturally be grateful for the earliest possible reply.

You will note a guarded reference to the Ulm Declaration at the end of the second paragraph.[3]

Yours ever,
p.p. GEORGE CICESTR:
(Dictated by the Bishop but not signed, owing to absence.)

98. From George Bell[1]

133

3rd May, 1934

My dear Bonhoeffer,

I got your letter with the seal of the German Church[2] this morning. It was posted to Winchester, Chichester having been misread for Winchester, so it reached me after I had sent my draft letter to you.[3] Comment is indeed unnecessary on the character of that seal.[4] Thank you too for the other information you give me in your letter of May 1st.

[1.] LPL, Bell Papers 42, 26; carbon copy, with handwritten note for the file: "German Church"; in original English, including errors. See also *NL*, A 42,2 (6); typewritten copy. Previously published in *GS* 1:189.

[2.] Bell enclosed a draft (not found) of his "Ascension Day message" (see 1/103); on the same day he also sent a copy of the same to Alphons Koechlin for approval (see Bell and Koechlin, *Briefwechsel*, 125), as well as copies to J. H. Oldham and Hans Schönfeld (see their replies in LPL, Bell Papers 5, 418, and 19, 246–47). [On Oldham's involvement in the preparation of this message, see also Clements, *Faith on the Frontier*, 292.—KC]

[3.] See 1/103, ed. note 4. [See also 1/92, ed. note 4.—KC]

[1.] LPL, Bell Papers 42, 27; carbon copy; in original English, including errors. See also *NL*, A 42,2 (7); typewritten copy. Previously published in *GS* 2:172.

[2.] See 1/95, ed. note 3.

[3.] See 1/97.

[4.] See 1/95, ed. note 3.

My trouble with my draft letter is that it is too long—amongst other things. But I am waiting for your comments.

Yours ever,

[George Cicestr]

99. To George Bell[1]

May 3rd, 1934

My Lord Bishop,

thank you very much for your most interesting letter.[2] I think it will be a very helpfull and important document in the present situation. May I just add a few words with regard to details:

You speak "of the loyalty (of the pastors) to what they believe to be Christian truth." Could you not say perhaps: to what *is* the Christian truth—or "to what we believe with them to be the Christian truth"? It sounds as if you want to take distance from their belief. I think even the Reichsbishop would be right in taking disciplinary measures against ministers, if they stand for something else but the truth of the Gospel (even if they believe it to be the truth)—the real issue is that they are under coercion on account of their loyalty to what *is* the true Gospel—namely their opposition against the *racial and political element as constituent for the Church* of Christ.[3]

Is not perhaps the word "one-sided" (page 2) misleading?[4] It could seem as if one possibly could sympathize with *both* sides at the same time and as if the difference between both sides were not ultimate, so that one just has to decide for either side. I am affraid, Heckel will make use of this "one-sided" in a way you do not want it to be used.

p. 3 "the introduction of racial distinctions" *and political principles*—could that be added?[5] It is always the same error—the swastica in the Church seal! Many sources of revelation besides and except Christ. Other constitutive norms for the Church than Christ himself.

[1.] LPL, Bell Papers 42, 28–29; handwritten; in original English, including errors. See also *NL*, A 42,1 (15); typewritten copy. Previously published in *GS* 1:189–91.

[2.] Of May 2, 1934, with the draft of the "Ascension Day Message" (1/97).

[3.] Bell then changed his text to conform to Bonhoeffer's objection (see 1/103, ed. note 3).

[4.] Reference unclear; Bell must have dropped the indicated passage (see 1/103).

[5.] Bell left this as "the introduction of racial distinctions" (see 1/103). In contrast to Bonhoeffer, Hans Schönfeld had suggested that the bishop drop this accusation as "a weak point in such statement" (reply of May 4, 1934; LPL, Bell Papers 5, 418).

Finally, I think the stimulating effect of your letter would be still a bit stronger if you would hint at the absolute necessity of unanimousness with regard to some crucial principles, and that any further cooperation would be useless and unchristian, if such unity would prove unreal. If there would be no word of that sort, Müller and his men will be released, for they would win time till August[6] and would not need to be afraid of any definite action from your side in the near future anymore. The policy of the more intelligent people in the Churchgovernment has always been: "discuss the problems as much as you want, but let us act"—the thing they are affraid of is not discussion but action. If they could gather from this letter that the ecumenic movement would leave them alone for a certain while, they would consider it a success for themselves. So I think it necessary not to give them the possibility of such an illusion (of which they would make any political use they can!).

Excuse my frank comments to your letter. You know that I am most thank-   135
full to you for giving me the chance of expressing my opinion to you so frankly.

I remain with great gratitude
Yours very respectfully
Dietrich Bonhoeffer

100. From Ernst Wolf[1]

Bonn, May 6, 1934

Dear Colleague Bonhoeffer,

It was Walter Dreß, your brother-in-law, who gave me your address. You may have heard from him, since I asked him a few weeks ago, before he visited you,[2] to tell you that the journal *Zwischen den Zeiten*[3] is going to resume publication as a monthly under the title *Evangelische Theologie*.[4] It will be based on what appeared in 1933 as *Blätter zur kirchlichen Lage*,[5] edited by H. Diem and P. Schempp, among

---

[6.] Until the ecumenical conference in Fanø.

[1.] BA Koblenz, NL Ernst Wolf 367, vol. 31; carbon copy.

[2.] Walter Dreß and his wife, Susanne, visited Bonhoeffer in London from March 22 until around April 19, 1934.

[3.] ["Between the Times"—KC] The bimonthly journal, founded in 1922 by Barth, Thurneysen, and Gogarten, and edited by Georg Merz, ceased publication in 1933, when Barth and Thurneysen withdrew their participation because of Gogarten's leanings toward the German Christians.

[4.] ["Evangelical Theology"—KC]

[5.] ["On the Church Situation"—KC]

others. After thinking it over for a long time, I yielded to the urging of K. Barth, among others, and have accepted the editorship together with a few other men.[6] The enclosure will give you their names as well as other details.

Our intentions are stated in a foreword that points the way ahead and thus represents a commitment.[7] I have nothing more to add to it at this time. You will be able to judge for yourself and on this basis to reply when I now ask if you would be willing to support us by joining with us in this effort.

136 There appears to be a not inconsiderable demand for a theological journal such as this one that we are planning, especially in the north and east of Germany. I constantly find new evidence of this. Thus it seems to me, especially since we have managed to get the approval of the Chamber of Literature to resume publication in spite of the ban,[8] that we are called upon to put into this all the effort that it will demand of us. It is the cause that weighs on us and this present situation, which leads me to approach you in spite of what I can imagine are the particularly heavy demands of your ministry.

I would appreciate it if you could let me know soon how you respond to this in principle.[9] Perhaps I can also hope for an actual contribution from you before too long.[10]

With all best wishes for you and for your work,
Yours respectfully,
Ernst Wolf

  Enclosures: 3[11]

[6.] In addition to Ernst Wolf, the editors included Wilhelm Niesel, Paul Schempp, and Wolfgang Trillhaas. For an account of the founding and orientation of *Evangelische Theologie*, see the articles by Ernst Wolf, Gerhard Sauter, and Helmut Gollwitzer in *Evangelische Theologie* 44 (1984): 101–47.

[7.] This foreword by Ernst Wolf ("Evangelische Theologie [1934], Vorwort der Herausgeber") was reprinted in *Evangelische Theologie* 44 (1984): 102–11.

[8.] On February 2, 1934, the Reich Press Guild extended the moratorium, during which no new newspapers or journals might be founded, until September 30, 1934. The Press Guild—like the Reich Chamber of Literature—had been constituted on September 22, 1933, as an instrument of *Gleichschaltung* [the official term for bringing everything into line with Nazi ideology and practice—KC] by Minister of Propaganda Goebbels.

[9.] See Bonhoeffer's reply of May 11, 1934 (1/104).

[10.] In August 1935, Bonhoeffer published in *Evangelische Theologie* the essay "Die Bekennende Kirche und die Ökumene" (*DBW* 14, 2/6) [previously published in English as "The Confessing Church and the Ecumenical Movement," *NRS*, 326–44—KC], and in June 1936 "Zur Frage nach der Kirchengemeinschaft" (*DBW* 14, 2/19.1) [previously published in English as "The Question of the Boundaries of the Church and Church Union," *Way to Freedom*, 75–96—KC].

[11.] Not extant.

101. Theodor Heckel to Baron Bruno Schröder[1]

Berlin-Charlottenburg, May 8, 1934

Dear Baron Schröder,

During our last conversation in London in February,[2] we agreed that, in order finally to clear up the situation brought about by your telegram to the Reich bishop[3] and the telegram from the London pastors to the church government,[4] you would put before the committee of the Association of Congregations my declaration to the London pastors, which had received their unanimous assent.[5]   137 Might I therefore perhaps inquire whether the committee has met by now, and what conclusions were reached as a result?

With respectful greetings,
Yours sincerely,
Heckel

102. From Erich Seeberg[1]

Berlin, May 9,1934

Dear Colleague Bonhoeffer,

I am happy to grant you a leave of absence for the coming summer semester;[2] but I must also inform you that if you require a leave of absence for the next winter semester as well, this must be requested from the minister.[3] I have not, however,

---

[1.] ADBC, Association of Congregations 4, 12; typewritten. See also *NL*, A 41,1 (34); typewritten copy. Previously published in *GS* 6:322. On the same sheet of paper, a handwritten note by the recipient: "Copy sent to Pastor Hermann [Johannesburg] 25/5/34—Answer *25/5/34*."

[2.] Before Heckel's return to Germany following his negotiations in London on February 8 and 9, 1934; see 1/74.1 and also *DB-ER*, 353.

[3.] Of January 9, 1934 (1/52).

[4.] Of January 6, 1934 (1/48).

[5.] Declaration of February 9, 1934. This statement had certainly not received the "unanimous assent" of all the pastors; indeed, Bonhoeffer and several of his colleagues had protested vigorously against it (see *DB-ER*, 353, and Schröder's reply of May 25, 1934 [1/112]).

[1.] *NL*, A 39,2 (6); typewritten; letterhead "Protestant Theological Faculty of the Friedrich Wilhelm University—The Dean." Previously published in *GS* 2:179.

[2.] Cf. 1/45 and 1/51.

[3.] Minister for Cultural Affairs Bernhard Rust (see *DB-ER*, 410).

lost hope that conditions in the church will gradually settle down, so that you will also feel inwardly that it is possible for you to return to Germany.

With greetings and best wishes,
Yours sincerely,
E. Seeberg
Dean

103. George Bell to the Members of "Life and Work"
(Ascension Day Message) [1]

A Message
regarding the German Evangelical Church
to the Representatives of the Churches
on the Universal Christian Council for Life and Work
from the Bishop of Chichester

I have been urged from many quarters[2] to issue some statement to my fellow members of the Universal Christian Council for Life and Work upon the present position in the German Evangelical Church, especially as it affects other Churches represented on the Universal Christian Council for Life and Work.

138

The situation is, beyond doubt, full of anxiety. To estimate it aright we have to remember the fact that a revolution has taken place in the German State, and that as a necessary result the German Evangelical Church was bound to be faced with new tasks and many new problems requiring time for their full solution. It is none the less true that the present position is being watched by members of the Christian Churches abroad not only with great interest, but with a deepening concern. The chief cause of anxiety is the assumption by the Reichbishop in the name of the principle of leadership of autocratic powers unqualified by constitutional or traditional restraints which are without precedent in the history of the Church. The exercise of these autocratic powers by the Church Government appears incompatible with the Christian principle of seeking in brotherly fellowship to receive the guidance of the Holy Spirit. It has had disastrous results on the internal unity of the Church; and the disciplinary measures which have been taken by the Church government against Ministers of the Gospel on account of

---

[1.] From "Minutes of the Universal Christian Council for Life and Work, Fanø, Denmark, Geneva 1934," 65–66; in original English, including errors. WCC Library, Geneva, BR 280.24 U 3 m. Previously published in *GS* 1:192–93. See also *NL,* A 42,3 (3); hectograph. [Also published in the *Times,* May 12, 1934.—KC]

[2.] See especially Bonhoeffer's letters urging Bell to write (1/79, 1/89, and 1/92).

their loyalty to the fundamental principles of Christian truth,[3] have made a painful impression on Christian opinion abroad, already disturbed by the introduction of racial distinctions in the universal fellowship of the Christian Church. No wonder that voices should be raised in Germany itself making a solemn pronouncement before the whole Christian world on the dangers to which the spiritual life of the Evangelical Church is exposed.[4]

There are indeed other problems which the German Evangelical Church is facing, which are the common concern of the whole of Christendom. These are such fundamental questions as those respecting the nature of the Church, its witness, its freedom and its relation to the secular power. At the end of August the Universal Council will be meeting in Denmark. The Agenda of the Council will inevitably include a consideration of the religious issues raised by the present situation in the German Evangelical Church.[5] It will also have to consider the wider questions which affect the life of all the Churches in Christendom. A Committee met last month in Paris to prepare for its work, and its report will shortly be published entitled, "The Church, the State, and the World Order."[6] I hope that this meeting will assist the Churches in their friendship with each other, and in their task of reaching a common mind on the implications of their faith in relation to the dominant tendencies in modern thought and society, and in particular to the growing demands of the modern State.

139

The times are critical. Something beyond conferences and consultations is required. We need as never before to turn our thoughts and spirits to God. More earnest efforts must be made in our theological study. Above all more humble and fervent prayer must be offered to our Father in Heaven.[7] May He, Who alone

---

[3.] The words "the fundamental principles of Christian truth" replace, in response to Bonhoeffer's objection (see 1/99), the distanced formulation of the original draft: "what they believe to be Christian truth."

[4.] This is an allusion to the Ulm Declaration of April 22, 1934, in which representatives of the Confessing Church from all over Germany, in protest against the unjust regime of the Reich Church, had declared themselves to be "the lawful Evangelical Church of Germany before the whole of Christendom" (see 1/92, 1/97, and 1/125).

[5.] Hans Schönfeld had tried in vain to dissuade the bishop from including this pointed emphasis on the German situation with reference to the conference theme. His alternative formulation was ". . . raised so urgently by the present world situation and the development of the different nations" (see 1/99, ed. note 5).

[6.] On the Paris conference, see 1/114, ed. note 4.

[7.] The call for "more earnest efforts . . . in our theological study" and "more humble and fervent prayer" "beyond conferences and consultations" was apparently included at Koechlin's suggestion in his reply of May 5, 1934 (see Bell and Koechlin, *Briefwechsel*, 126).

can lighten our darkness give us grace! May He, Who knows our weakness and our blindness, through a new outpouring of the Spirit enable the whole Church to bear its witness to its Lord with courage and faith!

(Signed) George Cicestr:
Ascensiontide 1934[8]

104. To Ernst Wolf[1]

May 11, 1934

Dear Professor Wolf:

Thank you very much for your letter.[2] I am delighted that you have found a way to fill the disturbing gap that was left when *Zwischen den Zeiten* went under.[3] I shall be glad to offer my help when you can use it[4] and wish you well with this great undertaking. May it help to clear away the darkness and to reveal many paths that have not yet been traveled. May it become that which we are all longing for—a courageous journal.

    Once again my sincere thanks, and all good wishes,

Yours sincerely,
Dietrich Bonhoeffer

105. From Théodore de Félice[1]

Geneva, May 11, 1934

Dear Friend,

The exact location of our study week[2] this summer has been determined. It is Fanø, near Esbjerg in Denmark. Given the available transportation, although our study week will begin on August 22 in the evening, it will not end until late morning on August 30, so that we can leave in the afternoon.

[8.] May 10, 1934.

[1.] *NL*, A 41,9 (23); handwritten copy of typewritten letter from London. Previously published in *GS* 6:294.
[2.] Of May 6, 1934 (1/100).
[3.] See 1/100, ed. note 3.
[4.] See 1/100, ed. note 10.

[1.] WCC Archives, World Alliance, Letters to Dietrich Bonhoeffer; carbon copy; written in French. Cf. Winterhager's reply of May 22, 1934 (1/109), and Bonhoeffer's of June 17, 1934 (1/115).
[2.] Fifth Ecumenical Youth Conference, August 22–29, 1934 (cf. 1/141).

I would like to know where you are in your negotiations for finding delegates for this study week. Since our study week is taking place in Denmark, we think that it is necessary for Mr. Sparring-Petersen, who is a member of our committee,[3] to collaborate fairly closely in the planning of our week. If you agree with this proposal, would you be kind enough to forward the enclosed letter to him, once you have read it yourself.

Would you personally be able to give a presentation on the third subject on the agenda, "What kind of action must we take, as individuals and as Christians, when the state comes into conflict with Christian principles?"[4] We thought that for each subject there would be two speakers.

Can you tell me what stage the preparations have reached for the theological meeting in Luxembourg?[5] Would you tell me at the same time if there would be any objection to announcing your lecture in advance in the Ecumenical Press Service, or if you consider it preferable not to mention it ahead of time.

Very cordially yours,
Th. de Félice

106. To George Bell[1]

May 15th 1934

My Lord Bishop,

your letter[2] has made a very great impression on me and on all my friends here who have read it. In its conciseness it strikes at the chief points and leaves no escape for misinterpretation. I am absolutely sure that this letter of yours will have the greatest effect in Germany and will indebt the opposition very much to you. And what I think is most important, this letter will help the opposition to see that this whole conflict is not only within the church,

[3.] The joint Youth Commission of the World Alliance and the Universal Council.

[4.] Talks on this theme were finally given on August 25 by Otto Dudzus and J. P. Ricoeur (see 1/141, pp. 203–4).

[5.] At the meeting of the Youth Commission in Paris, January 31–February 1, 1934, Bonhoeffer had been assigned to prepare an "Anglo-French-German theological conference" for young pastors. It was planned for early September, on the theme "The State from a Christian Viewpoint." (Minutes of Paris meeting, literary estate of Eberhard Bethge, Fanø file); see also Winterhager's reply of May 22, 1934 (1/109).

[1.] LPL, Bell Papers 42, 30; typewritten; in original English, including errors. See also *NL*, A 42,1 (16); typewritten copy. Previously published in *GS* 1:194. On the same paper is a note by Bell's office: "German Church—answered 16/5/34. Copy."

[2.] Bell's Ascension Day message to the members of the Universal Christian Council for Life and Work; see 1/103.

but strikes at the very roots of National-socialisme. The issue is the freedom of the church rather then any particular confessional problem. I am very anxious to learn what the effect on the Churchgovernment will be.

Once more I wish to thank you for your letter which is a living document of ecumenic and mutual responsibility. I hope, it will help others to speak out as clearly as you did.

I remain, My Lord Bishop, yours very respectfully,
Dietrich Bonhoeffer

142   **107. From George Bell**[1]

16th May, 1934

My dear Bonhoeffer,

I am very glad indeed to get your letter[2] and to know that my Message appeals to you so strongly, and I hope it may help to do the good you say.

I hear to-day from Keller, on his way back from Berlin, that he had two hours' conversation with Müller, Heckel and Jäger on May 11, on behalf of the Federal Council[3] of U.S.A., resulting in the promise of Jäger to suspend disciplinary measures of a non-political character, and a statement by Müller that they would try to do something for the victims of the Aryan paragraph.[4] That was before my Message was known, or the letter from the Presbyterian Alliance.[5]

Yours sincerely,
[George Cicestr]

[1.] LPL, Bell Papers 42, 31; carbon copy; in original English, including errors. See also *NL*, A 42,2 (8); typewritten copy. Previously published in *GS* 2:172.

[2.] Of May 15, 1934; see 1/106.

[3.] [The Federal Council of Churches in the United States, which became the National Council of Churches in 1950. The Federal Council had sent protests to German church leaders in Berlin about the "Aryan" paragraph within the church and about Nazi measures against the Jews more generally.—KC]

[4.] Cf. the "Report of Dr. Adolf Keller's visit to the Reich Bishop," LKA EKvW, 5,1, Fasc. 261/I.

[5.] Letter from the executive committee of the Reformed World Alliance to the Moderator of the Reformed Alliance, Hermann A. Hesse; see *Reformierte Kirchenzeitung* 84 (May 27, 1934): 175.

108. From Théodore de Félice[1]

Geneva, May 17, 1934

My dear sir and friend,

Enclosed please find the proposal for distributing the subsidies and also the free participation in the Study Week in Denmark.[2] You will notice that we have exceeded the amount allotted.[3] In order to balance the budget, we must count on the fact that there are always countries that don't send their delegates, and that is why this year we cannot allow subsidies not used by one country to be transferred to another.

143

May I remind you also that you must find from among your delegates someone who would be willing to treat the following subject for a quarter of an hour on the morning of August 23rd: "Church and state at the present time and the consequent difficulties for our ecumenical action in Germany."[4]

I intend to publish soon an invitation and program for the study week in English and in French. How many copies would you like?

Very cordially yours,
Th. de Félice

[1.] WCC Archives, World Alliance, Letters to Dietrich Bonhoeffer; carbon copy; written in French. Cf. Winterhager's reply (1/109) and Bonhoeffer's letter of June 17, 1934 (1/115).

[2.] Ecumenical Youth Conference in Fanø, August 22–29, 1934 (see 1/141).

[3.] According to the Minutes of the Paris meeting of the Youth Commission, January 31–February 1, 1934, in which Bonhoeffer participated (literary estate of Eberhard Bethge, Fanø file), 2000 Swiss francs, largely from the World Alliance budget, were available for the study week.

[4.] This report was given, right at the beginning of the Youth Conference, by Winterhager on behalf of the German delegation (see Winterhager's reply, 1/109, and the conference minutes, 1/141).

109. Jürgen Winterhager to Théodore de Félice[1]

Berlin, May 22, 1934

Dear Monsieur de Félice,

I have much pleasure in replying to both of your letters (May 11. and May 17.)[2] which P. Bonhoeffer has sent on to me. I find that there shall be three delegates[3] to the "semaine d'études." Myself being one of those three (according to P. Bonhoeffer's former statement). I shall send you the names and addresses of the other two within three weeks-time. Unless different instructions are coming from you, I shall also send that list of names to M. Sparring-Petersen—in the same way as I am going to forward your annexe-letter to him.[4]

Concerning the exposé of the third subject in the order, P. Bonhoeffer will write to you himself in a short time.

The rencontre théologique au Luxembourg[5] will take place during the *first week of September*. In the whole there will be ca. 12 delegates of the three nations concerned. When advertising this rencontre, you need not publish the names of the delegates, because all our oecumenic group members will be able to associate all necessary details about it on account of former informations. And in our letters and circulaires here, we just let it be known as the "Réunion franco-germano-britannique." That will do.

With reference to your first question in the 17.5 letter, I should like to let you know that P. Bonhoeffer has appointed his German representative (with whom M. Henriod has been recently—when in Berlin)[6] to deliver the short address on August 23, at Fanø. As to the last enquiry, we should like to ask for four exemplaires of invitation-programmes in English or French.

144

[1.] WCC Archives, Youth Commission of World Alliance, Félice's Correspondence; typewritten; in original English, including errors; typewritten letterhead: "Ecumenical Youth Commission" [in French and German]/"German Secretariat" [in German].

[2.] See 1/105 and 1/108. At the Youth Commission Meeting in Paris, January 31–February 1, 1934, Winterhager had been appointed as Bonhoeffer's assistant for the ecumenical youth work in Germany (literary estate of Eberhard Bethge, Fanø file, minutes); see *DB-ER*, 375.

[3.] These were the three official delegates, whose expenses were to be paid by the Youth Commission. Additional delegates could attend at their own expense (see Félice's reply of May 29, 1934, WCC Archives, Youth Commission of World Alliance, Félice Correspondence).

[4.] See 1/105.

[5.] Cf. 1/105, ed. note 5.

[6.] This refers to Winterhager himself.

With kindest regards from several members of Oecumenic Youth Groups in Germany,

Very sincerely yours,
Cecile[7]

110. To Julie Bonhoeffer[1]

May 22, 1934

Dear Grandmama,

I really have a guilty conscience, since I still haven't answered your last letter.[2] I had hoped things would quiet down somewhat after Easter, but there is little sign of that yet. Now that Pentecost is past I am again hoping for some peace and quiet. It is really hard to understand how so much can be going on in such a small congregation. But it has the effect that at the beginning a great many requests come in from all sorts of places, and then later there are fewer. It's only disagreeable for me because it keeps me from getting to my own work as I would like to do. Preaching every week still makes a lot of work for me, and I would like to take a break from it. But that's just it, one cannot do that, it cannot depend on whether one is in the mood or not. In any case, I find preaching much harder in summer than in winter. The newness of nature makes one forget so easily everything else that is not at all new. Just now it is quite lovely here. We had a church excursion yesterday and were outdoors all day, in an area[3] that is famous because at this time of year the whole forest floor is absolutely covered in blue, for hundreds of meters, by a kind of bellflower.[4] Furthermore, I was greatly surprised to find wild rhododendrons in the woods, a whole lot of them, hundreds of bushes growing close together. They were just coming into bloom, and probably in two weeks they will be a fabulous sight. It's a completely different climate here, very unpleasant in winter, but all the more beautiful in spring.

145

[7.] Winterhager's code name.

[1.] *NL*, A 39,4; typewritten. Excerpt in *GS* 2:181–83.

[2.] Not extant.

[3.] [This would most likely have been Epping Forest, just to the northeast of London, a favorite spot for outings from St. Paul's Church as for other London churches and Sunday schools in the 1930s, with special facilities provided for them there (information to KC from Ruth Colman, daughter of Frank Goetz and Doris Dickens, whose wedding Bonhoeffer conducted on May 3, 1934; see 3/9).—KC]

[4.] [The bluebell (*Endymion nonscriptus*), which flowers profusely in many parts of Britain in springtime, is relatively scarce on the European continent, hence Bonhoeffer's evident unfamiliarity with it.—KC]

It's still very uncertain how much longer I shall be here. I recently had a letter from E. Seeberg, the dean,[5] confirming my current leave of absence and informing me that if I want to extend it, I'll have to apply to the ministry for permission. That is very difficult to do, so I assume that I shall then have to make a final decision whether to return to an academic career. I'm not so tremendously keen on it anymore, and there seems no reason to suppose I shall feel any keener by this winter. It's just that I'm concerned about doing something for my students, but perhaps other ways will be open to me.

146

Before I tie myself down anywhere for good, I'm thinking again of going to India. I've given a good deal of thought lately to the issues there and believe that there could be important things to be learned.[6] In any case it sometimes seems to me that there's more Christianity in their "heathenism" than in the whole of our Reich Church. Christianity did in fact come from the East originally, but it has become so westernized and so permeated by civilized thought that, as we can now see, it is almost lost to us. Unfortunately I have little confidence left in the church opposition. I don't at all like the way they're going about things and really dread the time when they assume responsibility and we may be compelled yet again to witness a terrible compromising of Christianity. At the practical level I'm not yet certain how the plan for India is going to work out. There's a possibility—but please don't mention this to students etc.—that I might go to Rabindranath Tagore's university.[7] But I'd much rather go directly to Gandhi and already have some very good introductions from his best friends.[8] I might be able to stay there for six months or more as a guest. If this is ever arranged, and I can manage it financially, I would go in the winter.

Before that, however, I will come to Berlin during the summer holidays. I'm thinking of taking my holiday in August. Mama has been asking about my plans, so would you please send this letter on to her? At the beginning of August there is a student conference that I expect I shall have to lead. Then on August 23 a conference begins in Denmark[9] to which I definitely plan

---

[5.] Letter of May 9, 1934, see 1/102.

[6.] Cf. 1/94, ed. note 2.

[7.] Santiniketan, a religious college near Calcutta.

[8.] For example, C. F. Andrews (see 1/94, ed. note 1).

[9.] The Ecumenical Youth Conference was to begin on August 23, 1934 in Fanø, followed the next day by the joint conference of the Universal Christian Council for Life and Work and the World Alliance for Promoting International Friendship through the Churches (see 1/141). At the September 1933 World Alliance meeting in Sofia, Bonhoeffer had been assigned to prepare a position paper on the question of peace for the Fanø conference (see *DB-ER*, 314 and 376).

to go. I have to give a speech there, which I agreed to do over a year ago. In between I would like a restful time in the mountains somewhere and perhaps to go to Oberammergau. I have never seen the play there. Will you be in Friedrichsbrunn?[10] If so, I'll come there in any case.

So, this will give you some idea of what I am doing these days. I am able to   147 write so seldom because I have an awful lot of people who need something urgently, so that I have to write to them.

But I think about you very often and wish I could keep you company sometimes, when you are alone.

Much love and thanks to you, dear Grandmama,
Dietrich

111. To Jürgen Winterhager[1]

Dear Friend,

To answer your letter[2] briefly: at the moment, for two reasons, there is no question of my approaching the Reich Church government to ask that a vicar be assigned to me. (1) My request would be turned down, as was Schönberger's two weeks ago. (2) For the time being I am making no request of any kind whatever of a church government that I do not recognize and that does not recognize me—my position here has (fortunately!) not yet been confirmed![3] Schönberger has decided to bring over a vicar on his own responsibility, who will of course *not* get credit toward ordination. But the congregation simply *needs* the help and will underwrite it.[4] My case is different, since I have been here only six months and my predecessor[5] managed on his own for twelve years and was forty years older. You will not have thought the question you have underlined in red was *my* own, but it is Schönberger's question. It cannot be helped—he does not want someone

---

[10.] [Summer home of the Bonhoeffer family, in the Harz Mountains. See *DB-ER*, 24.—KC]

[1.] *NL*, A 41,9 (22); typewritten copy. Previously published in *GS* 2:179–80. According to *GS* 2:634, the original is in possession of Professor Winterhager, Berlin. According to a note, the envelope bore the postmark "Forest Hill, May 25, 1934, 7:30 P.M."

[2.] Not extant. Winterhager had apparently inquired as to whether he could come to London as a vicar.

[3.] Cf. 1/11.1, 1/50, and 1/125; also *DB-ER*, 329.

[4.] Schönberger's congregation, the Hamburg Lutheran Church, was the largest of the German expatriate congregations in London.

[5.] Friedrich Singer.

148   who "stands on the sidelines." His congregation is as good as a Party cell,[6] so I doubt whether it would suit Konstantin.[7] For my part, I could only invite you *personally*, and of course I'd be glad to do so. Officially there is no hope of it at present.

I have just received a letter from Seeberg[8] in which he told me that if I want to extend my leave from the university over the next winter, I must request it from the ministry. I have no doubt that this would be turned down, which would confront me with the definitive question: here, or the university, or something *entirely* different, such as India[9] or a monastic community.[10] Thus it is downright impossible for me to raise the issue of a vicar to my congregation, since I may already have to inform them in a few weeks that I am leaving.

It also seems much more important to me that we come to something concrete with our settlement plans.[11]

Did you see the *Times* for Saturday after Ascension? They printed Chichester's message.[12]

I was *very* pleased with the report of your work.[13] I am looking forward to the minutes.

Schönberger rang *just now*: he wants someone ideally to come *right away for one year*, or even *half a year*! Grant of three pounds toward travel—that almost covers the entire voyage. He wants an answer soon!

Yours as ever,
D[ietrich] B[onhoeffer]

[6.] I.e., a Nazi Party cell.

[7.] A cover name for Winterhager himself.

[8.] Of May 9, 1934; see 1/102.

[9.] Bonhoeffer was planning a period of study under Gandhi's auspices; see 1/158.

[10.] Cf. 1/133 and 147.

[11.] See Bonhoeffer's January 29, 1935, memorandum to the Youth Commission (1/199).

[12.] Reprint of Bell's Ascension Day message (see 1/103) in the *Times* of May 12, 1934.

[13.] Presumably about theological and ecumenical activities, for example, of Bonhoeffer's former group of students.

112. Baron Bruno Schröder to Theodor Heckel[1]

149

London, May 25, 1934

Dear Bishop Heckel:

Many thanks for your letter of May 8,[2] which I found on my return here.

In view of the state of ecclesiastical affairs in Germany, which is still very unsettled, the churches here are not at present in a position to make any reply. I hope that the time may soon come when unity will be restored in the Evangelical Church in Germany. We shall then have to reconsider the question of the churches over here. To obviate any misunderstanding, I would point out that there was no unanimous assent to the declaration of February 9.[3]

Meanwhile I remain
Sincerely and respectfully yours,
B[runo] S[chröder]

113. From the Diary of Julius Rieger[1]

June 9, 1934

Spoke with Bonhoeffer on the telephone. Eidem had a conversation with the Führer about ten days ago[2] and expressed to him his concern about the Lutheran Church. Eidem spoke for about twenty minutes, and then Hitler answered him very sharply, "in a tone as if he were giving a public speech." A revolution had taken place. Why was he bothering about affairs in Germany? and so on . . .

[1.] ADBC, Association of Congregations 4, 15; carbon copy. See also *NL*, A 41,1 (39); typewritten copy. Note for the file: "Copy sent to Park Street, Pastors Wehrhan, Schönberger, Rieger, and Bonhoeffer—25/5/34." The four London pastors had discussed the day before how Schröder might reply to Heckel. In a letter of the same date to the overseas pastor Johannes Herrmann in Johannesburg (Association of Congregations 8/1; see *NL*, A 41,1–37), Schröder described the attitude of the London congregations affirmed in the letter: "Up to now we have simply kept quiet and (i.e., with regard to Heckel's declaration of February 9, 1934) not made any move, our position being to wait until there should be more clarity in the current church situation."

[2.] See 1/101.

[3.] Heckel's declaration to the London Pastors' conference; see above 1/74.3; see also *DB-ER*, 353.

[1.] *NL*, A 41,9 (18); typewritten copy. Previously published in *GS* 6:324.

[2.] [Erling Eidem was the Lutheran archbishop of Uppsala, Sweden.—KC] Regarding his reception in the chancellery on May 2, 1934, see Eidem's account from memory in Nicolaisen and Kretschmar, *Dokumente zur Kirchenpolitik*, 2:127ff., and Scholder, *Churches and the Third Reich*, 2:77–79.

150   Jacobi and Hildebrandt phoned Bonhoeffer last Monday[3] to say that the Emergency League[4] is looking for someone to direct a training course for pastors, vicars, and students. Bonhoeffer was asked if he would accept this position.

June 19, 1934

In regard to the above-mentioned matter, Bonhoeffer has gone to Berlin[5] and will be back on Saturday the twenty-third.

114. From Hans Schönfeld[1]

Geneva, June 14, 1934

Dear Mr. Bonhoeffer,

In preparing for the joint working meeting of the Ecumenical Council[2] and the World Alliance,[3] it will be important for you to have a full set of the theses and papers that were presented at the ecumenical study conference in Paris. I am having these sent to you for your personal information.

These theses and papers, as well as a report on the discussions, are to be published at the beginning of July in a study book titled "The Church and the Problem of the State Today."[4]

[3.] On June 4, 1934.

[4.] The reference is to the Old Prussian Union Church Council of Brethren, appointed on May 29 in Barmen. The minutes of the council's meeting of June 15 (LKA EKvW, 5,1 no. 94) noted: "*Jacobi:* Our own seminary in Berlin (Bonnhöfer [*sic*])." At the July 4 meeting, planning for Old Prussian Union seminaries in Westphalia and Berlin-Brandenburg had reached the concrete stage. Jacobi reported: "Berlin-Brandenburg is looking for a suitable building. A director (Bonhöfer) is available." Finally, the minutes recorded the decision that "Bonhöfer can take up the post as director of the seminary in Berlin-Brandenburg as of January 1, 1935" (minutes as above; see also *DB-ER*, 410).

[5.] For a conversation with Karl Koch and Martin Niemöller, which also dealt with the problem of participation in the Fanø conference.

[1.] WCC Archives, Life and Work, Study Department, Study Conferences, Fanø 1934; carbon copy; file reference FA 287/34. See also *NL*, A 40,2 (1); typewritten copy. Previously published in *GS* 1:195–96.

[2.] [At that time, the Universal Christian Council for Life and Work in Geneva, the precursor of today's World Council of Churches.—KC]

[3.] In Fanø, August 24–30, 1934.

[4.] ["Die Kirche und das Staatsproblem in der Gegenwart"] This was published as no. 3 in the series Kirche und Welt (Research Department of Life and Work, Geneva 1934) and included contributions by Paul Althaus, Emil Brunner, and Wilhelm Menn. [The series evidently appeared only in German.—KC]

Following the recent meeting in Paris with representatives of our Administra-　151
tive Committee[5] and of the World Alliance, the Research Department was asked
to draw up some questions as guidelines for the discussion at the joint working
meeting in Denmark.[6] For the discussion on church and state on the first day, we
propose the following questions:

1. How does the church of Christ understand the nature and responsibility of
the state?

2. How does the church of Christ understand its relationship to the state, both
in regard to its freedom from and its commitment and obligations to the state?

3. Is the state, on the one hand, or the church, on the other, entitled to make
an unconditional claim for itself, and if so, in what sense?

The discussion will be so directed as to make clear the decisive significance of
these questions and the work to be done on them and will also go into the details
of the way in which the concrete tasks that they pose should be tackled during
the next two or three years.

For the second day's topic, "The church and the peoples of the world," we
have set the following two questions as guidelines of fundamental importance:

1. On what basis, and with what right, does the church have a responsibility
to speak on international problems? How is the relationship of ecumenicity to
internationalism properly understood?

2. By what means, and within what limits, does the church work to help in solving international problems?

We are in agreement that the discussion here should enter into major problems and tasks with regard to international law on a concrete level. You will find
particularly in the theses of Dr. W. Menn a number of basic ideas on this topic,
which are also being developed and amplified for the study book.[7] If you have
proposals and suggestions for the questions for this second day, I would appreciate hearing from you soon. Perhaps you have already heard that on the afternoon
of August 24 in Fanø we are planning a joint working session for the speakers with
representatives of the Research Commission of the Research Department, to plan　152
the course of the discussion in broad outline. I hope you will be able to take part

---

[5.] The five-member Administrative Committee carried on the day-to-day business of
Life and Work.

[6.] Schönfeld's formulation of the questions that follow does in fact refer to that of
Wilhelm Menn. In a letter to Schönfeld of April 19, 1934 (WCC Archives, Study Conferences, Paris 1934, Correspondence), Menn also made suggestions for the choice of discussion speakers, asking "Will Bonhoeffer be there? Will he perhaps attend the dubious World
Alliance Youth Conference?"

[7.] *Internationalität und Ökumenizität* (Internationalism and Ecumenicity), in Kirche
und Welt 3, 91–101.

in this meeting but would be grateful if we could receive your suggestions for it ahead of time.

Yours sincerely,
Hans Schönfeld

114a. Hardy Arnold to Eberhard Arnold[1]

Birmingham, June 14, 1934

My dear Father,

Today I am just writing briefly about two important things, because these last weeks I have here are rather hectic for me and I have to use my time well.

1. In London I met with Pastor Dr. Bonhoeffer, who is pastor of two German congregations in London.[2] He has only been there since October; before that he was lecturer in systematic theology in Berlin, but for well-known reasons[3] moved to London when he had the opportunity. Some time ago he wrote to me[4] asking if he might visit me here, or I him there, because he is interested in founding a community of brothers with some of his students, based entirely on the Sermon on the Mount,[5] and wanted to hear about our experience; he had heard about us through Niemoeller [sic].[6] So I met with him and two of his friends[7] and heard more about their plans.

Their idea is that of a Protestant monastery with things like spiritual exercises, confessional, etc. The assumption is that though they do not know the will of God for our time, they want to try to live exactly according to Jesus' words

---

[1.] Bruderhof Archives, Woodcrest, Rifton, N.Y.; handwritten; unpublished. German edited by Hans Pfeifer. The editors wish to express their gratitude to the Bruderhof Archives and its archivist, Emmy Barth, for permission to publish this and the other letters in this volume by Hardy and Eberhard Arnold.

[2.] The meeting took place on June 12, 1934. Bonhoeffer's time in England is also covered in *DB-ER*, 325–419.

[3.] This is an oblique reference to events in Nazi Germany. [But Bonhoeffer's reasons for coming to London were more complicated than what Hardy surmises; see Bonhoeffer's letter of October 24, 1933, to Karl Barth, 1/2.—KC]

[4.] Letter (not extant) of April 7, 1934, mentioned in Hardy Arnold's letter of April 27, 1934, to Bonhoeffer, 1/92a.

[5.] Wolf-Dieter Zimmermann, a senior member of Bonhoeffer's seminar in 1932–33, reported that such plans had been discussed in Bonhoeffer's seminar since the summer semester of 1932. See Bonhoeffer's correspondence with Wilhelm Stählin in *DBW* 12, 1/20, 1/99, and 1/100, as well as in *Dietrich Bonhoeffer Jahrbuch*, 1:84–88. In the summer of 1933, one idea that arose was to found a community with students in Romania (interview with Zimmermann, January 12, 2004).

[6.] Probably arranged by Franz Hildebrandt.

[7.] Herbert Jehle and Rudolf Weckerling; see Arnold's letter of June 15, 1934, to Edith Böker, 114b.

and by thorough study of the Bible and religious exercises to discern God's will. Unfortunately Bonhoeffer makes a distinction between theology students and lay persons, who might also be accepted, and while he does not entirely reject married participants, he is critical of the idea to the extent that he fears that the love between two persons and family cares would distract married participants from the essential object.

All these points ought to be discussed in depth. The time we had was unfortunately so short that each of us had to confine himself to listening to the other. The *essential* seems to me the fact that behind Bonhoeffer stands a group of sixty to seventy[8] young persons who are seriously struggling to recognize and to do God's will in our time and are prepared to do *everything* to further this cause. There is a group in Berlin, one in Bonn, and one in Tübingen.[9]

Now Dietrich Bonhoeffer wants to *visit* the Bruderhof[10] *in the middle of next week;*[11] he is coming to Germany especially in order to do so and at the same

---

[8.] These figures reflect the great hopes of Bonhoeffer and his friends at this time. In the same vein, Jehle said that "there were in Germany dozens of young theologians who were ready to stick their neck out" but also that "there was considerable despair over the few young men who were available for this" (Larry Rasmussen, "Interview with Herbert Jehle," *Bonhoeffer Jahrbuch*, 2:116 and 115). Weckerling also considered these figures too high (letter of August 27, 2003).

[9.] Presumably Bonhoeffer was thinking of Karl Barth's students in Bonn. On the Bonhoeffer circle in Berlin, see *DB-ER*, 207–10, and Heimbucher, "Christusfriede," 168ff. In a January 1935 letter to the Ecumenical Youth Commission, Bonhoeffer speaks of the successful activities of the "German Fanø group" in Heidelberg and Tübingen. He also mentions serious consideration of founding a "small Christian community," but only with the Berlin group. "This group would also make a definite stand for peace by conscientious objection" (1/199).

[10.] The Bruderhof was a settlement that grew out of a Christian community founded by Eberhard Arnold. The group refused to participate in society, for example, through military service and by membership in an established church. It tried to live according to the Sermon on the Mount, as a community under the direct guidance of the Holy Spirit, and practiced the communal sharing of goods. In 1920 it moved to a house in Sannerz, near Schlüchtern, Germany, and had been living on the income from the Neuwerk-Verlag in Schlüchtern, a publishing house for which Eberhard Arnold was the editor, as well as from its own farming. When Sannerz became too small, a new community, the so-called Rhön-Bruderhof, was founded at Neuhof near Fulda. Under persecution by the Nazis, the Bruderhof community left Germany, going first to England, then to Paraguay, and then to the United States and Canada after World War II. There are now six Bruderhof settlements in the United States, each with several hundred members. See the articles on "Eberhard Arnold" and "Bruderhof" by Hans Zumpe in *Religion in Geschichte und Gegenwart*, 2nd ed., 1:633 and 1425–26, as well as Arnold's *God's Revolution*. [For other works published by the Bruderhof in the United States, see http://www.bruderhof.com/us/E-books/E-books.htm and http://religiousmovements.lib.virginia.edu/nrms/Bruderh.html.—KC]

[11.] The visit to the Bruderhof never took place. On June 19, 1934, Bonhoeffer had a conversation with Karl Koch and Martin Niemöller about starting a seminary in Berlin-

time for negotiations with the Pastors' Emergency League, which is showing a profound interest in his plans.

He is going to *telephone* on Wednesday, probably from Berlin, to discuss everything with you briefly and what is the best way for him to get there. I think this is something very important. It would be wonderful if we could make common cause with this group. In any case, we must be prepared. They are very much looking to us in the Bruderhof, and the two other friends, who will be returning to Germany during the next month, have also promised to visit us.

Bonhoeffer is also planning with one of the two, Dr. Jehle,[12] to go to India in the autumn,[13] to spend half a year in Gandhi's community, which as you probably know practices complete sharing of goods but is strongly monastic and ascetic. It seems to me that Bonhoeffer has great hopes for this time there.

On the essentials we are in agreement with B[onhoeffer]: (1) no private property, putting all goods under the administration of the community;[14] (2) nonviolence. The only thing is that he does not seem to have grasped the issue of the church-community as being led by the Spirit of God. Perhaps you can help him. I gave him the chapter on the Holy Spirit from the *Innenland*.[15]

[. . .] My love to Mama and everyone,

Your son Heinrich

Brandenburg, and about his participation at Fanø. See 1/113, ed. note 5, and *DB-ER*, 410.

[12.] On these plans, see also Larry Rasmussen's interview of March 1, 1968, with Herbert Jehle, *Bonhoeffer Jahrbuch*, 2:110–23.

[13.] On Bonhoeffer's plans for India, see 1/94 and 1/110, ed. note 8; Bonhoeffer's letter of July 13, 1934, to Reinhold Niebuhr (1/127); and Rasmussen's interview with Jehle. Julius Rieger also reported on plans to go to India with Bonhoeffer; see his *Dietrich Bonhoeffer in England*, 27–28. In a letter of April 28, 1934, to Erwin Sutz, Bonhoeffer discussed questions of the Sermon on the Mount and the suffering resistance, 1/93.

[14.] [The German here is *Gemeinde*; in the Bruderhof movement, however, the word consistently used to translate this is "community."—KC]

[15.] Arnold, *Innenland*.

114b. Hardy Arnold to Edith Böker[1]

Birmingham, June 15, 1934

Dear Idel,[2]

[. . .] One of the most important things in London was meeting with Pastor Dietrich Bonhoeffer and two of his friends, Dr. Jehle[3] and Vicar Weckerling.[4] The three of them are planning, together with some motivated groups of young theology students in *Berlin, Bonn,* and *Tübingen* (!), to found a sort of Protestant monastic community, with confessions, spiritual exercises,[5] remaining unmarried as far as possible. Their planning is still a bit piecemeal, but they have good intentions of learning from others, from monasteries, from Gandhi's ashram, and *from us!* So next week Pastor Bonhoeffer will be visiting the Bruderhof,[6] he was so impressed with what I was able to tell him. If it is given to us to reach agreement and to unite with this group of fifty to seventy young people, it would be wonderful! Quite a few of them would need to visit us, here or there, and we them. In many things the group has very *clear* views, for example, on the issues of violence and private property. That there are still many things to be cleared up, and the whole project leans strongly toward *asceticism and self-denial,* can be explained by the year in which this little movement was born: *1933!* Flee from the midst of Babylon![7] The great shock and the terrible disappointment, which the N[ational] S[ocialist] revolution has meant for all those who thought they could permeate the state and our economic system etc. with a Christian spirit, is now driving them to monastic communism. However, beyond a solid core who would permanently live in

---

[1.] Bruderhof Archives; handwritten; unpublished. German edited by Hans Pfeifer. Publication by permission of the Bruderhof Archives, Woodcrest, Rifton, N.Y.

[2.] Hardy Arnold was engaged to be married to Edith Böker (Boeker).

[3.] The physicist Herbert Jehle was already part of Bonhoeffer's Berlin circle in 1932 (see Larry Rasmussen's interview with him in the *Bonhoeffer Jahrbuch,* 2:110–23) and in 1933–34 was taking a sabbatical at Cambridge. In 1938 he was awarded a research post in molecular and astrophysics at the University of Brussels. During the war he was arrested there by the Gestapo and sent to the concentration camp in Gurs, in the foothills of the Pyrenees; he was released with the help of the Quakers and the World Student Christian Federation. He was later professor at the University of Nebraska and George Washington University.

[4.] Rudolf Weckerling was then a student at Richmond Methodist College in London. [It was he who facilitated Bonhoeffer's contact with the college, which led to Bonhoeffer's visit there on October 4, 1934 (2/4).—KC]

[5.] See 1/93. See also *DBWE* 3:155–56 and *DBW* 12:199.

[6.] See 1/114a, ed. note 11.

[7.] Jer. 51:6. Cf. Bonhoeffer's letter of November 20, 1934, to Rößler, 1/172: "that it is high time to 'flee to the next town'" [Matt. 10:23]. See also *DBW* 8:432.

the order, they wish to always have a whole group of young theologians whom they are *training* before they go into pastorates (!).[8] The basis of this yet-to-be-founded order is to be the *Sermon on the Mount.* Through religious exercises and serious study, and through the attempt to begin to follow Jesus' words as a *rule,* the hope is to come nearer to the essential core of the truth of Christ, by being *open* right from the start about not yet knowing the will of God for our time. Thus the project is strongly theologically defined, for example, through the idea that thorough and constant reading of the Bible will protect them from error, in other words, from heresy (how they fear it!!).[9] One thing they clearly lack is the outpouring of the Holy Spirit, even the recognition of the need for this. (It occurs to me that [St.] Francis lacked this as well, as did the first brothers in his order. Thus a *rule* had to be set by *one* person, to which others then willingly and *humbly submit.* In our community, however, *order* grows out of the unanimity of the community under the guidance of the Spirit; it is not thought through and formulated ahead of time, but rather arises out of life *itself.* That is why we are not an *order* but a *community,* as long as the Spirit is with us.)

¶So Bonhoeffer's idea is the idea of a *Protestant order.*[10] Since he and his friends are looking to two things from which they want to learn, *Gandhi* and the *Hutterite* movement,[11] a lot depends on our being given the gift to testify to the living reality of our community, in words and actions. After Bonhoeffer has been to the Bruderhof, I will see him again in London (in early July), along with Dr. Jehle. He is the one I get on with best. On Tuesday[12] after the other two had to leave, we went for a long walk in Hyde Park. He is the least theological one, doctorate in engineering, *nice* fellow, Swabian from Stuttgart, twenty-seven years old. He invited me to Cambridge, and I will go there July 2–3, then to London until the tenth, then to *Paris.* (I am now going to prepare thoroughly for the project with the children.)

[8.] Thus, as early as June 1934, Bonhoeffer was thinking of a house of brethren and a seminary in conjunction with each other. Cf. 1/147; *DBW* 14, 1/24; and *DB-ER,* 460–62.

[9.] But see Bonhoeffer's well-differentiated thinking on "orthodoxy," 1/127.

[10.] See Bonhoeffer's remarks to his brother Karl-Friedrich in his letter of January 14, 1935: "The restoration of the church must surely depend a new kind of monasticism, which has nothing in common with the old but a life of uncompromising discipleship, following Christ according to the Sermon on the Mount. I believe the time has come to gather people together and do this" (1/193).

[11.] As a theology student, Eberhard Arnold reached the conclusion that infant baptism was unbiblical and should be rejected and had himself baptized. Because of this he was barred from taking his first set of theological examinations. During a long stay in the Tyrol in 1913–14, he became interested in the Anabaptist movement there and later contacted the Hutterites in Canada and affiliated the Bruderhof community with them. On a visit to Canada in 1930, he was baptized once more and ordained. Cf. Baum, *Against the Wind,* 47–50 and 189–205, as well as Arnold, *God's Revolution.* [See also the list of Bruderhof books in English, 1/114a, ed. note 10.—KC]

[12.] June 12, 1934.

Dr. Jehle also wants to come to Silum in early August, or to the Rhön-Bruderhof, from Stuttgart. This is very important, since he and Bonhoeffer plan to go to Gandhi in India in September, to spend half a year in his *order*. If they could first experience what *community* is (they are strongly influenced by Barth in unconsciously thinking all the things of the Spirit are *enthusiasm*)[13] then this journey wouldn't be necessary; although I am more and more inclined to think that sooner or later *our* community needs to send someone to Gandhi. His movement is without doubt the most positive living example today in the area of individual mysticism and the monastic thinking connected to that. Sooner or later we need to have a heart-to-heart talk with him. In view of the huge influence that his simple way of life has on many of the best people (even Jack Hoyland!),[14] it has become unavoidably necessary [to think about] the community's being sent to the *world*, to find those who are seeking and eager, everywhere—whether in Asia, Europe, or the North Pole. This needs to happen soon, it is becoming *more and more urgent* [. . .]

With much love to you all, yours,
Eberhard—Ha[rdy]

115. To Théodore de Félice[1]

London, June 17, 1934

Dear Mr. de Félice,

Thank you very much for the program of the Fanø Youth Conference,[2] which I shall ask Mr. Winterhager to forward straightaway. By the way, Mr.

[13.] [*Schwärmerei*: this was Luther's hostile description of the "radical" reformation movements of the sixteenth century such as the Anabaptists and those claiming direct prophetic inspiration, whether as individuals or as separated communities of believers. It remained a pejorative term in mainstream Protestantism to describe movements outside established church structures, characterized by unusually zealous piety and an emphasis on "spiritual gifts" rather than "pure doctrine" (cf. Helmut Rößler's reference to the "sanctification sects" and other groups in his letter of November 20, 1934, to Bonhoeffer, 1/172). A not dissimilar usage of "enthusiasm" appeared in eighteenth-century England in reaction to the evangelical revival and the rise of the Methodist movement, but in this case "enthusiasm" was seen as a threat to good manners and orderly society rather than representing a mistaken theology.—KC]

[14.] Jack Hoyland, a Quaker in Woodbrooke, was among those to whom C. F. Andrews referred Bonhoeffer. Cf. 1/94.

[1.] WCC Archives, World Alliance, Letters from Dietrich Bonhoeffer; photocopy of typewritten letter. See also *NL*, A 40,1 (4); photocopy. Previously published in *GS* 6:352. See the replies to letters from Félice of May 11 and 17, 1934, 1/105 and 1/108.

[2.] Ecumenical Youth Conference of August 22–29, 1934. [The starting date appears elsewhere as August 23; see 1/110, ed. note 9.—KC] A hectographed invitation in French, with agenda and travel information, is in the literary estate of Eberhard Bethge, Fanø file.

Winterhager's address is no longer in Berlin itself, but rather: "Erlenhaus Hermannswerder, Potsdam."

For the theology conference in Luxembourg,[3] the dates have now been set—it will be the week of September 2–8. We are already in communication with Toureille, Craske, and Kilborn.

For the presentation in Fanø on August 25 (Saturday), we have as the first speaker Mr. Dudzus, a theology student from Berlin, and, second, Miss Karding, a candidate in theology, also from Berlin.[4] The report on August 23 (Thursday)[5] will be given by Mr. Winterhager.

The German delegation will include (probably), in addition to myself, the following: Miss Karding and Mr. Kühn, postgraduate theology students; Miss Frik and Mr. Dudzus, undergraduate theology students; and Dr. Winterhager, vicar.[6]

153   I have also sent the invitation to the Hungarian student group whose letter you forwarded to me.[7] You should receive a reply soon from Budapest.

Yours sincerely,
Bonhoeffer

115a. Eberhard Arnold to Hardy Arnold[1]

Rhön-Bruderhof, near Fulda, June 24, 1934

[. . .] The Spirit of God has spoken among you, with the fierceness of the storm and refreshing like the wind, awakening you to life. I believe that, in these days of crisis in world politics, the hour is near when "many" will turn away from the

---

[3.] See 1/105, ed. note 5.

[4.] On the topic "What action should we take, as individuals and as Christians, when the State is in conflict with Christian principles?" Otto Dudzus was the German speaker (see 1/141).

[5.] On "Church and State at the present moment and the consequent difficulties for our ecumenical action in Germany."

[6.] The participants' list also includes as German delegates: Willi Brandenburg, Hilde Enterlein, Hans Kramm, Winfried Maechler, J. Speck, and Ernst Tillich (literary estate of Eberhard Bethge, Fanø file).

[7.] On June 8, 1934. For the cover letter from Félice inquiring whether, in Bonhoeffer's opinion as youth secretary, this student group could be invited, see WCC Archives, World Alliance, Letters from Dietrich Bonhoeffer; photocopy of typewritten letter. According to the participants' list, the following individuals from Budapest attended the conference: E. Fabinyi, N. Mackay, and E. Somos.

[1.] Bruderhof Archives; typewritten copy; unpublished; from Sannerz; June 24, 1934. Edited by Hans Pfeifer. Publication by permission of the Bruderhof Archives, Woodcrest, Rifton, N.Y.

"politics" of the state and seek a better way of justice, fellowship among nations, and peace for humankind. They will do this by turning to the "Politeia," which is none other than the one kingdom, the true kingdom of *God*.

May it also be given to us to come together in this power with Dietrich Bonhoeffer or perhaps with Dr. Jehle and also get to know their groups in Berlin, Bonn, and Tübingen. However, according to many experiences I have had at universities with such hopes, it can hardly be expected that sixty to seventy young people are actually prepared to assume such a total responsibility, for the sake of the act to which Jesus bore witness. Perhaps you should write back to me immediately whether we should write again to Dietrich Bonhoeffer in Berlin. We have already telephoned his mother, but perhaps she has not been able to deliver our message to him. [. . .]

So in this, as always, I can only put my heartfelt trust in the guidance of the Spirit, since I am certain that the unity of God, the love of Christ, and the mission of the Spirit is with you. In the joy of this faith, I embrace you

115b. Eberhard Arnold to Hardy Arnold[1]

To Eberhard Heinrich Arnold
Birmingham

My beloved Eberhard Heinrich,

[. . .] You have made it abundantly clear that the life of such a community cannot be built upon human planning, and least of all upon a primarily economic basis. The belief in unanimous community is so amazingly[2] unknown everywhere, because the third article of the Apostles' Creed, that of faith in the Holy Spirit and the work of the Spirit, has been totally lost to Christendom in general. Even in the case of Dietrich Bonhoeffer, who has not yet come to see us here although we telephoned him, the foundation of the renunciation of private property and holding of goods in common, as well as nonviolence, still seems to me, like many another such undertaking, to be quite far from the calling of the community by the Spirit of Jesus Christ.[3] This even though his declaration of intent to carry out the Sermon on the Mount, to live according to the words of Jesus, is very significant.

[1.] Bruderhof Archives; typed copy; unpublished; from the Rhön-Bruderhof, June 26, 1934. Edited by Hans Pfeifer. Publication by permission of the Bruderhof Archives, Woodcrest, Rifton, N.Y.

[2.] "amazingly" added by hand.

[3.] [Arnold's perception of a general lack of interest in the third article of the creed—the Holy Spirit—and of Bonhoeffer's own emphasis on the rule of Christ seemingly at the expense of the Spirit should be related to Bonhoeffer's stress on the significance of the *filioque* in the context of the Church Struggle. See 1/20, ed. note 33.—KC]

And again because of his monastic ideas and inclinations toward the East and India, like Leo Tolstoy and the Dukhobors,[4] it is all very questionable.[5]

[. . .] So in this, as always, I can only entrust you wholeheartedly to the guidance of the Spirit, since I am certain that the unity of God, the love of Christ, and the mission of the Spirit are with you. In the joy of this faith, I embrace you.

Your grateful Father

116. From Henry Watson Fox[1]

London, June 27, 1934

My dear Bonhoeffer,

The Archdeacon of Kingston,[2] (Archdeacon G. H. Marten) who is our Chairman, is speaking at the joint Council Meetings at Fano, Denmark, in August on the same subject as yourself, "The Church and the World of Nations."[3] He would very much like to have a talk with [you] on his treatment of the subject, if possible, some time next week, and suggests that you might lunch with him. Would you write or telephone to him and fix up a day and time when you could meet. His address is 11 Percival Road, East Sheen, S.W. 14, and his telephone number

---

[4.] "Spiritual wrestlers" in Russian. The Dukhobors were a religious society founded in the eighteenth century in southern Russia; they rejected the worship and dogmas of the Russian Orthodox Church and every other external authority. They followed a strict Christian ethic and were supported by Leo Tolstoy. Following a period of persecution in 1888–89, many emigrated to Canada.

[5.] It is understandable that Eberhard Arnold distanced himself from Bonhoeffer, since their ideas were quite different (cf. Hardy Arnold's letter of June 15, 1934, 114b, as well as his report on his encounter with Bonhoeffer, *Bonhoeffer Jahrbuch*, 2:105–9). The Bruderhof members undertake a lifelong commitment and live in settlements as completely withdrawn as possible from the surrounding society. Bonhoeffer, however, was planning an educational center intended to prepare students for resistance under dictatorship by orienting their lives completely to Christ. Nevertheless, Bonhoeffer was not unimpressed by his encounter with the Bruderhof movement. In Finkenwalde he adopted Eberhard Arnold's rule for the Bruderhof in Sannerz, that no member of the community might ever speak in a negative way about another who was absent. See Arnold, *God's Revolution*, 113–14, and *DB-ER*, 428.

[1.] *NL*, Anh. D 1,4 (10); handwritten; in original English, including errors. Fox was writing as general secretary of the British section of the World Alliance for Promoting International Friendship through the Churches on behalf of the chairman, George H. Marten.

[2.] Kingston-upon-Thames, a southwestern suburb of London, formerly a town with a royal history.

[3.] Marten's thesis paper for Fanø is in the WCC Archives, Life and Work, 324 (Study Conferences–Paris, April 1934).

"Prospect 3733." If you telephone, you will get him at 10 or 9.30 in the morning. If you could lunch with him, it would be in London and not at his home.

I am very glad to hear that you are back from Germany.[4]

Yours

H. W. Fox

117. To George Bell[1]

154

London S.E. 23, Juni 28th, 1934

My Lord Bishop,

The statement of Bishop Müller at Holle[2] (Hanover) in which he has threatened a procedure for High Treason for all those ministers who give any information in church matters abroad has caused much anxiety to Dr. Winterhager and to myself.—Bishop Müller's statement continues that "there is no emergency for faith" in present-day Germany.[3]

We consider this latter maintenance a vehement rejection and a very unsatisfactory reply to your Ascension Day Message[4] in which it was truly and clearly stated to what an extent the Christian faith was really endangered on account of the "German Christian" church government.

We therefore believe it to be very essential that now the Universal Christian Council again expresses its judgment. This oecumenic judgement and protest would not lose its substantial object if and when Bishop Müller had himself resigned at the time of its publication. We feel sure that the leaders of the church opposition and the great majority of steadfast Protestants in our country are more and more embarrassed by the first of the recent statements, i.e. the High Treason Threat. They will all consider the oecumenic witness and protest to be most helpful for all those who are otherwise left quite unprotected from threatening insult and great danger.

[4.] Bonhoeffer had been in Berlin June 18–24.

[1.] LPL, Bell Papers 42, 38; typewritten; in original English, including errors. See also *NL*, A 42,1 (17); typewritten copy. Previously published in *GS* 1:196-97.

[2.] Gauger, *Chronik der Kirchenwirren*, 2:221, reports a speech Müller delivered on June 26 in Halle but does not repeat the threat of prosecution for high treason; the reference probably is, in fact, to Holle, which is southeast of Hildesheim.

[3.] In the speech reported by Gauger (see ed. note 2), Müller is quoted as follows: "The warning that is sometimes sounded within the church these days, that our confession is in danger, is not only a lie, it is also incredibly stupid."

[4.] See 1/103.

155 The oecumenic witness will now be particularly helpful, if a statement of yours is to declare openly that any dispute and any information upon church matters is in the field of religious discussion only and has nothing to do whatever with state politics. And all the more important would be your statement now since through British press and broadcast the attention of many churches all over the world has more than ever been drawn to the frightening measures and threats of Bishop Müller. World Protestantism will surely expect very soon an open reply to those provocative attacks against the Ascension Day Message which was sent to all the Churches of Christ.

With many thanks and kindest regards from Dr. Winterhager, I am

Sincerely yours,
Dietrich Bonhoeffer

118. From George Bell[1]

Private
29th June, 1934

My dear Bonhoeffer,

I enclose a letter from Professor Fabricius to the Archbishop of Canterbury[2] which speaks for itself. The Archbishop has sent it to me, asking me to make any comments which occur to me for his consideration. I send this by express in the hope that it will reach you while Dr. Winterhager is staying with you. I should be glad if you could tell me something about Professor Fabricius, but more important if you would indicate what sort of comments you would think would be most likely to pierce Professor Fabricius' armour. The Aryan paragraph, unreserved homage demanded for the State, the use of force and prohibition of free elections, 156 and the introduction of the leadership principle with the autocratic powers given

---

[1.] LPL, Bell Papers 42, 39; carbon copy; in original English, including errors. See also *NL*, A 42,2 (9); typewritten copy. Previously published in *GS* 2:173.

[2.] In a June 19, 1934, letter on behalf of a "Central Office for Confessional Research and Ecumenical Relations" in Berlin, Fabricius [a member of the German Christians] had sought to refute the charge made at the Convocation of Canterbury, the Anglican provincial synod [for southern England—KC], that the Protestant church in Germany was endangered by false teachings and paganism (copy of letter in LPL, Bell Papers, 6, 66–72). He said that a strict distinction should be made between the sect known as the "German Faith Movement" and the "German Christians." He asserted that the latter "were faithful to the confessional foundation of the church in accordance with the Scriptures" and, furthermore, with regard to their national historical theology, were "in full agreement with the English people." In contrast, Fabricius argued, the church opposition of Barmen was based on a "Barthianism" that was contrary to the gospel.

to Bishop Müller, seem clear points to be made. But is Professor Fabricius likely to be influenced thereby?

I also enclose, so that if he likes Dr. Winterhager could take it with him to Berlin, a copy of a pamphlet just issued, with a report of the two speeches in Convocation.[3] Beyond giving my consent to the reproduction of the debate in Convocation I have had nothing to do with the preparation of the pamphlet, which is just out to-day.

Yours sincerely,

[George Cicestr]

119. To George Bell[1]

(Private)

June 29th, 1934

My Lord Bishop,

I am very grateful indeed for your letter and the excellent booklet[2] which have both reached me before Dr. Winterhager's departure. We find that this publication of the "Friends of Europe" will be *very helpful* to all Protestants in our country. We have sent it to our friends of the Emergency League[3] at once and have ordered several more copies.

I have then dealt with the enclosed letter[4] thoroughly.—Dr. Fabricius is an Assistant Professor in the University of Berlin. He is considered to be ill and much embittered.[5] His influence among the younger generation and his theological significance have always been very limited. There may be certainly some connection between his recent activities and Bishop Heckel's   157 foreign church office, but there does actually not exist any ecumenic basis of

---

[3.] *Protestantism in the Totalitarian State*, no. 12 in the Friends of Europe series, quotes excerpts from the debate (including the speeches by Headlam and Bell in the Upper House) and the resolutions adopted by the Convocation of Canterbury on June 7, 1934, as well as an essay on the developments in the Evangelical Church of Germany. On this convocation, see also the reports in the *Times* of June 8, 1934, reproduced in Bell and Koechlin, *Briefwechsel,* 132ff.

[1.] LPL, Bell Papers 42, 40; typewritten; in original English, including errors. See also *NL,* A 42,1 (18); typewritten copy. Previously published in *GS* 2:173–76.

[2.] See 1/118, ed. note 3.

[3.] Probably Franz Hildebrandt and Martin Niemöller.

[4.] Cf. 1/118, ed. note 2.

[5.] Fabricius suffered from severely impaired vision. At the discussion at the University of Berlin on June 22, 1933, he had been among the defenders of the German Christians, while Bonhoeffer had stood up for the Young Reformation movement (cf. *DB-ER,* 287).

his new "zentralstelle."[6] If there were not a tendency of the present church government possibly acting as an influence behind it, the letter itself had not to be taken very seriously. It is doubtful, at least, that Dr. Fabricius himself will be much influenced either by theological arguments or even facts.

I heartily disapprove of the whole tone and tenor of Dr. Fabricius's letter. Yet I have dealt with all the strange arguments contained therein, and after a long talk with Dr. Winterhager, I should like to submit to you the following points as possibly forming an outline to the answer, however shortly any answer should be stated in replying Dr. Fabricius's letter.

Dr. Fabricius maintains that there is a large difference between the official German Christians and the "German Faith Movement." In fact, this difference is extremely small! We may prove this by three statements:

1. Dr. Krause's party, affiliated to the "German Faith Movement" (*"sport palace"*) is still officially within the church "communion" and is entitled to send its representatives to both parish councils and governing bodies.[7]

2. An "ecclesiastic" member of the German Faith Movement (a curate) has recently (at an open meeting attended by Dr. Coch-Dresden, the Bishop of Sachsen) read the following "passage" from the Gospel according to St. John: "In the beginning was the Nation, and the Nation was with God, and the Nation was God; the same was in the beginning with God, etc."— Bishop Coch has not expressed one word of disagreement with this new version of the New Testament.[8] But several ministers of the opposition who witnessed this event have written to Bishop Müller and have asked him to correct the reading curate afterwards. But no such measure has been taken by Bishop Müller. In this way has a "version" of Scripture reading been authorized which could not be surpassed by anything else in heresy.

158

[6.] ["Central office," a reference to the organization Fabricius claimed to represent; see 1/118, ed. note 2.—KC]

[7.] Reinhold Krause, erstwhile head of the [Berlin] German Christians, whose speech helped provoke the uproar following the November 13, 1933, Sports Palace rally, was still an official member of the national synod—although he had since founded his own "German *Volkskirche*" and appeared as a speaker at rallies of the "German Faith Movement"—until he was excluded from the synod by August Jäger's decree on July 7, 1934 (cf. Scholder, *Churches and the Third Reich*, 2:100 and 218). [In the German edition of this note the reference is to "G. Krause," possibly a confusion with Gerhard Krause, one of Bonhoeffer's first seminarians at Finkenwalde, who came to disagree with Bonhoeffer over the issue of "legalization." See *DB-ER*, 617–18.—KC]

[8.] According to Gauger, *Chronik der Kirchenwirren*, 2:205, this took place at a student rally in the Ore Mountains [the *Erzgebirge*, on the Czech border—KC] on March 18, 1934, where a theological student had used this bastardized version of John 1:1–3 as the text for his address (see also *Junge Kirche* 2, no. 9 [May 5, 1934]: 379).

3. The High President of Brandenburg, Herr Kube, Member of the General Synod of the Church in Prussia and at the same time one of the responsible leaders of the German Christians, has concluded his latest Midsummer-Night speech in saying: "Adolf Hitler yesterday, to-day and for evermore!"[9]

We believe these three points to be sufficient proofs against Dr. Fabricius's ignorant statement.—We would also point out that his description of Karl Barth's theology is very superficial and inadequate and does not require much consideration. Moreover, Dr. Fabricius's reproach of the Barmen synod is drastic in extravagance as he wishes the Protestant Opposition to be responsible for introducing the leadership principle and for imitating the political methods of National Sozialism.[10] One should rather keep in one's mind that the initiative to the election of a Reichsbischof was never taken on *our* side and that it was not the opposition which elected Dr. v. Bodelschwingh. It was the old (conservative) church government which did that when still in power (early in 1933).[11] Neither Dr. v. Bodelschwingh himself nor the Free Synods have ever dreamt of securing leadership of any political bearing in the church.

Dr. Fabricius expresses himself a desire for information "in what behalf (which probably means, 'to what extent') the German Evangelical Church is in danger to cease to be fully Christian."[12] Now we should like to make Dr.   159 Fabricius conceive that the points which you, my Lord Bishop, stated in your letter to-day,[13] are all based upon facts which make it doubtful whether the German Church has not already ceased to be a Christian Church at all—the Aryan paragraph, unreserved homage demanded for the State, the use of force and prohibition of free elections, and the introduction of the leadership principle with the autocratic powers given to Bishop Müller.

[9.] This declaration by the Brandenburg regional leader (*Gauleiter*) at an assembly of the Hitler Youth—here apparently incorrectly dated—is documented in Gauger, *Chronik der Kirchenwirren*, 2:292.

[10.] Fabricius had claimed that the "Barmen brothers," in contradiction to their own subsequent theological declaration, had imitated the National Socialist "Führer principle" in the spring of 1933 by "appointing" Friedrich von Bodelschwingh as Reich bishop without "general elections."

[11.] On the events leading to Bodelschwingh's election by the representatives of the regional churches in May 1933, which at first amounted to an embarrassing setback for the German Christians in their demand for new general elections and for their candidate, Ludwig Müller, see Scholder, *Churches and the Third Reich*, 1:324–32.

[12.] This was [based on] Bell's choice of words in his speech in the Upper House of the Convocation of Canterbury (see 1/118, ed. note 3).

[13.] See 1/118.

Dr. Fabricius finally accuses the Protestant opposition of the same thing on account of which Bishop Müller has felt entitled officially to issue the High Treason Threat![14] We openly declare and emphasize that the Opposition Movement has never caused the foreign press to interfere in any question of political bearing.—On the other hand the Protestant opposition particularly enjoys and highly appreciates the intercession and the active assistance given by the world-wide fellowship of Christ.

The Protestants who wish to be loyal to Jesus Christ believe in a universal Church, and they will always remain grateful to the Church of England and other Churches because they have helped to keep that ecumenic faith strong.

When I was in Germany last week, I saw Praeses Koch.[15] He asked me to offer you his kindest regards and the expressions of his sincere gratitude and appreciation of all the help you have already given to our Protestant Movement, again and again.

With thanks and with kindest regards also from Dr. Winterhager,

Respectfully yours,
Dietrich Bonhoeffer

160   **120. To Max Diestel**[1]

London, July 1, 1934

Dear Superintendent Diestel:

Thank you very much for your letter.[2] I am very pleased that you are planning to stay with me here. I have arranged for a car to meet you on Sunday morning[3] at Liverpool Street Station, and have tried to explain to the driver

---

[14.] Fabricius had insinuated that the Barmen synod, although its declaration rejected all "human arrogance" (*Eigenmächtigkeit*), had been mobilizing the international press and church leaders abroad for its own purposes.

[15.] [Karl Koch, church president of the regional Westphalian church.—KC] In Berlin on June 19, 1934, at a discussion about the participation of Confessing Church representatives in the ecumenical conference in Fanø (see *DB-ER*, 377).

[1.] *NL*, Anh. A 7 (8); typewritten. Nothing more has been discovered about Diestel's plan to visit Bonhoeffer in London. It was probably related to the problems about German participation in the Fanø conference (on the discussions in the German branch of the World Alliance, see 1/125).

[2.] Not extant.

[3.] Probably Sunday, July 8, 1934.

how he may recognize you. In case it is needed, here is the license number of the car: TM *3384.*

If anything should come up before your journey that might prevent it, I trust I would receive a brief word from you.

Meanwhile I wish you a pleasant and restful holiday.

With my thanks and greetings as always,
Yours sincerely,
Dietrich Bonhoeffer

121. From Théodore de Félice[1]

Geneva, July 2, 1934

Dear Friend,

Naturally[2] I had sent all the corresponding members of the Youth Commission an announcement for the Fanø Study Week.[3] In response I received from Mr. Jaensch the enclosed letter.[4] I will leave it up to you to give it the appropriate follow-up. I didn't write anything to Mr. Walther Müller.

Moreover, Burlingham writes to me to ask what subsidy is planned for the English who are going to the theological conference in Luxembourg.[5] I am answering him that it is with you and Mr. Toureille that he has to make arrangements for sharing the 250 francs—which is the total available for this gathering.

161

Very cordially yours,
Th. de Félice

[1.] WCC Archives, World Alliance, Letters to Dietrich Bonhoeffer; carbon copy; in French.

[2.] This appears to be a response to a request from Bonhoeffer, which has not been found, for the prospectus to be sent to him.

[3.] Cf. 1/115, ed. note 2.

[4.] Of June 27, 1934; not extant. Apparently Jaensch asked to have a certain W. Müller invited to the Youth Conference (see Bonhoeffer's reply to Félice, 1/122).

[5.] Cf. 1/109.

121a. Hardy Arnold to Eberhard Arnold[1]

Birmingham, July 3, 1934

My only beloved Father,

[. . .] In London I shall also see Bonhoeffer and Dr. Jehle.[2] About the latter, I definitely feel that he is growing toward us. He will come to see us in August, in Silum or at the Rhön-Bruderhof, whichever is easier for him. I am looking forward to being together with him.

[. . .] I shall be meeting Pastor Bonhoeffer and Dr. Jehle, along with the young Pastor Weckerling from that Protestant monastically inclined group, on Tuesday.[3] I talked with Bonhoeffer on the telephone, and he said that his pastoral duties did not allow him to be away from London more than four days, so that he had not been able to visit us this time from Berlin, where he had spent less than three days. But he would like to catch up with us in August.

[. . .] My heartfelt greetings to everyone, in peace and unity.

From your lowly but very grateful son,
Eberhard Heinrich
[. . .]

122. To Théodore de Félice[1]

London, July 4, 1934

Dear Mr. de Félice,

Thank you for your kind letter[2] with the one from Mr. D. Jaensch enclosed. I should like to know whether this letter of June 27 was preceded by any correspondence, and who sent the Youth Commission's invitation to Mr. Jaensch. Neither he nor Mr. Müller is included in the youth delegation that

---

[1.] Bruderhof Archives; first page handwritten (only the salutation appears here); the remaining pages are typed copy. German edited by Hans Pfeifer. Publication by permission of the Bruderhof Archives, Woodcrest, Rifton, N.Y.

[2.] Hardy Arnold had written on June 29, 1934, to Edith Böker that another student of Bonhoeffer's had been present at a meeting of the Bruderhof movement in Woodbrooke on June 28, 1934. This was probably Jürgen Winterhager, who was in London at the time; see 1/118 and 1/119.

[3.] July 5, 1934.

[1.] WCC Archives, Letters from Dietrich Bonhoeffer; photocopy of typewritten letter. See also *NL*, A 40,1 (5); photocopy. Previously published in *Mündige Welt*, 5:227, and *GS* 6:352–53.

[2.] Of July 2, 1934; see 1/121.

we in Germany have already selected to go to Fanö.[3]—Before I can agree
to Mr. Jaensch's request that Mr. Müller be invited, we must somehow find
out about the latter's theology and position on church politics, as he is not
at all known to us. I shall, of course, ask Mr. Winterhager to look into this
personally.

I have, by the way, already written to tell Mr. Schönfeld[4] that the participation of our German youth delegation at Fanö will essentially depend
on whether representatives of the present Reich Church government are
to take part in the conference.[5] Our delegation members have in any case
agreed to stay away from any sessions in Fanö at which church government
representatives are present. It would be good if there could be clear general
awareness of this alternative that they face. And I hope that you, too, will
help us to get the ecumenical movement to state openly which of the two
"churches" in Germany it is prepared to recognize.

162

With regard to the theology conference in Luxembourg, which will take
place in the first week of September, it was agreed at the February meeting
in Paris[6] that, of the total fund of 250 francs, 100 francs each would be available to the German and English delegations, and to the French delegation,
50 francs.

Sincerely yours,
D. Bonhoeffer

123. From Théodore de Félice[1]

Geneva, July 6, 1934

Dear Sir,

Thank you very much for your letter of July 4.[2] I didn't tell you clearly enough
in my last letter that I hadn't taken any steps with the people in Germany for the
study week in Fanø, but I had only sent the enclosed mimeographed prospectus[3]
to the leaders whose addresses we have; it is in response to this that I received

---

[3.] See the names of the intended official delegation, 1/115.

[4.] Letter not extant. Henriod replied to it on July 7, 1934; see 1/124.

[5.] Handwritten note added in the margin: "This is confidential!"

[6.] Cf. 1/105, ed. note 5.

[1.] WCC Archives, World Alliance, Letters to Dietrich Bonhoeffer; carbon copy; in
French.

[2.] See 1/122.

[3.] See 1/115, ed. note 2.

the letter from Mr. Jaensch, which I did not answer, any more than I answered Walther Müller.

As far as the German participation in the conferences in Fanø, according to information from Mr. Henriod, there will be no member of the Reich Church government at the session of the Management Committee of the Alliance,[4] but for the mixed sessions, Monday and Tuesday,[5] Germany will be represented by various prominent people, of whom you will find a list enclosed. You will see that both tendencies are represented.[6]

163 As for the delegation for the Youth Commission session, it depends, as far as Germany is concerned, entirely on you or Winterhager; I don't know which side Stange,[7] who is a member of it, is on.

Thank you for the information about the theological conference.

Very cordially yours,
Th. de Félice

124. From Henry Louis Henriod[1]

7th July 1934

My dear Bonhoeffer,

Your letter to Schönfeld[2] arrived this morning. Schönfeld is away on his holiday until the end of the month. Therefore, according to your instructions I have opened your letter to him and this is my answer:

I fully appreciate and sympathize with the most delicate and painful situation in which German representatives will be at the meeting at Fanö, because of their

---

[4.] Meeting of the Management Committee (of the thirty-member Executive Committee), to which Bonhoeffer belonged, on August 28, 1934.

[5.] On Tuesday, August 28, 1934, Bonhoeffer was to give his lecture on "The Church and the Peoples of the World."

[6.] The list has not been found. However, see the names mentioned in Henriod's letter of July 7, 1934 (1/124); Bonhoeffer could hardly have been expected to agree with Félice that they represented "both tendencies."

[7.] Erich Stange was vice-chairman of the Youth Commission.

[1.] LPL, Bell Papers 19, 318–19; carbon copy, from Geneva; in original English, including errors. See also *NL*, A 40,2 (5); typewritten copy. Previously published in *GS* 1:197–200.

[2.] Letter from before July 4, 1934 (see 1/122, ed. note 4), written after discussion with Karl Koch and Martin Niemöller; not extant. Bonhoeffer had apparently "described the situation following Barmen and the political tension, and asked about the formation of the Fanø committees and the invitation to the Confessing Synod. In the case of an exclusive invitation to the Reich church, he would announce his own withdrawal" (*DB-ER*, 378). [On the background to the issue of participation at Fanø, see *DB-ER*, 372–81.—KC]

delicate relationships with their State authorities, because of the presence of an official Church delegation, because of the probable exposure of the inner German difficulties before an international gathering.

For the Management Committee of the World Alliance, that is to say for the sessions of the Commissions on August 22nd,[3] for the meeting of the Executive Committee on the 23rd, for the meeting of the Management Committee dealing with its business on August 24th, only those appointed by the German Branch of the World Alliance, and men like Siegmund-Schultze, Pastor Maas (if he comes) and yourself as members of a World Alliance Commission appointed on former meetings,[4] with the right to sit with the Management Committee, will be present. No other persons will be invited from Germany.

164

For the Council of Life & Work, the official delegation named by Bishop Heckel will be composed of Bishop Heckel himself, Dr. Wahl, Dr. Krummacher, Privatdozent Wendland, Prof. Hanns Koch, plus other standing members of the German representation on Life and Work: Prof. Deissmann, Dr. Simons, plus any substitutes, as have been appointed by the *Continental Section*[5] in the past, and who remain entitled to come: Vice-President Burghart (not coming); Dozent Theophil Mann (?); Generalsuperintendent Zoellner (?); Prof. Siegmund-Schultze (announced); Prof. Titius (announced); in addition, leaders and members of permanent commissions of Life and Work, such as Pastor Menn, Prof. Dibelius, Dr. Stange as members of the Administrative Committee (I have no indication whether he is coming or not) and yourself as member of the Youth Commission, Dr. Iserland who will represent the International Missionary Council and of course Schönfeld.

I quite agree with you that time will come when "this development will lead inevitably to the oikumene having to face the unambiguous question of which of the two churches in Germany it is going to recognize. It is important to gain a clear understanding ahead of time of the gravity of this decision."[6] But, to be able to make the choice you contemplate, the Universal Christian Council must be notified that there are two Churches and not one. Up till now no such indication has reached us; no request for recognition by any new organisation of Churches or Church. Furthermore, up till now the very leaders of the opposition like Dr. Koch, Niemöller and others have *urged* us not to severe our relationships with the official Church Government so as to maintain a right of pressure over them. If

[3.] Meetings of the Commissions on Finance and Minorities.

[4.] As a member of the Youth Commission, Bonhoeffer was entitled to attend meetings of the World Alliance's Executive Committee.

[5.] One of the five geographical area groups into which the Universal Council for Life and Work was divided.

[6.] [The section in quotation marks is evidently taken from Bonhoeffer's letter to Schönfeld, which has been lost (see ed. note 2). In his letter Henriod quotes the original German, here translated.—KC]

the Barmen Synod and present or future developments lead to the constitution of the Church distinct from the present recognised official Church, that you yourself have recognised when you announced your decision to accept the invitation of the German Congregation in London, and if and when this new Church asks for recognition by Life & Work, then, and only then, will the question of choice become possible for the Oecumenic Movement. This is at least my own understanding of the situation, which Schönfeld shares entirely according to our frequent conversations on the subject. This is still, I think, the point of view of the Bishop of Chichester, according to my knowledge; to ascertain this last point, I am sending him a copy of this letter to you.

If the present Church Government remains in power in Germany and is represented at the Fanö meeting, as they clearly indicate, and if after the debate on Church and State and the special session contemplated on the afternoon of August 25th, when the answer to the letter of the Bishop of Chichester of May 10th[7] is discussed, the official representatives of the Church express their desire to continue to be part of the Life & Work Movement and the meeting concur to this decision, as stated earlier in this letter, there will be no other alternative, no choice that we can make unless a move is made from Germany itself.

You will have noticed, I am aware, that there are a good many "if" in my letter, and things may turn in a different way. But I was anxious that you would fully understand where the responsibility rests with regard to the future relationships between Life & Work and the German Church.

Concerning the World Alliance, as long as the World Alliance in Germany in its present shape remains in existence, and as long as its leaders refuse to be incorporated into an official organ of the German Official Church, the World Alliance will not change its relationships and Fellowship. But in case Bishop Heckel or others declare disbanded the World Alliance and no protest or indication comes to us from the leaders of the German branch that they refuse to be suppressed, or even accept such a possible Gleichschaltung, then it would become very difficult for the World Alliance to take another attitude than the legal constitution of the World Alliance is concerned.

It goes without saying that my hopes and prayers are that the situation in Germany will evolve in such a way that either official or nonofficial Church of organisation in Germany will become free again to live and to act according to the principles of the Gospel only, and you can be certain that fellow-Christians and fellow-Christian organisations in other countries share to their utmost with

[7.] See 1/103.

Germany to remain true to the Gospel of Jesus Christ in the programme in the attitude of their leaders wherever they are.

Yours very sincerely,
[Henry Louis Henriod]

125. To Henry Louis Henriod[1]   166

July 12th 1934

My dear Henriod,

thank you very much for your letters.[2] I appreciate your readiness to understand our point of view and your sympathy with our difficulties. Thanks for your friendly words!—Now, your main point is, that the Confessional Church in Germany should notify[3] the Universal Council of its very existence. As I see it, that has been done long ago in Ulm[4] as well as in Barmen where the Confessional Synod made the official claim before the whole Christian world to be the true Evangelical Church in Germany. If this claim is at all taken seriously, then it includes the hope of recognition by the other churches. If I am right, the churches represented on the Universal Council have been *invited* to send their representatives and have not done so by their own initiative. I have discussed this point with the Bishop of Chichester recently and I learn, he has written to you already about it. You say: "if the Barmen Synod . . . lead to the constitution of the church distinct from the present recognised official church . . . then, and only then will the question of choice become possible for the ecumenic movement." I think, you are misinterpreting the legal construction of the Confessional Church at this point. There is not the claim or even the wish to be a Free Church beside the Reichskirche,[5] but there is the claim to be the only theologically and legally legitimate evangelical church in Germany, and accordingly you cannot expect this church to set up a new constitution, since it is based on the very constitution, which the Reichskirche has neglected. It follows, that according to my opinion, a move should be made by the Universal Council in the form of an official invita-

---

[1.] LPL, Bell Papers 42, 42; "Copy" typewritten by Bonhoeffer for Bell, with handwritten additions; from London; in original English, including errors. See also *NL*, A 40,1 (14); typewritten copy. Previously published in *GS* 1:200–202. For Bonhoeffer's accompanying letter, see 1/126.

[2.] Henriod's letter of July 7, 1934, and Félice's of July 6, 1934; see 1/124 and 1/123.

[3.] "Notify" replaces "apply."

[4.] On April 22, 1934; see 1/92, ed. note 4.

[5.] "Beside the Reichskirche" inserted later.

tion to the Confessional Synod to participate in the Ecumenic work of the
167   churches. You will realize, that it is exceedingly delicate for the Confessional
Church to make this move after having already once[6] declared before the
whole Christianity, what their claim is. So, I feel strongly, that legally and
theologically the responsibility for the future relationships between the German Church and the Ecumenic Movement rests with the Ecumenic Movement itself and its actions.

With regard to the World Alliance I may say, after having attended an
important meeting of it two weeks ago,[7] that it is out of question, that the
Reichskirche should be allowed to take over their business. There is a very
strong feeling against D. Heckel, so that even the possibility of staying away
from Fanö in case D. Heckel should be there is being seriously considered.

Finally, you will allow me to correct your statement concerning my recognition of the Reichskirche in my personal position. I am in no relation
whatever with the Reichskirche. I am elected merely by my congregation and
this election has neither been confirmed by the Reichskirche as it should
have been, nor would I accept such a confirmation at all. When I went over
to London, there was no Confessional Church, which had made the claim
it is making now—this having been one of the reasons why I left Germany.
Excuse this lengthy explanation, but I should not like to be misunderstood
by my friends.

The decree of Frick[8] is indeed of the greatest importance. I feel, it is
once more a great moment for the Ecumene to speak. This decree may mean
the definite suppression of Christianity as a place where public christian[9]
opinion can be formed.

I am glad you have found so quickly a substitute for me at Fanö and I am
sending you the documents[10] under separate cover. You will understand my
168   decision not to go to Fanö better. I frankly admit that I cannot agree with the
invitation of D.[11] Heckel without inviting the opposition.

[6.] "Already once" inserted later.

[7.] Meeting of the German branch of the World Alliance in Berlin on June 19, 1934
(see *DB-ER*, 377).

[8.] On July 9, 1934, the Reich Minister of the Interior had banned "until further
notice, without exception, all discussion of the church dispute through public assemblies,
pamphlets or leaflets," other than official pronouncements by the Reich bishop (see Nicolaisen and Kretschmar, *Dokumente zur Kirchenpolitik*, 2:150 [and Scholder, *Churches and the
Third Reich*, 2:219—KC]).

[9.] "Christian" inserted later.

[10.] Presumably the preparatory materials for the speakers (cf. 1/114).

[11.] [" D.," as also in the next sentence, is the German style for "Dr."—KC]

I have talked all these problems over with D. Koch and Niemöller on my trip to Berlin,[12] and we all agreed.

I hope to hear from you again,

Yours
[Dietrich Bonhoeffer]

126. To George Bell[1]

July 12th 34

My Lord Bishop,

herewith I send you a copy of my answer to Henriod.[2] What do you think about the Frick decree?[3] I hope that the pastors will this time dare to come up against the State. This treatment is unbearable. The decree itself seems to have come out of a very nervous and tense situation.[4]

May I hear what your decision is with regard to the Fanø conference and the German Opposition.[5]

Yours sincerely,
Dietrich Bonhoeffer

[12.] June 18–24, 1934.

[1.] LPL, Bell Papers 42, 41; handwritten; from London; in original English, including errors. See also *NL*, A 42,1 (19); typewritten copy. Previously published in *GS* 2:177.

[2.] Of the same date; see 1/125.

[3.] See 1/125, ed. note 8.

[4.] In a conversation with Bell two days later, Bonhoeffer said he considered it highly likely that "something will happen during the next few days," in the form of "a decisive step by either the church government or the state, raising its threatening hand [against us]" (Bell and Koechlin, *Briefwechsel*, 142).

[5.] On the question of whether representatives of the German Confessing Church could also be invited to the ecumenical conference, Bell had written on July 7, 1934, to Ammundsen and Koechlin asking their advice. He wrote: "I am given to understand (by Bonhoeffer, with whom I have discussed the matter) that if an invitation were to be presented to Praeses Koch it would be welcome, and that representatives would undoubtedly be sent" (*GS* 1:203; cf. Bell and Koechlin, *Briefwechsel*, 138–39; *DB-ER*, 379; Boyens, *Kirchenkampf und Ökumene*, 1:110-11).

169   **127. To Reinhold Niebuhr**[1]

London, July 13, 1934

Dear Professor Niebuhr,

You will be surprised to hear from me again after so long.[2] This is truly terrible, because during the past year I have often meant to write to you and ask your opinion about what is going on. My cousin was here a while ago[3] and talked a great deal about you. I also received a very kind invitation from your mother-in-law,[4] which unfortunately I was unable to accept. So there have been all sorts of reasons for me to think of you lately. However, there is a most particular reason why I am writing to you today. I need your advice and help in connection with some matters on behalf of emigrants.[5] Since I have been in London, of course, I have had a great deal to do with such matters. What I would like to ask today is whether you know of an organization over there to which students could turn (either Jews, or those expelled from the university for political reasons), which would make it possible for them to continue their studies or to be retrained for another profession, and what sort of organization it is. Here, a committee has recently been formed especially to help academics who have to emigrate, but it has almost

170   no money. Here in London I am especially concerned about a twenty-three-year-old man who used to be chairman of the Republican Student League, a law student,[6] who is really in need and for whom I cannot find a place. I don't think he is especially brilliant, but he simply must be helped. I would

---

[1.] Library of Congress Annex, Washington, D.C., Dept. of Manuscripts, Reinhold Niebuhr Papers, box 2, General Correspondence; typewritten; in German. See also *NL*, A 41,9 (12); photocopy. Previously published in *GS* 6:294–97. [Bonhoeffer had studied with Niebuhr at Union Theological Seminary, New York, 1930–31; see *DB-ER*, 159–60.—KC] As Niebuhr said in a 1968 interview with Larry Rasmussen, he advised Bonhoeffer not to study with Gandhi, saying that Gandhi was "an ethical liberal with philosophical footings at great distance from the *Weltanschauung* of a sophisticated German Lutheran; furthermore, Nazi Germany was no place for attempting the practice of nonviolent resistance. . . . Hitler's creed and deeds bore no resemblance to British ways and means. The Nazis would suffer none of the pains of conscience about using violence which the British did, and organized passive resistance would end in utter failure" (Rasmussen, *Dietrich Bonhoeffer*, 213). Bonhoeffer nevertheless pursued his plans for India; see 1/154.

[2.] The last contact had been Bonhoeffer's February 6, 1934, letter of recommendation for his cousin Hans Christoph von Hase (*GS* 6:259–61).

[3.] Hans Christoph von Hase had written from New York on March 30, 1934, that he was coming to London "around June 1" (*NL*, C 24).

[4.] Mrs. Keppel-Compton, an Englishwoman.

[5.] [Niebuhr was very active in helping refugees from Nazi Germany; Bonhoeffer may have known of this from his cousin. See Merkley, *Reinhold Niebuhr*, 155–57.—KC]

[6.] This was probably Kurt Berlowitz.

like to know whether there is a possibility in the States for him to carry on with his studies or to begin new ones, perhaps a scholarship or whatever. That is one case. Another is that of the author Armin T. Wegner—Tillich will certainly know him—very left-wing; he has had a terrible time in a concentration camp, a complete breakdown. He has not been able to find anything here and is in despair.

Please forgive me for troubling you with these things, but they are only a tiny part of what we are seeing here almost every day, and we end up standing there empty-handed, unable to help. My congregations support me in this work and are very understanding, which helps significantly.

The most recent events in Germany demonstrate in no uncertain terms where we are headed. I could only be amazed that there were no Protestant pastors among those who were shot on June 30.[7] In our circles we begin to understand more and more, especially since Frick's recent muzzling decree, that what we are now involved in is a new Kulturkampf.[8] What is strange is how long it takes for that possibility even to dawn on a Protestant pastor. And even now they are less willing to acknowledge this in Westphalia than here in Berlin. The danger of an orthodox, so-called intact church body[9] is very great in the West, and I consider it a serious possibility that some   171
day the state will find its best allies in this kind of church. An "orthodox" church is most certainly a much safer bet for the National Socialist state than Müller's church.[10] This is the very danger against which we have to protect ourselves, even though there is much to be said for orthodoxy. We are being very shortsighted here. A man like Müller will not be too embarrassed to subscribe to our entire orthodoxy, perhaps more or less honestly from his subjective viewpoint. The parting of the ways is not there but elsewhere, in the Sermon on the Mount.[11] It is high time to bring the focus back to the

---

[7.] The victims of the so-called Röhm putsch included, in addition to SA leaders, several prominent German Catholics (cf. Scholder, *Churches and the Third Reich*, 2:197).

[8.] On July 11, 1934, Karl Koch had objected to the Reich Ministry of the Interior "in the name of the Confessing Church, which alone legally represent[ed] the German Evangelical Church," that "by means of attacks by the state, the illegal government of the Reich bishop was being supported and artificially preserved in its opposition to the Protestant Church" (Gauger, *Chronik der Kirchenwirren*, 2:259). On the Frick decree, see 1/125, ed. note 8. The term *Kulturkampf* alludes to the struggle between the Prussian state and the Catholic Church between 1871 and 1887.

[9.] See 1/133, ed. note 5.

[10.] [Bonhoeffer and other radicals in the Confessing Church viewed the passivity of the conservative "intact" churches to be a greater long-term threat than the German Christians.—KC]

[11.] [The Sermon on the Mount would become increasingly important to Bonhoeffer upon his return to Germany in 1935, both in terms of shaping the model of the theological

Sermon on the Mount, to some degree on the basis of a restoration of Reformation theology,[12] but in a way different from the Reformation understanding. And precisely at this point the present opposition will divide once again. Until we get to that point, all we are doing is preparing for it. The new church that must come into being in Germany will look very different from the opposition church of today.[13]

For my part, I am planning to go to India quite soon to see what Gandhi knows about such things and what there is to learn there. I am just now waiting for a letter and an invitation from him.[14] Do you perhaps know some important people there to whom you could recommend me?

I am presently doing some writing about the question of the Sermon on the Mount etc.[15] I am halfway through your *Moral Man* etc.,[16] which I find very interesting, and plan to finish it during my holiday.

I remember with gratitude many happy times with you in New York. Please give my regards to your wife.

Yours very sincerely,
Dietrich Bonhoeffer

172   **128. To Hildegard Lämmerhirdt**[1]

Dear Miss Lämmerhirdt,

Thank your very much for your letter.[2] I will be writing to my friends in Berlin in the next day or two and am confident that there is enough work

---

community he created in Finkenwalde and, of course, as a central part of his reflections in *Discipleship* (see *DBWE* 4, chap. 6).—KC]

[12.] In particular, at the end of May 1934 the Barmen Theological Declaration, in rejecting the false doctrine of the German Christians, had reaffirmed the *solus Christus* of the Reformation.

[13.] [This entire paragraph presages a number of themes that would be central to Bonhoeffer's thought in the years that followed, including the belief he often expressed in prison that the church of the future would have to be very different. See, for example, his comment in his May 1944 baptismal sermon for Dietrich Bethge, *LPP*, 300.—KC]

[14.] On Bonhoeffer's preparations for his trip to India, see 1/54, 1/93, 1/94, 1/154, and 1/158.

[15.] First drafts for *Discipleship* (*DBWE* 4); cf. the comment in 1/93, ed. note 12, on "spiritual exercise."

[16.] *Moral Man and Immoral Society* (1932); cf. *DB-ER*, 268.

[1.] In possession of Hilde Lämmerhirdt, Brakel, Westphalia; typewritten, presumably from London, in July 1934.

[2.] Not extant.

to do there.[3] However, it doesn't make much sense to start now, since the decisive people will be away until the end of August, and work with the laity will only start up again in September at the earliest. I would also think it a good idea to get an impression again of what this sort of work is like, before you make any definite decision about a career. Unfortunately, based on what I have heard lately, I doubt very much that you would get any financial help for your expenses at the beginning. Could you perhaps, as a way of preparing a bit for the work you would like to do in Berlin, participate in one of the summer courses that must certainly be available at Bethel?[4] This would also give you a chance to see what Bethel is like. I think it possible that teaching the Bible in Berlin could turn out to be quite demanding, not least in terms of your knowledge of the Bible.

It is truly extraordinarily difficult these days to make firm decisions in any particular direction. Thus I do understand, to a degree, your worry about this. In the end, however, these worries and all such difficulties and annoyances in life are given us to spur us toward prayer. So they come from God and lead us back to God—and the great danger is that we won't let go of them but want to keep them to ourselves. Only then are they fruitless and destructive.

My plans for India are still very unsettled. I am currently waiting for a letter from there.[5]

I have pleasant memories of your time here in London and our good   173
conversations.

With all best wishes, I remain
Yours sincerely,
Dietrich Bonhoeffer

[3.] Hilde Lämmerhirdt had spent a year in London (1933–34) and was looking for a job in Germany. She was considering working as a catechism teacher in Berlin.

[4.] [In addition to its facilities for the disabled, the Bethel community in Westphalia had a theological college.—KC]

[5.] Cf. 1/127, ed. note 14.

129. From Hans Schönfeld[1]

July 16, 1934

Dear Pastor Bonhoeffer:

On behalf of Dr. Schönfeld, I would like to ask you please to be good enough to invite Dr. Wendland, a doctor of theology and lecturer at the University of Heidelberg, to the Youth Conference being held in September in Denmark.[2] Dr. Wendland is very interested in youth work, and his participation at this conference could be especially valuable, since he is one of the participants in the council meeting who are to speak during the discussion of the theme "Church and State."[3]

Sincerely yours,

(p.p.) Dr. Behrens

174   130. From Hermann Wolfgang Beyer[1]

Greifswald, July 30, 1934

Dear Pastor Bonhoeffer,

In going through my files from the time of my service in the Clerical Ministry of the German Evangelical Church, I have discovered the letter you wrote to me during that time[2] and realize that I did not reply to it then, since it only arrived just after my resignation from that position. I still feel compelled, nevertheless, to say a word to you about it, although on a completely personal basis. I can assure you that, during my time in the church government, your name was never mentioned to me in any connection whatever with foreign press reports about what was happening in the German church. Furthermore, on listening to what was being

---

[1.] WCC Archives, Life and Work, Study Department, Study Conferences–Fanö 1934; carbon copy. See also *NL*, 40,2 (2); typewritten copy. Previously published in *Mündige Welt*, 5:228, and *GS* 6:354. Probably from Geneva, written by Schönfeld's colleague Dr. Behrens.

[2.] Ecumenical Youth Conference on the island of Fanø, August 22–29, 1934. [Schönfeld cites September erroneously.—KC]

[3.] On July 17, 1934, the Church Foreign Office wrote to Geneva that Heinz-Dietrich Wendland and Theodor Heckel were planning together for the plenary discussion on August 27 in Fanø, since their presentations "were presumably . . . on about the same theological level." Furthermore, the Church Foreign Office would be very pleased if Wendland were invited to the Youth Conference: "I believe this could be helpful to the ecumenical cause in Germany" (Krummacher to Schönfeld, WCC Archives, as in ed. note 1). Bonhoeffer did not agree at all (see 1/136). In the end, Wendland appeared in Fanø as a speaker at the two plenary sessions on August 27 and 28, but not at the Youth Conference.

[1.] *NL*, A 41,9 (4); typewritten. Previously published in *GS* 2:156.

[2.] On January 6, 1934; see 1/47.

said around me, I never heard anything of the kind. Thus I do not know in what circles these slanderous remarks against you were circulated. I feel an obligation to tell you this even now and unquestionably do not need to assure you that if any such remarks had reached me, I would have refuted them vehemently. My entire engagement during that time was to hold the line for a clean and aboveboard attitude truly worthy of the church.

Yours sincerely and respectfully,
Beyer

131. To H. Fricke[1]

London, July 31, 1934

Dear Mr. Fricke:

I am writing to you today with an important request. Would you please do me the great kindness and take care of the enclosed payment to Pastor Bodelschwingh in Bethel? The confirmation from the Reich Bank has only just now reached me, after having been sent around to many different addresses. I know very little about banking matters and don't know how to proceed at this point. Would you be so kind as to help me out? In case you have any questions about this, would you please be so kind as to telephone my assistant, Dr. Winterhager? He knows all about this. I am leaving on holiday tomorrow and will only be back three weeks from now. In case it becomes complicated, I suppose it will have to wait for my return. This amount represents a donation collected by my two congregations.[2] So I suppose my name should be given as the sender, as pastor of the Sydenham and St. Paul's churches.

175

With many thanks for your help, and best wishes, I remain
Sincerely yours,
Dietrich Bonhoeffer

[1.] *NL,* A 41,9 (6); typewritten.

[2.] Bonhoeffer mentioned Bethel [the famous center for physically and mentally handicapped people in Bielefeld, Westphalia, led by Friedrich von Bodelschwingh—KC] in his sermon on 2 Cor. 12:9 for an evening service in 1934; see 3/19.

132. To George Bell[1]

London S.E. 23, 31st of July 34

My Lord Bishop

today I am coming to you with a great question. Dr. Wedell, a Non-Aryan very influential[2] lawyer of Düsseldorf, who is a very definitely Christian man and very activ in his congregation, has come to London for a holiday and is very much distressed about the situation of Non-Aryan Christian youth in Germany.[3] He feels it his duty to do something in this regard and he would very much like to see you, if possible, at any time here or in Chichester before Saturday[4] when he has to leave again for Germany. He is a very serious and conscientious man and if it could be done at all that he could see you—or if you cannot do it, perhaps that he could see somebody who could report you on it—it would be very helpfull for him. Dr. Wedell is married to a cousin of mine, who is "Aryan."[5] His address is: Rembrandt- Hotel, Thurloe Place, S.W.7. If you would be so kind as to let him know shortly, whether he might see you, I should be very gratefull to you. I shall be on holiday tomorrow. But if you cannot arrange it, he will understand it very well.

I saw Siegmund-Schulze yesterday, who was here for a few hours[6] and left for Danmark last night.

With many thanks I am, my Lord Bishop, Yours sincerely
Dietrich Bonhoeffer

133. To unknown recipients[1]

[. . .] I am following the development of the Church Struggle with growing concern. What sort of front is this that has suddenly popped up—Koch, Mei-

[1.] LPL, Bell Papers 42, 43; handwritten; in original English, including errors. See also *NL*, A 42,1 (20); typewritten copy. Previously published in *GS* 6:297–98.

[2.] "Very influential" inserted afterward.

[3.] [This reflects the situation at that point of Christians of Jewish descent, who were also affected by the Nazi racial laws.—KC]

[4.] On August 4, 1934.

[5.] Gertrud Wedell, née Bonhoeffer, from Elberfeld.

[6.] He had come to urge Bonhoeffer to attend the Fanø conference after all (cf. 1/134).

[1.] EZA, Best. 50, 254, Bl. 8; carbon copy. Note in pencil: "Bonhöffer circular letter." Apparently a partial copy of a letter from Bonhoeffer to theologian friends in Berlin. See *NL*, A 41,10; photocopy. Previously published in Bethge, "Besorgnis vor der Barmer Synode," in Norden, *Zwischen Bekenntnis und Anpassung*, 89–90. The formulations of some sentences are parallels, in some cases literally, of Bonhoeffer's reflections in his letters to Erwin Sutz

ser, Wurm[2]—for one thing, they are *in no way* the people whom *we* have in
mind, all decidedly "pastoral" types from before the war; for another, they
are certainly not offering a significantly clearer theology (though it may perhaps, or surely, be a more seriously *Christian* one) than those whom we would
like to get rid of over there.[3] This "cookery course"[4] I find just plain irresponsible. Might it not anyway be better and more true to our *being as church*
if the people in the so-called intact body of the church[5]—what does that   177
mean anyway? a body "holy and without spot or wrinkle"?[6]—perhaps didn't
come to the fore just now, but rather those from the Nazareth of Germany's
North or East, and not from the firmly founded Jerusalem of Westphalia.[7]
We are well aware, in any case, what that firm foundation actually looks like.
There could be no greater catastrophe now than a church-not-worthy-to-be-
church being followed by an arrogant, all too intact church. But it looks now
as though there is no stopping it any longer. All the more reason to keep

---

(April 28, 1934, 1/93) and Reinhold Niebuhr (July 13, 1934, 1/127). Cf. also the content
of his memorandum to the Ecumenical Youth Commission (January 29, 1935, 1/199). A
possible reference for dating this letter exists in a message addressed by the newly constituted Council of Brethren to "the Congregations and Brethren in the Diaspora" published
at the end of July 1934 (in *Junge Kirche* 2 [1934]: 675–76), which begins with the sentence
"The Church of the Lord is firmly founded!" The signatures of Koch, Meiser, and Wurm
head the list. Bonhoeffer is possibly making a sarcastic allusion to this declaration.

[2.] Since April 11, 1934, the activities of the church opposition had been coordinated
by the "Nuremberg committee," representatives of the Confessing Church synods in the
western and southern regional churches under the leadership of Karl Koch—excluding,
during the first weeks, the "radical" Pastors' Emergency League (see Scholder, *Churches and
the Third Reich*, 2:83–84).

[3.] The German Christian church government under Ludwig Müller.

[4.] [The German here, *Kochkurs* (cookery course), is a pun on "Koch's course" (in the
sense of leadership).—KC]

[5.] This refers to the representatives of the non–German Christian regional churches
of Bavaria, Baden, and Hanover [the so-called intact churches], in contrast to the "disrupted" regions of the Prussian church, where emergency bodies were formed to oppose
being forced under the governance of the "German Christians." [The "intact" churches
were the regional churches of Bavaria, Württemberg, and Hanover (and to some extent,
the churches of Baden and Lippe), in which the bishops had retained control of the governance structures, in contrast to the "disrupted" churches throughout Prussia, where, in
the wake of the July 1933 church elections, the heavy German Christian influence in the
church leadership compelled the church opposition to organize its own governance structures. See also 1/127 and Helmreich, *German Churches under Hitler*, 163–64 and 167.—KC]

[6.] Eph. 5:27.

[7.] "Nazareth" and "firmly founded Jerusalem" allude here to John 1:46 ["Can anything good come out of Nazareth?"] and Ps. 87:1 ["On the holy mount stands the city he
founded"]. [Here Bonhoeffer seems to be hoping that more opposition will emerge in the
regional churches of northern and eastern Germany, outside the intact churches and the
Prussian church (which included Westphalia); several of the northern and eastern regional
churches were German Christian strongholds.—KC]

our eyes open and know exactly what it is we are after. All the more reason to take hold of the New Testament issues that burn one's fingers.[8] All the more reason to be aware that only a totally clear, unambiguous, unshakable, matter-of-fact, and cheerful attitude can help us win the Church Struggle inwardly as well as outwardly. I believe that what has happened up to now has only been preliminary skirmishing. The second, real battle is coming and will break out somewhere else altogether, and we will no longer be able, or be allowed, to fight it out with the same fresh and cheerful militancy. Instead, this second struggle about Christianity will be won by those who can suffer all the way through it. It will lead to the complete splintering and shattering of the so-called opposition fronts held by those who seek to be Christians. It will lead to our complete isolation, it will make it impossible to confuse the church with the church-political community, and everything will be left to individuals once again, the way it was at the beginning. We shall rediscover ourselves as individuals, and through individual witness—and only so—shall we rediscover what discipleship means. Only then will it be clear what it means to confess our faith. Peter confessing his faith was Peter the disciple, Peter who was called to suffer.[9] For in the end, it is suffering alone that

178   will overcome the world, lift up the cross, and make it visible. All this is not hope for a new kind of Christian heroism, but it is this alone that will create the ground on which one can stand and credibly proclaim Christ. So it is altogether a secondary aspect, but this is precisely where we have all become so blind.

So all this is nothing other than a dialectical pointer toward the possibility of faith, discipleship, confession. Thus it stands (since this concept of possibility is not theologically permissible)[10] at the margin of theology, at the point where theology as a science has to focus on faith as a reality.

Only at this point do all thoughts of a monastic community[11] become right and meaningful. So most certainly not a Catholic one [. . .]

[8.] The reference is to the Sermon on the Mount and discipleship (cf. 1/93 and 1/127).

[9.] Cf. Matt. 10:13–28 and par., as well as the passages on Peter in *Discipleship* (*DBWE* 4:46 and 84–86).

[10.] Cf. *DBWE* 2:132 and *DBW* 10:373–75; see also Holl, *Luther*, 234–35. [Holl, a leading authority on Luther, had been one of Bonhoeffer's influential teachers at the University of Berlin; see *DB-ER*, 78–79 and 85–86.—KC]

[11.] Cf. 1/111, 1/147, and 1/199.

134. To Ove Valdemar Ammundsen[1]

August 8, 1934

My dear and esteemed Bishop,

Please forgive me for taking so long to reply to your kind letter.[2] But I did not want to do so until I had come to a firm decision. It has indeed become quite clear to me, through your letter and then through a conversation with Siegmund-Schultze, that I must go to Fanö, putting aside all personal reservations about it.[3] Now that an invitation has also been sent to President Dr. Koch,[4] and thus there has been a more or less formal declaration that   179 the conference will listen to us, the situation has become quite clear. Many thanks once again for your words; please always write to me when you have the feeling that I am doing something wrong. These ecumenical matters are for us Germans something that we only learn if we keep paying attention, gaining experience, and receiving help—and for this I thank you.

Now just a word about the conference itself. Personally, to be quite frank, I am more afraid of many of our own supporters, when I think of Fanö, than of the German Christians.[5] It's possible that many on our side may be terribly cautious for fear of seeming unpatriotic, not so much from anxiety as rather from a false sense of honor. Many people, even those who have been doing ecumenical work for quite some time, still seem incapable of realizing or believing that we are really here together purely as *Christians*. They are dreadfully suspicious, and it prevents them from being completely open. If only you, my dear Bishop, could manage to break the ice, so that these

---

[1.] Royal Library, Copenhagen, Ammundsen Archive; handwritten; possibly from London. See also *NL*, A 41,9 (1); typewritten copy. Previously published in *GS* 1:205–6.

[2.] Not extant. [But see *DB-ER*, 379–80, for Ammundsen's letter of July 11, 1934, to George Bell concerning Confessing Church representation at Fanø.—KC]

[3.] Bonhoeffer had announced that he would stay away from any sessions of the council at which representatives of the Reich Church government were present (see 1/122), and he had already decided not to give his speech to the plenary session (see 1/125); see also *DB-ER*, 376–77.

[4.] After consulting with Ammundsen and Koechlin (see 1/126, ed. note 5 [also *DB-ER*, 379–80, for Ammundsen's reply to Bell—KC]), Bell, as president of the Universal Council for Life and Work, had decided on July 18, 1934, to invite two representatives of the Confessing Synod of the German Evangelical Church to the assembly in August "as guests and as authoritative spokesmen in a very difficult situation" (*GS* 1:204 and Boyens, *Kirchenkampf und Ökumene*, 1:330 and 110, as well as Scholder, *Churches and the Third Reich*, 2:237).

[5.] [This is another reference to Bonhoeffer's reservations about the intact churches and their leaders, bishops Meiser, Wurm, and Marahrens, who were cautious about church politics. See his similar comments in 1/127 and 1/133.—KC]

people become more trusting and open. It is precisely here, *in our attitude toward the state,* that we must speak out with absolute sincerity for the sake of Jesus Christ and of the ecumenical cause. It must be made quite clear—terrifying though it is—that we are immediately faced with the decision: National Socialist *or* Christian. We must advance beyond where we stood a year ago[6] (I remember, you said so at the time!). However heavy and difficult it may be for us all, we must face this and go through with it, without trying to be diplomatic but speaking frankly as Christians. And we shall discover the way by praying together. I just wanted to say that.

In my opinion, a resolution ought to be drawn up—no good can come of evading it. And if the World Alliance in Germany should then be dissolved—well, all right, then we have acknowledged that we were to blame, and that's better than vegetating along in a state of insincerity. Only the *complete truth* and *complete truthfulness* can help us now. I know that many of my German friends think otherwise. But I do beg you to try to understand this idea.

180   How nice that we shall soon see each other—I am really looking forward to it. After the conference a small group of German students (about ten) and I are going to have a retreat in Denmark.[7]

I would very much like to go over to Copenhagen, where I could have the great pleasure of seeing your daughter[8] again. A very good friend of mine[9] works at the German embassy in Copenhagen. But I don't know yet whether I'll get there, either before or after the conference.

I've heard that you are in Germany these days.[10] It is so good to know that there are still people standing by us in spite of everything, and in prayer with us.

With sincere gratitude and esteem I remain,
As ever,
Dietrich Bonhoeffer

[6.] At the World Alliance meeting in Sofia, September 15–20, 1933 (see *DB-ER,* 311–16).

[7.] This probably meant the theology conference originally to have been held in Luxembourg, which then took place in Bruay (cf. 1/115 and 1/151).

[8.] Esther Ammundsen.

[9.] Hans Bernd von Haeften.

[10.] On August 10, 1934, Ammundsen met in Hamburg with leaders of the Confessing Synod, among them Bonhoeffer's friend Franz Hildebrandt (cf. Boyens, *Kirchenkampf und Ökumene,* 1:111).

135. From Théodore de Félice[1]

Geneva, August 11, 1934

My dear sir and friend,

Please note a few modifications in the Fanø schedule that I am enclosing,[2] about which I leave to you to inform your delegates.

As a result of a cancellation that occurred during vacation by someone else whom I had asked to be responsible and who was also on vacation, there is no longer anyone to treat the subject "The Christian and the State according to the Bible." Would you be willing to treat this subject? You would be doing us an enormous favor.

Aren't Latvia, Estonia, and Lithuania part of your region?[3] You know that we had planned to pay the expenses of a delegate from each of these countries, as well as a subsidy for each of them. Have you not found anyone? I just received three registrations from Hungary.[4] Have you not found anyone either for the   181 Netherlands; we had planned to pay the expenses for the delegate from that country, but not a subsidy.

I thank you in advance for your answer and I remain,

Very cordially yours,
Th. de Félice

136. To Théodore de Félice[1]

London, August 12, 1934

Dear Mr. de Félice,

You will already have heard from Schönfeld or Miss Marks that I should like to give my paper in Fanø after all, but in view of the present circumstances have altered the contents correspondingly.[2] Although I am now a delegate

---

[1.] WCC Archives, World Alliance, Letters to Dietrich Bonhoeffer; carbon copy; in French.

[2.] Not extant.

[3.] As Ecumenical Youth Secretary for Central and Northern Europe, Bonhoeffer was also responsible for the Baltic states.

[4.] Cf. 1/115, ed. note 7.

[1.] WCC Archives, World Alliance, Letters from Dietrich Bonhoeffer; typewritten. See also *NL*, A 40,1 (6); photocopy. Previously published in *Mündige Welt*, 5:228–29, and *GS* 6:354–56.

[2.] Cf. the theses on "The Church and the Peoples of the World: The Fundamental Principles of the World Alliance" (2/2), which Bonhoeffer had sent to Geneva a few days previously.

from the Evangelical Confessing Church (of Germany),[3] I wish to give the paper in my capacity *as Youth Secretary.*

Since I have not heard anything from you about plans for the *evenings* or worship services (morning and evening), I have put together a plan for the week, together with Mr. Winterhager, and have asked him to write up a draft for the daily schedule. I am enclosing a copy of this draft[4] and hope it is not in contradiction with your own plans.

182   In view of the extreme seriousness of the situation,[5] we are most anxious that you should not prepare a "festive evening" or any other form of light entertainment.[6] Some members of the German youth delegation will have been involved in very difficult church-political circumstances and do not know what lies in store for them and all other confessing Protestants after their return from Fanø and in the weeks to come.[7]

Dr. Wendland has not been personally invited to the *Youth* Conference by either Winterhager or myself,[8] since we have heard that he was, or may even still be (?), a member of the German Christian movement.[9] The ten

---

[3.] The participation of a Confessing Church delegation had become very uncertain (see Koch's letter to Bell, August 10, 1934, in Boyens, *Kirchenkampf und Ökumene,* 1:333–34) because of the tense political situation (see notes 5 and 7). In the August 10 letter to Bell, President Koch had therefore agreed that if necessary Bonhoeffer might represent the church opposition in Fanø (cf. O. V. Ammundsen, "Report of My Interview with D. Koch and His Friends," WCC Archives, Life and Work, Executive Committee, Fanø, August 1934, p. 3; also Bell and Koechlin, *Briefwechsel,* 144–45). However, Bonhoeffer's appointment to this role only seems to have had a "behind-the-scenes" effect at the conference itself.

[4.] Not extant.

[5.] Following the June 30, 1934, murders [of SA leader Ernst Röhm and his Party allies, whom Hitler perceived as a threat—KC], the church opposition was also subjected to open threats (see Ammundsen, "Report of My Interview with D. Koch and His Friends," WCC Archives, Life and Work, Executive Committee, Fanø, August 1934, p. 3). The murder of Austrian Chancellor Dollfuß by Nazi rebels on July 25 had intensified Germany's isolation abroad. Finally, in the early days of August, following the death of Reich President Hindenburg, Hitler had declared himself "Führer and Reich Chancellor of the German People" with the full powers of both.

[6.] [Bonhoeffer evidently had in mind the kind of occasion, standard then as now during such conferences, which would include singing, games, joke telling, and satirically humorous sketches.—KC]

[7.] It was reported to the leadership of the Confessing Church, as a threat from the Reich Ministry of Cultural Affairs, that a Confessing Church delegation would face the same "fate" as Röhm and his people (Ammundsen, "Report of My Interview with D. Koch and His Friends," WCC Archives, Life and Work, Executive Committee, Fanø, August 1934, p. 3; see also Roon, *Zwischen Neutralismus und Solidarität,* 69–70).

[8.] See 1/129.

[9.] Wendland's name appears as a signatory on the first appeal of the Young Reformation movement in May 1933 (see *DB-ER,* 281). In 1934 he had an ecumenical reputation as a defender of the "new Germany." Although he apparently considered himself as "belonging

members of our German youth delegation[10] all stand firmly in the Confessing Church. Besides the younger members, whose names Winterhager has already sent you, we have also invited, as (older) guests (that is, "honorary members") in our delegation, Pastor Forell (of Berlin, currently in Uppsala)[11] and Pastor Hildebrandt (Berlin-Dahlem).[12]

I would be grateful if you could inform me here at my London address as   183 to whether and where the members of the German delegation can be lodged together on Fanø, because some of them may already be in Esbjerg on the morning of August 22.

I had invitations sent to Holland and the Baltic countries several weeks ago. Since I received no answers from them, I assumed that the church offices there were in touch with you directly. The only ones who have written to me or to Winterhager up to now have been the Hungarians.

However, when I received your letter the day before yesterday, I sent follow-up letters right away by air mail. I myself am particularly interested to see who all will come from Austria.[13] Could you inform me ahead of time about that as well?

Regarding the paper on "The Christian and the State according to the Bible," I have asked one of our young Germans, Vicar Winfried Maechler, to undertake it. I hope he will find enough peace and quiet to prepare it in the short time that is left.[14]

Winterhager is ready and able to *translate immediately into English* all presentations by our German youth delegation. But I doubt that Mr. Dudzus will

---

to the Confessing side," he was quite willing to be recruited for the Church Foreign Office strategy for the conference (cf. Boyens, *Kirchenkampf und Ökumene*, 1:118 and 332; Roon, *Zwischen Neutralismus und Solidarität*, 69–70; and 1/129).

[10.] See 1/115, ed. note 6.

[11.] Winterhager had written to Bishop Bell on August 9, 1934: "Pastor Forell will be an honorary member of that German Youth Delegation as he has ever been in close touch with our oecumenic groups in Berlin. Moreover, we feel greatly obliged that your Lordship will also consider Pastor Forell's invitation to be a guest at some of the senior meetings" (*NL*, A 42,4–6).

[12.] Hildebrandt met with Bonhoeffer on Fanø on August 18–19, 1934, but did not stay for the conference (see 1/140, ed. note 2).

[13.] Bonhoeffer's particular interest in this probably concerned the Nazi putsch attempt in Vienna. The Austrian participant in the conference was Margarete Hoffer (see her report in *Die Kirchen am Werk* [a journal published by the ecumenical council—KC] [6/1934]: 8ff).

[14.] Maechler gave his paper at the morning session on August 24, 1934 (see 1/141).

be in a position to send his paper beforehand in writing (through the post) from Germany to Geneva.[15]

With greetings and best wishes, from Winterhager as well,

Yours sincerely,

D. Bonhoeffer

184   **137. From Hans Schönfeld**[1]

August 13, 1934

Dear Dr. Bonhoeffer:

I have recently seen your theses for your address in Denmark[2] and would beg you to adopt a more comprehensive approach to the theme "The Church and the Peoples of the World" or "Internationalism and Ecumenism," especially in your introductory words, than you have done in these theses.[3] In doing so, you will find the theses of Dr. W. Menn particularly suggestive; they have already been edited further, taking a cue from the results of the ecumenical study conference in Paris.[4] The study book itself, *The Church and the Problem of the State Today*, will unfortunately not be ready until the beginning of the conference itself, on Fanö. However, we trust that we may count on your participation in the speakers' meeting on August 24, at four in the afternoon, at which we will go through the plans for the discussions once again carefully. You have no doubt already received a number of the other important theses from the study conference in Paris.

With best wishes,

Yours respectfully,

Hans Schönfeld

[15.] Given the postal censorship in Nazi Germany, it was hardly possible to mail a paper on "What position should we take as individual Christians when the state enters into conflict with Christian principles?" (cf. 1/141).

[1.] WCC Archives, Life and Work, Study Department, Study Conference Fanø 1934; carbon copy; file ref. FA 353/34. See also *NL,* A 40,2 (3); typewritten copy. Previously published in *GS* 1:207.

[2.] "The Church and the Peoples of the World"; see 2/2.

[3.] When he sent the thesis papers to Wilhelm Menn on August 10, Schönfeld expressed himself more clearly: "I must say that I am rather horrified at what Mr. Bonhoeffer has submitted here, so narrowly limited to the problem of war. Even Zankow's theses, in his peculiar German, are of more value" (WCC Archives, Life and Work, Study Department, Study Conference Fanø 1934; carbon copy; file ref. FA 353/34).

[4.] See 1/114, ed. note 7.

138. From Théodore de Félice[1]

Geneva, August 16, 1934

Dear friend,

Your draft of a schedule, for which I thank you, has been compared to the one I had already established, and you will find enclosed the result that we arrived at, Mr. Henriod and myself.[2]

Indeed, we consider it necessary that on Monday and Tuesday[3] the youth also participate in the adult service in order for them all to be entirely in the same atmosphere. On the other hand, we cannot yet establish the time of the short evening services because we are waiting to ask the various prominent people at Fanø. 185

Finally, of the four subjects that you proposed for the "informal meetings" in the evenings, we have chosen two: "The Conflict of the Churches in Germany" and "Conscientious Objectors," but we are not officially assigning them a place in the program; it will be during the study week itself that we can see where it would be appropriate to place them, for I certainly think that the delegates will keenly want to discuss these subjects.

The subject "Confession of Faith" seems to me a bit outside the conference theme, and since Mr. A. Philip is not coming, he will not be able to treat the one on "Security and Peace." Besides, the program is already rather full.

You mention Dr. Weinland,[4] but there's no question of his coming to the youth conference; I never invited him and he is nowhere to be found on our list of registered delegates.

The guests you have invited, Forel[5] and Hildebrandt, will be housed with the youth; it goes without saying that the latter, like anyone beyond the three Germans who can come free, will be housed at their own expense. I am notifying the mission guesthouse that will have to lodge these people.

I thank you very much for having done what was necessary regarding the Netherlands and the Baltics.

From Austria it is Miss Hoffer who is coming.

[1.] WCC Archives, World Alliance, Letters to Dietrich Bonhoeffer; carbon copy; in French.

[2.] Not extant. This was undoubtedly a previous version of the hectographed "Program for the Study Week" [in French—KC] found in Bethge's literary estate, Fanø file.

[3.] August 27 and 28, 1934, the days for the plenary discussions on "The Church and the State Today" and "The Church and the Peoples of the World," which the youth were allowed to attend as auditors (see 1/141).

[4.] Refers to Heinz-Dietrich Wendland.

[5.] Birger Forell.

Thank you also for having been willing to look for someone to handle the subject "The Christian and the State according to the Bible."

You will see from the program that no festive gathering[6] is planned.

Anticipating the pleasure of seeing you again soon, dear friend, I remain,

Very cordially yours,
Th. de Félice

Enclosure[7]

186   **139. To Ove Valdemar Ammundsen**[1]

August 18, 1934

My dear, esteemed Bishop,

My friend Pastor Hildebrandt told me about your meeting in Hamburg.[2] I find it a great pity that our people are not coming.[3] In view of the most recent developments,[4] it now seems to me imperative that not only Life and Work but also the World Alliance should publish a resolution, perhaps even the same resolution. I know there are strong feelings against this,[5] but I shall do everything I can to counteract them. We dare not keep silent at this point.

I am writing now just to you, my dear Bishop, to ask your advice as to how I should proceed and, what is even more important, your help with this matter! I would so very much appreciate your assistance! I do hope you received my last letter.

Looking forward very much to seeing you, in sincere gratitude and esteem, I remain,

As ever,
Dietrich Bonhoeffer

[6.] [Cf. 1/136, ed. note 6.—KC]

[7.] Not extant.

[1.] Royal Library, Copenhagen, Ammundsen Archive; handwritten. See also *NL*, A 41,9 (1); typewritten copy. Previously published in *GS* 1:207–8. Probably from Fanø (see 1/140, ed. note 2).

[2.] See 1/134, ed. note 10.

[3.] See 1/136, ed. note 3.

[4.] See 1/136, ed. note 5.

[5.] See *DB-ER*, 381–82.

140. To Julie Bonhoeffer[1]

Dear Grandmama,

Again this year it turns out that, due to unexpected circumstances, I won't be able to come for your birthday. I am really sorry about this. It has been such a long time since I was there for your birthday. These are times in which one should really hold that much tighter to all one's personal ties than before, so it's hard when that isn't even outwardly possible. One feels more and more   187
what a great gift it is to be such a big family, and that we are so happy, so exceptionally happy with one another. And that you and my parents keep us all together as a family, as you do, well, it's hard to imagine what life would be like otherwise. My wish for you today, and for all of us, is that we may remain so, in spite of everything, for a long time to come. We all need it more than ever.

I have been so very sorry that our correspondence has been in spurts. Surely this is entirely my fault. There are always so many letters to write that there is never time for the ones I most want to write and to be able to take my time doing it. At the moment (since yesterday) I'm in Fanö, waiting for the conference to begin. Franz is here too and had lots to tell me,[2] including news of Mama and how she is helping our cause in all sorts of ways. I am certainly grateful to Mama for all she is doing, and it's just fabulous the way she looks after my students. I know they are all incredibly fond of her and look up to her, and that always makes me so happy. And I hope what is going on does not get to be too much for Papa, with all the many other things he has to do. Now they are having a short break; if only it could be a nice long holiday! For there are all sorts of things that they will yet have to go through.

[1.] *NL*, A 39,4 (5); handwritten; from Fanø, probably on August 19, 1934, but possibly on the 18th. Excerpted in *GS* 2:183 and *GS* 6:298–99.

[2.] In 1975 Franz Hildebrandt recalled: "Dietrich was a speaker at the World Alliance conference in Fanø in September [*sic*]; we met there, he coming from London, I from Berlin, before the conference began. After the Röhm bloodbath it was not advisable for any representative of the Confessing Church to be seen on the island, so I got away before Heckel and his satellites arrived. I was preaching at Forest Hill at the time when Dietrich, in the relative security of being an overseas pastor, was giving his famous talk on the Eighty-fifth Psalm. It was a text that preoccupied us intensively during those weeks" ("Errinerungen an Forest Hill," 37–38).

Franz brought me the news that Köhn[3] is interested in having me stay in London for another semester. That would mean turning down the seminary proposal[4]—at least I think so—which would be rather painful for me. But of course I completely understand Köhn's point of view. So I shall have to 188　write to Gerhard[5] about it. For the moment I am wondering how things here are going to turn out. I'm the only one of us here,[6] which I think is a bad mistake.

Now I must close; the sandstorm in this beach chair[7] makes it almost impossible to write. I'm hoping my parents will come to London in October!

All my best wishes for the next year, and for a happy birthday with the rest of the family!

With love and gratitude,
Dietrich

[3.] Code name for President Koch.

[4.] See 1/113, ed. note 4.

[5.] Jacobi.

[6.] Representing the Confessing Church; cf. 1/136, ed. note 3.

[7.] [Since Fanø was a seaside resort, the beach close by the conference center provided ample opportunities for relaxation, which no doubt partly compensated for the strictures against any "festive gathering" (see 1/136, ed. note 6, and 1/138, ed. note 6). Cf. the photographs in Bethge, Bethge, and Gremmels, *Life in Pictures* (centenary ed.), 82.—KC]

141. From the Report on the Fifth International Youth Conference[1]

[Opening session on organizational matters,
evening of August 22, 1934]

Thursday, August 23rd

After the devotional led by Bonhoeffer,[2] the 1st working session was opened at 9:45 P.M. under his chairmanship. D. B. Watson was appointed as secretary of the Conference.

Craske presented the general theme of the Conference: *"Church and State."*   189
[Craske's talk reproduced here]

The second of our secretaries in Berlin (Bonhoeffer's associate) made a statement on the condition of oecumenical activity in Germany.[3]

[1.] *Fanø Fellowship*, no. 1, October 1934, published quarterly by the Oecumenical Youth Commission (hectographic copy, 15 pages, handwritten at top of first page: "Nos. 1 & 3 in English No. 2 in Eng. & French"); WCC Archives, Ecumenical Youth Commission, Fanø Friendship. The English translation reproduced here is also contemporary. Only the passages that clearly concern the participation of Bonhoeffer and his students are reproduced here. The omitted sections are described briefly in square brackets. The conference report was compiled in autumn 1934 by Théodore de Félice on the basis of manuscripts of the speeches as well as discussion notes by D. B. Watson (these can be found in the literary estate of Eberhard Bethge, Fanø file, as well as in the WCC Archives, International Christian Youth Conference, Fanø, July [*sic*] 1934), which are quoted in the notes. In September–October 1934, Jürgen Winterhager reviewed the report before publication. Out of concern for the German participants, Winterhager deleted some names and toned down many of the formulations. Some of these have been reconstructed from the documents found in Geneva, as indicated in the notes. Winterhager also prepared a German translation (also in the WCC Archives, International Christian Youth Conference), after Bonhoeffer had said he was unable to do so. The German text of resolutions 2 and 4 has been published in *GS* 1:209ff. At the end it is noted that there were fifty-eight delegates at the Youth Conference, from Austria, Belgium, Czechoslovakia, Denmark, England, France, Germany, Hungary, India, Ireland, Japan, Madagascar, the Netherlands, Norway, Poland, Russia (an emigré), Scotland, Sweden, and the United States. [All footnotes in the German volume (pages 188–98) have been translated here.—KC]

[2.] Bonhoeffer conducted morning prayers, possibly based on Ps. 85:8[9], which was also the text for his speech at the main conference: "Let me hear what God the LORD will speak . . . " (see 2/3; also Heimbucher, "Christusfriede—Weltfrieden," chap. 2, § 5.1). E. C. Blackman reported soon after the conference: "We started in the right atmosphere, for at our devotions on the first morning Bonhoeffer reminded us that our primary object was not to commend our own views, national or individual, but to hear what God would say to us" (literary estate of Eberhard Bethge, Fanø file). Margarete Hoffer wrote: "At our first devotions we were urgently told, as the watchword for our entire conference, that our work cannot and must not consist of anything but listening together to what the *Lord* says, and in praying together that we may hear aright. Listening in faith to the words of the Bible, hearing one another as listeners who obey, this is the core of all ecumenical work" (*Die Kirchen am Werk*, no. 6 [Nov. 1934]: 8ff.).

[3.] According to Watson's notes, the speaker was Winterhager. The latter still felt too exposed by the formulation in the draft report that said, "One of our German friends

Kilborn reported on the situation in *Great Britain*.

[Kilborn's talk reproduced here]

In the course of the discussion, some points in the above addresses were made more precise.[4]

[Afternoon session with reports from the United States (B. S. Abernathy), from France (J. Martinesque), Scandinavia (W. A. Sparring-Petersen), and Hungary (N. Mackay) on the theme: "The Church and the State of today, and the difficulties that beset our oecumenical activities in various countries"]

190   Many questions were asked again.[5]

The day was closed after dinner by prayers led by Rajaobelina.

Friday, August 24th

Devotional was led by Toureille.

Then, under the chairmanship of de Félice, Maechler gave his address on "Christian and State according to the Bible."[6]

1. What is a Christian according to the New Testament? A [person] called by Christ, who has become a member of the body of Christ, is bringing the Kingdom into the world, and is a participant of the Kingdom, if loyal and obedient. Christ is

---

explained the situation of Church and State in Germany at present, and the resulting difficulties for our ecumenical action." (See Winterhager's urgent request for this to be changed in his letter of September 30, 1934, to Félice, WCC Archives, World Alliance, Letters from D. Bonhoeffer, no. 24.)

[4.] According to Watson, these included particularly the Church Struggle in Germany and the position the church opposition was taking on political issues. (German participants said, among other things, "Opposition of the Conf[essing] Synod not yet political, but will become that, if the uncompromising minority in the government becomes stronger—but as long as there is some liberty of conscience, one can be Christian and loyal Nazi and not make the opposition into a political question. . . . Conf. Synod have not yet worked out the full Christian attitude of church and state—have had to be content with very little up to now. Will soon have to settle this question.") [This illustrates how the Confessing Church, even at this point, confined its opposition to Nazism to questions affecting the church. It is not clear which German participants are being quoted or to whom the "uncompromising minority in the government" refers.—KC]

[5.] According to Watson's notes, the issue of "church and revisions of frontiers" was discussed with regard to Hungary. (In Hungary, as in the German Reich, nationalist forces were pushing for a "revision" of the 1919 Paris peace treaties and the territorial losses that had been imposed.) The assembly preparations were probably the source of the statement: "Oecumenical representatives prepared to tell the truth to the world, but do not foster any political opinions or actions."

[6.] Maechler's paper is reproduced from the detailed notes taken by Watson (WCC Archive, International Christian Youth Conference, Fanø 1934).

the suffering King who is actually reigning. Membership of each individual Christian depends on:

(a) hearing the Word of God and doing it;

(b) following Christ, in His suffering, and in the hope of the eternal promises.

2. What is the state according to the New Testament? The reign of a few mighty men, whose origin is force, not love. Because [humans] were perverted, force is necessary, in order to ensure the lesser of two evils. Christ says that the State is entitled to respect and financial support, but not to demand spiritual allegiance. [The] State has relative value. The end of the political order is war, revolt, and apocalyptic disaster.

3. Relations of Christian and State in the New Testament

a) Positively: State equals force, i.e., materialism. Christian equals love, i.e., spiritual element and idealism.

Despite [the] contrast there are positive relations between the two. The Roman state already protected St. Paul against persecutions. The State allows Christian[s] to enjoy certain privileges. It protects [them] as individual[s] in war and conflict. The Christian must be grateful for having order maintained.

b) Negatively: Both allegiances (spiritual and worldly) often conflict. If the conflict becomes a question of ultimate religion, the Christian will enjoy the membership of the Kingdom of God more than [human] society. There are no national barriers for a Christian, and yet national barriers of the world must be respected.   191

4. Can the Christian community and the State interchange functions, so to speak? [The] Totalitarian state takes over functions of the Church and adapts them to the State, changing its relative authority into actual authority. On its side, it is impossible for the Church to take over functions of the State, because it cannot use weapons of the World, but must trust in the spirit.[7]

The Conference divided itself into four international discussion groups to study those subjects.

> [Afternoon session with papers by F. W. Craske and S. Zankow on "The City of God"]

After dinner, the Conference took part in the divine service held at Nordby for all the oecumenical conferences.

Saturday, August 25.– Morning.

Devotional was led by Scharling.

Under the chairmanship of Zernov,[8] Ricoeur spoke on *"What position should we take as individual Christians, when the state enters into conflict with Christian principles?"*

[7.] Cf. Thesis 5 of the Barmen Theological Declaration.

[8.] [Nicolas Zernoff.—KC]

[Ricoeur's talk reproduced here][9]

Dudzus reported on the same subject as Ricoeur.[10] As soon as Church and State take themselves seriously, it is quite natural that they enter into conflict; it has always been so. The Church must remind the State of its limitations. The State has no absolute authority. This authority belongs only to God. The Church has a value and dignity by itself; it has the duty to preach the word of God.

But the church tends to become a part of the world instead of opposing the world. There is of course no question of taking an anarchical stand. We have duties to the country in which we live and notably the task to tell it the truth. But we must be prepared to be falsely charged with the imputations of raising political opposition.

192   In the times of its extremest loyalty to God, the Church has always been declared, by its most loyal representatives, to be [an] enemy of the state. Christians have to give their testimony even in suffering.

But we must always be careful that our decisions are dictated by faith, and never by political, cultural, sociological or other motives. We must also take care of the influence of our environment. The [balance] between [the alternatives of] individualism and socialism must leave us essentially indifferent, even if we are keenly interested in the one or the other. We have to keep ourselves away from all other motives than the Word of God.

The four discussion groups met afterwards to discuss the above questions.

Six draft resolutions had been given to the Secretariat of the Conference. They were referred to the Commission on resolutions. This Commission was composed of Blackman (Chairman), Tweedie-Stodart (Secretary), Martinesque, Scharling, Thyagaraju, Tillich, whose names had been proposed by the discussion groups. These draft resolutions were changed somewhat by the Commission, and then submitted to the national delegations, in order to let them present their comments before the plenary meeting.

[Evening session chaired by T. de Félice with discussion of resolutions I (on continued work of the Youth Conference in cooperation with Life and Work and the World Alliance), 2[11] (referred to the Commission on Resolutions), 3 (proposed theme for the next conference: "The Church"— rejected because it is in the province of Faith and Order), and 6 (instead

---

[9.] Detailed notes on Ricoeur's paper are in the WCC Archives, International Christian Youth Conference, Fanø, 1934.

[10.] The French manuscript of this paper is in the WCC Archives, International Christian Youth Conference, Fanø, 1934.

[11.] The French delegates Martinesque and Ricoeur submitted a "draft resolution" on the international character of the church, which was also supported by the Hungarian delegation (WCC Archives, International Christian Youth Conference, Fanø, 1934). See discussion of the revised version on pp. 206–7.

of a sermon, the main conference worship services should be centered on prayer and confession—passed on as a suggestion, not as a resolution. Evening prayers led by N. Mackay]

Sunday, August 25th [26th]

The Youth Conference took part in a visit with the adult conferences to Ribe and were present at the service in the cathedral [with Prof. Runestam of Uppsala preaching],[12] followed by luncheon [at Ribe] (at which some young delegates were asked to speak on behalf of the Youth Conference) and a visit to the town. On returning, they visited various interesting [social welfare] institutions in Esbjerg [and enjoyed an excellent coffee at Esbjerg town hall].

After dinner the conference held a long session—Chairman: Toureille—Vote-counters: Gerritsen and Matsuda. These officials did not take part in the voting.

193

Draft resolution Number 4 was brought before the meeting.[13] As the delegates were divided in opinion, it was decided that a separate vote should be taken for the 1st paragraph, 2nd paragraph and that the remaining paragraphs should be grouped together for a third vote.

The first paragraph was adopted unanimously.

A German delegate moved the suppression of paragraph 2, as its adoption would have meant that the German delegates had given their support to press attacks on Germany.[14] Paragraph 2 was adopted by 26 votes to 17, with two abstentions.

The remainder of the motion was adopted by 30 votes to 1, with 14 abstentions.

The following is the text of the resolution:

"The members of the 5th International Conference of Youth, meeting at Fanø, 22–29 August, where they have especially studied the problem of State from the Christian point of view,

"agree that the rights of conscience, undertaken in obedience to God's Word, exceed in importance those of any State whatever.

(Carried unanimously)

"They believe that the attacks upon these rights made in various countries justly provoke an ever growing condemnation by general public opinion.

(Carried: 26 for, 17 against, 2 abst[entions])

[12.] [This addition is in Winterhager's translation.—KC]

[13.] The draft for this resolution came from members of the French delegation. The typed text, headed "Projet de résolution" and signed by the French participants, had a final paragraph added in Jean Lasserre's handwriting (WCC Archives, International Christian Youth Conference, Fanø, 1934).

[14.] Watson's notes quote Ernst Tillich's objection as follows: "Very serious. If carried it implies German delegates are in favor of press attacks on Germany" (literary estate of Eberhard Bethge, Fanø file).

"They notice however that even those States which have inscribed in their law liberty of conscience, violate this law by severely punishing in one way or another, conscientious objectors.

"They are glad that an increasing number of states allow their conscientious objectors to replace military service by non-milit[ary] service (Denmark, Finland, Norway, Holland, Sweden).[15]

194 "They ask the other States to follow this example, and seeing that conscientious objection is a universal phenomenon[,] would say to the Governments wh[ich] are afraid to do this[,] on the ground[s] that in recognizing conscientious objection they would unilaterally weaken their fighting forces, that the institution of non-military service should be the object of an international convention.

"They request the World Alliance and the Universal Christian Council for Life and Work, directly and through the Churches with [which] they are in contact, to make urgent representation to Governments in order that young people who [push] the teaching of their Churches, as they understand it, to its final conclusions[,] should not be treated as criminals.

"They ask the Christian Churches not to [denounce] those of their members who in faithfulness to the Gospel refuse to bear arms, but to recognize them as their true children and to follow them with loving sympathy in their efforts of obedience to the Gospel."

(Carried: 30 for, 1 against, 14 abst[entions])

The resolution in its entirety was carried: 24 votes for, 12 against, 7 abstentions.

A new version of draft resolution No. 2[16] was brought into discussion. Various amendments dealing with minor points were adopted.

A Polish delegate, on behalf of his delegation, proposed the replacing in paragraph A of "any war whatsoever" by "aggressive war." A French delegate replied that this would change the whole spirit of the resolution. A Hungarian delegate declared that he and his fellow delegates were not in a position to vote on account of the political situation of Hungary,[17] but were fully in sympathy with those intending to vote [in favor]. The English delegation reminded the conference that, as the Bishops said in 1930, "War is evil." They [would] vote in this spirit.

A Polish delegate [announced that he shared the position taken by] the Hungarian delegate in view of the political and geographical situation of Poland.[18]

[15.] The draft resolution originally included "USSR (only for members of certain denominations)," but after discussion this was crossed out.

[16.] [Here the French version reads: "which had been referred back to the Committee the evening before."—KC]

[17.] See ed. note 5.

[18.] Watson noted: "The country is surrounded by Soviet-Russia–Germany" (literary estate of Eberhard Bethge, Fanø file).

A French delegate regretted the introduction of individual political cases in this discussion.[19] Another French delegate[20] [remarked that it is not the same thing to say] "War is evil" [as to say] "participation in war is evil."

The Polish delegation withdrew its amendment.

The Chairman announced that, as the original motion was in French, and as the English and German translations were not accurate, these versions would be revised according to the French text.

195

The following is the text of the resolution.

"Recent years have witnessed a strengthening of the sovereignty of the State and the attempt on the part of the State to become the only center and source of spiritual life. Most of the Churches have replied by mere academic protests, or they have shirked their responsibilities.

"On the basis of biblical revelation we affirm the universal nature of the church.

"(a) The Church has for its essential task the preaching of the Word of God. Therefore it could not be a function (even the highest function) of the nation. The Church works within the nation, but it is not 'of the nation.' It is independent, in its preaching, and therefore in its very existence, of merely national objectives. In particular it ought not to give its blessing to any war whatsoever. In face of the growing claims of the State the Church should abandon its attitude of passivity and, without fear of consequences, declare the will of God. Accordingly we urge the Churches to dissociate themselves from every Church which does not affirm this universalism, on the ground that it is not Christian.

"(b) The Church, although it should not enter political struggles, ought however, to urge its members to study social and political questions, with a view to action. This action, for which they are responsible individually, should have as its result the building up of a State where there is entire freedom for the Christian life.

"(c) When faced by concrete problems encountered in his individual life the Christian ought to make his choice in the light of this principle: 'We must obey God rather than men.'"

(The Resolution in its entirety was carried: 34 for, 0 against, 7 abstentions)

The Hungarian delegation explained that, as they represented the Federation of Hungarian Protestant Students, they were obliged to abstain, although they were in sympathy [with the resolution]. They were unable to condemn defensive war. A German woman delegate having [brought up] an incident on account of the abstentions,[21] the Chairman proposed a short time of prayer.

[19.] Watson noted: *"Ricoeur:* a great pity to try to introduce individual political cases under the strain of present situation" (literary estate of Eberhard Bethge, Fanø file).

[20.] Jean Lasserre.

[21.] According to Winfried Maechler's recollection, it was Hilde Enterlein who intervened at this point (Maechler, "Bonhoeffers Fanö-Friedensrede," 189).

Then Bonhoeffer reminded the Conference that we are one Church in spite of differences of opinion. We will build up the Church [together by] listening to God.
196   The remark that we are divided is not [made] as a reproach, but as a witness to the profound problem[s confronting] the Church. We are in deep sympathy with our Hungarian [friends]. Strong expression is a good thing, to show the real facts, but having said them we then join in common prayer, penitence and worship.[22]

A Polish delegate said that they agreed with [this] vision of the Church; no expression of opinions must be so strong as to destroy our real unity as one Church.

The Hungarian delegation then thanked Bonhoeffer on account of his speech and understanding. We have come here to collaborate as far as possible; we will work for the unity of the church.[23]

This moving session concluded at 12:30 A.M. with prayer.

197   *Monday, August 27th*

The Youth delegates were present at the devotional[24] and sessions of the adult conferences; the subject of the day was *The Church and the State of to-day*.[25]

[22.] Bonhoeffer's intervention in the face of this "apparent impasse . . . with little chance of decision" is reproduced fully in Watson's notes as follows: "Remember prayers of the first day [see ed. note 2—KC]. Situation of conference here is full of difficulty and challenge. We have been in danger of causing the conference to become merely a big show and to disguise under the outward form of resolutions, the main manifestation of our dependence. But we are one Church in spite of differences of opinions. Human attitudes will not build the Church, but the common listening to God. No doubt in all this that we are one Church. Must remember the disruption is one of our main temptations. But the building of the Church is seen in the common longing for the voice of God, and in cherishing this certainty of one Church. The remark that we are divided is not as a reproach but as witness to the profound problematics of the Church. There is suffering in the divided Church. We welcome the Hungarian speaker and are in sympathy with him and his people. We Germans understand the Hungarian feelings better than any other nation because of the similarity of our sufferings.—'The sharing of [Christ's] sufferings' [Phil. 3:10]. If we disagree with those whom we love, we suffer. It is the expression of the divisions of the Church which we love and we long to heal these divisions. Strong expression is a good thing to show the real facts. But having said them we then join in common prayer and penitence and worship" (literary estate of Eberhard Bethge, Fanø file; see also *DB-ER*, 390–91).
[23.] According to Watson's notes: "Thanks for Bonhoeffer's speech and understanding. We are part of the conception of one Church and are willing to further it. We have true fellowship in suffering and have come here to render co-operation as far as possible. In the critical and depressed state of Hungary, you will excuse our hesitation and recognize our will to common understanding and resolve to press towards the vision of the future of a united Church" (literary estate of Eberhard Bethge, Fanø file).
[24.] Led by F. W. T. Craske.
[25.] With George Bell presiding, the introductory speakers were Arvid Runestam, Marc Boegner, Prof. Vyschefslavzeff, Theodor Heckel, and J. H. Oldham (see WCC Archive,

At the afternoon meeting of these adult conferences, Blackman and Sturm presented resolution Number 2.[26]

> [Evening session of the youth conference with F. W. T. Craske in the chair; adoption of the resolution 5 (the Universal Christian Council to co-opt secretaries of the Ecumenical Youth Commission)[27] and reactions to the events of the day]

Winterhager expressed his gratitude for having been permitted to take part in the senior meeting. We must prepare ourselves to be worthy to take their place.[28]

Carter asked how we [shall] know what happens to our resolutions. De Félice answered [that] he [would] send word of them to all members of the Conference.

The evening devotional was led by Matsuda.[29]

Tuesday, August 28th

The Youth delegates took part in the devotional and meetings of the senior conferences. The subject of the day was: *The Church and the Peoples of the World.*[30]

In the afternoon session, Blackman and Lasserre, [accompanied] by a delegation of the Youth Conference, presented resolution Number 4.[31]

In these meetings with the senior delegates, Bonhoeffer and Toureille only, in addition to those already mentioned, had the opportunity to speak on behalf of youth. But Youth delegates sustained the speakers whose ideas were in agreement with the resolutions of the Youth Conference by their strong applause, keeping silent [reprovingly] when the contrary was the case.

"Minutes of the Meeting of the Council, Fanø, Denmark, 1934," published by the Universal Christian Council on Life and Work, Geneva, p. 38).

[26.] See p. 206.

[27.] Besides Bonhoeffer, F. W. T. Craske, Théodore de Félice, and Pierre Toureille were named at Fanø as members of the Universal Christian Council.

[28.] According to Watson's notes, Winterhager said: "Some of us have disapproved much of the plenary meeting; but we are grateful for permission to take part in it, because we can get to know something of the work of the elders, and prepare ourselves to be worthy to take their place" (literary estate of Eberhard Bethge, Fanø file).

[29.] [Here Félice inserted a note that some names of worship leaders were added to the minutes after the conference.—KC]

[30.] With Lord Dickinson presiding, the introductory speakers were George H. Marten, André Bouvier, Dietrich Bonhoeffer (see 2/3), and Stefan Zankow. Watson noted: "Plenary session with seniors. Morning: Striking speech by Bonhoeffer. Afternoon: Presentation of resolutions and a report by Lasserre" (literary estate of Eberhard Bethge, Fanø file).

[31.] See p. 205.

198   *Wednesday, August 29th*

The morning service was led by Burlingham.

The Conference met afterward in plenary closing session, also under [Burlingham's] chairmanship. It was first decided to break in[to] national groups to discuss what could be done in the future.

On resuming its deliberations, the Conference heard the *French delegation* exposing its suggestions:

[Position statement by the French delegation]

Germany: Oecumenical cooperation between German and Swedish youth groups is being continued. Small study circles in our Free Church Synod also carry on and [are] intensify[ing] the friendship work of the Northeast and central European secretariat. Moreover, we shall never cease to render our testimony individually. We ask for your prayers and thoughts, in order that our faith fail not.[32]

[Statements by the Scandinavian, Polish, Austrian, Indian, Belgian, and British delegations. Then de Félice, as Secretary of the Oecumenical Youth Commission, responded to various suggestions by the delegations. In conclusion, he said:]

We must put practically into effect our big resolutions relating to war and conscientious objectors:

(a) in fighting against the attempts to prepare the public mind for war, through the training of civilians in resisting air [raids], gas attacks, etc.

(b) in studying those factors leading to wars, and in combatting them;

(c) in thinking in advance, what we shall do in case of war;

(d) in making propaganda in favor of civil service as an alternative to replace military service.[33]

In the afternoon, a very impressive service, led by Craske, closed this splendid conference. [This Conference remains in the memories and the hearts of the delegates, as many letters received since the Conference testify, an outstanding milestone on the road of service.][34]

[32.] This passage was altered at Winterhager's request (see letter of September 9, 1934, from Winterhager to Félice, WCC Archive, World Alliance, Letters from D. Bonhoeffer; cf. ed. note 3). The minutes originally reproduced (in French) the following statement by Willy Brandenburg: "For lack of organization, we can only give our testimony individually. We ask you to pray and to think of us, that our faith may not fail."

[33.] Even the young ecumenists in Germany continued to work on this issue, despite the political risks. Besides Bonhoeffer's "Memorandum to the Ecumenical Youth Commission" (1/199), there is information about this in the "Report on the Question of Military Service" written by Winterhager in March 1935 for the German World Alliance meeting (see Heimbucher, "Christusfriede—Weltfrieden," chap. 3, §1.2).

[34.] [This last sentence is in the English but not the French version.—KC]

142. To Karl Koch[1]   199

Göttingen, Saturday, September 1

Dear President Koch:

May I please come to see you sometime between tomorrow and Tuesday[2] midday? I would like to discuss some issues from the last meeting,[3] from which I am just returning. On Tuesday I must return to my parishes. If you are to be away, I would be happy to speak with Brother Asmussen. There are all sorts of important questions to be dealt with. Tomorrow morning (Sunday), Professor Leibholz will telephone on my behalf, for your reply.

Yours most respectfully and sincerely,
Dietrich Bonhoeffer

143. From the Minutes of the Session
of the Reich Council of Brethren[1]

**Thirteenth Session of the Reich Council of Brethren
on September 3, 1934, in Würzburg, Hotel Excelsior–Railway Station**

[Previous agenda points: 1. Relationship of the Confessing Church to the State; 2. Relationship of the Confessing Church to the Reich Church Government; 3. Report and discussion on the founding assembly of the "Lutheran Council" in Hanover.]

4. Fanö   200

Pastor *Bonhoeffer*, who had arrived in the meantime,[2] reported on the conference of the Universal Council in Fanö, August 24 to 30, 1934.

[1.] LKA EKvW, 5,1, no. 767, fasc. 1; handwritten. See also *NL*, A 41,9 (9); typewritten copy. Previously published in *Mündige Welt*, 5:231. Stamped by recipient: "The President of the Confessing Synod of the German Evangelical Church, September 3, 1934."

[2.] September 4, 1934.

[3.] Probably the meeting of the Council of Brethren of the Pastors' Emergency League on August 31, 1934, in Berlin. Three days later, Asmussen informed the Reich Council of Brethren in Würzburg: "The Pastors' Emergency League has been meeting these last few days . . . and requests the Reich Council of Brethren . . . to address a word to the State" (Meiser, *Verantwortung für die Kirche*, 1:334).

[1.] LKA EKvW, 5,1, no. 704, fasc. 2; handwritten. Excerpted in *GS* 1:220–21. See also Meiser's record (*Verantwortung für die Kirche*, 1:329ff.), which breaks off *before* agenda point 4, "Fanö." According to the minutes, participants in the meeting were K. Koch, E. Fiedler, H. Asmussen, G. Weber, H. Meiser, T. Wurm, F. Müller-Dahlem, G. Jacobi, H. A. Hesse, J. Beckmann, K. Immer, W. Link, E. Klügel, and H. Meinzolt.

[2.] For the afternoon session at 3:40 P.M.

Three [*sic*] difficulties:

1. It was not clear for what reasons the representatives from the Confessing Church did not come.[3]

2. Are the Lutheran confessionalists not very significant, and do they not represent a breach in the Confessing front?[4]

3. Is the Confessing Synod a legal church? Why does it remain within the German Evangelical Church?

4. Contact with the ecumenical movement. Step to lift controls not taken by Hitler.[5]

Chichester[6] would be glad to come to Germany for September 23 if asked to do so.

Bonhoeffer recommends that the Confessing Synod reply to the message from the Universal Council.[7]

Communication, possibly an open letter, to Bishop Heckel.

Bonhoeffer was in Fanö as Youth Secretary of the World Alliance for Promoting International Friendship through the Churches, thus ex officio.

201   *Fiedler* pointed out that in *Das Evangelium im Dritten Reich*,[8] no. 35, the review of the church disciplinary measures is incorrect, and that this calls for a reply giving the exact numbers.

[3.] See 1/136, ed. note 3.

[4.] In itself this did indeed constitute a problem; cf. the third point on the agenda. ["Lutheran confessionalists" refers to the intact churches and their bishops. Although they had affirmed the Barmen declaration, soon afterward they began to push for a more moderate course. The "schism" did indeed finally come at the Dahlem synod, where delegates from the Lutheran churches voted against the emergency church law (*Notrecht*) passed at that meeting.—KC]

[5.] Permission for Confessing Church representatives to participate in the ecumenical conference (see Boyens, *Kirchenkampf und Ökumene*, 1:110–12 and 330–37).

[6.] George Bell.

[7.] Under protest and resistance from the German delegation headed by Heckel, the Fanø Conference had passed a resolution on August 30, 1934, on the church situation in Germany that contained a clear condemnation of the policies of the German Christian–dominated church government. The delegates to the Universal Council for Life and Work and the Executive Committee of the World Alliance for Promoting International Friendship through the Churches jointly declared their "grave anxiety" at the threat to "vital principles of Christian liberty" and said that "an autocratic church rule, . . . the use of methods of force, and the suppression of free discussion are incompatible with the true nature of the Christian Church." Finally, the resolution also said: "The Council desires to assure its brethren in the Confessional Synod of the German Evangelical Church of its prayers and heartfelt sympathy in their witness to the principles of the Gospel and of its resolve to maintain close fellowship with them." Previously published in Boyens, *Kirchenkampf und Ökumene*, 1:337–38. See also *DB-ER*, 382–83, and Scholder, *Churches and the Third Reich*, 2:240. Moreover, that same day President Koch was pointedly elected to the Universal Council, over Heckel's strenuous objections. There was no protest against the co-opting into the council, at the same time, of the youth secretary (and unofficial representative of the Confessing Church), Bonhoeffer.

Bonhoeffer urged that a man be appointed by the Confessing Synod to take charge of ecumenical affairs on its behalf.

Resolution: That the daily allowance for this session be fixed at thirty marks.

A report on Fanö is to be published at Oeynhausen.[9]

Resolution: George Bell is to receive a letter of thanks and an invitation.[10]

Bonhoeffer: Heckel has not, up to now, been co-opted into the Universal Council.[11] Five seats are held by Germans.

Bonhoeffer considers it unlikely that ecumenical guests could be invited by the Reich Church government to attend the consecration.[12] If extended, invitations would undoubtedly be declined; only the position of Popp and Glondys is in doubt.

[Following agenda points: 5. Other business, including the question of the loyalty oath; 6. Church government assignments; 7. Confessing Synod.]

Session adjourned at 8:28 P.M.

(signed) Dr. Fiedler

144. To George Bell[1]

Bruay en Artois (P. de Calais) 7. Sept. 1934

My Lord Bishop,

First of all, I want to thank you very much for the great help you have rendered to the cause of our Church at the Fanø Conference. The resolution in

---

[8.] This concerned the number of disciplinary measures in the German Evangelical Church; the German Christian body had denied that there were eight hundred. In its circular letter no. 14 of September 15, 1934, the Reich Council of Brethren presented a different picture. [*Das Evangelium im Dritten Reich* was a periodical published between 1932 and 1937.—KC]

[9.] "The World Conference on Fanø," published in Council of Brethren circular letter 14 (September 15, 1934): 7ff.

[10.] See 1/144.

[11.] Heckel was promoted at Fanø, however, as a member of the continental European group, to a position on the twenty-seven-member Executive Committee of the Universal Council. WCC Library, Geneva, BR 280.34 U 3m, "Minutes of the Universal Christian Council for Life and Work Fanø, Denmark, Geneva 1934," written in English, p. 58.

[12.] Installation of Reich Bishop Müller at the Berlin Cathedral on September 23, 1934.

[1.] LPL, Bell Papers 42, 45; typewritten, with typewritten letterhead: "Dietrich Bonhoeffer, (Conference oecumenique de la jeunesse [Ecumenical Youth Conference])"; in original English, including errors. See also *NL*, A 42,1 (21); typewritten copy. Previously published in *GS* 1:222.

202   its final form[2] has become a true expression of a brotherly spirit, of justice and truthfulness. And therefore the contents of the resolution will and must strike every one who reads it without prejudice.

Immediately after the Conference I went to Germany and met Präses Koch with the assembly of the whole Confessional Council.[3] I delivered there a detailed report on the Fanø Conference and I felt strongly that the resolution of Fanø had been met with the greatest appreciation. Moreover the Synod Council asked me to express to you in particular their deep gratitude. Präses Koch and the Council asked me to express to you at the same time their great desire to have the opportunity of meeting you when you are coming back from Sweden. If any time were convenient to you, Präses Koch would like to meet you at Hamburg. Other representatives of the Synod will come with him. Perhaps you would be so very kind as to send a short note to Oeynhausen.[4]

With deep thanks, I am, my Lord Bishop, Yours sincerely,
Dietrich Bonhoeffer

144a. Bishop Heckel to Bishop Dietrich[1]

Berlin-Charlottenburg 2
September 7, 1934

In reply to your letter of July 18, 1934, no. 4581, I am sorry to have to respond that considerable difficulties would stand in the way of employing Pastor Lebrecht, Groß-Zimmern, in service to a congregation abroad. In view of the composition of German colonies abroad and the attitudes of the overwhelming majority of their members toward the German fatherland, opposition to Pastor Lebrecht would develop as soon as it became known that he is not of the Aryan race. The resulting

---

[2.] See 1/143, ed. note 7.
[3.] See 1/143.
[4.] Cf. 1/148.

[1.] Unpublished, in possession of Marianne Lebrecht; typewritten. Reprinted in Gremmels and Pfeifer, *Dietrich Bonhoeffer Jahrbuch 2003*, 15–16. Included in a longer letter from Bishop Dietrich to Hans Lebrecht. Letterhead: "The Bishop of the Evangelical Church of Hesse-Nassau, Darmstadt, Mackensenstr. 40, Telephone 349 and 1108, October 1, 1934. Reply to no. 401." The text says: "Re: Employment of Pastor Lebrecht, Groß-Zimmern, in service to congregations abroad. To Pastor Lebrecht, Groß-Zimmern: In reply to your letter of April 5, 1934, I am sending you the following copy for your information. Signed (by hand) Dr. Dietrich." The copy, on the letterhead of the "German Evangelical Church, Church Foreign Office, Jebenstr. 3," has the ref. no. "A 2848" and is addressed to "The Bishop, Evangelical Church of Hesse-Nassau, Darmstadt," followed without salutation by the above text. [Ernst Ludwig Dietrich was an outspoken German Christian; he was bishop

shock to the unity of the colony must be avoided.[2] I therefore would not advise accepting this application for employment abroad, especially since I take the liberty of assuming, on the basis of your letter, that there is no objection to keeping this pastor in his present employment in your regional church.

(signed) Dr. Heckel

145. The Ecumenical Youth Conference to Ove Valdemar Ammundsen[1]

Bruay-en-Artois, September 8, 1934

Dear Bishop Ammundsen:

We would all like to thank you most sincerely for your kind greetings sent to us.[2] And we especially want to thank you once again for your confidence, your help, and the great legacy that you gave us at the Fanö conference, to   203 take with us for our future ecumenical work.

In constant gratitude and admiration, we remain[3]
Yours sincerely
For the delegation from   Germany   Dietrich Bonhoeffer
England   T. H. H. Kilborn
France   Jean Lasserre

---

of Hesse-Nassau from 1934 to 1936, when minister of church affairs Hans Kerrl established church committees to replace bishops in several regional church governments.—KC] This letter establishes that upon receiving Bonhoeffer's letter (1/85a), Lebrecht had applied through official channels to the Church Foreign Office. Edited by Hans Pfeifer. See also *DBW* 14, 1/8a.

[2.] Heckel uses this argument even though he knows better. He was well acquainted with the situation in London since his visit there in February 1934 (cf. 1/94 through 1/108, as well as Bonhoeffer's letter of April 1 to Lebrecht, 1/85a). In October 1933 Heckel had turned down Franz Hildebrandt's request in the same way, but without giving a reason. Furthermore, Heckel's choice of words (e.g., "colonies") betrays his political viewpoint.

[1.] Royal Library, Copenhagen, Ammundsen Archive; typewritten with handwritten addition. On the back is a handwritten note from Winterhager thanking Ammundsen for his letter. Ammundsen replied to "Mr. Bruay" (i.e., Winterhager) on December 19, 1934. See *Mündige Welt*, 5:237.

[2.] Not extant. The Ecumenical Youth Commission organized a "French-German-British theological conference" for young pastors in Lasserre's parish in Bruay, held September 4–8, 1934; see 2/3a as well as 1/151.

[3.] Bonhoeffer added the last line by hand.

146. From the Diary of Julius Rieger[1]

September 11, 1934

Bonhoeffer has found out from the Ministry of Justice[2] that on June 30 and July 1, 207 people were shot![3]

In Fanö, Birnbaum suddenly appeared by private airplane,[4] after Heckel had said, in the innermost circles of the Council (e.g., with regard to the Jewish question), that "it was not his province" to speak. Before that he had shown Siegmund-Schultze the door, with polite excuses that the latter's presence would prevent him from speaking. Then Birnbaum, who was allotted a quarter of an hour for his speech, used it for an absurd rigmarole about his personal experiences with people who became Christians because they were National Socialists. Heckel's lectures[5] (as was twice remarked) began very precisely but later became tangled up, confused, and obviously off the cuff.

204　　## 147. To Erwin Sutz[1]

London, September 11, 1934

My dear Sutz,

Thank you very much for your cards.[2] I got *both* of them. *Really* a pity that we did not see each other in Berlin. Just think, after the Fanö conference, where

---

[1.] *NL*, A 41,9 (18); typewritten copy. Previously published in *GS* 6:324.

[2.] Through his brother-in-law Hans von Dohnanyi.

[3.] The exact number of victims of the so-called Röhm putsch is not known to this day. In his speech to the Reichstag justifying his actions, Hitler spoke of seventy-seven deaths; historians' estimates today vary from eighty-five to two or three times that number.

[4.] Regarding this "grotesque interlude," see Scholder, *Churches and the Third Reich*, 2:240. [Birnbaum, a member of the High Church Council, had been dispatched to the conference by the German Christian officials after receiving a report that Heckel was not making a good impression there. Assuming that any significant event in Denmark must be taking place in the capital, he arrived in Copenhagen, only to learn that the venue was Fanø, some three hundred kilometers to the west, and chartered a seaplane to take him there.—KC] Cf. 1/167.2.

[5.] At the beginning of the conference on the afternoon of August 25, Heckel had given a one-and-a-half-hour position paper on ecumenical work, without going into the conflict in the German church. On August 27 he then presented his announced introductory paper on "Church and State." In the *Times* that day, Heckel's first lecture was described as "a brilliant ascent into the stratosphere of pure ecclesiastical dogma," a formulation that became a byword at the conference when referring to Heckel's speeches.

[1.] Literary estate of Erwin Sutz, Herrliberg, Switzerland; handwritten. See also *NL*, A 29,4 (14); typewritten copy. Previously published in *GS* 1:41–43.

[2.] Not extant.

I saw Jean,[3] I was with him in Bruay for three more days.[4] We enjoyed this time *very* much. There was so much to think about once again and to reminisce about.[5] I admire enormously the work Jean is doing. There is actually something of a sectarian fanaticism in this northern French Protestantism. It was the first time I have really seen a *totally* working-class congregation. The surrounding area with war-memorial tourist sites and cemeteries[6] and the terrible poverty of these mining towns make a dark background for preaching the gospel.

Now I am back again in our congregation, tormenting myself with trying to decide whether to go back to Germany as director of a preachers' seminary that is soon to be opened there,[7] stay here, or go to India.[8] I no longer believe in the university; in fact I never really have believed in it—to your chagrin! The next generation of pastors, these days, ought to be trained entirely in church-monastic schools, where the pure doctrine, the Sermon on the Mount, and worship are taken seriously—which for all three of these things is simply not the case at the university and under the present circumstances is impossible. It is also time for a final break with our theologically grounded reserve about whatever is being done by the state—which really only comes down to fear. "Speak out for those who cannot speak"[9]—who in the church today still remembers that this is the very least the Bible asks of us in such times as these?[10] And then there's the matter of military service, war,[11] etc., etc.

From now on, I believe, any discussion between Hitler and Barth would be quite pointless—indeed, no longer to be sanctioned. Hitler has shown himself quite plainly for what he is, and the church ought to know with whom it has to reckon. Isaiah didn't go to Sennacherib either.[12] We have tried often enough—too often—to make Hitler aware of what is going on. Maybe we've

205

[3.] Lasserre.

[4.] See 1/145, ed. note 2. [See also 2/3a.—KC]

[5.] Lasserre, Bonhoeffer, and Sutz had become friends as students at Union Theological Seminary in New York during 1930–31 (see *DB-ER*, 153–54).

[6.] In the region surrounding Bruay, a million soldiers [British, French, and German—KC] were killed in the Battle of the Somme in 1916.

[7.] See 1/113, ed. note 4.

[8.] Cf. 1/127, ed. note 14.

[9.] Prov. 31:8. [Cf. 1/62, ed. note 3.—KC]

[10.] Cf. the possibilities for church action in Bonhoeffer's essay "The Church and the Jewish Question" (*GS* 2:44–53; *DBW* 12, 2/13).

[11.] See the Fanø conference resolutions (1/141) and the papers Bonhoeffer gave at the main conference (2/2 and 2/3).

[12.] See 2 Kings 19 and Isaiah 37. Cf. 1/93.

not yet gone about it in the right way, but then Barth won't go about it the right way either. Hitler is not in a position to listen to us; he is *obdurate*, and as such he must compel *us* to listen—it's that way round. The Oxford movement[13] was naive enough to try and convert Hitler—a ridiculous failure to recognize what is going on. *We* are the ones to be converted, not Hitler.

I would love to have about three months of quiet to do some writing[14] but don't see my way to it yet. What are you up to? What sort of man is Brandt?[15] I don't understand how any man can stay on in Hitler's entourage, unless he is either a Nathan[16] or else shares the guilt for what happened on June 30[17] and July 25,[18] and for the lie served up on August 19[19]—and shares the guilt for the next war! Please forgive me, but for me these things are really *so* serious, I don't feel like being witty about them anymore. Write to me what you think about all this! I would love it if we could talk about whether you perhaps see things quite differently—and about other things, about theology and the parish and the Sermon on the Mount.

206 Is Barth going to stay in Switzerland now?[20]

Let me hear from you again. Forgive me for this mad letter.

As ever your old friend,
D[ietrich] B[onhoeffer]

[13.] See 1/8, ed. note 20.

[14.] Bonhoeffer was working on the first drafts of *Discipleship* (*DBWE* 4); cf. 1/93.

[15.] Karl Brandt, Hitler's personal physician, whom Sutz had met on an Alpine tour.

[16.] This is an allusion to Nathan, the prophet and preacher of repentance in 2 Sam. 7 and 1 Kings 1.

[17.] The date of the so-called Röhm putsch murders; see 1/146, ed. note 3.

[18.] The assassination of Austrian Chancellor Engelbert Dollfuss; see 1/136, ed. note 5.

[19.] After Hindenburg's death on August 19, 1934, Hitler combined and personally assumed the offices of Reich president and Reich chancellor and had this confirmed through a "referendum" in which 89.9 percent of the vote was affirmative.

[20.] Barth had learned during his holiday on the "Bergli" that the police in Munich had confiscated copies of his series Theologische Existenz Heute (see Prolingheuer, *Der Fall Karl Barth*, 22–23).

148. To Hans Asmussen[1]

Dear Brother Asmussen,

Have you received a letter from Bell in which he asked if he could meet you in Hamburg on September 26?[2] I had a letter from him today in which he is a bit concerned[3] that perhaps something has been lost in the post. He asked for a meeting point. His telegraph address is Autoklub Stockholm. I know from previous conversations that he would be keen to meet Niem. and Jak.[4] among others, and I think it would be very good if they could come. By the way, a good interpreter will be needed.

Yours as ever,
Bonhoeffer

148a. Wilhelm Lütgert to Adolf Schlatter[1]

Bergstr. 3, Neubabelsberg, October 4, 1934

Dear and honored friend,

We here are so concerned about the events in the Württemberg regional church[2] that I wanted to write to you, because these events confront us with a question that is perhaps the same for you in Swabia. We were quite surprised that the

---

[1.] LKA EKvW, 5,1, no. 767, fasc. 1; typewritten, presumably from London, around September 20, 1934. Cf. 1/144.

[2.] There was a six-hour discussion in Hamburg on September 26, 1934, between Bell and Karl Koch, Hans Asmussen, Eberhard Fiedler, and Paul Humburg as representatives of the Confessing Synod (see Bell and Koechlin, *Briefwechsel*, 147; also Bell's letter of October 10, 1934, to Koch, LKA EKvW, 5,1, no. 320).

[3.] Letter not extant.

[4.] Martin Niemöller and Gerhard Jacobi.

[1.] LKA Stuttgart, Best. D 40/429; typewritten with handwritten salutation and signature.

[2.] By the decree of September 3, 1934, the church of Württemberg was to be incorporated into the German Evangelical Church. The German Evangelical Church's "legal administrator," August Jäger, appeared in Stuttgart on September 8 for this purpose. Anyone who did not bow to the change was placed on leave. A commissioner was put in charge of the church administration, and on September 14, Bishop Theophil Wurm was replaced by a "clerical commissioner" and on September 15 placed under house arrest. Forty superintendents, 82 percent of the pastors, the majority of congregations, and the theological faculty in Tübingen backed Wurm, so that this attempt at incorporation ultimately failed. See Schäfer, *Die Evangelische Landeskirche in Württemberg*, 3:524–672. [See also Scholder, *Churches and the Third Reich*, 2:245–47.—KC]

steamroller[3] that is paving a straight horizontal highway clear across Germany for the bishops' cars has now arrived in Swabia as well. It appears that up to now you have been spared the traffic accidents due to this automobile business, which have cost so many people their lives. Here they have led the young theologians to begin carving out a road closed to automobile traffic.[4] And that is what gives me pause. In stark contrast to everything that the press is spreading about unchallenged, our young theologians here have developed a deep abhorrence toward the bishops' church policies, and those close to me are on their way to burning all their bridges behind them:[5] withdrawing from the official theological examinations, to be examined instead by a commission formed for this purpose; setting up their own preachers' seminary, with my former assistant,[6] a Barth scholar who is in London at present, as director; having themselves ordained by the president of the Confessing Church synod here;[7] and being assigned to pastorates by the Confessing Church.

¶In doing this, they insist that they do not wish to start a free church but only want to set up an organization[8] to minister to the congregations deprived of it. That the Confessing Church synod has no pastors to provide, that pastors who take up pastorates anywhere outside the regional church would be expelled by

---

[3.] Lütgert used this image of a "steamroller" to describe the policies that the German Christian–led Reich Church government used to incorporate the regional churches. "Traffic accidents" probably refers to arrests, suspensions, bans on speaking, and internal divisions resulting from German Christian policies.

[4.] This is Lütgert's description of the alternative training system that the Confessing Church was creating for pastors, at the urging of young theology students and pastors who recognized only the Councils of Brethren as their church government. The Confessing Church developed its own committees to oversee examinations, field work in congregations, preachers' seminaries, ordinations, and assignments to pastorates. See Scherffig, *Junge Theologen im "Dritten Reich"*; as well as Ludwig, "Die 'Illegalen' im Kirchenkampf," 22–70.

[5.] Ernst Tillich, who was Lütgert's assistant during Bonhoeffer's leave, invited students, vicars, and assistant preachers of the Confessing Church in Berlin-Brandenburg to found a "Fellowship of Young Theologians" on September 24. On that day, forty-five of them signed the declaration of commitment to the fellowship, which after Tillich's departure from Berlin was led by Christoph von Hase, Hans Herbert Kramm, and Elimar Kintzel, joined in November by Albrecht Schönherr, Joachim Kanitz, and Wolfgang Büsing (LKA EKvW, Best. 5,1–124, 1. See also Ludwig, "Die 'Illegalen' im Kirchenkampf," 49–55). One of the first members was Klaus Block, later Lütgert's son-in-law. Irmgard Block, née Lütgert, later recalled heated arguments about the Confessing Church and Bonhoeffer in her family. (Information given to the German editors by Hartmut Ludwig, October 30, 1996.)

[6.] On July 4, 1934, the Old Prussian Council of Brethren decided that Bonhoeffer should be director of the preachers' seminary for Brandenburg; this existed in Finkenwalde from 1935 to 1937 [see *DB-ER*, 411 and 419–24—KC].

[7.] Pastor Gerhard Jacobi of the Kaiser Wilhelm Memorial Church in Berlin.

[8.] The Confessing Church claimed to be the legitimate German Evangelical Church. It was established as an independent organization through the resolutions of the first

the police, as was done to one of my nephews,[9] who was dismissed although a legitimate pastor—all that does not bother them. They don't recognize the church law, and they hope that their numbers will make the church government reconsider. That would indeed amount to starting a free church, and the example of the Old Lutherans,[10] who started under very similar circumstances and who have now dried up to a swampy pond, doesn't frighten them because they don't know the story. The leaders of the church opposition are brave officers, but that does not make them field commanders. They keep pointing to the example of Bavaria, Württemberg, and Rhineland-Westphalia. How things stand in western Germany, and what concrete goal is being pursued there, isn't clear to me because the press is being forced to keep quiet about it. All the older and more experienced people are warning them, but these youths, with their courage, which gladdens one's heart, and their inexperience, which does not, are turning a deaf ear to the warnings as if they were infirmities of old age. The danger is truly great. There are at least forty of the best, most serious and capable we have who are about to take this step and thereby step into a vacuum. The principle I am advocating is opposition, but without separation. But the boundaries between the two are becoming fluid. How do things stand where you are? What is the opposition planning to do? I am afraid not of the quarrel but rather of pointless sacrifices like that of Langemark,[11] which are glorified but made in vain because of faulty leadership. I am in complete agreement with everything you wrote to me. But how do things stand with the theological younger generation there? Colleagues are being intimidated by heavy threats and bans on speaking, and one really does not know what one should be doing. Requests for audiences[12] are not accepted or even answered. For our declaration with regard to Schmitz and Soden,[13] we cannot find either an outlet

---

confessional synod of the Old Prussian Union Church on May 29, 1934, and the second confessional synod of the German Evangelical Church, held in Berlin-Dahlem on October 19–20, 1934.

[9.] Name not found.

[10.] The Old Lutheran free church was founded in the early nineteenth century after its members refused to accept the church union and order of service introduced by Prussian king Friedrich Wilhelm III (see Werner Klän's article on the Old Lutherans in *Religion in Geschichte und Gegenwart*, 4th ed., 1:379–81).

[11.] In October and November 1914, Langemark had been the scene of a battle that inflicted some of the greatest losses of World War I; 45,000 students and schoolboys, mostly volunteers, met their death because of flawed military policies.

[12.] [With officials.—KC]

[13.] On August 13, 1934, some fifty college teachers declared their solidarity with the theology professors Otto Schmitz in Münster and Hans von Soden in Marburg, who were sent into early retirement for their role in the Church Struggle. The measures against Soden were rescinded on October 24; Schmitz became director of the Confessing Church preachers' seminary in Westphalia (see Dinkler, Dinkler-von Schubert, and Wolters, *Theologie und Kirche im Wirken Hans von Sodens*, 103–5).

that will publish it or a channel through which to submit it. Please write to me briefly how things stand with you, and what sort of advice you are giving to young pastors, students, and candidates for examination.[14] The situation is naturally connected closely to the political situation, and that makes it more difficult. The peace in which to do our work is being destroyed, but actually the stormy times in the church, and in any sort of spiritual life, have always been the fruitful times.

(handwritten) Yours sincerely,

W. Lütgert

149. From the Diary of Julius Rieger[1]

October 5, 1934

Chichester has a friend who went to see Hitler. He told him about the devastating effects the German church dispute has had in England. Hitler asked for suggestions. The friend came back to Chichester with this, and now Chichester has asked Bonhoeffer's opinion.[2] We are agreed that state intervention on Hitler's part would only be possible if it took the form of replacing his old spokesman (L. Müller) with a new one. Müller was given the job at the time[3] to sort things out, which he has not succeeded in doing. Now someone else must be given the same assignment. Perhaps this man could be a competent lawyer who has the confidence of the confessional front. Advantages:

1. If Hitler gives this order, everything must be done according to the Führer's wishes.

2. The new official would be in a position to reverse the mistakes through legal channels and to help the opposition attain the entitled response to their demands.

3. Extraordinarily favorable impression abroad, if the National Socialist Führer were to solve the most difficult problem—namely, the church problem (cf. Mussolini and Catholicism).[4]

207 (margin)

[14.] It is not known whether Schlatter replied. The problem Lütgert is addressing here, an independent training program for Confessing Church pastors, existed only in the Confessing Church in the Old Prussian Union provincial churches, but never in Württemberg.

[1.] *NL*, A 41,9 (18); typewritten copy. Previously published in *GS* 6:324–25.

[2.] See also Bonhoeffer's advice in his letter of October 24, 1934, to Bell (1/155).

[3.] After the defeat of the church opposition in January 1934 [following the church leaders' meeting with Hitler—KC]; see Scholder, *Churches and the Third Reich*, 2:43–44.

[4.] In 1929 the Lateran treaties helped to bring about a "peace settlement" between the Roman Catholic Church and Mussolini's fascist regime in Italy.

150. From Théodore de Félice[1]

Geneva, October 12, 1934

Dear friend,

I am sending you separately the French report on the youth conference in Fanø.[2] I absolutely want to have a German edition of it appear, just as I am going to publish an English edition of it. It would not be at all right to have it only in one language. But unfortunately it is absolutely impossible for us in Geneva to translate this text into German, given our limited resources in personnel. I am therefore asking you if you can provide a rendering of this text in German.[3] I have put a line next to the passages that do not need to be translated, because they already are.

You probably know that as far as the German contributions to the discussion are concerned, I submitted my text to your assistant, who made all the useful cor-   208 rections, since I hadn't received an answer from you.[4]

With my fondest memories of Fanø,
Most cordially yours,
Th. de Félice

151. To Théodore de Félice[1]

London, 13. Okt. 34

My dear de Félice,

may I ask you to let me have *some information* about this mischievous Bruay Conference.[2] I have not heard a word from Toureille, no explanation whatsoever, *why the French delegation has never arrived.*[3] I do not think it right, to

---

[1.] WCC Archives, World Alliance, Letters to Dietrich Bonhoeffer; carbon copy; in French.

[2.] See 1/141.

[3.] See Bonhoeffer's reply of November 20, 1934 (1/174, esp. ed. notes 4 and 5).

[4.] To Félice's letter of September 11, 1934 (WCC Archives, World Alliance, Letters to Dietrich Bonhoeffer), in which he had asked some questions regarding the format of the minutes.

[1.] *NL*, A 40,1 (7); photocopy of handwritten letter from the WCC Archives (but not found there); in original English, including errors. Previously published in *Mündige Welt*, 5:337, and *GS* 6:356.

[2.] See 1/153; a report on this conference was previously published in *Mündige Welt*, 5:235–37.

[3.] On September 9, 1934, Winterhager had reported to Geneva that the German and British participants in the Bruay conference had waited in vain for the French delegation

leave that point quite undiscussed, it caused much concern among German and British young people.

Yours ever
Dietrich Bonhoeffer

152. George Bell to Edward Keble Talbot[1]

16th October, 1934

My dear Father,

A friend of mine, who is German Pastor in London, a young man, Pastor Bonhoeffer, has been asked to undertake the training of theological students on behalf of the Confessional Synod in Germany. He is an excellent theologian who was introduced to me by Professor Adolf Deissmann as one of his best men of recent years. He is very anxious to have some acquaintance with our methods in England, both with regard to training for the ministry and with regard to Community life. He expects to leave England at the end of December.[2] I have promised to give him one or two introductions, and I venture to ask you whether it would be possible for you to let him come and stay, some time in the middle of the week, at a convenient date to yourself, between now and the end of the year.[3] He cannot get away during the week-ends, but two or three nights in the middle of the week would be very possible and a very great kindness to him, and incidentally to our friends in Germany. He speaks English perfectly.

Yours sincerely,
[George Cicestr]
Rev. Father E. K. Talbot
Sent also to: Father O'Brien
                Father Tribe
                Rev. Eric Graham
                Principal of Wycliffe Hall
                Canon Tomlin of St. Augustine's, Canterbury

209

that had registered to participate. Since no cancellation had been sent, doubts arose as to whether Toureille had even asked his delegation to come (WCC Archives, Youth Commission, Félice Correspondence).

[1.] LPL, Bell Papers 42, 46; carbon copy; in original English, including errors. See also *NL,* A 42,3 (6); typewritten copy. Previously published in *GS* 2:184. See Reginald Tribe's favorable reply of October 18, 1934, to Bell, *NL,* A 42,4 (7).

[2.] On Bonhoeffer's plans to visit Gandhi in India at the beginning of 1935, see 1/154 and 1/158.

[3.] These visits finally took place in March 1935. [See *DB-ER,* 412.—KC]

153. From Théodore de Félice[1]

Geneva, October 17, 1934

My dear friend,

Thank you for your letter of the 13th.[2] Upon receipt of the report from Winter-hager,[3] I had written to Toureille. My letter crossed one from him in which he explained the following: "Upon my return from Denmark, I was ill in Louvain, then again here (Congénies), when I arrived. Therefore I was unable to go to Bruay, and what is even more disappointing: no Frenchman was able to go there, neither Professor Leenhardt, neither Jean Bosc, nor Helmlinger. I am so sorry about it. I had a feeling this would happen after the scuffle that took place about this issue in Fanö."

I think that having written this letter to me he deemed it useless to answer the   210
one I had written to him on the same subject.

Very cordially yours,
Th. de Félice

154. George Bell to Mahatma Gandhi[1]

22nd October, 1934

Dear Mr. Gandhi,

A friend of mine, a young man, at present German Pastor in London, Pastor Bonhoeffer, 23 Manor Mount, London, S.E. 23, is most anxious that I should give him an introduction to you. I can most heartily commend him. He expects to be in India for the first two or three months of 1935. He is intimately identified with the Church opposition movement in Germany. He is a very good theologian, a most earnest man, and is probably to have charge of the training of Ordination candidates for the Ministry in the future Confessional Church of Germany. He wants to study community life as well as methods of training. It would be a very great kindness if you could let him come to you.

Yours sincerely,
[George Cicestr]

[1.] WCC Archives, World Alliance, Letters to Dietrich Bonhoeffer; carbon copy; in French.

[2.] See 1/151.

[3.] See 1/151, ed. note 3.

[1.] LPL, Bell Papers 42, 49; carbon copy; in original English, including errors. See also *NL*, A 42,3 (9); typewritten copy. Previously published in *GS* 2:185. See Gandhi's reply of November 1, 1934, to Bonhoeffer, 1/158.

155. To George Bell[1]

24th October 1934

My Lord Bishop,

thank you very much indeed for your introductions to the various religious Communities.[2] I am making a plan now and will answer the kind invitations myself. I hope to see them all before Christmas.[3]

211   With regard to the recent and long-expected events in the German Church,[4] I am afraid that Hitler will try to postpone a decision as long as possible—perhaps even till after the Saar election.[5] I could imagine him saying that he would not interfere in the Church conflict, not even in the situation of a schism. He would leave it all to the Church and, of course, in fact[6] leave it to some S.A. etc. groups to interfere on their own initiative and so to terrorise the True Evangelical Church in Germany. I have been thinking much about your question, what Hitler could do in case he was willing to settle the conflict.[7] From his point of view I can only see the one way of dismissing Jäger and Müller and nominating a representative of the Opposition—possibly a lawyer, not a theologian, Dr. Flor of the Reichs-gericht,—with the special task to restitute legal and confessional conditions in the Church. After a certain period of vacancy a new Reichsbishop could be elected by a legal National Synod. This Interim however should last for at least one year, so that the greatest excitement may have passed by.[8] There is a certain difficulty of Hitler nominating a theologian, who would become Reichsbishop afterwards. We have always disapproved of the nomination of Müller, not only personally but also fundamentally. He may nominate a lawyer, but he has just to confirm a theologian. The fact that Hitler has

----

[1.] LPL, Bell Papers 42, 50; typewritten; in original English, including errors. See also *NL*, A 42,1 (22); typewritten copy. Previously published in *GS* 2:177–78.

[2.] See Bell's letter of October 16, 1934, to E. K. Talbot (1/152).

[3.] Bonhoeffer was only able to make these visits in March (see *DB-ER*, 412).

[4.] After the police arrested Bishops Wurm and Meiser in early October, the second national Confessing Synod was convened in Dahlem. It met on October 20 and 21, 1934, definitively renounced obedience to the German Christian leadership, and declared the formation of an emergency church government. [See Scholder, *Churches and the Third Reich*, 2:258–68.—KC]

[5.] The January 13, 1935, plebiscite on the return of the Saarland to Germany.

[6.] "In fact" inserted afterward.

[7.] See 1/149.

[8.] On November 16, 1934, Bell passed this proposal for an interim period of church government under a lawyer's leadership to Hitler's envoy [in London—KC], Joachim von Ribbentrop (see Bell and Koechlin, *Briefwechsel*, 173).

consulted the Reichsminister Gürtner (of Justice) last Saturday[9] perhaps indicates a move in this direction.

I thank you once more very much for your great kindness and remain yours very respectfully and sincerely

Dietrich Bonhoeffer

156. From G. H. Saunders[1]   212

London, October 24th., 1934

Dear Sir,

At the request of Dr. J. H. Rushbrooke,[2] President of the above Council, I have pleasure in sending you herewith copy of a resolution passed at the last meeting of our Executive Committee.

I am, Yours faithfully,

G. H. Saunders

[9.] Bonhoeffer probably knew of this October 20, 1934, conversation through his brother-in-law Hans von Dohnanyi. Hitler's consultations with Gürtner were decisive in changing his policy toward the church, according to Klaus Scholder. See Scholder, *Churches and the Third Reich*, 2:278.

[1.] ZEKHN 35/45; typewritten; in original English, including errors; letterhead: "National Council of the Evangelical Free Churches—Memorial Hall, Farringdon Street, London E. C. 4." See also *NL*, A 40,6 (4); photocopy. The letter contains a handwritten note from Bonhoeffer Mr. Asmussen: "Dear Mr. Asmussen, this is for the J.K. [the journal *Junge Kirche*—KC] or whatever you like. It is not to be confused with the resolution of the 'Council' that was printed in the last issue. Yours, D. Bonhoeffer." Bonhoeffer had previously sent the council declaration he mentions to *Junge Kirche*, where it was published in the no. 10, 1934 issue (letter from W. L. Robertson of October 11, 1934, *NL*, A 40,6 [3]). President Koch responded to both resolutions with a letter of thanks on November 29, 1934 (*NL*, A 40,6 [5] and [6]).

[2.] [Rushbrooke, a leading British Baptist figure with an intimate knowledge of Germany, held the full-time position of general secretary of the Baptist World Alliance. The alliance had (amid misgivings among many Baptists in Britain and the United States) held its Fifth World Congress in Berlin in August 1934, during which Rushbrooke led a delegation to see Reich Bishop Müller to seek assurances that the German Baptists and other free churches would not be coerced into a single German Protestant church. Müller readily gave these assurances. See Clements, "A Question of Freedom? British Baptists and the German Church Struggle," in Clements, *Baptists in the Twentieth Century*, 96–113.—KC]

[Enclosure:][3]

Resolution of the Executive Committee
of the National Council of the Evangelical Free Churches.
Passed at its Meeting of September 21st. 1934
Churches in Germany

That this Executive of the national council of the Evangelical Free Churches asso-
ciates itself with the resolutions on the ecclesiastical and religious situation in
Germany passed at the meeting of the Universal Council on Life and Work held
recently at Fanoe, Denmark,[4] and, impressed with the vital evangelical issues
concerned, assures its brethren in Germany who are standing for the preservation
of the liberties of Christ's Church and Gospel,[5] of the sympathy and the prayers
of the Evangelical Free Churches of this Country.

157. From the Diary of Julius Rieger[1]

October 25, 1934

213

A few days ago Chichester went to see Bismarck (first secretary at the German Embassy in London) and painted the darkest possible picture for him of the
present situation. The next day Canterbury called on Hoesch (ambassador in
London).[2] There is no holding back the masses of the church people.[3] A conference of bishops (of the Church of England) was imminent, which was to make a
decision on the German church issue.[4] These resolutions have apparently now

---

[3.] *NL*, A 40,6 (2); typewritten copy.

[4.] See the minutes of the meeting of the Council of Brethren, 1/143, ed. note 7.
[Several British participants from free churches attended Fanø.—KC]

[5.] [The emphasis on the "liberties" of the church and Christianity was characteristic
of much of the Anglo-Saxon Protestant perspective on the Church Struggle, whereas for
the Confessing Church itself it was the truth-content of the gospel that was at least as much
at issue. See Clements, "A Question of Freedom? British Baptists and the German Church
Struggle," in Clements, *Baptists in the Twentieth Century*, 96–113, and Bonhoeffer, "Protestantism without Reformation," in *No Rusty Swords*, 92–118, and *DBW* 15, 2/6.—KC]

[1.] *NL*, A 41,9 (18); typewritten copy. Previously published in *GS* 6:325.

[2.] Regarding the conversations of October 12 and 16, 1934, during which the bishops
[Bell and Lang] made demands and set ultimata, see Scholder, *Churches and the Third Reich*,
2:264–65 and 276, and *DB-ER*, 394.

[3.] An example was the massive protest against the dismissal of Bishop Meiser (see
Scholder, *Churches and the Third Reich*, 2:251 and 257–58).

[4.] The English bishops were to hold their regular assembly on October 24, 1934, at
which—as the archbishop explained to Hoesch—he, Canterbury, was expected to "initiate a
position statement by the English clergy on the events in the German church, and he could

been adopted by the bishops' assembly but not made public. The entire proceedings have purposely been kept secret, and this has obviously been done by order of the Foreign Office and at the request of the German Embassy. The Foreign Office said (by telephone in reply to a report by Hoesch)[5] that changes are to be expected in the next few days.

158. From Mahatma Gandhi[1]

November 1, 1934

Dear friend,

I have your letter.[2] If you and your friend[3] have enough money for return passage and can pay your expenses here, say, at the rate of Rs.[4] 100 per month each,   214 you can come whenever you like. The sooner the better so as to get the benefit of such cold weather as we get here. The Rs. 100 per month I have calculated as the outside limit for those who can live simply. It may cost you even half the amount. It all depends upon how the climate here agrees with you.

With reference to your desire to share my daily life, I may say that you will be staying with me if I am out of prison[5] and settled in one place when you come. But otherwise, if I am travelling or if I am in prison, you will have to be satisfied

---

not avoid doing this" (according to a telegram from Hoesch to the foreign minister in Berlin, which was forwarded to the Reich chancellery) (BA Koblenz, Akten der Reichskanzlei, Akten zur deutschen auswärtigen Politik, C III, 1, 474).

[5.] On October 22, 1934 (see note 4). After receiving a communication from the Ministry of Foreign Affairs in Berlin, Hoesch was able to inform the archbishop of a pending German governmental announcement on the church conflict, thereby preventing him from needing to take a position on it quickly.

[1.] NL, Anh. C 1; in original English; printed in and photocopied from *The Collected Works of Mahatma Gandhi*, vol. 59 (September 16–December 15, 1934) (Ahmedabad: Navajivan Trust [published in Delhi by the director, Publications Division, Ministry of Information and Broadcasting, Government of India; printed by Shantilal Harjivan Shah, 1974], 273 [no. 286]. Addressed to "Pastor Dr. Dietrich Bonhoeffer, Esq., 23 Manor Mount, S.E. 23, London." At lower left a note: "From a copy: Pyarelal Papers. Courtesy: Pyarelal."

[2.] Not extant. Regarding the background, see also Bell's letter to Gandhi, 1/154, as well as those of C. F. Andrews to Bonhoeffer, 1/94; Bonhoeffer to Niebuhr, 1/127; and Bonhoeffer to Sutz, 1/147.

[3.] It is unclear whether this refers to Julius Rieger or to Herbert Jehle; both later reported having made plans with Bonhoeffer, possibly at different periods (cf. *DB-ER*, 408; Rieger, *Dietrich Bonhoeffer in England*, 27; Jehle, unpublished report of 1963/64, in possession of Ulrich Kabitz, Munich).

[4.] Rupees.

[5.] In the preceding years Gandhi had been in prison several times, most recently in August 1933. At this time he was struggling especially against the caste system and in solidarity with the untouchables.

with remaining in or near one of the institutions[6] that are being conducted under my supervision. If you can stay in any of the institutions I have in mind and if you can live on the simple vegetarian food that these institutions can supply you, you will have nothing to pay for your boarding and lodging.

Yours sincerely,

[Gandhi]

159. The Secession of the German Evangelical Congregations in Great Britain from the Reich Church[1]

159.1 Minutes Taken by Dietrich Bonhoeffer on behalf of St. Paul's Church[2]

Special Parish Meeting
Christ Church, November 5, 1934, 8 P.M.

Present: Representatives of the congregations of St. Paul's, Sydenham, St. George's, St. Mary's, and Hull. Pastors Wehrhan, Schönberger, Rieger, Bonhoeffer, Schreiner, Steiniger, Boeckheler. Pastor Wehrhan presiding.

The session was opened with a prayer for the proper composure and strength to make a decision in this solemn moment for the church. Pastor Wehrhan explained that we had been invited in light of the necessity for the congregations here to take a stand with respect to the events in the church in Germany. We are responsible for ourselves, and now that the decision has been made in Germany to establish the Confessing Church, we must decide whether to remain subject to the church regime [Kirchenregiment] of Reich Bishop Müller. Pastor Bonhoeffer gave a talk on the church situation in Germany; Pastor Rieger spoke on the effects the church dispute has had in other countries. Both presentations led to the conclusion that action must be taken now, and that our Christian consciences could not responsibly make a decision to remain under the present Reich Church government [Reichskirchenregierung].

215

[6.] Gandhi's main center of activities at the time was the Sarbamati Ashram in Ahmedabad (northwest India).

[1.] In addition to the documents concerning this meeting that are reproduced here, there also exist notes taken by Martin Böckheler (see *NL*, D 13), which are quoted to supplement Bonhoeffer's speech [in 1/159.2, ed. note 10—KC].

[2.] ADBC, Minute Book of St. Paul's Church, 125–26; handwritten. See *NL*, A 41,3 (1); photocopy and typewritten copy.

After some questions and suggestions, the entire assembly agreed unanimously to go on record, with a resolution to the effect that the assembled representatives of the congregations declare that *they consider themselves as belonging inwardly*[3] *to the Confessing Church*, and that they will take up with the authorities of the Reich Church and the Confessing Church[4] the necessary negotiations arising from this. This decision is to be communicated to these authorities. The session was adjourned at 9:30 P.M.

Dietrich Bonhoeffer, Pastor[5]

159.2 Minutes on behalf of the Association of Congregations[6]   216

Minutes
of the Joint Meeting of Pastors and Elders
of the Protestant Congregations in England, November 5, 1934

1. The meeting was called to order at 8 P.M. by Pastor Wehrhan. Pastor Böckheler from Hull led the opening prayer; the response was the singing in unison of the first stanza of the hymn "O Holy Spirit, Come to Us."

[3.] The meaning of this formulation later became a point of contention. See, for example, 1/168 and 1/183. [The German word translated here as "inwardly" is *innerlich* and can certainly be interpreted in more than one way. It might, for example, be seen as indicating an "inner oneness of spirit" with the Confessing Church but without necessarily implying any outward, formal, or organizational manifestation of this "belonging." This is unlikely, however, since the whole issue of "confession" that united the church opposition, both in Germany and in Britain, was a very public affair requiring a definite decision with concrete consequences. More likely behind it is the understanding, held by Bonhoeffer and his allies, of the Confessing Church as the sole and rightful embodiment of the German Evangelical Church as it had existed before the Nazi rise to power and to which the congregations in Britain had belonged for years. Note that the resolution does not actually speak of the congregations in Britain "joining the Confessing Church" (although in practical organizational terms that is what would have to follow; see 1/162). Rather, as in Bonhoeffer's eyes, if they were remaining true to the confessional basis of the German Evangelical Church, as distinct from the Reich Church with its dominant "German Christian" ethos, then ipso facto they logically belonged to the Confessing Church, hence the "inwardly"—or one might almost say "intrinsically." See also note 7.—KC]

[4.] "The Confessing Church" replaces "the Foreign Office."

[5.] These minutes bear, in the margin, the signatures of fifteen representatives of congregations (some of which are difficult to decipher): G. Henne, C. Blumenstock, J. Streitberger, G. Eisemann, H. Weber, H. Klugmann, P. Grandyot, E. Henne, Fr. Strobel, H. Hirsch, C. Compton, Fr. Ph. Schlarb, G. Neubert, A. Wolford, W. Neubert.

[6.] ADBC, GV 1, 13.48; typewritten, no author indicated. See also *NL*, A 41,3 (3); typewritten copy. Previously published in *GS* 6:326–69. Probably the minutes were provided "in great haste" by Pastor Schönberger's vicar, Benjamin Locher, and sent by Schönberger on November 6, 1934, to Baron Schröder (ADBC, GV 1, 10.4; see also *NL*, A 41,1 [45]).

2. *Pastor Bonhoeffer* then reported on what is taking place in our home church.

Since Saturday, October 20, the situation in the Evangelical Church has become clearer. The so-called church opposition, including the Pastors' Emergency League, the large southern German churches, and the church of Hanover have constituted themselves as a free church[7] and have communicated this to the Reich Church and the state.[8] Thus there are now two churches: the Reich Church and the Confessing Church.

The following is a brief overview of church events since our last meeting:

1. Report of a meeting of the southern German bishops in the office of the Reich bishop on January 27, 1934,[9] and their reaffirmation of confidence in the Reich bishop's promises to remove the Aryan paragraphs and to reinstate the pastors who had been dismissed.[10] [However,] the consequence was that the Aryan paragraphs were reinstated and pastors and bishops were dismissed without good reason. The breach of these promises culminated in the unconstitutional incorporation of the southern German regional churches into the Reich Church.[11]

2. The next step, in response, was to set up emergency synods. This soon occurred throughout the country, until at the end of May the first national synod of the Confessing Church was held,[12] where the regional churches of Württemberg, Bavaria, and Hanover once more participated as a united front. This was also the organized declaration of war toward the Reich Church.[13]

3. Oberheid left, and Jäger was installed as a bigger gun.[14] Then came the report of the brutal use of violence in Württemberg and Bavaria in connection

217

[7.] The term "free church" did not correspond to the self-understanding of the synod; it said in its message that the Reich Church government had "separated itself from the Christian Church" and that the synod's own "Council of Brethren of the German Evangelical Church" was now the rightful governing body; see Scholder, *Churches and the Third Reich,* 2:267–68. [The situation in practice, however, was to remain structurally more ambiguous. At no point were there really two completely separate, independent churches.—KC]

[8.] On the decisions of the Dahlem Confessing Synod of October 19–20, 1934, see Scholder, *Churches and the Third Reich,* 2:267–69.

[9.] For more about the negotiations, see Scholder, *Churches and the Third Reich,* 2:43; other church leaders were present in addition to the southern German bishops.

[10.] Böckheler's notes say, "Once again the bishops, in full self-abnegation, supported Müller." In this they were evidently swayed by Hitler's reception two days earlier, at which the contents of a bugged telephone conversation of Niemöller's were read aloud, placing the opposition church leaders in a very embarrassing position. On this, see Scholder, *Churches and the Third Reich,* 2:39–43.

[11.] In the spring of 1934; see Scholder, *Churches and the Third Reich,* 2:53–74.

[12.] Held in Barmen, May 29–30, 1934.

[13.] According to Böckheler: "Seven thousand Emergency League pastors, (two thousand German Christian pastors), the rest undecided."

[14.] In March 1934 Heinrich Oberheid was named as the Reich bishop's chief of staff. August Jäger was appointed on April 12, 1934, as "legal administrator" of the German

with the attempts by the Reich Church government to incorporate the regional churches there.[15] The result was great outrage, with Confessing Church gatherings and declarations of loyalty to the bishops throughout the country.

In addition there was Jäger's unwise remark at the church office in Stuttgart, where he spoke of the creation of a national church as the long-term goal of the Evangelical Church.[16] Similarly, in Hanover, Müller declared himself in favor of "one German church free from Rome."[17] The high point of these lies was the proclamation and celebration of the unification process on the occasion of the Reich bishop's installation.[18]

4. Report on the Fanø conference.[19]   218

5. Under the pressure of the above events, the entire opposition gathered on October 20 and declared itself to be the only rightful church.[20] This amounted to a clear statement that we mean the Christian Church, and not a heathen entity dressed up as Christianity. As a sign thereof, this was followed on the same day by the ordinations of young graduates in theology.[21]

Evangelical Church. The previous year Jäger had played an ignominious role as state commissioner for the churches in Prussia; see *DB-ER*, 366.

[15.] [The "brutal use of violence" should perhaps be taken metaphorically rather than literally, implying physical violence. Jäger tried to take over those churches; the two bishops were briefly placed under house arrest and released as soon as popular protests made Jäger back down. See Scholder, *Churches and the Third Reich*, 2:244–52.—KC]

[16.] Böckheler notes, "With Germanness [*Deutschtum*] as the tie that binds (not the confession)." See Scholder, *Churches and the Third Reich*, 2:246.

[17.] On September 18, 1934, Reich Bishop Ludwig Müller stated: "What we want is a German Church free from Rome. The goal for which we are fighting is one state, one Volk, one church!" (Scholder, *Churches and the Third Reich*, 2:253). Scholder also describes the strong reactions aroused by this declaration, including that of the Reich minister of foreign affairs, particularly in connection with the approaching Saar plebiscite.

[18.] In the Berlin Cathedral on September 23, 1934. See Scholder, *Churches and the Third Reich*, 2:256–57.

[19.] Böckheler notes: "Fanø conference: rejection of all dictatorship by force in Christian churches. Our struggle in the church is not a political but a Christian struggle, not a political reaction in ecclesiastical form." On the Fanø conference, see 1/141 and 1/143.

[20.] This occurred at the Dahlem Confessing Synod, October 19–20, 1934; see Scholder, *Churches and the Third Reich*, 2:266–69.

[21.] Böckheler notes: "October 20: Confessing Church declares itself to be the only rightful church of the gospel, having waited with enormous patience until schism became unavoidable, but no other responsible course possible before God. Antichrist in Reich Church (cf. the Reformation). Relief at being clear before God and our conscience. Free church established in faith. Bishops have joined free church (under President Koch). Ordinations the next day." Following the synod, church president Koch ordained five candidates in Dahlem (see Niesel, *Kirche unter dem Wort*, 44).

6. In the meantime Bishops Wurm, Meiser, and Marahrens have been received by Hitler,[22] and Hitler has declared his intention that the state on principle would keep its distance from all church groups. This amounts to saying that there will be no infringement on church development.

That means that today, saying no to the Confessing Church means saying yes to the Reich Church.[23]

3. Next, *Pastor Rieger* spoke on "The Implications of the Church Struggle in England."

1. England in general.

The events of the past one to one and a half years have enormously changed the attitude in England toward Germany. This change can be explained by the lack of understanding of measures taken by the state and especially by events in the German Evangelical Church. This mood of hostility toward Germany seems to be hardening in the English-speaking countries. Public opinion speaks of the Germans of 1933–34 as brutal heathens who have fallen away from the Christian God. In recent months well-educated people have also begun to take offense at what is going on in Germany. Furthermore, the political popular press has been making the most of the events in the church; there are also the Sunday church papers that regularly summarize the news from the popular papers.

2. The English churches.[24]

It is no secret that all the Protestant churches in England are opposed to the German Evangelical Church. There is no local or national church in England that has not reported the events with abhorrence, protest, mockery, and derision.[25]

3. Questions regarding the German colony and congregations.

In the German congregations, too, the church dispute is felt to be an enormous embarrassment, indeed, as an overwhelming test of fortitude for all Germans, both in Germany and in England, which is becoming well-nigh unbearable. To

219

[22.] On October 30, 1934; see Meier, *Der evangelische Kirchenkampf,* 1:511; and Scholder, *Churches and the Third Reich,* 2:282.

[23.] Böckheler notes: "All our sufferings won't frighten us. If we don't stand with the Confessing Church, we have said yes to Müller's church. Aren't things already clear enough? either the national church, or Jesus Christ alone."

[24.] On the initiatives by English church leaders toward the church policies of the German state during the weeks before this meeting, see Scholder, *Churches and the Third Reich,* 2:263–64.

[25.] Crossed out by hand: "This attitude was expressed in Fanø."

our great sorrow, we fear that the actions of the Reich Church government will only damage the esteem in which the Third Reich is held.[26] German journalists, officials, and business people also share this feeling. Germany is also suffering economically because of the Reich Church. English people no longer want to buy goods marked "Made in Germany." So Müller is sabotaging Hitler's work of rebuilding in every way.

I know what a big step it is to say no [to] this church. But I believe it is a necessary step, for the sake of Protestant Christianity, the German people, and the Third Reich. The decision rests with you.

I would like to close with the words of the Lord Bishop of Chichester: (see *Junge Kirche* 1934, no. 12, p. 512, last paragraph).[27]

4. Regarding the legal aspect, *Pastor Schönberger* made the following observations:
So that we will not in future be expected to toe the line of a church to which we do not inwardly belong, I propose that the English congregations form a special 220
association, as an independent entity that is part of the church federation, and which cannot be overruled without its own consent. The Association of Congregations must be recognized as an independent body.

The following questions must also be considered:

a) Does the new church guarantee subsidies?

b) Does the new church grant the right of congregations to call and to dismiss their own pastors?

I therefore request that contacts be made with the Reich Church and the Confessing Church, and that we then have another meeting to make decisions.

5. Then *Pastor Wehrhan* read aloud a resolution composed in accordance with the will of the assembly, which was signed by all the elders and pastors. It reads as follows:[28]

The elders assembled here in Christ Church declare that they inwardly[29] hold

---

[26.] [It is difficult to determine the extent to which this may be a tactical statement, but it certainly portrays the distinction, made by most in the church opposition at the time, between opposition concerning church politics and political opposition against the Nazi regime.—KC]

[27.] Rieger quoted the final sentence of Bell's Ascension Day message as it appeared in *Junge Kirche*, see 1/103.

[28.] Böckheler notes: "*Vote*. All except two or three for the Confessing Church." A note added later (1975): "Not clear whether these were votes against or abstentions. Cannot remember their names anymore."

[29.] [See 1/159.1, ed. note 3. The wording of the resolution as recorded here differs slightly from the record in 1/159.1 but in essential respects is the same, including the word "inwardly" (*innerlich*).—KC]

[30.] Originally "the confession"; corrected by hand.

the same position as the Confessing Church[30] and that they will immediately take up the necessary negotiations with the church authorities (Foreign Office of the Reich Church, and the Confessing Church) arising from this.

A proposal was also unanimously agreed that two or three gentlemen be sent to conduct the negotiations at Oeynhausen and Berlin.[31]

6. The meeting was concluded with the chorale "Stay with us, with your grace . . ." and the benediction.

160. Baron Bruno Schröder and Friedrich Wehrhan to the Church Foreign Office[1]

London S.W.13, November 10, 1934

221   The German Evangelical congregations in Great Britain have been extremely pleased to hear that, on the basis of the Führer's declarations, the conscious profession of loyalty to the Third Reich and its Führer does not imply adherence to

---

[31.] Bonhoeffer, Schönberger, and Wehrhan left for Oeynhausen and Berlin on November 25, 1934. See 1/162 and 1/178.

[1.] ZEKHN 35/45; carbon copy, unsigned, on letterhead of the Association of German Evangelical Congregations in Great Britain and Ireland, addressed as follows: "To the Church Foreign Office, attention of Bishop Heckel, Berlin Charlottenburg"; a typewritten copy with names of the signatories (typed in later) is in the files of St. George's Church, London. See also *NL*, A 41,1 (47); typewritten copy. Previously published in *GS* 2:186–87. The literal text of this message is also enclosed in a letter (ADBC, GV 1, 9.6; see also *NL*, A 41,1 (46) of November 9, 1934, from Pastor Rieger to Baron Schröder, which says in part, "I am sending you . . . the two proposals as we drafted them together yesterday at your apartment" (whether "we" includes others besides Baron Schröder and Rieger is unknown). The second draft is of Baron Schröder's personal cover letter to Heckel; whether it was sent to Berlin in this form is unknown.

[2.] The source for this statement has not been discovered. It could have been a rumor, perhaps deliberately started, following Hitler's October 30, 1934, reception [of the church leaders—KC] (see, e.g., Helmut Rößler's letter of November 16, 1934, 1/168). In this connection, a notice in the *Times* of September 29, 1934, referring to a report sent by its "German diplomatic and political affairs correspondent," is also interesting. Following the installation of the Reich bishop, this official government publication [this is probably a reference to an official statement by the Nazi regime—KC] reaffirmed the Reich government's "Declaration of Neutrality" on December 1, 1933, toward the "quarrel in the Protestant church," which stated that Hitler did not consider himself a religious reformer; National Socialism was purely a political renewal movement that did not dream of involving the religious sphere; the new state was striving for "reconciliation" with both churches and recognized their right to organize their own religious life (see J. Gauger, *Chronik der Kirchenwirren*, 2:318–19). It is possible that both of the opposing church groups were happy to use this report in defending themselves against state interference.

any one church group.[2] These congregations have been based, some of them for centuries, on the Bible and the confession and therefore consider the Confessing Church to be the rightful successor of the German Evangelical Church Federation that they joined in 1928[3] so as to preserve their connections with the church at home.

The representatives of the German Evangelical congregations who met on November 5, 1934, in the German Evangelical Christ Church have therefore unanimously resolved to communicate the foregoing to the Church Foreign Office in Berlin and at the same time to enter into negotiations with the Confessing Church in Oeynhausen.[4]

[Baron Bruno Schröder]
[Pastor Fr. Wehrhan]

222

161. From the Minutes Book of St. Paul's Church[1]

Quarterly Meeting
November 12, 1934, at 7 P.M., St. Paul's Church

Present: Messrs. G. Henne, Streitberger, Weber, Klugmann, Neubert, Wolford, Hirsch, E. Henne, Schlarb, Dickens, C. Compton, Strobel, Klotz, Pastor Bonhoeffer

The meeting was opened with prayer. The minutes of the last meeting were read and approved. The treasurer presented the account books, which were examined and found to be in order. Mr. Henne reported some news received in his correspondence. Repairs to the heating system have been completed. Mr. Kleinschmidt is to be requested to pump the organ bellows. The worship services for Christmas and New Year's Eve are to be held on December 23 and 30, respectively. The meeting was adjourned with prayer at 8 P.M.

Dietrich Bonhoeffer, Pastor[2]

[3.] Rieger reviews this history in "Die deutschen evangelischen Gemeinden."
[4.] See 1/159.

[1.] ADBC, Minute Book of St. Paul's Church; handwritten by Bonhoeffer. See *NL*, A 41,3 (1); photocopy and typewritten copy.
[2.] This is followed by the signatures of fifteen council members (not all of which correspond to the attendance list at the beginning).

162. Friedrich Wehrhan to Karl Koch[1]

London S.W.13, November 13, 1934

Dear Mr. President,

223
It is an honor for me to send you enclosed a copy of the letter[2] that we have sent to the Church Foreign Office in Berlin, for your information and with the request for your response. Please reply to us as soon as you possibly can.[3] Pastor Schönberger and Pastor Bonhöfer have been delegated to open, if possible in person, the necessary negotiations for the congregations here to join the Confessing Church. Please be so kind as to let me know when it would be convenient for you to receive them.

Since the way has thus been opened for our congregations abroad to join the Confessing Church, it would be advisable to set up without delay an office that corresponds to the Church Foreign Office in Berlin.

I am also enclosing the minutes of the assembly of elders of our churches, on the basis of which we wrote our letter to Berlin.[4]

I remain, with all best wishes for God's blessing,
Respectfully and sincerely yours,
F. Wehrhan, Pastor

[1.] ZEKHN 35/45; typewritten, signed by hand, on letterhead of the Association of German Evangelical Congregations in Great Britain and Ireland; a corrected copy with accompanying letter from Wehrhan is in the files of St. George's Church, London. See also *NL*, A 41,2 (9); typewritten copy. Previously published in *GS* 2:187. At the same time, Wehrhan also sent a personal letter to Koch in which he pointed out that, should Heckel come over to the Confessing Church side and take a leadership position there, this would "cause us to question seriously our adherence to that church," since "we here have suffered too much from his dishonest attitude" (*GS* 2:187; see also *NL*, A 41,2 (10); previously published in *Mündige Welt*, 5:150–51). He wanted Koch "to be . . . in no doubt . . . about the position taken by almost all the pastors and congregations in Great Britain."

[2.] See 1/160.

[3.] Koch's reply was sent on November 15, 1934 (copy: ADBC, GV 1, 13.50; *NL*, A 41,1 [48]). It contains no real position, but Koch says he is glad of the support shown and asks Bonhoeffer and Schönberger to get in touch with him as soon as they arrive in Germany.

[4.] Enclosed was the congregational assembly's resolution of November 5, 1934, somewhat stylistically polished (see 1/159.2) with the signatures of forty-six representatives of St. Paul's, Sydenham, St. Mary's, St. George's, and Hamburg Lutheran Churches (all in London) and from the Hull, Liverpool, South Shields, and Newcastle congregations.

163. The German Embassy in London
to the Ministry of Foreign Affairs[1]

Bishop Heckel phoned Prince Bismarck[2] early this morning and told him that he had been informed that the German Evangelical churches here, in close collaboration with Baron Schröder, had unanimously resolved to join the Confessing Church.[3] Indicating his belief that this could result in unfavorable international repercussions, Heckel asked Bismarck to contact Baron Schröder in order to   224
delay for the time being this step, which he described as at best premature in view of the fact that the clarification of internal German church affairs had not yet been completed.

Bismarck replied that the embassy had not been informed of such a decision on the part of the Evangelical churches here, and further that he would be unable, without instructions from the Ministry of Foreign Affairs, to undertake on his own initiative what Bishop Heckel was asking. However, he said that he would inform himself about the matter and report to the Ministry of Foreign Affairs.

Inquiry directed meanwhile to Pastor Wehrhan here has revealed that all the Evangelical churches here, together with Baron Schröder, decided a few days ago to send a letter to the Church Foreign Office, declaring that they had unanimously resolved to join the Confessing Church and to open negotiations with the Oeynhaus synod.[4] This letter was sent yesterday to the Church Foreign Office, for the attention of Bishop Heckel, and should arrive tomorrow.[5] There is no plan to make the letter public here.

I request that Bishop Heckel be informed and that I be provided with any necessary guidance on this point.

Hoesch

[1.] BA Koblenz, Files of the Reich Chancellery, R 43 II 163, p. 94; typewritten. See also *NL*, A 41,6 (5). Typed above the text: "Telegram (Geh. Ch. V.). London, November 13, 1934, 7 P.M., received November 13, 1934, 9:45 P.M. No. 310 of November 13." Above this, handwritten: "To RK 10241³⁴." The document is also stamped "The Reich Chancellor has been informed" and initialed by Reich Chancellery chief Lammers (November 16). Some sections have been underlined by an unknown hand (not reproduced here). Previously published in *Mündige Welt*, 5:151, and (in part) *DB-ER*, 396–97.

[2.] Otto Christian, Prince von Bismarck.

[3.] See 1/159.

[4.] Refers to the leadership of the Confessing Synod (President Koch) in Bad Oeynhausen.

[5.] Clearly refers to the letter of November 10, 1934, from Baron Schröder and Pastor Wehrhan; see 1/160.

164. Theodor Heckel to the German Pastors Abroad[1]

Berlin-Charlottenburg, November 14, 1934

Confidential

My Brothers,

Our church is in the midst of a grave struggle! The resignation of the former legal administrator[2] was an unmistakable symptom of crisis; it was in no way a solution.

225 Throughout all the conflicts until now, the Church Foreign Office has been able to preserve the independence of German church work abroad in the face of the demands of factions and opinions within the church. This independence and unity will be upheld whatever the circumstances. Thus it is not as though our German churches abroad had to choose between different groups within the home church or had to make decisions themselves with regard to church politics. The German Evangelical Church abroad is called upon to act in concert, in unity and unanimity, since it is in greater danger from the erroneous decisions of individuals than any one of them, looking out from his particular outpost, can judge. Affiliation with the Foreign Office of the home church does not indicate that one has taken a political stance within the church for or against a particular church system. The work of the churches abroad, like the Church Foreign Office, stands over and above these contradictions. But no claim is made on the personal inner convictions and attitude of any one of our colleagues.

I would beg you, my colleagues in the ministry, to believe me if I say no more than that I am struggling as best I can, within the responsibilities of my office and in my sincere commitment to the German Evangelical congregations abroad, for a genuinely ecclesiastical solution to our problems. In the course of the past days and weeks, I have discussed openly and frankly with the Reich bishop[3] the need for a genuinely ecclesiastical decision. With the consent of all my colleagues, I made some specific suggestions. At this moment of decision for our church, I ask for, indeed, I rely on, your trust and patience. Our congregations abroad must not be torn apart by individual decisions of the moment.[4] We must pray and wrestle together in committed unity, so that after these years of struggle among German Protestants there may be a true church within and beyond the borders of Germany!

Dr. Heckel

[1.] ADBC, GV 1, 4.17; typewritten, signed by hand, the word "confidential" also handwritten. See also *NL*, A 41,2 (11); typewritten copy. This is presumably the document that was enclosed with Heckel's letter of November 16, 1934, to Baron Schröder (see 1/167.1).

[2.] August Jäger, who resigned on October 29, 1934.

[3.] Ludwig Müller

[4.] Refers obviously to the Londoners' resolutions of November 5, 1934 (cf. 1/159).

165. To Christine von Dohnanyi[1] 226

Dear Christel,

Thank you very much for your letter! As for Richter's job,[2] I think at the moment Lotte Leu[3] is applying for it.

This is just a quick note because I have had two conversations with Mama, yesterday and today, which I didn't quite understand. Yesterday evening she seemed to me to be very depressed about something, but of course I couldn't guess what it might be. She said Papa was worn out with a cold—is there something more to it than that? Today when I was saying to Franz Hildebrandt that Mama seemed so depressed yesterday, she came on the phone herself and said I must have been mistaken; she had just felt so alone in the house yesterday. But her voice sounded to me the same as yesterday, and I don't think I am mistaken about that. Do you know what this is about? Is somebody sick, or is there some other worry? Or is she perhaps worried about me? I hope not—she had a time like this several years ago, didn't she, when she was so often depressed about some illness she was afraid she had herself. This now reminds me of that time. Please let me know right away what it is, if you know yourself. It's really making me uneasy. Please write me all about it—I'd much rather know now than to wait the eight days until I get there,[4] not knowing what's going on.

How are things at your house? I'm very glad you enjoyed the pictures.[5] There are lots of good engravings to be had here. My best to Hans—and this year I would like my birthday present in advance from him; I don't want to wait till February. And I'd like a good big one, by Christmas at the latest![6]

Warmly,
Dietrich

[1.] *NL,* A 39,4 (8); handwritten, from London; undated but according to Eberhard Bethge probably from November 1934. Previously published in *GS* 6:300–301.

[2.] Presumably Lothar Richter.

[3.] Charlotte Leubuscher.

[4.] Bethge believes that this refers to a trip to Berlin in late November 1934.

[5.] Possibly a birthday gift to Christel, whose birthday was on October 26.

[6.] Perhaps an unclear, coded reference to an anticipated political event.

227   **166. To Gerhard Leibholz**[1]

Dear Gert,

I'm really sorry I gave you all such a fright the other night. What an outrageously stupid thing to do. But it was really nice to talk with you and to hear that you are all right. So first I want to wish you all the best for the next year—plenty of quiet times, on one hand, and, on the other, plenty of changes; it's hard to know which one wishes for more. I'm really sorry about the worries you are having with the children.[2] Sabine wrote me about them.—Please tell her thank you from me for her nice letter and the little package!—But in such a case why not put the children in the car and send them straightaway to the family in Berlin? That's what I really don't understand.

I'm coming to Berlin next week,[3] and then in January for a longer stay, though not yet[4] permanently—on leave from my job here. No telling what I'll be doing after that point.[5] I feel quite settled here, but of course it's not going to be my life's work. I'm reluctant to leave, but it's more to do with quite ordinary feelings of security, which one must not allow to get the upper hand, or else life isn't worth much at all anymore, and not enjoyable either. So, I'll see you soon! Forgive me for this short note; I have to go out, and I want you to get it on time.

Love and best wishes to all of you!
Dietrich

[1.] *NL*, A 39,4 (7); photocopy; handwritten, undated, obviously written from London for Leibholz's birthday on November 15, 1934; original in possession of Sabine Leibholz, Göttingen. Previously published in *GS* 6:301–2.

[2.] This refers to the difficulties the pro-Nazi atmosphere created for the Leibholz children at school (see Leibholz-Bonhoeffer, *Bonhoeffers*, 87–89.)

[3.] Bonhoeffer left for Berlin on the evening of November 25, 1934.

[4.] "yet" inserted after the sentence was written.

[5.] These two sentences evidently refer to plans to become director of a Confessing Church theological seminary.

167. Theodor Heckel to the Association of Congregations in London[1]   228

167.1. Cover Letter to the Chairman Baron Bruno Schröder[2]

Berlin-Charlottenburg, November 16, 1934

Dear Baron Schröder,

I am taking the liberty of sending you enclosed my reply to the letter of November 10[3] from the Association of Congregations. I also would like to thank you in return for the thanks expressed to me in your cover letter of the same date.[4] However, I will not conceal from you that this declaration by the congregations would have better expressed a concern for the overall work of the church on behalf of Germans abroad that I represent had it been preceded by a personal contact and open discussion. The German Evangelical congregations in Great Britain emphasize that they are grounded in Bible and confession, a statement that can only be commended and to which the Church Foreign Office has certainly never taken exception. However, in my view that should have given rise to the simple obligation to clarify the matters in question in a form that would have expressed more than a merely legalistic conception of the mutual relationship.

I am also taking the liberty, my dear Baron, of enclosing for you a confidential circular letter, which I sent on November 14[5] to all clergy of congregations abroad that belong to the German Evangelical Church. You will be able to gather from this letter the basic attitude that underlies my leadership of the Church Foreign Office, as well as my view of the current situation.

Most respectfully yours,
Dr. Heckel

[1.] ADBC, GV 1, 4.16; typewritten. See also *NL*, A 41,1 (50); typewritten copy.

[2.] On Heckel's personal stationery, with a handwritten note at the top, apparently by the office receiving it: "Copy sent to Pastor Wehrhan 19/11/34" as well as "Answer 27.11.34."

[3.] Cf. 1/160.

[4.] Only a draft found; see 1/160, ed. note 1.

[5.] See 1/164.

229   **167.2 To the Association of Congregations**[6]

Berlin-Charlottenburg, November 16, 1934

From the letter of November 10 from the German Evangelical congregations in Great Britain and Ireland,[7] which was received here on November 14, I believe I am to understand that the representatives of the German Evangelical congregations in Great Britain have the intention of withdrawing their congregations from the German Evangelical Church. That this comes without any prior personal contact and open discussion with the Church Foreign Office and is expressed in such a brief communication, out of proportion to the momentous consequences of this step, pains me very deeply. Furthermore, I cannot escape the impression that this declaration in the name of the congregations in Great Britain is based on insufficient information and erroneous presuppositions.

The Association of Congregations appears to assume that there are now two Evangelical Churches standing side by side in Germany, and that they have to decide in favor of one or the other, namely, the German Evangelical Church and the "Confessing Church." The association predicates the legitimacy of the latter. This is an error. The so-called Confessing Church is not a church in a legal sense. It could be called a movement within the church that grants itself self-governing authority. The "Confessing Church" lacks the definitive and permanent form and constitution required for an independent legal entity. Finally, it is of the essence of the matter that there has been no public and legal recognition by the state.

The conclusion that was drawn in your letter of November 10 with regard to the rightful succession does not stand up in any sense. There can be no question but that the rightful successor to the German Evangelical Church Committee[8] is the German Evangelical Church (according to art. 2 of the Reich law on the Constitution of the German Evangelical Church, signed by the Führer as Reich chancellor on July 14, 1933—see Reich Legal Gazette I 1933, p. 471)—a fact that is not contested by any faction.[9] To date there has been no amendment to this law.

230   The previous relationships of the German Evangelical congregations abroad were thus at the time automatically transferred to the German Evangelical Church. The

---

[6.] On letterhead of the Church Foreign Office, addressed to "the Association of German Evangelical Congregations in Great Britain and Ireland, attention of Baron Bruno von Schröder, London E.C. 3." Sender's reference: "A8438."

[7.] See 1/160.

[8.] ["Committee" is here clearly a mistake. Regarding a later correction to "Federation," see 1/183, ed. note 3.—KC]

[9.] The Confessing Church, however, stated at Barmen and Dahlem that it no longer recognized the Reich Church as the rightful church. See Scholder, *Churches and the Third Reich*, 2:145–50 and 267–72.

legal presupposition of your letter is therefore in contradiction with the legal and constitutional basis of the church as sanctioned by the Reich chancellor.

Permit me to point out, furthermore, that the Association of Congregations, according to its own statutes, does not have the power to make binding decisions with regard to the relationship of the congregations belonging to the German Evangelical Church or of clergy belonging personally to the German Evangelical Church, nor to publish statements on behalf of the congregations in such a matter (cf. no. 1c of the Statutes of the Association of Congregations of September 12, 1927, referring also to Declaration I appended to the statutes). Therefore, if the congregations believe they are in a position to take the responsibility of seceding from the German Evangelical Church, the appropriate body in each individual congregation must make the decision to dissolve its membership in the German Evangelical Church, according to the requirements of §15 of the Church Federation Law of June 17, 1924, on the relationship to the Church Federation of German Evangelical church communities, congregations, and clergy outside Germany.[10]

Dr. Heckel

168. Helmut Rößler to the German Evangelical Pastors Abroad[1]

Heerlen, November 16, 1934
Confidential

Dear Colleagues, dear Brothers,

I take the liberty of writing to you in connection with the circular letter of November 14 from Bishop Heckel of the Foreign Office,[2] which you must have received   231 by now. I want to add a simple word of collegial solidarity, as a German Evangelical pastor in the diaspora who, most probably like all of you, has been following the church events in our fatherland with the strongest emotions, and who feels the need to examine his conscience with regard to the decisions being made in our church today and our responsibilities toward ourselves and our congregations.

[10.] In the event of the dissolution of a church community or a congregation's membership in the church federation, this paragraph provided for a declaration to be made "by a decision of its constitutional representatives" (see *Das Recht der EKD*, 127).

[1.] *NL*, A 41,9 (19); photocopy of typewritten letter with handwritten corrections; sender's address top left as follows: "German Evangelical Church of Heerlen, Holland"; previously published in *GS* 6:329–34. According to Roon (*Zwischen Neutralismus und Solidarität*, 137), this letter is based on Heckel's thinking, at some points somewhat altered by Rößler. In his reply of November 20, 1934 (see 1/172), Bonhoeffer immediately expressed his suspicion that Heckel's Foreign Office had a hand in this. Regarding the background, see also Roon, 136–38.

[2.] See 1/164.

During the critical days of the past week, I had to make a business trip to Berlin to negotiate with the Church Foreign Office about a small church building our congregation has just finished constructing, which was dedicated last Sunday. This gave me the opportunity to learn in detail about the state of the critical disputes in our church. I would like to pass along my impressions to you, along with my thoughts about them, not to try to influence you in any way, but only out of a sense of duty toward you as my colleagues in the ministry who are feeling the same uncertainties and inner distress as I myself, and who, I may assume, will be as grateful as I would be in your place for a word of enlightenment to help you make up your own minds about it all.

The impression I received of the situation of last week (November 4–11) is the following:

Since the fall of the legal administrator, Dr. Jäger, there has been a second wave of resistance against the Reich bishop, this time on a much broader front. The Confessing Synod has been joined by the associations within the church (Home Mission, Gustav Adolf Society, etc.), the Lutheran Council, and most of the Protestant theological faculties in rejecting the present church government.[3] All these groups are agreed on this *negative* judgment. Even within the ranks of the German Christians, negative positions on this point are widespread. The front rank for the other side is being maintained by the German Christians and those among them who hold church government and church leadership positions, although it must not be overlooked that there are serious differences among these people. For example, the national church movement in Thuringia recently distanced itself again from the present church government, and some German Christians in other regions of Germany have taken note and are already joining it in doing so.

As an indication of how serious the situation is, the Confessing Synod is proclaiming that circumstances call for emergency law, on the authority of the Reich Ministry of Justice, which it justifies by insisting that all the legislation enacted by Müller's church government since the implementation of the new church constitution has been invalid. The synod proposes to put in place a fundamental legal reconstruction, in total disregard of the existing church government, on the basis of the church constitution of July 11, 1933.[4] On the other side, Hitler has declared on behalf of the state and out of profound disappointment about the course of the Church Struggle, a neutral and impartial attitude toward the Church Struggle as such.[5] Although it will have been considerably relieved by this declaration, the

---

[3.] See Schmidt, *Martin Niemöller im Kirchenkampf,* 238.

[4.] President Koch had negotiated without noticeable success on November 2, 1934, with Justice Minister Gürtner to obtain official recognition of the emergency church law proclaimed in Dahlem (cf. Meier, *Der evangelische Kirchenkampf,* 1:513).

[5.] See 1/160, ed. note 2.

Confessing Synod can hardly hope, in view of the statement made last week by Interior Minister Frick, to be accorded corporative rights by the state.[6]

This is a matter for serious anxiety, that the Third Reich might disassociate itself altogether from church affairs. In that case the Church Struggle might well end in a drift toward the establishment of free churches, as in America, in which event the tie that has existed since Luther's day between the Evangelical Church and the German state would cease to be, and the fateful common cause between the German Evangelical Church and the Third Reich would be disbanded. Whether we in Germany would then find ourselves with one or more free churches, in place of the federation represented by the present German Evangelical Church, is of minor importance compared with the certain prospect that state subsidies for all church bodies and activities—the Protestant theological faculties, confessional schools, and work among the German communities abroad—would be in jeopardy. It would therefore seem obvious at present that a total victory for the Confessing front would mean the end of the national church [Volkskirchentum] and the beginning of the growth of free churches—perhaps even a definitive ecclesiastical schism within German Protestantism.

It appears that there is only one way to avoid the possibility of such disastrous consequences for the German Evangelical Church: a legal reorganization of the existing church government that preserves the continuity of the unified church constitution and administration and its tie to the state authorities. In order to do this, a decision is required of the Reich bishop, which Bishop Heckel and other men have been struggling to obtain, up to now without success.

233

This is the situation within which we must understand the position of the Church Foreign Office. Its leadership has been completely devoted to defending the independence of the German Evangelical congregations abroad. (Bishop Heckel responded to the question put to him in the Hague, "Who will assure us that there will be no encroachment on the independence of the congregations abroad?" by saying, "If there is any encroachment on it, it will be because I am no longer standing where I stand today!")[7] The Foreign Office has been careful to safeguard integrity in church administration. Consequently, up to now we who are abroad can thank God that we have largely been spared the internal dissensions within the church. For we know that, for the most part, the German congrega-

---

[6.] According to Meier, *Der evangelische Kirchenkampf,* 1:512, on November 6 Frick had received the Reich bishop and various German Christian bishops loyal to him and declared to them that the basic law enacted through the church elections in 1933 was recognized and unassailable. On the same day, all publications concerning Evangelical Church matters were banned, except for official announcements by the Reich Church government (cf. also Gauger, *Chronik der Kirchenwirren,* 2:366).

[7.] At a meeting of German Protestant pastors abroad in February 1934 (see Roon, *Zwischen Neutralismus und Solidarität,* 139).

tions abroad will stand or fall on the basis of a solution for German Protestantism that really applies to the whole church. So, in the face of the danger described above, the Church Foreign Office has to keep in mind that our work abroad cannot be based on the good will of one or more free churches. The office is in a particularly difficult situation, and anyone who has seen this at close range must plead on its behalf for understanding.

I can well understand that many colleagues in the ministry might have a sense of belonging inwardly to the Confessing Church[8] and would not understand why they shouldn't simply give way to it. But as things are now, to do so would be to stab the Church Foreign Office in the back, just when, aware of its ultimate responsibility for German Protestantism worldwide, it is struggling to find a real solution for the *whole* church that does not necessitate the complete disintegration of what now exists. There must be no confusion between such an overall solution and the idea of a compromise (such as some middle ground between Koch and Kinder).[9] What we are talking about is whether and how the government of the whole church (of which the last pillars left standing are the Old Prussian Union church administration and the Church Foreign Office in Berlin) can, in continuity, be placed in new hands. We cannot simply walk away and leave these fortifications at the mercy of the embattled Reich bishop, as the Confessing Synod believes it can do, without unleashing a catastrophe. Anyone who is aware of such a responsibility for the whole cannot decide by simply following his heart. Furthermore, the Confessing Church itself does not so far appear to have found a positive way to avoid breaking up the whole church or to assure, by legal means, the continuity of its work. What we are hearing is that the Confessing Synod unfortunately is torn by profound differences of opinion regarding both the situation in general and the appropriate way forward, which are impairing its powers of decision.[10]

Under the pressure of these events and of his sense of responsibility, Bishop Heckel seized the initiative some time ago and in the last few days has been calling insistently for a definite change. It is clear that this means he is definitely distancing himself from the ecclesiastical system that exists at present. However, he knew he had to abandon all reservations and set forth the situation in all its seriousness, all the way to the inevitable conclusion for the top level.

234

[8.] For this formulation, especially the use of the word "inwardly," see the London resolution of November 5, 1934, (1/159) and Heckel's December 10, 1934, letter to the Association of Congregations (1/183).

[9.] Karl Koch was president of the Confessing Synod; Christian Kinder was the national leader of the German Christians.

[10.] This refers to the conflict over the establishment of an "emergency church government" as well as the Reich Council of Brethren elected in Dahlem (see minutes of the Reich Council of Brethren meeting of November 9, 1934, according to Meiser, *Verantwortung für die Kirche*, 348–57).

This being the position, individual demonstrative acts by congregations abroad[11] could do more harm than good, quite aside from the fact that congregations abroad that intervene in internal German church disputes may at any time easily incur accusations of treason and have a hard time refuting them.[12] We all have good reason not to burden the forces struggling for a genuinely ecclesial resolution in Germany with any shadow of reproach from abroad for being "reactionary," thereby bringing them under yet more pressure. This would be to achieve the very opposite of what we must fight for today—a unified German Evangelical National Church[13] within the Third Reich and for the sake of Protestant German culture worldwide.

I come to the conclusion of my impressions and thoughts: We have now been going along with the Church Foreign Office for a year and under its leadership have been able to preserve the independence of our work against all onslaughts, which is still by far the best way for us to serve our people throughout the world. It seems to me that what is called for in the *present* critical moment is not to hinder or endanger the unity of the church's mission abroad in this ultimate hour as it commits itself to finding a solution for the whole church. We have not yet reached the point where the Church Foreign Office expects us to choose between the German Christians and the Confessing Church! So I ask my colleagues in the ministry to bear with me while I offer this advice:

235

Refrain as long as possible from making decisions, and if they cannot be postponed, do not in any case announce them without contacting the Church Foreign Office!

Confidentially, I would like to let you know that if, after conscientious study, the Church Foreign Office makes a decisive change, we will be informed immediately. That will be the moment for *united* action by the congregations abroad. Our ultimate responsibility, which is ours as congregations abroad through the fact of our existence on behalf of the entire German Evangelical Church, is to wait patiently and prayerfully, ready to take action but waiting for the call, to fight and to suffer through this time with one another and with our congregations.

United with you in the one ministry to the Church of Jesus Christ, in the love we share for our Volk[14] and Reich, I beg you, my brethren in the ministry, to treat this letter confidentially, and remain as one among many,

Yours sincerely,

Rößler

[11.] This obviously refers to the course taken in London; see the preceding documents.

[12.] Heckel had already aroused indignation by using this argument in February 1934 in London; see 1/74.1.

[13.] [German *Volkskirche*—KC]

[14.] [Regarding *Volk*, see the editor's introduction, pp. 4–5.—KC]

169. To George Bell[1]

Nov. 17th 34

My Lord Bishop,

thank you very much for your letter.[2] It has upset me very much indeed. I was certain that the translation of the mentioned article[3] had reached you on Sunday the 4th! What happened was this: I was so busy the week before the 4th that I did not get ready with the translation until Saturday evening. But knowing that it would be too late to post it then and that you were wanting it on Sunday, I asked a young German, to go to Chichester *personally* and bring the translation to the Palace, on Sunday morning. Train and fare[4] question was settled and [I] felt quite a relief that everything would work out well in spite of my delay. Ever since I have not heard from this young man anymore. But I had no doubt, that everything was in order. Now the content of your letter is rather disconcerting. I shall probably not be able to get in touch with the messenger until Monday morning, since he has not got telephone and I do not even know his exact address. I hope that nothing happened to him.

236

But I must apologize, first of all, to you for this mischievous response to your kind request for the translation. I am very sorry indeed and I do not know, how to make up for it—moreover since I cannot understand how it could happen at all.

Please, excuse me, My Lord Bishop! As soon as I get to know anything about it, I shall let you know.

I am Yours very respectfully and thankfully
Dietrich Bonhoeffer

I am going to Germany the next week or the week after. The german congregations here have joined the Confessional Church.[5] I am very happy about it.

D.B.

[1.] LPL, Bell Papers 42, 51; handwritten, from London; in original English, including errors. See also *NL*, A 42,1 (23); typewritten copy.

[2.] Letter unknown.

[3.] This reference is unclear.

[4.] Misspelled in the original as "fair."

[5.] See 1/159.

170. From the *Gemeindebote* [1]

**Brahms's German Requiem
in St. Paul's Church**

The choir of St. Paul's Church will sing the German Requiem by Brahms on Remembrance Sunday,[2] November 25, at 6:30 P.M. during the worship service. We hope that German Protestants in London will not miss this unique opportunity to hear this work sung by a German church choir in a German church. We therefore cordially invite you to this evening at our church. Our choir director is Mr. E. A. Seymour, F.R.C.O.[3]   237

Pastor Dr. Dietrich Bonhoeffer[4]

171. From George Bell [1]

19th November 1934

My dear Bonhoeffer,

very many thanks for your letter.[2] I do not think anybody came personally to Chichester with the translation, but please do not upset yourself about it. It didn't put me out in any serious way at all. I only hope, that the MS is not lost, nor the travelling expenses.

I shall be deeply interested in hearing of your visit to Germany. The danger I see at this present moment is the splitting of the German Evangelical Church into sections. I do most earnestly hope that the common front may be maintained and that the Church will be a consolidated body. Tell me when you go, in case it is possible to see you actually beforehand.

Yours ever
[George Cicestr][3]

[1.] ADBC, *Gemeindebote für die deutschen evangelischen Kirchen in Großbritannien*, November 18, 1934, p. 5. See also *NL*, 41,8 (3); typewritten copy.

[2.] [See 1/17, ed. note 2.—KC]

[3.] [F.R.C.O: Fellow of the Royal College of Organists. This is an indication, together with the nature of the Brahms work, of the high level of musical accomplishment in St. Paul's Church (cf. 1/84, and the reference by Bonhoeffer to "the most beautiful activity of our Church, in the church choir" in the wedding sermon of May 3, 1934, 3/9).—KC]

[4.] According to Bethge, Bonhoeffer himself took part in this concert before leaving for Germany the same evening (*DB-ER*, 463).

[1.] LPL, Bell Papers 42, 52; carbon copy; from Chichester; in original English, including errors.

[2.] Of November 17, 1934, see 1/169.

[3.] For Bonhoeffer's reply on November 21, 1934, see 1/175.

172. To Helmut Rößler[1]

London, November 20, 1934

My dear Rössler,

238

And so the two of us meet again![2] in such an official way—and, once again, on opposite sides of an issue. What a pity that we haven't seen each other personally or written to each other in the meantime. Thus your letter I received today[3] came like a bolt out of the blue for me. I really and truly hadn't expected this—that you had listened to Heckel's siren song and his terminology such as "decision on behalf of the whole church" and "American free churches." If you had seen these churches, you would admit that they are not so despicable, certainly less so than Müller's church, the "national church"[4] that we have never had and never will in *that* form. And there is even everyone's favorite cheap shot, "treason against our fatherland." That you fell under the spell of these siren songs, like an innocent youngster—I'm amazed and wish I could still be that innocent. I was, for a long time, especially with regard to the Foreign Office, until I got to know it better, last year before I left, then in February here, in March in Berlin, and in August in Fanö.[5] Now I know these voices, and I know that objectively there is nothing behind them except the attempt to avoid making the decision that is demanded. The subjective side, Heckel's character and his good or not-so-good personal intentions, can be left out of the account altogether, or be left for a personal conversation that is not subject to so many misunderstandings, one hopes soon. But from an objective viewpoint there seems to me no doubt that Heckel's path, and he is not the first to follow it, is the path that Meiser and Wurm and many others have finally realized is the wrong one, and from which they have now deliberately departed, admitting that they were mistaken.[6] To put it briefly, it is the path of good tactics but not the path of faith. (I fear for the time when it becomes a good tactical choice to join the Confessing Church. Then we shall be astonished to see who all turn up there!)

[1.] Archiv der Evangelischen Kirche im Rheinland, Düsseldorf, Literary estate of Helmut Rößler, file 10.3; typewritten and handwritten. See also *NL*, A 41,9 (20). Previously published in *GS* 6:334–37. See the reply, 1/181.

[2.] Helmut Rößler and Bonhoeffer had been friends as students; see the references in *DBWE* 9, *DBW* 10, *DBW* 11, and *GS* 1:51–65 [see also *DB-ER*, 111, 122, 137, 165—KC].

[3.] See 1/168.

[4.] [German *Volkskirche*—KC]

[5.] See *DB-ER*, 321, 347–54, 364–66, 382–85, and in the present volume 1/74 and 1/82.

[6.] On January 27, 1934, Meiser and Wurm had stood "firmly with the Reich bishop" but then on March 13 protested vehemently to Hitler against the church policies of the Reich bishop (see Scholder, *Churches and the Third Reich*, 2:44 and 70–71).

Dear Rößler, I was in Germany during the first half year of the Church
Struggle, have been back about every eight to ten weeks since, and have had   239
any number of visits from pastors and theological students from there. So I
know the *arguments* in favor of Heckel's line by heart. But the line is false. It
is not we who would "stab the Church Foreign Office in the back" but rather
the Foreign Office itself that is betraying our congregations abroad to a pseudochurch for the contemptible purpose of getting the pastors paid. Please
don't forget that, after all the violence and brutality and slander in Württemberg,[7] the bishop of the Foreign Office gave his bishop's blessing to the
Reich bishop, who was responsible for those things, in the form of a biblical
introduction[8] to his service of installation![9] This, instead of refusing to
associate himself with the powers of darkness—what does Christ have to do
with Beliar?[10] So if we are talking here sentimentally about the personal
sacrifice that this cause demands and even portraying such a betrayal with a
halo of martyrdom around it, that only shows how far the poison has worked
its way in and that it is high time to "flee to the next town."[11] In the face of
facts and visions[12] such as these, our actions should not be decided by the
question[13] of what might follow[14] nor by the sorry and indecent question
of whether they could be considered treasonable. What is called for here is
an immediate, uncompromising No. There *is* no more communion between
us and this kind of a church, and since that is so, we should say so. We have
waited long enough.

In February we had the Foreign Office here.[15] They knew what our   240
concerns were. Since then we have heard nothing about the Foreign Office
standing up for the integrity of the church. Instead, there has been one
humiliation after another from the anti-Christian church regime. Moreover,

---

[7.] In September the church government of Württemberg had been accused of financial irregularities, and Bishop Wurm had been suspended (see Scholder, *Churches and the
Third Reich*, 2:246–47).

[8.] The words "in the form of a biblical introduction" have been added by hand.

[9.] Installation of Ludwig Müller as Reich bishop at the national meeting of German
Christians on September 23, 1934, in the Berlin Cathedral.

[10.] 2 Cor. 6:15: "What agreement does Christ have with Beliar? Or what does a
believer share with an unbeliever?"

[11.] Cf. Matt. 10:23.

[12.] Previously miscopied and published in *GS* as "judgments" [very similar to an old
word for "visions" in German—KC]; cf. "visions and revelations" in 2 Cor. 12:1.

[13.] "Our actions should not be decided by the question" replaces "it is not a question."

[14.] Cf. the verse that Bonhoeffer was fond of quoting from Theodor Storm's
"Sprüchen" (Sayings): "The one asks, What comes next? / The other only, Is it right? /
This is what makes the difference / between the free man and the thrall" (Storm, *Gesam-
melte Schriften*, 1:148).

[15.] See 1/74.

it is not true that Heckel has kept the congregations abroad free of the German Christians' poison. I know, and can document it with the definitive testimony of a colleague, that Heckel told a colleague who was going to South America that he had to become a German Christian! Furthermore, he has defended that church regime when he was here and to ecumenical partners as well. We have on record, in our minutes of the meeting with him here, that he tried to make the state and Adolf Hitler responsible for the sorry state of affairs in the church—and then it is the opposition that is accused of treason! I am not a National Socialist, but I know that Heckel has strayed far from the path, in the company of those who are. He demanded a written declaration from me that I would withdraw from all ecumenical activities. He ordered me to fly to Berlin for this purpose, but of course he didn't get my signature![16] Finally, if one really looks at this "situation of the whole church," one should draw the right conclusions and realize that the supposed integrity of the Church Foreign Office cannot allow it to preserve its tie with a church regime that is so unchristian. What kind of illogical congregationalism[17] is that—one of convenience? In any case, there is no credible excuse for the use of *tactics* when it comes to a central decision in and of faith. That is what this is all about. Here in London we hope that we have made such a decision; since then we feel confident, whatever may happen. It was no longer possible to act otherwise.

Now to a personal question. Did Heckel ask you to write this letter, or did he know you were writing it? Its scope is too precisely directed toward us here in London for us not to suspect this.[18] Furthermore, we thought we detected that the envelopes had been addressed on the Foreign Office typewriter! I would regret this alliance very deeply. Why doesn't Heckel write himself, instead of using roundabout ways? But, as I said, these are only suspicions.

241

I used to have quite good relations with Heckel—almost a friendship,[19] so this whole business is doubly painful for me. On a human basis I sometimes fccl terribly sorry for him. But there's nothing for it; we have chosen separate ways. And now I am honestly afraid that our friendship too, yours and mine, is threatened by such a parting of the ways. So I am asking you,

---

[16.] Cf. *DB-ER*, 365–66, as well as Bonhoeffer's letters to Heckel of March 18, 1934 (1/82) and to Sutz of April 28, 1934 (1/93).

[17.] Refers to the doctrinal independence of each local congregation of the Congregational churches in the United States.

[18.] Handwritten from this point.

[19.] See *DBW* 11:93–94.

could we not get together some time? We could clear up so many things! I look forward to your reply soon. Best regards to your wife.

As ever,
Dietrich Bonhoeffer

173. The German Evangelical Pastors' Association in Great Britain to All Pastors Abroad[1]

Dear Brothers,

In reaction to Dr. Heckel's confidential circular letter of November 14,[2] we would like to put forward the following for consideration by all German congregations abroad:

We will not go into the attempts made by Dr. Heckel in his letter to deprive us of our right to make decisions for ourselves, but we agree with him that today "the German Evangelical Church abroad is called upon to act in concert, in unity and unanimity."[3] But when he says that to remain affiliated with the Church Foreign Office does not imply taking a position for or against one church system or another, we cannot help but point out that during Dr. Heckel's negotiations with us in London in February of this year[4] he did try to extract from us an unconditional declaration of confidence in Reich Bishop Müller and the Reich Church. His participation with the German Christian bishops, and only with them, in the installation ceremony of the Reich bishop[5] does indeed indicate a strong church-political position on behalf of the German Christian system.

We believe that we as clergy abroad, whose first and last responsibility is that toward our congregations, must ourselves have the last word with regard to "the need for a genuinely ecclesiastical decision." We must do so "within the responsibilities of (our) office and in (our) sincere commitment to the German Evangelical congregations abroad."

242

[1.] Files of St. George's Church, London; typewritten copy with corrections by hand; without date, names of addressees, or signature; from the text, a date in late November and names of addressees may be deduced. See also *NL*, A 41,2 (12); typewritten copy. Previously published in *GS* 2:188–89. Nothing more is known about the authorship or Bonhoeffer's role.

[2.] See 1/164.

[3.] This and the subsequent section in quotation marks are direct quotes from Heckel's letter (1/164).

[4.] February 8–9, 1934; see 1/74 and *DB-ER*, 348–54.

[5.] On September 23, 1934, in the Berlin Cathedral. [See also 1/159.2, p. 233.—KC]

Consequently, on the twelfth of this month[6] we in Great Britain made a decision and sent the following letter to the Church Foreign Office in Berlin, with a copy to the Confessing Synod in Bad Oeynhausen:

[Here follows the text of the letter of November 10.][7]

This we have done on the basis of our bond with the gospel according to the Scriptures and the confessions of the Reformation, and our responsibility toward church and nation. We could no longer run away from making a decision. To make *none* at all would have amounted to a decision in favor of the German Christian church regime. We have therefore dissolved our tie with this church regime and will shortly be opening negotiations with the Confessing Synod.

In making this decision, we had our responsibility toward the entire Protestant church community abroad very clearly in mind. Our congregations have grown in the soil of the pure gospel, and only because of this have they been able to survive for centuries despite wars and hardships. They have been the strongest link between the German community abroad and the homeland. But this they can be only if they serve our people abroad in love, following the example of our Lord Jesus Christ and not the commands of a dictatorship. We wish to pursue this ministry with even greater zeal today, since the Führer's hard battle has brought about the unity of the German nation.

We pray that our congregations abroad may now awaken and recognize their duty to free the church of Martin Luther and the people of the Reformation[8] from unchristian deeds of violence within the church and blatant errors of doctrine and so bring the church back to its position of honor in the eyes of our nation and the world.

243

Brethren abroad,

The gospel commands us to be truthful and united, and the Führer of our people desires both from us. Let us stand together in this struggle, which we take up not for our own sake but rather for the sake of the church and the German people. Let us enter into negotiations with the Confessing Church as the rightful successor to the German Evangelical Church Federation, which we joined in the past for

---

[6.] Probably a typing error, since it should be the "fifth of this month."

[7.] See 1/160.

[8.] "The church of Martin Luther and the people of the Reformation" were written in by hand to replace "the German Evangelical Church and the German people."

the sake of unity. We call upon you to make your position known immediately, so that we can begin broadly based negotiations without further delay.

We ask for your prayers that the Lord God may bless our beloved German church and may use us, in our weakness, to accomplish his will.

In greetings of fellowship,
The German Evangelical Pastors' Association in Great Britain
President   Recording Secretary

174. To Théodore de Félice[1]

20th of Nov. 34

My dear de Félice!

Thanks ever so much for your letters.[2]

1.) As I shall not be in London but in Berlin in January, Paris would rather be more suitable to me for the meeting.[3]

2.) I have made various attempts to spare some time for the desired translation.[4] But it was absolutely futile. Excuse this delay, but less to keep [you]   244 waiting any longer, I ask you to ask Winterhager for the translation.[5] He is in Berlin now.

All good wishes to you.

Yours ever
Dietrich Bonhoeffer

[1.] WCC Archives, World Alliance, Letters from Dietrich Bonhoeffer; photocopy of handwritten letter from London; in original English, including errors. See also *NL*, A 40,1 (8). Previously published in *Mündige Welt*, 5:240.

[2.] Presumably of October 12 and 17, 1934 (1/150 and/or 1/153) and/or possibly another letter that has not been found.

[3.] Meeting of the Ecumenical Youth Commission, which was eventually held in Paris in February 1935 (see also 1/192, 1/196, and 1/199).

[4.] This refers to the translation into German of the report on the Fanø Youth Conference, which Félice had requested on October 12, 1934 (cf. 1/150).

[5.] Félice then wrote to Winterhager on November 23, 1934 (see WCC Archives, Youth Commission, Félice's correspondence), requesting this translation and sending him the English version, which by then had been completed.

175. To George Bell[1]

Nov. 21st 34

My Lord Bishop,

thank you very much indeed for your kind words.[2] I am, however, still upset about this mischievous translation affair, all the more as I cannot get in touch with the mentioned young man. He has moved from his address, apparently. Now I am fortunately still in the possession of the periodical which you sent to me. So I shall start at once with a new translation, if it [is] still of any use to you. I should be only too glad, if it is not too late and if you allow me to do the job in the next two or three days. Would you just drop me a line? Please, believe me, I shall be *very glad* indeed to do it again, only in order to make up for this unfortunate affair.

I remain
Yours very thankfully
Dietrich Bonhoeffer

245   **176. Baron Bruno Schröder to Theodor Heckel**[1]

London, November 27, 1934

Dear Bishop Heckel:

My thanks for your letter of November 16,[2] which was directed to me personally.

I greatly regret that you are of the opinion that the congregations and I were wrong to send you our decision without prior consultation with you.

Previous experience had led us to conclude that discussions of the sort that took place earlier this year must necessarily prove unfruitful.

This step was taken after long and careful consideration, and no discussion could have influenced us to decide otherwise.

Yours sincerely and respectfully,
B[runo] S[chröder]

[1.] LPL, Bell Papers 42, 32–34; handwritten, from London; in original English, including errors. See also *NL*, A 42,1 (24); typewritten copy.

[2.] Letter of November 19, 1934; see 1/171.

[1.] ADBC GV 1, 4.19; typewritten copy, with handwritten notice "Copy," signed "BS"; typewritten notice added at the top: "Copies sent to Pastors Wehrhan, Schönberger, Rieger, and Bonhoeffer 3/12/34." See also *NL*, A 41,1 (55); typewritten copy.

[2.] See 1/167.

177. Theodor Heckel to Baron Bruno Schröder[1]

Berlin, November 28, 1934

I have not yet received any reply to my letter of November 16, 1934,[2] ref. A 8438. In replying to the communication received from the Association of Congregations, I was naturally assuming that the Association of Congregations would not take any further steps without contacting me. However, I have now learned from the weekly newsletter in the Rhineland, *Unter dem Wort*,[3] no. 47, of November 25, that the Association of Congregations has already made its announcement, based on a false interpretation of the law, to the Council of Brethren of the Evangelical Church of the Old Prussian Union or to other bodies in the Confessing movement. I would like to point out once again that the Association of Congregations is not legally in a position to make binding declarations on behalf of individual congregations and clergy affiliated with the German Evangelical Church with regard to their relationship with the church. I therefore find myself compelled, as long as I receive no further reply from the Association of Congregations in the immediate future, to inform the individual congregations and clergy affiliated with the German Evangelical Church in England of the correspondence to date from my point of view.

Dr. Heckel

246

[1.] ADBC GV 1, 4.20; typewritten; letterhead of the Church Foreign Office, sender's ref. "A 8550"; address: "To the President of the Association of German Evangelical Congregations in Britain and Ireland, Baron Bruno Schröder, London E.C.3"; without salutation; at the top a typewritten note evidently by the recipient's office [in English—KC]: "Copies sent to Pastors Wehrhan, Schönberger, Rieger and Bonhoeffer 3/12/34." See also *NL*, A 41, 1 (56); typewritten copy. Previously published in *GS* 2:190.

[2.] See 1/167.2.

[3.] ["Under the Word." Cf. 1/183, ed. note 5.—KC]

178. Minutes of a Discussion between London Pastors and the Leadership of the Confessing Synod in Berlin[1]

Transcript of the discussion[2] between President Dr. Koch and Church Councilor Breit,[3] on the one hand, with Pastors Wehrhan, Schönberger, and Bonnhöfer[4]

Wehrhan begins: We have firm plans, since we have made a firm decision to withdraw from the Reich Church as soon as we get home. All the congregations in England are ready to take this step. We are still in doubt only about whether to become affiliated anywhere else. Our intention is to make ourselves totally independent. If we eventually affiliate with the church again, it will be only on condition that we do not have to deal with Bishop Heckel anymore. For us Germans abroad, Heckel has become completely intolerable. That has been our experience in England for the past five years, but especially since February of this year.

In February when Heckel visited us, he expected us to sign a declaration that we would submit ourselves to the Müller government.[5] He threatened those who refused to sign with the confiscation of their passports. While the pastors in England were assembled to meet with him, Heckel produced a prepared statement, but we never discussed it. However, after the meeting was over, he told Pastor Schönberger to write at the bottom of this statement, "This declaration was unanimously agreed to by all the German Protestant pastors in England."[6] According to his own words, Heckel's leadership of the Foreign Office has been conducted so as to keep the church dispute away from the congregations abroad. Thus he also asked the pastors abroad to refrain from making any statements on the church dispute. It became impossible for us to keep this stance, because he

247

[1.] ZEKHN 35/45; typewritten, the last page on letterhead of the president of the Confessing Synod, Bad Oeynhausen. See also *NL*, A 41,7; carbon copy (of copy) and (partly) typewritten copy. Previously published in *Mündige Welt*, 5:153–55. Cf. also Bonhoeffer's and Schönberger's presentation to the Foreign Office on December 5, 1934, 1/180.

[2.] This conversation probably took place on November 28, 1934, in Berlin. This can be deduced from a carbon copy among Bonhoeffer's papers of a November 26, 1934, letter from Hans Asmussen to the president of the Old Prussian Union Church, Dr. Ehlers, and from Pastor Wehrhan's November 22, 1934, letter to Präses Koch from London (ZEKHN 35/45; see also *NL*, A 41,2 [13]), announcing the visit of the London pastors, which bears a handwritten note, evidently by the recipient: "Dahlem Wednesday afternoon."

[3.] Hans Asmussen obviously also took part in the conversation as head of the Provisional Church office and ecumenical officer of the Confessing Synod (see *Mündige Welt*, 5:153–55).

[4.] Bonhoeffer's name was spelled this way throughout but has been corrected in the rest of the text by the German editor.

[5.] See 1/74.

[6.] See 1/74.1, also *DB-ER*, 352–53.

was continually working on the basis of information that was factually untrue. He even passed these false assertions to the foreign press. For example, he said that in Germany there had been no dismissals from office, only leaves of absence. The man here who has decisive influence in ecumenical matters[7] has said that he no longer has confidence in Bishop Heckel's integrity.

The pastors from England then gave several more examples supporting this impression.[8]

Koch: Do you take full responsibility for these statements?

Wehrhan: Baron Schröder[9] says Heckel told us a pack of lies.

Breit: For what constituency do you claim to be speaking?

Wehrhan: Pastor Schreiner[10] is the only one of us in England who takes a different view. But at an assembly of our congregations, even Pastor Schreiner called for disassociation from the Reich Church government and explicitly agreed to it. Practically all our congregations want to withdraw from the Reich Church. When   248 the proposal was made to the assembly at which all the congregations in England were represented, it was greeted with thunderous applause.

Bonhoeffer: All the congregations in England inwardly[11] take the same position as the Confessing Synod. The only question is, how shall we go about affiliating with it?

Breit: Do you make the condition that, even in a future disposal of the church issue in Germany, Heckel must under no circumstances be on the church staff?

Answer: Yes.

Breit: In what form do you see your future affiliation?

Answer: We stand on the same ground as the Confessing Synod. It is only the form about which we are not sure.

Breit: We would consider it desirable for you to join the Confessing Synod at some future point.

[7.] Possibly Bishop Bell. [But this could also be J. H. Oldham, who at the Fanø conference in August 1934 had added to his already long list of ecumenical roles the chairmanship of the Research Committee of Life and Work and thereby was now effectively the organizer of the conference on "Church, Community, and State" being planned for Oxford in 1937. He was in close and continual contact with George Bell, as well as with Bonhoeffer, and not least on the German participation in the preparations for Oxford. On December 14, 1934, he wrote to Bell: "I very much distrust Heckel and this is part of the difficulty" and was repeating the same comment two years later. See Clements, *Faith on the Frontier*, 299 and 303.—KC]

[8.] I.e., the pastors from England who were present.

[9.] "Schröder" is written in by hand.

[10.] Pastor K. H. Schreiner, the German pastor in Liverpool, had expressed his doubts about breaking relations with the Reich Church, both to the Foreign Office (see *NL*, A 41,6 [6]) and to Baron Schröder (see ADBC, GV 1, 11; handwritten; *NL*, A 41,1 [49]; copy).

[11.] [See 159.1, ed. note 3.—KC]

Wehrhan: That is also our thinking. But in any case it would be important to us to have a new form of affiliation. We would like to be autonomous.

Bonhoeffer: The congregations abroad that are financially dependent take the same position as ourselves, but they aren't free to decide because of their financial dependence.

Pastor Schönberger from London then reported that in the London congregations and some others there is unanimous agreement that their congregations should withdraw from the current Reich Church government. On the question that then arose as to how the German congregations abroad should be joined together independently of the Reich Church's Foreign Office and of Bishop Heckel, who is unacceptable to the said congregations, Pastor Schönberger made the following confidential observations, with the consent of his colleagues Bonhoeffer and Wehrhan:

All the congregations in England have expressed in writing that they inwardly stand on the same ground as the Confessing Church. Pastor Schönberger sees the practical consequences as follows: An attempt will be made from London to gather all the German Evangelical congregations abroad together into one organization, without, for the time being, the further step of legal affiliation with the German Evangelical Confessing Church. Pastor Schönberger, as cultural warden of the National Socialist German Workers' Party in England, has obtained the approval of Gauleiter Bohle[12] of Hamburg for this organization of the congregations, so that there is no foreign policy obstacle to such an undertaking.[13] An attempt should be made, with the Gauleiter's approval, to establish ties between this new Foreign Office in London and an office of the German government that could possibly make the necessary funds available. The Confessing Church is asked not to establish any Foreign Office on its own, but to remain in unspoken agreement to leave the functions of such an office to the German pastors' committee that is to be established in England.

Pastor Schönberger is to serve as liaison to the Party, and Pastor Bonhoeffer as liaison to the Confessing Church. All inquiries reaching the Confessing Church that concern German Protestants abroad should please be referred to the gentlemen in London.

Pastor Asmussen shared the information that a plan had already been discussed in Oeynhausen to set up such a Foreign Office at a German Protestant location abroad, since it would be easier to overcome certain difficulties from there than

[12.] [A *Gauleiter* was the top regional Nazi official; Bohle was *Gauleiter* not only of Hamburg, but of the Party *Auslandsorganisation*, which kept surveillance over Germans living abroad.—KC]

[13.] This contradicts Bohle's own view; see 1/180, ed. note 3.

from within Germany. He understood Pastor Schönberger's remarks to mean that this new, to-be-created Foreign Office and the German Confessing Church would stand together ecclesiastically and confessionally but should not be bound by a contract. However, there should be a gentlemen's agreement that possible questions of precedence that are of concern to the German Evangelical Confessing Church be resolved in consultation with both sides together.

179. To Karl Koch[1]

Berlin, December 1, 1934

Dear President Koch:

Before I return to London, permit me to say a very brief word on the question of Karl Barth's oath.[2]

I am convinced that our ecumenical partners will see this as the turning point of the current developments in the church in Germany. If the new church regime[3] cannot find a word of solidarity or a plea for understanding to make on Barth's behalf, this will seriously threaten the interest in the Confessing Church that has been shown thus far by the ecumenical community. It will create the impression that we are deviating from the original, true line followed by the Confessing Church and will alienate people from our position. I know that the eyes of all Protestants are fixed on the new church regime, awaiting its decision, and feel that it is my responsibility to let you know about this.

Most sincerely and respectfully yours,
Dietrich Bonhoeffer

[marginal note: 250]

[1.] ZEKHN 35/45; typewritten, signed by hand; see also LKA EKvW, 5,1, 431/II, and *NL*, 41,9 (10); typewritten copy. Previously published in *GS* 6:303 and *Mündige Welt*, 5:238. For the reply, see 1/184.

[2.] Karl Barth had declared—in vain—that he was prepared to take the official's oath, if the additional phrase he proposed, "insofar as I can responsibly do so as a Christian," were recognized. The question here is whether the Confessing Church would support him in making this qualification. Cf. Prolingheuer, *Der Fall Karl Barth*, 65–75 [and Busch, *Karl Barth*, 255–58—KC].

[3.] The Provisional Church Government of the German Evangelical Church, constituted on November 22, 1934, under the leadership of Bishop August Marahrens. See Prolingheuer, *Der Fall Karl Barth*, chaps. 3 and 4, 27–75 [and Scholder, *Churches and the Third Reich*, 2:291—KC].

180. The Ministry of Foreign Affairs
on the Presentation by Dietrich Bonhoeffer and Gustav Schönberger[1]

Note for the File

Two Protestant pastors in London, citizens of the German Reich, Schönberger (cultural warden of the NSDAP in London) and Bonhöfer, presented the following plan to me and LR Freudenberg,[2] claiming that they had discussed it already with Gauleiter Bohle[3] in Hamburg and received his general agreement to it.

251

The two gentlemen pointed out that the German Evangelical congregations in London had broken off their relationship to the Reich Church, since they inwardly stand on the foundation of the Confessing Synod. They said they had lost all confidence in the Reich bishop as well as in Bishop Heckel of the Church Foreign Office. Various German congregations abroad, e.g., in South Africa, were turning to the London group for the same reasons, the two pastors said, and it was to be expected that other Protestant congregations abroad that had lost confidence in the Reich Church government would do the same.

¶To prevent the German congregations abroad from falling away one by one and to enable the German Evangelical congregations abroad to support one another, the two pastors proposed the founding of a German expatriate church,

---

[1.] Political Archive, Auswärtigen Amt (Ministry of Foreign Affairs), Berlin [correction], VI A, Evangelische Angelegenheiten (Protestant Affairs), file ref. 2, vol. 9; typewritten, signed by hand; "Copy for the file," dictation ref. VI A 5455 Re; missing in NL. Previously published in *Mündige Welt*, 5:345. According to an accompanying note, this text was forwarded to the foreign minister, who gave his consent but said he wanted "nothing to do with this matter." Copies were sent to the German embassy in London, the general consulate in Pretoria, the Nazi Party overseas organization in Hamburg, and the Church Foreign Office. Cf. also Heckel's response, 1/203, and the discussion between the London pastors and the Confessing Synod [leaders], 1/178.

[2.] Adolf Freudenberg (LR is an abbreviation for *Legationsrat*, or legation officer) reports briefly on this visit in Zimmerman, *I Knew Dietrich Bonhoeffer*, 166. [Freudenberg subsequently left government service because of his wife's Jewish ancestry. See also the index of names.—KC]

[3.] Ernst-Wilhelm Bohle, Nazi Party regional governor [*Gauleiter*, see 1/178, ed. note 12—KC] in Hamburg and director of the Party's overseas organization, wrote to the Ministry of Foreign Affairs on December 21, 1934, (no. 5788) after receiving these notes, that he had "in no way given his approval" to Schönberger's plans and had referred him "to the Führer's deputies, telling him that he must also present his concern to the Ministry of Foreign Affairs." He further stated that the overseas organization of the Party had initially refused to deal with church matters, but that he was also of the opinion that the dangers "described" by Pastor Schönberger did indeed exist and must "definitely be thoroughly investigated." Bohle wrote that Schönberger had explained these thoughts to him "in Berlin," but he did not mention Bonhoeffer. It is therefore unlikely that Bonhoeffer took part in the conversation with Bohle, even though the these notes by the Ministry of Foreign Affairs initially suggest it.

which must be fully independent of both the Reich Church government and the Confessing Synod, so as not to be drawn into the unfortunate church dispute. The two gentlemen had in mind that the administration of the proposed new German expatriate church be carried out from London, but of course there must be a certain connection with the mother country. The two gentlemen thought that either the National Socialist Party or the Ministry of Foreign Affairs could be considered as their bridge to the homeland. During the conversation, however, they said they would only consider the Ministry of Foreign Affairs as an administrative liaison office. They said that the group in London considers it necessary to have a contact with the Ministry of Foreign Affairs and does not want to do anything without its consent.

The two pastors from London were told that the conditions under which   252
their plan could be carried out did not exist at this time. We said that the Foreign Ministry was well aware of the serious repercussions of the church dispute on the German Evangelical congregations abroad, but that the situation within the Reich was still developing. We said that as long as this had not been settled, there was no purpose even in considering a plan such as the two gentlemen had presented. The idea of a withdrawal of all the German Evangelical congregations abroad from the Reich Church appeared extremely dubious to us, since every move toward independence carried the great danger that the German congregations abroad would become spiritually alienated from the mother country. Thus I could not imagine that the overseas office of the NSDAP in Hamburg had given its agreement to this plan. In our opinion to move the governance of those German congregations outside the Reich to a location abroad would contravene the principles of current policy. Indeed, it is essential for spiritual and cultural influences to continue to come from the Reich and, in church matters, from its church. In our opinion there was no possibility for the administration of all the German Protestant churches abroad to be carried out from London, since it was clear that from London one had a very one-sided view of developments inside the Reich, especially church issues, mainly through the eyes of the English press or through news received indirectly from the Reich. Furthermore, it was very doubtful whether the interests of all the German congregations abroad were really the same as those of the congregations in London, which had always had their own particular viewpoint.

With respect to the proposal from the two gentlemen, that the Ministry of Foreign Affairs assume the administrative relationship with the German congregations abroad, I therefore had to state, at least on behalf of this office, that the Ministry of Foreign Affairs would under no circumstances be prepared to undertake a responsibility in an area outside its competence as an office of the Reich government. Some concrete examples were given to demonstrate the impossibility of the proposal.

All in all, the plan presented by the two gentlemen seemed very inadequately thought out and in many ways self-contradictory. Messrs. Schönberger and Bonhöfer appeared, in making this request, to be motivated by a very strong animosity toward the Church Foreign Office in particular.

To the two gentlemen's question as to how they should respond to any further inquiries from German congregations abroad, I replied that, in the interest of preserving cohesion between the mother country and the German community abroad, we would necessarily expect that there be no further propaganda for the plan that had been presented to me, in any case from London, and that inquiries should be answered in such a way as to reassure the persons concerned.

253

Berlin, December 5, 1934[4]

Roediger

181. From Helmut Rößler[1]

Heerlen, December 6, 1934

My dear Bonhoeffer,

I'll begin my answer at the end: would you be able to be, and remain, friends with a Communist? Yes! With a Frenchman? Yes! With a Mohammedan, a Hindu, or a heathen of the Batak faith? I would think so. With a Christian, a German, who "betrays the gospel"??—well, I don't think that's what I am. But I protest with all my might against seeing the relation between the opposing sides in the church today as the fulfillment of Matt. 10:35.[2] The differences may lie deep as an abyss, but they have absolutely no effect on blood relationships and bonds of friendship; they are poles apart in matters of the mind, but not of faith! So even if you were a fanatic of the Confessing Church, while I saw the Lord's promise today as being offered by the poor, really *poor* Lazarus (theologically, intellectually, and in human terms) that the German Christians represent, I would not take this to mean any destruction of our relationship with each other. I could not make any sense of that at all. My opinion of intellectual differences and battles is much too low, compared

---

[4.] It is not known when this conversation actually took place; it may have been several days earlier.

[1.] Archiv der Evangelischen Kirche im Rheinland, Düsseldorf, Literary estate of Helmut Rößler, file 10,3; carbon copy, with illegible passages corrected by hand and a handwritten note at the top: "My (painful) parting of the ways with D. Bonhoeffer in the Church Struggle." See also *NL*, A 41,9 (21); photocopy without this addition. Previously published in *GS* 6:337–40. Reply to Bonhoeffer's letter of November 20, 1934, 1/172.

[2.] "For I have come to set a man against his father, and a daughter against her mother, and a daughter-in-law against her mother-in-law."

with my high estimation of the true mystery of our calling and mission in history, to allow me to think otherwise.

2. Of course I wrote my circular letter[3] by agreement with Heckel, to give 254 my brothers in the ministry abroad some insight into the struggles and the position of *our* church authorities. I am in no way ashamed of this "alliance," not even if it leaves me open to the charge of being too ambitious. If you felt that the scope of the letter had an impact on you, that shows how much we needed to look at these things from a viewpoint outside Germany, but different from that of England.

3. If you are going to call me an innocent youngster, then I will have to call you a naïve child, if you equate the Confessing Church with Christ and Müller's government with Belial. Only once in your letter did you mention any foreboding that the Confessing Church could also be a tactical path that attracts all sorts of people. How can it escape your notice that this is already the case, that it is already a collection of the most disparate minds, from neo-Protestantism[4] to the sanctification sects and fanatics of the confessions, all working together? The Confessing Church isn't any more the true church than the German Christian Church. The true church lies hidden within each of them.

4.[5] You write about a betrayal of our congregations abroad to a pseudochurch for the contemptible purpose of getting pastors paid and added that you were confident of having made your decision. Can you hold it against me if I say that back to you and point out that your confidence is based (objectively, not subjectively!) in good part on just this contemptible pastors' pay, which puts you in England in a position of knowing you aren't dependent on any assistance?[6] It's odd that only the congregations in England (and not even all of them) feel that they have to break off relations with the Church Foreign Office, while the responses I have received so far from all the other congregations abroad agree with what I said. That is just why your decision is *not* a real one—because it is not a life-or-death issue for your congregations, the way it is for most of the others. So you think you 255

[3.] On this, see also 1/168, ed. note 1.

[4.] A collective term for the theological currents in the Protestant church that were open to the intellectual and cultural influences of the nineteenth century (esp. that of Schleiermacher).

[5.] In the original this paragraph was also numbered 3. The numbering of all further paragraphs has been adjusted accordingly.

[6.] Until long after World War II, the London congregations and some others as well continued to be independent of subsidies from Germany. A "United German Church Fund," established in 1928, had the accumulated funds from the treasuries of defunct German Evangelical congregations, thus providing additional resources beyond the money raised by the existing congregations themselves (cf. Rieger, "Die deutschen evangelischen Gemeinden," 104).

can make a more cool-headed and correct judgment, but the truth is that for you the decision is blurred into a systematic one, not an existential Either/Or.

5. What is promising about Heckel's position for so many of us in the crush of the Either/Or is that it offers just what we are hoping and secretly longing for, the vision of a church that is equally distant from both the German Christians and the Confessing Church, the church that is to come. It is also because he has the courage to stay sober, while almost everyone else is overenthusiastic, if not a blind fanatic. What this sobriety means is this: separating oneself from an established church is always a matter of madness about something, a rebellion based on a devout life or devout thinking, whereas reformation only takes place in that one day you find yourself outside, not because you got up and marched out.[7] You can only march out into another church, a "next town,"[8] which is basically just as human as the church you left behind. And in this case it can be done only by putting at stake the continued existence of numerous congregations that cannot survive without some continuity between old and new in the same church. A decision to stand fast, when everyone is crying breakup and catastrophe, can be reproached only for being a tactic and seems to me more courageous—and more faithful—than to march out and feel relieved that one has been faithful to one's confession. "Some people believe in their confession, and others confess their belief"[9]—even among the devil's folk!

6. We here in Holland who are backing Heckel are especially aware of a warning from the history of this country where we are working and a call to pass the warning on to others. There was a precursor of what is now happening in Germany exactly one hundred years ago in Holland, when the "Gereformeerden" left the Reformed Church.[10] The spiritual powerlessness of the Dutch churches now in the life of the people is most distressing. This division had only one beneficiary:

[7.] On the question of whether to separate from the Reich Church or to wait to be "thrown out," see Bonhoeffer's correspondence with Karl Barth of September 9 and 11, 1933 [*DBW* 12, 1/96 and 1/97—KC] (*GS* 2:126–30). Bonhoeffer had asked for Barth's opinion as to whether the time had not come to initiate the separation, since the "Jewish Christians" had already been "thrown out." Barth nevertheless advised waiting.

[8.] Matt. 10:23; cf. 1/172, ed. note 11.

[9.] The source of this quotation is not known.

[10.] [In 1834 a major secession took place from the national Reformed Church of the Netherlands (Nederlandse Hervormde Kerk, NHK) to form the Christian Reformed Church, joined in 1886 by followers of Abraham Kuyper in a further secession from the NHK to form the Reformed Churches of the Netherlands (Gereformeerde Kerken in Nederlandse). These secessions in a "free church" direction were motivated by a resurgent Calvinism dissatisfied with the rationalism and liberalism allegedly prevailing in the NHK.—KC]

Rome. I am sending you the theses of Pastor Fischer in Amsterdam.[11] He used to be a pillar of the Confessing Church, but withdrew, justifying his action on the   256 basis of Dutch church history. The result was these theses, which he wrote after doing research in the files and sources, fresh from this experience. He presented the theses at our last pastors' conference, and we all agreed with him fully.

7. Over against these basic views and line of thinking, individual actions, including errors of judgment on Heckel's part, if you like, do not seem to me to carry much weight. Your letter is full of such details, which can only be evaluated at all in relation to a basic attitude, given that even the best of us makes mistakes.

8. In conclusion I will say to you that I could never feel at home in the Confessing Church, even in the absence of all the other doubts regarding the survival of the congregations abroad. In its approach the Confessing Church is a church of restoration, which means that historically it is already dead because it is closed rather than open toward the future. For me the Reformation confessions have only limited validity, if their day is not already past. God has given us too much genuine theological insight in the time since then for us to continue in extenso regarding these confessions as our own. I even consider the division of our people into Catholics, Protestants, and the Third Confession[12] to be limited; we could go beyond it. A new Reformation is on its way. We are now in the century of the reform councils, and in one hundred years perhaps the swan will take flight![13] This means that in principle I see more promise on the side of the Thuringian German Christians, for instance, even though they are still so rapturous, than in a restoration secessionist church, which no longer has the will to think of our whole people. A Confessing Church as Koch[14] sees it would be the church of a Council of Basel or of Constance! Today again we are not far from burnings at the stake on issues of conscience, as you are surely aware. The Confessing Church folk themselves sometimes put frightening pressure on people's consciences.

[11.] Pastor J. H. R. Fischer was originally close to the Confessing Church but later came more strongly under Heckel's influence. His theses warned the Confessing Church against splitting off, on the basis of church history in the Netherlands. On his role, see Roon, *Zwischen Neutralismus und Solidarität*, 141.

[12.] Under the Nazi regime one could indicate one's confession as "Protestant," "Catholic," or "God-believing" (*gottgläubig*). Of those choosing this third option, many belonged to Alfred Rosenberg's "German faith movement" (cf. *Junge Kirche* 1934, 216ff.). ["God-believing" was a catchphrase in Nazi Germany that referred to people (including Nazis) who had left the church but considered themselves religious.—KC]

[13.] [This is evidently an allusion to how Martin Luther recalled the words attributed to Jan Hus, the Czech "proto-reformer," who, when burned at the stake in 1415, said: "Today you are burning a goose, but from these ashes a swan will take flight." Luther dared to suggest that his own Reformation was a fulfillment of Hus's prophecy.—KC]

[14.] Karl Koch was president of the Confessing Synod.

I will close *for now*, having simply marked out my position in our discussion. How are you personally? I hope we will soon be able to have a good talk; we really need it.

Yours sincerely,
H[elmut] R[össler][15]

257   **182. Theodor Heckel to Baron Bruno Schröder**[1]

Berlin-Charlottenburg, December 10, 1934

My letters of November 16 and 28—A 8438[2] and A 8550[3]—still remain unanswered. In the meantime I have learned from reliable sources that, contrary to what was stated in your letter of November 10 to the Church Foreign Office,[4] the decision made on November 5, 1934, by the representatives of the German Evangelical congregations in Great Britain assembled at Christ Church said only that the congregational councils inwardly stand on the ground of the Confessing Church and will immediately take up with the church authorities (Foreign Office of the Reich Church and Confessing Church) any necessary matters arising from this.[5] In this decision, the stress is on the word "inwardly." It does not mention the legal interpretation set out in your letter of November 10. Furthermore, it is plainly stated that the representatives of the congregations wanted negotiations undertaken with the Foreign Office of the German Evangelical Church, among others. I do not know to what extent the president of the association was empowered to depart from this decision.

My suspicion that the decision of the congregational councils' representatives is based on insufficient information and erroneous assumptions has been fully confirmed. I repeat once and for all that no Confessing Church has been legally constituted in addition to the German Evangelical Church, and that there has been no official recognition of the Confessing Synod by the state.

[15.] The closing and initials in the NL document (apparently a copy of the carbon copy later found among Rößler's papers) were added by hand, presumably later by the author.

[1.] ADBC, GV 1, 4.22; typewritten copy; addressed "To the President of the Association of German Evangelical Congregations in Great Britain and Ireland, Baron Bruno von Schröder, London E.C.3"; no salutation; sender's ref. A 8663 (the same as the following letter, 1/183); neither was found in EZA. See also *NL*, A 41,1 (59). Previously published in *GS* 2:191–92.

[2.] See 1/167.2.
[3.] See 1/177.
[4.] See 1/160.
[5.] See 1/159.1.

Unfortunately, I note that two representatives of the London congregations, Pastors Schönberger and Bonhoeffer, spent some time in Berlin without deeming it necessary even to try to discuss matters with the Church Foreign Office. I am aware of the proposals that they made in official quarters in Berlin with respect to the reorganization of church work abroad,[6] proposals that the said persons   258 are in no way legally entitled to make and which, moreover, represent a plan that is wholly illegitimate on both ecclesiastical and national grounds. I can only warn against any further pursuit of such ideas.

Under the present circumstances I see myself obliged to inform all the congregations of my correspondence with their Association of Congregations.

(signed) Dr. Heckel

183. Theodor Heckel to the German Evangelical Congregations in Great Britain[1]

Berlin-Charlottenburg, December 10, 1934

In a letter of November 10, the Association of German Evangelical Congregations in Great Britain and Ireland informed the Church Foreign Office of the following:
"..."[2]

I replied to the association on November 16— A 8438—as follows:
"..."[3]

I have not yet received any reply from the Association of Congregations.

In the meantime I have learned from reliable sources that, contrary to what was stated in the letter of November 10 from the association to the Church Foreign Office, the decision made on November 5, 1934, by the representatives of the German Evangelical congregations in Great Britain assembled at Christ Church said only that the congregational councils inwardly[4] stand on the ground

---

[6.] See 1/178 and 1/180.

[1.] ADBC, GV 1, 4.23; hectographed, signed by hand, sender's ref. A 8663; addressed "To the Council of Christ German Evangelical Church in London, att. Baron Bruno von Schröder, London E.C.3"; apparently sent to Baron Schröder together with the preceding letter (1/182; cf. also the last paragraph of that letter). See also *NL*, A 41,1 (60); copy.

[2.] Here the letter (1/160) regarding the "secession resolution" is quoted in full.

[3.] Here the letter (1/167.2) is quoted in full (with no attention called to a correction: the German Evangelical Church is now described as the rightful successor of the German Evangelical Church *Federation* and not of the Church *Committee*).

[4.] [On the meaning of *innerlich*, here translated as "inwardly," see 1/159.1, ed. note 3. Nothing more clearly demonstrates the vast gulf between Heckel's thinking and that of the Confessing pastors, running throughout this letter, than his minimalist understanding of what "inwardly" implies. Quite apart from his ideological prejudices, Heckel is thinking only in narrowly legal, in contrast to theological, terms.—KC]

of the Confessing Church and will immediately take up with the church authorities (Foreign Office of the Reich Church and Confessing Church) any necessary
matters arising from this. In this decision, the stress was on the word "inwardly."
It does not mention the legal interpretation set out in the letter of November

259   10. Furthermore, it is plainly stated that the representatives of the congregations
wanted negotiations to be undertaken with the Foreign Office of the German
Evangelical Church.

In my reply to the communication received from the Association of Congregations, I naturally assumed that the Association of Congregations would not take any
further steps without contacting me. However, I have now learned from the weekly
newsletter in the Rhineland, Unter dem Wort, no. 47, of November 25,[5] that the
Association of Congregations has already made its announcement, based on a misinterpretation of the law, to the Council of Brethren of the Evangelical Church of
the Old Prussian Union or to other bodies in the Confessing movement.

Furthermore, two representatives of the London congregations, Pastors
Schönberger and Bonhoeffer, have been in Berlin during the last few days without
deeming it necessary even to try to discuss matters with the Church Foreign
Office. Instead, they entered into negotiations with offices of the Party and the
state[6] and with representatives of the Confessing Synod.[7] They made proposals
concerning a reorganization of all overseas German church work to an important
office in Berlin that go far beyond the relations of the German Evangelical congregations in Great Britain to the German Evangelical Church.[8] If these proposals
were to be carried out, the result would represent an unthinkable and deeply
regrettable development on both ecclesiastical and national grounds. From what I
hear, the proposed plans were rejected by the office to which they were submitted. The extent to which the two gentlemen's procedure was authorized by the
congregations in England is not altogether clear to this office.

In view of these circumstances, I find myself obliged to make direct contact
with all the congregations individually, asking for a response from each. That the
decision made by the congregational councils' representatives on November 5,
even in the corrected version reproduced above, is based on insufficient information has been fully confirmed. I repeat once and for all that no Confessing
Church has been legally constituted in addition to the German Evangelical Church,
and that there has been no official recognition of the Confessional Synod by the

---

[5.] A brief report on a meeting of the Council of Brethren of the Evangelical Church
of the Old Prussian Union, on November 16, 1934, in Berlin-Dahlem, at which a letter
from the German congregations in England was read "in which they declare that they [saw]
the Confessing Church as the rightful church in Germany." [See 1/177, ed. note 3.—KC]
    [6.] See 1/180.
    [7.] See 1/178.
    [8.] See 1/178 and 1/180.

state. However, I will be candid in saying to the congregational councils that I   260
can understand completely, in such a complicated situation, that it is possible for
decisions, even far-reaching ones, to be made on the basis of false information. It
is far from my intention to reproach you for it. On the other hand, I hope that
the above clarification will convince all congregations that the decision of November 5 does not do justice to the situation and is not the way forward for you. I
would like to emphasize that my effort has been—as has been recognized with
gratitude by the overwhelming majority of German Evangelical congregations and
churches abroad—to keep the influences of church politics and factions out of
our German church work abroad. We have been successful in the effort to keep
our German Evangelical congregations and churches abroad from being ensnared
in this unfortunate ecclesiastical dispute, which is tearing our church apart. However, this requires that the congregations themselves refrain from taking sides in
the dispute, as long as their own constitutional and confessional foundations are
not affected. The legal principles governing relations with the German Evangelical
congregations and churches abroad, the confessional status of the congregations,
and freedom of conscience for the clergy and church members have always been
guaranteed conscientiously by the Church Foreign Office and thus by the German
Evangelical Church. Thus there is no real reason to dissolve relations with the
German Evangelical Church. Moreover, the position of the German Evangelical
congregations abroad demands that, in every decision they make, they show consideration for the honor of our German people and fatherland.

I ask that each congregational council make its decision, based on the above
considerations, calmly and objectively. For the sake of clarity I hereby summarize
the essential legal points, mentioned in my previous letter, which need to be considered by vestries in making a decision: The view expressed by the Association
of Congregations in its letter of November 10, that the Confessing Synod is the
rightful successor to the German Evangelical Church Federation, in consequence
of which the congregations are joining the Confessing Synod, is incorrect. The
congregations are already part of the rightful successor to the German Evangelical
Church Federation, which is the German Evangelical Church. If congregations wish
to secede from the German Evangelical Church, each individual congregation must
make a specific declaration to this effect, according to the requirements of §15 par.
2 of the Church Federation Law of June 17, 1924, on the connection of German
Evangelical Church communities, congregations, and clergy outside Germany to
the Church Federation. According to §15 par. 3 of the same law, such action on   261
the part of congregations would invalidate all existing obligations of the German
Evangelical Church toward its clergy, particularly with regard to pensions.[9] Since
no other legally constituted national church exists to which they might adhere,

---

[9.] See Merzyn, *Das Recht der EKD*, 127.

congregations making such a decision would terminate *absolutely all* their rights in the home church.

I should be grateful if each vestry would please oblige by sending me a statement of its position.

To the best of my knowledge, the action of the Association of Congregations does not have the approval of the Liverpool, Bradford, South Shields, and Newcastle congregations.

Dr. Heckel

184. From the Provisional Church Administration[1]

Berlin, December 11, 1934

Dear Brother Bonhoeffer,

In reply to your letter,[2] I enclose a copy of the original statement from the Provisional Church Administration regarding the oath. I will write later concerning the rest.

In haste, with my best wishes,
Yours sincerely,[3]

[Excerpt from presumed] Enclosure:[4]
[. . .]
At this point in time, we are able to say the following regarding our position:

The oath to be sworn to the Führer, Adolf Hitler, which invokes the name of God, conveys the seriousness of one's commitment to loyalty and obedience as a responsibility before God, which is its proper foundation. Through the reference to God, it excludes any action that is contrary to the commandments of God according to the testimony of Holy Scripture.

With this understanding, we hold to the words of our Lord: "Give therefore to the emperor the things that are the emperor's, and to God the things that are

262

[1.] ZEKHN 35/45; carbon copy; on letterhead: "Provisional Administration of the German Evangelical Church, Am Johannestisch 5, Berlin." See also *NL*, A 41,9 (11); "copy of copy." Previously published in *Mündige Welt*, 5:238.

[2.] Letter to Karl Koch of December 1, 1934, 1/179.

[3.] It is not clear who signed this letter, possibly Koch or Asmussen.

[4.] Presumably the enclosure mentioned in the letter, but not found, was an excerpt from a letter to a student in Göttingen named Harms (according to Prolingheuer, *Der Fall Karl Barth*, 275). Koch sent this "provisional statement" on December 12, 1934, to "the state authorities"; on December 13, against the will of the Provisional Church Administration, it was made public in Westphalia (cf. Prolingheuer, *Der Fall Karl Barth*, 87 and 223–24).

God's" and the apostolic interpretation "We must obey God rather than any human authority" and "Let every person be subject to the governing authorities."[5]

We would point out to you that this statement is a provisional one and is therefore not to be made public.

185. Draft of a Letter to the Church Foreign Office[1]

185.1 Introductory Statement by Edward Crüsemann

December 13, 1934

Draft

To your letter of December 10, 1934,[2] I take the liberty of replying that the statement of November 10[3] by the Association of German Evangelical Congregations in Great Britain and Ireland did not have the character of a secession from the German Evangelical Church established under the law of July 15, 1933. The purpose of the statement was rather to deny recognition of the present church regime under Reich Bishop Müller, as well as its subordinate bodies.

(Here follows Bonhoeffer's draft)

185.2 Dietrich Bonhoeffer's Draft[4]

The chairman of the congregational council of . . . Church in . . . has been authorized to inform the Church Foreign Office of the German Evangelical Church of the following decision:

"Excerpt from the Minutes of . . . Church in . . . , Meeting of the congregational council on [date]. Present: . . . The presence of a quorum was confirmed according to paragraph . . . of the church constitution.

263

. . .

[5.] Matt. 22:21; Acts 5:29; and Rom. 13:1.

[1.] Files of St. George's Church, London; typewritten, with a handwritten note by Eberhard Bethge: "Drafted by Mr. Crüsemann, acknowledged by him; 23.8.57." Previously published in *GS* 2:192 with the notation: "result of the deliberations of the London pastors on the procedure to be followed by each individual congregation." See also *NL*, A 41,1 (61).

[2.] See 1/183.

[3.] See 1/160.

[4.] This (typewritten) text was found, together with the one by Crüsemann (1/185.1), in the files of St. George's Church; it is assumed to be Bonhoeffer's draft mentioned by Crüsemann. Except for a few slight changes, it agrees with the resolution quoted in the minutes of January 4, 1935, which follow (1/186).

[Agenda point] . . .) The congregational council declares unanimously that it refuses to recognize the present church government led by the present Reich bishop, Ludwig Müller. The . . . congregation can no longer tolerate the authority of a church government whose aims and methods are contrary to the most elementary principles of the Protestant faith. The congregational council declares further that the un-Protestant actions of the Reich Church government during the past eighteen months have done very serious harm to the reputation abroad of the German Reich. The congregational council emphasizes that it is prepared to recognize the constitution of a German Evangelical Church as laid down by the Reich law of July 15, 1933, as a legal basis for affiliation and continues to consider itself bound by its relationship to a German Evangelical Church that has this foundation.

. . ."

This excerpt verified as correct

(place and date)

. . . ,

Chairman of the Congregational Council

of . . . Church in . . .

186. Minutes of an Extraordinary Meeting
of the Congregational Councils of St. Paul's and Sydenham Churches[1]

Friday, January 4 [1935]

Extraordinary Joint Meeting
of the Congregational Councils of St. Paul's and Sydenham
in the Sacristy of St. Paul's Church, 7 P.M.

Present: A quorum of the councils of St. Paul's and Sydenham, and Pastor Bonhoeffer.

264　　　The meeting was opened with prayer. The pastor explained why he had asked the councils to meet together. The situation of the church dispute in Germany made it necessary to make a final decision. The German Protestant pastors in London had held several serious discussions with the president of the Association of Congregations and felt that the time had come to ask the congregational councils for a free and unambiguous statement of their

---

[1.] ADBC, Minute Book of St. Paul's Church, 127; handwritten by Bonhoeffer; see also *NL*, A 41,3 (1). Previously published in *GS* 2:192–94.

position. The immediate cause for concern was a letter from Bishop Heckel in Berlin[2] that was addressed directly to the councils, bypassing the pastors. This procedure must be seen as an attempt to drive a wedge between councils and pastors. The pastor then reported on the correspondence between Bishop Heckel and Baron Schröder that preceded the bishop's letter to the councils. Following the pastor's detailed report on the situation, and after a lengthy, free, and serious discussion among the members of the two councils, the following resolution[3] was adopted:

"The congregational councils of St. Paul's and Sydenham Churches, assembled here together, unanimously declare that they refuse to recognize the present government of the church under the present Reich bishop, L. Müller. The congregations of St. Paul's and Sydenham can no longer tolerate the authority of a church government whose aims and methods are contrary to the most elementary principles of the Protestant faith. The congregational councils declare further that the un-Protestant actions of the Reich Church government during the past eighteen months have done serious harm to the reputation abroad of the German Reich. The congregational councils emphasize that they are prepared to recognize the church constitution as laid down by the Reich law of July 15, 1933, as a legal basis for affiliation and continue to consider themselves bound by their relationship to a German Evangelical Church that has this as its foundation."

This resolution was adopted unanimously. In consideration of the political situation it was not to be communicated to Berlin until after the Saar plebiscite,[4] at a time to be determined jointly by the four London pastors.

The pastor emphasized once again that the decision just made represented only the conclusion to the actions of the councils up to this point. He thanked all those present for coming and closed the meeting with a prayer.

The meeting was adjourned at 9:15 P.M.

Dr. Dietrich Bonhoeffer, Pastor[5]

265

[2.] See 1/183.

[3.] On this resolution, cf. 1/185.

[4.] January 13, 1935.

[5.] Followed by the (partly illegible) signatures of G. Henne, C. Blumenstock, V. Streitberger, G. Eisemann, H. Weber, H. Klugmann, P. Grandyot, E. Henne, Fr. Strobel, H. Hirsch, C. Compton, F. Ph. Schlarb, G. Neubert, A. Wolford, W. Neubert.

187. To Baron Bruno Schröder[1]

London, January 7, 1935

My dear Baron,

First of all, my very best wishes for a blessed new year. God grant that you may be able to work with as much love, wisdom, and strength on behalf of his church in this year as in the last. I am certain that all the steps we undertook for the sake of the church in the past year, in which we were guided by your patience, which was certainly tried, and your nonetheless clear powers of judgment, will prove to have been a blessing for our congregations and our home church. I thank you for all that you have done, knowing that my friends in the Confessing Church join me in gratitude to you.

The great concern I bring to you today is one in which I am only the message bearer. The president[2] of the International Missionary Council, J. H. Oldham, D.D., asked me urgently to come and see him three days ago. It concerned the following: the entire German mission work[3] is facing catastrophe. Because of the foreign exchange ordinances,[4] all the German missions are threatened with total collapse in the coming weeks and months. The missionary societies have been fighting for their lives since June. The mission stations abroad used to receive about thirty thousand pounds a month, but during the past half year this has been reduced to a tenth of that amount, and by December nothing more was coming from Germany. Two months ago, two mission directors from Berlin were here to talk with Dr. Oldham about possible relief measures. The International Missionary Council is hoping, although nothing is certain yet, to be able to raise a one-

266

[1.] SBL, Family Papers, box FS 12/3/4 Miscellaneous–Pastor Boeckheler (successor to) Pastor Bonhoeffer; typewritten; at the top a handwritten note, probably by the recipient: "Answer 11/1/35." See also *NL*, Anh. A 25,1 (1).

[2.] [Oldham (see 1/178, ed. note 7) was actually general secretary, not president, of the International Missionary Council. The president was John R. Mott. On Oldham's collaboration with Bonhoeffer, see Clements, *Faith on the Frontier*, 296–302. See also 1/190, 1/191, and 1/206.—KC]

[3.] The "German mission work" probably refers to all the German organizations that had missionary efforts abroad, which were largely under the umbrella of the German Missions Council. [This is indeed the case. On the crisis in German missions after the Nazi rise to power and Oldham's efforts to assist them, see Clements, *Faith on the Frontier*, 290–96.—KC]

[4.] In the early years of National Socialist rule, a series of decrees placed severe restrictions on foreign exchange allocations and thus on transfers of funds abroad. See Schulz, "Die Anfänge des totalitären Maßnahmenstaates," 361–62.

time grant of fifty thousand pounds. The British Bible Society has been sending thirty thousand marks a month from here to the mission stations, and
this amount is then paid by the missionary societies into the British Bible
Society's bank account in Germany. So it is mainly problems in transferring
funds that threaten to destroy the German mission work.

¶Dr. Oldham, who is a great friend of Germany and German theology, is pessimistic about all this, but is tirelessly doing what he can to prevent the catastrophe. He has now asked me if I know anyone who might
be approached for help in German circles here. He knew of you, my dear
Baron, and your views and your activities. He was very happy when I mentioned your name and asked if I might write to you[5] and ask for your advice
and help. He would be glad to come and see you in person, if you would like,
and discuss the situation in detail with you. We both felt that this is such a big
and important matter that we need to consult you, that is, that we should not
fail to advise you of such a serious situation.

This is the sense in which you will understand this letter. A great Christian   267
ministry is at stake. May God give us strength and insight to intercede and
to help.

With admiration and gratitude, I remain
Yours sincerely,
Dietrich Bonhoeffer

188. To George Bell[1]

January 7th, 35

My Lord Bishop,

I must apologize for answering so late. The foggy weather last week kept me
in bed and made me absolutely unable to work. Thank you very much for
your kind letter.[2] You had given me the address of the young German girl[3]
before and I have forwarded it to my friend Pastor Jacobi.

[5.] "write to" was inserted in Bonhoeffer's handwriting.

[1.] LPL, Bell Papers 42, 55 and 56; handwritten; in original English, including errors.
See also *NL*, A 42,1 (25); typewritten copy. Previously published in *GS* 2:195–96.

[2.] Not extant.

[3.] Not identified.

I have not had any important news from home. I think they do not want to go on with their fight before the Saar plebiscite.[4] The thing that occupies me most in the present moment is the question what could be done for the refugees from the Saar, who will number about 30–50 thousand.[5] I am thinking of taking a few children and giving them into the homes of my people in the congregation. But how is the whole problem going to be solved, not individually but fundamentally? I enclose a copy of a "memorandum"[6] by one of the refugees who is here with his family and is trying to find some sort of work in the office of a lawyer, he himself having been a well known and very serious lawyer in Nürnberg.

With regard to the idea of sending some British clergymen over to Germany for the time after the Saar plebiscite, I still believe, it could be very helpful indeed. I do not think Rev. Cragg[7] could be offended. Pastor Forell from Sweden, who is devoting most of his time for the cause of the[8] Confessional Church, asked himself for such a delegation from Sweden. But it might be, of course, that this Swedish delegation would be sufficient for the time being.

Do you still think of the plan of an official British delegation to the Confessional Church on behalf of world-peace?[9] The more I think of this idea, the [more] it strikes me as most important and helpful.

At the beginning of a new year I wish to thank you most sincerely and heartily for all you have done for us in the last year. May God bless all your work and all the fellowship he is establishing through your work between our churches. Your work will never be forgotten in the history of the German Church.

I remain Yours gratefully
Dietrich Bonhoeffer

[4.] On January 13, 1935, deciding that the Saarland [which was then part of France— KC] should be returned to Germany and become part of the Reich.

[5.] The source of this very high estimate is not known. According to von zur Mühlen, *"Schlagt Hitler,"* 249, about eight thousand persons in all fled the Saarland following the plebiscite.

[6.] See *NL*, A 42, 1 (25).

[7.] R. H. Cragg, chaplain at the British embassy in Berlin; he sometimes transmitted confidential letters through the diplomatic post.

[8.] "Cause of the" replaces "opposition."

[9.] Cf. Bell's reply (1/189) and Hildebrandt's letter to Koch (1/191) as well as Bell and Koechlin, *Briefwechsel,* 185ff., in which Koechlin advises against this plan.

189. From George Bell[1]

8th January, 1935

My dear Bonhoeffer,

Very many thanks for your letter[2] and the enclosure. I am very sorry you have been poorly, and do hope you are better now. I wrote to Praeses Koch[3] and asked him if the sending of a group of five or six English Churchmen to talk with German Churchmen about peace and friendship between our two countries would be embarrassing or welcome. I sent the letter through Mr. Cragg.[4] I also said that I did not think it would do for the Universal Council to be mixed up in it, as that had concerned itself with the Church question. After some delay I had a short letter back.[5] He says that he would like five or six English Churchmen to come out to Germany but he wants them to be connected with the Universal Council, and he wants them to discuss the grave German Church questions. He does not say a word about peace and Anglo-German friendship. I am rather perplexed, for that was not at all what my lay friend was proposing to finance. I have written to Mr. Cragg to that effect. In the meantime I am in touch with Dr. Cross on the bare possibility of my being able to send him out to Berlin for a few days after seeing me, and to come back with a report; but I do not really know whether this will be feasible.

269

I heard from Archbishop Eidem yesterday and I gather that Ehrenstrom is going to Berlin almost at once. I have not heard from Henriod about the proposed office of the Youth Committee at Berlin,[6] but I do not know why he is so long in answering, except that the Christmas holidays were rather long at Geneva.

Praeses Koch suggested that the party should go out to Berlin, if it went, about January 20th. I am going away to the Isle of Wight for a week on Saturday, and shall be in London on January 21st for most of that week. Thank you for what you have done about the young German girl. I do understand your principal occupation at the present moment with the question of what can be done for refugees from

<hr>

[1.] LPL, Bell Papers 42, 57; carbon copy; from Chichester; in original English, including errors. See also *NL*, A 42,2 (10); typewritten copy. Previously published in *GS* 2:196–97.

[2.] Of January 7; see 1/188.

[3.] On December 15, 1934; LPL, Bell Papers 6, 498, carbon copy.

[4.] See 1/188.

[5.] Of December 28, 1934; LPL, Bell Papers 6, 521; copy on letterhead and with Koch's handwritten signature in LKA EKvW, 5,1, no. 768, fasc. 2.

[6.] The German Ecumenical Youth Commission, whose work was being carried on mainly by Winterhager, worked out of the office of the Swedish legation pastor, Birger Forell, and used his communication privileges to send uncensored messages abroad via Sweden. See *GS* 2:197.

the Saar. Do you really think that they will number 30,000 to 50,000?[7] I wish one could think of some method of dealing with the problem fundamentally.

Thank you so very much for all your kind words about my poor efforts. I appreciate them greatly,

Yours ever,

[George Cicestr]

270   **190. From Baron Bruno Schröder**[1]

January 11, 1935

Thank you very much for your kind words and good wishes in your letter of January 7.[2] I am quite touched by what you said about me and only hope that the little I am able to do for our Confessing Church will be of service.

What you say about the German missions is very serious, and I completely agree that something must be done to prevent a total catastrophe. My youngest sister, Mrs. von Diest, is closely connected with the mission office in Liebenzell, so I have heard from there the same concern that it is well-nigh impossible to transfer funds to foreign countries.

What you say about Mr. J. H. Oldham is in any case encouraging, and I am gladly ready to meet him with you to discuss relief measures, such as the possibility of raising fifty thousand pounds. That would constitute a good fund, but how can fifty thousand pounds be raised in view of the requests coming from every quarter? These are unfortunately not times in which to collect large sums of money. I myself would certainly be glad to make my modest contribution. But we can discuss all this when I have the pleasure of meeting with you and Mr. Oldham.

In the meantime I remain, with all best wishes for the New Year,

Yours sincerely and respectfully,

B[runo] S[chröder][3]

[7.] See 1/188, ed. note 5.

[1.] SBL, Family Papers, box FS 12/3/4 B Miscellaneous–Pastor Boeckheler (successor to) Pastor Bonhoeffer; initialed carbon copy, from London [without salutation]. See also *NL*, Anh. A 35,2 (2).

[2.] See 1/187.

[3.] See the reply, 1/195.

191. Franz Hildebrandt to Karl Koch[1]

Berlin-Dahlem, January 12, 1935
Re: Correspondence with the Lord Bishop of Chichester

Dear President Koch:

Bonhoeffer has just written to me and seems rather worried. He said that your reply to Chichester's offer[2] to send a delegation here to discuss peace issues— referring evidently to the World Alliance problems at Fanö—sounded as though you were expecting a discussion of the *ecclesiastical* dispute, and this is *not* what the English side had in mind in this particular context. So Chichester doesn't quite know what to do, because he thinks his plan would be of benefit to us and has got all sorts of people interested in it (e.g., Dr. Oldham).

¶Bonhoeffer has promised that you will write to him again, to clear up what was perhaps only a linguistic misunderstanding and state your response to the plan for a peace delegation. Since Brother Müller[3] has just told me that the attitude in Oeynhausen toward this idea also was very positive, I don't mind mentioning to you that Bonhoeffer asked that there be a *prompt* reply to Chichester. In case this is to be sent, like my letter,[4] not through the post but rather in care of Cragg,[5] it would no doubt be best for Brother Müller to bring it here from Oeynhausen on Wednesday.

I remain yours sincerely and respectfully,
Hildebrandt

271

[1.] ZEKHN 35/45; typewritten, signed by hand, on letterhead of "The Council of the Evangelical Church of the Old Prussian Union." See also *NL*, A 42,4 (9); typewritten copy. Previously published in *Mündige Welt*, 5:233. The text is crossed out by hand and marked "B. Syn" [Confessing Synod].

[2.] On this, see Bonhoeffer's letter of January 7, 1935, to Bell (1/188, esp. cd. note 9) and Bell's letter of January 8, 1935, to Bonhoeffer (1/189).

[3.] Friedrich Müller [one of the pastors of the Confessing congregation] in Dahlem.

[4.] This probably refers to the above-mentioned letter from Bonhoeffer to Hildebrandt.

[5.] See 1/188, ed. note 7.

192. To Théodore de Félice[1]

defelice 2 rue montchoicy geneve =
sorry: coming unlikely winterhager deputee excuse delay being ill =
bonhoeffer 23 = manor mount se 23 london =[2]

272　**193. To Karl-Friedrich Bonhoeffer**[1]

January 14, 1935

Dear Karl-Friedrich,

I wish you rather belatedly[2] a happy new year. I was very pleased with the pictures of the children you sent me for Christmas. Since unfortunately I have seen so little of them, pictures help to fill the gap. Thank you also for your Christmas letter. I wanted to ring you on Christmas Eve, but it took so long to get a connection that night that nothing came of it. How are you getting along in Leipzig? I had actually been hoping you would stay in Frankfurt—it's more attractive for passing through than Leipzig—but Leipzig is closer. We really have hardly seen each other at all in the last few years, so the days together recently were very good ones for me. Perhaps I seem to you rather fanatical and mad about a number of things. I myself am sometimes afraid of that. But I know that the day I became more "reasonable," to be honest, I should have to chuck my entire theology. When I first started in theology, my idea of it was quite different—rather more academic, probably. Now it has turned into something else altogether. But I do believe that at last I am on the right track, for the first time in my life. I often feel quite happy about it. I only worry about being so afraid of what other people will think as to get bogged down instead of going forward. I think I am right in saying that I would only achieve true inner clarity and honesty by really starting to

[1.] WCC Archives, World Alliance, Letters from Dietrich Bonhoeffer; photocopy of a telegram; in original English. The date sent is not clear; although the typed text (originated "London 4531 21 13 1–23 S") seems to indicate January 13, 1935, a note above, in unknown handwriting, says "15.1.35." However, it is also possible that the telegram was not sent until January 23, since this is the date of Bonhoeffer's letter of apology (cf. 1/196).

[2.] The concern is the meeting of the Ecumenical Youth Commission, which was originally planned for January 31–February 1 in Paris and then postponed. See also Théodore de Félice's letter of January 29, 1935, to Bonhoeffer (WCC Archives, World Alliance, Letters to Dietrich Bonhoeffer) as well as 1/174, 1/196, and 1/199.

[1.] *NL*, A 39,4 (5); handwritten. Excerpted in *GS* 3:24–25.
[2.] Karl-Friedrich Bonhoeffer's birthday was on January 13.

take the Sermon on the Mount seriously.[3] Here alone lies the force that can
blow all this hocus-pocus sky-high—like fireworks, leaving only a few burnt-   273
out shells behind. The restoration of the church must surely depend on a
new kind of monasticism, which has nothing in common with the old but a
life of uncompromising discipleship, following Christ according to the Sermon on the Mount. I believe the time has come to gather people together
and do this.

Forgive me for these rather personal ramblings, but they just came to me
as I thought about our time together recently. And after all, we *do* have an
interest in each other. I still have a hard time thinking that you really find all
these ideas of mine completely mad.[4] Things do exist that are worth standing up for without compromise. To me it seems that peace and social justice
are such things, as is Christ himself.

I recently came across the fairy tale of "The Emperor's New Clothes,"[5]
which really is relevant for our time. All we are lacking today is the child who
speaks up at the end. We ought to put it on as a play.

I hope to hear from you soon—in any case, my birthday is coming soon.

Warm greetings to you all,
Dietrich

194. The German Evangelical Pastors in London
to the Church Foreign Office[1]

London, January 21, 1935

With reference to your letter of December 10, 1934,[7] the undersigned pastors hereby protest against any attempt, even though unsuccessful, by the Reich

---

[3.] On the significance of the Sermon on the Mount for Bonhoeffer, see also his letters
of April 28, 1934, to Sutz (1/93) and of July 13, 1934, to Niebuhr (1/127).

[4.] [Karl-Friedrich, the eldest of the Bonhoeffer brothers, was a physicist by profession
and a socialist by political commitment (see Leibholz-Bonhoeffer, *Bonhoeffers*, 17–19). The
apparent distance between the scientific and the theological outlook, allied with differing
sociopolitical perspectives (though note the affirmation of "social justice" two sentences
later), may at least partly account for the almost apologetic tone at several points in this
letter.—KC]

[5.] The fairy tale by Hans Christian Andersen.

[1.] Files of St. George's Church, London; typewritten; addressed "To the Church Foreign Office of the German Evangelical Church, Berlin-Charlottenburg 2, Jebenstrasse 3."
See also *NL*, A 41,2 (14); typewritten copy. Previously published in *GS* 2:194. The names
of the authors are unknown; also unknown is whether this letter was actually mailed; the
source information in *GS* 2 refers to it as a "drafted reply."

[2.] See 1/183.

Church government to drive a wedge between congregations, on the one hand, and pastors and their honored president of the Association of Congregations, on the other. This is the sentiment of the congregational councils as well as of the pastors themselves.

274   They do not feel called upon to enter into a discussion of the specific points mentioned in your letter—some correct, some incorrect, some liable to be misunderstood—that were passed to an office of the Reich Church government by an irresponsible private informer.

They protest once and for all and hereby warn the Foreign Office of the Reich Church government against any suggestive statement that impugns the political and patriotic convictions of the pastors. They point out that any further such insinuations will provoke serious consequences.

195. To Baron Bruno Schröder[1]

London, January 21, 1935

My dear Baron,

Many thanks for your kind reply[2] to my inquiry with regard to Dr. Oldham's visit to you. Oldham himself has now written to you, and I think my presence will not be needed at your discussion.

It is really quite embarrassing for me to have to turn to you today with another request. This time I will really understand if you have to say no, but still I must at least ask. In the autumn I came to you with Pastor Rieger about the needs of German Protestant refugees (of Jewish origin or with political problems). At that time you were so kind as to help us with fifty pounds each, and I don't know what I would have done without this aid during the first months of winter. Now these funds have long since been exhausted, and in the meantime my parishioners have truly helped me. As of today, frankly, as a result of these needs my personal bank account is completely empty. That I could manage, except that I know there are two people expecting money

275   from me tomorrow, who otherwise will have nothing to eat, and in three days there will again be others. What should I do? I have told these people that this cannot go on, and they understand, but they can find no other source despite all their efforts, and they are Protestant Christians with nowhere else to turn for help.[3] In view of this desperate situation, my dear Baron, I can

---

[1.] SBL, Family Papers, box FS 12/3/4 Miscellaneous–Pastor Boeckheler (successor to) Pastor Bonhoeffer; typewritten with handwritten corrections; at the top a note from the recipient: "Answer 23/1/35." See *NL*, Anh. A 35,1 (3).

[2.] See 1/190.

[3.] "And they are . . . for help" added by hand.

think of nothing else to do but to ask once again whether you are able to help. You will understand how difficult it is to see such misery before one's eyes and to stand there empty-handed. Please forgive my request!

With most sincere gratitude and respect, I am yours as ever,
Dietrich Bonhoeffer

196. To Théodore de Félice[1]

London, S.E. 23, January 23, 1935

My dear de Félice,

To my great regret, I suddenly find that I will not be able to come to the Paris meeting.[2] I have some drastically urgent matters in my congregations and simply cannot get away. I am terribly sorry, especially since I had so many things to discuss with you this time. My question now is, would you prefer me to write a brief memorandum[3] and send it to you? Or would you rather have Winterhager come? His travel from Berlin would be pretty expensive, however. Please let me know right away. Is there even money available for the travel costs of a substitute?

With best regards and all good wishes,
Yours ever,
Dietrich Bonhoeffer

197. From Baron Bruno Schröder[1]   276

London, January 23, 1935

Dear Pastor Bonhoeffer,

I received your kind letter of January 21 this morning.[2]

The situation of the German refugees is indeed a sad one, and I would be glad to help. However, as things are, I have to pay income tax on such donations. I

[1.] WCC Archives, World Alliance, Letters from Dietrich Bonhoeffer; photocopy of typewritten letter. See also *NL*, A 40,1 (9). Previously published in *GS* 6:356–57 and *Mündige Welt*, 5:240.

[2.] Meeting of the Joint Secretariat of the Ecumenical Youth Commission on February 15, 1935, which at this point was still being planned for January 31–February 1 (cf. 1/174, 1/192, and 1/199).

[3.] See 1/199.

[1.] SBL, Family Papers, box FS 12/3/4 B Miscellaneous–Pastor Boeckheler (successor to) Pastor Bonhoeffer; initialed carbon copy. See also *NL*, Anh. A 35,1 (4).

[2.] See 1/195.

therefore make it a rule to direct all such cases to the Society of Friends of Foreigners in Distress;[3] their Mr. Cable is very devoted to this cause. I can then make contributions to the society, which for me are tax-free and enable me to save 50 percent. I can also do so through the German Society of Benevolence.[4] This seems to me the only way in which I can do something to help, so please let me know whether this can serve your purpose.

Meanwhile I remain, with best wishes,
Yours respectfully,
B[runo] S[chröder]

198. To Baron Bruno Schröder[1]

London, January 28, 1935

My dear Baron,

Many thanks for your kind letter.[2] I am infinitely grateful for your willingness to help us once again in supporting refugees. I have given thought to the ways of doing this that you suggested and have also discussed them with my colleague, Pastor Rieger. In his opinion, the Society of Friends of Foreigners in Distress has yet to become involved in refugee work and has not considered it to be among its areas of activity. Of course, this does not exclude working through this society in case it received special funds for the purpose. As for the Benevolence Society, Pastor Rieger has the impression that they are too decidedly Reich-German in their aims to be considered for our purpose. I must add, however, that I cannot judge for myself, not knowing enough about the work of either organization.

So may I please just inquire whether it would be possible to avoid the income tax, in the same way as by making contributions to these two societies, if the money were directed to the fund for the poor of Sydenham or St. Paul's Church, or to a special fund set up by them? Aren't churches also included under this regulation? The ideal advantage of this solution would be that it would then be German Evangelical congregations that would be giving the aid, while in the other case it would be an English society, at least not a church organization. I think this would make a very important difference

---

[3.] Donations to this aid and welfare organization were tax-exempt.
[4.] See ed. note 3.

[1.] SBL, Family Papers, box FS 12/3/4 Miscellaneous–Pastor Boeckheler (successor to) Pastor Bonhoeffer; typewritten, with handwritten salutation and signature. See also *NL*, Anh. A 35,1 (5).
[2.] See 1/197.

to those receiving the support, which until now has partly been expressed by the fact that some of these people have found their way back to church for the first time in years and continue coming to services. Receiving aid from the church does put a more substantial obligation on the recipient to use it responsibly. If it were possible to make this solution work, I do think it would help people spiritually more than any other way. But in case it should not work this way, I will send a list of people whom I am no longer able to support to the organizations you have indicated, asking that they care for them.[3]

With sincere gratitude and admiration, I remain

Yours respectfully,
Dietrich Bonhoeffer

199. Memorandum to the Ecumenical Youth Commission[1]

278

29th. Jan 1935

Dear friends,

I am very sorry indeed to be prevented from coming to your meeting.[2] I am having some particularly difficult cases in the congregations which render my absence impossible. Please, excuse me and take my heartiest whishes for a successful conference.

My report on the work done since Fanö can be summed up in a few words. The German Fanö group has been doing a great deal of propagandistic work in the respective universities. A very encouraging step forward could be taken in Tübingen and in Heidelberg. Some of the speeches delivered at Fanö were mimeographed and spread among the students. There seems to be (mostly perhaps under the influence of the steadily growing military spirit) a readiness to take seriously the christian message of peace. In Berlin a group of students of various nationalities met under the auspices of the youth commission in the house of the Swedish pastor Forell and had a very satisfactory meeting; it is also there that a group of young Christians are seriously considering the possibility of starting a small christian community in the form of a settlement or any other form on the basis of the Sermon on the Mount. It is felt that only by a clear and uncompromising stand Christianity

---

[3.] The remainder of the letter handwritten.

[1.] WCC Archives, World Alliance, Letters from Dietrich Bonhoeffer; photocopy of typewritten text, dated and signed by hand, from London; in original English, including errors. See also *NL*, A 40,1 (10). Previously published in *GS* 6:357–59 and *Mündige Welt*, 5:240–41.

[2.] On February 15, 1935, in Paris; cf. 1/174, 1/192, and 1/196.

can be a vital force for our people. It is also felt that the developments of the Church dispute in Germany are tending more and more towards a sort of conservative Christianity which of cause would go very well with the rather conservative spirit which is steadily growing under the present Reichswehr and Industry regime. This group would also make a definite stand for peace by conscientious objection. The question which it has not yet succeeded to find an answer to, is whether in case of war a service in a sanitary group[3] would be Christianly justifiable. I should be thankful if you could just let us have your opinion about it, as it is very important for us to hear your point.

.   Winterhager made a trip of 6 weeks through Sweden and established new contacts there. We would like to propose if we may a baltic conference in the forthcoming summer.

I am in favour of an international youth conference, and I should be glad if the question of conscientious objection would be one of the subjects under discussion. I feel that one of the weaknesses of our cause is the lack of a common and definite attitude in the very crucial question. We should march on whatever the older people think and do.

Finally, would you be willing to help me to find some young students or pastor for the Seminary which I am supposed to start in the near future on behalf of the Confessional Synod. I should like to have the ecumenic aspect of it made clear from the beginning. We are now thinking if we could combine the idea of a Christian community mentioned above with the new Seminary. At any rate would the support from the ecumenic movements be most valuable for the carrying out of our plans. I know of similar ideas in England among some student groups, is there anything like this in France or Switzerland or anywhere else? Perhaps we could get in contact with one another then?

One of the special topics I should like to propose for the youth conference is: the use of coercion, its right and its limitations. Before this fundamental question is given an answer to, the theoretical basis of pacifism is very weak.

I hope to hear of you soon.

With all good wishes I am yours ever
Dietrich Bonhoeffer

[3.] [Bonhoeffer means an ambulance or medical unit (*Sanitäter*).—KC]

200. To Otto Piper[1]   280

February 3, 1935

Dear Professor Piper,

From your letter, I gather that you never received the card I sent you three weeks ago, asking you to substitute for me[2] *today*, since I had to go to Paris. I had to guess a bit on the address and hope I have got it right this time. In any case, I didn't go to Paris, so it was no problem. Unfortunately, I no longer need a substitute for the tenth through the twenty-fourth either, since there will be a confirmation and the things that go with it. Would you be available for March 3? I am flying to Germany tomorrow for three days.

With best regards,
Dietrich Bonhoeffer

201. Minutes of a Meeting of the Congregational Council[1]

Fourth Quarterly Meeting
Monday, February 11, 7 P.M. in St. Paul's Church

Present: Messrs. Henne, Blumenstock, Streitberger, Eisemann, Weber, Klugman, Grandyot, Henne, Hirsch, Compton, Schlarb, Neubert, Wolford, Neubert

The meeting was opened with a scripture reading and prayer. The minutes of the last meeting were read, approved, and signed. The treasurer presented the account books, which were examined and found to be correct. In the name of the council, the pastor expressed thanks to Mr. Henne for his sacrificial devotion to this work. Mr. Henne reported on recent correspondence. The pastor asked that a special collection for Winter Aid[2]   281 be approved. This collection is normally planned for the second Sunday in Advent. This year a collection for Winter Aid will be taken up following the pastor's last sermon on March 10. The pastor asked for permission also to take up a collection once again for German Protestant refugees in need.

[1.] *NL*, A 41,9 (16); photocopy of handwritten original (in possession of Professor Joseph Burgess, Philadelphia).

[2.] Piper was a German émigré [in England—KC] and had no permanent job, so he depended on working as a substitute preacher.

[1.] ADBC, Minute Book of St. Paul's Church; handwritten by Bonhoeffer. See also *NL*, A 41,3 (1); photocopy and typewritten copy.

[2.] [Winterhilfe, a relief program operated under the Third Reich.—KC]

The pastor then asked the council to grant him six months' leave, in order to answer a call from the leadership of the Confessing Church in Germany to set up a theological seminary.[3] Provisions will be made for a substitute pastor. The council showed full understanding for this request and granted the pastor a leave extending from March 15 to September 15. The pastor expressed his most sincere thanks to the council.

¶The meeting was adjourned with a prayer at 8:30 P.M.

Dietrich Bonhoeffer, Pastor[4]

202. To Baron Bruno Schröder[1]

[London] S. E. 23, February 11, 1935

My dear Baron,

When I returned from Germany last Friday, I was told that I had received several telephone calls from your bank during my absence. I don't know whether this had to do with the problem of the German refugees about which we have been corresponding. I would like to offer for your consideration another possibility, besides the ones mentioned in my last letter,[2] a so-called Refugees Committee for Professional Workers that is connected with the Quakers. The director is Mrs. Mary Ormerod, c/o Friends House in Euston Road. Would there be any question of making donations through this committee?[3] I should be very grateful if I could either come and talk with you personally or hear from you during the next few days.

I am, as ever, most respectfully yours,
Dietrich Bonhoeffer

282

[3.] The seminary was initially set up in April in Zingst on the Baltic seacoast but soon moved in June to Finkenwalde, east of Stettin. Bonhoeffer's granted leave eventually became a definitive departure. See *DBW* 14 and 15.

[4.] This is followed by the signatures of thirteen council members (not all of which correspond to the attendance list above).

[1.] SBL, Family Papers, box FS 12/3/4 B Miscellaneous–Pastor Boeckheler (successor to) Pastor Bonhoeffer; typewritten, signed by hand. See also *NL*, Anh. A 35,1 (6).

[2.] Of January 28, 1935; see 1/198.

[3.] Bonhoeffer had expressed certain reservations about the two charities proposed by Baron Schröder in the latter's letter of January 23, 1935, (1/197) and was apparently hoping that this suggestion would make it easier for Schröder to give the requested help.

203. Theodor Heckel to the Ministry of Foreign Affairs[1]

Berlin-Charlottenburg 2, February 15, 1935

I should like to express my most sincere thanks to the Ministry of Foreign Affairs for your note sent to me with your letter of December 14, 1934, ref. VI A 5455,[2] regarding Pastor Schönberger's plan[3] for creating an independent German church abroad, and for the reply of December 21, 1934, from the National Socialist German Workers' Party's overseas organization, forwarded to me with your letter of January 24, 1935, ref. VI A 5788.[4] Both these communications were received here with great interest. With regard to the final paragraph of the letter from the NSDAP's overseas organization, permit me to point out that the Church Foreign Office had already informed the councils of the German Evangelical congregations in Great Britain, in a circular letter of December 10, 1934,[5] about the negotiations with the Association of Congregations there and asked for their response. In response the German Evangelical congregations in Liverpool, South Shields, and Newcastle have sent resolutions from their respective councils expressing explicit confidence in the Church Foreign Office and its director. The church council in Bradford had already expressed similar sentiments even before the circular letter (see my letter of December 1, 1934, ref. A 8586). Moreover, none of the individual congregations in London has so far sent a negative reply to my circular letter. Now that eight weeks have gone by, any such explicit responses from the London congregations are no longer expected for the time being. The Martin Luther Federation[6] in Erlangen has recently been upsetting our work by trying, without any consultation with the Church Foreign Office, to move toward the establishment of an (international?) Lutheran church in England. I shall respectfully welcome any further information about this.

283

Dr. Heckel

[1.] Auswärtigen Amtes/Politisches Archiv, Berlin, VI A, Evangelischen Angelegenheiten (Protestant Affairs), file ref. 2, vol. 10; typewritten, signed by hand, on letterhead of the Church Foreign Office, sender's ref. A 6333/35; addressed "To the Ministry of Foreign Affairs in Berlin W.8," with two stamps indicating receipt: "AA rec'd 16 Feb. 1935 Nm" and "For. Ministry VI A 789, rec'd 18. Feb. 1935." Previously published in *Mündige Welt,* 5:347.

[2.] See 1/180.

[3.] Bonhoeffer is not mentioned here, although he is mentioned in the Ministry of Foreign Affairs note for the file (but not in the letter from Gauleiter Bohle [see 1/178, ed. note 12—KC]).

[4.] See 1/180, ed. note 3.

[5.] See 1/183.

[6.] The Martin Luther Federation maintained national organizations in Poland and Switzerland, and there were Lutheran churches in South Africa, Australia, the Netherlands, and Alsace associated with it. The extent of its efforts in England at the time is not known.

204. To Baron Bruno Schröder[1]

[London] S. E. 23, March 3, 1935

My dear Baron,

Your letter[2] has made me indescribably happy. Surely all of us are filled with gratitude that you have succeeded in finding this way of helping our church in this crucial hour of need. May God continue to bless his work and to give you strength and a joyful heart that you may bring such happiness—and more than that—to other people as well.

Next week, unfortunately, I shall have to come and say goodbye to you, since I shall be moving to Düsseldorf[3] to become director of the Confessing Church's theological seminary. At the moment I am taking six months' leave for this purpose but expect that it will be extended.

United with you in Christ's service, in gratitude and admiration, I remain,
Yours sincerely,
Dietrich Bonhoeffer

284

205. To Friedrich Siegmund-Schultze[1]

March 13, 1935

Dear Professor Siegmund-Schultze:

Thank you very much for your letter.[2] I am afraid there are no prospects for this young teacher at a German school here in London, as everything is controlled by the Party. Even Wehrhan is Pg.[3] and very nervous. Couldn't something perhaps be done at an English school through the Academic Assistance Council?[4] Don't you yourself have any connections there? It is always difficult to help someone who is still in Germany. Even the emigrants

---

[1.] SBL, Family Papers, box FS 12/3/4 B Miscellaneous–Pastor Boeckheler (successor to) Pastor Bonhoeffer; handwritten. See also *NL*, Anh. A 35,1 (10).

[2.] Letter of March 1, 1935 (in SBL); see *NL*, Anh. 35,2 (9), with which Baron Schröder enclosed a copy—not found—of a letter from his representative in Berlin, which apparently confirmed the possibility of financial help for the German missions. Cf. Bonhoeffer's request for aid in his letter of January 7, 1935 (1/187).

[3.] For a time there was a plan to locate the seminary in the Rhineland; see *DB-ER*, 422.

[1.] EZA 51/H II b 1,2; handwritten.

[2.] Inquiry of March 4, 1935, from Siegmund-Schultze (EZA 51/H II b 1,2) about the possibility of a teaching position in London for a young man.

[3.] Pg. was the abbreviation for *Parteigenosse* [literally Nazi "party comrade."—KC]

[4.] This was an aid organization founded in 1933 (known after 1936 as the Society for the Protection of Science and Learning) that, with varying success, found places for

who are already here we only manage to support by dint of great efforts. I am sorry to have so little to offer in a positive vein.

I remain, as always, yours respectfully,
Dietrich Bonhoeffer

206. To Joseph H. Oldham[1]

London S. E. 23, 13th March 1935

Dear Dr. Oldham:

I shall leave London for a visit to various theological colleges Saturday next. I shall probably have to be in Germany about the middle of April; before that 285 I hope to be in London once again for a few days. If it would ever suit you I should be very thankfull indeed for giving me an opportunity to see you once more before I leave for good.

The conference of young theologians to which I had been invited interested me very much and I hope to hear from Mr. Patrick something as to the time and the place of the conference.[2]

May I add that I have been very glad to hear that my cousin Professor Charlotte Leubuscher is working in one of your committees. I know she appreciates your great kindness very much indeed and I wish to tell you how satisfactory it is to me to know that she is under your friendly care.

I was so happy to hear that your conversation with Baron Schröder was so successfull.[3]

Thanking you once again for all you have done for me
I remain, dear Dr. Oldham, yours ever
Dietrich Bonhoeffer

German émigré scientists, including Otto Piper (see 1/200) at English universities and colleges. For teachers there were almost no job prospects.

[1.] New College Library, Edinburgh, J. H. Oldham files, file "Germany"; typewritten, signed by hand; in original English, including errors.

[2.] [Most probably this would have been one of the consultations in preparation for the Oxford 1937 conference on "Church, Community, and State," the studies for which Oldham was now coordinating.—KC]

[3.] On the preparations for this conversation, see 1/187, 1/190, and 1/195.

207. To "Ernst"[1]

Dear Ernst,

I'm now on the third stage of my journey, in Mirfield.[2] The second I spent with the Quakers in Birmingham.[3] I liked it very much there. (breaks off at this point)

286   **208. To Baron Bruno Schröder**[1]

London, March 15, 1935

My dear Baron,

The bearer of this letter is my friend Philip Cromwell Esq., the solicitor whom I recently mentioned to you. I confirmed his son a few weeks ago[2] and enjoy a very friendly relationship with the whole family. You were so kind to agree to see him, and I am sincerely grateful to you for this. About the concern that he has, which I briefly mentioned to you the other day, he can best tell you himself.

I thank you for everything you have done for me during the past year. I shall always remember it.

With all best wishes I remain, as ever,
Yours sincerely,
Dietrich Bonhoeffer

By the way, I have also written to my father.

[1.] *NL,* A 41,9 (25); picture postcard from Stratford-upon-Avon, unaddressed and undated, presumably of March 1935. Previously published in *GS* 6:302. The addressee was probably Ernst Cromwell, whom Bonhoeffer had confirmed on February 24, 1935, in London, and who apparently went to meet Bonhoeffer during his journey at the beginning of April (cf. letter of March 31, 1935, from his father, Philipp Cromwell, to Bonhoeffer [*NL,* C 23]).

[2.] Visit to the Community of the Resurrection (Father Talbot); see 1/152; also *DB-ER,* 412 [and Julius Rieger, "Contacts with London," in Zimmermann, *I Knew Dietrich Bonhoeffer,* 95–96.—KC]

[3.] Cf. 1/94 and *DB-ER,* 412. [The Quaker center at Selly Oak, Birmingham, is Woodbrooke. Note also Bonhoeffer's contacts with Hardy Arnold of the Bruderhof community, who was living in Birmingham at that time. Cf. 1/92a, 1/114a, 1/114b, 1/115a, and 1/115b.—KC]

[1.] SBL, Family Papers, box FS 12/3/4 Miscellaneous–Pastor Boeckheler (successor to) Pastor Bonhoeffer; typewritten, signed by hand. See also *NL,* Anh. A 35,1 (12).

[2.] Cf. 1/207, ed. note 1.

209. To Theodor Heckel[1]

London, March 25, 1935

Dear Bishop Heckel,

The congregational councils of Sydenham and St. Paul's Churches, at their last meeting, have granted me six months' leave and have appointed the present pastor in Hull, M. Böckheler, as my substitute. He will take up his   287
duties on April 1.

I remain sincerely and respectfully yours,
Dietrich Bonhoeffer
For the church councils: St. Paul's Church   Sydenham Church
                             G. Henne   P. Voigt

210. To Mr. Ryder (Office of Baron Bruno Schröder)[1]

30th of March 1935
Edinburgh[2]

Dear Mr. Ryder,

Thank you for your letter[3] which reached me only here. When I saw Baron Schröder last to say good-bye to him before leaving for Germany I asked him, if he would do me a last favour, namely to allow my friend, Philipp Cromwell, lawyer, to come to see him in a personal matter. The Baron at once kindly consented (with the words: "auf Ihre Empfehlung jeden")[4] and I thanked him. So I hope the Baron will be able to see him. Mr. Ph. Cromwell is a close friend of mine.

[1.] EZA 5/1316; handwritten by Bonhoeffer, with signatures of the council representatives; addressed "To the Church Foreign Office, Berlin-Charlottenburg, Marchstr. 2, for Bishop Dr. Heckel"; reception stamp: "German Evangelical Church, received March 30, 1935"; various illegible handwritten comments and initials. Previously published in *GS* 6:289 and *Mündige Welt*, 5:134.

[1.] SBL, Family Papers, box FS 12/3/4 B Miscellaneous–Pastor Boeckheler (successor to) Pastor Bonhoeffer; handwritten; in original English, including errors. See also *NL*, Anh. A 35,4.

[2.] [As part of his tour of religious communities and theological colleges, Bonhoeffer was in Edinburgh, Scotland, to visit Professor John Baillie, who had been one of his teachers at Union Theological Seminary, New York, in 1930–31. See *DB-ER*, 416.—KC]

[3.] Letter of March 21, 1935 (SBL, as in ed. note 1; see also *NL*, Anh. A 35,1 [13], in which Ryder inquires who Mr. Cromwell is and what he wants).

[4.] ["Anyone whom you recommend"—KC]

May I just add a question: would you kindly let me know if and when the Charity Fund Committee has decided on my question about help for refugees.[5] The meeting was supposed to have taken place some time ago and the need is urgent.

Yours sincerely
D. Bonhoeffer

288 **211. To Baron Bruno Schröder**[1]

London, April 15, 1935

My dear Baron,

I am leaving today and as my last action here would like to send you once more my sincere and cordial greetings.

At the same time, permit me to renew once again my request that the concern I first brought to you some time ago be kept in mind. At that time you agreed that at the next meeting of the charity you would speak in favor of a certain transfer of funds to Sydenham Church for its work with Christian refugees from Germany. I would be sincerely grateful to you for granting this request.

With all good wishes for you, I remain
Sincerely and respectfully yours,
Dietrich Bonhoeffer

[5.] On the question of aid to refugees, see the preceding correspondence, esp. 1/195, 1/197, 1/198, and 1/202.

[1.] SBL, Family Papers, box FS 12/3/4 Miscellaneous–Pastor Boeckheler (successor to) Pastor Bonhoeffer; typewritten, signed by hand. See also *NL*, Anh. A 35, 1 (16). Addressed to "Baron Henry Schröder, Esq.," apparently an error made by the church secretary. The banking house Schröder used this name, but at that time no one else in the family was named Henry.

PART 2
Reports and Lectures

1. 1933–1934 Annual Report of the German Evangelical Church of Sydenham, London[1]

Phil. 1:18: "Just this, that Christ is proclaimed in every way."

What role do the changes that occur in the life of a congregation play over against the one thing that never changes, come what may, "Just this, that Christ is proclaimed in every way"? A pastor leaves, another one comes—what difference does that make, in view of the fact that each of them is nothing if not a messenger of one and the same Lord and kingdom, that in every case the only important thing is the fulfilling of the eternal mission, "Just this, that Christ is proclaimed in every way"? Personality, sympathy, or antipathy notwithstanding, here in the church of Jesus Christ we are concerned with more important, more significant, more urgent things—not with the pastor, but with Christ, "that Christ is proclaimed in every way." Here there is no longer like or dislike but rather belief or unbelief—that is the fearful choice.

We live in an age that is freeing itself of various kinds of illusions. The church, too, can no longer entertain illusions. In the church, too, it is a matter of all or nothing. It must know on whom it should depend and on whom it should not. Better a small troop that is prepared for action than a great army where potential deserters have crept in. This is true for the church as well. It is about belief and unbelief, obedience or disobedience, discipleship or desertion, Christ or the idols in our lives.

The days are over in which we thought we had time, in the pulpit, to bring in all sorts of edifying literature, philosophy, everyday wisdom, and politics. The time the church has is short. Who knows whether tomorrow may not already be too late for that which is not said and heard today. This is a time for decision. The thirty minutes that the pastor has each week in which to speak to the congregation really do not allow time for aesthetics or politics—and why do we need these? People who are looking for such things can find them much better elsewhere at any time. There have always been pastors who succeeded in gathering an interested audience around them, but it was not a congregation they were building. We want to be a congregation and not an audience. Anyone who has understood what it means to be a member of a believing community, rather than of an audience, knows what a liberation that is for a person. Those who are just looking for interesting

---

[1.] *NL*, A 41,8; printed as an eight-page brochure by the Finsbury Press, London, presumably in April 1934. On the front and back covers are handwritten explanations of the photos, showing the church and the parish house, in Sabine Leibholz's handwriting (see Bethge, Bethge, and Gremmels, *Life in Pictures* [centenary ed.], 72 and 73). Partially published in *GS* 2:164–66.

ideas in general will not be looking to the church. And anyone who does not bring something to the church will not receive anything either. But whoever is looking for a place where the talk is not about society, not about all sorts of everyday matters, not about economics or politics, but only and uniquely about Christ, his will, and his comfort—even if only two or three are gathered together—let that person come to church. And let him not just come once a year, either—there is no blessing or promise in such church attendance—but rather come again and again and help us become a congregation where "Christ is proclaimed in every way."

It makes little material difference whether the attendance at a worship service is large or small. The so-called success of a pastor is really concerned least of all with the number of worshipers. But I would still like to ask: Does the average attendance of 40 during the last few months really correspond to the 140 names listed in the directory, representing some 280 persons who could come? Does a Sunday School attendance of six children, a confirmation class consisting of two children from one family, and a total of 42 contributing members, when the minimum contribution is as low as ten shillings and sixpence,[2] truly reflect the circumstances of this congregation? Or are there some inhibitions and obstacles, which with good will could be cleared out of the way? Do we really want it on our conscience that we have denied our growing children that which means more for their lives than perhaps even we ourselves suspect? Are we so sure of our situation and what we are doing that we think we can do without it for our own selves? I believe it is my duty as pastor to pose this question once again in all seriousness. No one is forced to do anything here, but we each carry this responsibility for ourselves, alone before God.

For the past year, there is the following to report: The congregational assembly was held on May 22, 1933. Pastor Singer presented a draft for the fifty-eighth annual report, which was accepted and ready to be sent for printing. The treasurer[3] presented the accounts for the year, with the information that, to his regret, expenses had obliged him to withdraw £250 from the congregation's reserves. The accounts were agreed for printing.[4] The negotiations with regard to a successor for Pastor Singer have been concluded. After many years' faithful service, Pastor Singer has retired from his position as pastor of the church and left London on October 21, 1933. He

[2.] [In today's decimal coinage, fifty-two and one-half pence sterling (approximately two U.S. dollars at that time).—KC]

[3.] Paul Voigt.

[4.] This probably refers to the treasurer's report for the year 1932–33. The treasurer's report appended to this annual report shows Sunday collections of up to £88, for a total of £504, of which £213 was allotted for the pastor's salary.

returned to his home town of Herrenberg in Swabia,[5] with the gratitude of the congregation for all the faithful love and work that he performed during his service here. A strong expression of the affection in which he was held by both his congregations was the overflowing crowd at his farewell party in St. Paul's Church, at which Sydenham Church presented him with a fine gift, for which a collection had been taken, as a sign of devotion and thanks.

On October 22, his successor, Pastor *Dr.* Dietrich Bonhoeffer, lecturer at the University of Berlin, took up his duties as pastor. For his first sermon he took as his text 2 Cor. 5:20.[6] On Sunday, November 12, a congregational assembly duly and unanimously elected him pastor of the congregation.[7]

On Christmas Eve at 4 P.M. a Christmas service was held in the church, at which the children from the newly established Sunday school presented a nativity play. It was a pleasure to see the children doing their part in service to the congregation. The church choir, which had been started during Advent under the direction of Mr. Whitburn, sang old familiar Christmas hymns. The attendance was very large that evening.　　294

¶The church choir sings every Monday evening at 8:30 P.M. at the vicarage and would be pleased to have more good voices join its ranks.

On Good Friday[8] afternoon a Passion prayer service was held in the church, with the children participating, the choir singing, and some younger members, mainly from St. Paul's Church,[9] presenting an old Passion play.

The congregation thanks everyone who has helped in serving the church during the past year!

In February the new hymnal for congregations abroad was introduced, a welcome innovation to all those who are concerned about our worship and about true church music. The new hymnals are now available for purchase.

On Palm Sunday, Ingrid Elisabeth and Gerhard Eduard Cruesemann were confirmed in our church. The texts they chose were Mark 9:23[10] and Rev. 2:10. [11]

It has pleased the Lord of life and death to call from our congregation into everlasting life the master baker G. Brenner and Mrs. Küch, after long and hard illness. The peace and comfort of God, which the world cannot give, be with all those who are in mourning for these losses. This is the congregation's prayer for them.

[5.] [In southern Germany.—KC]

[6.] See 3/1.

[7.] See the minutes of the election, 1/11.1.

[8.] March 30, 1934.

[9.] The Reformed church [in Aldgate—KC] of which Bonhoeffer was also pastor.

[10.] "All things can be done for the one who believes."

[11.] "Be faithful until death, and I will give you the crown of life."

May the Lord of our congregation give each of us a pure heart and a joyful spirit, and make us steadfast and faithful, throughout changing times, in this one thing—"Just this, that Christ is proclaimed in every way."

In the name of the congregational council:
Pastor *Dr.* Dietrich Bonhoeffer

295   **2. Theses Paper for the Fanø Conference**[1]

The Church and the Peoples of the World
The Fundamental Principles of the World Alliance[2]

Summary

1. The destiny of the Alliance is determined by the following: whether it regards itself as a Church or as a society with a definite purpose. The World Alliance is a Church as long as[3] its fundamental principles lie in obediently listening to and preaching the Word of God. It is a society, if its essential object is to realise aims and conditions of whatever kind they may be. It is only as a Church that the World Alliance[4] can preach the

---

[1.] WCC Archives, World Alliance, box 212.008, "World Alliance–Conference–Fanø Aug. 1934"; *NL*, A 40,3 (3). English translation originally reprinted in *GS* 1:444–46. This is the official English translation made at the time, following the mimeographed German version (*NL*, A 40,3 (1), which was reprinted in *DBW* 13:295–97. [It should be noted that this English translation was organized somewhat differently (as a numbered outline) than the German text. Page numbers from the German edition have been inserted at the appropriate places.—KC] Bonhoeffer sent his theses in early August 1934 to the Research Department of the Ecumenical Council in Geneva. His original draft exists in typewritten carbon copy (*NL*, A 40,3 [2]). In Geneva the mimeographed copies were made as well as this translation into English and one in French (*NL*, A 40,3 [4]), which are closely related to that text. Wordings in the first (carbon copy) German version that were altered in the mimeographed version [and for the English translation—KC] are noted throughout, since it cannot be ruled out that they go back in part to Bonhoeffer's corrections. Regarding the background of this text, see 1/114, 1/124, 1/125, 1/134, 1/136, and 1/137.
[2.] The original subtitle in the carbon copy was "Provisional Draft for a Theological Basis for the Work of the World Alliance" (see *DBW* 13:295). The change was probably made by Hans Schönfeld; see his letter of August 13, 1934, 1/137. As early as 1932 Bonhoeffer had submitted a lecture and thesis "Toward a Theological Foundation for the Work of the World Alliance"; see *GS* 1:140–61 [and *DBW* 11, 2/14—KC].
[3.] "The World Alliance is a Church as long as" replaces "It is church when" in the original carbon copy.
[4.] "The World Alliance" replaces "it" in the original carbon copy.

Word of Christ in full authority to the Churches and nations. As a society it stands without authority with innumerable other societies of the same kind.

2. The work of the World Alliance means work of the Churches for peace amongst the nations. Its aim is the end of war and the victory over war.

3. The enemy of work for peace is war. War must be understood
   a) as a conscious action of the human will, for which it is fully responsible;
   b) as the work of the evil powers of this world, enemies of God, similar to diseases,[5] catastrophes, etc;
   c) as the revelation[6] of a world which has fallen under the law of death. 296

4. Corresponding to this, the justification of war takes the following three forms:
   a) War—according to the conscious will of its leaders—works for the maintenance of the State and future peace, this is its moral justification;
   b) War is an irresistible event, over which no man has any power (so-called realism or, rather, naturalism);
   c) War reveals an heroic world of sacrifice.

5. Secular pacifism answers:
   a) the pacific welfare of humanity will not be brought about by means of war. War cannot be justified morally on that basis;
   b) a rational organisation must be created which will hold back the powers leading to war;
   c) war must be suppressed so as to reveal the world as a good world.

6. These two arguments are of equal value and are equally unchristian. They are not Christ-inspired but inspired by a desired or non-desired picture of the world.

7. The Christian Church answers:
a) The human will must be confronted with the[7] commandment: Thou shalt not kill. God does not exempt us from obeying His commandments. Man by his transgressions will be guilty before God. The God of the Sermon on the Mount will judge him. To the objection: The State must be maintained: the Church answers: Thou shalt not kill. To the objection: War creates peace: the Church answers: This is not true, war creates destruction. To the objection: The nation [Volk] must defend itself:

[5.] "Similar to" replaces "like" in the original carbon copy.
[6.] "The revelation of" replaces " revealing" in the original carbon copy.
[7.] "Divine" is omitted in the original carbon copy.

297 the Church answers: Have you dared to entrust God, in full faith, with your protection in obedience to His commandment? To the objection: Love for my neighbour compels me: the Church answers: The one who loves God keeps His commandments. To the question: What shall I do then? the Church answers: Believe in God and be obedient. But to the secular pacifism the Church answers: The motives of our actions are not the welfare of humanity, but obedience to God's commandments. Even if war meant the good of humanity, God's commandment would remain steadfast.

b) The powers of evil will not be broken by means of organisations, but by prayer and fasting (Mark 9:29). Any other attitude under-estimates these powers and regards them as naturalistic or materialistic. The spirits of hell will be banished only by Christ Himself. Neither fatalism, nor organisation, but prayer! Man, feeling responsible for peace, although subject to evil powers, is being led to recognise that help and the solution[8] will be brought about by God alone. Prayer is stronger than organisation. It is easy to hide the burden of evil and struggle by organisation. (Not against enemies of blood and flesh . . . (Eph. 6:12.)[9]

c) War revealing as it does a world under the law of death shows also that the abolition of war would only be the suppression of a horrible symptom, but would not cut the root of the evil itself. It is not pacifism that is the victory which overcomes the world (1 John 5:4) but faith, which expects everything from God and hopes in the coming of Christ and His Kingdom. Only then will the cause of evil—that is to say, the Devil and the demons—be overcome.

[8.] "The solution" (*Lösung* in German mimeographed version) replaces "redemption" in the original carbon copy. Cf. *GS* 1:158 [and *DBW* 11, 2/14, p. 344—KC].

[9.] The original copy adds the words "Not against flesh and blood . . ." The entire verse reads: "For our struggle is not against enemies of blood and flesh, but against the rulers, against the authorities, against the cosmic powers of this present darkness, against the spiritual forces of evil in the heavenly places" (NRSV).

3. Address to the Fanø Conference: English Transcription[1]

The Church and the Peoples of the World

"I will hear what God the Lord will speak: for he will speak peace unto his people, and to his saints" (Psalm 85:9).[2] Between the twin crags of nationalism and internationalism ecumenical Christendom calls upon her Lord and asks his guidance. Nationalism and internationalism have to do with political necessities and possibilities. The ecumenical Church, however, does not concern itself with these things, but with the commandments of God, and regardless of consequences it transmits these commandments to the world.[3]

Our task as theologians, accordingly, consists only in accepting this commandment as a binding one, not as a question open to discussion. Peace on earth[4] is not a problem, but a commandment given at Christ's coming. There are two ways of reacting to this command from God: the unconditional, blind obedience of action, or the hypocritical question of the Serpent: "Yea, hath God said . . . ?"[5] This question is the mortal enemy of obedience, and therefore the mortal enemy of all real peace. "Hath God not said . . . ? Has God not understood human nature well enough to know that wars must occur in this world, like laws of nature? Must God not have meant that we should talk about peace, to be sure, but that it is not to be literally translated into action? Must God not really have said that we should work for peace, of course, but also make ready tanks and poison gas for security?" And then perhaps the most serious question: "Did God say you should not

---

[1.] *NL*, A 40,5 (2); hectograph; previously published in *International Fellowship of Reconciliation, News Letter* no. 60 (October 1948) and in *GS* 1:447–49. At the end of the text is the comment: "Dietrich Bonhoeffer gave this address in the late summer of 1934, at the meeting of the Ecumenical Council of Christian Churches in Fanø, Denmark." Biblical citations follow the King James Version. [For Bonhoeffer's original German text, see *DBW* 13:298–301 (2/3.1), which reproduces *NL*, A 40,5 (1) and *GS* 1:216–19. Citations for this English transcription are from DBW 13:302–4, with some pertinent additional material inserted from the citations to the German document on pp. 298–301. It is possible that the English text reproduced here was prepared by Bonhoeffer himself. In the summer of 1933 Bonhoeffer was asked, as international youth secretary, to make this presentation (see *DB-ER*, 314). For further German secondary literature on this paper, see *DBW* 13 2/3.1, 298, ed. note 1.—KC]

[2.] [Ps. 85:8 KJV—KC]

[3.] Here the German text has the sentence: "As a member of the ecumenical movement, the World Alliance for Promoting International Friendship through the Churches has taken up God's call to peace and sends this command out to all peoples."

[4.] Luke 2:14; possibly also an allusion to Otto Dibelius's 1929 book, *Friede auf Erden?*

[5.] Gen. 3:1; cf. also the interpretation in *Creation and Fall, DBWE* 3:103–10.

protect your own people? Did God say you should leave your own a prey to the enemy?"

303   No, God did not say all that. What He has said is that there shall be peace among men—that we shall obey Him without further question, that is what He means. He who questions the commandment of God before obeying has already denied Him.

There shall be peace because of the Church of Christ, for the sake of which the world exists. And this Church of Christ lives at one and the same time in all peoples, yet beyond all boundaries, whether national, political, social, or racial. And the brothers who make up this Church are bound together, through the commandment of the one Lord Christ, whose Word they hear, more inseparably than men are bound by all the ties of common history, of blood, of class and of language. All these ties, which are part of our world, are valid ties, not indifferent; but in the presence of Christ they are not ultimate bonds. For the members of the ecumenical Church, in so far as they hold to Christ, His word,[6] His commandment of peace is more holy, more inviolable than the most revered words and works of the natural world. For they know that whoso is not able to hate father and mother for His sake is not worthy of Him,[7] and lies if he calls himself after Christ's name. These brothers in Christ obey His word; they do not doubt or question, but keep His commandment of peace. They are not ashamed, in defiance of the world, even to speak of eternal peace. They cannot take up arms against Christ himself—yet this is what they do if they take up arms against one another![8] Even in anguish and distress of conscience there is for them no escape from the commandment of Christ that there shall be peace.

How does peace come about? Through a system of political treaties? Through the investment of international capital in different countries? Through the big banks, through money? Or through universal peaceful rearmament in order to guarantee peace? Through none of these, for the single reason that in all of them peace is confused with safety. There is no

---

[6.] The English version here lacks a phrase with which this sentence begins in the German version: "There shall be peace because Christ is in the world, that means . . ." (*DBW* 13:299).

[7.] Allusion to Matt. 10:37 and Luke 14:26; cf. also the interpretation in *DBWE* 4:92–99 and 197.

[8.] Friedrich Siegmund-Schulze had used a similar argument in a lecture in 1929/30: "An injury to a Christian brother means an injury to a member of the body of Christ, an injury to the body of Christ himself" (Siegmund-Schultze, "Was kann die Kirche für den Frieden tun?" 3).

way to peace along the way of safety. For peace must be dared. It is the great venture. It can never be made safe. Peace is the opposite of security. To demand guarantees is to mistrust, and this mistrust in turn brings forth war.   304 To look for guarantees is to want to protect oneself. Peace means to give oneself altogether to the law of God, wanting no security, but in faith and obedience laying the destiny of the nations in the hand of Almighty God, not trying to direct it for selfish purposes. Battles are won, not with weapons, but with God. They are won where the way leads to the cross. Which of us can say he knows what it might mean for the world if one nation should meet the aggressor, not with weapons in hand, but praying, defenseless, and for that very reason protected by "a bulwark never failing"?[9]

Once again, how will peace come? Who will call us to peace so that the world will hear, will have to hear? so that all peoples may rejoice? The individual Christian cannot do it. When all around are silent, he can indeed raise his voice and bear witness, but the powers of this world stride over him without a word. The individual church, too, can witness and suffer—oh, if it only would!—but it also is suffocated by the power of hate. Only the one great Ecumenical Council of the Holy Church of Christ over all the world can speak out so that the world, though it gnash its teeth, will have to hear, so that the peoples will rejoice because the Church of Christ in the name of Christ has taken the weapons from the hands of their sons, forbidden war, and proclaimed the peace of Christ against the raging world.

Why do we fear the fury of the world powers? Why don't we take the power from them and give it back to Christ? We can still do it today. The Ecumenical Council is in session; it can send out to all believers this radical call to peace. The nations are waiting for it in the East and in the West. Must we be put to shame by non-Christian peoples in the East? Shall we desert the individuals who are risking their lives for this message? The hour is late. The world is choked with weapons, and dreadful is the distrust which looks out of all men's eyes. The trumpets of war may blow tomorrow. For what are we waiting? Do we want to become involved in this guilt as never before?

[9.] Allusion to Martin Luther's hymn "A Mighty Fortress Is Our God." [The English version here lacks a parenthetical remark found in the German (*DBW* 13:300): "Gideon: . . . the people with thee are too many . . ." (Judg. 7:2 KJV) Here God himself sees to the disarmament!—KC] See also Bonhoeffer's sermon of February 26, 1933 (DBW 12, 3/5).

305

"What use to me are crown, land, folk and fame?
They cannot cheer my breast.
War's in the land, alas, and on my name
I pray no guilt may rest."

M. Claudius[10]

We want to give the world a whole word, not a half word—a courageous word, a Christian word. We want to pray that this word may be given us, today. Who knows if we shall see each other again another year?

3a. Report on the Theological Conference in Bruay-en-Artois, September 15, 1934[1]

A Theological Statement from Young Ecumenists regarding the Task of the Church Today
Report on the Theological Conference in Bruay
Geneva, 15 September 1934

Quelques Nouvelles
No. 2   15 septembre 1934

Report issued by Dr. D. Bonhoeffer on behalf of the six delegates assembled in the Theological Conference at Bruay en Artois.
4–8 August[2] 1934
Delegates present:

Germany:	D. Bonhoeffer	Great Britain:	E. C. Blackman
	W. Maechler		T. H. Kilborn
	J. W. Winterhager		(Mrs. E. Kilborn, Guest)
France:	J. Lasserre		

[10.] Bonhoeffer has rephrased the first line of this last verse of Matthias Claudius's "Kriegslied" (War song) from *Wandsbecker Boten.* Cf. Henkys, *Gefängnisgedichte,* 15. [Claudius's line reads: "What use to me are crown, land, gold, and fame?" Bonhoeffer has replaced "gold" with "folk."—KC]

[1.] Typewritten manuscript; previously published in *Mündige Welt,* 5:235–37, and *Dietrich Bonhoeffer Jahrbuch,* 2:93–96. WCC, Youth Commission of World Alliance for Life and Work, Félice correspondence 1935, Documents 1935. This is the original English translation of the report. See also the introduction to this report by Victoria J. Barnett, *Dietrich Bonhoeffer Jahrbuch,* 2:89–92.

[2.] The month should be September.

The Theological Conference had been prepared in order to provide a compensation for the Franco-German Conference which had been arranged for, but could not take place in 1933.[3] The subject of that conference was to be formed by the actual situation, and the German representatives of the Oecumenical Youth Groups had suggested the following as an outline for the Conference discussions as well as for a statement to be submitted to the Universal Christian Council: "Ein theologisches Wort aus der oekumenischen Jugend zur Aufgabe der Kirche heute."[4]

In a circular issued by the Berlin (North and Central European) Secretariat in June 1934, it was suggested that the preparation for all delegates (whose list being ready in July) should run along the two following lines: Church and State; Justice and Love.

The Paris session of the Youth Commission (Jan. 31 and Feb. 1st 1934) had issued the project that the Conference should take place at Luxembourg. In consequence several letters were written by the Berlin Secretariat to the Rev. Jakoby. But there was only a very uncertain reply from that Luxembourg Church representative. It was not before the middle of August that the Rev. Jakoby wrote a second letter to express, at last, that for the month of September there seemed to be no possibility of accommodation at Luxembourg whenever the delegates might be willing to come there.

When all the preparations had been much complicated by that very late statement of Rev. Jakoby, M. le Past. Jean Lasserre kindly offered the house of his congregation to the Youth Commission as a Conference place. So the German and French Youth Secretaries (MM. Bonhoeffer and Toureille) made an agreement (at Fanø) that all Luxembourg delegates should be asked to come to Bruay (Lasserre) instead of Luxembourg, according to M. Lasserre's offer.

[3.] As youth secretary of the World Alliance, Bonhoeffer had been involved since 1933 in the planning of the German-French conference of young theologians, which was foreseen for the end of July 1933 in Luxembourg or France (see *DBW* 12, 1/52, 1/59, 1/61, and 1/70). Because this date ultimately fell during the turbulent days preceding the church elections in the Old Prussian Union church, he cancelled the conference on short notice (see *DBW* 12, 1/74). Now a meeting of young theologians from Germany, France, and England was rescheduled for 1934 in Luxembourg (the decision was made on January 31–February 2 at a youth commission meeting in Paris; see 1/105, ed. note 5). Because of organizational difficulties, this conference had to be rescheduled on short notice for Bruay-en-Artois, the parish of Jean Lasserre, Bonhoeffer's friend from his studies in New York (cf. 1/109, 1/115, and 1/122). Bonhoeffer was very annoyed that, contrary to expectations, no French delegation participated in the conference (cf. 1/151 and 1/153).

[4.] The final paragraph of this document, which is in quotation marks, is the "theological statement" referred to here.

In spite of this arrangement there came to Bruay not a single delegate of those appointed by the French Youth Secretary, two of whom had been asked to prepare and deliver speeches. The proceedings of the whole conference were much hampered by the fact that there appeared no Frenchman except M. Lasserre who could himself only act as a substitute member.

Apart from the actual contribution rendered to the Home Mission work of M. Lasserre's congregation by the British and German delegates,[5] the following statement can be considered as the result of the Theological Conference.

The discussions took place on the content of the Christian Gospel and on *the ultimate authority for us Christians in proclaiming the Gospel.*

One group affirmed the truth of Article 9 of Dr. Oldham's Fanö[6] Theses on Church and State that the essence of the Christian Gospel was the *supremacy of the personal;*[7] that the origin and authority are ultimately to be found in the life and mind of the Christian community which may or may not be at any given time the organised Christian Church.[8]

Another group affirmed the ultimate authority to be the Word of God as revealed in the Old and New Testaments.[9]

Because of these two different affirmations the relations between Church and State were also viewed in different ways.

The first group was inclined to make no final separation between Church and State, since the supremacy of the personal could be concerned in either.

The other group drew a sharp distinction between the Church as really being the living body of Christ (in the full meaning attached to it in the New Testament) and the State as being only God's institution for preserving his fallen creation from chaos.

These different views did not represent final differences as between the groups, since individual members found a measure of agreement although they could not find adequate language to express that agreement fully.

The agreement, however, was brought about to such an extent that the following *Resolution* was carried and is now being submitted to the Universal Christian Council and to the World Alliance so that these senior organisa-

---

[5.] The German and British delegates participated in "street preaching" in Bruay. See Kelly, "Interview with Jean Lasserre," 57.

[6.] The different spellings of Fanø/Fanö occur in the original document.

[7.] See Joseph H. Oldham, "Die Kirche und der Staat," in Althaus, *Die Kirche und das Staatsproblem der Gegenwart,* 214–16. See also Clements, *Faith on the Frontier,* 290–94.

[8.] Coming only weeks before the Dahlem synod, this statement was an indication of the radical "Dahlemite" line being taken by Bonhoeffer and his colleagues.

[9.] Presumably this was the position taken by Bonhoeffer and his students.

tions might consider the publishing of that resolution (in addition to the resolutions taken by the International Youth Conference at Fanø[)].

> "The Church although it cannot enter into the political struggle in an official capacity ought, however, through its members to study social and political questions with a view to action on their part either individually or in groups. Such an action should be based upon the responsibility of the church members for the social order according to the Will of God. The aim of this action should be building up of a State where there is entire freedom for the Christian life (the guidance of which should clearly be recognised in such Scripture passages as Matthew V–VII, Acts V. 29, etc.). Further there are many ways in which the Church, *within its own membership*, can and should reproduce the Christian life to-day: e.g., church unity, community living, settlement of disputes between church members without going to law, liberal education. As representing and proclaiming the voice of Christ ever remains the primary task of the Church throughout the world, the Church should not neglect its obligation to point out and to criticize those attainments of human society which are not in accordance with the Will of God as revealed in the Bible."

This resolution was agreed to by all the delegates stated[10] underneath:
MM Blackman, Bonhoeffer, Kilborn, Lasserre, Maechler, Winterhager

---

[10.] The original text incorrectly has "states."

4. Lecture on the Theology of Karl Barth and the Situation in Germany (Transcript)[1]

Tonight we had a visit from Dietrich Bonhoeffer of the University of Berlin, one of the leading young Barthian theologians and one of the most important figures in the German Church situation. He gave us a splendid talk on Barth's theology and the situation in Germany. He dealt mainly with the question of what is the ultimate authority and during the course of his speech he examined all the recognised authorities which he classified as follows:

Logical Authority	– Reason
	– Philosophy
	– Doctrine
Psychological Authority	– Experience
	– Conscience
Historical Authority	– Church
	– Bible
	– Orthodoxy—the Faith

306   I. *The Logical Authority* wrecks itself on human wisdom. The incarnation contradicts the logical principle of identity—either A or not A. Either man's way or God's way: man's thoughts or God's. That God should become man contradicts all reason and logic.[2]

2a. *The Psychological Authority.* The "German Christians" claim that they have received a new revelation in the new State of National Socialism (new in 1933 A.D.!). Thus God spoke in Christ—and in Hitler. The argument is as follows: The Christian message is an appeal of God to human experience. I can't proclaim a thing I don't know. Reply:—but if I know a thing by experience I do away with faith—and faith justifies. Faith can only exist where there is no experience. Indeed

---

[1.] In possession of Keith Clements; typed copy of a handwritten entry in the diary of John Wright of October 4, 1934; in original English, including errors. Wright was at that time a student at Richmond College [London], a seminary of the Methodist Church. Bonhoeffer's visit had been arranged by Rudolf Weckerling, who was then studying at Richmond College (*DB-ER*, 412). On July 1, 1970, Wright sent the typed copy to Keith Clements, adding a note: "I was so immature at the time that I would not [this word has been omitted in *DBW* 13—KC] like to rely on the accuracy of my reporting." Bonhoeffer had lectured once before on Barth's theology abroad, in 1930–31 in New York; that lecture was before the beginning of the Church Struggle and was decidedly different (cf. *DBW* 10, 2/17).

[2.] [By this time Bonhoeffer was using the term *Menschwerdung* (God becoming human); cf. Bonhoeffer's 1933 Christology lectures, *DBW* 12, 2/b–12.—KC]

faith proves to be true when it denies all human reason—faith then is trust[3] in defense of reason—(to seek a standpoint in the air, as I put it).[4]

2b. *Conscience.* There is no conscience in Paradise. Conscience assumes the knowledge of good and evil which is proper to the fallen state of Adam.[5] Conscience then is fallen and it aims to justify oneself by one's better self—which is sin. Thus it is not the voice of God but of the devil and hence has no authority.

3. *Historical Authorities.* Be it an infallible church, Book or Doctrine, all these assume that there is a spot in the world which is not fallen and thus exempt from sinfulness. But the only part of the world free from sin and its positive correlative is Christ Jesus, His only Son our Lord, and He alone is ultimate authority. This is seen perfectly in the cross where God's will crosses out all human will and effort. Hence the cross is a judgement. Thus the word of the cross which is foolishness[6] and a stumbling block[7] is the ultimate authority.

That is roughly the substance of the address.[8]

5. 1934–1935 Annual Report of the German Evangelical Church of Sydenham, London[1]   307

"For we cannot do anything against the truth,
but only for the truth." 2 Cor. 13:8

For another whole year, the preaching of Christ as the truth that makes us free has gone out to our congregation, and the sacraments of communion with this same Christ have been received. Whether they have encountered

---

[3.] [Incorrectly transcribed "hust" in *DBW* 13.—KC]

[4.] The comments in parentheses appear to be Wright's personal reactions.

[5.] Cf. *DBWE* 1:107–8; *DBWE* 3:87 and 128–29; *DBWE* 4:107; [and *DBWE* 6:277, 302–3 and 322—KC].

[6.] Cf. 1 Cor. 1:18 and 23.

[7.] Cf. 1 Pet. 2:8.

[8.] In his letter to Keith Clements, John Wright continued: "Then I record a question I raised and I have a suspicion that the answer recorded was more of JW than DB." Then he quoted again from his diary: "Many other questions came—on experience and conscience and a few on politics in Germany and on the purpose of preaching. Afterward I had a word with him and saw him off." [Evidently not all who heard the lecture at Richmond were impressed. To students for whom the chief contemporary challenges to theology lay in evolutionary science and psychology, Bonhoeffer came over almost as a biblical literalist. For his part, Bonhoeffer was unforgettably moved by the memorial boards commemorating the missionary pioneers sent out to Africa and elsewhere from the college. Cf. *DB-ER*, 412, and Bethge, Bethge, and Gremmels, *Life in Pictures* (1986 ed.), 138.—KC]

[1.] ADBC; printed brochure. On the cover: "Report on the Sixtieth Year of the German Evangelical Church of Sydenham, London S.E., April 1, 1934 to March 31, 1935."

faith, led people to God, whether they have strengthened those who were failing and comforted the sorrowful, brought liars and hypocrites to justice, humbled the proud and given fresh heart to those who have been humbled, God alone knows. If only two or three have received help, the work has not been in vain. The kingdom of heaven reckons not with masses but rather with the few.

For us the past year has been particularly marked by the events taking place in our home church. It has been the scene of an unparalleled struggle between powers of heresy, which turned away from the pure gospel of Jesus Christ as our only Lord and used brute force against pastors and bishops of Christ's church, and the host of those who had no other weapon, and desired no other, than the confession of Christ as Lord of lords. Out of necessity and faith, the confessing pastors and congregations have flocked together into the Confessing Church, which in the face of every threat has set up its own church government and refused to obey any longer the anti-Christian church government under the present Reich bishop. This challenge has also come to us here in our congregation. All of us here knew that we could no longer keep silent. Our London congregations, along with most of the other German congregations in England, have taken a firm stand together on the

308   ground of the Confessing Church and informed the appropriate authorities that we have done so. We needed to express our solidarity with our struggling and suffering brethren in our homeland, for the sake of the gospel and our conscience. A congregational assembly of our church unanimously approved[2] the steps taken by our congregational council.[3] No one can foresee the consequences this decision will have for us. But it is not this that we should worry about, but rather about our responsibility to the gospel as Christians and as Germans. We must be deeply grateful that council, congregation, and pastor were all able to make this decision together. For we can do nothing against the truth but only for the truth.

Special collections were taken: one for Bethel,[4] one for the victims of the mine disaster in Wales[5] and the earthquake disaster in Japan. For these

---

Reprinted in *GS* 2:200–202. The following annual report (1935–36) mentions that Bonhoeffer's draft for the report presented here had been accepted at the annual congregational assembly on May 20, 1935.

[2.] No documentation of this action has been found.

[3.] Cf. 1/186.

[4.] Cf. both the sermon on 2 Cor. 12:9 (3/19, ed. note 14) and the letter of July 31, 1934, to H. Fricke (1/131).

[5.] See also the sermon for the first Sunday of Advent 1933 on Luke 21:28 (3/4). [This was actually a mining accident in Derbyshire; see 3/4, ed. note 3.—KC]

we received letters of sincere thanks. Several times I have requested help for Christian German refugees in London who were in need,[6] and I have been grateful again and again for the loving response that I and these persons have received.

I am writing this report in Germany, where I am director of a new theological seminary that the leaders of the Confessing Church were obliged to set up and called me to lead. The education of a new generation of pastors is a matter of survival for the Confessing Church. When I was asked to apply for this position, the congregational council and I were of one opinion that such a request simply could not be refused at such a time as this. So for the time being I am on six months' leave from our congregation in order to do this work, which has now begun, though under unusual circumstances. On March 10, I took leave of the congregation temporarily. Pastor Böckheler from Hull has been asked to stand in for me. I never expected the time to say good-bye would come so quickly.

We owe a debt of gratitude to our esteemed Mrs. D. Schlund for the fine new lighting system that has been installed in the choir of the church and for the renovation of the antiquated light fixtures in the nave as well as for repairs to damaged areas on the inside walls of the church. 309

Those baptized this year were Ursula Marianne Willnow and Clive Ernst Otto Quitmann.

Those confirmed were Ernst Cromwell, Rudolf Eppenstein, Wolfgang Valentin, and Hans Heinrich Treviranus.

Those who died and received a church burial were Gertrud Lütgens (April 7, 1934), Mrs. Luise Delp (August 6, 1934), Mr. G. Brenner, Mr. Reinhardt Baelz (February 11, 1935).

We commend our dear departed ones into God's faithful hands and pray for those whom they leave behind in sorrow that the God of all comfort will grant them that peace which the world cannot give.

On December 7, 1934, Pastor Friedrich Singer died of a heart attack at Hornegg Sanatorium near Heilbronn.

We shall honor his wish that nothing be written about him after his death. As he always thanked his congregations with all his heart for their love and friendship shown to him, so our congregation remembers its faithful shepherd with sincere gratitude and is deeply saddened by his untimely death.

[6.] See minutes of the meeting of St. Paul's congregational council on February 11, 1935 (1/201).

"Blessed are those slaves whom the master finds alert when he comes; truly I tell you, he will fasten his belt and have them sit down to eat, and he will come and serve them" (Luke 12:37).

May it always be so in our church.—"For we cannot do anything against the truth, but only for the truth."

With gratitude, I remain faithfully yours,

In the name of the congregational council:

Dietrich Bonhoeffer, *Pastor*

PART 3
Sermons and Meditations

1. Sermon on 2 Corinthians 5:20
London, Nineteenth Sunday after Trinity, October 22, 1933[1]

2 Cor. 5:20: So we are ambassadors for Christ, since God is making his appeal through us; we entreat you on behalf of Christ, be reconciled to God.

Every change of pastors in a congregation is bound up with all sorts of human emotions. If all is well and as it should be in the congregation, it is painful to see the pastor who has served there faithfully leave. There are so many things that bind a good congregation and a good pastor. How could it be otherwise, when he has spoken with[2] his congregation Sunday after Sunday about the ultimate matters of life and death? When he has celebrated the Lord's Supper with the believers, with those who mourn, the poor in spirit, those who hunger and thirst, the peacemakers, and the long-suffering?[3] When he has searched day by day in the homes of his parishioners, to find one soul that longs for love, for strength, justice, peace, and freedom, and when he then is able to speak not only about people searching for their God but also about God's seeking out human beings in the midst of their uncertainty, their questions and hesitations and the burdens they carry, in the midst of their loneliness—and when, there in the stillness, such a soul opens and reveals itself to [the] neighbor and to God? How near the pastor comes to his congregation at such times, at least to the part of the congregation that is alive! How much he knows about their hardships and difficulties that no one else will ever know; how much he carries, silently and humbly, with his congregation, and brings it before God in prayer, as the faithful shepherd of his flock.

¶Yes, when all is well between pastor and congregation, then it is very understandable to be overcome by human sadness when the time comes to part. The church members look toward the future with some reservations and somewhat worriedly, somewhat fearfully. How is it going to be with the new one? Will things feel the same with him? Will he have the same understanding of his ministry or perhaps an entirely different one? For both pastors, of course, the same sort of thoughts and questions arise. So a moment like this is brimming and loaded with feelings of the most personal sort: pain, joy, worry, confidence.

[1.] Literary estate of Elisabeth Bornkamm; handwritten. See also *NL*, A 43,1; photocopy. Previously published in *GS* 5:491–98 and *PAM* 1:380–87. This is Bonhoeffer's first sermon as new pastor in London, after he had moved into the parsonage in Forest Hill on October 17, 1933.

[2.] "With" replaces "to."

[3.] An allusion to the Beatitudes in the Sermon on the Mount, Matt. 5:3–11.

So it would be good if, at a moment like this, we let ourselves be lifted up above the very personal level and take a broader, larger-scale view of things. A change of pastors is a situation in which we get stuck in our very personal feelings, but we should be encouraged to see something much larger, which does not concern persons at all, neither the old one nor the new one, but rather concerns the mission that is entrusted to both of them, no matter who they are.[4] What matters is the one who gives the orders, not the one who carries them out, only the master, rather than the servant. The one thing that is really necessary is that this master's mission be carried out, whether it causes pastors to break down or not; or whether they are often rather strange people, perhaps because they know more than others about the strange things in life; whether they can win people over easily, or whether they have a hard time with themselves and others. If only the mission is carried out, in preaching and in life, if only the pastor's sole concern is to devote his life to this master and this commission.

For the congregation, however, this means that at this point everything depends on its being led to let go of the issue of the person and to look instead to the Lord of the church; to pay attention to the preaching rather than the preacher; and to have only one question: Is this truly the gospel of our God[5] that we are hearing? Or is it the kind of arbitrary thinking that human beings invent, which blossoms today and withers away tomorrow like 315   the grass of the field?[6] There is really only one question for a congregation to ask of its pastor: Is he offering us the eternal word of God, the word of life, wherever he can, in the pulpit and in daily life? Or is he giving us stones instead of bread?[7] Is he giving us placebos that are perhaps more pleasant to take but do not satisfy our souls? Give us bread that fills our hungry souls! This should be the daily plea with which the congregation stands before its pastor, just as the pastor should stand before God and pray for this gift for his congregation as their pastor, their shepherd.

Between you and your pastor there should be only Christ. The one important matter between you and your pastor, wherever we meet, whether in serious or joyful moments, is always Christ.

So then, we are ambassadors for Christ. . . . That means that we do not work under our own authority. We do not send ourselves on mission. Nor are we ourselves the guarantors of what we have to say, for Christ alone guarantees the truth of the gospel. We preach because we are called and sent by

---

[4.] Cf. James 2:1–10.
[5.] "God" replaces "Lord Jesus Christ."
[6.] Cf. Matt. 6:30 [and Isa. 40:7—KC].
[7.] Cf. Matt. 7:9.

Christ; it is Christ who gives us the mission of delivering his message. And all our words serve but to keep our eyes on one goal, and to point toward it: toward Christ, toward the Lord, toward the Word of God, which is beyond all our words, which God speaks at any time and in any place, touches and enters human hearts and brings fear and comfort to them, whenever and wherever God wants. Not our word, but God's Word: yet even so, God's Word speaking through ours.

¶This is what makes a sermon something unique in all the world, so completely different from any other kind of speech. When a preacher opens his Bible and interprets the word of God, a mystery takes place, a miracle: the grace of God, who comes down from heaven into our midst and speaks to us, knocks on our door, asks questions, warns us, puts pressure on us, alarms us, threatens us, and makes us joyful again and free and sure. When the Holy Scriptures are brought to life in a church, the Holy Spirit comes down from the eternal throne, into our hearts, while the busy world outside[8] sees nothing and knows nothing about it—that God could actually be found here. Out there they are all running after the latest sensations, the excitements of evening in the big city, never knowing that the real sensation, something infinitely more exciting, is happening in here: here, where eternity and time meet, where the immortal God receives mortal human beings, through the holy Word, and cares for them, where human souls can taste the starkest terrors of despair and the ultimate depths of God's eternity.

316

Why do they not know this? How is it possible that thousands upon thousands of people are bored with the church and pass it by? Why did it come about that the cinema really is often more interesting, more exciting, more human and gripping than the church? Can that really be only the fault of others and not ours as well? The church was different once. It used to be that the questions of life and death were resolved and decided here. Why is this no longer so?

It is because we ourselves have made the church, and keep on making it, into something which it is not. It is because we talk too much about false, trivial human things and ideas in the church and too little about God. It is because we make the church into a playground for all sorts of feelings of ours, instead of a place where God's word is obediently received and believed.[9] It is because we prefer quiet and edification to the holy restlessness of the powerful Lord God, because we keep thinking we have God in our power

---

[8.] "Into our hearts, while the busy world outside" replaces "into the midst of our busy street, which."

[9.] Cf. Luther, *Ecclesia est creatura verbi* [the church is a creature of the word](WA 6:560) [and *The Babylonian Captivity of the Church, LW* 36:107—KC].

instead of allowing God to have power over us, instead of recognizing that God is truth and that over against God the whole world is in the wrong. It is because we like too much to talk and think about a cozy, comfortable God instead of letting ourselves be disturbed and disquieted by the presence of God—because in the end we ourselves do not want to believe that God is really here among us, right now, demanding that we hand ourselves over, in life and death, in heart and soul and body. And finally, it is because we pastors keep talking too much about passing things, perhaps about whatever we ourselves have thought out or experienced, instead of knowing that we are no more than the messengers of the great truth of the eternal Christ.

317　　Every empire in this world sends out its ambassadors. Their job is to give visible expression throughout the world to the will and the might of their empire. They are not meant to be anything other than representatives, in this way, of their home empire and their lord. The German ambassador or the French ambassador is supposed to be the quintessential German or Frenchman. This has nothing to do with him as a person, but concerns only his mission. And in order to carry out their mission, ambassadors are vested with all the authority of their empire. They speak and act on behalf of their lord.

And so the unseen Lord of the eternal kingdom and of the church sends his ambassadors into this world, giving them a mission that is greater than that of any other, just as heaven is greater than earth, and eternity·is greater than time. And the authority that this Lord gives his ambassadors is that much greater than all the authorities in this world. God's eternal word, God's eternal judgment, God's justice and God's grace, God's anger and God's mercy, salvation and damnation, reconciliation through Christ—these words are placed in the hands of the ambassadors of Christ as the most sacred and precious of goods, which they are called to administer through the grace of God. They will be required to give a full account to their Lord, the Shepherd of shepherds, for every word they have spoken in his name in his church; as the shepherds of the flock, they will have to carry the blame and the responsibility. This is the ultimate meaning of the pastoral ministry!

But, we ask, what human being can do this? Who can fulfill this commission? Who can carry this burden without breaking down under it? No human being can, not even the most devout. Nobody would presume to demand such a commission. But because it is a commission, because Christ must be preached, and woe to us if we do not preach his gospel,[10] we are carried by this obligation, this commission. We cannot do otherwise, even when we do

---

[10.] 1 Cor. 9:16.

it badly and not as we should,[11] even when we keep breaking down under this burden and making mistakes. But then we need to know that the congregation is shouldering the burden with us, helping us, standing by us, pointing out our mistakes and praying for us, and forgiving us our sins. No pastor can do his job properly if it is not given to him to know this. Many a pastor has failed because he wanted to carry his congregation, but the congregation did not carry him. A congregation that does not pray for the ministry of its pastor is no longer a congregation. A pastor who does not pray daily for his congregation is no longer a pastor.

    Our text sums up in one brief sentence the message that we are to convey: "We entreat you on behalf of Christ, be reconciled to God." What that means we cannot describe fully today. For every sermon is basically an interpretation of that sentence. That one short sentence will only be revealed in its full meaning when the end of the world is near and the last sermons are being preached, and when Christ himself comes to lead us into all truth.

    "We entreat you on behalf of Christ." Christ asks through us. He does not bark orders at us, he who is the Lord of all the world. He who has all power and authority does not force us.[12] Christ, who[13] could make anyone do anything, comes to us as one who asks, as a poor beggar, as if he needed something from us. That he comes to us in this way is the sign of his love. He does not want to make us contrary but rather wants to open our hearts so that he can enter. It is a strange glory, the glory of this God[14] who comes to us as one who is poor, in order to win our hearts.

    And what Christ asks of us, too, is so strange that we cannot[15] get over our astonishment: "Be reconciled to God." This means nothing less than let a king give you his kingdom, take heaven as a gift. Let the Lord of lords of all the world give you his love, and be his friends, his children, those whom he protects. Come, surrender yourselves to him and to his will, and you will be free from every evil, from all guilt, and from all bondage. You will be free from your own selves, you will have found your way home, you will be at home with your Father.

    We are unreconciled persons—that is our secret, which only Christ knows. We are persons who are not reconciled, which is why we are so worried, self-centered, unfriendly, distrustful, why we are untruthful and cowardly, why we are lonely, and why we are guilty. Be reconciled to God—give God the right

318

319

[11.] Uncertain reading.

[12.] Crossed out: "even if he might want to"; cf. Matt. 28:18.

[13.] Crossed out: "as Lord of the world."

[14.] Replaces "Christ."

[15.] Replaces "can hardly."

to rule over you, and in finding God you will also find your brother and your neighbor again; be reconciled to God, and you will also be reconciled with your brother. Look into the abyss of your soul. Let Christ ask you whether you are reconciled with God or whether you have fallen away and are not at peace with God, and then look up at him, see and return to your God. Give God your unreconciled and irreconcilable heart. And God will give you a new heart.

O Lord, give all of us new hearts, open and obedient to you: hearts that love our neighbor and pray to you for our church. Lord, give us a good beginning; open your fatherly heart to us and lead us, one day, home to your kingdom of eternal reconciliation, through Christ the Lord! Amen.

2. Sermon on 2 Corinthians 5:10
London, Repentance Day,[1] November 19, 1933[2]

2 Cor. 5:10: For all of us must appear before the judgment seat of Christ, so that each may receive recompense for what has been done in the body, whether good or evil.

Nothing can remain a secret, nothing stays hidden. As a German proverb says, "No story is so cleverly made but the sun will bring it to light one day."[3] That means this sun of ours, which is always bringing out into the light things that have taken place in the darkness—quite suddenly, to the great surprise and horror of everyone concerned. We clap our hands to our foreheads and say, how could such a thing be possible, and are terribly disappointed and strike terribly moralistic attitudes, while in the quiet of our hearts we ourselves are afraid of what the sun may find out. Sometimes it only takes a moment for a person's entire life and fate and secret to be laid bare. All it takes is for some strong hand unwittingly to pick up some old stone and to

320

[1.] [German *Bußtag.*—KC]
[2.] Literary estate of Elisabeth Bornkamm; handwritten. See also *NL,* A 43,2; photocopy. Previously published in *GS* 4:154–59 and *PAM* 1:387–94. On the first page, the opening words of hymns have been noted in Bonhoeffer's handwriting: "Wenn wir in höchsten Nöten sein [When in the hour of deepest need (*Lutheran Book of Worship,* no. 303)—KC] . . . Es ist gewisslich [The day is surely drawing near (*Lutheran Book of Worship,* no. 321)—KC] . . .Wachet auf [Wake, awake, for night is flying (*Lutheran Book of Worship,* no. 31)—KC].
[3.] [See the Grimms' story "The Bright Sun Brings It to Light," in which a tailor robs and murders a Jew for a few farthings; his crime remains a secret for many years until he casually repeats in his wife's hearing what the dying Jew had said: "The bright sun will bring it to light." The story is soon all over the town, and the tailor is brought to trial and condemned. See *Grimms' Fairy Tales and Household Stories,* 252–53.—KC]

see underneath it a swarm of filthy vermin and creatures of the dark that had hidden themselves here from the sunlight and are now exposed in all their frightening ugliness and trying to scurry away.

¶Such stones can lie around unnoticed for years until some clumsy foot knocks them aside. And such stones, under which no one expects to find anything, are quickly and easily seized upon as hiding places by these dark creatures of our hearts. But the dark things are still afraid; they tremble at every approaching step for fear of being exposed. Afraid of what actually? Other people—who most probably are in the same boat, all condemned together, but nonetheless pointing their long fingers at one another until their own secrets come to light.

¶Yet the course of this world often seems unjust, to the extent that not everything comes to light—only something here and something there, which allows everyone else to be so terribly morally outraged, as long as they have a shred of hope that it won't happen to them, certainly not because they have nothing to hide. So the proverb is not entirely right after all. And because it is not, all humanity can be divided into those whose secrets have come to light and those whose secrets have not. The latter are counted as moral and decent, while the former are considered immoral and despicable.

However, it is possible to live more or less discreetly. To be more discreet in this sense means to know how to stay in the shadows, to keep those things hidden in thoughts and feelings that someone else makes visible through actions. And the state of affairs in this world is that the sun can bring deeds to light, but not thoughts.

But how terribly mistaken we would be if we were satisfied simply to have realized this and therefore just went on living quietly, discreetly—but rotten in our innermost core.   321

The Day of Repentance and our text have more to say than the proverb. This text would not make a proverb. Proverbs must be moralistic and show at least one group of people that they are in the right. Our text does not do that; it doesn't say anyone is in the right. It is not moralistic at all, but rather thoroughly realistic. This text sheds light on the Day of Repentance, such a bright, glaring, dazzling light that it frightens us out of our wits. The Day of Repentance is not really a dark day, but rather a day of alarming brightness and transparency, uncontrollably light filled. In nature there are sometimes such days, when the air is so incredibly transparent that we can make out details that are usually shrouded in haze and distance. The Day of Repentance is this sort of day. Let us talk about this bright Day of Repentance. There is a sun here that has something to bring to light, but this sun, this light that reaches unsparingly into every corner and uncovers what is hidden, is Jesus Christ. And that changes everything.

The Day of Repentance is the day on which we are reminded in a truly unspectacular way—by a word from the Bible—that at the end of our existence, all our life will be uncovered and laid bare. "All of us must appear before the judgment seat of Christ."

We are people of today. Our way of living and thinking is not the Christian way; thus we have settled for a double self-deception about our lives that allows us to live in a certain degree of peace. One deception is in thinking that what has happened, what we have done in the past, has sunk into the dark depths of oblivion—that as long as we and others have more or less forgotten about it, it will stay forgotten. In other words, we live in the belief that forgetting is the ultimate and strongest power. Eternity means oblivion! The other deception under which we live is that we think we can decide between what is hidden and what is revealed, between what is secret and what is public. Each of us lives a public, visible life revealed to all, and in a completely separate compartment each of us has a hidden, secret life of thoughts, feelings, and hopes that no other person ever knows. We would be paralyzed with fear at the idea that all the thoughts and feelings we have had in just one day might suddenly lie open to the eyes of the world. We live under the very natural assumption that what is hidden stays hidden.

Yet here we see our lifelong comfortable assumptions unmasked, revealed as completely unjustified illusions. Eternity is not oblivion, but rather memory—eternal memory. Whatever happens in time, happens in this world, is preserved for all eternity. It leaves unavoidably immortal footprints.[4] This is why our forebears left us the image of the Book of Life, in which our lives are recorded.[5] The blank page has been written on. Nothing has been forgotten. For everything we do is done in the sight of the everlasting God; this is why it is preserved for all eternity. It makes no difference whether we have forgotten or not. God does not forget.

And another thing: for God there is no difference between what is hidden and what is secret.[6] To God, everything is as transparent as light. "For darkness is as light to you," says the psalm.[7] Because God is light,[8] because God is openly revealed, then we must also be in the light and stand revealed before God. That is why, before God, there are no secrets. That is why every secret will be revealed to God; that is why the end of all things means the revelation of all mysteries, the mysteries of God and those of humankind.

[4.] Crossed out: "it is written into God's plan."
[5.] Rev. 20:12.
[6.] Instead of "secret," Bonhoeffer must have meant "revealed."
[7.] Evidently an allusion to Ps. 139:12.
[8.] Cf. 1 John 1:5.

"For all of us must appear before the judgment seat of Christ, so that each may receive recompense for what has been done in the body, whether good or evil." That goes against our innermost human nature. We all have things to hide; we have lifelong secrets, worries, ideas, hopes, desires, passions—about which no one else in the whole world knows. There is nothing we are more sensitive about than when people[9] touch on such areas with their questions. And here it says in the Bible, against everything we think of as fair play, that one day at the end we will have to stand revealed before Christ, with all that we are and have been, and not only before Christ but also before all the other people standing there with us. And all of us know that we may be able to stand trial in many a human court, but not in that of Christ. "Lord, who could stand? . . ."[10]

Christ will judge. His spirit will distinguish between the spirits. He who was poor and powerless when he lived among us will in the end pass judgment on the whole world. For each person, therefore, there is only one essential question in life: what position do you take toward this Spirit—how do you stand toward this man Jesus Christ? Toward any other spirit, toward any other person, there are several possible positions to take. The ultimate decision does not depend on these. Toward Jesus Christ, there can only be an absolute Yes or an absolute No. For Christ is the Spirit against which every human spirit will be tested. Christ alone is the one whom no one can avoid, no one can pass by—even when we think we can stand on our own and be our own judge. No person is his or her own judge. Christ alone is the judge of humankind. No person is the judge over anybody else—Christ alone is the judge of us all, whose judgment is everlasting. And whoever has tried to pass him by here on earth without clearly saying Yes or No, will at the hour of death, at the moment when our lives are weighed for all eternity, have to stand face to face with Christ, to look into his eyes. His question will then be: have you lived in love toward God and your neighbor, or have you lived for yourself? Here there will be no escape, no excuses, no talking yourself out of it . . . here your whole life lies open to the light of Christ, "so that each may receive recompense for what has been done in the body, whether good or evil."

What a fearful moment that is to think about, when the book of our whole lives is opened, when we come face to face with what we have said and done against God's commandments, when we stand face to face with Christ and cannot defend ourselves. Lord, who could stand?

323

324

[9.] Crossed out: "and the church."
[10.] Ps. 130:3.

But the Bible is never intended to terrify us. God does not want human beings to be afraid, not even of the Last Judgment. We are to know about all this so that we can understand about life and its meaning. God lets people know about it now, today, so that today we can lead our lives in the open awareness and the light of the Last Judgment. We are to know for only one reason—so that we human beings will find the way to Jesus Christ, so that we will turn from our evil ways, turn back and seek to encounter Jesus Christ. God does not want to frighten people but sends us the word about the judgment only so that we will reach out more passionately, more hungrily for the promise of God's grace. It is so that we will recognize that by ourselves we do not have the strength to stand before God, that before God we must certainly pass away, but that in spite of everything God does not want us to die, but rather wants us to live.

Christ sits in judgment. That is truly a serious matter. Yet Christ sits in judgment, which also means that we are judged by the merciful one who lived among tax collectors and sinners, who was tempted as we are,[11] who carried and endured our sorrows, our fears, and our desires in his own body, who knows us and calls us by our names.[12] Christ sits in judgment, which means that grace is the judge, and forgiveness, and love—whoever clings to them has already been acquitted.[13] Those, of course, who want to be judged by their own works, Christ will judge and pass sentence based on those works. But we should be joyful when we think about that day. We need not tremble and hold back, but give ourselves gladly into his hands. Luther dared even to speak of it as that dear day of judgment.[14] So as we leave worship on the Day of Repentance, let us be not downcast but joyful and confident. Come, Judgment Day, we look forward to you with joy, for then we shall see our merciful Lord and clasp his hand, and he will receive us with open arms.

325

What about the "good and evil" about which Christ will ask us on that final day? The good is nothing other than our asking for and receiving his grace. The evil is only fear and wanting to stand before God on our own and justify ourselves. To repent, therefore, means to be in this process of turning around, turning away from our own accomplishments and receiv-

---

[11.] Heb. 4:15.

[12.] Cf. Isa. 43:1.

[13.] [Cf. what Bonhoeffer, eleven years later, was to write of himself to Eberhard Bethge in one of his last known letters from prison, on August 23, 1944: "My past life is brim-full of God's goodness, and my sins are covered by the forgiving love of Christ crucified" (*LPP*, 393).—KC]

[14.] For example in a sermon in 1539: "Therefore the Day of Judgment will be a time of rejoicing for you, far more so than the wedding day is for the bride; for this terrible Day has been converted into a happy and desirable Day for you" (*LW* 22:385).

ing God's mercy. Turn back, turn back! the whole Bible calls to us joyfully. Turn back—where? To the everlasting mercy of the God who never leaves us, whose heart breaks because of us, the God who created us and loves us beyond all measure. God will be merciful—so come then, Judgment Day. Lord Jesus, make us ready. We await you with joy. Amen.

3. Sermon on Wisdom 3:3
London, Remembrance Sunday,[1] November 26, 1933[2]

Wis. 3:3: . . . but they are at peace.

Two questions have brought us to church today, questions about which we human beings are never satisfied. They drive us from one place to another and burn continually within our souls, so that we never find rest on this earth. And now here in church they are seeking the answer, the truth, the solution to the riddle: Where have our dead gone? Where shall we be after our own death?

¶The church claims to have the answer to this final, most impossible question that people have. Indeed, the only reason the church exists is that it knows the answer to this ultimate question. If it did not know how to speak with all humility, but also with all conviction in this matter, then it would be nothing more than a pathetic society of the hopeless and the desperate, trying to interest one another in their sufferings and being a burden to one another. But that is just what Christ's church is not. We are here to talk not about our sufferings but about our salvation—not about our skepticism but about our confident hope. Skepticism is of no interest to us—it is never what people do not believe that is interesting, but rather that people do believe and hope, and what they believe—that alone is the important part. Church is the place of unshakable hope.

326

Where have our dead gone? Here we are today, remembering their death; in memory we see them again before us—those whom we loved—as we saw them that last time. That image has stayed with us like no other. We can feel again the way in which, at that sight, we totally forgot our own selves, how infinitely vain and empty our own lives appeared to us in that hour; how our gaze was fixed as if spellbound on that dear person, so inexplicably still, who could only remain silent about the mystery that he or she had now discov-

[1.] German *Totensonntag.* See 1/17, ed. note 2.
[2.] *NL*, A 43,3; typewritten copy, with handwritten corrections, probably by Eberhard Bethge. Previously published excerpt in *GS* 4:160–65 and *PAM* 1:394–402. Cf. 1/17.

ered. The person has gone over, has set out on the road from which no one comes back, and is now in a hallowed state of knowing and seeing that which is given to no living person. He or she has become an earth dweller as never before, sleeping quietly in the earth—but is also so far away from the earth, and marked by another world, as he or she never was in life. Today perhaps we must think of long, tormented hours, of illness and struggle and agitation—until death came, and all was very still and quiet. We remember how we sat dazed and stupefied by the bed, not yet understanding what had really happened, only needing to ask the same question over and over in the same tone: What happened? Where are you? And perhaps we were still asking the same question as we carried the dead person to the grave, and perhaps today it is still the same question that we call after him or her: Where are you? Where are you?

Perhaps we have long since resigned ourselves to the fact that it is all over for these persons, that they have sunk back into the nothingness from which they once came. But still our love cannot stop looking for them, from asking everywhere if anyone knows where our dear one has gone. A cry of pain rises from the depths and echoes through the world: the mother calling her child, the child its mother, the husband his wife; friend calls to friend, brother to brother, love weeps for its lost beloved: Where are you? Where are you, our dead whom we love?

327

In silence you went away from us, left us alone, and went into a strange land that no one knows. Why don't you speak to us? Where are you? Do you have to wander now, eternally, from one life to another? Are you all alone in the cold night of the grave, or are you forced to wander about in torment, finding no rest? Are you close by, around us? Do you have to suffer as we do, or perhaps much more dreadfully than we do? Are you longing for home, for warmth, for love, for us? Or is death like sleep for you, eternally dreaming and dozing, a weary sleep? Speak to us, why are you so far away?

But they do not speak. And when people think they have been able to call up the spirits of the dead in occult seances, there may well be all sorts of things going on between heaven and earth that we cannot know or comprehend, but one thing is certain: it is not our dead who appear here. They have been taken away from us—they are in the hand of God, and no torment will ever touch them.[3] We cannot torment them with our tears and pleas and conjuring. They do not speak. They are forever silent.

But who will answer our question? Who has an answer to love's questioning? Not even the church can make the dead speak or can call up their spir-

---

[3.] Wis. 3:1.

its. But what is the church to say to the mother who comes to it for refuge, asking about her child? What can it tell the child about his or her mother? What does it tell the wife, or the dear friend? It does not point to where the dead are, it does not say this or that about them. It does not point toward the world of the occult or show us the way into the world of the dead. It points only toward God. The world of the occult is still a human world that we can reach; it is accessible through all sorts of magic. But the realm of God is beyond all human worlds. No one can tell us about it but God and the one whom God sent, Christ. This is the world in which we must look for our dead.

¶So when someone comes to the church with the burning question, where are my loved ones who have died? he or she is told first of all to turn to God. There is no way to know anything about the dead without believing in God. God is the Lord of the dead; their fate is in God's hands. Only those who know about God will know anything about their dead loved ones. But this then also means that questions about the dead should not be asked self-ishly. It is not we who are the lords of the dead. Whoever wants to ask about them and really get an answer, whoever is not to be satisfied with small comfort, must dare to approach God and ask directly. And God will answer. For it is God's will to be revealed to human beings who come and ask, who are longing for the word, the answer, the truth of God, who believe it when they receive it. To them, God will speak of this mystery.

Now, today, the God of peace and everlasting love is telling this mystery anew to the congregation that is God's own, and only to the congregation. It is for those who believe in God, and God tells it to the congregation as an ultimate certainty: Those whom you seek are with me, and they are at peace. The realm of God is peace, the final peace after the final struggle. God's peace means rest for those whom life has made weary; it means safety and security for those who have wandered without anyone to care for and watch over them; home for the homeless, calm for those who are worn out with struggling, relief for tormented and wounded hearts, consolation for those who are distressed and weeping, the chance to sleep for those trembling with exhaustion . . . God's peace is like a mother's hand consolingly stroking the forehead of her sobbing child. As a mother comforts her child, so I will comfort you.[4] Your dead are comforted with God's own comfort: it is God who has wiped away their tears and put an end to their restless pursuits—they are at peace.

Above the beds of the dying, where strong and restless lives are fighting fearfully toward death, until with a heavy sigh it is all over . . . the word is

328

[4.] Isa. 66:13.

clearly heard: "But they are at peace."

At the last moments of those who have sinned greatly, for whom death seems to hold the awful horrors of damnation, who are in despair with remorse and repentance, Christ himself appears and closes their eyes as they die, and says: "But they are at peace."

Over the coffins of children and the elderly, over the coffins of the devout, who in simple faith in their last hour placed their hope only in Christ, the angels sing: "But they are at peace."

While we who are left behind see only suffering and fear and anguish and self-reproach and remorse, where we see only hopelessness and nothingness, God says: "But they are at peace."

God's "But . . ." is set over against all our thinking and seeking. It is God's "But . . ." that does not leave the dead to die but awakens them and draws them close. It is God's "But . . ." that makes death into a sleep from which we awaken into a new world. It is God's "But . . ." that brings the dead into paradise. "Truly, I tell you, today you will be with me in Paradise,"[5] says Christ to the thief who hangs next to him on the cross and repents. "But" they are at peace—this truly means not something that is self-evident but rather something completely new, the ultimate of ultimates, and it is God who makes it happen. Not our peace, but God's peace.

Let it be said again: there is no room here for selfish questioning. All our knowledge and all our hope come only from looking to God, whom we trust to do everything and whose word we believe: I am the resurrection and the life.[6] Because I live, you also will live.[7] And we can never hear about this realm of God, which is not our world, about this kingdom of peace into which our loved ones who have died have gone ahead of us, without an immeasurable longing that steals over us, an indescribable homesickness for that world, like children waiting to go into the room where the Christmas tree is—where there will be joy in fullness and blessed stillness.[8] No one has yet believed in God and the kingdom of God, no one has yet heard about the realm of the resurrected, and not been homesick from that hour, waiting and looking forward joyfully to being released from bodily existence.

Whether we are young or old makes no difference. What are twenty or thirty or fifty years in the sight of God? And which of us knows how near he

---

[5.] Luke 23:43.

[6.] John 11:25.

[7.] John 14:19.

[8.] Cf. verse 12 of Paul Gerhardt's hymn "Die güldne Sonne" (The golden sun): "Joy in fullness and blessed stillness await me there in heaven's garden fair."

329

or she may already be to the goal? That life only really begins when it ends[9] here on earth, that all that is here is only the prologue before the curtain   330 goes up—that is for young and old alike to think about. Why are we so afraid when we think about death? Why are we so anxious when we imagine lying on our deathbed? Death is only dreadful for those who live in dread and fear of it. Death is not wild and terrible, if only we can be still and hold fast to God's Word. Death is not bitter, if we have not become bitter ourselves. Death is grace, the greatest gift of grace that God gives to people who believe in him. Death is mild, death is sweet and gentle; it beckons to us with heavenly power, if only we realize that it is the gateway to our homeland, the tabernacle of joy,[10] the everlasting kingdom of peace.

Perhaps we say, I am not afraid of death, but I am afraid of dying. How do we know that dying is so dreadful? Who knows whether, in our human fear and anguish, we are only shivering and shuddering at the most glorious, heavenly, blessed event in the world? Whether we are only like a newborn baby, wailing as it first sees the light of this world? What about all the strange things we experience at the bedsides of dying persons—are they not evidence of this? What does it mean when such a person, after long struggling and wrestling and being afraid, at the last moment suddenly opens his or her eyes wide, as if seeing something glorious, and cries out, God, that's beautiful![11] We ask, what does this mean?

Yes, death is indeed frightening, bony old Death with his scythe, inviting one person after another to the dance of death, ready or not—if a person does not have faith, if he or she is not among the righteous of whom our scripture says: But they are at peace.

Death is hell and night and cold, if it is not transformed by our faith. But that is just what is so marvelous, that we can transform death. When the fierce apparition of the death's head, which frightens us so, is touched by our   331 faith in God, it becomes our friend, God's messenger; death becomes Christ himself. Yes, these are great mysteries. But we are allowed to know about them, and our life depends on them. Those who believe will have peace,

---

[9.] [Cf. Bonhoeffer's last recorded words, to Payne Best, on April 8, 1944, on being taken from Schönberg for court-martial and execution at Flossenbürg: "This is the end— for me the beginning of life" (*DB-ER*, 927, and *DBWE* 16, 1/239).—KC]

[10.] The German word here is *Freudenzelt*. The hymn "O Ewigkeit, du Donnerwort" (Eternity, O thunderous word), by Johann Rist, ends with the words: "Into your tabernacle of joy (*Freudenzelt*) be pleased to take me, Jesus, Lord."

[11.] Franz Hildebrandt, who heard this Remembrance Day sermon in person, recalled this passage in his June 1945 memorial address broadcast on BBC radio (Bethge, *Bonhoeffer-Gedenkheft*, 14).

death will not frighten them;[12] it can no longer touch them, for they are in the hand of God, and no torment will ever touch them.

Many are those who have tried to make a friend of death; but at the last hour it proved disloyal to them, it became their enemy. There is only one way to have death as a friend, and that is the way of faith. And then, then death becomes our best friend. Then one day, as we lie dying, we will hear the word of God ring out: "They are at peace." And our eyes will overflow with joy when we see the kingdom and its peace.

Perhaps it sounds childish to you that we speak this way. But in the face of such things as these, can we do otherwise than talk like children? In the face of these things can we be anything other than children, who really have no idea what it is about? And would we really want it otherwise? Would we want to be otherwise when we come into God's kingdom and are allowed to share in that day of joy? Look at children when they are full of joy and decide for yourself if you want to be better than that, and whether we should be ashamed to be so. "As a mother comforts her child, so I will comfort you."[13]

Jesus has called us children of the resurrection.[14] Homesick children, that is what we are when all is as it should be with us.

> Then through this life of dangers
> I onward take my way;
> But in this land of strangers
> I do not think to stay.
> Still forward on the road I fare
> That leads me to my home.
> My Father's comfort waits me there,
> When I have overcome.[15]
> Amen.

[12.] "Frighten them" replaces "cause them agony."

[13.] Isa. 66:13.

[14.] Luke 20:36.

[15.] Verse 6 from the hymn by Paul Gerhardt, "Ich bin ein Gast auf Erden" (I am a visitor on earth) [English translation by Catherine Winkworth in *The Chorale Book for England*, 1865—KC].

4. Sermon on Luke 21:28
London, First Sunday in Advent, December 3, 1933[1]

332

Luke 21:28: Now when these things begin to take place, look up[2] and raise your heads, because your redemption is drawing near.

You all know about accidents in mines. In the last few weeks we have had to read over and over in the papers about such an accident.[3] The men who have to go down every day into the mine shafts, deep into the earth, to do their work are constantly in danger that some day one of the tunnels will collapse or that they will be buried alive by an underground explosion. Then they are down there in the earth, where it is dark as night, left all alone. Their fate has caught up with them.

¶This is the moment that even the bravest miner has dreaded all his life. Shouting can do no good, no more than raving and running head-on into the wall. Neither will it help to exhaust his strength in efforts to get out. But the more a human being realizes that he is totally helpless, the more he rages, while around him all remains silent. He knows that up above people have come running, that women and children are crying—but the way is blocked; he cannot reach them. Nothing is left for him but his final moments. He knows that people are working feverishly up there. His mates are digging with dogged energy through the rock toward the ones who are trapped. Perhaps here and there some will still be found and rescued, but down here in the depths of the farthest shaft there is no hope anymore. All that remains now is torment, waiting for death.

¶But then, suppose he should suddenly hear a faint sound, as if of knocking, of hammering, of rocks breaking, and then of faraway voices calling, calling into the emptiness and darkness; and this banging and digging gradually gets louder, until suddenly, with a mighty blow, the hammering comes close

---

[1.] Literary estate of Elisabeth Bornkamm, handwritten. See also *NL,* A 43,4; photocopy. Partially reproduced in *GS* 4:166–70 and *PAM* 1:402–9.

[2.] [The NRSV reads "stand up," whereas the German Bible reads "look up" (*sehet auf*). Because Bonhoeffer uses the latter image in his sermon, the German meaning has been followed here.—KC]

[3.] [*DBW* 13 here refers to a "major accident in November 1933 in a mine in Wales." The accident nearest in time to this date, however, occurred on Sunday, November 19, 1933, at Grassmoor near Chesterfield in Derbyshire, England, when an underground explosion killed fourteen miners: "The men were trapped by a fall of roof and gassed a mile underground and over a mile from the pit shaft. . . . Bands of rescuers in gas masks descended the pit immediately, some in their 'Sunday' clothes, and worked three hours with pick and shovel before the first body was reached" (front-page item in *News Chronicle,* November 20, 1933).—KC]

333   by, echoing back, and at last a friend's deep voice, one of his mates, shouts
his name: Where are you? Help is coming!

¶Then all at once the despairing man leaps up, his heart almost bursting
with excitement and waiting, and screams with all his might: "I'm here, here,
help me!—I can't get through, I can't help, but I'm waiting, I'm waiting, I
can hold on till you come. Just come soon . . ." And he listens, beside himself
with concentration, as each blow comes nearer. Each passing second seems
like an hour. He can't see anything at all, but he can hear the voices of his
helpers. Then a last, wild, desperate hammer blow rings in his ear. Rescue is
at hand, only one more step and he will be free . . .

¶You know, don't you, why I am talking about this on this first of Advent?
What we have been talking about here is Advent itself. This is the way it is;
this is God coming near to humankind, the coming of salvation, the arrival
of Christ . . . look up and raise your heads, because your redemption is drawing near.

To whom might these words be spoken? Who would be interested in hearing them? Who would get excited on hearing something like this? Think of
a prison. For many years, the prisoners have borne the humiliation and punishment of being in prison. They have endured the misery of heavy forced
labor, until they have become a burden to themselves. Often one or another
of them has tried to escape but was either caught and dragged back again,
and then it was even harder, or he was hunted down and shot. The rest bear
their fate and their chains with sighing and tears. Then suddenly a message
penetrates into the prison: Very soon you will all be free, your chains will be
taken away, and those who have enslaved you will be bound in chains while
you are redeemed. Then all the prisoners look up, in chorus, with a heart-
breaking cry: Yes, come, O Savior![4]

Think of the sick. Think of someone who is tormented by an incurable
disease, dying slowly, slowly in unspeakable pain, longing only for the end of
this misery. And then comes the day when the doctor can say to him or her,
quietly and firmly: "Today you will be released." Then the mortally ill person
lifts his or her head joyfully, looking toward this release.

334   *And now think of the people* who are oppressed, not by outward imprisonment or physical disease, but by a heaviness in their souls. Think of the people with secrets, of whom we were speaking on Repentance Day,[5] people
living with guilt that has never been forgiven, for whom the meaning of life

---

[4.] [Cf. Bonhoeffer's reflections on his own prison experience in Tegel ten years
later, in his letter to Eberhard Bethge of November 21, 1943: "Life in a prison cell may
well be compared to Advent; one waits, hopes, and does this, that, or the other . . . the
door is shut, and can be opened only *from the outside*" (*LPP*, 135).—KC]

[5.] See 3/2, p. 327.

has been lost and with it all the joy of life. Think of us ourselves, trying to live in obedience to Christ and failing again and again. Think of the son who can no longer look his father in the eye, the husband who cannot face his wife; think of all the [. . .],[6] deep brokenness and hopelessness[7] that grows out of all these situations. Then let us hear the words again: Look up and raise your heads, because your redemption is drawing near. You shall be free from all that, the anguish and fear in your souls will come to an end. Salvation is near. (As a father says to his child: Look up here, not down at the ground; look at me, I'm your father . . . this is what it says in the gospel: look up and raise your heads, because your redemption is drawing near.)

So then, whom is this text actually addressing? People who know that they are unredeemed people, that they are in bondage and in chains, that they are in the power of a slave driver, so that they have to work without wages—people like the man trapped underground, like the prisoners, who are still watching and waiting for freedom, for true redemption—those people who would like to be redeemed people. Those to whom it is *not* addressed are all those who have become so used to their condition that they no longer even notice that they are prisoners, who, for so many practical reasons, have settled for being unredeemed—who have become so indifferent and dull that they don't even react if someone calls to them: Your salvation is near!

¶It is not for the well-satisfied with their full stomachs, this word of Advent, but rather for the hungry and the thirsty. *It knocks at their door*, powerfully and insistently. And we hear it, just as the miner trapped in the mine heard and followed with all the energy he had left, every hammer blow, every new stage as the rescuer approached. Is it even imaginable that he would have paid attention to anything else, from the moment when he heard the first knocking—anything except his approaching liberation? What the first of Advent   335
says is no different: Your redemption is near! It is knocking at your door now; can you hear it? It wants to make its way through all the rubble and hard stone of your life and of your heart. That will not happen very fast. But he is coming, Christ is clearing his way toward you, toward your heart. He wants to take our hearts, which have become so hard, and soften them in obedience to him. He keeps calling to us during these very weeks of waiting, waiting for Christmas, to tell us that he is coming, that he alone will rescue us from the prison of our existence, out of our fear, our guilt, and our loneliness.

Do you want to be redeemed? That is the one great, decisive question that Advent puts to us. Is there any remnant burning in us of longing, of recognition of what redemption could mean? If not, then what do we want from

---

[6.] Handwriting undecipherable.
[7.] "Hopelessness" replaces "humiliation."

Advent? What do we want from Christmas? . . . a little sentimentality, a little inward uplifting . . . a nice atmosphere? But if there is something in us that wants to know, that is set on fire by these words, something in us that believes these words—if we feel that once more, once more in our lives, there could be a complete turning to God, to Christ—then why not just be obedient and listen and hear the word that is offered us, called out to us, shouted in our ears? Redemption is near, don't you hear? Wait, wait just a moment longer, and you will hear the knocking grow louder and more insistent from hour to hour and from day to day. Then Christmas will come, and we will be ready. God is coming to us, to you and me—Christ the Savior is born.

Perhaps you will say yes, this is what you have always heard in church, and nothing ever really happened. Why didn't anything happen? Because we didn't want it to happen, we didn't want to hear or to believe; because we said: it may be that one or another of those who were trapped are saved, but as for us, so deeply buried, so distant, so out of the habit of these things, surely the Savior will never reach us. We aren't really devout; we don't have any gift for religious belief—we'd like to, but this just doesn't speak to us.

336 ¶But with all that we are only talking ourselves out of it. How can we tell, if we haven't ever tried it?[8] If only we really wanted to—if it weren't all just talk and trying to get out of it—then we would finally, finally begin praying and pray that this Advent would come into our hearts too. Let us not deceive ourselves. Redemption is near, whether we know it or not.[9] The question is only: Will we let it come in to us too, or will we refuse it entry? Will we let ourselves be caught up in this movement, which is coming down to earth from heaven, or will we close ourselves off from it?[10] Christmas is coming, with or without us[11]—it is up to each of us to decide.[12]

That such a genuine Advent produces something quite different from a fearful, petty, downtrodden, weak sort of Christianity, such as we often see, and which often tempts us to be scornful of Christianity itself, that is made clear by the two powerful challenges that introduce our text. Look up, lift your heads! Advent makes people human, new human beings. We, too, can become new human beings at Advent time.

[8.] Uncertain reading.

[9.] Crossed out: "it can get through the hardest rock."

[10.] Crossed out: "Sie ist auf der Bahn" (It is on the way); cf. the closing words of the Advent hymn, "Nun jauchzet all, die Frommen" (Now rejoice, all ye faithful), by Michael Schirmer: "hold your lamps ready, at your posts be steady, he is on the way."

[11.] Crossed out: "or against us."

[12.] Crossed out: "Many people would be ashamed to become Christians. They say it is such an outdated, childish, depressing affair."

¶Look up, you there who are staring emptily[13] down at the earth, who are transfixed by the little events and changes taking place on the surface of this earth. Look up at these words, you who have turned away from heaven in disappointment. Look up, you whose eyes are heavy with tears, with weeping for that which this world has mercilessly snatched away from us. Look up, you who feel so loaded down with guilt that you cannot[14] raise your eyes—look up, your redemption is drawing near. Something different is happening from what you see every day, something much more important, infinitely greater and mightier—if only you would take it in, be on the watch for it, wait just a moment longer, wait, and something completely new will break into your lives. God will come to you, Jesus is coming to take you for his own, and you will be redeemed people. Look up, be on the watch, keep your eyes open, watch, and wait for your redemption, which is drawing near.

337

Lift up your heads, the host of you who are bowed down, humiliated, despondent, like a beaten army with heads hanging. The battle is not lost—raise your heads, the victory is yours! Take courage, fear not, do not be worried or anxious. Be of good cheer, be assured of the victory, be strong, be valiant [männlich]. This is no time to shake your head, to doubt and look away—freedom, salvation, redemption is coming. Look up and wait! Raise your heads! Be strong and without fear!—for Christ is coming.

Again let us ask: Can we hear it now, the knocking, the driving, the struggling forward? Can we feel something in us that wants to leap up, to free itself and open up to the coming of Christ? Do we sense that we are not just talking in images here, but that something is really happening, that human souls are being raised up, shaken, broken open, and healed? That heaven is bending near the earth, that the earth is trembling and people are desperate with fear and apprehension and hope and joy? That God is bending down to humankind, coming to us where we live? Can the trapped miner pay attention to anything but the hammering and knocking of his rescuers? Can anything be as important to us as paying attention to this same hammering and knocking of Jesus Christ in our lives? Can we do anything, amid whatever is happening, other than to stop and listen, to tremble and reach out to him? Something is at work, within us too. So let us not block the way but rather open up to him who wants to come in. Once when Luther was preaching on our text during Advent, in the middle of winter, he announced: "Summer is near, the trees want to burst forth in blossom. It is springtime."[15] Whoever has ears to hear will hear.[16] Amen.

[13.] "Emptily" replaces "fixedly."
[14.] "Cannot" replaces "do not wish to."
[15.] WA 10, I/2, 114 and 120.
[16.] "Will hear" replaces "let them hear." Cf. Matt. 13:43.

338 **5. Sermon on Luke 1:46–55**
London, Third Sunday in Advent, December 17, 1933[1]

Luke 1:46–55:

> And Mary said,
> "My soul magnifies the Lord,
>   and my spirit rejoices in God my Savior,
>   for he has looked with favor on the lowliness of his servant.
>   Surely, from now on all generations will call me blessed;
> for the Mighty One has done great things for me,
>   and holy is his name.
> His mercy is for those who fear him
>   from generation to generation.
> He has shown strength with his arm,
>   he has scattered the proud in the thoughts of their hearts.
> He has brought down the powerful from their thrones,
>   and lifted up the lowly;
> he has filled the hungry with good things,
>   and sent the rich away empty.
> He has helped his servant Israel,
>   in remembrance of his mercy,
> according to the promise he made to our ancestors,
>   to Abraham and to his descendants forever."

The song of Mary is the oldest Advent hymn. It is also the most passionate, the wildest, and one might almost say the most revolutionary Advent hymn that has ever been sung. This is not the gentle, tender, dreamy Mary as we often see her portrayed in paintings. The Mary who is speaking here is passionate, carried away, proud, enthusiastic. There is none of the sweet, wistful, or even playful tone of many of our Christmas carols, but instead a hard, strong, relentless hymn about the toppling of the thrones and the humiliation of the lords of this world, about the power of God and the powerlessness of humankind. This is the sound of the prophetic women of the Old Testament—Deborah,[2] Judith,[3] Miriam[4]—coming to life in the mouth of Mary. Mary, who was seized by the power of the Holy Spirit, who humbly

---

[1.] Literary estate of Elisabeth Bornkamm; handwritten. See also *NL,* A 43,5; photocopy. Previously published in *GS* 5:498–504 and *PAM* 1:409–15.

[2.] Cf. Judg. 4 and 5.

[3.] Cf. Jth. 8–16.

[4.] Cf. Exod. 15:20–21.

and obediently lets it be done unto her as the Spirit commands her, who lets the Spirit blow where it wills[5]—she speaks, by the power of this Spirit, about God's coming into the world, about the Advent of Jesus Christ.

¶She, of course, knows better than anyone else what it means to wait for Christ's coming. She waits for him differently than does any other human being. She expects him as his mother. He is closer to her than to anyone else. She knows the secret of his coming, knows about the Spirit, who has a part in it, about the Almighty God, who has performed this miracle. In her own body she is experiencing the wonderful ways of God with humankind: that God does not arrange matters to suit our opinions and views, does not follow the path that humans would like to prescribe. God's path is free and original beyond all our ability to understand or to prove.[6]

                                                       339

There, where our understanding is outraged, where our nature rebels, where our piety anxiously keeps its distance—that is exactly where God loves to be. There, though it confounds the understanding of sensible people, though it irritates our nature and our piety, God wills to be, and none of us can forbid it. Only the humble believe and rejoice that God is so gloriously free, performing miracles where humanity despairs and glorifying that which is lowly and of no account.[7] For just this is the miracle of all miracles, that God loves the lowly. God "has looked with favor on the lowliness of his servant." God in the midst of lowliness—that is the revolutionary, passionate word of Advent.

¶It begins with Mary herself, the carpenter's wife: as we would say, a poor working man's wife, unknown, not highly regarded by others; yet now, just as she is, unremarkable and lowly in the eyes of others, regarded by God and chosen to be mother of the Savior of the world. She was not chosen because of any human merit, not even for being, as she undoubtedly was, deeply devout, nor even for her humility or any other virtue, but entirely and uniquely because it is God's gracious will to love, to choose, to make great what is lowly, unremarkable, considered to be of little value. Mary, the tough, devout, ordinary working man's wife, living in her Old Testament faith and hoping in her Redeemer, becomes the mother of God. Christ, the poor son of a laborer from the East End of London, Christ is laid in a manger . . .

    [5.] Cf. John 3:8.

    [6.] "In her own body . . . or to prove" inserted subsequently. The remainder of this insert, crossed out: "just as a king does not first become regal only when he sits on his throne, but also when he goes incognito among his people and when no one can forbid him to do so. So God, too, freely chooses which paths to take."

    [7.] "There, where our . . . and of no account" marks the continuation and end of the insertion.

340 ¶God is not ashamed of human lowliness but goes right into the middle of it, chooses someone as instrument, and performs the miracles right there where they are least expected. God draws near to[8] the lowly, loving the lost, the unnoticed, the unremarkable, the excluded, the powerless, and the broken. What people say is lost, God says is found; what people say is "condemned," God says is "saved." Where people say No![9] God says Yes! Where people turn their eyes away in indifference or arrogance, God gazes with a love that glows warmer there than anywhere else. Where people say something is despicable, God calls it blessed. When we come to a point in our lives where we are completely ashamed of ourselves and before God; when we believe that God especially must now be ashamed of us, and when we feel as far away from God as ever in all our lives—that is the moment in which God is closer to us than ever, wanting to break into our lives, wanting us to feel the presence of the holy and to grasp the miracle of God's love, God's nearness and grace.[10]

"Surely, from now on all generations will call me blessed!" sings Mary joyfully. What does it mean to call her blessed, Mary, the lowly maidservant? It can only mean that we worship in amazement the miracle that has been performed in her, that we see in her how God regards and raises up the lowly; that in coming into this world, God seeks out not the heights but rather the depths, and that we see the glory and power of God by seeing made great what was small. To call Mary blessed does not mean to build altars to her, but rather means to worship with her the God who regards and chooses the lowly, who "has done great things for me, and holy is his name." To call Mary blessed means to know with her that God's "mercy is for those who fear him from generation to generation," who are amazed as we reflect on the ways of God,[11] who let the Spirit blow where it wills, who obey it and say humbly, together with Mary: Let it be with me according to your word.[12]

341 When God chooses Mary as the instrument, when God decides to come in person into this world, in the manger in Bethlehem, this is not an idyllic family occasion but rather the beginning of a complete reversal, a new ordering of all things on this earth. If we want to be part of this event of Advent and Christmas, we cannot just sit there like a theater audience and enjoy all the lovely pictures. We ourselves will be caught up in this action, this reversal of all things; we will become actors on this stage. For this is a play in which each

---

[8.] "Draws near to" replaces "loves."
[9.] "No!" replaces "Out!"
[10.] "When we come to a point . . . nearness and grace" inserted subsequently.
[11.] "Are amazed . . . ways of God" replaces "give honor to God."
[12.] Luke 1:38.

spectator has a part to play, and we cannot hold back. What will our role be? Worshipful shepherds bending the knee, or kings bringing gifts? What story is being enacted when Mary becomes the mother of God, when God comes into the world in a lowly manger?

¶The judgment and redemption of the world—that is what is happening here. For it is the Christ Child in the manger himself who will bring that judgment and redemption. It is he who pushes away the great and mighty of this world, who topples the thrones of the powerful, who humbles the haughty, whose arm exercises power against all who are highly placed and strong, and whose mercy lifts up what was lowly and makes it great and glorious. So we cannot come to this manger in the same way as we would approach the cradle of any other child. Something will happen to each of us who decides to come to Christ's manger. Each of us will have been judged or redeemed before we go away.[13] Each of us will either break down or come to know that God's mercy is turned toward us.

What does this mean? Is it not just a figure of speech, the way pastors exaggerate a beautiful, pious legend? What does it mean to say such things about the Christ Child? If you want to see it as just a way of speaking, well, then go ahead and celebrate Advent and Christmas in the same pagan way you always have, as an onlooker. For us it is not just a figure of speech. It is what we have said: that it is God, the Lord and Creator of all things, who becomes so small here, comes to us in a little corner of the world, unremarkable and hidden away, and wants to meet us and be among us as a helpless, defenseless child—not as a game or to charm us, because we find this so touching, but to show us where and who God really is, and from this standpoint to judge all human desire for greatness, to devalue it and pull it down from its throne.[14]

342

The throne of God in the world is set not on the thrones of humankind but in humanity's deepest abyss, in the manger. There are no flattering courtiers standing around his throne,[15] just some rather dark, unknown, dubious-looking figures, who cannot get enough of looking at this miracle and are quite prepared to live entirely on the mercy[16] of God.

For those who are great and powerful in this world, there are two places where their courage fails them, which terrify them to the very depths of their souls, and which they dearly avoid. These are the manger and the cross of Jesus Christ. No one who holds power dares to come near the manger; King

---

[13.] "Each of us . . . go away" replaces "will have encountered grace or judgment."
[14.] Crossed out: "Where is Christmas here."
[15.] Crossed out: "who are afraid of his great power."
[16.] "On the mercy" replaces "on such lowliness on the part of."

Herod also did not dare. For here thrones begin to sway, the powerful fall down, and those who are high are brought low, because God is here with the lowly. Here the rich[17] come to naught,[18] because God is here with the poor and those who hunger. God gives the hungry plenty to eat, but sends the rich and well-satisfied away empty. Before the maidservant Mary, before Christ's manger, before God among the lowly, the strong find themselves falling; here they have no rights, no hope, but instead find judgment.

And even if today they think nothing will happen to them, it will come tomorrow or the next day. God puts down the tyrants from their thrones; God raises up the lowly. For this Jesus Christ came into the world as the child in the manger, as the son of Mary.

In eight days we will celebrate Christmas, for once really as the festival of Jesus Christ in our world. Before that, there is something we must clear up, something very important in our lives. We need to make clear to ourselves how, from now on, in the light of the manger, we are going to think about what is high and what is low in human life. Not that any of us are powerful persons, even if we would perhaps like to be and don't like to have that said to us. There are never more than a few very powerful people. But there are many more people with small amounts of power, petty power, who put it into play wherever they can and whose one thought is: keep climbing higher! God, however, thinks differently, namely, keep climbing down lower, down among the lowly and the inconspicuous, in self-forgetfulness,[19] in not seeking to be looked at or well regarded or to be the highest. If we go this way, there we will meet God himself. Each of us lives among persons who are the so-called higher-ups and others who are the so-called lowly. Each of us knows someone who is lower in the order of things than we ourselves. Might this Christmas help us learn to see this point in a radically different way, to rethink it entirely, to know that[20] if we want to find the way to God, we have to go, not up to the heights, but really down to the depths among the least of all, and that every life that only wants to stay up high will come to a fearful end?

God is not mocked.[21] It does not escape God's notice that we celebrate Christmas from year to year without taking it seriously. And we can count on God's word. At Christmas, when the Holy One, full of power and glory, lies

[17.] Crossed out: "and well-satisfied."

[18.] "Come to naught" replaces "become helpless and without hope"; crossed out: "and are sent away empty."

[19.] "Self-forgetfulness" replaces "selflessness."

[20.] Crossed out: "all our contrariness."

[21.] Gal. 6:7.

in the manger, the mighty will be brought down from their thrones if they do not at last turn again and repent.

It is an important matter for a Christian congregation to come to an understanding of this point, and having realized it, to draw the consequences for its members' life together. There is reason enough here to reconsider a number of things in our own congregation in this light.

Who among us will celebrate Christmas rightly? Who will finally lay down at the manger all power and honor, all high regard, vanity, arrogance, and self-will? Who will take their place among the lowly and let God alone be high? Who will see the glory of God in the lowliness of the child in the manger? Who will say with Mary: The Lord has looked with favor on my lowliness. My soul magnifies the Lord, and my spirit rejoices in God my Savior. Amen.

6. Meditation on Luke 9:57–62   344
London, New Year's Day, January 1, 1934[1]

Beginning with Christ

Luke 9:57–62: As they were going along the road, someone said to him, "I will follow you wherever you go." And Jesus said to him, "Foxes have holes, and the birds of the air have nests; but the Son of Man has nowhere to lay his head." To another he said, "Follow me." But he said, "Lord, first let me go and bury my father." But Jesus said to him, "Let the dead bury their own dead; but as for you, go and proclaim the kingdom of God." Another said, "I will follow you, Lord; but let me first say farewell to those at my home." Jesus said to him, "No one who puts a hand to the plow and looks back is fit for the kingdom of God."

"The road to hell is paved with good intentions"—this saying is found in many different countries. But it is not the worldly wise, impertinent statement of someone who refuses to do better. No, it rather reveals a profound Christian insight. Anyone who knows nothing better to do on New Year's Day than to make a list of bad things he or she has done and then decide from now on—how many such "from now ons" have we heard before!—to start off with better intentions is still far from being a Christian.

¶ *First* of all, such a person thinks that a good intention is enough for a new beginning. That is, he or she supposes that one can make a new start

---

[1.] *Gemeindebote für die deutschen evangelischen Kirchen in Großbritannien*, no. 1, January 7, 1934; see also *NL*, A 43,19; typewritten copy. Previously published in *GS* 4:171–74 and *PAM* 1:416–19. Cf. the interpretation in *DBWE* 4:59–61 and 115.

entirely on one's own, whenever one wants to. This is an evil illusion. It is God alone who makes a new beginning with a person, when God is pleased to do so, and not the human being who undertakes to do it with God. So a new beginning is not something one can do for oneself. One can only pray for it to happen. As long as people rely only on themselves and try to live that way, that is still the old way, the same way as in the past. Only with God is there a new way, a new beginning. And we cannot command God to do anything; all we can do is pray. But we can pray only when we have realized that there is something we cannot do for ourselves, that we have reached our limit, that someone else must be the one to begin.

¶ *Second*, if you are relying entirely on your own good intentions, you have no idea where they come from. You had better take another look. Our so-called good intentions are nothing other than the products of a weak and fearful heart, which is afraid of bad deeds and sins and is arming itself with all too human weapons to fight these powers. But anyone who is afraid of sin is already fully caught up in it. Fear is the net spread by the Evil One, in which we can easily become entangled and brought to a fall. If we are afraid, we have already fallen in, just as someone who is overcome by fear during a difficult mountain climb is sure to stumble.

So nothing comes of making good resolutions out of fear or anxiety. They will not bring us to a new beginning. The road to hell is paved with good intentions.

How do we find our way to a new beginning? Our text tells us about a young man who is obviously very taken with Jesus, who perhaps has been waiting a long time for a chance to express his enthusiasm. Now here comes Jesus into the town, and the enthusiast runs to meet him, stands in front of him, and says: I will follow you wherever you go. He wants to make the first move himself: with glowing devotion he offers himself, thinking he will be able to do everything asked of him and to leave everything behind, for this man. But Jesus demurs, suspicious of this enthusiasm. Do you know what you are doing? Do you know who I am, and where following me is going to lead you? Do you know that I need not someone who throws himself at me with enthusiasm, but rather someone with a firm, unshakable faith based only on my having called you? Have I called you? Are you coming simply and only in answer to my call? You are enthusiastic; you want to make a new beginning: think about what you are doing and whom you are daring to approach and remember that enthusiasm is only one step away from embarrassment!

Jesus himself calls to the second person in the story. This is someone living in the past, hanging onto some significant grief that he cannot forget. This person no longer looks forward to the future but would rather fade away into the past and into the world of the dead. Jesus' call is to step forward, out of all that. The person hesitates, wants to go back once more. No, "Let the dead bury their dead"—leave the past behind, free yourself—now or never. Christ calls you to a new beginning—take your chance, just because it is he! Now, today, because Christ is moving on—go with him, answer his call, now!

The third person surely would like to go with Christ. This is someone who takes it seriously and therefore surely can be allowed to attach a small condition to the offer to come and follow Jesus. "Please let me first . . ." Certainly I want to come, but surely you understand, Lord, I just need to do this and that "first." No, Christ doesn't understand, doesn't want to understand. "No one who puts his hand to the plow . . ." A man guiding a plow does not look back, but he also doesn't look way ahead into the unpredictable distance—only as far as the next step he has to take. Looking back is not the Christian thing to do. Leave your fear, worry, and guilt behind. Look up at the one who has given you a new beginning. Through him you will forget everything else.

The coming year will have its share of fear, guilt, and hardship. But let it be, in all our fear, guilt, and hardship, a year spent with Christ. Let our new beginning with Christ be followed by a story of going with Christ. What that means is beginning each day with him. That is what matters.

7. Sermon on Jeremiah 20:7   347
London, Third Sunday after Epiphany, January 21, 1934[1]

Jer. 20:7:

> O LORD, you have enticed me,
>   and I was enticed;
> you have overpowered me,
>   and you have prevailed.

Jeremiah was not eager to become a prophet of God. When the call came to him all of a sudden, he shrank back, he resisted, he tried to get away. No, he did not want to be a prophet and a witness for this God. But as he was running away, he was seized by the word, by the call. Now he cannot get

---

[1.] Literary estate of Elisabeth Bornkamm; handwritten. See also *NL*, A 43,8; photocopy. Previously published in *GS* 5:505–9 and *PAM* 1:425–30. This sermon was composed in the tense days before Hitler's reception for the church leaders. Bonhoeffer had tried through various appeals to influence the outcome of this event. See 1/55–1/62 [and *DB-ER*, 342–45—KC].

away anymore, it's all up with him, or as one passage says, the arrow of the Almighty has struck down the hunted game.[2] Jeremiah is his prophet.

It comes over a person from the outside, not from the longings of one's own heart; it does not rise up out of one's most unseen[3] wishes and hopes. The word that confronts us, seizes us, takes us captive, binds us fast, does not come from the depths of our souls. It is the foreign, the unfamiliar, unexpected, forceful, overpowering word of the Lord that calls into his service whomsoever and whenever God chooses. Then it is no good trying to resist, for God's answer is: Before I formed you in the womb I knew you.[4] You are mine. Fear not! I am your God, I will uphold you.[5]

¶And then all at once this foreign, this faraway, unfamiliar, overwhelming word becomes the incredibly familiar, incredibly near, persuading, captivating, enticing word of the Lord's love, yearning for his creature. It has thrown a lasso over the person's head, and there is no getting away anymore. Any attempt to struggle only shows even more how impossible it is, for the lasso will only pull tighter, a painful reminder of one's captivity. So the person is now a captive and must simply follow the path ordained for him or her. It is the path of someone whom God will not let go anymore, who will never again be without God: this means the path of someone who will never again, come good or evil, be God-less.

This path will lead right down into the deepest situation of human powerlessness.[6] The follower becomes a laughingstock,[7] scorned and taken for a fool, but a fool who is extremely dangerous to people's peace and comfort, so that he or she must be beaten, locked up, tortured, if not put to death right away. That is exactly what became of this man Jeremiah, because he could not get away from God. He was accused of fantasizing, being stubborn, disturbing the peace, and being an enemy of the people, as have those in every age even up to the present day who were seized and possessed by God—for whom God had become too strong.

¶Imagine how Jeremiah would have preferred to talk differently—how gladly he would have joined with others in shouting "Peace" and "Well-

348

[2.] "Or . . . game" replaces "God has 'set me as a mark for his arrow'"; cf. Lam. 3:12–13.

[3.] "Unseen" replaces "secret."

[4.] Jer. 1:5.

[5.] Echoes of Isa. 41:10 and 43:1; cf. also J. S. Bach's cantata "Fürchte dich nicht" (Fear not) (BWV 153.3).

[6.] "Will lead . . . powerlessness" replaces "is an extremely dangerous path."

[7.] [Cf. the continuation of the verse on which the sermon is based, but not quoted in the opening text, Jer. 20:7b: "I have become a laughingstock all day long; everyone mocks me."—KC]

being!"[8] where there was in fact strife and disaster.[9] How happy he would have been to have kept quiet and agreed that they were right to say so. But he simply couldn't; he was compelled and under pressure, as if someone were breathing down his neck and driving him on from one prophecy of truth to the next and from agony to agony. He was no longer his own master, no longer in control of himself. Someone else had power over him and possessed him; he was possessed by another. And Jeremiah was just as much flesh and blood as we are, a human being like ourselves. He felt the pain of being continually humiliated and mocked, of the violence and brutality others used against him. After one episode of agonizing torture that had lasted a whole night, he burst out in prayer: "O Lord, you have enticed me, and I was enticed; you have overpowered me, and you have prevailed."

God, it was you who started this with me. It was you who pursued me and would not let me go, and who always appeared in front of me wherever I went, who enticed and captivated me. It was you who made my heart submissive and willing, who talked to me about your yearning and eternal love, about your faithfulness and might. When I looked for strength you strengthened me; when I looked for something to hold onto, you held me; when I sought forgiveness, you forgave my guilt. I would not have wanted it thus, but you overcame my will, my resistance, my heart. God, you enticed me so irresistibly that I gave myself up to you. O Lord, you have enticed me, and I was enticed. I had no idea what was coming when you seized me—and now I cannot get away from you anymore; you have carried me off as your booty. You tie us to your victory chariot and pull us along behind you, so that we have to march, chastened and enslaved, in your victory procession. How could we know that your love hurts so much, that your grace is so stern?

¶You have overpowered me, and you have prevailed. When the thought of you grew strong in me, I became weak. When you won me over, I lost; my will was broken; I had too little power; I had to follow the way of suffering, I could no longer resist, I[10] could no longer turn back; the decision about my life had been made. It was not I who decided, but you who decided for me. You have bound me to you for better or worse. God, why are you so terrifyingly near to us?

Today in our home church, thousands of parishioners and pastors are facing the danger of oppression and persecution because of their witness for

349

[8.] [German *Heil*. Cf. the cry in Nazi rallies, "Sieg Heil!" and the salutation "Heil Hitler!"— KC]

[9.] Cf. Jer. 6:14: "They have treated the wound of my people carelessly, saying, 'Peace, peace,' when there is no peace."

[10.] Crossed out: "didn't have enough strength."

the truth.[11] They have not chosen this path out of arbitrary defiance, but because they were led to it; they simply had to follow it—often against their own wills and against their own flesh and blood. They followed it because God had become too strong for them, because they could not withstand God any longer, because a door had closed behind them, and they could no longer go back beyond the point where they received the word, the call, the command of God. How often they must have wished that peace and calm and quietness would finally return; how often they must have wished that they did not have to keep on threatening, warning, protesting, and bearing witness to the truth! But necessity is laid upon them. "Woe to me if I do not proclaim the gospel!"[12] God, why are you so close to us?

Not to be able to get away from God is the constant disquieting thing in the life of every Christian. If you once let God into your life, if you once allow yourself to be enticed by God, you will never get away again[13]—as a child never gets away from its mother, as a man never gets away from the woman whom he loves. The person to whom God has once spoken can never forget him entirely but will always know that God is near, in good times and in bad, that God pursues him, as close as one's shadow. And this constant nearness of God becomes too much, too big for the person, who will sometimes think, Oh, if only I had never started walking with God! It is too heavy for me. It destroys my soul's peace and my happiness. But these thoughts are of no use; one cannot get away, one must simply keep going forward, with God, come what may. And if someone thinks he can no longer bear it and must make an end of things—then he realizes that even this is not a way to escape from the presence of God, whom he has allowed into his life, by whom he has been enticed. We remain at God's mercy; we remain in God's hands.

Yet at this very point, when someone feels unable to go any further on the path with God, because it is too hard—and such times come to each one of us—when God has become too strong for us, when a Christian breaks down under God's presence, and despairs, then God's nearness, God's faithfulness, God's strength become our comfort and our help. Then we finally, truly recognize God and the meaning of our lives as Christians. Not being able to get away from God means that we will experience plenty of fear and despair, that we will have our troubles, but it also means that in good times and in bad we can no longer be God-less. It means God with us everywhere we go, in times of faith and times of sin, in facing persecution, mockery, and death.

[11.] For the events of the preceding months, see, for example, 1/73.
[12.] 1 Cor. 9:16.
[13.] Crossed out: "you will be driven by God."

¶So why be concerned about ourselves, our life, our happiness, our peace, our weakness, our sins?[14] If only the word and the will and the power of God can be glorified in our weak, mortal, sinful lives, if only our powerlessness 351 can be a dwelling place for divine power. Prisoners do not wear fancy clothes; they wear chains. Yet with those chains we glorify the victorious one who is advancing through the world, through all humankind. With our chains and ragged clothes and the scars we must bear, we praise the one whose truth and love and grace are glorified in us. . . . The triumphal procession of truth and justice, of God and the gospel, continues through this world, pulling its captives after it in the wake of the victory chariot.

Oh, that God would bind us at the last to his victory chariot, so that we, although enslaved and in chains, might share in the holy victory! God has persuaded us, become too strong for us, and will never let us go. What do our chains matter, or our burdens,[15] our sins, sorrows, and death? It is God who holds us fast and never lets us go. Lord, entice us ever anew and become ever stronger in our lives, that we may believe in you alone, live and die to you alone, that we may taste your victory.

8. Sermon on Psalm 98:1
London, Cantate Sunday, April 29, 1934[1]

Cantate
Ps. 98:1: O sing to the Lord a new song . . .

Today, on Cantate Sunday, let us speak about how we can praise our God through song and music. The God of Jesus Christ and how this God is worshipped by God's congregation here in music—let's talk about that.

Those of us who can remember the first time we ever went to church certainly remember above all the thunderous sound of the organ, which made an unforgettable impression and will be associated with[2] worship for all time

---

[14.] Crossed out: "We are captives, we are bound."
[15.] Crossed out: "That is our confidence and strength."

[1.] Literary estate of Elisabeth Bornkamm; handwritten. See also *NL*, A 43,9; typewritten copy. Previously published in *GS* 5:510–15 and *PAM* 1:440–46. [This sermon is of particular interest because of Bonhoeffer's love of music and his own musicianship. He was an accomplished pianist and as a youth had nearly opted for music rather than theology as a career. See *DB-ER*, 24–25, 32, 37, 328; Bonhoeffer's discussion of the "polyphony" of life in *LPP*, 303; and the treatment of this theme in Bonhoeffer in de Gruchy, *Christianity, Art, and Transformation*.—KC]
[2.] Crossed out: "our first."

352   for us. Half startled, half afraid, half awed, and half inwardly drawn toward it—so we might describe the turmoil in our soul at that moment. Heaven must be like that, when the angels and the saints are singing, up there before the throne of God. Who doesn't hear echoes of this first encounter with the music of the church, even today?

But perhaps there are also some of us who have belonged since childhood to those Reformed churches that do not allow an organ or any musical instrument in God's house, so as not to demean or obscure through human interference the glory of God's word as it is proclaimed through the Holy Scriptures.[3] These people might be feeling the sound of the organ as an impermissible human attempt to proclaim the glory of God in some way other than through God's word. They may be feeling a quiet anxiety and horror when they hear music in church.

A story is told about the great Italian Renaissance poet Petrarch, that one day he was looking down from a mountain in northern Italy at the blossoming countryside and was overcome by the feeling: O God, how beautiful, how beautiful this world is! But the next moment he crossed himself, took out his prayer book, and began to say his prayers.[4] Here is a person who is frightened by the beauty of this world and of this earth and in his fear runs away from it. He refuses to love this world in its splendor more than the one who created it, the creation more than its Creator. How incredibly dangerous it is for anyone to stand in St. Peter's in Rome, to hear and to love the heavenly voices of the Sistine Chapel choir[5]—if we do not hear and love the true voice of God[6] in the simplicity of the biblical language. How near it is to blasphemy, to take the man in a carpenter's smock, with his plain, clear,

353   simple, functional words, and celebrate him with such a rich and splendid human work of art that it makes us forget the poverty and humility of Jesus Christ.

To love God's creation more than we love God—this is the profound danger and temptation for all those who would love music for the sake of God. So let us not by any means despise those who avoid such dangers by letting God's word alone be heard in their churches. They are very serious about

---

[3.] In their early days the Reformation in Zurich under Zwingli and to a less radical extent Dutch Calvinism did not permit organ music in worship [and derivatively, the English Puritans and Separatists and the Scottish Presbyterians were for a long time hostile to any form of music in church except congregational psalm singing—KC].

[4.] Petrarch's famous account of his ascent of Mount Ventoux on April 26, 1336, is found in his *Epistolae.*

[5.] A trip to Rome in 1924 had made indelible impressions on Bonhoeffer (see *DBWE* 9:88, 91, and 107, and also *DB-ER*, 56–65).

[6.] Replaced "the Father."

it, with much knowledge of the uniqueness and exclusiveness, the irreplace-ability[7] and sobriety of the divine revelation. The word of God needs no ornamentation.

Let us keep this clearly in mind: the word of God, as it comes to us in [the] Bible and in the proclamation of his gospel, does not need ornamentation. It is clothed in its own glory, its own beauty—that certainly is true. But like exceptional human beauty, even the word of God cannot escape being adorned by those who love it. However, like every adornment of true loveliness, adorning the word of God cannot be anything other than letting its own beauty shine even more gloriously. Nothing foreign to it, nothing false, nothing artificial, no glittering trinkets or cosmetics, nothing that conceals its intrinsic beauty, but rather that which reveals it and makes it visible, should be used to adorn it.

Those who have loved this word of God throughout two thousand years have not let themselves be prevented from bringing the finest they had with which to adorn it. And[8] what could be the finest if not that which is unseen, namely, an obedient heart? But out of these obedient hearts grew the visible work and audible song to the glory of God and Jesus Christ. And here we have a book that contains fifteen hundred years of such singing to the glory of Jesus Christ.[9] Some artificial and unsuccessful adornments are found in it, as well as some that are incomparably noble and honorable.[10] And it is really a shame how little we often know of the very finest of our human heritage that lies hidden here and how seldom we turn to it.

But how can we find a key by which to distinguish the genuine and good from the false and miscarried art? Let us take an allegory: the human soul is a harp and the word of God, as it touches the soul, is the harpist. It is the purity of the harp strings and the extent to which they are well tuned that makes the melody sound pure and clear as it comes forth from the soul in praise of the harpist. And how often the strings are out of tune, how often they produce discord, how often what comes out of our mouths sounds as

354

[7.] Uncertain reading: German *Unersetzlichkeit*; but perhaps *Widersetzlichkeit* ["unruliness" or "contrariness"—KC].

[8.] Crossed out: "yet this word has shaken off every adornment" [replacing "refused every adornment"].

[9.] Bonhoeffer had introduced into his parishes the *Gesangbuch für die deutschen Auslandsgemeinden* (Hymnal for German parishes abroad) in the revised version published in the early 1930s. See 2/1, p. 303.

[10.] Cf. Bonhoeffer's lecture [about the history of German hymns—KC] on the occasion of the 1936 Berlin Olympics, "The Inner Life of the German Evangelical Church" (*GS* 4:385–90 and *DBW* 14, 2/21).

though all the strings are broken, and only a wild, wailing, tormented, discordant screech comes from our lips.

Certainly it can also happen that a storm sweeps across the strings and makes them sound—a storm of passion, of rebellion or outrage against one's fate, or perhaps a quiet moaning and crying—and then the song, the music that is heard is rather a glorification of ourselves, our passions, our love, our hate, our despair, our grief, and our sense of power.

This is what makes the great and crucial difference: whether it is God who is the harpist, or our own sufferings and passions—whether our singing and music making is to the glory of God and Jesus Christ alone, or whether it is the human being who is its measure and its focus. Bach wrote at the top of all his manuscripts: *soli deo gloria*, or *Jesu juva*, and it is as though Bach's music was nothing other than the untiring praise of God. Beethoven's music, on the other hand, seems to be nothing but the eternal expression of human suffering and passion. That is why we listen to Bach in church, and not to Beethoven.[11]

This profound contrast can be found all through our hymnal. There are many hymns in it that glorify the moods, longings, and feelings of human beings much more than the acts of God. But equally there are other hymns that focus on nothing other than the glory, power, love, and grace of God, in which human beings and their presumed greatness vanish altogether. These are very essentially the hymns of the Reformation era. Here the greatness of God and God's miraculous deeds come through with elemental power; human beings appear small but magnificent, made worthy to praise and worship this all-powerful God. Try comparing hymns written before 1680[12] with those of pietism, and the difference is inescapable.

Tolstoy once said that the czar should not allow Beethoven to be played by good people, since his music stirs up people's passions too deeply and thus puts people at risk. Luther, on the other hand, often said that music was the best thing we have, next to the word of God.[13] They each had something different in mind: Tolstoy was thinking of that music which glorifies human-

---

[11.] [For a positive appreciation of Beethoven by Bonhoeffer, however, see his comments in *LPP*, 240.—KC]

[12.] Replaces "up to the early 1700s."

[13.] See particularly Luther's letter to Ludwig Senfl of October 4, 1530: "Indeed I plainly judge, and do not hesitate to affirm, that except for theology there is no art that could be put on the same level with music, since except for theology [music] alone produces what otherwise only theology can do, namely, a calm and joyful disposition. Manifest proof [of this is the fact] that the devil, the creator of saddening cares and disquieting worries, takes flight at the sound of music almost as he takes flight at the word of theology" (*LW* 49, II, 428).

kind, Luther of music to the glory of God. And Luther knew that this latter music has dried innumerable tears, brought joy to the depressed, satisfied desires, raised up those who were cast down, strengthened the troubled; that it has brought forth tears again out of stubborn hearts and compelled great sinners to repentance in the face of God's goodness.

O sing to the Lord a *new* song. The emphasis is on the word *new*. What is this new song, if it is not a song that makes someone a *new* person, when a person leaves darkness and worry and fear behind and breaks forth into new hope, new faith, new confidence? The new song is the one that awakens God's presence anew in us—even if it is a very old song, of the God who, as Job[14] says, "gives songs in the night."[15] The song of praise in the night of our lives, of our suffering and our fear, in the night of our death[16]—this is the new song. The song[17] that calls the foolish to stop and think, the sinner to turn around, the homeless to come home, the stubborn to weep, and those who weep to rejoice—the song that calls the infant to God at baptism, calls boy and girl to confess their faith at confirmation, calls bride and groom to obedience and faithfulness, and announces the hope of the resurrection at the bedside of the dying and by the open grave—this is the new song of Christ, the Lord and Savior.

O sing to the Lord a new song—and yet all our songs are only a reflection of the song of songs, which sings of eternity before the throne of Jesus Christ or, like the images in the Bible, speaks of the shouts of joy—"Holy!" and "Hallelujah!"—from the angels in heaven and all the saints to the Father, the Son, and the Holy Spirit.[18] The hope of Christians in every time has never imagined this eternity in God without its being filled with[19] an ocean of sound, of harps and singing. Images are only images, yet they have their rightness. Why should not we, here and now, look forward to that new song that will embrace us when we finally close our eyes, the purest, sweetest, hardest, and most violent of all songs. O sing to the Lord a new song—yes, Lord, we come with songs on our lips. Let your song grow strong when ours fall silent, let the angels play when we drop our hands; when we lie on our deathbed, let your song resound, which no mortal can hear. Lord, we hasten to join in your new song. *Jesu juva*—help us, Jesus. Amen.

356

[14.] Job 35:10.

[15.] [German Luther Bible version. NRSV translates "gives strength in the night."—KC]

[16.] [Cf. how Bonhoeffer was to draw strength in his imprisonment from reciting psalms and (especially Gerhardt's) hymns. See *LPP*, 27, 40, 128, and 368.—KC]

[17.] Crossed out: "that calls the sinner to repentance."

[18.] Cf. Isa. 6:3; Rev. 14:2–3 and 19:1–7.

[19.] "Filled with" replaces "bathed in."

357 **9. Marriage Sermon on Ruth 1:16–17**
London, May 3, 1934[1]

Ruth 1:16–17: ... for whither thou goest, I will go; and where thou lodgest, I will lodge: thy people shall be my people, and thy God my God: Where thou diest, will I die, and there will I be buried: the LORD do so to me, and more also, if ought but death part thee and me.[2]

This day of your marriage is indeed a day of great joy, not only for you, but also for your families, for your friends and for this congregation. It is— humanly spoken—the most joyful moment in man's[3] life to find another man's love. To love and to be loved—this is the height of human happiness, this seems to be the ultimate meaning of life, the only experience which is fulfilling all human longing, striving, hope and desire. Man hungers after love.[4] Everything seems empty and useless to him if there is no love in one's life and everything becomes great, important and colourful through love. But also God hungers after love, he wants to love and to be loved. That is the kinship of man and God; and it is therefore that man cannot help thinking of God whenever he is experiencing love in his life. God himself is love.[5] He loves and he wants to be loved.

Still our love is not God's Love. For God's love is never selfish, seeketh not her own, beareth all things, believeth all things, endureth all things. God's love never faileth[6]—but our love—how soon does it fail, how selfish, how impatient is it! Our love needs to be sanctified and purified in its very depth by God's love.

We know what [a] serious and daring word it is if a man promises his love, his faithfulness and his truth to another man.[7] We know how weak and unsteady man's nature is and how little he knows about the true meaning of

---

[1.] *NL*, A 43,21; handwritten; in original English, including errors. Bonhoeffer's literary estate also includes a typewritten copy with a heading in Eberhard Bethge's handwriting: "Wedding of Frank Goetz and Doris Dickens on May 3, 1934, in the German Reformed St. Paul's Church, London. Ruth 1:16–17."

[2.] [King James Version. Bonhoeffer presented a Bible, signed by himself, to the bridal couple at the service; it is now in the possession of their daughter Ruth Colman (letter of Ruth Colman to KC, December 30, 2003).—KC]

[3.] [Throughout this English sermon it is clear that whenever Bonhoeffer speaks of "man" he is speaking inclusively of male and/or female, as with the German *Mensch*, "person." Cf. the German translation of this sermon in *DBW* 13:508–10.—KC]

[4.] "After love" replaces "to love and be loved."

[5.] Allusion to 1 John 4:16.

[6.] Allusion to 1 Cor. 13:5–8.

[7.] [See ed. note 3.—KC]

love and faithfulness. We do not want to close our eyes before the fact that every marriage is a great venture, indeed comparable only to the venture of Christian faith and obedience of God. But as soon as men realize what they are enterprising[8] when they want to get married, they lift their eyes up to God who alone is the true love and faithfulness. You have come here to ask God for his help, for his strength, for his advice. Only with his help you can dare to promise what you will have to promise now before Him and His congregation. The meaning of this promise is expressed in the word which I have read to you: "*Whither thou goest,* I will go, where thou lodgest, I will lodge."—Whither thou goest—do we realize what that means? do we know which way life will force us to go, do we know where the future will compel us to lodge? Whither thou goest—I will go. What is the only basis for such a promise? *Thy people shall be my people* and thy God my God—this is the answer. Thy people . . . this has a special meaning for you both—both of you are of the same descent, both of you of the same nationality—and it is with deep thankfulness that you look back today to what these streams of influence have meant to you from your childhood on—and having this in common you will go through many difficulties of life more easily than many others.

But still deeper than that—*thy God is my God.* Husband and wife may have everything in common,—if they disagree in this very crucial and most personal point, their marriage will be a hard, not to say an almost impossible task. To be married in a true christian sense means to be able to pray together. We thank God, that he has been with you all your life-time, that he has made you faithful members of his congregation. You were baptized, you were confirmed in this church, you have been taking part for many years in the most beautiful activity of our Church, in the church-choir, it is true to you that you may say to one another today: Thy God is my God. You will take all your love, all your faithfulness from Him who alone makes life worth living and love worth loving. In this service you will service each other. Life is service—love is service—marriage is service—it is God's will that we serve him by serving our neighbour. If ought but death shall part thee and me— that is the ultimate word man can say to each other. May God, the Lord of all life, the Father of all love, bless this word on your life and make it real to you in the years to come. This is our prayer.[9]

358

359

[8.] "Enterprising" replaces "daring."

[9.] On another sheet is an apparently alternate conclusion: ". . . of a marriage. If ought but death shall part thee and me—that is the ultimate word a man can speak to another man. This congregation, your parents your friends are praying with me that God may bless this word on your life and make it real to you in the years to come . . . Text . . . Amen."

10. Sermon on 1 Corinthians 2:7–10
London, Trinity Sunday, May 27, 1934[1]

May 27, 1934   **Trinity**   **1 Cor. 2:7–10**

But we speak God's wisdom, secret and hidden, which God decreed before the ages for our glory. None of the rulers of this age understood this; for if they had, they would not have crucified the Lord of glory. But, as it is written [Isa. 64:4],

> "What no eye has seen, nor
>   ear heard,
>   nor the human heart conceived,
> what God has prepared for those
>   who love him"—

these things God has revealed to us through the Spirit; for the Spirit searches everything, even the depths of God.

The lack of mystery in our modern life means decay and impoverishment for us. A human life is of worth to the extent that it keeps its respect for mystery.[2] By honoring mystery, we keep within us some of the child we used to be. Children keep their eyes wide open, wide awake, because they know that they are surrounded by mystery. They don't yet have this world figured out; they haven't yet learned to make their way by avoiding its mysteries, as we do. We do away with mystery, because we sense that it takes us to the limits of our existence—because we want to master everything and have it at our disposal. That is just what a mystery will not let us do. Anything *mysterious* is *uncanny* for us—we cannot do anything with it. We are not *at home* with it; it points toward another kind of "being at home."[3]

¶However, to live without mystery means not to know anything about the secrets of our own lives or those of other people, or of the world's secrets. It means passing by that which is hidden within ourselves, other people, and the world, staying on the surface, taking the world seriously only to the extent to which it can be *calculated* and *exploited*,[4] never looking for what is behind the world of calculation and of gain. To live without mystery means not to see the most important things that happen in life, even to deny that

360

[1.] Literary estate of Elisabeth Bornkamm; handwritten. See also *NL*, A 43,10; typewritten copy. Reprinted in *GS* 5:515–20 and *PAM* 1:446–51.

[2.] A previous beginning to this sermon, crossed out, says: "Human beings have value to the extent that they keep their respect for mystery."

[3.] [In these last two sentences Bonhoeffer is using a wordplay in German: *Geheimnis* (mystery), *unheimlich* (uncanny), *daheim* (at home), *Daheimsein* (being at home).—KC]

[4.] "Exploited" replaces "used."

they exist.[5] It is our refusal to know that a tree has roots in the dark realm of the earth, that everything living here in the light has come forth from the dark, secret place of the womb, and that all our thoughts, too, all our spiritual life, also come from a hidden, secret, dark place, like our body, like everything that lives. *That the roots of all that is clear and obvious and understandable lie in mystery*, that is what we do not want to hear. If we do hear it, then we want to get to the bottom of this mystery, to calculate and explain it. We want to dissect it, and we thereby only succeed in killing the life in it and still do not find the mystery. The mystery remains a mystery. It eludes our grasp.

¶However, *mystery does not mean simply not knowing something*. The greatest mystery is not the most distant star; to the contrary, the closer something is to us, the better we know it, the more mysterious it becomes to us. The person farthest away from us is not the most mysterious to us, but rather the neighbor. And the mystery of that person will not be diminished for us the more we find out him or her; instead, he or she will become ever more mysterious to us, the closer we come together. The very deepest mystery is when two persons grow so close to each other that they *love* each other. Nowhere in the world can a human being sense the power and the splendor of the mysterious as deeply as here. When two people know everything about each other, the mystery of their love becomes infinitely great between them. Only within this love do they understand each other, know all about each other, fully recognize each other. And yet the more they love each other and know about each other through love, the more they realize the mystery of their love. Thus knowledge does not dispel the mystery but only deepens it. *That the other person is so close to me, that is the greatest mystery.*[6]

Why are we saying all this today, on the day when we are supposed to be talking about God the *Holy Trinity*? We say it to draw attention, in a very human way, to that concept that we are always losing sight of and without which there is simply no way to come near to understanding the idea of God the Holy Trinity—that is, the concept of mystery.

"But we speak God's wisdom, secret and hidden . . ." The thoughts of God are not obvious to us; we cannot arrive at them by common sense.[7]

361

[5.] "Not to see the most important things that happen in life" replaces "to deceive ourselves on purpose."

[6.] [Cf. what Bonhoeffer writes ten years later in prison, in his "Outline for a Book": "The transcendental is not infinite and unattainable tasks, but the neighbor who is within reach in any given situation" (*LPP*, 381; *DBW* 8, 4/187, p. 558). Indeed, this whole sermon makes for suggestive reading as a preliminary to Bonhoeffer's exploration of a "religionless Christianity" in the prison writings, where a renewed understanding of "mystery" is an important theme. Cf. *LPP*, 135, 158, and 282.—KC]

[7.] ["Common sense": Bonhoeffer actually uses the term in English here.—KC]

God cannot simply be grasped in the way we might expect to do it; instead, the church speaks of the *secret and hidden wisdom of God.* God lives in mystery. To us, God's very being is mystery, from everlasting to everlasting; a mystery because it speaks of a home in which we cannot—not yet—be at home. All the thoughts that we can ever think about God should never be for the purpose of solving this mystery, making God easily understandable and no longer mysterious for everyone. Instead, all our thinking about God must serve only to make us see how completely beyond us and how *mysterious* God is, to make us glimpse the mysterious and hidden wisdom of God in all its mystery and hiddenness, rather than making it any less so—and thus perhaps give us a glimpse of the mystery of that home from which it comes. Every dogma of the church only points to the mystery of God.

362   But the world is blind to this mystery. It wants to have either a God whom it can calculate and exploit or else no God at all. The mystery of God remains hidden from the world. The world does not want it. Instead, it makes its own gods according to its wishes and never recognizes the mysterious and hidden God who is near at hand. "None of the rulers of this world understood this . . ." The rulers of this world[8] live by calculation and exploitation; that is how they come to be great rulers in the eyes of the world. But they do not understand mystery; only children do.

¶The world carries an unmistakable sign that proves it is blind to the mystery of God: the cross of Jesus Christ. If they had recognized him, "they would not have crucified the Lord of glory." That is the unrecognized mystery of God in this world: Jesus Christ. That this Jesus of Nazareth, the carpenter, was the Lord of glory in person, that was the mystery of God. A mystery, because here on earth God became poor and lowly, small and weak, out of love for humankind; because God became a human being like us, so that we might become divine; because God came to us, so that we might come to God. God who becomes lowly for our sake, *God in Jesus of Nazareth—that is the secret and hidden wisdom* . . . "what no eye has seen, nor ear heard, nor the human heart conceived"—God's glory in lowliness and poverty, in his love for humankind. That God did not remain far above human beings but rather comes *close* to us and loves us, *God's love and closeness—that is the mystery of God, the holy mystery prepared for those who love God.*[9]

[8.] [Although the NRSV translation of this passage uses "of this age," the German Bible and Bonhoeffer here use *dieser Welt,* "of this world."—KC]

[9.] A passage crossed out by Bonhoeffer follows: "God's love, God's revelation, Jesus Christ—all this is the expression of God's mystery. But only those who love God share in this mystery of God's love in Jesus Christ. *The mystery is being loved by and loving God.* There

That it is the one God, Father and Creator of the world, who in Jesus 363
Christ loved us even unto death, who in the Holy Spirit opens our hearts to
receive and to love that one God; that there are not three Gods, but only
one, who envelops, creates, and redeems the world from beginning to end;
and that in each of these God is fully God, as Creator and Father, as Jesus
Christ and as the Holy Spirit—that is *the depth of deity,* which we *worship as a
mystery* and *understand as mystery.*

For in all our speaking we can only point to this mystery, God revealed
in the lowliness of Jesus Christ and in the gift of the Holy Spirit to the
whole world. God's self-glorification expressed in love—that is God's essential mystery.

When we say, at the beginning of our worship service, "In the name of
God, the Father, the Son, and the Holy Spirit," we are appealing to this mystery of the love of God.

For hundreds of years the church has been teaching about God the Holy
Trinity. But this is anything but a rationalistic hardening of religion;[10] to
the contrary, it is our continuing effort to point in every way we can toward
the mystery of the living God.

What the doctrine of the Trinity means is immensely simple, so that any
child can understand it. There is *truly only one* God, but this God is perfect
love, and as such God is Jesus Christ and the Holy [Spirit]. The doctrine
of the Holy Trinity is nothing but humankind's feeble way of praising the
mighty, impetuous[11] love of God, in which God glorifies himself and
embraces the whole world in love. It is a call to adoration, to reverence, to
love in which we lose ourselves in God. All glory be to the Father, and to the
Son, and to the Holy Spirit, now and forever. Amen.

---

is no greater mystery in the whole world than this, that God loves us and that we may
love God, and it is not to be compared with any human love, as the Creator cannot be
compared with the creature. The Creator of the world loves you—that's not common
sense, that is mystery, incredible mystery, which only those who are loved by God understand. The mystery is being loved by and loving God; but being loved by God means Jesus
Christ, and loving God means the Holy Spirit. The name of the mystery is therefore
Christ and Holy Spirit, the name of God's mystery is Holy Trinity. 'God has revealed this
to us through *his* Spirit. For the Spirit searches everything, even the depths of God.' No
human eye, no human ear, no human heart can receive God's word, speech, and mystery,
only the Holy Spirit, who is given to us. God's mystery in Christ is so great that it can only
be recognized by those who receive Christ and the Spirit of understanding."

[10.] Cf. Harnack, *Reden und Aufsätze*, 1:254: "The symbol actually contains only titles.
In this sense it is imperfect; for no confession is perfect which does not paint the Savior
before our eyes and make an impression on our hearts."

[11.] Uncertain reading.

364 **11. Baptismal Homily on Joshua 24:15**
London[1]

Joshua 24:15—as for me and my house, we will serve the Lord.[2]

This is not a mere word or a phrase, but it means something very definite. It is a great and joyful day, indeed, when mother and child together give their lives into the hands of Jesus Christ. This common act will bind their lives together much closer than anything else. This day means, indeed, a new start in life. It means a life not ruled by one's own will and desire, but ruled by the will and command of Christ himself. It means the recognition that there must be a superior will above our own will, and superior power above our own power. From now on, your house shall have only one Lord, Jesus Christ, only one will, the will of God, only one spirit, the Holy Spirit. There is no room left for selfishness and egoism—for, [as] for me and my house we will serve the Lord. There would be something wrong with this day if there would not be a real change in your homelife from now on. For Jesus has come to dwell with you and wherever Jesus comes he changes lives and houses.

There are a great many who would say—for me and my house, we will serve our own will, the smoothness[3] in life, wealth, and so on. But, it would be only too short-sighted not to see that neither money or anything else can help us if our soul [is] in need of help. Our soul needs something else, something strong—our soul needs God.—Nobody can foretell the future, and it is no use doing it. But however dark it seems to be, there is only one man who is free from every fear—the man who believes that God is his help.

This baptism is not a formal act or ceremony, but it is God's own word and promise to be with you, to love you, to forgive you all sins, to help you in every need, to sanctify your life, to make you holy and innocent, to make you
365 a child of God. If you believe that God will forgive you and make you holy and help you—then he will forgive you and help you in all your life-time. Do not undertake it easily to become a Christian. It means much, it means everything. Faith matters. Faith means eternal life. We pray that the peace of God which passes all understanding[4] be with you and your child and your house now and ever. Amen.

[1.] *NL*, A 43,22; handwritten; in original English, including errors; Bonhoeffer's literary estate also has a typewritten copy. Bethge's note on the copy, that the occasion was the baptism of Ursula Marianne Willnow, daughter of a consulate secretary in the German embassy, on June 24, 1934, in the Sydenham church, is probably incorrect, since at that baptism Bonhoeffer probably preached in German.

[2.] [Bonhoeffer used the King James Version in this sermon.—KC]

[3.] Uncertain reading; perhaps "success."

[4.] Allusion to Phil. 4:7.

12. Sermon on Luke 13:1–5
London, Sixth Sunday after Trinity, July 8, 1934[1]

Luke 13:1–5   July 8, 1934

At that very time there were some present who told him about the Galileans whose blood Pilate had mingled with their sacrifices. He asked them, "Do you think that because these Galileans suffered in this way they were worse sinners than all other Galileans? No, I tell you; but unless you repent, you will all perish as they did."

Perhaps this text frightens you, and you think it sounds only too much[2] like the news of the day—too dangerous for a worship service. In church we would rather get completely away from the world of the newspapers and the latest sensations. That's right, that is what we are doing here, really getting away from this world. But we want to do it in such a way that it cannot jump on us again almost as soon as we are out the church door and take us captive and oppress us; instead, we want to leave the worship service having *overcome*   366 it.[3]

[1.] Literary estate of Elisabeth Bornkamm; handwritten. See also *NL*, A 43,11; photocopy. Reprinted in *GS* 5:521–27 and *PAM* 1:452–60. It was Bonhoeffer's first sermon after hearing of the murders committed by the Nazis in connection with the so-called Röhm putsch [on June 30 and July 1, 1934, which received instant and wide coverage in the British press, prompting widespread shock and horror. The victims of the putsch included Hitler's rivals in the party, but also the respected Catholic leader Erich Klausener and several others—KC]. Cf. Bonhoeffer's letter of July 13, 1934, to Reinhold Niebuhr (1/127); also 1/146 [on Bonhoeffer's private information that as many as 207 persons had been killed, as reported to him by his brother-in-law Hans von Dohnanyi in the Ministry of Justice—KC].

[2.] "Too much" replaces "rather."

[3.] Bonhoeffer crossed out the next two and a half pages, which said: "As human beings we stand in the midst of the events of this world of ours—we today more than any previous generation. We experience not only the events of our individual lives, of our city and country, but are also drawn into things that are happening in other countries and even the whole world. We cannot get away from them. We are moved, carried along, shaken by them—and if our senses are not dulled by all these many impressions, we feel ever more strongly the close ties that bind all human life together. But we are very different in our personal reactions to these events. Some say it is not Christian and not right to get too deeply involved with life's convulsions—that this is only the world and has nothing to do with the Christian faith. So don't get involved in things that have nothing to do with you, keep your fingers and your eyes away from all the things of the world. Such [people] sometimes make a very [replaces 'rather'] strange distinction—as citizens they are indeed involved in things, sometimes very intensely, but as Christians they want nothing to do with them." The next part was first outlined by Bonhoeffer in words and phrases: "Others see the events . . . the issue of guilt . . . we are fortunate in having a scripture passage that shows how Jesus reacts

367 So it cannot really be our purpose to "get away" from these things by closing our eyes to them or forgetting them as quickly as possible, even for a little
while; but rather to know the position we should take on them *as Christians*.
What matters is not *that* we get away from these things but rather *how* we get
away from them.

There are people who cannot bear to go to a funeral—or rather, do not
want to go. Why not? Because they are afraid of the shock of being that close
to a dead person. They don't want to see this side of human life, and they
think that if they don't look at it, they have managed to get rid of the thing
itself altogether.

There are even people who think themselves particularly *devout* if they
do not see the dark side of life, if they close themselves off from the catastrophes of this world and just lead their own tranquil, pious lives in peaceful
optimism.

But it can never do any good to fool oneself into ignoring the truth, for
in deceiving oneself about the truth of one's own life, one is certainly deceiving oneself about God's truth as well. And it is certainly never pious to close
the eyes that God gave us to see our neighbor and his or her need, simply to
avoid seeing whatever is sad or dreadful.[4] So it can certainly never be the
right way to try to get rid of the things that frighten and depress us.[5]

There is also another way, a much more human and serious way of dealing with these things—but that also turns out to be a very unchristian way.

---

to such news. How does Jesus read the newspaper . . . as an illustration of the human
attitude toward God . . . repentance . . . issue of guilt here too . . . but for *every* person . . .
not judge and think and grasp and accuse, but *repent* . . . Why? because *called by God* . . .
solidarity in guilt . . . Repentance overcomes the world, because God is seen to be right." A
written text follows that was subsequently crossed out as well: "Others are so affected by the
events and the shocks of this life that they can no longer find rest, that for every accident,
every catastrophe they have to ask who is guilty and will only calm down when they think
they have found out who it is. The question of who is right and who is wrong is the central
one for us [replaces: 'concerns us in these cases']. And we all know that it is possible to go
on endlessly about these sorts of questions. But such talk is fruitless in the end and does
not take things seriously enough. We always want to have someone on whom we can unload
all our moral indignation, and someone else who we think is in the right, to whom we can
express all our moral sympathy, in whom we can recognize ourselves and believe that we
too are in the right. To see only in black and white, so that we ourselves can be on the side
of light. But everyone knows that there is no end to such questions, and that here everyone
can see himself or herself as being in the right. It is fruitless, after all, to see things in this
way—we are only scratching the surface, even though we think we are being very serious.
Thus it is also a very unchristian way. We learn this from the text that we have just read."

[4.] "Are closed . . . dreadful" replaces "are misused in such a way that we see only
ourselves."

[5.] The sentences that follow are crossed out: "That is a weak and cowardly way to
behave, but it is true that few among us will think so. The contrast to the person who

Let us take a simple example: suppose we see an accident happen in the street. We see someone get run over. We are unspeakably shocked and stand there stunned for a moment. But then our first thought is: *Whose fault is it?* This is an everyday example of a very common attitude. When something terrible happens to us personally or to our family or our nation [Volk], our first question when we have recovered from the shock is: *Whose fault is it?*[6] And now we cannot rest, our thoughts go back and forth, in our mind's eye we see all the people who are in any way involved with this accident, and we keep examining them more closely and insistently, asking in a more and more embittered way, Whose fault is it? Who is right? Who is wrong? Human beings are moralists through and through. They want to accuse one person and exonerate the other. They want to be the judges of what happens. And *this is their way of dealing with a terrible disaster—by saying that one person is right and the other wrong.* Whether we are thinking of small happenings in our lives or great catastrophes like wars and revolutions, it is the same everywhere. What people want is to be the judge.—Now let us just stop here for a moment.

It is immeasurably valuable for us that Luke—alone among the Gospel writers—has preserved for us the report[7] of how Jesus reacted to such news of a catastrophe that had hit his country, a sensation for the newspapers, we might say, and what he had to say about it.

Jesus was told by eyewitnesses that Pilate had ordered the execution of several Galileans, that is, compatriots of Jesus, apparently as rabble-rousers and enemies of the state. The executions had taken place under circumstances that made the blood of devout Jews boil:[8] the condemned persons were said to have been seized while making their sacrifices in the temple in Jerusalem and thus to have been killed within the temple domain. Truly a report guaranteed to make feelings run high, if anything would, to stir up judgment and counter-judgment and start an energetic political discussion. It must have gone back and forth: Pilate was right—Pilate was wrong; the Galileans were victims of a tyrant—the Galileans got the punishment they deserved. But the prevailing view seems to have been that the Galileans would not have met such a terrible fate, such a fearsome death, if they had not been guilty. Some serious transgression must have been involved, for

368

369

---

refuses to attend funerals is the one who feels best when surrounded by sensational happenings, who prefers the air of the catacombs to the fresh breeze outdoors. Then there is a more general and much shrewder way . . ."

[6.] Crossed out: "Who is in the right?"

[7.] "The report" replaces "the story."

[8.] "Made the blood of devout Jews boil" replaces "inflamed the hearts of devout Jews."

otherwise God would not have allowed such a dreadful thing to happen. This was the interpretation of serious and pious persons; they believed that even this event could not be separated from the fact that a God exists, from whom all things come, for good or evil, and whose judgments are just. All one could now do was to turn away with a shudder from these punished sinners, who had become the target of God's wrath. This was how people dealt with this event.

This was the official view, we would say, of the daily press. And now Jesus begins by joining them in the idea that in any case one cannot separate God from this terrible event; that ultimately it is not Pilate who is at work here, but rather that God alone is at work in this world, in both good and evil. But this very thought, that the hand of God is in this, means something entirely different for Jesus than what it means for public opinion.[9]

Not a word does he say about Pilate, whether he was right or wrong; not a word about the Galileans, not a word of political judgment, not a word of moralistic judgment. This is very clear: Jesus does not judge! Jesus does not say which side is right, especially not to the pious, who have interpreted this event so earnestly and moralistically. *Jesus says "No"* to them.

"Do you think that because these Galileans suffered in this way they were worse sinners than all other Galileans? *No, I tell you.*" Jesus says No to the devout, he says No to their attempt to deal with this dreadful event by judging. Jesus says *No*—meaning, first of all, *stop* all your advice and interpretations, your know-all judgments. . . . Stop trying to put these things behind you in all these ways—*stop*—for these things are too enormous; God is at work here . . . I tell you *No* . . . that means that this is *God's holy mystery*, and human beings are not meant to presume upon it. So away with all your judgments[10] and saying who is right, one side or the other, be still and silent. . . . Here this is God's holy mystery.

And after Jesus has commanded them to be silent and reverent, after God has become visible behind his stern "No," he then proceeds to attack those

370

[9.] The next page is crossed out: "Not a word does he say about Pilate, whether he was right or wrong; not a word of moralistic judgment. This must be clear to us: . . . Jesus does not judge! Jesus does not say which group of human beings is right. Why? Because, behind this earthly political event, Jesus sees God—and what he does not see is that God decides that one is right and the other is wrong, but only brings out one point: *Repent,* all of you! For Jesus this shocking newspaper report of terrible events is God's ever-new, unmistakable call to us to repent. It is the living illustration of that which he preached, that before God human beings must repent and humble themselves and submit themselves to God's justice. 'Do you think that because these Galileans suffered in this way they were worse sinners than all other Galileans? No, I tell you; but unless you repent, you will all perish just as they did.'"

[10.] "Judgments" replaces "interpretations."

who have immediately rushed to judgment. "Do you think . . . No; but unless you repent you will all likewise perish . . . Siloam . . ."

What is Jesus doing here? On the occasion of this report Jesus is doing one and the same thing he did throughout his life: calling people to repentance. Here is God—therefore repent. For Jesus, then, this shocking newspaper report about the terrible things that happened in the temple is nothing other than a renewed call from God to all who can hear, in unmistakable terms, to repent and to turn back. It is for him a palpable, living illustration for his preaching that human beings must humble themselves before the mystery and power of God and repent and submit themselves to God's justice.

Now we are on dangerous ground. Now we are no longer bystanders, onlookers, judges of these events, but we ourselves are being addressed; we are affected. This has happened for us, God is speaking to us, this is all about us.[11]

And therefore, first of all: Do not judge, so that you may not be judged![12]   371
Do not set yourselves up as being better than those Galileans or that Pilate. In the face of such terrible acts of God, do not say with pride, "God, I thank you that I am not like other people. . . . "[13] Instead, pray silently within yourselves, "God, be merciful to me, a sinner."[14]

Jesus too raises the question of guilt. But he answers it differently. It is not Pilate or the Galileans who are meant here, but we, we ourselves. In the face of terrible human catastrophes, Christians are not to assume the arrogant, know-all attitude of looking on and judging, but rather are to recognize: this is my world in which this has happened. This is the world in which I live, in which I sin by sowing hate and lovelessness day by day. This is the fruit of what I and my brothers have sown—and these people here, these Galileans and Pilate, are my brothers, my brothers in sin, in hate and evil and lovelessness, my brothers in guilt. Whatever happens to them is meant for me too; they are only showing me God's finger pointed in anger, pointed at me as well.[15] So let us repent and realize *our* guilt and not judge.[16]

[11.] Crossed out: "Therefore, since nothing happens without God, you had better hear in this event the living voice of God calling you!"

[12.] Matt. 7:1.

[13.] Luke 18:11.

[14.] Luke 18:13.

[15.] "Pointed at me as well" replaces "which is patient with me."

[16.] Crossed out: "But isn't that a rather unproductive attitude or view to take? No, precisely the opposite is true. It is only through repentance that the world may be overcome, that evil will be overcome by good."

It is hard to think like this, and it is even harder to believe—as we must believe—that it is this attitude alone which can overcome the world, that only through repentance can the world be renewed. So isn't it fruitless to think this way? Does it make anything better? Yes, it does; it makes *everything* better. How so? Because through our repentance, God's grace can find its way back to us; because in our repentance no human being can be in the right, but rather God alone is right in all God's ways, whether in making us know fear or in showing us mercy.

A great man of our time—who is not a Christian,[17] but it is tempting to call him a heathen Christian—tells a story, in his autobiography,[18] that took place when he was director of a school. He was doing everything in his power for these young people, and one day within this school community an injustice was done, which shook him to the core. However, he took this not as an occasion that called for him to judge or to punish anyone but only as a call to repentance. So he went and spent long days in repentance, with fasting and all kinds of self-denial. What did this mean? It meant first of all that in the guilt of his pupils he saw his own guilt, his lack of love, patience, and truthfulness. Then, it meant that he knew that there could be room for the Spirit of God only in the spirit of humble realization of guilt. Finally, it meant the recognition that faith and love and hope could be found only in repentance. We have not yet believed enough; we have not yet loved enough—can we be judges? Jesus speaks: *I tell you, No.*

It is a quiet journey, a strange and slow-moving journey, which leads through repentance to newness of life. But it is the only way that is God's way. And if we have realized this and go home with it from church and are serious about it, only then have we overcome the world we find in the newspapers, the world of terror and the world of judgment.

Lord, lead your people to repentance, beginning with us![19]Amen.

[17.] "Not a Christian" replaces "a heathen."
[18.] Gandhi, *His Own Story*, 186–88.
[19.] Sentence replaces "Lord, renew the world, beginning with me!"

13. Sermon on Matthew 11:28–30
London, Late September 1934[1]

Matt. 11:28–30

"Come to me, all you that are weary and are carrying heavy burdens, and I will give you rest. Take my yoke upon you, and learn from me; for I am gentle and humble in heart, and you will find rest for your souls. For my yoke is easy, and my burden is light."

373

Since the day when Jesus spoke these words, there should no longer be any-one on earth who is so forsaken and alone as to say of himself or herself: Nobody has ever asked about me; nobody has ever wanted me or offered to help me. Whoever has heard these words of Jesus even once in his or her life and still talks that way is lying, is showing contempt and scorn for Jesus Christ and not taking his words seriously. For Christ was calling *everyone* who labors and is heavy-laden. His was not a narrow circle; it was no intellectual or spiritual-religious aristocracy that he gathered around him. Instead, he made his circle as wide as possible, so wide that no single person could say with a good conscience that he wasn't being addressed, since he wasn't among those who labored and were heavy-laden. This is just what is so amazing about this call: it really puts every human being in the embarrassing situation of admit-ting that they too are called and meant, indeed, perhaps they in particular.

Those who labor and are heavy-laden—who are they? Jesus intention-ally says nothing here that sets any limit. People are laboring and heavy-laden if they feel that way—in truth, including those who do not feel that way because they do not want to feel it. Laboring and heavy-laden certainly describes those men and women and children who outwardly have a hard lot in life and heavy work to do, those whom, we might say, have been placed by chance into the dark side of life, into servitude and into outward and moral misery. I have seldom felt so strongly that I was among those who labor and are heavy-laden as in the mining town in northern France where I have just been on holiday.[2] It is a joyless, driven, humiliated, abused, and soiled exis-tence, which is inherited and passed on from fathers to children and chil-dren's children. Wherever people experience their work as God's curse[3] on humanity—there you will find those who labor and are heavy-laden.

[1.] Literary estate of Elisabeth Bornkamm; handwritten. See also *NL*, A 43,12; type-written copy. Reprinted in *GS* 5:527–33 and *PAM* 1:465–71. The date follows a note on the first page of the manuscript in someone else's handwriting.

[2.] In Bruay-en-Artois, visiting Jean Lasserre; see *DB-ER*, 392, and 1/147.

[3.] Cf. Gen. 3:17–19; cf. also *DBWE* 3:133–34.

But it is all too easy for us to see such people only among those who are outwardly poor. Jesus certainly searched for and found those who were struggling hardest and carrying the heaviest burdens, not among the poor but among the so-called rich. Think of the rich young man whom it is said Jesus loved, who "went away sorrowful" because he was not strong enough to follow Jesus.[4] There is hardly a more depressing realization for a person than to see that, while outwardly he has everything he could want, inwardly he is hollow and empty and superficial; that all his possessions will not buy him the most important things in this earthly life: inner peace, joy of spirit, a loving marriage, and family life. How much unspeakable inner suffering, lives weighed down by the heavy debts that wealth brings, is found in the homes of those who seem so fortunate!

¶No, those who labor and are heavy-laden do not all look the way Rembrandt drew them in his "Hundred Guilder"[5] picture—poverty-stricken, miserable, sick, leprous, ragged, with worn, furrowed faces. They are also found concealed behind happy-looking, youthful faces and brilliantly successful lives. There are people who feel utterly forsaken in the midst of high society, to whom everything in their lives seems stale and empty to the point of nausea, because they can sense that underneath it all, their souls are decaying and rotting away. There is no loneliness like that of the fortunate.

But even those who are so intoxicated with their busy lives that they do not seem to feel how alone they are, who do not think about whether they are laboring and heavy-laden, are actually so. It has the opposite effect for them, because at the bottom of their hearts they know or suspect that this is also their condition, but they are afraid to admit it. So they throw themselves even more madly into their supposedly happy lives and keep running away from every word that might speak the truth to them. They do not want to be considered as those who labor and are heavy-laden, but in Jesus' eyes they are doubly so.

Everyone, all of you is what it means—Come to me, *all* who labor and are heavy-laden. The latter words are meant, *not as a limitation* on who is included in "all," but as a *statement* about them. Who would want to say, when Jesus calls, that this has nothing to do with them? Who would want to say they know nothing about the state of laboring and being heavy-laden?

When people come to the end of their inner strength and have become a burden to themselves, when they do not want to go another step, are afraid of the next hill looming ahead, are weighed to the ground by some kind of

----

[4.] Matt. 19:16–22; cf. *DBWE* 4:68–71.
[5.] [Rembrandt's famous etching *Christ Healing the Sick*, 1642/45.—KC]

guilt, and feel betrayed and deceived by the whole world—then no[6] words, no ideals or dreams one builds for the future will help. They need only one thing: a human being who can be trusted completely, unconditionally; someone who understands everything, listens to everything, bears with everything, who believes, who hopes, who forgives all things[7]—someone to whom one can say, You *are* sweet rest and gentle peace, my longing, yes, and my heart's ease[8]—someone in whose presence our sorrows are dispelled, our hearts open in love without words; someone who quietly takes away our burden and all the strain and anxiety[9] and thus redeems our souls from their bondage in this world.

¶But who has someone like that? Where can such a person be found? This is the miracle above all miracles, that everyone has and can find such a person, that this person himself is calling us to come to him, inviting us, and offering himself. This person who is our rest, our peace, who refreshes and redeems us, is Jesus Christ alone. He alone is fully human, and in being truly human is also God, and Redeemer, and peace, and rest. Come to me, all who labor and are heavy-laden, and *I* will give you rest. Everything depends on this "I"—not as an idea, not as a word, not as a preacher, but *I,* Jesus the human being, who knows each one of us, who has suffered and struggled though everything that we have to suffer, the human person Jesus, our Redeemer.

There are two possible ways to help someone who is bowed down under a[10] burden. One can either remove the entire weight of it, so that from now on the person has nothing to carry anymore, or one can help carry it, so that it becomes lighter and easier to carry. Jesus does not go the first way. Our burden is not taken away. Jesus, who himself carried his cross, knows it　　376 is part of being human to carry our cross, to shoulder our burden, and that only with our burden, and not without it, will we be sanctified. The burden that God has laid on someone's shoulders, Jesus will not take away. But he lightens our load by showing us how better to[11] carry it.

"Take my yoke upon you, and learn from me . . . " A yoke is itself a burden, a burden added to the weight of the other burden, but it has the peculiarity of being able to lighten the load. A burden that would otherwise crush a person down to the ground can be made bearable by using a yoke. We know

---

[6.] Crossed out: "fine."

[7.] Cf. 1 Cor. 13:7.

[8.] First verse of Friedrich Rückert's poem "Come In to Me." [The Schirmer edition of Schubert's setting of "Du bist die Ruh'" has this translation by Theodore Baker: "Thou art sweet Peace and tranquil rest, I long for thee to soothe my breast."—KC]

[9.] Crossed out: "all uncertainty."

[10.] Crossed out: "heavy."

[11.] "Better to" replaces "one ought to."

this from pictures of people carrying water with a yoke over their shoulders and of draught animals with a yoke that makes it possible for them to pull heavy loads without experiencing pain and torment and without injuring themselves. Jesus wants to put us human beings under such a yoke, so that our burdens will not be too heavy. "My yoke," he calls it—for it is the yoke under which he learned to carry his burden, his load, which is a thousand times heavier than any of ours, because it is all our burdens together that he is carrying. "Take my yoke upon you" means "come with me under my yoke"—yoked together with him, so that we can no longer pull away, and with all those who want to be yoked together with Jesus—yoked together until the day when the yoke will be lifted entirely from our shoulders.

"Learn from me . . . " see how I carry this yoke, and do it the same way. "Learn from me; *for I am gentle and humble in heart.*" This then is the yoke he carries, *his gentleness and lowliness,* and it is the yoke that we are to take upon ourselves, which Jesus knows[12] will help to make our burdens light. To be "gentle" means not to kick against the goads,[13] not to rebel against the burden, not to bump against it and rub ourselves sore, but to be quiet and patient and carry the load that has been put on us, knowing that it is God who lays the burden on us and will help us to go on. "*. . . gentle and humble in heart.*" To be humble means to give up one's own will entirely, not to try to get one's own way, but to be happier when the other's will is done than when mine is done. To be humble means to know that we are servants of God, and that it is the servants' job to carry the load—but it is also to know that we have a good master, who will some day lift the load from our shoulders, after this burden has sanctified and humbled and purified us.

377

Whoever will bear this yoke, and learn from it, receives a great promise: "*. . . and you will find rest for your souls.*" This is the end, this peace is the last, although we experience it already here under the yoke of Jesus, yoked together with him in gentleness and lowliness. But only at the end, when every burden falls away, will we experience the longed-for perfect rest.

As we look ahead to that blessedness, as we hope for our release[14] from toil and guilt, we can already hear Jesus saying, today, ". . . For my yoke is easy, and my burden is light . . ." Woe to anyone who plays games with these words, making it seem that Christ's cause is an easy one. The person who really understands what it is about is the one who shrinks back in horror from the seriousness and the dreadfulness of the cause of Christ, who does not dare to approach it for fear of what it means for our real lives. But once

[12.] "Knows" replaces "says."
[13.] This echoes Acts 9:5 [in the KJV, although not NRSV—KC] and Acts 26:14.
[14.] "Release" replaces "liberation."

someone has grasped the meaning of Jesus Christ and his will for us, then we must certainly say to that person, go now to Jesus himself, take his yoke upon you, and you will see that everything, everything changes, that all your fear and horror disappears, and that all at once, for the person who is with Jesus, it is true: "my yoke is easy . . ."

In conclusion, there is still one question remaining between us, which we have to call by its name so that it will not confuse us. Some say: Jesus is dead . . . how shall we go to him . . . how will he comfort us, how will he help us? What else can we answer but this: No, Jesus is living, living here in our midst. Look for him, here or at home, call to him, ask him, beg him, and suddenly he will be there with[15] you, and you will know that he lives. You cannot see him, touch him, or hear him, but you will know that he is there, helping and comforting you, and only he. And you will take his yoke upon you and be joyful and wait with longing for the final rest in him.

> A short while yet, and it is won.
> Of painful strife there will be none.
> Refreshed by life-streams, thirsting never,
> I'll talk with Jesus, forever and ever.[16]

378

14. Sermon on 1 Corinthians 13:1–3
London, Twentieth Sunday after Trinity, October 14, 1934[1]

1 Cor. 13:1–3   October 14, 1934

If I speak in the tongues of mortals and of angels, but do not have love, I am a noisy gong or a clanging cymbal. And if I have prophetic powers, and understand all mysteries and all knowledge, and if I have all faith, so as to remove mountains, but do not have love, I am nothing. If I give away all my possessions, and if I hand over my body so that I may boast, but do not have love, I gain nothing.

The reasons that have moved me to preach this series of sermons on the thirteenth chapter of the first letter to the Corinthians are these: First, this

---

[15.] "Be there with" replaces "come to."

[16.] Søren Kierkegaard's epitaph. [Bonhoeffer cites a somewhat free German version of the original Danish. Translation of this German version by Isabel Best and Keith Clements.—KC]

[1.] Literary estate of Elisabeth Bornkamm; handwritten. See also *NL*, A 43,13; typewritten copy. Reprinted in *GS* 5:534–42 and *PAM* 1:472–81. First of a four-week series of sermons on the thirteenth chapter of 1 Corinthians.

chapter is one that we need in our congregation, just as it was needed by the church in Corinth. What does it mean, after all, to be a Christian church-community, if in all the fine things that happen here, one thing is not completely clear, indeed self-evident—that the members of a church-community are to love one another? What image is the congregation offering, to itself and to the world, if not even this first obligation is being taken seriously. If there was one human thing about the first Christians that pagans found con-

379 vincing, it was quite simply that they could physically see with their own eyes that two neighbors, or a master and his slave, or estranged brothers suddenly were no longer against each other but rather with and for each other. So it really made a difference, outwardly and visibly, that they had become Christians. But do we think this means that, since we are already Christians, nothing more needs to change? Wouldn't it be better to say that if we too were to become Christians, many things in our own lives would suddenly change? Would not these words of judgment also apply to a congregation . . . and if everything happened just so in our congregation, if we all came to church and did all sorts of good deeds—"but had not love, we would be nothing"?

The second reason I had for choosing this text is the particular situation of our German churches. Whether or not we want to see it, whether or not we think it is right, the churches are caught up in a struggle for their faith such as we have not seen for hundreds of years. This is a struggle—whether or not we agree—over our confession of Jesus Christ alone as Lord and Redeemer of this world.[2] But anyone who inwardly and outwardly joins in this struggle for this confession knows that such a struggle for faith carries a great temptation with it—the temptation of being too sure of oneself, of self-righteousness and dogmatism, which also means the temptation to be unloving toward one's opponent. And yet this opponent can never truly be overcome if not through love, since no opponent is ever overcome, except by love. Father,[3] forgive them; for they do not know what they are doing—how many people have truly been overcome by these words of Jesus! Even of the most passionate battle for the faith it could well be said: " . . . *but had it not love, it would be nothing.*"

This brings us to the third reason: the Protestant church has been able to

380 proclaim with unparalleled confidence the victory and the power of faith in the Lord Jesus Christ alone and thus has caused the world to hear again the message of the Bible in its purity. But who still hears this word of faith the

---

[2.] This sentence replaces: "And despite all that is difficult and depressing about it, we are thankful for this struggle, which has awakened the churches to be ready for their Lord." Cf. 1/93, p. 135.

[3.] "Father" replaces "Lord," as in Luke 23:34.

way it is meant to be heard?—that what it really means is that God is to be *loved* above all?[4] To love God does not just mean that when things are going badly for us, we say: God will help us again! That truly amounts to a feeble and puny faith. To love God means to rejoice in God, to think and pray gladly to God, to love being alone in God's presence, to wait impatiently for God, for every word and every request; it means not causing God sorrow but rejoicing simply that there is God, that we can know and have and speak with and live with God. To love God—and for love of God, to love our brethren as well—in our disillusioned Protestant church do we still understand this?[5] Can we hear it without saying that it is simply pietism—and what if it were? Does not this same declaration stand above the Protestant church, which preaches of faith alone: ". . . but had it not love, it would be nothing"?

In everything I am now going to say, let us keep one thing in mind: that we are not going to look at other people but rather look within *ourselves* and ask whether *we* have love. Who knows—maybe that neighbor of ours who seems such a lone wolf, so odd, self-centered, not friendly at all, might turn out to be full of longing to love greatly—only it takes a long, long time for the ice to break and set his or her heart free. And who knows whether all our efforts to be friendly, and what we say to others about this person, only do all the more to prevent the true breakthrough to the great love for God and for others. So let us look only at ourselves and hear what is said as being meant just for us.

In the first place it is very simple, what is being said here—that a human life is only meaningful and worthwhile to the extent that it has love in it, and that a life is nothing, is meaningless and worthless, when it is without love. A life is worth as much as the love in it. Everything else is nothing at all, a matter of indifference, unimportant. All the good and bad, big and little things are unimportant. Only one thing is asked of us—whether we have love.   381

We have all had the experience[6] of standing at the grave of someone about whom we could think of absolutely nothing to say, where we simply felt terribly depressed: how unspeakably poor this person's life was, how meaningless, how much time and effort was lost here. For this person had no one to love and was not loved by anyone. We watch dully, without pain or tears, as this life is finally laid to rest, as it may perhaps have longed to be. This was a skinflint, a jealous, tyrannical person who only knew and wanted and looked

---

[4.] Echoes Luther's explanation of the First Commandment in his Small Catechism (Kolb and Wengert, *Book of Concord*, 481–85).

[5.] "Disillusioned" replaces "sober."

[6.] "Had the experience" replaces "known the feeling."

out for himself, who hated other people and thought they got in the way of the happiness that he never actually found. This was someone who remained alone and lonely—one cannot but wonder if he must remain alone for all eternity. These are the graves that perhaps distress us the most, for they preach to us in the most simple and vivid way the meaning of the words ". . . but have not love, I am nothing."

And then there are the graves where a mother, a faithful father, a happy child passes before our eyes, and standing all around are those who have known this person's love. There are an enormous number of them, including many whom the others do not know, but they themselves know why they are there. And our voices are lifted up and will not be silent, in praise of the love that was glorified in this human life.

These are very simple experiences in life from which we begin to have an idea why Paul sings the praises of love so exclusively. Any life without love is really nothing, not worth living, but where love is, the meaning of life is fulfilled. Compared with love, the rest really does not matter: good luck or bad luck, poverty or riches, honor or shame, being at home or far away, life or death—what meaning do they have for people who dwell in love? They do not know, it makes no difference to them; all they know is that good luck or bad, poverty or wealth, honor or shame, home and foreign lands, life and death are all given so that they can love all the more strongly, purely, and fully. Love is the one thing that is beyond all differences, comes before all differences, and remains within all differences. Love is strong as death.[7]

382

[7.] Song of Sol. 8:6. The paragraph that follows is crossed out: "From this last it becomes clear to us that this hymn of praise to love is not particularly a matter of the good bourgeois class morality that we take for granted, but something that cuts across our well-ordered bourgeois ideas of life. When the last 'judgment' or 'saving word' is pronounced on our lives, if it really depends on whether a person loved or not—if love is really all or nothing for God—then the world suddenly looks quite different. Suddenly a lot of things [replaces 'everything'] that counted as great in this world fall away into that nothingness, that emptiness, that annihilation of all life. Everything that spoke to us of power and honor and might, of desire and possession, which was high up in this world, is put down, judged, destroyed by this one word from the New Testament. It is nothing, absolutely nothing. The world order is turned upside down if we take this statement seriously: and have not love, I am nothing. But with the world—and now we are really getting to the point—has to go also our piety, our Christianity, or religious life in all its seriousness. The things we have been saying so far are taken for granted by the majority; they don't even need to [be] said. But they would be altogether misunderstood if we stopped there and just stood over against the fallen world as a saved remnant of churchgoers, the devout. No, this word cuts through our own ranks as well, our church and our piety. This is where we finally recognize the sharpness in this word love, which protects it from being misunderstood, the tremendous aggressive power in it that is lifted up precisely against the pious and brings them down from their false thrones."

Love makes everything else petty; whatever seems great is really pitiful and crumbles to nothing, a picture of misery. What is the value of a life of pleasure, honor, fame, and brilliance compared to a life lived in love?[8] But we must not stop even there, for this question is amazingly powerful and insists on continuing: what is, furthermore, the value of a pious and moral[9] life, a disciplined life of sacrifice and self-denial, if it is not a life lived in love?

As we read this text, images arise before us of people who are so serious and able, so dedicated and zealous in their life of faith that humankind can be proud, we can be proud of them, and we imagine that the Creator too must be proud. We look up to these people in awe and admiration; we bow completely before them and would never venture a word of criticism of them, since they seem beyond our common humanity, alone in their exalted greatness. And then comes the terrible spectacle in which these mighty ones, whose seriousness and devoutness we can never match, are seized and brought down[10] by one little word—"and had not love." They who seemed everything to us are made as nothing before God, whose light of truth streams over them and from whom they cannot hide the truth that, despite all their exalted power, the hearts within them were stony and cold.[11]

383

"And if I speak in the tongues of mortals and of angels . . ." About what? About that which is sacred to me in life, and important and serious.—To whom? Indeed, to those to whom I want to make these things real, those whom I want to win over to this sacred cause. Let us suppose, then, that we can do this, speak of the greatest and holiest things in such a way that we forget everything else and are carried away by enthusiasm. Suppose, too, that we have a unique gift for expressing our feelings in words, feelings that others can only carry silently inside them. Suppose we speak thus with one another in complete honesty and devotion. Yet still—"If I speak in the tongues of mortals [and of angels], and do not have love, I am nothing, a noisy gong or a clanging cymbal."

¶That devastates and paralyzes us like a bolt of lightning. That is the possibility we hadn't foreseen, that even our holiest words could become unholy, godless, and mean, if there is no heart in them, if they are without love. So it is possible for that which is given to us human beings in order that we may create the most intimate communion among ourselves, the power of the *Word*, to become unholy if the love is torn out of it and it becomes self-serving and self-absorbed. A noisy gong, a clanging cymbal—a hollow roar, empty

---

[8.] Crossed out: "A devastated life."
[9.] "Moral" replaces "disciplined."
[10.] "Seized and brought down" replaces "knocked down."
[11.] Echoes of Ezek. 11:19 and 36:26 and of Hauff's fairy tale "The Cold Heart."

384   chatter, without heart or soul—that is what can become of our words. That is
what they do become, for the other person—even our most sacred, solemn,
truthful assertions, even our declarations of love, if they are not spoken in
love. So this is the first thing: the one who speaks solemn, pious words, if he
or she does not pass the test of love, turns out to be a noisy gong or a clanging
cymbal, a nothing; while the one who is perhaps slow of tongue, with stutter-
ing speech, like Moses,[12] or whose mouth may be closed and dumb,[13] can
be saved by his or her love. The word without love—that is the first point.

But deeper than the word lies insight, knowledge of the mysteries of
this world and the one beyond, devoted and prayerful thinking on God,
contemplation of things past and present, and illumination of things to
come. Are these not also forms of the devout life, awe inspiring for us? How
much sacrifice and self-denial are demanded of us to arrive at truth and
insight[14]—"and if I have prophetic powers, and understand all mysteries
and all knowledge. . . ." When we hear these words, are we not seized by a
great longing—if I only had these, then my thirst would be satisfied; if I knew
why I must go this way and why another must go that way, if I could discover,
here and now, the hidden ways of God—wouldn't that be blessedness? Then
it says again, "but have not love, I am nothing." Insight, knowledge, truth
without love is nothing—it is not even truth, for truth is God, and God is
love. So truth without love is a lie; it is nothing. *Speaking the truth in love,*" says
Paul in another letter.[15] Truth just for oneself, truth spoken in enmity and
hate is not truth but a lie, for truth brings us into God's presence, and God
is love. Truth is either the clarity of love, or it is nothing.

But we have left out a little phrase in between, one that opens up[16] a
385   terrible riddle to us: "and *if I have all faith,* so as to remove mountains . . . but
have not love, I am nothing." "If I have all faith . . ." What does that mean,
what chord does that strike within us? All faith, all confidence, certitude that
I am with God and God is with me in all the sorrows and anxieties of my
life—all faith, so that I no longer have to be afraid of what tomorrow may
bring—is this not what we pray for every day? That would be enough for us,
that we could hold onto until the end of our lives. And yet here it comes
again, *but have not love, I am nothing.* What a baffling thing—imagine a person who had all faith and still did not love, did not love God and his or her
brother or sister! What a dark abyss we are looking into now—a faith that is

---

[12.] Exod. 4:10.
[13.] Cf. Matt. 9:32–33.
[14.] Crossed out: "the great theologians of all time, people who have insight about
God."
[15.] Eph. 4:15.
[16.] "Opens up" replaces "seems to open up."

self-glorifying and self-centered in its very foundations, in which I am only looking out for myself; a godless faith—believing, not for the sake of God, but for my own sake. God keep us from such an abyss, such superstition, which fools us into thinking that we are with you—when we are really far away from you, God. Who will help us escape such danger?

Now there is no holding back—it keeps getting[17] worse, to our despair. Not only is there faith without God and without love, but also good deeds that look like works of love but have nothing to do with love. If I give every-thing I have to the poor—if I deny myself and make sacrifices as only love can do and still "have not love" but rather make the sacrifices out of a heart full of vanity and selfishness, *thinking that such sacrifices would fool God and my neighbor about what kind of heart I have*—I gain nothing.

So what can the devout person give, in the end, beyond his or her naked life itself as a sacrifice for God and for Christ, as a martyr? If I give my body to be burned, if I give proof of how seriously devout I am and seal it with my death—if I become a martyr for God's cause—God, what grace it would be to die for you!—but have not love, I truly gain nothing. If I appear to love God to the extent of sacrificing my life, but still do not really love God |386| but only myself and my dream of martyrdom and the fame it will bring. . . . The judgment applies even to the martyr[18]—the lack of love plunges him or her into nothingness.[19]

Who can understand this? We might indeed say, who doesn't understand it? Which of us does not see that, in all these instances,[20] we are the ones who talk big and have knowledge and faith and do good deeds and sacrifice ourselves only for our own sake,[21] without love, without God? Which of us does not see that God must condemn such doings—because God is love and wants only our whole, undivided love—and nothing more?

¶What then is love, this love of God and the other person? It is not words, or knowledge[22] or faith, not deeds of love or the sacrifice of our lives, in the way we think of it. Do we have love? Has judgment already been passed on us too? Let us call upon love, that it may come from God's very self and[23] snatch us from the pit of destruction. O God of all love, come into our con-fused hearts and save us, because you love us, through love. Amen.

[17.] "Keeps getting" replaces "can become even."

[18.] "The martyr" replaces "me then."

[19.] On this theme, see also his thoughts on a martyrdom "without love," *DBWE* 4:180.

[20.] "In all these instances" replaces "again and again."

[21.] "For our own sake" replaces "for their own sake."

[22.] Crossed out: "truth."

[23.] Crossed out: "and sanctify us" (uncertain reading).

15. Sermon on 1 Corinthians 13:4–7
London, Twenty-first Sunday after Trinity, October 21, 1934[1]

1 Cor. 13:4–7   October 21

Love is patient; love is kind; love is not envious or boastful or arrogant or rude. It
does not insist on its own way; it is not irritable or resentful; it does not rejoice in
wrongdoing, but rejoices in the truth. It bears all things, believes all things, hopes
all things, endures all things.

387   Last Sunday we learned that,[2] despite all our ideals, our seriousness, our
knowledge, and our faith, even our good deeds and sacrifice, our lives are
worth *nothing* if we do not have that one thing that Paul calls love.[3] So it
could be that our whole life is meaningless, even if we do our full duty, earnestly and with all our might—because it is done not out of love but out of
pride or fear or the vanity of our hearts. And that all our piety is not worth
a penny either, if people say of it that it "has not love."[4] But if all human
life and activity amount to nothing without love, we are confronted with the
question: What *is* this love on which everything depends?[5] What is this love,
without which all of us are *nothing?*

It is true that no one lives entirely without love. Every person has love
within him or her and knows its power and passion. Each of us knows, furthermore, that it is this love that makes our whole life meaningful; that without
this love that we know and have, we could just throw away all our lives—they
would no longer be worth living. However, this love, with its power and passion and meaning, which everyone knows, *is self-love—our love for our own
selves.* This is what fulfills us and gives us energy to be active and inventive;
it is that without which life would not be worth living. So we do know love,
but only in a fiendishly distorted way, as in a mirror—as self-love. But this
self-love is love that has gone wrong, that has fallen away from its origin. It

---

[1.] Literary estate of Elisabeth Bornkamm; handwritten. See also *NL*, A 43,14; typewritten copy. Reprinted in *GS* 5:542–49 and *PAM* 1:482–89.

[2.] Replaces "The last question that we considered last Sunday was that."

[3.] "If we . . . love" replaces "if it is not love that gives all meaning and worth to our
lives."

[4.] "If people . . . 'has not love'" replaces "if its source is not love."

[5.] Crossed out: "Can there be such a thing as a life so poor that there is no love to be
found in it? Is there such a thing as a person of whom people say he or she 'has not love'? Is
it really so special? Do all people really know and experience and have it in their lives? Isn't
love rather that which everyone is looking for in order to be happy? And doesn't everyone
find it eventually in one way or another? Isn't it actually a truism that it is love alone that
makes life meaningful? So what then is this love, without which all of us are *nothing?*"

is self-satisfied and is therefore condemned never to bear fruit—a love that is really hatred of God and my brother and sister, because they could only disturb me within the tight little circle I have drawn around myself. It has all the same power, the same passion, the same exclusiveness of real love—here   388 or there. What is totally different is its goal—myself, rather than God and my neighbor.

But self-love is also clever. It knows that it is only a distorted likeness of love's original image. So it pretends, veils itself, and dresses itself up in a thousand different forms, trying to look like real love—and it succeeds so well that human eyes can hardly tell the difference between the real thing and the fake. Self-love disguises itself as love of our neighbor or our country, as public charity, as love of humankind, trying not to be recognized for what it really is.[6] Yet Paul cuts through all of self-love's attempts to cloud the issue and to deceive and compels it to face its proper responsibility by drawing for it, for us, his picture of what God considers real love.[7]

Each of the characteristics listed here can be interpreted somewhat differently on its own. But taken all together, there is no doubt that they break the spell of self-love and let the love of God and one's neighbor become a reality. But where is this taking place? It doesn't say *a loving person* does this or that, but rather says *love* does this or that. Who is this love? Whom are we talking about? How do we know it?

Before we answer that, let us listen to what is being said. *"Love is patient and kind. . . ."* That means love can wait a long, long time, till the very end. It doesn't become impatient, doesn't try to hurry things or force them to happen. It expects to wait a good long time.[8] It is confident only of being able finally, finally to overcome the other's resistance.[9] Being patient and waiting, continuing to be kind and loving, even if it doesn't seem to serve any purpose, is the only way to overcome a human being. That is the only way to loosen the chains that bind every person, the chains of fear of the other, of the fear of a radical change, of a new life. Friendliness often seems totally inappropriate, but *love is patient and kind*—it waits, the way one waits   389 for someone who has lost the way, waits and rejoices whenever he or she finally gets there.

For that reason love is not jealous—but self-love is jealous. It wants something for itself, it wants to win over and possess the other person for itself, *it* wants

---

[6.] Crossed out: "But God recognizes it and sees through it."

[7.] Crossed out: "If we must nevertheless try to define real love as opposed to self-love, this will be done through a whole series of statements about what real love does."

[8.] "Expects . . . time" replaces "does not count on receiving love back from the other person."

[9.] Crossed out: "that he or she will give in."

something from that person. But *love* doesn't want anything *from* the other person—what it wants is everything for that person. It doesn't want to possess the other person, especially not to have him or her jealously all to itself. It only wants to love the other person, because it cannot do otherwise; it only wants the person for his or her own sake. It wants nothing from other people but desires everything for them. Jealousy, which supposedly enhances and safeguards love, actually destroys love, soils and desecrates it.

Because love is not jealous, because it seeks nothing for itself, it therefore doesn't try to make anything of itself —it would rather be wholly inconspicuous or not really be seen at all. It does not call attention to itself, or put on airs, or try to be anything special—it is not boastful; it is not arrogant or rude. We do everything to point out what is special about our love; we play the roles of[10] the saint, the innocent, the fool, or even the martyr with our love. We try to make the other afraid that we might suddenly withdraw our love; that is, we play games with our love, we use it to treat others any way we like.[11] We are ready and able to break the rules of decency and custom, modesty and reserve, in order to get attention for our love. *But love is not rude*—it does *not* do all those things that we do in the guise of love. It does not do them, because *it does not insist on its own way.* It wants nothing for itself, really and truly—it forgets itself and does not see itself, any more than our eyes can see themselves.

¶What love might want, if it tried to get its own way—at least what in any
390   case we are looking for when we love someone—is at least to be loved back or some degree of gratitude for our love. But even what we might think belongs to love, what it deserves, *it does not insist on* having for itself. For it is just when it does not so insist—not even surreptitiously and secretly—that perhaps it will find what it seeks. Love is happy and grateful when others find what they are looking for; and it looks on without envy when the other person loves someone else, the way a good mother rejoices when her child finds someone to love with his or her whole heart, even when the mother herself has to stand back.[12]

Even when the other person turns out to be sinful and spiteful, love does not become bitter, because it is not looking to receive kindness. It is thinking not of itself at all but only of the other. It grieves over the other's nastiness, is saddened by it, and loves him or her all the more, but does not become

---

[10.] Inserted: "the roles of."

[11.] Crossed out: "we want attention for it, we want to be noticed, we break the rules, we behave like wild things."

[12.] Crossed out: "But she is the very one who is not looking for anything for herself, but rather . . ."

bitter. When our whole life seems bitter because we are not loved in return, love says to us: you haven't yet really loved someone if you let his or her hate or inattentiveness destroy your love; otherwise you would be free of bitterness. You allow yourself to become bitter, but love never does. *It doesn't let the bad things count.* Wherever we think that justice demands that we keep count of good and bad and determine it—there, love is blind, knowingly blind; it sees the bad, but doesn't count it, rather forgives—and only love can forgive. It forgets, instead of bearing grudges. If we could only understand that one thing: love does not bear grudges. It meets the other person each day anew, with new love. It forgets what went on yesterday—it is even willing for others to be scornful and think it is being foolish. It never loses faith but simply goes on loving.

So don't right and wrong make any difference to love? No, love does *not* rejoice at injustice, but it does rejoice in the truth. It wants to see things as [they] are. It would rather see clearly the hate and injustice and lies that are there than all sorts of charming masks that only serve to cover up the hate and make it even uglier. Love wants to create and to see clear relationships. It rejoices in the truth—for only truth enables love to love again, anew.

Now comes the great summing-up, which we hardly dare to expound, because it is so immensely deep and vast and serious. *Love bears all things, believes all things, hopes all things, endures all things.* The focus here is on *all things*—there is no compromising here; it really means *anything.* Perhaps once, in a great moment of our lives, we might say to someone, I'd do anything for you, I'd give up anything for you, I'd bear anything, together with you.[13] But even as we say it, we are silently setting the one great condition: As long as you will do the same for me. For love, no such condition exists. Love's "anything" is not subject to any circumstances—it is, unconditionally, *all things.*

391

Love bears all things—that means it cannot be frightened by any evil. It can look upon and take in all the horror of human sin. It doesn't look away from what is unbearable; it can stand the sight of blood. Love can stand anything. No guilt, no crime, no vice, no disaster is so heavy that love cannot look at it and take it upon itself, for it knows: love is still greater than the greatest guilt.

Love believes all things—and because of that *it can be fooled but is still in the right.* Because of that, one can betray love and lie to it, but still it stands. But who would be foolish enough to believe everything? Isn't that just asking others to take me for a fool? Yes, it would be foolish if I had in mind getting

---

[13.] Crossed out: "until the first test comes and we . . ."

anything for myself with my love. But if I really and truly do not want anything out of it for myself, just to love unconditionally, boundlessly, without prejudice—then it is not foolish at all. Then it is *the* way to overcome other persons, the way to make them begin to wonder, until they turn around and come back. Love believes *all things*, because it cannot do otherwise than to believe that in the end the very final word will be that everyone, yes, everyone, is called to be overcome by love.

¶Has it ever happened to you that you were talking with someone who was considered really bad, someone whom nobody expected ever to do anything right or honest, but you listened to him or her and believed in what he or she was saying? And then the person simply broke down, just from being believed, and said to you, "You are the first one who has believed me in a long time." And that then that person really took heart from your belief in him or her—even if he or she had just been lying to us. On the other hand, can you remember the despair of someone whom we didn't trust, but who we found out later had been telling us the truth, and who, because of our mistrust, had come to doubt his or her entire faith? After these experiences, one understands why love does not make any distinctions but with open eyes believes all things—or with blind eyes, sees the true future.

Love hopes all things. It never gives up on anyone, knowing the day will come when the lost one will turn back, will have to return to the love he or she has denied, broken up, shaken off, forgotten, when the sickness finally yields and the person stands erect, healed. Love is like the doctor at the bedside who "doesn't give up hope" for the patient, and this hope makes the patient take heart. And because love has no other desire than that the patient take heart, it will *never* give up on him or her but will keep hoping all things—not just for individual persons, but for a whole people and for a church. If one has not love, then to hope for all things is crazy recklessness and overoptimism. But to hope for all things out of love is the power that a people [Volk] and [a] church need in order to stand upright again. This is what we are called to do—to hope so unconditionally that our loving hope can empower others.

Anyone who believes and hopes all things for the sake of love, for the sake of helping people stand tall again, must be patient and suffer. The world will take him or her for a fool, and perhaps a dangerous fool, because this foolishness challenges the malicious forces and brings them out. Yet the malicious can only be fully loved when they come out into the light. *Therefore: love endures all things*—and is blessed in its endurance, for this endurance makes it grow ever greater and ever more irresistible. Love that only has to endure a little will stay weak. Love that endures all things will gain the victory.

Who is this love—if it is not he who bore all things, believed all things, hoped all things—and indeed, had to endure all things, all the way to the cross? Who was never looking for his own gain, never became bitter, and never kept count of the evil done to him—and thus was overpowered by evil? Who even prayed for his enemies on the cross[14] and thereby totally over-   393
came evil? Who is this love, which Paul was talking about, other than Jesus Christ himself? Who else could it be, if not he? What better symbol could there be, standing over this entire passage, than the cross?

16. Sermon on 1 Corinthians 13:8–12
London, Twenty-second Sunday after Trinity, October 28, 1934[1]

1 Cor. 13:8–12   October 28, 1934

Love never ends. But as for prophecies, they will come to an end; as for tongues, they will cease; as for knowledge, it will come to an end. For we know only in part, and we prophesy only in part; but when the complete comes, the partial will come to an end. When I was a child, I spoke like a child, I thought like a child, I reasoned like a child; when I became an adult, I put an end to childish ways. For now we see in a mirror, dimly, but then we will see face to face. Now I know only in part; then I will know fully, even as I have been fully known.

In troubled times, if we stop to ask ourselves what will really come of all our agitation, when our thoughts go back and forth from one idea to another; what will come of all our worries and fears, all our wishes and hopes, in the end—and if we are willing to have an answer from the Bible[2]—what we will hear is: There will be just one thing in the end, and that is the love that was in our thoughts, worries, wishes, and hopes. Everything else ends and passes away—everything we did not think, and long for, out of love. All thoughts, all knowledge, all talk that has not love comes to an end—*only love never ends.*

Now if we are aware that something will come to an end, then it is prob-   394
ably not even worth starting. Life is too short and too serious for us to have time to waste, to spend on things that will only come to an end. Now and then we realize this for ourselves with shattering clarity. On New Year's or on our birthday, when we look back at what we have done during the past

---

[14.] Cf. Luke 23:34.

[1.] Literary estate of Elisabeth Bornkamm; handwritten. See also *NL*, A 43,15; typewritten copy. Reprinted in *GS* 5:549–55 and *PAM* 1:489–95.

[2.] "If we . . . Bible" replaces "if we are willing to have Christianity's answer."

year or in the period of our lives just past, we are sometimes horrified to see that we have done nothing of lasting value.[3] All our worries and efforts, all the things we have thought and said, have long since died away to nothing. Nothing is left—except perhaps an act of love, a loving thought, a hope for someone else, which may have occurred almost by chance, perhaps without our even being aware of it.

Where this is leading is clear: everything, all our knowledge, insight, thinking, and talking should in the end move toward and turn into love. For only what we think because of love, and in love, will remain, will never end.

Why must everything else come to an end, and why does only love never end? Because only in love does a person let go of himself or herself and give up his or her will for the other person's benefit. Because love alone comes not from my own self but from another self, from God's self. Because it is through love alone that God acts through us—whereas in everything else it is we ourselves who are at work; it is *our thoughts, our speaking, our knowledge*—but it is God's love. And what is ours comes to an end, all of it—but what is of God remains. Because love is God's very self and God's will; that is why it never ends, it never doubts, it stays its course. It pursues its way with sure steps, like a sleepwalker, straight through the midst of all the dark places and perplexities of this world. It goes down into the depths of human misery and up to the heights of human splendor. It goes out to enemies as well as to friends, and it never abandons anyone, even when it is abandoned by every-

395   one. Love follows after its beloved through guilt and disgrace and loneliness, all of which are no part of it; it is simply there and never ends. And it blesses every place it enters. Everywhere it goes, it finds imperfection and bears witness to perfection.

Love desires to enter into the world of our thoughts and our understanding. Understanding is the most like love. This is because its object is the other; it goes toward the other. Knowledge wants to grasp and understand and explain the world and other people and the mysteries of God. There is no human being who does not take part in the search for understanding. Human beings are fundamentally creatures who seek to understand, who must try to understand, even against their own will, even when thinking is not their calling and not their personal goal.[4] There are the great questions on which each person tries out his or her capacity to understand and comes to understand the limits of our understanding. These questions are: What is

---

[3.] "We . . . value" replaces "we would be very glad to be able to name some things, which will last, which will not come to an end and pass away."

[4.] Crossed out: "To be human is to seek knowledge."

a person's own path that he or she should follow through life? What is the other person's path? What is the path of God, which underlies all our human paths? There is no one who is not familiar with these questions and does not have to keep asking them, but there is no one who would be able to answer them on the strength of his or her own ability to understand.

All the solutions that people in this world have tried, which we try every day, are imperfect; they will all pass away. No one knows this better than someone who has done a lot of thinking and knows a great deal. Today there is no one who knows it better than those who, not so long ago, were so proud and confident in their success—physicists and other scientists.[5] And this truth was recognized by one of the greatest thinkers of all time as the end and the beginning of all wisdom, when he said: *I know that I know nothing.*[6] That was indeed the end; that was his final certainty.

But beyond this certainty, Paul recognized an infinitely greater certainty: Our knowledge is imperfect—but when that which is perfect comes, the imperfect will end. That which is perfect is love. Understanding and love are the imperfect and the perfect. And the more longing for perfection there is in the person who seeks knowledge, the more loving he or she will be. *Perfect understanding is perfect love.* This is a strange but very profound and true statement by Paul. 396

Perhaps someone will ask: But what does understanding have to do with love in the first place? Knowledge means precisely the objective, factual kind of knowing, without any personal opinion entering into it. Certainly that is true. But in order even to be able to see something, we need to love it. If we are indifferent toward a person or a thing, *we will never understand it.* We will always misunderstand a thing or a person we hate. Only a person whom we *love can we fully know.* We will know only as much about a person as we love in him or her.

¶The so-called worldly wise person, who is reckoned to be a good judge of people, actually knows and understands nothing about them. He or she has a trick of knowing about people's evil inclinations and being especially wary of them—but must do this precisely because this person does not understand people. Imagine that someone whom we do not find likable has done something to us that surprises us, and then that someone whom we love very much has done something that we simply cannot understand. In the first case we will immediately have all sorts of explanations for the bad motives

[5.] On the "shaking" of scientific thought by the quantum and relativity theories, cf. *GS* 5:186 (*DBW* 11, 2/3, p. 146).

[6.] The words of Socrates (Plato, *Apologia* 23 A).

that led him or her to such an action; while, on the other hand, we will end-lessly search and ask, and indeed invent excuses, in an effort to understand why the person we love acted the way he or she did. We will certainly finish by knowing this second person better than we know the first.

All real understanding is a piece of love, even if it is[7] a love that is still all wrapped up in vanity and self-centeredness and thirst for fame. But it has within it a longing for the perfection that will come when the imperfect has passed away, when perfect truth, knowledge, and love will dawn on us.

"*But when the perfect comes,* the imperfect will *pass away*"—it doesn't hap-pen gradually, as if the imperfect could grow up into the perfect. Instead, the perfect, which the imperfect can never achieve, simply *comes* by itself. It will come, in complete freedom, in the perfection of its power, and the imperfect will stop, will break up, as a reflected image breaks up when one sees the reality.

It is a surprising image that we have here, in which childhood is compared to imperfect knowledge and mature adulthood to the perfection of love. "*When I was a child,* I spoke like a child, I thought like a child, I reasoned like a child. . . ." Knowing without loving is childish, childish reasoning, a child-ish attempt to become master of the world in a sneaking way. Proud knowl-edge without love is like the bragging of a stupid youngster who does not deserve to be taken seriously, at which a mature adult can only smile. "When I became a man, I gave up childish ways." We would have said it exactly the other way around—childishness is knowledge with love in it, and maturity is realistic knowledge without love. But Paul says that love is the thing that shows mature insight, true knowledge, adulthood. The way of love is the way an adult acts. This makes the distinction clear between this sort of love and any sort of passion, weakness, or sentimentality. Love means truth in the eyes of God; it means perfect knowledge in the eyes of God.

Then another image: "For now we see in a mirror. . . ." The thoughts of God are only seen in the world as if reflected in a mirror. We see them only as if in mirror writing. And God's mirror writing is hard to read. It says that the great is small and the small is great, that right is wrong and wrong is right, that a promise awaits the hopeless while judgment awaits those who are full of hope; it says that the cross signifies victory and death signifies life. We can read God's mirror writing in Jesus Christ,[8] in his life and sayings and dying.

[7.] Crossed out: "imperfect."

[8.] Crossed out: "who is the perfect mirror of God." On this interpretation, cf. the final chapter of *Discipleship*, "The Image of Christ" (*DBWE* 4:281–88).

¶ "For now we see in a mirror *dimly*. . . ."—seeing the cross dimly, in God's mirror writing, makes it really hard to recognize and to understand. That is the way we see now, certainly—"*but then* face to face." "*But then*," when the perfect comes breaking in, when the mirror of this world is shattered and the glorious light of God surrounds us. "*But then*," at the end, at our end, in the hour of our dying and ceasing and departure. "*But then*," face to face. . . . Then all will be clear, and perfect love will be with us. "*Face to face*"—to see God as God truly is; not only to believe in love but to see it and feel it, touch it and experience it, to live in its blessedness. "*Blessed are* the pure in heart, for they will *see God*"[9]—then, face to face.

398

"Now I know in part; then I shall understand fully, even as I have been fully understood." The answer is in that last phrase, "even as I have been fully understood." That is the only reason why I may hope to understand fully and to experience perfection—that I am understood by God, by love, by that which is perfect. God's light seeks out my eyes; God's love seeks my heart. God has long since known me and loved me—that is why I am so irresistibly drawn to God, to know God and to love God in return. That is why I press on so urgently toward God, toward perfection, even though I know only in part. I could never know God if God had not first known me. God and the human creature recognize each other. They see each other face to face, they know about each other, they know about their love for each other; they know that they cannot and should not be without each other. And now they are with each other and in each other, one in knowledge, one in the blessed mystery of their love. The human creature sinks down to the ground and stretches out his or her hands,[10] and is no longer his or her self, but is in God. That is perfection.[11] Amen.

[9.] Matt. 5:8.

[10.] Crossed out: "forgets himself or herself."

[11.] "Perfection" replaces "the end." Cf. Bonhoeffer's last recorded words, on April 8, 1945: "This is the end—for me the beginning of life" (*DB-ER*, 927. [See also 3/9, ed. note 9.—KC])

399 **17. Sermon on 1 Corinthians 13:13**
London, Reformation Sunday, November 4, 1934[1]

1 Cor. 13:13   Reformation Sunday, November 4, 1934

And now faith, hope, and love abide, these three; and the greatest of these is love.

This series of sermons was very intentionally planned so that this text would fall on Reformation Sunday. With this we wish to say that the church that has spoken, as probably no other has done, about the power and the salvation and the victory of faith in Jesus Christ alone, the church that is so great in its faith, must be even greater in its love. On the one hand, then, we want to look back to the original Reformation; on the other, we want to respond actively to a danger and degeneration that has threatened Protestantism since its beginnings. For the message of the faith that alone saves and redeems has become hardened, a dead letter,[2] because it has not been kept alive by love. A church may have great faith—the most orthodox beliefs, the firmest loyalty to its confession—but if it is not even more[3] a church of pure and all-embracing[4] love, it is good for nothing.

¶What does it mean to believe in Christ, who was himself love, if I still hate? What does it mean to confess Christ as my Lord in faith if I do not do his will? Such a faith is not faith but hypocrisy. It does nobody[5] any good to protest that he or she is a believer in Christ without first going and being reconciled with his or her brother or sister—even if this means someone who is a nonbeliever [gottlos], of another race, marginalized, or outcast.[6] And the church that calls a people [Volk] to belief in Christ must itself be, in the midst of that people, the burning fire of love, the nucleus of recon-
400   ciliation, the source of the fire in which all hate is smothered and proud, hateful[7] people are transformed into loving people. Our churches of the

---

[1.] Literary estate of Elisabeth Bornkamm; handwritten. Cf. *NL*, A 43,16; photocopy; partially reproduced in *GS* 5:555–60 and *PAM* 1:496–501.
[2.] "A dead letter" inserted.
[3.] "Even more" inserted.
[4.] "Pure and all-embracing" inserted.
[5.] Crossed out: "and no church."
[6.] Matt. 5:24. Cf. also *DBWE* 4:66. The following is crossed out: "Our hearts have been gratified by the news that our home church has found its way out of a badly confused situation."
[7.] "Proud, hateful" inserted.

Reformation have done many mighty deeds, but it seems to me that[8] they have not yet succeeded in this greatest deed, and it is more necessary today than ever.

"And now faith, hope, and love abide, these three . . ." "Faith"—that certainly means that no person and no church can live by the greatness of their own deeds, but rather they live by the mighty deeds of God alone, past and present,[9] and (this is the decisive thing) that God's great works remain hidden, unseen in the world. It is just not the same for the church as it is in the world and the history of the peoples. In the world it is important to be able to point to the great things one has done, but the church that did that would be showing that it has become enslaved to the laws and the powers of this world. *The church of success* is truly far from being *the church of faith.*

¶The deed that God has done in this world, the source of life for all the world ever since, is the cross of Golgotha. This is what God's "success" looks like, and this is what the successes of the church and of individual Christians will look like, if they are acts of faith. That faith abides—this means that it remains true that *humankind must live by that which is unseen,* that we do not live by our own visible work, but rather by the invisible act of God. The believer sees error and believes in truth, sees guilt and believes in forgiveness, sees death and believes in eternal life, or sees nothing—and yet believes in the work and the grace[10] of God. "My grace is sufficient for you, for power is made perfect in weakness."[11]

¶So it is with the church of the Reformation. It can never live by its own action, not even those performed in love. Instead, it lives by that which it has not seen yet believes.[12] It sees doom yet believes in salvation; it sees false teaching yet believes in God's truth; it sees betrayal of the gospel yet believes in God's faithfulness. The church of the Reformation is never the visible communion of saints but rather the church of sinners, which believes, against all appearances, in grace and lives only by that grace. "If you want to be a saint, get out of the church,"[13] Luther once exclaimed. Church of sinners—church of grace—church of faith—that's what it is. "So faith

401

[8.] "It seems to me that" inserted.

[9.] "No person . . . present" replaces "nothing in life depends on the greatness of what human beings do, but the only really great deeds in our lives must be done by God alone."

[10.] "And the grace" inserted.

[11.] 2 Cor. 12:9. Quotation inserted in text.

[12.] "Yet believes" inserted. Cf. John 20:29: "Blessed are those who have not seen and yet have come to believe."

[13.] Source not found.

abides"—because it lives before God and only from God.[14] There is only one sin, and that is to live without faith.

But a faith that bravely[15] clings to the unseen and lives by it, as if it were already here and now, hopes at the same time for the age of fulfillment and of seeing and having.[16] It hopes with the certainty of a hungry child whose father has promised him or her bread, who can wait for a while, but in the end really wants to have that bread; or like someone listening to music, who is willing to stay with it through a dark tangle of dissonances, but in the certainty that dissonance will resolve into harmony; or like a patient who takes a bitter drug so that it will finally take away the pain. Faith that has no hope is sick. It is like a hungry child who will not eat or [a] tired person who will not go to sleep. As surely as a person believes, surely he or she will also hope.

¶And hope is nothing to be ashamed of, hope beyond all bounds. Who would want to talk about God, without hope—the hope of seeing God someday? Who would want to talk about peace and[17] love among[18] humankind without wanting to experience[19] them someday, for all eternity? Who would want to talk about a new world and a new humanity without the hope of sharing in them oneself? And why should we be ashamed of our hope? It is not our hopes of which we will one day have to be ashamed, but our puny and fearful lack of hope, which doesn't trust God in anything, which in false humility fails to reach out for God's promises when they are given, which is
402   resigned to this life and cannot rejoice in God's eternal power and glory. "We bid you be of hope!"[20] "Hope does not disappoint us."[21] The more a person dares to hope, the greater he or she will become in his or her hope. Through hope, people grow—if it is hope in God alone and in God's power alone. So hope abides.

"And now faith, hope, and love abide, these three; and the greatest of these is love."

Again we hear the echo of the first verses of this chapter: . . . and if I have all faith, so as to remove mountains . . .—and we can add: and if I have all hope but have not love, I am nothing.[22] For the greatest of these is love.

[14.] "And only by the grace of God" added.
[15.] Uncertain reading, could also be "really."
[16.] "And having" added.
[17.] "Peace and" inserted.
[18.] "Among" replaces "for."
[19.] "Wanting to experience" replaces "experiencing."
[20.] Johann von Goethe, from the poem "Symbolum" (1815). English from Thomas Carlyle, *Critical and Miscellaneous Essays*, 4:482.
[21.] Rom. 5:5.
[22.] Cf. 1 Cor. 13:2. Cf. also the sermon of October 14, 1934, 3/14.

What can be greater than to live in faith *before* God? What can be greater than to live one's life *toward* God? What is greater is the love that lives *in* God.[23] "Walk before me!"[24] "He who abides in love, [abides] *in* God."[25] What is greater than the humility of faith, which never forgets how infinitely far the Creator is from the creature; what is greater than the confidence of hope, which longs for the coming[26] of God and the moment of seeing God's reality? What is greater is the love that here and now is sure of God's presence and nearness everywhere, that clings to God's love and knows that his love desires nothing other than our love. What is greater than faith, which hopes for and holds fast to its salvation in Christ and will be justified by him? What is greater than hope, which is prepared at any moment[27] for the blessedness of death and of going home? What is greater is the love that serves,[28] forgetting everything for the sake of the other, and even gives up its own salvation in order to bring it to the brethren—for those who lose their love for my sake will find it.[29]

Faith and hope abide. Let no one think it possible to have love without faith and without hope! Love without faith would be a stream without a   403 source.[30] That would mean that one could have love without Christ. *Through faith alone we are justified* before God, through hope we are prepared for our end, and through love we are made perfect.

Through faith alone we are justified—our Protestant church is built on this sentence. To the human question, how can I stand before God? Luther found the one answer in the Bible: if you believe in God's grace and mercy through Jesus Christ. To the question of how human beings can be justified before God, the answer is through grace alone, through faith alone. We would be entirely right if, here at the end, we turned the first sentence of the chapter around and said, *and if I have all love, so as to accomplish all good works*, but have not *faith*, I am nothing.[31] Faith alone justifies—but love makes perfect.

Faith and hope enter into eternity transformed into the shape of love. In the end everything must become love. Perfection's name is love.[32] But the

---

[23.] This sentence added.
[24.] Cf. Gen. 17:1.
[25.] Cf. 1 John 4:16. These last two quotes inserted.
[26.] "Coming" replaces "nearness."
[27.] "At any moment" inserted.
[28.] "That serves" inserted later.
[29.] Cf. Matt. 10:39: "those who lose their *life* . . ."
[30.] This sentence added.
[31.] Cf. 1 Cor. 13:2.
[32.] Taken from the beginning of the paragraph and inserted here.

sign of perfect love in this world bears the name cross. That is the way that perfect love must go in this world, must go over and over again. That shows us first of all[33] that this world is ripe, even overripe, for its destruction; only God's indescribable patience can wait for the end time. Second, it shows us that the church in this world remains the church under the sign of the cross. In particular, the church that wants to become the church of God's visible glory, here and now, has denied its Lord on the cross. Faith, hope, and love together lead us through the cross to perfection. [34]

404   When we go out the doors of this church now, we enter into a world that is longing for the things we have spoken of here[35]—not simply for the words, of course, but for the reality. [36] Humanity, [37] betrayed and disappointed a thousand times over, needs faith; humanity, wounded and suffering, needs hope; humanity, fallen into discord and mistrust, needs love. Even if we no longer have any compassion for our own poor[38] souls, which are truly in need of all three, do at least have compassion for your poor fellow human beings. They want to learn from us how to believe again, to hope, to love again; do not deny them. On this Reformation Sunday, let us hear the call—believe, hope, and above all, love—and you will overcome the world.[39] Amen.

[33.] "First of all" inserted later.

[34.] "It shows us . . . perfection" replaces "We cannot doubt that a world in which love is hung on a cross is nearing its end. We believe in it, we hope in it, that [crossed out: 'God'] the new world will come, that peace and love will be among humankind and worship, that all hate, all death, all torment, all violence, all misery must end and the kingdom must come that is ruled by love."

[35.] Crossed out: "a world that is poor in faith, hope and love."

[36.] The following sentence crossed out: "The world in which we live is poor, really poor in faith. It believes in that which it can touch [uncertain reading] and take hold of and understand—it lives a life between pride and resignation, without faith."

[37.] "Humanity" here and in the following three instances replaces "the world."

[38.] "Poor" inserted later.

[39.] Cf. 1 John 5:4.

**18. Sermon for Evening Worship Service on Proverbs 16:9
London, 1934[1]**

Proverbs 16:9. A man's heart deviseth his way: but the Lord directeth his steps.[2]

Whenever I have come to a foreign country and to a german congregation abroad, there was one question which struck me most; and this question was: how did all these people here come to this place? On which way were they led? Which were the multifarious motives and which was the strange destiny that brought them here? Did not chance and incalculable circumstances play a great role in their lives? Was it not very often that only quite a small cause became all important for the whole of their lives? But—on the other hand—there must have been very often an extremely strong, inflex- 405 ible, incomparable willpower which made its way and struggled through every sort of difficulties and finally reached its aim. Just imagine that each of us should get up and tell us how he got to this country, to this city, to this place.—I am sure all of us would be simply amazed about the strange and wonderful ways on which men are being led—and it would undoubtedly be a good thing for all of us to learn again what we forget so quickly, to survey the wonders of our lives hitherto. There would be no one who could not tell of great plans and hopes in his life, of many defeats and disappointments, of happiness and misery, of loneliness and fellowship, of restlessness and work, and perhaps of final peace and tranquillity which he had found after so long a wandering and struggle. Some of us are in the midst of their way, some are just beginning, others have been crudely interrupted and have to make a new start, the majority of us, however, will rather have to look back into the past than forward into the future. But no one has reached the end, we still have to go on wandering our road and no one knows where his road is leading him tomorrow.

But there has always been an interesting observation which made me think: it is striking how often you hear from young and old people when they tell you their lifestory and their plans—the old german proverb: "Jeder ist seines Glückes Schmied"[3]—*everyone forges his own luck.* This saying seems

---

[1.] *NL*, A 43,6; handwritten; in original English, including errors; presumably preached during 1934 in St. Paul's Reformed Church in London. Previously published (with language corrections) in *GS* 4:174–79. According to Eberhard Bethge, an evening service was held in English once a month at St. Paul's.

[2.] [King James Version.—KC]

[3.] According to Büchmann's *Geflügelte Worte*, this sentence is attributed to the Roman consul Appius Claudius, 307 B.C.E.

to express the experience of many of us to a great extent. It lies all with me and you, if we make our life a success or a failure, if we are happy or not, it depends altogether on my willpower, my work, my sacrifices, my temperament and my gifts, if we are content or if we are always discontented and grumbling against our fate—so they claim to know.

"Jeder ist seines Glückes Schmied." There is *the boy* who dreams of the time when he will be grown up, who dreams of the future and of success, of work [?] and honour and fame, of adventure and happiness—"how shall I attain it?" he asks himself day and night—and what answer could be prouder and simpler and more encouraging than this word: everyone forges his own luck? Strike the iron while it is hot![4] I suppose there is no boy whom these words would not stimulate to still greater hope and impatience.

There is the *grown-up* man who has experienced it often enough: it is you who must do it, you alone, you must struggle through, you must keep cheerful and optimistic even if everything is against you—"you must forge your luck."

And there is finally the *old man* who looks backward, who has seen much of this world, who perhaps started his life as a poor small boy and whose life was a success and who may pass away with the proud statement and advice: everyone forges his own luck.

But among all these unanimous voices there is one other voice which perhaps seems strange and foreign to us; it is the voice of the old wise king Salomo: "*A man's heart deviseth his way, but the Lord directeth his steps.*" This word is indeed the strictest contradiction to that old popular saying. It really makes all the difference if a man lives of the basis of this biblical or that popular proverb. It makes indeed all the difference if a man attempts to live on its own ideas, plans and devices and believes them to be the ultimate reality—or if a man realizes that neither his ideas and wishes nor even his highest willpower may destine his life, but that there exists some other unknown, unseen and hidden element which alone matters, which is behind every thing, which makes history of men and nations, which is the ultimate reality—called God Almighty. Our life is not a simple straight line, drawn by our own will and mind, but life is something which is composed of two different lines, two different elements, two different powers—life is composed of man's thoughts and Gods ways and in reality there is not even such a thing as man's way at all—for: "a man's heart deviseth his way"—that is to say it is only a devised way, a way in ideas, in theory, in illusion—but there is only one real way which we are bound to go inevitably and this is God's way.

406

[4.] This sentence added later.

The difference between these two ways is, that man wants to foresee the whole of his life at once, but God's way goes only step by step. "A man's heart   407 deviseth his way: but the Lord directeth his *steps*." This, of course, seems very unsatisfactory to man. Man wants to look over his life from the beginning to the end. But God does not allow it. He wants man to go step by step, guided not by his own ideas of life, but by God's word, which comes to him on every step whenever man asks for it. There is no word of God for the whole of our life. God's word is new and free today and tomorrow, it is only applicable to the very moment in which we hear it. God wants us to go step by step in order to drive us to Himself for help again and again.

Since we recognize that we cannot discover the mystery of our future *in reality*, we are trying to do it either in our imagination or with calculation. But life can never be calculated. Life is beyond the realm of figures and ideas, life laughs at every attempt to calculate it, for life comes from God Himself, who cannot be calculated in his plans, who is free to do whatever he pleases.—Life is dark and beyond the grasp of human understanding, so are man's ways and fates. Who understands them? Who interprets them?

Let me call your attention to an example which has occupied my mind since I was a boy. The most thoughtful game which man has ever invented, the game of chess, is a most wonderful symbol of human life. Life is like game of chess against a superior partner. There are two partners who join the game; each one deviseth his way to win the game. But it is the weaker one who will soon make the following observation: he has his plan, he seems to go on, to succeed; the partner is yielding, his moves seem to be quite insignificant, he does not even appear to understand my—the weaker player's—intentions, he is yielding more and more, so that I do not even pay any attention anymore to his moves. But suddenly, just before I intend to make the last decisive moves, I am faced with my own disaster, I must recognize that my partner has already won the game before I had understood one of his moves. And it is only now, when the game is over and when my defeat is evident, that I begin to understand gradually every single move of my partner and I begin to realize why he appeared so slow, so hesitating. Now I understand all the apparently insignificant moves which led so necessarily to my defeat.

You understand what I am trying to say. Man is the loser. God is the win-   408 ner, but God lets man make a start, lets him go on, succeed, and he seems to be entirely passive, his countermoves seem quite insignificant. We seldom notice them at all. So we go on proud and selfconscious and certain of our success and final victory. But God can wait, he waits sometimes years and years, he suffers us going on for years and years and does not appear to see that we are going on the wrong way,[5] in the hope that man finally will understand his moves and surrender his life to him. But once in every man's life—and it may be only in the hour of his death—God crosses man's way so that man *cannot* go any further, that he must stop and recognize in fear and trembling[6] God's power and his own weakness and misery,—that he must surrender his life to him who is the victor, that he must ask for mercy; for nothing but mercy can help him.

It is only in these great moments of our life that we understand the meaning of God's guidance of our life, of God's patience and God's wrath[7] and it is only then, that we recognize that these hours in which God has crossed our way are the only hours which matter in our life, which make our life worth living.

Man's plans are crossed by God's way and this crossing *points to that place* in the world where all human desires, ideas and ways were crossed by God's way—it points to the Cross of Christ—two directions, two ways, one crossed through the other—man's will crossed and crucified by God's will; man's defeat—God's victory; man's end—God's beginning; man's crucifixion—God's kingdom. Only the way of man which leads to the Cross is the way which is directed by God step by step—and which finally must lead[8] through this Cross to the life ever-lasting. Amen.

[5.] "He suffers . . . way," inserted later, along with an illegible further addition, perhaps "God waits."

[6.] Cf. Phil. 2:12, as well as Søren Kierkegaard's work *Fear and Trembling.*

[7.] "Of God's patience and God's wrath" inserted later.

[8.] "And which finally must lead" replaces "directed and leading."

19. Sermon for Evening Worship Service on 2 Corinthians 12:9
London, 1934 (?)[1]

"my strength is made perfect in weakness"[2]
2 Cor. 12:9

All philosophy of life has to give an answer to the question which presents itself everywhere in the world: what is the meaning of weakness in this world, what is the meaning of physical or mental or moral weakness?[3] Have we ever thought about it at all? Have we ever realized that ultimately our whole attitude toward life, toward man and God depends on the answer to this problem? Even if we have never faced this question intellectually, do we know that actually[4] we are bound to take[5] an attitude towards it every day? What has remained unconscious with us,[6] shall become conscious now, conscious in the light of the word of God. There is a certain inclination in human nature to keep off from all problems that might make us feel uncomfortable in our own situation. We like to leave these questions in the darkness of subconscious action rather than to put it into the light of a clear and responsible intellectual attitude. We are all dealing with the problem of weakness every day, but we feel it somewhat dangerous to give account of our fundamental attitude. But God does not want us to put our head into the sand like ostriches, but he commands to face reality as it is and to take a truthful and definite decision.

Someone might ask: why is this problem of weakness so all-important? We answer: have you ever seen a greater mystery in this world than poor people, ill people, insane people—people who[7] cannot help themselves but who have just to rely on other people for help, for love, for care. Have you ever thought what outlook on[8] life a cripple,[9] a hopelessly ill man, a socially   410

[1.] *NL*, A 43,7; handwritten; in original English, including errors; probably preached during 1934 at St. Paul's Church (for possible indication of date, see ed. note 14). Previously published (with language corrections) in *GS* 4:179–82.

[2.] [King James Version.—KC]

[3.] "Physical . . . weakness" replaces "physically [replaces 'bodily'] or mentally or morally weak man."

[4.] Replaces "practically."

[5.] "Bound to take" replaces "taking."

[6.] Crossed out, in order: "ever since," "hitherto," "up to now."

[7.] "Poor people . . . people who" replaces "a man who physically or mentally weak."

[8.] The text says "of."

[9.] In this and the following passage, Bonhoeffer is clearly distancing himself from the Nazi ideology, which at that time had authorized the sterilization of persons with disabilities under the "Law for the Prevention of Genetically Ill Progeny" and eventually led

exploited man, a coloured man in a white country, an untouchable[10]— may have? And if so, did you not feel that here life means something totally different from what it means to you and that on the other hand you are inseparably bound together with the unfortunate people, just because you are a man like them, just because you are not weak but strong, and just because in all your strength[11] you will feel their weakness?[12] Have we not felt that we shall never be happy in our life as long as this world of weakness from which we are perhaps spared—but who knows for how long—is foreign and strange and far removed from us, as long as we keep away from it consciously or subconsciously?[13] (Bethel!)[14]

Let us be truthful and not unreal, let us ask the question: What is the meaning of weakness in this world? We all know that Christianity has been blamed ever since its early days for its message to the weak. Christianity is a religion of slaves,[15?] of people with inferiority complexes; it owes its success only to the masses of miserable people whose weakness and misery Christianity has glorified. It was the attitude towards the problem of weakness in the world which made everybody to followers or enemies of Christianity. Against the new meaning which Christianity gave to the weak, against this glorification of weakness, there has always been the strong and indignant protest of an aristocratic philosophy of life which glorified strength and power and violence as the ultimate ideals of humanity. We have observed this very fight going on up to our present days. Christianity stands or falls with its revolutionary protest against violence, arbitrariness and pride of power and with its apologia for the weak.—I feel that Christianity is rather doing too little in showing these points than doing too much. Christianity has adjusted itself much too easily to the worship of power. It should give much more offence, more shock to the world, than it is doing. Christianity should [. . .][16] take a

411

---

to euthanasia for those considered "unworthy of life." Cf. also 1/68, ed. note 3 (letter of February 2, 1934, from Bonhoeffer's father).

[10.] "A socially exploited man" and "an untouchable" inserted later.

[11.] Uncertain reading.

[12.] "And just because . . . weakness" inserted later.

[13.] Crossed out: "This world of weakness is the thorn in our flesh."

[14.] Added later as a note in the margin, perhaps in relation to a letter of July 31, 1934, in which Bonhoeffer asked H. Fricke to send a donation from his London congregations to Friedrich von Bodelschwingh, director of the clinics and nursing homes at Bethel, Sarepta, and Nazareth near Bielefeld (see 1/131). This could indicate the date of this sermon.

[15.] This phrase was coined by Friedrich Nietzsche; see his *Beyond Good and Evil*, 204–37, and *On the Genealogy of Morals*, 36–43. Cf. also *DBWE* 9, 3/2, p. 491, ed. note 1, and 3/15, p. 529, ed. note 2.

[16.] Illegible insert.

much more definite stand for the weak than to consider the potential moral right of the strong.

In the middle between the christian and the aristocratic view there is a great variety of attempts to mediate between them. The most dangerous of these positions is the very common attitude of benevolence and beneficience.[17] There the seriousness of the problem is not [at] all recognized. Weakness to them[18] is nothing but imperfection. But this includes, of course, that the higher value in itself is strength and power. Strength and weakness are considered [. . .][19] in the proportion of the perfect and in the imperfect. Here Christianity must protest. With all due respect for the real sacrifices that have been made in such a benevolent attitude, it must be said frankly that this approach is wholly wrong and unchristian,[20] for it means condescension instead of humility. Christian love and help for the weak means humiliation of the strong before the weak, of the healthy before the suffering, of [thc] mighty before the exploited. The Christian relation[21] between the strong and[22] the weak is that the strong has to look *up* to the weak and never to look down. Weakness is holy, therefore we devote ourselves to the weak. Weakness in the eyes of Christ is not the imperfect one[23] against the perfect, rather is strength the imperfect and weakness the perfect. Not the weak has to serve the strong, but the strong has to serve the weak, and this not by benevolence but by care and reverence. Not the powerful is right, but ultimately the weak is always right. So Christianity means a devaluation of all human values and the establishment of a new order of values in the sight of[24] Christ. 412

Here we have arrived at the last question: What is the reason for this new conception[25] of the meaning of weakness in the world? Why is suffering holy? Because God has suffered in the world from man, and wherever he comes, he has to suffer from man again. God has suffered on the cross. It is therefore that all human suffering and weakness is sharing God's own suffering and weakness in the world. We are suffering: God is suffering much

---

[17.] Corrected several times. One version plainly said "attitude of a benevolent and beneficient one to the weak." See also the following note.

[18.] "To them" replaced by an illegible correction. "To them" referred to the "benevolent and beneficient one(s)" mentioned in the sentence before the last one.

[19.] Illegible insert.

[20.] Replaces "dangerous."

[21.] Replaces "attitude."

[22.] The text says "to."

[23.] The text says "over" instead of "one."

[24.] "In the sight of" replaces "before."

[25.] Uncertain reading.

more. Our God is a suffering God.[26] Suffering conforms man to God. The suffering man is in the likeness of God. "My strength is made perfect in weakness" says God. Wherever a man in physical or social or moral or religious weakness is aware of his existence and likeness[27] with God, there he is sharing God's life, there he feels God being with him, there he is open for God's strength,[28] that is God's grace, God's love, God's comfort, which passeth[29] all understanding and all human values.[30] God glorifies himself in the weak as He glorified himself in[31] the cross. God is mighty where man is nothing.[32]

413   **20. Sermon on Mark 9:23–24**[1]

Mark 9:23–24: "If you are able!—All things can be done for the one who believes." . . . "I believe; help my unbelief!"

To a person who is in what appears, to human eyes, to be a hopeless situation, Jesus says this: if you could believe. Then everything in your life would be different. Then you wouldn't be standing here so timidly, so desperately, because then you would know that nothing is impossible for you. These words are spoken to a father whose child, in human terms, is incurably ill, who would do anything to help his son and yet must look on helplessly while the child is destroyed. The father has tried everything he can think of and finally has come to Jesus' disciples;[2] and now only one way is left, one that

---

[26.] "We are suffering . . . suffering God" added later, replacing "Suffering opens the eyes of man to God and to his presence." [Cf. this theme in Bonhoeffer's later prison writings, e.g., his letter of July 16, 1944: "The Bible directs man to God's powerlessness and suffering; only the suffering God can help" (*LPP*, 361).—KC]

[27.] "Likeness" replaces "conformity."

[28.] "Is sharing . . . open for" inserted later, replacing "receives from."

[29.] Allusion to Phil. 4:7 in King James Version.

[30.] "Which passeth . . . values" added later.

[31.] "In" replaces "on."

[32.] Crossed out: "so we may see God's glory."

[1.] *NL*, A 33,9; handwritten; undated. Previously published in *GS* 4:88–92 and *PAM* 1:430–36; in *GS* it is classified among the Berlin sermons. Otto Dudzus, however, thinks that because of the watermark of the paper used, this sermon belongs to the same period as the London sermon on 2 Cor. 12:9 (3/19). On the other hand, certain aspects of the content speak against London, for example, Bonhoeffer's remark that he had seen "a play about the life of St. Francis" "a few weeks ago." See also ed. note 4.

[2.] "The father has tried everything he can think of and finally has come to Jesus' disciples" replaces "The father may have tried everything."

he treads in fear and trembling, the way that causes everyone to tremble, the first time we walk it—the *way to Jesus.*

Why would we rather take any other way than the way to Christ[3] himself when something goes wrong in our lives? Why do we avoid really choosing this way? Why do we shudder and turn away? Because we know that we will have to answer a mighty question, and this question is: Can you believe? Can you believe in such a way that your whole life becomes, or will become, one great act of trust in God, of daring to believe in God? Can you so believe that you never look to left or right but do what you have to do for God's sake? Can you so believe that you obey God? Can you believe? If you could believe, then yes, help would be at hand. Then nothing would be impossible for you any longer.

How often we are terrified by our own lack of faith. Oh, if only I *could*   414 believe! At the bedsides of those who are sick and dying, at the edge of despair over myself and others, this is the cry that rises up in me: oh, if only I *could* believe! Yet when we have the chance to observe the life of someone who lived and died in faith, as I did a few weeks ago when I saw a moving play about the life of St. Francis,[4] then we are totally convinced that this is the only way that is worthwhile—just to live the way Christ wants us to, without worrying about what is going to happen to us personally.[5] Then it takes hold of us irresistibly: if only I could believe, yes, then my whole life really would be different. Then I would be free, perhaps even somehow happy, because nothing would be impossible for me anymore. "I can do all things through him who strengthens me, Jesus Christ."[6]

We do believe in all sorts of things, far too many things in fact. We believe in power, we believe in ourselves and in other people, we believe in humankind. We believe in our own people [Volk] and in our religious community, we believe in new ideas[7]—but in the midst of all those things, we do not believe in the One[8]—in God. And believing in God would take away our faith in all the other powers, make it impossible to believe in them. If you believe in God, you don't believe in anything else in this world, because you

---

[3.] "Christ" replaces "Jesus."

[4.] In 1931 Chr. Kaiser Verlag published, as no. 30 in the series Münchener Laienspiele, *Ein Spiel vom Heiligen Franz* (A play about St. Francis), by Otto Bruder (the pseudonym for Otto Salomon), 3rd ed. (1st and 2nd eds. published by Neuwerkverlag). It is not known when or where Bonhoeffer saw this play.

[5.] "To us personally" inserted afterward.

[6.] Cf. Phil. 4:13.

[7.] This sentence added later.

[8.] "In the midst of all those things, we do not believe in the One" replaces "we do not believe."

know it will all break down and pass away. But you don't need to believe in anything "else," because then you have the One who is the source of all things, in whose hands everything comes to rest.

¶We know the victories that can be won by a person who truly believes in himself or herself, or who believes in any power or idea[9] in this world to the point of total self-surrender to it and living it out. Such a person can accomplish superhuman things, impossible things. How much greater will be the victory of the person whose faith is not in some subjective illusion but in the living God! The miracles of Jesus, the effect that he had on people, were nothing other than his faith! *We* should be the ones to live by such faith. How ashamed we must be when we look at our lives, even compared to the accomplishments of people who had faith in the things of this world. Oh, if only we could believe!

¶Why can we not believe? What are the obstacles to our faith? There are as many answers to that as there are unbelieving people. One would cite intellectual difficulties, another would plead not having a "gift for religion," for another it would be a hard experience of life, a generally pessimistic outlook, and so on. There is no lack of reasons that we can put forward to excuse ourselves. No human being ever lacks these, even when everything else is lacking. But the *one* honest answer to this question is that we basically do not *want* to believe. I know we feel offended if someone says that. We say we must have tried a hundred times over in our lives to believe, and even now we still want to, but it is just that way for us in particular—we really, even with the best will in the world, just simply *cannot* believe. This is not true; it is all a sham, even though we may not be consciously aware of it. What is true[10] is that in all these despairing and strained efforts to believe, what we really wanted was not to believe. That is, we didn't want that which is the first requirement of faith, namely, to surrender ourselves totally, not to think of ourselves anymore, to extinguish completely our need for recognition and recognize God alone, to put our trust and dare to believe in God alone. We would surrender what was uncomfortable to us, but not that which we cared about![11] To have faith means to trust and to dare *unconditionally*, and that we didn't want; we wanted to set conditions, and thereby we missed the whole point, and our whole effort was not genuine. *We did not want to believe.*

[9.] "Or idea" inserted later.

[10.] The punctuation in the original is uncertain here: "it is true" could be construed as concluding the previous sentence (after being crossed out and written in again), but it makes more sense if it belongs to the next sentence, as opposed to concluding the previous one and contradicting its opening words.

[11.] Sentence added later.

If someone comes with pious arguments proving that the Bible says there   416
are people whom God has predestined not to be able to have faith but rather
to be objects of wrath that are made for destruction,[12] our answer is, That
may be true, but how do you know that you are one of them? Who told you
that? How do you know that it is not actually your fault that you refuse to
believe, when God has never stopped calling you? You want to have faith—all
right, isn't that enough to show that God is calling you, that [you] are supposed to have faith and that you can believe if you will only trust in him? *We
do not want to believe.*

But Jesus says: if you could believe. There is longing and infinite compassion in these words. If only you would decide to take this step that you have
wanted all your life to take and never did, to believe. If only you would give
yourself up, quite simply and in everything that is most personal and specific
to you, and let Jesus be your Lord.

All things are possible for the one who believes. Here we are talking about
an incurable illness, which is really supposed to be broken through faith
in the power of God and in fact is broken. We stand amazed; we look for
excuses, ways it could have happened: suggestive influences or unconscious
psychotherapy. Christ says no, none of that; it was faith, it was God.

All things. People who study the human mind know that the thing that
seems least possible is to break through a mental pattern or mental compul-
sion that has a person in its grip, to turn the person in a different direction.
Jesus says, *All things.* People who live lives of religious devotion know that we
have no hope of combating our sins, our selfishness, our weaknesses,[13] as
long as we rely on ourselves alone,[14] that nothing is more desperate than
a human being's struggle against sin. Jesus says, all things are possible for
those who believe. The most hardened and stubborn sinner becomes a new
being, free from all fear,[15] all compulsiveness, all evil habits, if he or she   417
will only believe—that is, will dare to put his or her trust in God. The most
melancholy person becomes joyful, the most timid soul becomes outgoing,
the most diffident and lukewarm character is suddenly glowing with [new]
life—"if only you could believe."

All things are possible—We can think of so many times when we turned to
God wanting to believe,[16] when we prayed and called to God to help us, if it

---

[12.] Rom. 9:19–23.
[13.] "Our selfishness, our weaknesses" inserted later.
[14.] Here the phrase "a short time—then once more" has been added later.
[15.] "Fear" replaces "guilt" (uncertain reading).
[16.] Uncertain reading; might also be "turned to God full of belief."

be his will—and we did not receive the help, at least not in the way we asked for it. All things—is it really true?

Doesn't that almost mean that faith can *compel* God? Yes, that is indeed what it means! But that is just what is so incredible, that God *wants* to be compelled by our faith—not by our complaining and lamenting and worrying and sighing, but by our faith. That almost sounds blasphemous—but could it be true? Isn't *God's will*, after all, the place where every true[17] faith must meet its limit? What does it mean, to believe in God, if not to make room for God's will, what God wills for us, for the world? Can there then be anything at all that is not possible, if it is God's will? And don't we know very well what God's will is for our lives? Don't we know very well what God's will is for our people [Volk] and for our church? Shall we not dare at last, in faith, to let God's will for us be done?

You answer:[18] Lord, I believe; help my unbelief! The promise that Jesus has given to the one who believes draws this father out beyond his own limitations, compels him to believe. Jesus himself compels the man to have faith, so that he says, Lord, I believe—I believe what you say, I believe that your word and your promise are true. I believe, *when I am looking at you*, when I hear the words, when I see. But *when I am looking at myself*, then, dear Lord, *help my unbelief*. When I am besieged, when everything in me resists such a promise—reason, history, the world, my experience—help my unbelief.

We are being asked whether we believe. We are being called upon—oh, if only you could believe! To us the promise is given: all things are possible. *Looking at these words*, is there any answer we can make, other than: Lord, I believe—and looking at our own nature, is there any prayer we can make, other than: Lord, help my unbelief. No one can escape this paradox. Do you believe? I believe—help my unbelief, which is [there] anew every day. Who is ready to say, I believe, in the face of the temptations we experience every hour? Lord, we want to dare it, at your word—but our faith cannot make it happen; only you can. Not we ourselves, not even our faith, but you alone—for you, nothing is impossible. Lord, help my unbelief! Amen.

418

[17.] "True" inserted.
[18.] Uncertain reading.

21. Funeral Address on Luke 2:29–30
London, 1934 (?)[1]

St. Luke 2:29–30. Lord, now lettest thou thy servant depart in peace [. . .] : For mine eyes have seen thy salvation.[2]

A life, full of joy and full of suffering, has come to its end. Death came as friend and took away all pain and anxiety from her; and we stand in solemn thankfulness before God, who in his mercy has put an end to this suffering. She is released, God has wiped away all tears from her eyes, she is with him in eternal rest. Five daughters and sons have lost their loving mother who had sacrificed her life for them, a great number of families have lost a faithful friend, and our congregation has lost one of its true and active members. There must have been much love in this life, much loyalty to old friends, much true devotion to the christian church—our gathering here is, indeed, a living proof for it.—But there is no human word of comfort strong enough to those who have been afflicted most of all by this dead. It is Gods own word   419 alone which helps us to the right vision of things and which gives us a brave and quiet heart in such troubled times. Lord, now lettest thou thy servant depart in peace—death of a Christian means peace for body and soul, and we all feel strongly,[3] it must be wonderful to have peace after a life in labour and sorrow. No human life finds true peace in this world, the other world is the world of peace; and we long for the time when all pious[4] souls will meet again in that restful world to come.

"Mine eyes have seen thy salvation." There are many things that the eyes of an old woman have seen. Many joyful and happy days in marriage and family, many wonderful things in the growing up of her children and grandchildren. She saw generation[s] coming and passing, she saw the joys of youth, the duties of married life, and the burdens of old age. Her eyes saw love and fellowship, but her eyes also saw the dark shadows of life. Her eyes had seen enough to be closed for ever. But they would not have seen all, they would not even have seen the most important thing in life—if one could not say—mine eyes have seen Thy salvation. Only the man who can say so, joyfully and thankfully, can close his eyes in peace. They have shown him whatever a man is granted to see by the Almighty, they have shown him a glimpse

---

[1.] *NL*, A 43,23; handwritten; in original English, including errors; the person and date of the funeral are unknown, but probably delivered in London in 1934.

[2.] [King James Version.—KC]

[3.] "Feel strongly" replaces "understand."

[4.] "Pious" replaces "our."

of the world to come, of the world where there is no sin, no pain, no labour anymore. We thank God that he has opened her eyes to see him, that he has revealed his true life to her that she could bear her suffering in faith and hope. In taking leave from the mortal body which we loved, we praise God that He has saved her soul and has let her depart in peace, that he has shown her salvation. May God grant us a life at the end of which we might speak as our dear sister could speak: "Lord, now lettest thou thy servant depart in peace; for mine eyes have seen thy salvation." Amen.

420   **22. Fragment of a Wedding Sermon**[1]

. . . we will find the peace of God. There are three great things that preserve the peace of God: the readiness of each person to sacrifice for the other, to pray and to forgive sins. What gives us the strength to do this? Because God has made peace with us, therefore we have peace, even when it does not at all appear to be so, and therefore we have hope. Therefore you, too, will have peace in your marriage, because Christ has come to dwell with you. And your marriage will become like a piece of the church,[2] dwelling in the peace of God in this world and the next. Amen.

23. Bible Reading and Prayer on 1 Corinthians 4:20 and James 2:13–17[1]

"For the kingdom of God depends not on talk but on power."[2]

"For judgment will be without mercy to anyone who has shown no mercy; mercy triumphs over judgment. What good is it, my brothers and sisters, if you say you have faith but do not have works? Can faith save you? If a brother or sister is naked and lacks daily food, and one of you says to them, 'Go in peace; keep warm and eat your fill,' and yet you do not supply their

---

[1.] *NL*, A 43,24; handwritten; there is also a copy of it in Bonhoeffer's literary estate in unknown handwriting.

[2.] Cf. *DBWE* 3:100 and 125, and *DBWE* 4:234, 249, and 264–65, with reference to Eph. 5:22–33.

[1.] *NL*, Anh. A 6 (6); handwritten; found in Bonhoeffer's copy of the Old Prussian Union Church program statement. On the back, the following note in English indicates it stems from the London period: "We stand at the frame of a man whose life was a life of labour."

[2.] 1 Cor. 4:20.

bodily needs, what is the good of that? So faith by itself, if it has no works, is dead."[3]

Lord, do not allow us to go around spouting empty words and pious sayings,[4] but show us that it is better to love than to produce words and better to obey than to argue. We are always trying to escape from your commands with words and various pious sayings. Hold us fast, take us captive, compel us to obey your word, which is valid for today. May we do today what we can do today, and may we do it in faith and so begin this year,[5] Lord, in humility. Our Father . . .

421

[3.] James 2:13–17.
[4.] Uncertain reading.
[5.] Illegible word.

HANS GOEDEKING, MARTIN HEIMBUCHER,
AND HANS-WALTER SCHLEICHER

EDITORS' AFTERWORD
TO THE GERMAN EDITION

I

The decision to leave Germany and become a pastor abroad, taking charge   422
of two German congregations in London, did not come easily to Dietrich
Bonhoeffer. He could not count on more than a few friends and like-minded
colleagues to understand his motives. A few days after arriving in London,
he tried to explain his reasons in a letter to Karl Barth,[1] saying that he had
always wanted to be a pastor. But he could not accept a pastorate in his Prussian home church without giving up his "unconditional opposition" to the
German Christian dominated church and "abandoning [his] solidarity with
the Jewish Christian pastors." He also found himself "in some way [he didn't]
understand" in radical opposition to all his friends and becoming increasingly isolated in his views. "And so I thought it was about time to go into the
wilderness for a spell, and simply work as a pastor."

Bonhoeffer here justified his decision to the theologian who—in agreement and disagreement—had become the definitive authority for him since
the beginning of the 1930s.[2] He acknowledged that he had been afraid to
ask Barth's advice and had only informed him of the decision after going
away, because he wanted to remain free to make his own decision. And Barth
replied plainly enough indeed: "And now that you have come to me with this
after the fact, I truly cannot do otherwise than call to you, 'Get back to your

---

[1.] Letter of October 24, 1933, 1/2.
[2.] On the relationship between Barth and Bonhoeffer, see *DB-ER*, 175–86.

post in Berlin straightaway!'"[3] Neither Bonhoeffer nor Barth could foresee at the time how many consequences Bonhoeffer's move to London would have for the church opposition as well as later for the political opposition in Germany.

In any case, Bonhoeffer's acceptance of the pastorate in London represented an interruption in the academic career that he had begun with great success. He did not in fact close the door behind him forever, taking only a leave of absence from the Berlin University faculty.[4] Yet during the time in London his fundamental doubts about the value of pursuing academic theology grew, particularly given the situation at that time. "I no longer believe in the university; in fact I never really have believed in it," he wrote in September 1934 to his friend Erwin Sutz.[5] At the same time, the events of the Church Struggle compelled him constantly to rethink the basic questions about the nature of the church—the topic of his dissertation in 1927—and these now demanded to be tested in concrete church practice.

Barth's fear that Bonhoeffer was trying to withdraw from the Church Struggle by going abroad is contradicted by the letter that Bonhoeffer wrote, before he left for London, to Theodor Heckel, the senior consistory official in the Reich Church government who was responsible for pastors abroad. "I am not a German Christian and cannot honestly represent the German Christian cause abroad. Of course, my first duty would be as pastor to the German congregation. But I believe that my connections with leading circles in the English churches resulting from ecumenical work, as well as my personal interest in the ecumenical task of the churches, would make it inevitable that I be called upon to take a position on issues of the German church and the German Christians, because people will approach me with questions about it. . . . I would rather be obliged to give up going to London than to arouse any lack of clarity about my position."[6]

This is an early indication, clearly expressed to the Church Foreign Office, of what Bonhoeffer's two main activities were to be in London, besides his work as a local pastor: the Church Struggle and ecumenical relations. Bonhoeffer had no intention of withdrawing into the quiet of a remote parsonage but was determined to use his ecumenical connections on behalf of the Church Struggle. That a twenty-seven-year old academic should succeed within a short time in persuading not only his influential ecumenical friends but also the German congregations in England and his fellow pastors to take

---

[3.] Letter of November 20, 1933, 1/16.
[4.] See 1/45.
[5.] Letter of September 11, 1934, 1/147.
[6.] Letter of October 4, 1933, *DBW* 12, 1/107.

influential positions on the German Church Struggle and to maintain them at least during the months he was in England is impressive testimony to this young man's persuasive powers.

II

It may be useful to sketch the political situation in the church in Germany as it was when Bonhoeffer left for London. At the beginning of April 1933, after organized acts of violence against Jewish businesses, the so-called Aryan paragraph was announced as part of the Law for the Reconstitution of the Civil Service, which excluded Jews from the civil service. A few days earlier, German Christians had declared at their "Reich conference" in Berlin that persons of "alien blood" did not belong in the pulpit and should not be allowed to be married at German Protestant altars. In June the general super-intendents of the Old Prussian Union Church [comprising the provinces of Berlin, Brandenburg, the Rhineland, and Westphalia] were suspended, and August Jäger was appointed state commissioner of the Protestant Church. In July a constitution for a new national Protestant Church was promulgated with Hitler's signature, and national church elections were called at short notice. Through massive involvement of the National Socialist Party appara-tus, the German Christians gained more than 70 percent of the votes. Then, in September, the general synod of the Old Prussian Union introduced the Aryan paragraph into the church as well, and on September 27 at the national synod in Wittenberg, Ludwig Müller was made Reich bishop.

Certainly these developments did not take place unopposed. At the first election for Reich bishop on May 27, 1933, the opposition did succeed in electing Friedrich von Bodelschwingh, against Ludwig Müller, the Ger-man Christian candidate. Barely one month later, however, Bodelschwingh resigned after Jäger's appointment. In the months that followed, there were university rallies, protest delegations, services of atonement and prayer, and even visits by representatives of ecumenical organizations in Geneva. After the opposition had been defeated in the church elections in July, the ques-tion arose as to what possibilities remained for practical resistance to the new church policies, and—as a prerequisite—for a clear formulation of the church's nonnegotiable confessional foundation in the Reformation. Pre-liminary work began on the Bethel Confession.

Unlike many others, Dietrich Bonhoeffer realized early the fundamen-tal significance of discrimination against "non-Aryans" for the church as well as for the rest of society. He actively opposed it from the beginning. In April 1933 he was already writing an essay, "The Church and the Jewish Question," in which he made it clear that the questions raised pertained not

425

only to the fate of a few "Jewish Christians" but also to the very nature of the church itself. At the university in June, in front of two thousand students, he debated the Aryan paragraph with Emanuel Hirsch and others. In July he went to the Gestapo to protest their search of one of the offices of the Young Reformation League and was threatened with imprisonment in a concentration camp. In August he helped to formulate the Bethel Confession but ultimately refused to sign the final version because he felt it had been watered down too much compared with the original draft, particularly in its theological rejection of anti-Semitism. And in September he worked with Martin Niemöller to prepare for the founding of the Pastors' Emergency League. He continually raised the question—together with his friend Franz Hildebrandt, who was directly affected by the Aryan paragraph—as to whether responsible pastors should not resign from their positions and convene as a free church, but hardly any of his supposedly like-minded colleagues agreed.

426   In view of this situation and the fact that, for Bonhoeffer, the crucial struggle was not about church policy issues of the day but concerned the very foundations of the church itself, his decision to go abroad had definite consequences.

III

When Dietrich Bonhoeffer went to London, it was not the first time he had served in the ministry, nor was it the first congregation abroad in which he had worked. He had served as vicar in Barcelona in 1928–29 and since the autumn of 1931 had been student chaplain at the Technical College in Berlin-Charlottenburg; he had also taught a confirmation class in the Berlin-Wedding district in 1931–32. Thus he was familiar with the duties of a pastor and was attracted to them in many ways. But it is one thing to be the vicar who sometimes substitutes for the pastor in leading worship, in administering the sacraments, or in social ministry, or to minister to a very specific sector of society as a student chaplain—it is quite another to be *the* pastor responsible for two congregations. The duties that awaited Bonhoeffer in London also included some that were unique to congregations abroad, since they had a particular social role in offering companionship with compatriots.

Bonhoeffer took over two congregations in London: the United congregation of Sydenham in the south of the city, whose members were mainly prosperous, and in the east the two-hundred-year-old Reformed St. Paul's Church, most of whose members came from working-class families. For many at St. Paul's, German had already become a foreign language, so that now and then Bonhoeffer was called upon to preach in English there.

Bonhoeffer's first impression of these two churches, when he came there as a candidate in July 1933, was of "congregations in rather a neglected state."[7] Soon after he assumed his duties, he tried to introduce a series of innovations: Sunday school classes, youth groups, presentation of nativity and passion plays, festive worship services on special days, a new hymnal.[8] That these initiatives did not always meet with full approval is certainly not surprising in view of the usual tendency to conservatism in congregations abroad.   427

There is comparatively little documentation of Bonhoeffer's social ministry during this period. But there is plenty of testimony to his heartfelt concern for the refugees who were arriving in increasing numbers from Germany. He wrote to the bishop of Chichester on their behalf,[9] persuaded the congregational councils to take up collections for the emigrants,[10] and went several times to Baron Schröder for help.[11] He contacted Reinhold Niebuhr in New York when the Communist writer Armin T. Wegner arrived in London, having just been released from a concentration camp, to find out if there was a possibility for him to make a living in the United States.[12] Above all, he also gave generously out of his own pocket to relieve the hardships of the new arrivals during their first days.

Bonhoeffer put a great deal of effort into preparing his sermons. In a letter to his grandmother he confessed that preaching every Sunday was not easy for him.[13] The manuscripts that have survived show that not only was he very demanding of himself as a preacher but he also expected his listeners to digest an often strong message. For the congregation, it was quite a change from the "mild, folksy, pious sermons of his predecessor" to the penetrating and theologically sophisticated interpretations of the young lecturer in systematic theology.[14]

However, in many of these sermons Bonhoeffer also gave proof of a pastoral capacity for empathy. The sermon for Remembrance Sunday in 1933 shows a mature humanity that one would hardly expect from a twenty-seven-year-old (and it also left a deep impression on his friend Hildebrandt,   428

[7.] See his letter to Karl Barth, 1/2.

[8.] Several indications of such activities are found in the Sydenham *Gemeindebote*; see, e.g., 2/1.

[9.] See, for example, the letter of January 7, 1935, 1/188.

[10.] Cf. 1/201.

[11.] See 1/187.

[12.] See 1/127.

[13.] Letter of May 22, 1934, 1/110.

[14.] See *DB-ER*, 330.

who was present).[15] Also intensely vivid was the Advent Sunday sermon in which Bonhoeffer compared the approaching hope of salvation with that of a miner trapped underground who hears his rescuers coming nearer.[16] It was preached only days after a mine accident in Wales had been in the headlines.[17]

At first glance, one might wonder why Bonhoeffer did not relate his preaching more directly to the political and church events back home that were affecting him so deeply. However, the method of "linking" with historical events had become inadmissible for Confessing Church preachers because of its misuse in the theology of the German Christians. Nevertheless, and perhaps precisely *because* Bonhoeffer refused to use direct "topical" references in his sermons, his listeners could hardly have been in doubt about the intensity of their preacher's contemporary concern.

In this light, the manuscript of his sermon for July 8, 1934, following the June 30 killings (in the wake of the so-called Röhm putsch) in Germany, makes gripping reading.[18] It is full of fresh starts, pages of crossed-out sections and corrections, which testify to the degree to which Bonhoeffer was torn between these deeply disquieting events and the strict homiletic standards he set for himself. In the face of this literal "wrestling" to go beyond political indignation to a passionate call to repentance—directed not toward Hitler and the National Socialists but rather toward himself, the congregation, and the whole church—secondary categories like "political" or "apolitical" are not adequate to classify Bonhoeffer's preaching. And members of the congregation who had "ears to hear" would have understood why this preacher, right after the highly official protest letter from the London pastors had been sent to Berlin in January 1934, gave voice to his most personal confession through his sermon on Jeremiah 20:7: "God, it was you who started this with me. It was you who pursued me . . . who always appeared in front of me wherever I went, who enticed and captivated me. It was you who made my heart submissive and willing, who talked to me about your yearning and eternal love, about your faithfulness and might. . . . When you won me over, I lost; my will was broken; I had too little power; I had to follow the way of suffering . . . I could no longer turn back; the decision about my life had been made. It was not I who decided, but you who decided for me. You have bound me to

429

[15.] 3/3; see also Hildebrandt, "Erinnerungen an Forest Hill (1933–1934)," 38.

[16.] 3/4.

[17.] [The accident nearest in time to the date of this sermon actually occurred in Derbyshire, England. See 3/4, ed. note 3.—KC]

[18.] 3/12.

you for better or worse. God, why are you so terrifyingly near to us?"[19] We also learn from some of the letters that Bonhoeffer wrote to friends during these months that the possible personal consequences of a decisive opposition to National Socialism were already quite clear to him.[20]

IV

It must soon have been clear to Bonhoeffer, there in London, that not a few of his friends in Germany missed him. Their thoughts were similar to those of Karl Barth, who had written in that letter of November 20: "I can only and shall always have the same answer: And what of the German church? And what of the German church?—until you are back in Berlin, manning your abandoned machine gun like a loyal soldier."[21]

When he received this letter, however, Bonhoeffer was already involved once again in the German Church Struggle—if now from England. On November 13, at the German Christians' mass rally in the Berlin Sports Palace, the top Nazi district official, Dr. Krause, had called for "liberation from the Old Testament with its Jewish money morality and from these stories of cattle-dealers and pimps,"[22] thereby arousing widespread indignation, even among some German Christians. Through telephone calls, telegrams, and letters, Bonhoeffer and Hildebrandt intervened in the increasingly fierce disputes and the shaping of opinion within the church opposition.[23] They 430 saw the Church Struggle as a challenge to decide between the false and the true church. And only a few weeks after arriving in England, Bonhoeffer had an opportunity to present his view of the situation in Berlin at the annual conference of German pastors in England.[24] Although he could not prevent the pastors' decision to send a delegation to the planned installation of the Reich bishop, he did persuade them to have this delegation carry a declaration to the Reich Church government in which they clearly threatened to dissolve their ties with the Reich Church.[25]

That first action was soon followed by others: telegrams of protest to the church leadership and letters to government offices, even to the Reich presi-

---

[19.] 3/7, p. 351.
[20.] Cf. 1/93 and 1/133.
[21.] 1/16, p. 40.
[22.] [Cited in *DB-ER*, 335.—KC]
[23.] See *DB-ER*, 335–38; also 1/21–1/27.
[24.] See 1/20.1.
[25.] 1/20.2.

dent, in the name of the pastors or of the Association of German Congregations.[26] These were backed up by numerous telephone calls, which in addition to sharing information helped to stiffen the spines of the opposition and encourage them. The statements of telephone and telegram charges that have been found among Bonhoeffer's papers come to more than twenty-five pounds for January through March 1934 alone,[27] a considerable sum in those days—a circumstance in which the London post office, unsure what to do, reacted by reducing the amount the foreign pastor had to pay.[28]

The documents presented in this volume illustrate the problems of the time as well as the clarity with which Bonhoeffer judged these developments and the determination with which he confronted the official policies of the church. When Theodor Heckel traveled to London in February 1934 to pour oil on the troubled waters, a storm blew up instead. Opposing positions on theological principles and on church policy were taken in the ensuing discussion. But when Heckel then tried to apply pressure by insinuating that the pastors were aligning themselves with treasonous activities, Bonhoeffer and two colleagues left the meeting. He was no longer willing to continue the conversation under the circumstances.[29]

A particular success for Bonhoeffer's efforts was surely the decision of the German Protestant churches in England to secede from the Reich Church, on November 5, 1934.[30] For the congregations themselves this had hardly any practical consequences, but it drew attention within the church in Germany and among congregations abroad, even if the overseas congregations in England were the only ones to make such a clear decision in the conflict between their loyalty to the church policies in their homeland, on one hand, and their confession, on the other. That this occurred so decisively was due primarily to Dietrich Bonhoeffer. He was able to persuade the congregations and his colleagues that the Church Struggle was actually about *principles* of faith that had to be given more weight than any national or "folk" ties. With Bonhoeffer's departure, however, the critical momentum for maintaining this position was lost. The decision to secede from the Reich Church was never executed in a legal sense. Two years later it did lead to a dispute between the Church Foreign Office and the two congregations for which Bonhoeffer had been directly responsible. There were also considerable dif-

431

[26.] See, for example, 1/27, 1/48, 1/52, 1/56.
[27.] *NL*, Anh. D 1,9.
[28.] See *DB-ER*, 327–28.
[29.] See 1/74.1.
[30.] See 1/159.

ficulties between St. George's Church in London, where Julius Rieger was pastor (and where Franz Hildebrandt found a position as assistant pastor in 1937), and the authorities in Berlin.[31] None of the other German churches in England, however, pursued the issue of separation from the Reich Church and its possible consequences any further.

V

432

Two circumstances were favorable to Bonhoeffer's opposition activities in England. First, the German congregations there were more independent of the Reich Church than those in Germany or in other countries. Second, Bonhoeffer had opportunities for close contacts with influential ecumenical figures, who could offer outside support to the Confessing Church in its struggle.

Soon after his arrival in London, Bonhoeffer activated his ecumenical contacts. At the beginning of November 1933, he made the acquaintance of George Bell, the bishop of Chichester. This meeting was followed by a lively correspondence and numerous personal encounters between Bell and Bonhoeffer. Bell also recommended Bonhoeffer to other church leaders and politicians because of his outstanding knowledge of the German situation. The trust that quickly developed between the bishop and the young German theologian became a personal friendship in the months that followed. Bonhoeffer was able to approach Bell with extensive requests and proposals without fear of being misunderstood. For his part, Bell adopted Bonhoeffer's view of the Church Struggle with respect to important issues that, with the discriminating judgment of an experienced ecumenist, he could interpret to great advantage. The bond between Bell and Bonhoeffer was to remain significant beyond the years 1933–35, both personally and politically. In the spring of 1939, anticipating his military conscription orders, Bonhoeffer—determined to exercise conscientious objection to military service under Hitler's state—sought Bell's spiritual counsel.[32] In 1942 in Sigtuna, Sweden, Bonhoeffer informed Bell about the names and objectives of the resistance group around Ludwig Beck and Carl Goerdeler, which was preparing a coup. His purpose was to obtain a positive signal through Bell from the British government for this group, in order to make it easier for those in the German opposition who were still hesitant to act.[33] Finally,   433

[31.] See *DB-ER*, 405–6, and Gerhard Niemöller, "Die deutschen evangelischen Gemeinden in London und der Kirchenkampf," 141–46.

[32.] See *DB-ER*, 638–39.

[33.] See *DB-ER*, 757–70.

Bonhoeffer's last recorded words were a message to Bell, on April 8, 1945, the day before his execution: "[T]ell him that this is for me the end, but also the beginning—with him I believe in the principle of our Universal Christian brotherhood which rises above all national hatreds and that our victory is certain—tell him, too, that I have never forgotten his words at our last meeting."[34]

Bonhoeffer decisively used his personal contact with Bell, like his ecumenical contacts in general, in the service of radical opposition to the German Christian church regime. It was he who provided the impetus for Bell's "Ascension Day Message"[35] in the spring of 1934, which prepared the way for the declaration of solidarity with the Confessing Church by the ecumenical conference in Fanø. On April 15, 1934, Bonhoeffer conveyed to Bell the "outcry" of a German friend: "In the present moment there depends everything, absolutely everything on the attitude of the Bishop of Chichester."[36] August Jäger had been appointed "legal administrator" of Ludwig Müller's "Clerical Ministry," and the Reich bishop was trying through "peace declarations" to take the wind out of the sails of the church opposition. Bonhoeffer, however, was quite familiar with the people who were doing these things as well as their aims and would permit no illusions about any possibility of reaching agreement with this church regime. On the contrary, he feared that the desire to broaden the "oppositional front" might come at the price of losing the church resistance's unambiguous stand.[37] Thus Bonhoeffer tried from the outside, through the ecumenical movement, to push for more clearly defined alternatives. The difficulty was that with this he made demands on ecumenical partners from which even many of his German friends recoiled.

434   Both at home and abroad, Bonhoeffer was demanding refusal of *any* cooperation, not only with the German Christians but also with those such as Heckel who tried to take positions "between the two fronts." And while "naive, starry-eyed idealists like Niemöller" still considered themselves to be "the real National Socialists"[38]—although this would change radically in the course of the year 1934—Bonhoeffer refused to allow political prudence to rule in church and ecumenical matters. During the preparations for the Fanø conference, he alerted his Geneva colleagues that members

---

[34.] Letter of October 13, 1953, from Payne Best to George Bell (*DBWE* 16, 1/239, p. 469). See also the lecture Bell delivered on May 15, 1957, in Göttingen, previously published in *GS* 1:399–413 (see esp. p. 412); see also *DB-ER*, 927.

[35.] 1/103.

[36.] 1/89.

[37.] See 1/133.

[38.] Letter from Bonhoeffer to Erwin Sutz, April 28, 1934, 1/93.

of the German youth delegation would not attend sessions at which representatives of the Reich Church government were present.[39] He was also uncompromising in turning away German pastors who wanted to attend the youth conference if he was not sure of their position on the church situation.[40] And he implored ecumenical leaders not to yield to the temptation of political or strategic restraint, which had so often paralyzed the church opposition in Germany. With respect to the Fanø conference, he wrote Danish bishop and World Alliance leader Valdemar Ammundsen: "It is precisely here, *in our attitude toward the state*, that we must speak out with absolute sincerity for the sake of Jesus Christ and of the ecumenical cause. It must be made quite clear—terrifying though it is—that we are immediately faced with the decision: National Socialist *or* Christian."[41]

Both in the Confessing Church and in his ecumenical work, Bonhoeffer fought for the enforcement of the confessional decision, and he demanded a readiness to accept the political consequences. In 1933 he was virtually the only figure to contemplate the possibility of direct conflict with the unjust state on the "Jewish question" as a consequence of church solidarity with the Jewish Christians. Not only should a "council" judge between true and false doctrines, but if necessary it should also provide a defense against the effects of destructive policies. Bonhoeffer now called for comparable action at the ecumenical level in the cause of peace. The Fanø conference was taking a "conciliar" decision by standing up for the Confessing Church over against the German Christian church regime. Here again Bonhoeffer came with the demand—for many at the conference, a utopian one—that the ecumenical movement, as "the Church of Christ in the name of Christ," should take "the weapons from the hands of [the peoples'] sons"—that is, in the face of the threat of war, call for conscientious objection to military service.[42]

435

Bonhoeffer's activities and demands in the Church Struggle and in the ecumenical sphere should not be seen as stemming only from the political farsightedness of one whose contacts, in both Germany and England, extended into government circles. Ultimately they can only be explained in the light of his christological understanding of the church. "Christ existing as community"—the concept that Bonhoeffer expressed with this short phrase in his dissertation—had been tried in the fire of seven years' experience, as encouraging as it was frustrating, of church reality at home and abroad. It now had a profound existential meaning for him. As hesitant and

---

[39.] Letter of July 4, 1934, to Théodore de Félice, 1/122.
[40.] Letter of August 12, 1934, to Théodore de Félice, 1/136.
[41.] Letter of August 8, 1934, 1/134.
[42.] "The Church and the Peoples of the World," 2/3.

ambiguous as the Confessing Church in Germany might appear, for Bonhoeffer this was the reality confessed to in words of the Barmen Theological Declaration: "The Christian Church is the congregation of the brethren in which Jesus Christ acts presently as the Lord in Word and sacrament through the Holy Spirit."[43] And though the ecumenical realm might be haunted by many *theologumena* over which students of Luther and Barth could only shake their heads, nonetheless, an ecumenical conference must be expected, in common prayer and common decision, in repentance and obedience, to be a place where the church becomes visible. Of course, it would do so in the same way as every other form of the church, in brokenness, yet as that *una sancta* that was to bring hope to the nations.[44] Such expectations and such a promise remain, to this day, challenges that the ecumenical movement has yet to meet.

436

VI

It is striking that hardly any academic theological documents by Bonhoeffer exist from the entire period of his stay in London, although there is a wealth of them from the periods immediately before and after. There was probably little time for such work between his parish work, the Church Struggle, and ecumenical meetings. We know that in the spring of 1934 he was particularly preoccupied by the Sermon on the Mount, since he wrote to his friend Sutz on April 28: "Please write and tell me sometime how you preach about the Sermon on the Mount. I'm currently trying to do so."[45] The sermons in question, which have not been preserved, are clearly connected with first drafts on "discipleship." The following summer Bonhoeffer mentioned that he was working on some writing having to do with the Sermon on the Mount.[46] He seems to have made use of this work, at the end of his time in London, in preparing his New Testament lectures on "discipleship" at the preachers' seminary, which in turn gave rise to the book published in 1937.

A long-cherished wish of Bonhoeffer's came to the fore during his last months in London, in connection with the work he was to take up in the preachers' seminary: his desire to visit India and especially to meet Mahatma Gandhi. Bonhoeffer was interested in the combination of a *vita communis*

[43.] From the third thesis of the Barmen declaration, in Cochrane, *Church's Confession under Hitler*, 240.

[44.] Cf. Bonhoeffer's 1935 essay "The Confessing Church and the Ecumenical Movement," *DBW* 14, 2/6.

[45.] 1/93.

[46.] See 1/127.

with political resistance work, with which, in his view, the "heathen" Gandhi put Western Christianity to shame.[47] During 1934 Bonhoeffer apparently made two attempts to get in touch with Gandhi, first through Gandhi's friend   437
C. F. Andrews and later through Bishop Bell. Herbert Jehle was included in the first plans he made in the spring and summer.[48] At that point Bonhoeffer was considering taking more time off from his activities in the Church Struggle. But by autumn he was thinking of it entirely in terms of his preparations for the seminary at Finkenwalde. He then planned to go to India for only a few weeks, together with Julius Rieger, to gain stimulating ideas for the "life together" and training of his ordination candidates in the seminary.[49] When it later became impossible for him to carry out his India plans, he and Rieger visited several spiritual and monastic communities in England. The beginnings of his intense concern with the issues of "life together" certainly date from this period.

The year and a half during which Bonhoeffer worked in London definitely have their place in the continuity of his life's path and are in no way to be regarded as an unessential interval. None of the concerns that had moved and preoccupied him in the foregoing years was forgotten or put aside during this time, and few of the driving forces of his life in London remained without consequences later on, whether for himself, the church, or the political scene. Whereas previously in Berlin he had been surrounded by a relatively large number of like-minded people, even though he increasingly felt himself to be isolated, in London he first had to seek out his allies. He did this, however, surprisingly quickly, and it must have helped him overcome the uncertainty about his future path that he felt during his first months in London.

During his absence from Germany, the politics and church policy goals of those in power became clearer, the fronts more sharply defined, and the prospects for the future gloomier. These developments confirmed more and more Bonhoeffer's judgment and conviction as to what was most important   438
in that situation. Looking back on the time in London, he could see two high points: the Fanø conference and the decision of his congregations in London to secede from the Reich Church. Despite these successes, when Bonhoeffer went home he did not go primarily as a church policy maker and ecumenical leader. Instead, he was committed above all to the training of young pastors—although indirectly and fundamentally this was to

---

[47.] See 1/54, 1/127, and 2/3.

[48.] Cf. 1/93, 1/110, 1/111, 1/127; also Jehle, "Auf der Seite der Verfolgten."

[49.] Cf. 1/154 and 1/158; also Rieger, *Dietrich Bonhoeffer in England*, 27–32, and *DB-ER*, 407–9.

make an influential contribution to both church policy and the ecumenical movement. After Bonhoeffer had supported the beginnings of the church opposition movement "with all [his] might," he now turned to the task of awakening and strengthening the forces for "an opposition of a very different kind."[50] For Bonhoeffer, concentrating on a spiritual task within the church could never mean a quietist retreat from political responsibility, any more than going to London had meant that. The way was being prepared for political steps with entirely new dimensions, for which Bonhoeffer's various activities during the London years and their interrelatedness provided a foundation and background experience. From 1933 to 1935, Bonhoeffer proved himself, as theologian and as Christian, to be above all a "man for his times" who was prepared to assume great personal risks and sacrifices for the sake of both church and society.

[50.] Cf. 1/93.

APPENDICES

Appendix 1.
Chronology 1933–1935

1933	October 14	Germany leaves the League of Nations.	441
	October 17	Beginning of his London ministry	
	October 22	Sermon on 2 Cor. 5:20	
	October 24	Letter to Karl Barth defending his decision to go to London	
	November 13	Sports Palace rally of the German Christians in Berlin, with Reinhold Krause's speech	
	November 19	Sermon on 2 Cor. 5:10. First suspensions in Germany from the ministry	
	November 21	Bonhoeffer's first visit to Bishop Bell in Chichester	
	November 26	(Day of Remembrance) Sermon on Wis. 3:3	
	November 27–30	Ministry conference in Bradford/Yorkshire	
	December 3	(1st Sunday in Advent) Sermon on Luke 21:28	
	December 17	(3rd Sunday in Advent) Sermon on Luke 1:46–55	
	December 20	Protestant Youth groups subsumed into the Hitler Youth	
1934	January 4	Ludwig Müller's "muzzling decree"	
	January 21	Sermon on Jer. 20:7	
	January 25	Hitler's reception of the Protestant church leaders	
	January 31	Bonhoeffer attends ecumenical youth commission meeting in Paris	
	February 8–9	Church Foreign Office delegation led by Heckel visits London	

429

	February 13	Bonhoeffer attends Council of Brethren meeting in Hanover before going on to Berlin, where he becomes ill
	February 21	Heckel appointed bishop, overseeing the Church Foreign Office
	March 1	Ludwig Müller places Martin Niemöller in involuntary retirement
	March 6	Complaint about Bonhoeffer to the Church Foreign Office; Bonhoeffer attends independent synod meeting in Berlin-Brandenburg
	March 22–ca. April 19	Suzanne and Walter Dreß visit London
	April 12	August Jäger named "legal administrator" of the German Evangelical Church. Beginning of compulsory incorporations of regional churches into the Reich Church
442	April 22	Ulm declaration issued by the confessional front
	April 29	(Cantate Sunday) Sermon on Ps. 98:1
	May 3	Marriage sermon on Ruth 1:16–17
	May 10	Bishop Bell's Ascension Day message to the ecumenical world
	May 27	(Trinity Sunday) Sermon on 1 Cor. 2:7–10
	May 29–31	Reich confessing synod in Barmen; Barmen Theological Declaration
	June 18	Bonhoeffer in Berlin; discusses participating in the Fanø meeting with Karl Koch and Martin Niemöller
	June 24	Baptismal sermon on Josh. 24:15
	June 30	Röhm putsch
	July 8	Sermon on Luke 13:1–5
	July 9	Wilhelm Frick forbids public statements about the Protestant church dispute
	July 25	Austrian president Dollfuss murdered
	August 2	Reich president Hindenburg dies; Hitler personally assumes both the presidency and the chancellorship
	August 18–30	Bonhoeffer arrives in Fanø
	August 20	Bernhard Rust orders all civil servants to take a loyalty oath; Karl Barth refuses to swear the oath as is

August 22	Ecumenical youth conference begins in Fanø
August 24–25	"Lutheran Council" founded
August 28	Bonhoeffer's peace speech at the ecumenical conference of the World Alliance for Life and Work in Fanø
August 30	Resolution in support of the Confessing Church passed in Fanø under protest by Bishop Heckel
September 3	Bonhoeffer attends Reich Council of Brethren meeting in Würzburg; reports on Fanø
September 4–8	Bonhoeffer visits Jean Lasserre in Bruay-en-Artois; French-German-British youth conference
September 23	Installation of Reich Bishop Ludwig Müller
End of September	Sermon on Matt. 11:28–30
October 6–12	Bishops Wurm and Meiser placed under house arrest
October 14	Sermon on 1 Cor. 13:1–3
October 16	At the German embassy in London, archbishop of Canterbury Cosmo Lang threatens to break ecumenical ties with the Reich Church
October 19–20	Second Reich Confessional Synod in Dahlem; synod declares a state of emergency church law and establishes emergency governance of the Protestant church
October 21	Sermon on 1 Cor. 13:4–7
October 26	August Jäger resigns
October 28	Sermon on 1 Cor. 13:8–12
October 30	Confessing bishops visit Hitler: Bishops Marahrens, Meiser, and Wurm cleared
November 1	Invitation from Mahatma Gandhi
November 4	(Reformation Day) Sermon on 1 Cor. 13:13
November 5	German Protestant congregations in England break with the Reich Church government
November 20	Church incorporation law rescinded; Reich Church project collapses
November 22	First provisional church administration of the Confessing Church is established. Karl Barth and Martin Niemöller resign in protest from the Reich Council of Brethren

443

	November 25	Bonhoeffer sings in the chorus of the Brahms Requiem and then travels to Berlin, where he negotiates with Westphalian church president Karl Koch and the Ministry of Foreign Affairs
	December 22	Karl Barth loses teaching position in Bonn
1935	January 4	Congregational councils of St. Paul's and Sydenham refuse to recognize the Reich Church government through acceptance of the German Evangelical Church constitution
	January 13	Saar plebiscite
	January 29	Bonhoeffer's memorandum to the ecumenical youth commission
	February 4	Bonhoeffer travels to Berlin for three days
	February 11	Bonhoeffer requests a leave of absence from St. Paul's from March 15 to September 15, 1935, to direct a Confessing Church preachers' seminary
	February 24	Confirmation service in Sydenham
	March 10	Farewell sermon in London
	March 16	Universal compulsory military duty instituted in Germany
	March 25	Bonhoeffer informs the Church Foreign Office of the six-month leave of absence he has been given from the London congregations
444		
	March 26	Bonhoeffer visits the Anglican monastery in Kelham
	March	Bonhoeffer visits the "Community of Resurrection" in Mirfield
	March 30	Bonhoeffer in Edinburgh
	April 12	Bonhoeffer returns to London
	April 13	Confirmation of Hans-Heinrich Treviranus in Sydenham, London
	April 15	Bonhoeffer meets with George Bell in London; return to Germany

Appendix 2.
Unpublished Material from Bonhoeffer's Literary Estate
1933–1935

---

1. Letters and Documents   445

Addressee or Content	*Date*	NL *Reference*
To Miss Luce		
(Baron Schröder's secretary)	December 1, 1933	A 41,1 (12)
To Walter Dreß	ca. January 6–12, 1934	*NL* S. Dreß in possession of Andreas Dreß, Bielefeld
Excerpts from the council meeting minutes of the St. Paul's Church (German Reformed) in London	May 7 and July 30, 1934	
Entry in Mrs. Flemming's visitor book	May 27, 1934	Anh. D 1,6 (1)
To Herbert Jehle (postcard)	September 17, 1934	A 41,9 (7)

2. Reports and Lectures

Theme	*Date*	*First Publication*
F. Hildebrandt, Ten Theses for the Free Churches	April 1934	*GS* 1:167

3. Sermons and Meditations
—No additional material—

Appendix 3.
Texts Published in *Gesammelte Schriften* and in *DBWE 13*

GS	*DBWE* 13		
1:39–41	134–36	2:138–39	28–29
1:41–43	216–18	2:139	37
1:181–83	151–55	2:139–40	43
1:182–83	64–65	2:142	74–75
1:184–85	118–19	2:142–43	87–88
1:185–86	120–21	2:143–44	88–89
1:187–89	128–30	2:144	89
1:189	139	2:145	115
1:189–91	140–41	2:145	116
1:192–93	144–46	2:146	117–18
1:194	147–48	2:147–18	49–50
1:195–96	156–58	2:149–50	52–53
1:196–97	167–68	2:150	54–55
1:197–200	176–79	2:150–51	55
1:200–202	179–81	2:151–52	56
1:205–6	191–92	2:152–54	65–67
1:207	196	2:154–55	75–76
1:207–8	198	2:156	186–87
1:216–19	307–10	2:157–58	81–82
1:220–21	211–13	2:158	77
1:222	213–14	2:159–60	83–84
1:444–44	304–306	2:160–62	121–22
1:447–47	307–310	2:162–63	131
		2:164–66	301–304
		2:169	130–31
2:130–34	21–24	2:170	132–133
2:134–37	39–41	2:171	137–38

2:172	139	5:542–49	382–87
2:172	148	5:549–55	387–91
2:173	168–69	5:555–60	392–96
2:173–76	169–72		
2:177	181	6:220	72–73
2:177–78	226–27	6:288	74
2:179	143–44	6:288–89	119
2:179–80	153–54	6:289	297
2:181–83	151–53	6:290–91	42–43
2:184	224	6:291–93	92–95
2:185	225	6:293–94	99
2:186–87	236–37	6:294	146
2:187	238	6:294–97	182–84
2:188–89	255–57	6:297–98	188
2:190	259	6:298–99	199–200
2:191–92	270–71	6:300–301	241
2:192	275–76	6:301–2	242
2:192–94	276–77	6:302	296
2:194	285–86	6:303	363
2:195–96	279–80	6:304–7	44–49
2:196–97	281–82	6:307–8	82
2:200–202	315–18	6:308	84
		6:308–9	90
3:24–25	284–85	6:309–10	91–92
		6:310–12	102–4
4:88–92	404–8	6:312–19	104–13
4:154–59	326–31	6:322	143
4:160–65	331–36	6:322–23	123
4:166–70	337–41	6:323	124
4:171–74	347–49	6:324	216
4:174–79	397–400	6:324	155
4:179–82	401–4	6:324	138
		6:324–25	222
5:491–98	321–26	6:325	228–29
5:498–504	342–47	6:326–29	231–36
5:505–9	349–53	6:329–34	245–49
5:510–15	353–57	6:334–37	252–55
5:515–20	360–63	6:337–40	266–70
5:521–27	365–70	6:341	33
5:527–33	371–75	6:341–43	25–26
5:534–42	375–81	6:343–46	30–33

6:346–47	33–34	6:352–53	174–75
6:347–49	70–71	6:354	186
6:349	90	6:354–56	193–96
6:349–50	126	6:356	223–24
6:350–51	126–27	6:356–57	287
6:352	163–67	6:357–59	289–90

BIBLIOGRAPHY

1. Archival Sources and Private Collections

Dietrich Bonhoeffer's papers and personal library, as well as correspondence from others and relevant material in other archives, have been cataloged in the *Nachlaß Dietrich Bonhoeffer* volume compiled by Dietrich Meyer and Eberhard Bethge. All such citations in *DBWE* are indicated by *NL*, followed by the corresponding reference code within that published index. Not all this material is part of the actual Bonhoeffer Nachlaß in the Staatsbibliothek in Berlin; footnote citations of *NL* material from other archives also give the numbering from the respective archive. All the material listed in the Meyer and Bethge catalog, however, has been included on microfiches at the Bundesarchiv in Koblenz and in the Bonhoeffer collection at Burke Library, Union Theological Seminary, New York. The designation *NL Bibl.* in some bibliographic records indicates that a copy of the book was found in Bonhoeffer's personal library.

Archiv der Evangelischen Kirche im Rheinland, Düsseldorf
Archives of the Dietrich Bonhoeffer Church, Sydenham, London (ADBC)
    Bestand Gemeinde-Verband
      (Records of the Congregational Association)
    Kirchenbücher und Protokolle, Sydenham and St. Paul
Archives of the German St. George's Church, London
Archives of the World Council of Churches, Geneva (WCC Archives)
    World Alliance
    Youth Commission of World Alliance
    Life and Work, Study Department
Auswärtigen Amtes/Politisches Archiv, Berlin (formerly in Bonn)
    Bestand: VI A, Ev. Angelegenheiten
Bruderhof Archives, Woodcrest, Rifton, New York

439

Bundesarchiv Koblenz (BA Koblenz)
 Nachlaß Erich Seeberg
 Nachlaß Ernst Wolf
 R 43 II163: Akten der Reichskanzlei
Evangelisches Zentralarchiv, Berlin (EZA)
 Bestand 5: Kirchliches Außenamt
 Bestand 50: Kirchenkampf Archiv
 Bestand 51: Ökum. Archiv (Sammlung Siegmund-Schultze)
Karl Barth-Archiv, Basel
Lambeth Palace Library, London (LPL)
 Bell Papers, Volume 42 (Dietrich Bonhoeffer) and Volume 5
Landeskirchliches Archiv der Evangelischen Kirche in Westfalen,
 Bielefeld (LKA EKvW)
 Bestand 5,1: Archiv Wilhelm Niemöller
Landeskirchliches Archiv Stuttgart (LKA Stuttgart)
Library of Congress, Washington, D.C.
 Papers of Reinhold Niebuhr
National Library of Scotland, Edinburgh
 Holdings: ACC 9251 (Papers of Professor Franz Hildebrandt)
New College Library, Edinburgh
 J. H. Oldham files
Royal Library, Copenhagen
 Ammundsen Archive
Sammlung Sutz, Herrliberg, Switzerland
Schroders Bank, London, Archives (SBL)
 Holdings: Family Papers
Staatsbibliothek zu Berlin
 Nachlaß Dietrich Bonhoeffer (Nachlaß 299)
Zentralarchiv der Evangelischen Kirche in Hessen und Nassau,
 Darmstadt (ZEKHN)
 Bestand: 35/45

Private Collections (locations at the time of German *DBW* publication)
 Eberhard and Renate Bethge, Wachtberg-Villiprott
 Elisabeth Bornkamm, Heidelberg
 Ulrich Kabitz, Munich
 Hildegard Lämmerhirdt, Brakel/Westphalia
 Sabine Leibholz, Göttingen
 Rudolf Weckerling, Berlin

2. Literature Used by Bonhoeffer

Bell, George K. A. *Die Kirche von England (Ecclesia I)*. Translated by Dietrich Bonhoeffer, Elisabeth Reinke, and Berta Schulze. Edited by Friedrich Siegmund-Schultze. Gotha: Klotz, 1934. Originally published as *A Brief Sketch of the Church of England* (London: Student Christian Movement, 1929).

Die Bibel oder die ganze Heilige Schrift des Alten und Neuen Testaments nach der deutschen Übersetzung D. Martin Luthers (The Bible or entire Holy Scripture of the Old and New Testaments according to the German translation of Dr. Martin Luther). Edition commissioned by the German Evangelical Church Conference. Mitteloktav-Ausgabe. Stuttgart, 1911. *NL-Bibl.* 1 A 6.

Brunner, Emil. *Das Gebot und die Ordnungen: Entwurf einer protestantisch-theologischen Ethik*. Tübingen: J. C. B. Mohr (Paul Siebeck), 1932. *NL-Bibl.* 4.6. Translated by Olive Wyon as *The Divine Imperative: A Study in Christian Ethics* (Philadelphia: Westminster Press, 1947).

Deutsche Theologie. Periodical published by W. Kohlhammer Publishers in Stuttgart, 1934–43. After 1944: *Theologische Rundschau*.

Niebuhr, Reinhold. *Moral Man and Immoral Society: A Study in Ethics and Politics*. New York: Charles Scribner's, 1932. *NL-Bibl.* 4.33.

Protestantism in the Totalitarian State. Friends of Europe 12. London: Friends of Europe, 1934.

Wurmbach, Adolf. *Wir sind die drei Könige mit ihrem Stern*. Edited by Rudolf Mirbt. Münchener Laienspiel Verlag 50. Munich: Chr. Kaiser Verlag, 1930.

3. Literature Mentioned by Bonhoeffer's Correspondents

Althaus, Paul, et al. *Die Kirche und das Staatsproblem in der Gegenwart* (The church and the problem of the state today). Kirche und Welt: Studien und Dokumente 3 (Church and world: studies and documents). Papers presented by Paul Althaus, Emil Brunner, and V. A. Demant at an ecumenical study conference, Paris, April 1934. Geneva: Research Department, Universal Christian Council for Life and Work; Berlin: Furche-Verlag, 1934.

Barth, Karl. *Lutherfeier, 1933*. Theologische Existenz heute 4. Munich: Chr. Kaiser Verlag, 1933.

———. *Reformation als Entscheidung*. Theologische Existenz heute 3. Munich: Chr. Kaiser Verlag, 1933.

Benedix, Roderich. *Die zärtlichen Verwandten: Lustspiel in drei Aufzügen* (The gentle relatives: A comedy in three acts). 1864. Reprint, Leipzig: P. Reclam Verlag, 1904.

Hildebrandt, Franz. *EST: Das lutherische Prinzip* (EST: The Lutheran principle). Göttingen: Vandenhoeck & Ruprecht, 1931.

Künneth, Walter, and Helmuth Schreiner, eds. *Die Nation vor Gott: Zur Botschaft der Kirche im Dritten Reich* (The nation before God: On the church's message in the Third Reich). 1933. 3rd ed. Berlin: Wichern Verlag, 1934.

Nichols, Beverly. *Cry "Havoc."* 4th ed. London: Jonathan Cape, 1933.

Scheler, Max. *Vom Ewigen im Menschen.* 1923. 3rd ed. Berlin: Der neue Geist Verlag, 1933 (popular edition). Translated by Bernard Noble from the 4th German edition as *On the Eternal in Man* (London: SCM, 1954).

Stapel, Wilhelm. *Der christliche Staatsmann: Eine Theologie des Nationalismus* (The Christian statesman: A theology of nationalism). Hamburg: Hanseatische Verlagsanstalt, 1932.

4. Literature Consulted by the Editors

Akten zur deutschen Auswärtigen Politik 1918–1945. Series C, *1933–1937.* Vol. 3: *Das Dritte Reich: Die ersten Jahre*; part 1: *June 14 to October 31, 1934.* Göttingen: Vandenhoeck & Ruprecht, 1973. Translated as *Documents on German Foreign Policy, 1918–1945, from the Archives of the German Foreign Ministry* (Washington, D.C.: U.S. Government Printing Office, 1949).

Arnold, Eberhard. *God's Revolution: Justice, Community, and the Coming Kingdom.* 2nd ed. Farmington, Pa.: Plough, 1997.

———. *Innenland.* Berlin: Furche Verlag, 1918. Translated as *Inner Land: A Guide into the Heart and Soul of the Bible.* 2nd ed. (Farmington, Pa.: Plough, 1999).

Barnett, Victoria. *For the Soul of the People: Protestant Protest against Hitler.* New York: Oxford University Press, 1992.

Baum, Marcus. *Against the Wind: Eberhard Arnold and the Bruderhof.* Translated by the Bruderhof Communities. Farmington, Pa.: Plough, 1998. Originally published as *Stein des Anstoßes: Eberhard Arnold 1883–1935* (Moers: Brendow, 1996).

Beckmann, Joachim, ed. *Kirchliches Jahrbuch für die Evangelische Kirche in Deutschland 1933–1944* (Church yearbook of the Evangelical Church in Germany 1933–1944). 2nd ed. Gütersloh: C. Bertelsmann, 1976.

Bell, George, and Alphons Koechlin. *Briefwechsel 1933–1954* (Correspondence 1933–1954). Edited by Andreas Lindt. Zurich: EVZ Verlag, 1969.

Bergen, Doris. *Twisted Cross: The German Christian Movement in the Third Reich.* Chapel Hill: University of North Carolina Press, 1996.

Bethge, Eberhard. *Bonhoeffer-Gedenkheft.* Berlin: Haus & Schule, 1947.

———. *Dietrich Bonhoeffer: Theologe, Christ, Zeitgenosse: Eine Biographie.* Munich: Chr. Kaiser Verlag, 1967; 7th ed. 1989. Translated by Eric Mosbacher, Peter Ross, Betty Ross, Frank Clarke, and William Glen-Doepel as *Dietrich Bonhoeffer: A Biography,* under the editorship of Edwin Robertson, revised and edited by Victoria Barnett, based on the 7th German edition (1st Fortress Press ed., Minneapolis: Fortress Press, 2000).

Bethge, Eberhard, Renate Bethge, and Christian Gremmels, eds. *Dietrich Bonhoeffer: Sein Leben in Bildern und Texten.* Munich: Chr. Kaiser, 1989. Original English translation by John Bowden: *Dietrich Bonhoeffer: A Life in Pictures* (Fortress Press, 1986). 2006 centenary edition translated by Brian McNeil as *Dietrich Bonhoeffer: A Life in Pictures* (Philadelphia: Fortress Press, 2006).

Bonhoeffer, Dietrich. *Dietrich Bonhoeffer Werke.* 17 vols. Edited by Eberhard Bethge et al. Munich: Chr. Kaiser/Gütersloher Verlagshaus, 1986–99. Translated as *Dietrich Bonhoeffer Works*, Victoria J. Barnett, Wayne Whitson Floyd Jr., and Barbara Wojhoski, general editors. 17 vols. (Minneapolis: Fortress Press, 1996–).

Vol. 1: *Sanctorum Communio: Eine dogmatische Untersuchung zur Soziologie der Kirche.* Edited by Joachim von Soosten. Munich: Chr. Kaiser Verlag, 1986; 2nd ed., Gütersloh: Chr. Kaiser/Gütersloher Verlagshaus, 2005. Translated by Reinhard Krauss and Nancy Lukens as *Sanctorum Communio: A Theological Study of the Sociology of the Church,* edited by Clifford J. Green (Minneapolis: Fortress Press, 1998).

Vol. 2: *Akt und Sein: Transzendentalphilosophie und Ontologie in der systematischen Theologie.* Edited by Hans-Richard Reuter. Munich: Chr. Kaiser Verlag, 1988; 2nd ed., Gütersloh: Chr. Kaiser/Gütersloher Verlagshaus, 2002. Translated by Martin Rumscheidt as *Act and Being: Transcendental Philosophy and Ontology in Systematic Theology,* edited by Wayne Whitson Floyd Jr. (Minneapolis: Fortress Press, 1996).

Vol. 3: *Schöpfung und Fall: Theologische Auslegung von Genesis 1–3.* Edited by Martin Rüter and Ilse Tödt. Munich: Chr. Kaiser Verlag, 1989; 2nd ed., Gütersloh: Chr. Kaiser/Gütersloher Verlagshaus, 2002. Translated by Douglas Stephen Bax as *Creation and Fall: A Theological Exposition of Genesis 1–3,* edited by John W. de Gruchy (Minneapolis: Fortress Press, 1996).

Vol. 4: *Nachfolge.* Edited by Martin Kuske and Ilse Tödt. Munich: Chr. Kaiser Verlag, 1989; 2nd ed., Gütersloh: Chr. Kaiser/Gütersloher Verlagshaus, 1994; 3rd ed., 2002. Translated by Barbara Green and Reinhard Krauss as *Discipleship,* edited by Geffrey B. Kelly and John D. Godsey (Minneapolis: Fortress Press, 2001).

Vol. 5: *Gemeinsames Leben. Das Gebetbuch der Bibel.* Edited by Gerhard Ludwig Müller and Albrecht Schönherr. Munich: Chr. Kaiser Verlag, 1987; 2nd ed., Gütersloh: Chr. Kaiser/Gütersloher Verlagshaus, 2002. Translated by Daniel W. Bloesch and James H. Burtness as *Life Together* and *Prayerbook of the Bible,* edited by Geffrey B. Kelly (Minneapolis: Fortress Press, 1996).

Vol. 6: *Ethik*. Edited by Ilse Tödt, Heinz Eduard Tödt, Ernst Feil, and Clifford Green. Munich: Chr. Kaiser Verlag, 1992; 2nd ed., Gütersloh: Chr. Kaiser/Gütersloher Verlagshaus, 1998. Translated by Reinhard Krauss and Charles West, with Douglas W. Stott, as *Ethics*, edited by Clifford J. Green (Minneapolis: Fortress Press, 2004).

Vol. 7: *Fragmente aus Tegel*. Edited by Renate Bethge and Ilse Tödt. Gütersloh: Chr. Kaiser/Gütersloher Verlagshaus, 1994. Translated by Nancy Lukens as *Fiction from Tegel Prison*, edited by Clifford J. Green (Minneapolis: Fortress Press, 2000).

Vol. 8: *Widerstand und Ergebung* (Resistance and submission). Edited by Christian Gremmels, Eberhard Bethge, and Renate Bethge, with Ilse Tödt. Gütersloh: Chr. Kaiser/Gütersloher Verlagshaus, 1998.

Vol. 9: *Jugend und Studium: 1918–1927*. Edited by Hans Pfeifer, with Clifford Green and Jürgen Kaltenborn. Munich: Chr. Kaiser Verlag, 1986; 2nd ed., Gütersloh: Chr. Kaiser/Gütersloher Verlagshaus, 2005. Translated by Mary Nebelsick, with the assistance of Douglas W. Stott, as *The Young Bonhoeffer: 1918–1927*, edited by Paul Matheny, Clifford J. Green, and Marshall Johnson (Minneapolis: Fortress Press, 2001).

Vol. 10: *Barcelona, Berlin, Amerika: 1928–1931* (Barcelona, Berlin, New York: 1928–1931). Edited by Reinhart and Hans Christoph von Hase, with Holger Roggelin and Matthias Wünsche. Munich: Chr. Kaiser Verlag, 1991; 2nd ed., Gütersloh: Chr. Kaiser/Gütersloher Verlagshaus, 2005.

Vol. 11: *Ökumene, Universität, Pfarramt: 1931–1932* (Ecumenical, academic, and pastoral work: 1931–1932). Edited by Eberhard Amelung and Christoph Strohm. Gütersloh: Chr. Kaiser Verlagshaus, 1994.

Vol. 12: *Berlin: 1932–1933*. Edited by Carsten Nicolaisen and Ernst-Albert Scharffenorth. Gütersloher: Chr. Kaiser/Gütersloher Verlagshaus, 1997.

Vol. 13: *London: 1933–1935*. Edited by Hans Goedeking, Martin Heimbucher, and Hans-Walter Schleicher. Gütersloh: Chr. Kaiser/Gütersloher Verlagshaus, 1994.

Vol. 14: *Illegale Theologenausbildung: Finkenwalde 1935–1937* (Theological education at Finkenwalde: 1935–1937). Edited by Otto Dudzus and Jürgen Henkys, with Sabine Bobert-Stützel, Dirk Schulz, and Ilse Tödt. Gütersloh: Chr. Kaiser/Gütersloher Verlagshaus, 1996.

Vol. 15: *Illegale Theologenausbildung: Sammelvikariate: 1937–1940* (Theological education underground: 1937–1940). Edited by Dirk Schulz. Gütersloh: Chr. Kaiser/Gütersloher Verlagshaus, 1998.

Vol. 16: *Konspiration und Haft: 1940–1945*. Edited by Jørgen Glenthøj, Ulrich Kabitz, and Wolf Krötke. Gütersloh: Chr. Kaiser Gütersloher Verlagshaus, 1996. Translated by Lisa Dahill, with supplementary material translated by Douglas W. Stott, as *Conspiracy and Imprisonment:*

1940–1945, edited by Mark S. Brocker (Minneapolis: Fortress Press, 2006).

Vol. 17: *Register und Ergänzungen* (Index and supplements). Edited by Herbert Anzinger and Hans Pfeifer, assisted by Waltraud Anzinger and Ilse Tödt. Gütersloh: Chr. Kaiser/Gütersloher Verlagshaus, 1999.

————. *Gesammelte Schriften* (Collected writings). Edited by Eberhard Bethge. 6 vols. Munich: Chr. Kaiser Verlag, 1958–74.

————. *No Rusty Swords: Letters, Lectures, and Notes, 1928–1936.* Translated by Edwin H. Robertson and John Bowden. London: Collins; New York: Harper & Row, 1965.

————. *Predigten—Auslegungen—Meditationen* (Sermons, interpretations, meditations). 2 vols. Vol. 1: *1925–1935.* Vol. 2: *1935–1945.* Edited by Otto Dudzus. Munich: Chr. Kaiser, 1984, 1985.

————. *The Way to Freedom: 1935–1939.* Edited and introduced by Edwin H. Robertson. Translated by Edwin H. Robertson and John Bowden. New York: Harper & Row, 1966.

————. *Widerstand und Ergebung: Briefe und Aufzeichnungen aus der Haft.* Edited by Eberhard Bethge. Munich: Chr. Kaiser, 1951; expanded ed., 1970, 1985. Translated by Reginald H. Fuller as *Letters and Papers from Prison*, edited by Eberhard Bethge, translation revised by Frank Clark et al., additional material translated by John Bowden for the enlarged edition published in London (London: SCM, 1971; New York: Macmillan, 1972; New York: Simon & Schuster, 1997).

Bonhoeffer, Karl. "Lebenserinnerungen, geschrieben für die Familie" (Life memories, written for the family). In *Karl Bonhoeffer zum Hundersten Geburtstag am 31. März 1968* (To Karl Bonhoeffer, on the one hundredth anniversary of his birth, March 31, 1968), edited by J. Zutt, H. Scheller, and E. Straus, 8–107. Berlin: Springer, 1969.

Boyens, Armin. *Kirchenkampf und Ökumene: Darstellung und Dokumentation* (Church Struggle and Oikumene: Description and documentation). Vol. 1: *1933–1939.* Vol. 2: *1939–1945.* Munich: Chr. Kaiser, 1969, 1973.

Bruder, Otto. *Ein Spiel vom Heiligen Franz* (A play about St. Francis). 3rd ed. Münchener Laienspiele 30. Munich: Chr. Kaiser Verlag, 1931.

Büchmann, Georg. *Geflügelte Worte: Der Zitatenschatz des deutschen Volkes* (Familiar quotations: The treasury of citations of the German people). Completely revised and edited by Gunther Haupt and Winfried Hofmann. 38th ed. Berlin: Haude & Spener, 1993.

Busch, Eberhard. *Karl Barths Lebenslauf nach seinen Briefen und autobiographischen Texten.* 4th ed. Munich: Chr. Kaiser Verlag, 1975. Translated by John Bowden as *Karl Barth: His Life from Letters and Autobiographical Texts* (Grand Rapids, Mich.: Wm. B. Eerdmans, 1994).

Carlyle, Thomas. *Critical and Miscellaneous Essays.* 5 vols. New York: Charles Scribner's Sons, 1900.

Claudius, Matthias. *ASMUS omnia sua secum portans oder Sämtliche Werke des Wandsbecker Boten* (ASMUS omnia sua secum portans or collected works of the Wandsbeck messenger). Berlin: S. Fischer, 1941. Reprint of the first edition (1775–1812), Munich: Siebenstern, 1976.

Clements, Keith, ed. *Baptists in the Twentieth Century.* London: Baptist Historical Society 1983.

———. *Bonhoeffer and Britain.* London: Churches Together in Britain and Ireland, 2006.

———. *Faith on the Frontier: A Life of J. H. Oldham.* Geneva: World Council of Churches; Edinburgh: T. & T. Clark, 1999.

Cochrane, Arthur C. *The Church's Confession under Hitler.* Philadelphia: Westminster, 1962.

Cooper, John M., and D. S. Hutchinson, eds. *Complete Works of Plato.* Indianapolis: Hackett, 1997.

de Gruchy, John W. *Bonhoeffer for a New Day: Theology in a Time of Transition.* Grand Rapids: Wm. B. Eerdmans, 1997.

———. *Christianity, Art, and Transformation: Theological Aesthetics in the Struggle for Justice.* New York: Cambridge University Press, 2001.

de Gruchy, John W., and Steve de Gruchy. *The Church Struggle in South Africa.* Twenty-fifth anniversary edition. Minneapolis: Fortress Press, 2005.

Dibelius, Otto. *Friede auf Erden? Frage, Erwägungen, Antwort* (Peace on earth? Question, considerations, response). Berlin: Furche Verlag, 1930.

Dietrich Bonhoeffer Jahrbuch. Series. Gütersloh: Chr. Kaiser Verlag, 2003–.

Dinkler, Erich, Erika Dinkler-von Schubert, and Michael Wolter, eds. *Theologie und Kirche im Wirken Hans von Sodens: Briefe und Dokumente aus der Zeit des Kirchenkampfes, 1933–1945* (Theology and church in the actions of Hans von Soden: Letters and documents from the era of the Church Struggle, 1933–1945). Göttingen: Vandenhoeck & Ruprecht, 1984.

Evangelisches Kirchengesangbuch in den Gliedkirchen der Evangelischen Kirche in Deutschland (EKG) (Protestant hymnal for the member churches of the Evangelical Church of Germany). Kassel: Bärenreiter Verlag, 1951–.

Falcke, Heino. *Vom Gebot Christi, daß die Kirche uns die Waffen aus der Hand nimmt und den Krieg verbietet: Zum konziliaren Weg des Friedens. Ein Beitrag aus der DDR* (On Christ's commandment that the church remove the weapons from our hands and prohibit war: On the conciliar path of peace. A contribution from the German Democratic Republic). Stuttgart: Radius, 1986.

Gandhi, Mahatma. *Collected Works.* 100 vols. Delhi: Publications Division, Ministry of Information and Broadcasting, Government of India, 1958–94.

———. *Mein Leben.* Edited by C. F. Andrews. Translated by Hans Reisiger.

Leipzig: Insel Verlag, 1930; Frankfurt: Suhrkamp Verlag, 1983. Originally published as *His Own Story* (London: George Allen & Unwin, 1930).

Gauger, Joachim. *Chronik der Kirchenwirren* (Chronicle of the confusion in the church). 3 vols. Vol. 1: *Vom Aufkommen der "Deutschen Christen" 1932 bis zur Bekenntnis-Reichssynode im Mai 1934* (From the emergence of the "German Christians" 1932 to the Confessing Reich synod in May 1934). Vol. 2: *Von der Barmer Bekenntnis-Reichssynode im Mai 1934 bis zur Einsetzung der Vorläufigen Leitung der Deutschen Evangelischen Kirche im November 1934* (From the Barmen confessional Reich synod in May 1934 to the installation of the Provisional Church Administration of the German Evangelical Church in November 1934). Elberfeld, 1934–35

Goethe, Johann Wolfgang von. *Werke*. Hamburger Ausgabe. Edited by Erich Trunz. 13th ed. 14 vols. Munich: C. H. Beck, 1982. Translated as *Goethe's Collected Works* (Princeton, N.J.: Princeton University Press, 1994–).

Gollwitzer, Helmut. "Zum Weg der Zeitschrift." *Evangelische Theologie* 44 (1984): 137–47.

Gordon, Ernst. *And I Will Walk at Liberty: An Eye-Witness Account of the Church Struggle in Germany 1933–1937*. Edited by J. C. B. Gordon. Bungay (Suffolk): Morrow, 1997.

Gremmels, Christian, and Hans Pfeifer, eds. *Dietrich Bonhoeffer Jahrbuch 2003*. Gütersloh: Chr. Kaiser Verlagshaus, 2003.

Gremmels, Christian, and Ilse Tödt, eds. *Die Präsenz des verdrängten Gottes* (The presence of the suppressed God). Internationales Bonhoeffer Forum 7. Munich: Christian Ktaiser Verlag, 1987.

Grimms' Fairy Tales and Household Stories. Translated by H. B. Paull and L. A. Wheatley. London: Frederick Warne, 1868–89. An electronic version of over 200 of the tales (including "The Bright Sun Brings It to Light") based on the translation by Margaret Hunt (1884), edited by William Barker, can be found on the Web page www.ucs.mun.ca.

Harnack, Adolf von. *Reden und Aufsätze* (Speeches and essays). 1904. Vol. 1. 2nd ed. Giessen: Ricker, 1906.

Heimbucher, Martin. "Christusfriede—Weltfrieden: Dietrich Bonhoeffers kirchlicher und politischer Kampf gegen den Krieg Hitlers und seine theologische Begründung" (The peace of Christ—world peace: Dietrich Bonhoeffer's ecclesiastical and political struggle against Hitler's war and its theological grounding). PhD diss., Göttingen, 1991.

Helmreich, Ernst Christian. *The German Churches under Hitler: Background, Struggle, and Epilogue*. Detroit: Wayne State University Press, 1979.

Henkys, Jürgen. *Dietrich Bonhoeffers Gefängnisgedichte: Beiträge zu ihrer Interpretation* (Dietrich Bonhoeffer's prison poems: Toward an interpretation). Munich: Chr. Kaiser Verlag, 1986.

Hildebrandt, Franz. "Erinnerungen an Forest Hill (1933–1934)" (Memories of Forest Hill, 1933–34). In *100 Jahre Deutsche Evangelische Gemeinde Sydenham* (Centenary of the German Evangelical Church of Sydenham), 35–38. London, 1975. Excerpt published in *IBG-Rundbrief* 21 (March 1986) (Newsletter, International Bonhoeffer Society, German Section).

Holl, Karl. *Gesammelte Aufsätze zur Kirchengeschichte* (Collected essays on church history). Vol. 1: *Luther.* 1921. 2nd and 3rd eds. Tübingen: J. C. B. Mohr (Paul Siebeck), 1923.

Huber, Wolfgang. "Ein ökumenisches Konzil des Friedens—Hoffnungen und Hemmnisse" (An ecumenical council of peace—hopes and hindrances). *Ökumenische Existenz heute* (Ecumenical existence today) 1 (1986): 101–47.

Jehle, Herbert. "Auf der Seite der Verfolgten" (On the side of the persecuted). Unpublished manuscript in the possession of Ulrich Kabitz.

Kelly, Geffrey B. "An Interview with Jean Lasserre." *Union Theological Seminary Quarterly Review* 27, no. 3 (Spring 1972): 149–60.

Kierkegaard, Søren. *Furcht und Zittern.* Translated by Emanuel Hirsch. Düsseldorf: E. Diederichs Verlag, 1962. Translated by Alastair Hannay as *Fear and Trembling* (New York: Penguin Books, 2006).

Die Kirchen am Werk (The churches at work). Periodical published by the Universal Christian Council for Life and Work and the World Alliance, 1933–38.

Kirche und Welt. Series published by the Research Department of Life and Work, Geneva 1934.

Kolb, Robert, and Timothy J. Wengert, eds. *The Book of Concord: The Confessions of the Evangelical Lutheran Church.* Translation of *Die Bekenntnisschriften der evangelisch-lutherischen Kirche* by Charles Arand, Eric Gritsch, Robert Kolb, William Russell, James Schaaf, Jane Strohl, and Timothy J. Wengert (Minneapolis: Fortress Press, 2000).

Künneth, Walter. "Echte Fronten." *Junge Kirche* (October 1933): 238–42.

Kupisch, Karl. *Studenten entdecken die Bibel: Die Geschichte der Deutschen Christlichen Studenten-Vereinigung* (Students discover the Bible: The history of the German Student Christian Association). Hamburg: Furche Verlag, 1964.

Lebrecht, Marianne. *Verschweigen oder kämpfen: Ein Pfarrer und seine Gemeinde im Kirchenkampf 1933–1945* (Stay silent or resist: A pastor and his congregation in the Church Struggle 1933–1945). Study Group on Church and Israel, Evangelical Church in Hesse and Nassau 18. Heppenheim, 2001.

Leibholz-Bonhoeffer, Sabine. *Vergangen, erlebt, überwunden: Schicksale der Familie Bonhoeffer.* Wuppertal-Barmen: Kiefel, 1968. Translated as *The Bonhoeffers: Portrait of a Family* (Chicago: Covenant, 1994).

Ludwig, Hartmut. "Die 'Illegalen' im Kirchenkampf." In *Predigtamt ohne Pfarramt? Die "Illegalen" im Kirchenkampf,* edited by Karl-Adolf Bauer. Neukirchen-Vluyn: Neukirchener Verlag, 1993.

Luther, Martin. *Werke: Kritische Gesamtausgabe* (Weimarer Ausgabe = WA). 58 vols. Weimar: H. Böhlau, 1883–. Translated as *Luther's Works,* vols. 1–30 edited by Jaroslav Pelikan, vols. 31–55 edited by Helmut Lehmann, complete works on CDROM (Minneapolis: Fortress Press; St. Louis: Concordia, 2002).

Lutheran Book of Worship. Minneapolis: Augsburg, 1978.

Maas, Hermann. "Die Weltbundtagung auf Fanø in Dänemark" (The World Alliance conference in Fanø in Denmark). In *Ökumenisches Jahrbuch 1934/35* (Ecumenical yearbook 1934/35), edited by Friedrich Siegmund-Schultze, 211–18. Zurich: M. Niehans, 1936.

Macfarland, Charles S. *The New Church and the New Germany: A Study of Church and State.* New York: Macmillan, 1934. 2nd ed. New York: AMS Press, 1983.

Maechler, Winfried. "Bonhoeffers Fanö-Friedensrede zwischen Pazifismus und Widerstand" (Bonhoeffer's Fanø peace speech between pacifism and resistance). *Die Zeichen der Zeit* (The signs of the time) 38 (1984): 189–90.

Maiwald, Birger. "Eine biographische Notiz: Theodor Heckel" (A biographical note: Theodor Heckel). In *Kirchengemeinschaft—Anspruch und Wirklichkeit: Festschrift für Georg Kretschmar* (Ecclesiastical community— claims and reality: Festschrift for Georg Kretschmar), edited by W. D. Hauschild, Carsten Nicolaisen, and Dorothea Wendebourg, 189–233. Stuttgart: Calwer Verlag, 1986.

Mayer, Rainer. "Was wollte Dietrich Bonhoeffer in Fanø? Zur aktuellen Diskussion um ein Friedenskonzil" (What did Dietrich Bonhoeffer want in Fanø? The current discussion concerning a peace council). *Theologische Beiträge* (Theological contributions) 19 (1988): 73–89.

Meier, Kurt. *Der evangelische Kirchenkampf: Gesamtdarstellung in drei Bänden* (The Protestant church struggle: An overview in three volumes). Vol. 1: *Der Kampf um die "Reichskirche"* (The struggle for the "Reich Church"). Göttingen: Vandenhoeck & Ruprecht, 1976.

Meiser, Hans. *Verantwortung für die Kirche: Stenographische Aufzeichnungen und Mitschriften 1933–1955.* Vol. 1: *Sommer 1933 bis Sommer 1935* (Responsibility for the church: Stenographic notes and records 1933–1955, vol. 1: Summer 1933 to summer 1935). Edited by Hannelore Braun and Carsten Nicolaisen. Arbeiten zur kirchlichen Zeitgeschichte (Works on contemporary ecclesiastical history) series A, vol. 1. Göttingen: Vandenhoeck & Ruprecht, 1985.

Merkley, Paul. *Reinhold Niebuhr: A Political Account.* Montreal: McGill-Queen's University Press, 1975.

Merzyn, Friedrich, ed. *Das Recht der EKD* (The laws of the Evangelical Church of Germany). 2nd ed. Hanover: Luchterhand, 1956.

Meyer, Dietrich, and Eberhard Bethge, eds. *Nachlaß Dietrich Bonhoeffer: Ein Verzeichnis. Archiv—Sammlung—Bibliothek* (Dietrich Bonhoeffer's literary estate: A bibliographical catalog. Archive, collection, library). Munich: Chr. Kaiser Verlag, 1987.

Moore, David, ed. *Celebrating Critical Awareness: Bonhoeffer and Bradford 60 Years On: Conference Papers and Proceedings.* Bradford, England: Methodist Church Touchstone Centre, 1993.

Müller, Christine Ruth. *Bekenntnis und Bekennen: Dietrich Bonhoeffer in Bethel (1933). Ein lutherischer Versuch* (Confession and confessing: Dietrich Bonhoeffer in Bethel (1933). A Lutheran attempt). Studienbücher zur kirchlichen Zeitgeschichte (Studies on contemporary history and the church) 7. Munich: Chr. Kaiser Verlag, 1989.

Die Mündige Welt. (The world come of age). Vol. 5: *Dokumentation zur Bonhoeffer-Forschung 1928–1945* (Documents on Bonhoeffer research 1928–1945). Edited by Jørgen Glenthøj. Munich: Chr. Kaiser Verlag, 1969.

News Chronicle. 26 vols. Illustrated. No. 26247 (June 2, 1930)–no. 34126 (November 19, 1955). London: Daily News, 1930–1955.

Nicolaisen, Carsten, and Georg Kretschmar, eds. *Dokumente zur Kirchenpolitik des Dritten Reiches* (Documents regarding the church politics of the Third Reich). Vol. 1: *Das Jahr 1933* (The year 1933). Vol. 2: *Vom Beginn des Jahres 1934 bis zur Errichtung des Reichsministeriums für die Kirchlichen Angelegenheiten am 16. Juli 1935* (From the beginning of 1934 to the establishment of the Reich Ministry for Church Affairs on July 16, 1935). Munich: Chr. Kaiser Verlag, 1971, 1975.

Niemöller, Gerhard. "Die deutschen evangelischen Gemeinden in London und der Kirchenkampf" (The German evangelical parishes in London and the Church Struggle). *Evangelische Theologie* (Evangelical theology) 19 (1959): 131–46.

Niemöller, Wilhelm. *Die Evangelische Kirche im Dritten Reich: Handbuch des Kirchenkampfes* (The evangelical church in the Third Reich: Handbook of the Church Struggle). Bielefeld: Ludwig Bechauf, 1956.

———. *Kampf und Zeugnis der Bekennenden Kirche* (Struggle and witness of the Confessing Church). 1948. Bielefeld: Ludwig Bechauf, 1949.

Niesel, Wilhelm. *Kirche unter dem Wort: Der Kampf der Bekennenden Kirche der Altpreußischen Union 1933–1945* (The church under the Word: The struggle of the Confessing Church of the Old Prussian Union 1933–1945). Arbeiten zur Geschichte des Kirchenkampfes (Studies on the history of the Church Struggle) 11. Göttingen: Vandenhoeck & Ruprecht, 1978.

Nietzsche, Friedrich, *Beyond Good and Evil: Prelude to a Philosophy of the Future.* Translation of *Jenseits von Gut und Böse* by Walter Kaufmann. 1966. New York: Vintage Books, 1989.

————. *On the Genealogy of Morals and Ecce Homo.* Translation *of Zur Genealogie der Moral* and *Ecce Homo* by Walter Kaufmann and R. J. Hollingdale. New York: Random House, 1967.

Norden, Günther van. *Der deutsche Protestantismus im Jahr der nationalsozialistischen Machtergreifung* (German Protestantism in the year of the National Socialist seizure of power). Gütersloh: Gütersloher Verlagshaus Mohn, 1979.

————. *Kirche in der Krise: Die Stellung der evangelischen Kirche im nationalsozialistischen Staat im Jahre 1933* (Church in crisis: The position of the Protestant Church in the National Socialist state in 1933). Düsseldorf: Presseverband der Evangelischen Kirche im Rheinland, 1963.

————, ed. *Zwischen Bekenntnis und Anpassung: Aufsätze zum Kirchenkampf in rheinischen Gemeinden, in Kirche und Gesellschaft* (Between confession and conformity: Essays on the church struggle in Rhineland parishes, in church and society). Cologne: Rheinland Verlag, 1985.

Petrarch. *Epistolae.* Translated by Craig Kallendorf as *Selected Letters* (Bryn Mawr, Pa.: Thomas Library, Bryn Mawr College, 1986).

Prolingheuer, Hans. *Der Fall Karl Barth: Chronographie einer Vertreibung 1934–1935* (The case of Karl Barth: Chronicle of an expulsion 1934–1935). 1977. 2nd ed. Neukirchen-Vluyn: Neukirchener Verlag, 1984.

Rasmussen, Larry. *Dietrich Bonhoeffer: Reality and Resistance.* New edition. Louisville: Westminster John Knox, 2005.

Die Religion in Geschichte und Gegenwart (Religion in history and the present). 5 vols. Tübingen: Mohr, 1909–13; 2nd ed., 1927–31; 4th ed., 1998–2000.

Reuter, Hans-Richard, ed. *Konzil des Friedens: Beiträge zur ökumenischen Diskussion* (Council of peace: Contributions to the ecumenical discussion) I. Texte und Materialien der FEST (Protestant Institute for Interdisciplinary Research), series A, no. 24. Heidelberg, 1987.

Rieger, Julius. "Die deutschen evangelischen Gemeinden in England nach dem Kriege" (The German evangelical parishes in England after the war). In *Auslanddeutschtum und evangelische Kirche, Jahrbuch 1933* (Germans living overseas and the Evangelical Church, 1933 yearbook), edited by Ernst Schubert. Munich: Chr. Kaiser Verlag, 1933.

————. *Dietrich Bonhoeffer in England.* Berlin: Lettner-Verlag, 1966.

Roberts, Richard. *Schroders: Merchants and Bankers.* London: Macmillan 1992.

Roggelin, Holger. *Franz Hildebrandt: Ein lutherischer Dissenter im Kirchenkampf und Exil.* (Franz Hildebrandt: A Lutheran dissenter in the Church Struggle and in exile). Göttingen: Vandenhoeck & Ruprecht, 1999.

Roon, Ger van. _Zwischen Neutralismus und Solidarität: Die evangelischen Niederlande und der deutsche Kirchenkampf 1933–1942_ (Between neutrality and solidarity: Protestant Holland and the German Church Struggle 1933–1942). Studien zur Zeitgeschichte (Studies on contemporary history) 24. Stuttgart: Deutsche Verlags-Anstalt, 1983.

The Round Table: A Quarterly Review of the Politics of the British Commonwealth. 1910–48. Since 1983: _The Commonwealth Journal of International Affairs._

Sauter, Gerhard. "Was heiß 'Evangelische Theologie'?" _Evangelische Theologie_ 44 (1984): 112–37.

Schäfer, Gerhard. _Die evangelische Landeskirche in Württemberg und der Nationalsozialismus: Eine Dokumentation zum Kirchenkampf_ (The regional Protestant church in Württemberg and National Socialism: Documentation of the Church Struggle). 6 vols. Vol. 2: _Um eine Deutsche Reichskirche 1933_ (The question of a German Reich Church 1933). Vol. 3: _Der Einbruch des Reichsbischofs in die Württembergische Landeskirche 1934_ (The intrusion of the Reich Bishop into the regional Württemberg church in 1934). Stuttgart: Calwer Verlag, 1972, 1974.

Scherffig, Wolfgang. _Junge Theologen im "Dritten Reich": Dokumente, Briefe, Erfahrungen_ (Young theologians during the "Third Reich": Documents, letters, experiences). 3 vols. Neukirchen-Vluyn: Neukirchener, 1989–94.

Schmidt, Jürgen. _Martin Niemöller im Kirchenkampf_ (Martin Niemöller in the Church Struggle). Hamburger Beiträge zur Zeitgeschichte (Hamburg contributions to contemporary history) 8. Hamburg: Leibniz-Verlag, 1971.

Schmidt, Kurt Dietrich, ed. _Die Bekenntnisse und grundsätzlichen Äußerungen zur Kirchenfrage_ (The confessions and statements of principle on the church question). Vol. 2: _Das Jahr 1934_ (The year 1934). Göttingen: Vandenhoeck & Ruprecht, 1935.

Scholder, Klaus. _Die Kirchen und das Dritte Reich._ Vol. 1: _Vorgeschichte und Zeit der Illusionen 1918–1934._ 1977. 2nd ed. Frankfurt: Propyläen/Ullstein, 1980. Translated by John Bowden as _The Churches and the Third Reich_, vol. 1: _Preliminary History and the Time of Illusions, 1918–1934_ (Philadelphia: Fortress Press, 1988). Vol. 2: _Das Jahr der Ernüchterung 1934: Barmen und Rom._ 1985. 2nd ed. Berlin: W. J. Siedler, 1988. Translated as _The Churches and the Third Reich_, vol. 2: _The Year of Disillusionment 1934: Barmen and Rome_ (London: SCM Press, 1988).

Schubert, Franz. _Twenty-four Favorite Songs._ New York: G. Schirmer, 1895, 1923.

Schulz, Gerhard. "Die Anfänge des totalitären Maßnahmenstaates" (The beginnings of the totalitarian state measures). In _Die nationalsozialistische_

Machtergreifung: Studien zur Errichtung des totalitären Herrschaftssystems in Deutschland 1933/34 (The National Socialist seizure of power: Studies on the establishment of the totalitarian system of rule in Germany 1933/34), edited by Karl-Dietrich Bracher, Wolfgang Sauer, and Gerhard Schulz. Ullstein Taschenbuch 2993. 1960. Frankfurt/Berlin: Ullstein, 1974.

Siegmund-Schultze, Friedrich. "Was kann die Kirche für den Frieden tun?" (What can the church do for peace?). Lecture delivered in Aarau. Private printing. Gotha: 1929/30.

Storm, Theodor. *Gesammelte Schriften* (Collected writings). 1877. 6th ed. Braunschweig: G. Westermann, 1891.

Strohm, Christoph. *Theologische Ethik im Kampf gegen den Nationalsozialismus: Der Weg Dietrich Bonhoeffers mit den Juristen Hans von Dohnanyi und Gerhard Leibholz in den Widerstand* (Theological ethics in the struggle against National Socialism: Dietrich Bonhoeffer's path into the resistance with the jurists Hans von Dohnanyi and Gerhard Leibholz). Heidelberger Untersuchungen zu Widerstand, Judenverfolgung und Kirchenkampf im Dritten Reich (Heidelberg studies on resistance, persecution of the Jews, and the Church Struggle in the Third Reich) 1. Munich: Chr. Kaiser Verlag, 1989.

Von zur Mühlen, Patrik. *"Schlagt Hitler an der Saar!": Abstimmungskampf, Emigration und Widerstand im Saargebiet 1933-1935* ("Defeat Hitler at the Saar!": Voting struggles, emigration, and resistance in the Saar region). Bonn: Verlag Neue Gesellschaft, 1979.

Weizsäcker, Carl Friedrich von. *Die Zeit drängt: Eine Weltversammlung der Christen für Gerechtigkeit, Frieden und die Bewahrung der Schöpfung* (Time is short: A world assembly of Christians for justice, peace, and the preservation of creation). Munich: Hanser Verlag, 1986.

Winkworth, Catherine. *The Chorale Book for England.* London: Longman, Green, Longman & Roberts, 1863. Reprint, Grand Rapids: Christian Classics Ethereal Library, 2002.

Wolf, Ernst. "Evangelische Theologie [1934]: Vorwort der Herausgeber" (Protestant theology: foreword by the editor). Reprinted in *Evangelische Theologie* 44 (1984): 102–11.

Zimmermann, Wolf-Dieter, ed. *Begegnungen mit Dietrich Bonhoeffer.* 1964. 4th ed. Munich: Chr. Kaiser Verlag, 1969. Translated by Käthe Gregor Smith as *I Knew Dietrich Bonhoeffer* (1966; London: Fontana Books, 1973).

Zwischen den Zeiten. Periodical. Munich: Chr. Kaiser Verlag, 1923–33. After 1933: *Evangelische Theologie.*

Index of Scriptural References

Index of Names

This index lists people mentioned in this volume, including authors and editors of literature cited in the notes. It provides brief profiles of the people listed and differs from the German edition by also including information about those whose work began after 1945, as well as additional information of interest to readers of the English edition. It does not include personal names that appear in book titles or only in the bibliography. When possible, dates of birth and death have been provided.

1908, fellow at the Punjab University; 1913, joined Tagore's Institute Santiniketan, Bengal, later vice president there; 1913–14, accompanied Gandhi to South Africa; worked in various capacities for the Indian government; author of several books on Gandhi; 1932, first met Bonhoeffer at joint conference of Life and Work and the World Alliance at Gland, Switzerland; moved close to Quaker belief and practice but in later life resumed role as Anglican priest—136–37, 163, 425

Anzinger, Hervert: editorial assistant *DBW* 13—16

Appius Claudius: 307 BCE., Roman consul—397

Arnold, Eberhard (1883–1935): German Protestant revivalist; 1920s, founder of Bruderhof pacifist community—13, 133, 158–60, 164–66, 174

Arnold, Hardy: son of Eberhard Arnold and member of the Bruderhof community in England; 1934, student at Birmingham university in England, met with Bonhoeffer in London; 1939, wrote a famous pacifist statement (*The Call of the Hour*) that referred to that earlier conversation—13, 133–34, 158–60, 161–63, 164–65, 174, 296

Asmussen, Hans Christian (1898–1968): 1923, pastor, Flensburg; 1925, Albersdorf/Dithmarschen; 1932, Hamburg-Altona; 1933, suspension; 1934, forced retirement; 1934, member of the Reich Confessing Church Council of Brethren; 1935–36, director and lecturer at the Confessing seminaries in Berlin and Elberfeld; 1936, pastor, Berlin-Lichterfelde; 1941, arrested and convicted in the collective trial against the examination board of the Old Prussian Union Council of Brethren; 1943, assistant pastor, Württemberg; 1945, president of the chancellery of the Evangelical Church of Germany; 1948, provost, Kiel; 1955, retired—211, 219, 227, 260, 262, 274

Atkinson, Henry A. (1877–1960): U.S. sociologist and pastor in the Congregationalist Church; head of the Church Peace Union; until 1932, general secretary, then until 1946, international secretary of the World Alliance for Promoting International Friendship through the Churches; 1928, general secretary of the Universal Christian Council for Life and Work; September 1933, participated in the conference of the World Alliance for Promoting International Friendship through the Churches, Sofia—31

Bach, Johann Sebastian (1685–1750): German church musician and composer—356

Baelz, Reinhardt: February 11, 1935, Bonhoeffer officiated at his funeral—317

Baillie, John (1886–1960): Scottish theologian; 1930–34, taught at Union Theological Seminary, New York, where Bonhoeffer was among his stu-

Bruay, France; 1935–44, general secretary of the French Student Christian Federation; 1944–55, Reformed pastor, Meaux; 1952, professor of dogmatics, Paris—225

Bouvier, André: Swiss Reformed pastor; spoke at the plenary session of the ecumenical Council for Life and Work in Fanø—31, 209

Boyens, Armin: German Protestant minister, church historian, and ecumenist—25, 65, 88, 115, 120, 123, 132, 181, 191, 192, 195, 212

Brahms, Johannes (1833–97): German composer—251

Brandenburg, Willi (Willy) (1909–42): from Berlin; 1934, participated in the Fanø youth conference; 1936–37, participated in the fourth Finkenwalde session; 1938, ordained; ministry in Pätzig/Neudamm (Neumark); 1942, killed in action on the eastern front—164

Brandt, Karl (1904–48): 1934–44, Hitler's personal physician; 1948, executed—218

Breit, Thomas (1880–1966): 1908, pastor, Augsburg; 1914–18, military chaplain; 1925, church dean, Hof, Bavaria; 1933–45, senior church official in Munich and representative of Bavarian bishop Meiser; 1934, member of the Reich Council of Brethren and the council of the German Evangelical Church; 1934–36, member of the Provisional church administration; director, Lutheran Council; 1936–38, Lutheran Secretariat, Berlin—260–63

Brenner, G. (died toward the end of 1933): baker, member of the congregational council, St. Paul's Church in London; Bonhoeffer officiated at his funeral—68, 101, 303, 317

Brown, A.: member of the congregational council, German congregation, London-Sydenham—28, 67

Brown, William Adams (1865–1943): U. S. Presbyterian pastor, theologian, and ecumenist; 1898–1936, professor of systematic and practical theology at Union Theological Seminary, New York; 1933, participant at the conference of the World Alliance for Promoting International Friendship through the Churches in Sofia—31

Bruder, Otto: see Salomon, Otto

Brunner, Emil (1889–1966): Swiss Reformed theologian, one of the founders of dialectical theology; 1924–53, professor of systematic and practical theology, Zurich—87, 126, 135

Buchman, Frank (1878–1961): U. S. theologian of German-Swiss descent; 1908, following a conversion he helped found the Oxford Group movement (after 1938, this became the Moral Rearmament movement; after 1945, called the Caux movement)—32

Büchmann, Georg (1822–84): German philologist—397

Burgess, Joseph: professor in Philadelphia; owner of one of Bonhoeffer's

movement, including Faith and Order and Life and Work; pioneer of form criticism—89, 177

Dibelius, Otto (1880–1967): German pastor and church leader; 1921, senior consistory councillor and member of the High Consistory responsible for school affairs;1925, general superintendent of the Old Prussian province of Mark Brandenburg (Kurmark); active in the ecumenical movement and the Confessing Church; 1933, placed on forced leave by German Christian church authorities; 1937, arrested briefly and released; 1945–66, bishop of Berlin-Brandenburg; 1949–61, chair of the governing council of the Evangelical Church of Germany—307

Dickens, C.: member of the congregational council, St. Paul's, London—29, 101, 237

Dickens, Doris: see Goetz, Frank and Doris

Dickinson, Sir Willoughby (1859–1943): British parliamentarian and ecumenist; head of the London county council; secretary and later president and honorary president of the World Alliance for Promoting International Friendship through the Churches; 1931–35, president of its International Council; 1934, participated in the plenary session of the ecumenical Council for Life and Work in Fanø—209

Diels, Rudolf (1900–1957): 1933, head of the Gestapo, Berlin; 1934, governmental president, Cologne; 1936–43, Hanover; 1944, imprisoned temporarily by the Gestapo—31

Diem, Hermann (1900–1975): German theologian; 1934–50, pastor, Ebersbach, and director of the Württemberg Ecclesiastical-Theological Society, which had ties to the Confessing Church; 1950, teaching appointment; 1957, professor of church law and regulation, Tübingen—141

Diest, Mrs. von: youngest sister of Baron Bruno Schröder from Liebenzell; active in the mission society there—282

Diestel, Karl Julius Max (1872–1949): German theologian, ecumenist; 1903, pastor, Dettingen/Hohenzollern; 1914, Berlin; 1925, superintendent for church district Koelln-Land 1, to which the Grunewald parish belonged; 1931, governing secretary, German section of the World Alliance for Promoting International Friendship through the Churches; after 1933, member, Confessing Church Council of Brethren, Berlin-Brandenburg; 1946–48, general superintendent, Berlin, and pastor, Kaiser Wilhelm Memorial Church, Berlin—172–73

Dietrich, Ernst Ludwig (1897–1974): prominent German Christian; 1934–36, bishop of Hesse-Nassau (appointed by Reich Bishop Müller); 1936, removed from office by Minister of Church Affairs Hans Kerrl, who established a church committee to govern several regional churches—214–15

Dinkler, Erich (1909–81): German theologian, church historian, and philosopher; scholar of Christian antiquity—221

Dinkler-von Schubert, Erika (1904–2002); scholar of Christian antiquity; honorary professor, Heidelberg—221

Dohnanyi, Christine (Christel) von, née Bonhoeffer (1903–65): Dietrich Bonhoeffer's sister; 1925, married Hans von Dohnanyi; participant in the resistance movement against the National Socialist regime; 1943, arrested and temporarily held in custody—60, 241

Dohnanyi, Elisabeth (Elsa) von, née Kühnwald (1877–1946): mother of Hans and Grete von Dohnanyi; divorced from Ernst von Dohnanyi; pianist—61

Dohnanyi, Hans von (1902–45): son of the composer Ernst von Dohnanyi; brother of Margarete Bonhoeffer; 1925, married Christine, née Bonhoeffer; from 1929, consultant in the Reich Ministry of Justice; 1932, attorney, Hamburg; 1933, consultant to the president of the Reich Court; 1934, personal consultant to Reich Minister of Justice Gürtner; 1938, Reich court counselor in Leipzig; August 25, 1939, appointed to the central division in the Military Intelligence Office of the High Military Command; head of the political department in Major General Hans Oster's office; with General Oster one of the leaders in the resistance against Hitler; April 5, 1943, arrested; 1945, executed in Sachsenhausen concentration camp—60, 216, 241, 365

Dollfuss (Dollfuß), Engelbert (1892–1934): Austrian politician; 1932, federal chancellor; May 25, 1934, shot to death during a National Socialist coup— 218, 194

Dove, John: editor of the British periodical *The Round Table*—72

Dreß, Andreas: youngest son of Susanne and Walter Dreß; professor of mathematics, Bielefeld University—433

Dreß, Susanne (Susi, Suse), née Bonhoeffer (1909–91): Dietrich Bonhoeffer's sister; 1929, married Walter Dreß; mother of Michael and Andreas—60, 76, 86, 141, 430

Dreß, Walter (1904–79): 1929, married Susanne, née Bonhoeffer; 1938, Confessing Church pastor, Berlin-Dahlem and lecturer at the seminary, Berlin; professor of church history, Berlin—13, 60, 75, 76–77, 85, 86, 100, 141, 430

Dudzus, Otto (1912–2000): one of Dietrich Bonhoeffer's students; studied theology, initially in Bonn; also studied in Rostock; summer semester 1933, attended Bonhoeffer's lectures on Christology; 1934, participated in the Fanø youth conference; 1936–37, participated in the fourth Finkenwalde session; summer 1937, participated in the fifth Finkenwalde session; 1937–38, (illegal) vicar with Günther Harder in Fehrbellin; from

the German Democratic Republic; church provost (emeritus), Erfurt—11

Félice, Theódore de (1904–2005): studied theology in Strasbourg and Paris; 1929–30, Reformed pastor, Mars (Ardèche); 1930–36, secretary of the International Committee of Christian Youth Associations, Geneva; 1933–36, secretary of the youth commission of the ecumenical Council for Life and Work and of the World Alliance for Promoting International Friendship through the Churches; 1934–45, president of the Alliance of Religious Socialists, Romance language section; 1936–41, studied law and international relations, Lyon and Geneva; 1939–70, general secretary of the International League against Slavery (FAI); 1945–70, governmental delegate, Canton of Geneva—8, 11, 38, 58, 60, 71, 90, 98, 146–47, 149, 151, 163–64, 173–76, 193–98, 201, 202, 204, 209, 223–24, 225, 257, 284, 287

Fezer, Karl (1891–1960): 1920, city pastor, Tübingen; 1926, professor of practical theology, Tübingen; 1930, full professor of practical theology and supervisor, Protestant seminary, Tübingen; May–September 1933, member of the German Christians; July–September 1933, member of the provisional leadership of the German Evangelical Church; 1956–59, professor, Tübingen—44, 49, 69, 94

Fiedler, Eberhard (1898–1947): 1934, lawyer with the Reich Court in Leipzig; May 1934, member of the Reich Council of Brethren; October 1934, member of the Advisory Council of the German Evangelical Church; summer 1934, director of the legal section, Confessing Church central office, Bad Oeynhausen; November 1934, legal member and director of the church chancellery of the first Provisional church administration; 1936, resigned for health reasons; after 1945, official of the upper regional court in Gera—211, 219

Fischer, J. H. R. (Hans) (1906–70): student of Karl Barth in Münster and acquaintance of Bonhoeffer; 1931, Berlin; 1933, assistant pastor, Bochum-Weitmar; participated in work on the Bethel Confession; 1934, dismissed by the German Christian leadership; June 1934, pastor of the German Reformed church (Hervormde Kerk), Amsterdam; 1940, pastor of the German overseas church in Rotterdam (under the Church Foreign Office); worked with refugees during the war; later revived the German Seamen's Mission in Rotterdam—269

Flor, Wilhelm (1882–1938): church lawyer; 1923–31, upper regional court official and honorary member of the Evangelical Consistory, Oldenburg; 1931, Reich court official, Leipzig; member of the Saxon Council of Brethren; October 1934, member of the Reich Council of Brethren of the first Provisional church administration (because he was prohib-

sor of theology; 1925, lecturer in systematic theology, Jena; 1931–35, professor of systematic theology, Breslau; 1933, favored German Christians, break with Karl Barth; 1935–53, professor, Göttingen—36, 69, 93, 141

Goltz, Hannah Countess von der, née von Hase (1873–1941): sister of Bonhoeffer's mother; wife of Rüdiger von der Goltz—61, 85

Goltz, Rüdiger Count von der (Uncle Rudi) (1865–1946): husband of Hannah, née von Hase; Prussian career military officer; in World War 1, major general and commander of the Baltic division; 1918, liberated Finland from Soviet troops—61, 85

Gordon, Ernst Heinrich (anglicized in 1940: Ernest Henry) (1909–91): 1932–33, one of Bonhoeffer's first students in Berlin; 1933–34, participated in the preachers' seminary, Wittenberg; October 1933, member of the Pastors' Emergency League; December 1934, ordination; by summer 1937, expelled from four congregations because of his Jewish ancestry; November 1937, fled to Switzerland; January 1939, fled to England; joined Anglican Church; 1940, ordination as priest; 1977, retired—125

Göring, Wilhelm Hermann (1893–1946): National Socialist politician; 1933, Prussian minister president; January 30, 1933, prominent role in forming Hitler's government; occupied various ministerial offices; 1935, Reich minister of aviation 1940, Reich marshal; after World War 2, sentenced to death at the Nuremberg trials; 1946, committed suicide before execution—90, 106

Graham, Eric (1888–1964): 1929, principal, Cuddesdon College near Oxford; 1944, bishop of Brechen—224

Grandyot, V. (or P.): member of the congregational council, St. Paul's Church, London—231, 277, 291

Gregor, Christian (1723–1801): poet, songwriter, and from 1789, bishop of the Moravian (Herrnhut) community—95

Gremmels, Christian: German professor of social ethics and Protestant theology; author of works on Bonhoeffer; member of *DBW* editorial board—11, 200, 214, 301, 315

Gürtner, Franz (1881–1941): jurist and member of the German National Peoples' Party; 1922, Bavarian justice minister; 1932–41, Reich minister of justice—227, 246

Haeften, Hans-Bernd von (1905–44): confirmed with Bonhoeffer; 1930–33, manager of the Stresemann foundation; from 1933, member of the Confessing Church; 1933, joined the Ministry of Foreign Affairs; cultural attaché in Copenhagen (renewed contact with Bonhoeffer); 1935, in Vienna; 1937, legation secretary, Bucharest; 1940, reporting legation officer in the cultural section of the Ministry of Foreign Affairs, Berlin;

from 1941, active member of the Kreisau circle; 1943, deputy head of the information section, later of the cultural section in the Ministry of Foreign Affairs; participated with his brother Werner in preparations for July 20, 1944; arrested immediately after the failed coup; August 15, 1944, executed in Plötzensee—192

Haenchen, Ernst (1894–1975): 1927, lecturer, Tübingen; professor of systematic theology, Giessen; November 1933, left the German Christians after the Sports Palace rally; winter 1933–34, worked with Hermann Beyer when the latter was clerical advisor to the Reich Ministry for Church Affairs; 1939–46, professor of New Testament, Münster—69

Häfele, Walter (1900–1935): 1926, pastor, Emmendingen/Baden; vicar for urban ministry; from 1930, pastor, Berlin —33

Hancock, Eric Gray: 1934, at the behest of Jürgen Winterhager, sent Bonhoeffer a pacifist book for his birthday—99

Hansen, Wilhelm: 1928, ordained, Rehme/Oeynhausen-South; 1930, German pastor in Manchester, England; 1934, Bradford—50

Harms, Hans Heinrich (1914–2006): 1934, theology student, Göttingen; 1960–67, senior pastor, Hamburg; 1967, bishop, Oldenburg—274

Harnack, Adolf von (1851–1930): influential church historian and liberal theologian; 1876, professor of church history, Leipzig; 1879, Giessen; from 1888, Berlin; 1890, member of the Prussian Academy of Science; 1905–21, general director of the Prussian state library; 1911, cofounder and first president of the Kaiser Wilhelm Society for the Advancement of the Sciences; 1914, ennobled; Bonhoeffer already knew Harnack as a neighbor in Grunewald, attended his seminar, and delivered the student eulogy at the memorial after Harnack's death—363

Hase, Hans Christoph von (1907–2005): Bonhoeffer's cousin; 1933–34, fellowship, Union Theological Seminary, New York; 1934, pastor, Berlin-Wilmersdorf; 1934–37, military chaplain, Jüterborg; 1937, Rostock; 1947, pastor, Marburg; 1954, Herford; 1957–73, director of the central office, Diaconical Welfare and Social Agency of the Evangelical Church of Germany, Stuttgart; coeditor of *DBW* 10: *Barcelona, Berlin, Amerika 1928–1931*—182, 220

Hase, Pine von: married Benedikt von Hase, the brother of Bonhoeffer's mother—100

Hasse (or Hesse), Otto: one of Bonhoeffer's Berlin confirmands—62

Hauff, Wilhelm (1802–27): German author of historical and satirical novels, fairy tales, stories, poems—379

Havaz, Andrea: staff member, Conference of European Churches—16

Headlam, Arthur Cayley (1862–1947): 1923–45, bishop of Gloucester; 1922–45, head of the Council on Foreign Relations of the Church of

1932, general secretary of the World Alliance and (until 1938) of the ecumenical Council for Life and Work; September 1933, participated in the Sofia conference; 1946–51, managing director, Ecumenical Institute of Bossey near Geneva—31, 33, 60, 70–71, 87, 119, 120, 123, 176–81, 197, 281

Herrmann, Johannes Hugo: German pastor; 1919, ordination; 1920, pastor, Groß-Nossin, Pomerania; 1925, pastor, Johannesburg, South Africa; 1955, retired—155

Hess, Rudolf Walter Richard (1894–1987): National Socialist politician; 1933, Reich minister; 1941, prisoner of war after voluntary flight to England; 1946, sentenced at Nuremberg to life in prison—264

Hesse, Hermann Albert (1877–1957): 1902, pastor, Duisburg; 1909, Bremen; 1916–46, Wuppertal-Elberfeld; from 1929, director of the Reformed preachers' seminary there; April–June 1933, Reformed representative of the German Evangelical Church Federation ("Kapler committee" for reforming the German Evangelical Church); 1934, member, Reich Council of Brethren; 1934–46, moderator of the Reformed Alliance; 1943, in the Dachau concentration camp—148, 211

Heydorn, A. F.: congregational council member, Sydenham congregation in London—67

Hildebrandt, Franz (1909–85): German pastor and close friend of Dietrich Bonhoeffer; 1927, met Dietrich Bonhoeffer; 1931, doctoral work and vicar assignment; 1933, assistant pastor, Klein-Machnow, Berlin; September 1933, resigned after the "brown synod"; until January 1934, with Dietrich Bonhoeffer in the parsonage, London; 1934, assistant to Martin Niemöller, Berlin-Dahlem; 1935–37, lecturer at the Confessing seminary, Berlin; 1937, emigrated to England after brief imprisonment; 1938, assistant pastor, St. George's, London; 1939–46, pastor to German Protestant refugees in Cambridge; 1946–51, Methodist minister, Cambridge; 1953, professor of theology, Drew University, Madison, New Jersey; 1968, left the Methodist conference; 1969–83, chaplain, Marie Curie Fairmile Nursing Home, Edinburgh, Scotland —16, 22, 23, 27–28, 41, 52–53, 56, 60, 65–67, 75, 82, 86, 92–95, 100, 101, 125, 156, 158, 192, 194, 195, 197, 198, 199, 200, 215, 241, 280, 283, 335, 416, 417, 419

Hindenburg, Paul von (1847–1934): general field marshal; 1925–34, president of Germany—83–84, 85, 87, 88, 89, 90, 105, 107, 194, 218

Hirsch, Emanuel (1888–1972): 1921–45, professor of church history, Göttingen; after 1936, also professor of systematic theology; 1933, National Socialist sympathizer, supporting member of the SS, and preeminent theological advisor to the German Christians; 1934–43, editor of the German Christian periodical *Deutsche Theologie*; after 1937, NSDAP mem-

versity trustee, Kiel; after 1945, businessman in Hamburg—248

Kintzel, Elimar (1908–94): "illegal" Confessing Church pastor—220

Kittel, Gerhard (1868–1948): German New Testament scholar, sympathetic to National Socialism; 1921, appointed professor, Greifswald; 1926, Tübingen; 1935, participated in the German Lutheran Day, Hanover; 1939–43, professor, Vienna and Tübingen; 1945, dismissed and arrested by the occupation authorities—36, 69

Kittel, Helmuth (1902–84): 1930–36, lecturer and professor of religious education, Hamburg-Altona, Kiel, Lauenburg, Danzig; professor of New Testament and religious education, Münster; member of the German Christians until the November 1933 Sports Palace rally; 1946, professor, Celle; 1953, Osnabrück; 1963–70, Münster—69

Klän, Werner: author of study on the "illegal" pastors in the Confessing Church—221

Klausener, Erich (1885–1934): German politician and head of Catholic Action, Berlin; murdered during the Röhm putsch—365

Kleinschmidt: member of German Reformed St. Paul's Church, London—237

Klotz, K.: member of the congregational council, German Reformed St. Paul's Church, London—29, 68, 101, 237

Klotz, Leopold: publisher—26

Klügel, Eberhard (1901–66): 1929, assistant pastor; 1931, worked with the Berlin City Mission and as an advisor to the Evangelical Press Association for Germany; chaplain in the regional association for Inner Mission, Hanover; 1933, pastor, Bennigsen; 1933, member of the Council of Brethren of the Pastors' Emergency League; 1937–50, head of the preachers' seminary in Erichsburg; 1943–46, advisor to Bishop Marahrens; 1950, member of the regional church council in Hanover; 1959, church superintendent of Hanover—211

Klugmann, H.: member of the congregational council, German Reformed St. Paul's Church, London—29, 68, 101, 231, 237, 277, 291

Knak, Siegfried (1875–1955): 1901, pastor, Pomerania; 1910–20, inspector, Berlin Mission Society; 1921–49, director, Berlin Mission Society; from 1950, professor of mission studies at the seminary, Berlin, and at the University of Halle —46

Koch, Hans: professor, Königsberg; August 1934, participated in the Fanø conference—177

Koch, Karl (1876–1951): 1904, pastor, Westphalia; 1916–49, Bad Oeynhausen; 1919–33, representative in the Prussian parliament (German National People's Party); 1927, church superintendent in Vlotho and president of the Westphalian provincial synod; 1930–32, member of the

national Parliament; 1934, member of the provisional church administration of the German Evangelical Church; 1934–43, president of the
Old Prussian and Confessing Synods of the German Evangelical Church;
1945–49, president of the Westphalian regional church—46, 53, 106,
129, 156, 172, 176, 177, 181, 188, 189, 191, 200, 211, 219, 227, 233, 238,
246, 247, 260–63, 269, 274, 281, 283, 430

Koechlin, Alphons (1885–1965): Swiss theologian and ecumenist; 1910, pastor, Stein/Rhein; 1921, Basel; 1923, head of the Basel Mission; 1936–59,
its president; from 1925, member of the Universal Christian Council
for Life and Work; 1926–47, vice president of the World Alliance of the
YMCA; 1934, participated in the conference in Fanø; maintained close
contact with George Bell during the Church Struggle; 1940–54, member
of the executive committee of the World Council of Churches; 1933–54,
church president; 1940–54, executive committee member of the World
Council of Churches; 1941–54, president of the Swiss Protestant Church
Federation; October 1945, participated in the Stuttgart conference—80,
81, 116, 139, 181, 191, 280

Kolb, Robert: Missions Professor of Systematic Theology and director of the
Institute for Mission Studies at Concordia Seminary, Saint Louis—108,
372

Kramm, Hans Herbert (1910–55): vicar in Potsdam, Sweden, and Berlin
(with Birger Forell); 1932–33, member of Bonhoeffer's circle of students in Berlin; 1934, participated in the ecumenical youth conference
in Fanø, and 1935 in Chamby; from February 1935, ecumenical adviser
with the Confessing Church; 1936, curate, London and Copenhagen;
1936, hospital chaplain, Berlin; 1938–39, fellowship at Oxford; 1941, pastor, German Lutheran St. Mary's Church, London; 1953, pastor, Lüne-
burg—164, 220

Krause, Gerhard: one of Bonhoeffer's first seminarians at Finkenwalde—
170

Krause, Reinhold (1893–1980): 1932, joined the NSDAP; 1932–33, district
head and spokesperson for Protestant church questions; 1932–33, head
of the German Christians for Berlin; member of the provincial synod
and of the Old Prussian General Synod (Mark Brandenburg); cofounder
of the German National People's Party in Berlin-Pankow; after November 13, 1933, relieved as district head after his Sports Palace speech and
dismissed from all church offices; 1945–50, interned in Landsberg/
Warthe and Buchenwald; 1951–58, secondary school teacher—46, 69,
170, 419, 429

Krummacher, Friedrich-Wilhelm (1901–74): 1928, pastor, Essen-Werden;
1934, senior church official and bishop, Church Foreign Office, German

INDEX OF SUBJECTS

Editors and Translators

Victoria J. Barnett (MDiv, Union Theological Seminary, New York) is general editor of the *Dietrich Bonhoeffer Works*, English edition, and director of church relations at the United States Holocaust Memorial Museum. She is the author of *Bystanders: Conscience and Complicity during the Holocaust* (Greenwood Press, 1999) and *For the Soul of the People: Protestant Protest against Hitler* (Oxford University Press, 1992) and the editor and translator of the new revised English edition of *Dietrich Bonhoeffer: A Biography*, by Eberhard Bethge (Fortress Press, 2000), as well as *And the Witnesses Were Silent: The Confessing Church and the Jews*, by Wolfgang Gerlach (University of Nebraska Press, 2000). In addition to numerous book chapters and articles, she is the author of the essay on Bonhoeffer on the U. S. Holocaust Memorial Museum Web site.

Isabel Best is a 1961 graduate of Oberlin College, where she studied English literature, French, and German. She has lived, studied, and worked in France, Germany, and Switzerland for over twenty-five years. She served ten years on the office staff of the Conference of European Churches in Geneva, Switzerland. Since earning a Diploma in Translation from the Institute of Linguists, London, in 1996, she has worked as a freelance translator for international organizations in Geneva, including the World Council of Churches, where her husband is employed.

Keith Clements was born in Sichuan, China, in 1943. He studied natural sciences and theology at Cambridge, continued theological studies at Oxford, and was ordained to the Baptist ministry in Great Britain in 1967. He served Baptist congregations in England for ten years before becoming a tutor at Bristol Baptist College in 1977 and a part-time lecturer in the Department of Theology and Religious Studies at Bristol University, where he was also awarded a doctorate. From 1990 to 1997, he was secretary for international affairs in the Council of Churches for Britain and Ireland. He then served from 1997 to 2005 as general secretary of the Conference of European Churches, Geneva. He has written extensively on modern church history and theology, and his publications include two previous books on Bonhoeffer, *A Patriotism for Today* (2nd ed., 1986) and *What Freedom?* (1990), together with a companion to the present volume, *Bonhoeffer and Britain* (2006).

Douglas W. Stott is a freelance editor and translator. A graduate of Davidson College, Northwestern University, and Emory's Candler School of Theology, he also studied in Germany at the Philipps University in Marburg and at the University of Stuttgart. His translation credits include several volumes of the *Theological Dictionary of the Old Testament* and the *Exegetical Dictionary of the New Testament*; commentaries for the Old Testament Library; *DBWE* 10, *Barcelona, Berlin, New York: 1928–1931*, and *DBWE* 14, *Theological Education at Finkenwalde: 1935–1937*; F. W. J. Schelling's *Philosophy of Art*. He was also on the translation team of volume 1 of *Religion Past and Present*. He is currently preparing an annotated English edition of the correspondence of Caroline Schlegel-Schelling.

Barbara Wojhoski studied art history at New York University, ancient history at the Philipps University in Marburg, Germany, and anthropology at Georgia State University, and has participated in archaeological excavations of Late Woodland Period sites in Arkansas. She has been a full-time freelance editor since 1995 for academic and denominational presses and has worked on projects ranging from a dictionary of the Miami-Illinois language to contemporary fiction translated from German to theological commentaries and philosophical works.